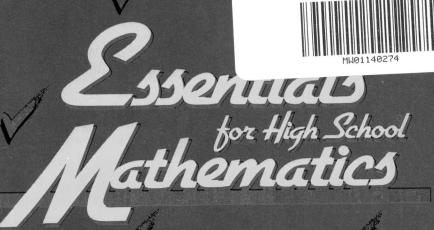

Essentials for High School Mathematics

Martin P. Cohen
Gerald H. Elgarten
Francis J. Gardella
Wendy S. Lewis
Joanne E. Meldon
Marvin S. Weingarden

TEACHER CONSULTANTS
Earlette Kinest
David R. Marchand
Exie L. Nicholas
Kaz Ogawa
Jean Bush Ragin
Mattie A. Whitfield

Houghton Mifflin Company **BOSTON**

Atlanta   Dallas   Geneva, Illinois   Palo Alto   Princeton   Toronto

Authors

Martin P. Cohen, Professor of Mathematics Education, University of Pittsburgh, Pittsburgh, Pennsylvania.

Gerald H. Elgarten, Assistant Professor of Secondary School Mathematics Education, City College of the City University of New York.

Francis J. Gardella, Supervisor of Mathematics and Computer Studies, East Brunswick Public Schools, East Brunswick, New Jersey.

Wendy S. Lewis, Mathematics Teacher, Royal High School, Simi Valley, California.

Joanne E. Meldon, Mathematics Teacher, Taylor Allderdice High School, Pittsburgh, Pennsylvania.

Marvin S. Weingarden, Supervisor of Secondary Mathematics, Detroit Public Schools, Detroit, Michigan.

Teacher Consultants

Earlette Kinest, Mathematics Teacher, McKinley Senior High School, St. Louis, Missouri.

David R. Marchand, Assistant Professor of Mathematics, Venango Campus, Clarion University of Pennsylvania, Oil City, Pennsylvania.

Exie L. Nicholas, Mathematics Teacher, Wichita Falls High School, Wichita Falls, Texas.

Kaz Ogawa, Instructional Adviser in Mathematics and Computer Science, Senior High Schools Division, Los Angeles Unified School District, Los Angeles, California.

Jean Bush Ragin, Mathematics Teacher, Baltimore City Public Schools, Patterson High School/The Gilman School Upward Bound Program, Baltimore, Maryland.

Mattie A. Whitfield, Mathematics Teacher and Chairperson of the Mathematics Department, Boca Raton High School, Boca Raton, Florida.

1992 Impression

Copyright © 1989 by Houghton Mifflin Company. All rights reserved.

No part of this work may be reproduced or transmitted in any form or by any means, electronic or mechanical, including photocopying and recording, or by any information storage or retrieval system without the prior written permission of Houghton Mifflin Company, unless such copying is expressly permitted by federal copyright law. Address inquiries to Permissions, Houghton Mifflin Company, One Beacon Street, Boston, MA 02108.

Printed in U.S.A.

ISBN: 0-395-39359-0

CDEFGHIJ–D–9654321

contents

UNIT 1 WHOLE NUMBERS

CHAPTER 4
DIVIDING WHOLE NUMBERS   69

CHAPTER 5
ORDER OF OPERATIONS AND NUMBER THEORY   93

UNIT 2   FRACTIONS

CHAPTER 6
FRACTION CONCEPTS   117

UNIT 3   DECIMALS

vi   Contents

CHAPTER 14
METRIC MEASUREMENT 293

Computer: Programming in BASIC **319**

Competency Test: Decimals **320**

Cumulative Review, Chapters 1–14 **322**

UNIT 4 RATIO, PROPORTION, AND PERCENT

CHAPTER 15
RATIO AND PROPORTION 323

CHAPTER 16
PERCENTS 345

CHAPTER 17
MORE PERCENTS 371

UNIT 5   STATISTICS AND PROBABILITY

CHAPTER 18
STATISTICS   397

CHAPTER 19
PROBABILITY   419

UNIT 6   ALGEBRA AND GEOMETRY

CHAPTER 20
INTEGERS   441

CHAPTER 21
SOLVING EQUATIONS   463

CHAPTER 22
PERIMETER AND AREA   485

Beginning a mathematics book is something like
beginning a long hike. Addition and subtraction
of whole numbers makes a good starting point.

CHAPTER 1

ADDING AND SUBTRACTING WHOLE NUMBERS

1-1 WHOLE NUMBERS AND PLACE VALUE

There are ten **digits** in our number system: 0, 1, 2, 3, 4, 5, 6, 7, 8, and 9. The position of a digit in a number is very important. We say that the **place** of the digit determines its **value**. A **place value chart** shows the place of each digit in a number. We can use the chart to give the value of the digit.

billions 1,000,000,000	hundred millions 100,000,000	ten millions 10,000,000	millions 1,000,000	hundred thousands 100,000	ten thousands 10,000	thousands 1000	hundreds 100	tens 10	ones 1
7	1	8	3	5	2	4	0	9	6

example 1

Give the value of each of the following digits in the chart above.

a. 4   **b.** 8

solution

a. 4 is in the thousands' place. Its value is 4000.
b. 8 is in the ten millions' place. Its value is 80,000,000.

your turn

Give the value of the underlined digit in each number.

1. 78,0<u>3</u>1,020,135
2. 4<u>4</u>,081,295,000
3. 104,8<u>9</u>5,121
4. 3,821,047,35<u>6</u>
5. <u>5</u>6,229,003
6. 9<u>0</u>7,343,816

    Commas separate large numbers into groups of three digits, called **periods.** We use the names of the periods to read a large number.

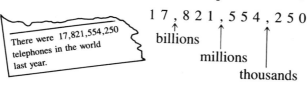

17 , 8 2 1 , 5 5 4 , 2 5 0   You read:

billions
   millions
      thousands

seventeen *billion,*
eight hundred twenty-one *million,*
five hundred fifty-four *thousand,*
two hundred fifty

A number may be written either in *words* or as a *numeral.*

example 2

Write 2,150,400,008 in words.

solution

word form: two billion, one hundred fifty million, four hundred thousand, eight
short word form: 2 billion, 150 million, 400 thousand, 8

your turn

Write the word form of each number.

7. 84,502,003   **8.** 36,524,800,000   **9.** 17,413,934,228

Write the short word form of each number.

10. 518,329,070,004   **11.** 21,753,003,916   **12.** 102,763,094,251

example 3

Write the numeral form of the following number.

eight hundred twelve billion, ninety-two million, six thousand, thirty-three

solution

Write the short word form. Leave a blank space for each empty place.

812 billion, __ 92 million, __ __ 6 thousand, __ 33

Fill in the blank spaces with zeros.

812 billion, 0 92 million, 0 0 6 thousand, 0 33

The **numeral form** is 812,092,006,033.

your turn

Write the numeral form of each number.

13. 107 billion, 49 million, 543 thousand, 6   **14.** 69 million, 4 thousand, 337
15. ninety-seven billion, fifty thousand, eight   **16.** one million, five thousand, twelve

practice exercises

practice for example 1 (page 2)

Give the value of the underlined digit in each number.

1. 47,560   **2.** 1,283,014   **3.** 832,005   **4.** 6,000,715
5. 1843   **6.** 417,547,002   **7.** 14,283,504   **8.** 711,012,300,552

Write the word form of each number.

9. 315   **10.** 3002   **11.** 27,921   **12.** 806,003

13. 4,925,016   **14.** 11,528,920   **15.** 201,987,000,000   **16.** 51,328,418,782

Write the short word form of each number.

17. 1,006,003   **18.** 206,003,927   **19.** 87,000,294,036   **20.** 500,140,000,488

21. 9081   **22.** 7001   **23.** 2,200,000,000   **24.** 60,000,000,006

Write the numeral form of each number.

25. 9 million, 40 thousand, 56   **26.** 2 million, 100 thousand, 13

27. five thousand, seventy-three   **28.** ten billion, sixty-four thousand

29. two hundred seventy-three billion, nine hundred six million, four

30. eight billion, ten million, two hundred thousand, thirty-two

Match the numeral form of each number with its word form.

31. 6004   **A.** sixty thousand, four hundred

32. 6040   **B.** six hundred forty thousand

33. 60,004   **C.** six thousand, forty

34. 60,400   **D.** six hundred thousand, forty

35. 600,040   **E.** six thousand, four

36. 640,000   **F.** sixty thousand, four

37. Recently there were 3,339,756,324 dollar bills in circulation. Write the short word form of this number.

38. One million, three hundred sixty thousand people saw the Chinese exhibit. Write the numeral form of this number.

review *exercises*

Find each sum.

1. 8 + 7   **2.** 9 + 6   **3.** 9 + 8   **4.** 8 + 4

5. 5 + 9   **6.** 8 + 6   **7.** 5 + 8   **8.** 9 + 4

9. 4 + 7   **10.** 9 + 9   **11.** 8 + 3   **12.** 9 + 7

1-2 ADDING WHOLE NUMBERS

There were 39,837 tickets to the football game sold in advance. Another 7465 tickets were sold at the gate. The numbers were added to announce that 47,302 tickets were sold in all.

To add two or more whole numbers, use the following method.

1. Line up the addends vertically. Digits with the same place value should be in the same column.
2. Add the digits in the ones' column. If the sum is 10 or more, rename.
3. Continue column-by-column from right to left.

```
  1  1  1 1
  3 9, 8 3 7   ⟍ addends
+   7, 4 6 5   ⟋
  4 7, 3 0 2   ← sum
```

example 1

Find each sum.

a.
```
  7 3 4     ⬅ No renaming
+1 6 2         is needed.
  8 9 6
```

b.
```
    1  1
    9 3 1
+   2 8 4
  1 2 1 5
```

c.
```
    2 2 1
  $ 2 8 7 9
      5 7 4
+     8 9 2
  $ 4 3 4 5
```

your turn

Find each sum.

1.
```
  1416
+6272
```

2.
```
  37,788
+  6,079
```

3.
```
  $58,904
+ 73,298
```

4.
```
  $1954
   846
+  648
```

example 2

Find each sum.

a. 28 + 72 + 94

b. $4018 + $65 + $397

solution

a.
```
  1 1
    2 8     ⬅ Rewrite the
    7 2        addition in
+   9 4        vertical form.
  1 9 4
```

b.
```
      1 2
  $ 4 0 1 8
        6 5
+     3 9 7
  $ 4 4 8 0
```

your turn

Find each sum.

5. 56 + 19 + 42

6. 125 + 319 + 546

7. $735 + $8 + $46

8. $804 + $6122 + $27

9. 12 + 49 + 83 + 65

10. 9 + 37 + 132 + 55

Adding and Subtracting Whole Numbers 5

You may add two numbers in any order. This is the **commutative property of addition.**

$$2 + 5 = 7 \quad \text{and} \quad 5 + 2 = 7$$

When you add three numbers, you may group as shown below. This is the **associative property of addition.**

$$(3 + 6) + 8 = 9 + 8 = 17 \quad \text{and} \quad 3 + (6 + 8) = 3 + 14 = 17$$

You can use these properties to add numbers *in any order* and *in any groups of two.*

example 3

Use the properties of addition to find each sum.

a. $9 + 6 + 1 + 4 + 8$

b. $325 + 29 + 105$

solution

a. $9 + 6 + 1 + 4 + 8$ ← Group numbers whose sum is 10.

$10 + 10 + 8 = 28$

b.
$$
\begin{array}{r}
\overset{1}{3}\,2\,5 \\
2\,9 \\
+1\,0\,5 \\
\hline
4\,5\,9
\end{array}
$$
← Add $5 + 5$ first.
$5 + 5 = 10$
$10 + 9 = 19$

your turn

Use the properties of addition to find each sum.

11. $7 + 9 + 3$ **12.** $4 + 7 + 16$ **13.** $5 + 6 + 7 + 4 + 5$

14. $15 + 8 + 5 + 7 + 2$ **15.** $149 + 17 + 21$ **16.** $506 + 97 + 114 + 23$

practice exercises

practice for example 1 (page 5)

Find each sum.

1. $\begin{array}{r}328 \\ +461\end{array}$	**2.** $\begin{array}{r}4172 \\ +2624\end{array}$	**3.** $\begin{array}{r}22{,}558 \\ +68{,}936\end{array}$	**4.** $\begin{array}{r}52{,}095 \\ +39{,}033\end{array}$
5. $\begin{array}{r}\$29{,}879 \\ +\ 70{,}311\end{array}$	**6.** $\begin{array}{r}\$49{,}671 \\ +\ 83{,}709\end{array}$	**7.** $\begin{array}{r}\$129 \\ 58 \\ +\ 925\end{array}$	**8.** $\begin{array}{r}\$8732 \\ 920 \\ +\ 859\end{array}$

practice for example 2 (page 5)

Find each sum.

9. $187 + 57 + 14$ **10.** $281 + 56 + 193$ **11.** $\$246 + \$109 + \$513$

12. $\$3025 + \$311 + \$629$ **13.** $47 + 159 + 236 + 24$ **14.** $562 + 117 + 25 + 139$

Use the properties of addition to find each sum.

15. $4 + 8 + 6 + 7 + 2$
16. $19 + 5 + 3 + 1 + 5$
17. $27 + 63 + 12 + 28$
18. $85 + 34 + 15 + 16$
19. $18 + 3 + 9 + 31 + 27$
20. $34 + 13 + 7 + 6 + 21$

mixed practice (pages 5–6)

Find each sum.

21.
$$\begin{array}{r} 129 \\ 58 \\ +922 \\ \hline \end{array}$$

22.
$$\begin{array}{r} 1469 \\ 8495 \\ +\ 376 \\ \hline \end{array}$$

23.
$$\begin{array}{r} \$509 \\ 117 \\ +\ \ 38 \\ \hline \end{array}$$

24.
$$\begin{array}{r} \$5532 \\ 9568 \\ +\ \ 741 \\ \hline \end{array}$$

25.
$$\begin{array}{r} 25{,}490 \\ +48{,}927 \\ \hline \end{array}$$

26.
$$\begin{array}{r} 36{,}008 \\ +\ 9{,}978 \\ \hline \end{array}$$

27.
$$\begin{array}{r} \$18{,}516 \\ +\ 50{,}086 \\ \hline \end{array}$$

28.
$$\begin{array}{r} \$19{,}725 \\ +\ 83{,}187 \\ \hline \end{array}$$

29. $103 + 27 + 139$
30. $210 + 109 + 211$
31. $79 + 120 + 231$
32. $751 + 604 + 359$
33. $874 + 200 + 926$
34. $119 + 970 + 511$
35. $\$5 + \$90 + \$15$
36. $\$38 + \$17 + \$2$
37. $\$25 + \$19 + \$15 + \$11$
38. $\$17 + \$13 + \$3 + \$7$
39. $\$918 + \$972 + \$198$
40. $\$224 + \$672 + \$156$

41. Kim has 28 French coins, 57 English coins, and 13 Canadian coins in her collection. What is the total number of coins in her collection?

42. Len's rare Asian stamp is valued at $42. His African stamp is valued at $89. What is the total value of these two stamps?

review *exercises*

Give the value of the underlined digit in each number.

1. 50<u>8</u>
2. 67<u>8</u>0
3. 52,<u>8</u>64
4. <u>8</u>1,147
5. <u>6</u>30,492
6. 891,<u>0</u>47
7. 4<u>2</u>1,567,809
8. 714,<u>8</u>29,220,617

mental math

To add $46 + 27$ mentally, think of 27 as $20 + 7$.
$$46 + 20 = 66 \qquad 66 + 7 = 73$$

◄── **Think: 6 + 7 = 13, and 66 + 7 is greater than 70.**

Add mentally.

1. $52 + 43$
2. $48 + 21$
3. $25 + 46$
4. $37 + 18$
5. $77 + 24$
6. $65 + 37$
7. $125 + 34$
8. $262 + 315$

1-3 ESTIMATING SUMS

It is often important to know how to **estimate**. One way to estimate a sum is to add the **front-end** digits.

SELECTED STYLES MARKED DOWN

Do I have enough money to pay for these? Did I get the correct change?

---

example 1

Estimate by adding the front-end digits.

a. 53,279
    +21,987

b. 4267 + 3149 + 2403

solution

a.   53,279
       +21,987   **The word *about***
    about 70,000 ◄──   **indicates that the**
                        answer is an estimate.

b. 4267 + 3149 + 2403
         about 9000

your turn

Estimate by adding the front-end digits.

1. 2243 + 3049
2. 63,497 + 42,986
3. 219,368 + 621,422
4. 32 + 41 + 12
5. 307 + 214 + 517
6. 2167 + 4209 + 1096 + 2349

    Each estimated sum in Example 1 is less than the exact sum. You can often get a closer estimate if you **adjust** the sum of the front-end digits.

---

example 2

Estimate by adjusting the sum of the front-end digits.

a. 336 + 221 + 469 + 285

b. 2964 + 3426 + 319 + 3289

solution

a.   336
        221 ⟩about 100
        469 ⟩about 100
       +285
      ─────
       1100   +   200
           about 1300

b.   2964 ──about 1000
        3426
         319 ⟩about 1000
       +3289
      ─────
       8000   +   2000
           about 10,000

Estimate by adjusting the sum of the front-end digits.

7. 307 + 248 + 345 + 103

8. 3333 + 1922 + 2301 + 1357

9. 2644 + 3385 + 2541 + 502

10. 24,999 + 10,892 + 10,902 + 15,901

practice exercises

practice for example 1 (page 8)

Estimate by adding the front-end digits.

1. 421 + 316 + 104

2. 507 + 219 + 428

3. 2067 + 3192 + 1045 + 2166

4. 426,822 + 609,324

5. 12,216 + 41,891 + 63,822

6. 6042 + 7294 + 9004 + 5179

practice for example 2 (pages 8–9)

Estimate by adjusting the sum of the front-end digits.

7. 219 + 580 + 345 + 162

8. 841 + 96 + 222 + 343

9. 26,892 + 33,004 + 302

10. 14,021 + 34,098 + 2022

11. 6931 + 3504 + 2987 + 4581

12. 22,567 + 32,521 + 12,517 + 32,416

mixed practice (pages 8–9)

Estimate each sum.

13. 553 + 763

14. 273 + 522

15. $393 + $143 + $264

16. $631 + $244 + $335

17.
```
  264
  387
  431
+  92
```

18.
```
  2419
  1274
  3625
+  718
```

19.
```
$22,791
 34,067
 14,228
+   826
```

20.
```
$441,106
 192,018
  54,992
+  3,167
```

21. A gold charm costs $129, a silver necklace costs $239, and a quartz watch costs $175. Which two items together cost about $300?

22. Mary added 68,471 + 732,105 + 879 on her calculator. The display was ⌐901455⌐. Explain how you can tell the answer is wrong.

review exercises

Find each difference.

1. 11 − 6
2. 13 − 4
3. 15 − 7
4. 12 − 5
5. 11 − 3
6. 14 − 8
7. 17 − 8
8. 16 − 9
9. 18 − 9
10. 12 − 4
11. 15 − 9
12. 13 − 5

1-4 SUBTRACTING WHOLE NUMBERS

In one year there were 14,642 cars registered in Springfield. In the same year there were 3715 registered trucks and buses. If you subtract, you find that 10,927 more cars were registered than trucks and buses.

To subtract two whole numbers, use the following method.

1. Line up the numbers vertically. Digits with the same place value should be in the same column.
2. Subtract the digits in the ones' column. If 10 more ones are needed, rename.
3. Continue column-by-column from right to left.

$$
\begin{array}{r}
\scriptstyle 3 \ \ 16 \ \ 3 \ 12 \\
1\,4,\,6\,4\,2 \\
-\ \ \ 3,\,7\,1\,5 \\
\hline
1\,0,\,9\,2\,7 \leftarrow \textbf{difference}
\end{array}
$$

We say that addition and subtraction are **inverse operations.** This means that one operation "undoes" the other. You can check a difference by adding.

$$
Check: \begin{array}{r}
1\,0,\,9\,2\,7 \\
+\ \ 3,\,7\,1\,5 \\
\hline
1\,4,\,6\,4\,2 \ \checkmark
\end{array}
$$

example 1

a.
$$
\begin{array}{r}
6\,4\,9 \\
-1\,2\,5 \\
\hline
5\,2\,4
\end{array}
$$
← No renaming is needed.

b.
$$
\begin{array}{r}
\scriptstyle 6 \ 13 \\
8\,7\,3\,5 \\
-\ \ \ 1\,8\,2 \\
\hline
8\,5\,5\,3
\end{array}
$$

c.
$$
\begin{array}{r}
\scriptstyle 3 \ 12\,15 \\
\$\,2\,6,\,4\,3\,5 \\
-\ \ 1\,2,\,2\,9\,7 \\
\hline
\$\,1\,4,\,1\,3\,8
\end{array}
$$
← Rename twice in the tens' place.

your turn

Find each difference.

1.
$$
\begin{array}{r}
2658 \\
-\ \ 405 \\
\end{array}
$$

2.
$$
\begin{array}{r}
7193 \\
-1548 \\
\end{array}
$$

3.
$$
\begin{array}{r}
\$16,438 \\
-\ \ 7,642 \\
\end{array}
$$

4.
$$
\begin{array}{r}
\$45,240 \\
-\ 17,589 \\
\end{array}
$$

example 2

a.
$$
\begin{array}{r}
\scriptstyle 5 \ 9 \ 10 \\
6\,0\,0 \\
-1\,4\,2 \\
\hline
4\,5\,8
\end{array}
$$
← Rename one of the hundreds as 9 tens, 10 ones.

b.
$$
\begin{array}{r}
\scriptstyle 3 \ 9 \ 9 \ 15 \\
\$\,4\,0\,0\,5 \\
-\ \ \ \ 5\,7\,8 \\
\hline
\$\,3\,4\,2\,7
\end{array}
$$

your turn

Find each difference.

5.
$$
\begin{array}{r}
300 \\
-\ 29 \\
\end{array}
$$

6.
$$
\begin{array}{r}
4003 \\
-1582 \\
\end{array}
$$

7.
$$
\begin{array}{r}
\$7020 \\
-\ 6478 \\
\end{array}
$$

8.
$$
\begin{array}{r}
\$80,001 \\
-\ \ 6,443 \\
\end{array}
$$

example 3

Find each difference.

a. $6159 - 4532$ **b.** $30,010 - 4829$

solution

a.
$$\begin{array}{r} \overset{5\ \ 11}{6\cancel{1}59} \\ -4\ 5\ 3\ 2 \\ \hline 1\ 6\ 2\ 7 \end{array}$$
← Rewrite the subtraction in vertical form.

b.
$$\begin{array}{r} \overset{2\ 9\ \ 9\ 10\ 10}{\$\ \cancel{3}\ \cancel{0},\ \cancel{0}\ \cancel{1}\ \cancel{0}} \\ -\ \ \ 4,\ 8\ 2\ 9 \\ \hline \$\ 2\ 5,\ 1\ 8\ 1 \end{array}$$

your turn

Find each difference.

9. $496 - 25$ **10.** $78,124 - 8096$ **11.** $900 - 433$ **12.** $4006 - 32$

practice exercises

practice for example 1 *(page 10)*

Find each difference.

1.
$$\begin{array}{r} 167 \\ -\ 83 \end{array}$$

2.
$$\begin{array}{r} 858 \\ -761 \end{array}$$

3.
$$\begin{array}{r} \$3241 \\ -\ 2193 \end{array}$$

4.
$$\begin{array}{r} \$6429 \\ -\ 457 \end{array}$$

5.
$$\begin{array}{r} 8947 \\ -3059 \end{array}$$

6.
$$\begin{array}{r} 39,813 \\ -35,927 \end{array}$$

7.
$$\begin{array}{r} \$61,290 \\ -\ 4,891 \end{array}$$

8.
$$\begin{array}{r} \$53,380 \\ -\ 17,419 \end{array}$$

practice for example 2 *(page 10)*

Find each difference.

9.
$$\begin{array}{r} 704 \\ -359 \end{array}$$

10.
$$\begin{array}{r} 500 \\ -309 \end{array}$$

11.
$$\begin{array}{r} \$1000 \\ -\ 585 \end{array}$$

12.
$$\begin{array}{r} \$2800 \\ -\ 1694 \end{array}$$

13.
$$\begin{array}{r} 80,061 \\ -17,889 \end{array}$$

14.
$$\begin{array}{r} 16,020 \\ -2,059 \end{array}$$

15.
$$\begin{array}{r} \$70,005 \\ -\ 30,986 \end{array}$$

16.
$$\begin{array}{r} \$90,010 \\ -\ 42,295 \end{array}$$

practice for example 3 *(page 11)*

Find each difference.

17. $344 - 59$

18. $736 - 527$

19. $8011 - 852$

20. $6010 - 1837$

21. $12,931 - 6495$

22. $61,004 - 15,987$

23. $\$5147 - \$1973$

24. $\$6005 - \$4322$

25. $\$7200 - \$14$

26. $\$4183 - \$98$

27. $\$57,000 - \$891$

28. $\$61,182 - \$914$

mixed practice (pages 10–11)

Find each difference.

29.	319 −129	**30.**	8341 −6032	**31.**	$8020 − 734	**32.**	$5005 − 899
33.	6142 −1091	**34.**	3763 − 764	**35.**	$53,090 − 980	**36.**	$5070 − 88

37. 83 − 34   **38.** 601 − 366   **39.** 901 − 62

40. 4500 − 2847   **41.** 190 − 47   **42.** 3892 − 3591

43. $3500 − $1250   **44.** $1104 − $837   **45.** $10,742 − $5924

46. $30,000 − $668   **47.** $5943 − $56   **48.** $90,135 − $17,082

49. In a recent year 2,966,763 people lived in Los Angeles. In the same year 1,594,086 people lived in Houston. How many more people lived in Los Angeles than in Houston?

50. There are forty-two thousand seats in a stadium. Thirty thousand, nine hundred seven seats have been sold in advance for a concert. How many seats are still available?

review *exercises*

Find each sum or difference.

1. 43 + 88   **2.** $96 − $48   **3.** 501 − 322

4. 291 + 6035   **5.** 18,515 + 40,690   **6.** 33,214 − 8097

7. $7200 − $1496   **8.** $6921 + $576   **9.** 60,904 − 7291

10. 4 + 679 + 83   **11.** 6 + 9 + 7 + 4 + 1   **12.** 84 + 32 + 68 + 16

calculator corner

If you understand place value, you can use addition and subtraction on a calculator to correct an incorrect number in one step.

example   Enter 497,846. Correct it to 407,846 in one step.

solution   497846 − 90000 = 407846   ◄— **Decrease the ten thousands' place by 9.**

Enter the first number. Correct it to the second number in one step.

1. 2775 → 2075   **2.** 15,386 → 15,306   **3.** 60,451 → 68,451

4. 306,217 → 346,217   **5.** 189,793 → 589,793   **6.** 65,829,410 → 62,829,410

1-5 ADDITION AND SUBTRACTION PHRASES

Many English words and phrases suggest the operation of addition. Others suggest subtraction. The chart lists some examples.

Addition		Subtraction	
plus	more than	minus	fewer than
sum	altogether	difference	reduced by
total	combined	decreased by	how much more
increased by		less than	how much less

example 1

Find each number.

a. twenty-six more than nine

b. 46 decreased by 12

solution

a. *More than* suggests addition.

$9 + 26 = 35$

b. *Decreased by* suggests subtraction.

$46 - 12 = 34$

your turn

Find each number.

1. eighty increased by four
2. eighteen less than fifty
3. the sum of 18 and 59
4. 1001 reduced by 929

A **variable** is a symbol used to represent a number. We often use letters like *x*, *n*, and *a* as variables. An expression that contains a variable is called a **variable expression.**

example 2

Write each phrase as a variable expression. Use *n* as the variable.

a. $\underbrace{\text{a number}}_{n} \underbrace{\text{increased by}}_{+} \underbrace{\text{ten}}_{10}$

b. twelve less than a number

$n - 12$

◄ Be careful of the order in a subtraction phrase.

your turn

Write each phrase as a variable expression. Use *x* as the variable.

5. sixty subtracted from a number
6. five hundred more than a number
7. the total of a number and eighteen
8. seventy minus a number

Adding and Subtracting Whole Numbers 13

practice exercises

practice for example 1 (page 13)

Find each number.

1. 43 more than 25
2. 55 increased by 9
3. fifteen minus twelve
4. forty-five less than ninety
5. the total of seventeen and thirty
6. six less than twenty-six
7. 345 reduced by 309
8. 289 fewer than 1003
9. the sum of 100 and 131
10. 1027 more than 1760
11. 156 fewer than 200
12. ninety-eight plus twenty

practice for example 2 (page 13)

Write each phrase as a variable expression. Use y as the variable.

13. seventeen more than a number
14. the sum of a number and one
15. seven less than a number
16. a number decreased by twelve
17. a number plus fifty-three
18. eighty-seven increased by a number
19. nineteen minus a number
20. seventy decreased by a number
21. the total of a number and nine
22. sixty-two more than a number
23. forty-six reduced by a number
24. a number increased by forty-two

mixed practice (page 13)

**Match each phrase with the correct variable expression.
Each expression will be used more than once.**

25. nineteen less than a number t
26. the total of a number t and nineteen
27. a number t minus nineteen
28. a number t decreased by nineteen
29. nineteen more than a number t
30. nineteen fewer than a number t
31. nineteen reduced by a number t
32. a number t increased by nineteen
33. a number t and nineteen combined
34. nineteen decreased by a number t

A. $t + 19$
B. $t - 19$
C. $19 - t$

Write three different phrases for each variable expression.

35. $y + 81$
37. $14 + c$
38. $z - 100$

39. Aubrey is thirteen years older than Tom. Tom is *t* years old. Write a variable expression for Aubrey's age.

40. Donna has twenty books. Mattie has *m* fewer books than Donna. Write a variable expression for the number of books that Mattie has.

41. Julio has *q* quarters. He has six fewer nickels than quarters. Write a variable expression for the number of nickels that Julio has.

42. Mai has *n* nickels, *d* dimes, and *p* pennies. Write a variable expression for the combined number of nickels, dimes, and pennies that she has.

review *exercises*

Write the word form of each number.

1. 6032   **2.** 14,008   **3.** 121,043,200   **4.** 17,008,502,076

Find each sum or difference.

5.
$$17,819 \\ + \ 6,541$$

6.
$$80,005 \\ -13,267$$

7.
$$\$4215 \\ - \ \ \ 793$$

8.
$$\$1762 \\ + \ \ \ \ \ 48$$

mental math

To subtract 199 from 476 mentally, first subtract 200, then add 1.

$$476 - 200 = 276 \qquad 276 + 1 = 277$$

Add or subtract mentally.

1. 184 − 99   **2.** 563 − 299   **3.** 437 + 99   **4.** 654 + 299

5. 965 − 499   **6.** 3275 + 1999   **7.** 5164 − 2999   **8.** 1687 + 3999

You can solve some problems in mathematics by using a strategy called **trial and error.** A "trial" means that you make a reasonable guess of the answer. Then you check your guess. If your first guess is an "error," you at least eliminate one possible answer. You may even get some information that will lead you to the correct answer.

At the right is an addition problem in which some of the digits are missing. Each digit from 1 to 9 can be used only once. Use trial and error to place the missing digits correctly.

1-6 VARIABLE EXPRESSIONS

If you are asked to find the sum $36 + 55$, you add the numbers. The answer is 91. If you are asked to find the sum $n + 7$, you cannot add until you are given a **value** to replace the variable. Then you can **evaluate** the variable expression.

example 1

Evaluate each expression for the given value of the variable.

a. $x - 67$, when $x = 92$

b. $n + 27 + n$, when $n = 43$

solution

a.
$$\left.\begin{array}{c} x - 67 \\ 92 - 67 \end{array}\right\} \quad \begin{array}{r} 92 \\ -67 \\ \hline 25 \end{array}$$

b.
$$\left.\begin{array}{c} n + 27 + n \\ 43 + 27 + 43 \end{array}\right\} \quad \begin{array}{r} 43 \\ 27 \\ +43 \\ \hline 113 \end{array}$$

your turn

Evaluate each expression for the given value of the variable.

1. $89 + a$, when $a = 22$

2. $79 - m$, when $m = 62$

3. $y + y$, when $y = 76$

4. $c + 18 + c$, when $c = 57$

A variable expression may contain more than one variable.

example 2

Evaluate each expression when $x = 19$, $y = 15$, and $z = 22$.

a. $x - y$

b. $z - y$

c. $x + y + z$

solution

a.
$$\left.\begin{array}{c} x - y \\ 19 - 15 \end{array}\right\} \quad \begin{array}{r} 19 \\ -15 \\ \hline 4 \end{array}$$

b.
$$\left.\begin{array}{c} z - y \\ 22 - 15 \end{array}\right\} \quad \begin{array}{r} 22 \\ -15 \\ \hline 7 \end{array}$$

c.
$$\left.\begin{array}{c} x + y + z \\ 19 + 15 + 22 \end{array}\right\} \quad \begin{array}{r} 19 \\ 15 \\ +22 \\ \hline 56 \end{array}$$

your turn

Evaluate each expression when $a = 30$, $b = 9$, and $c = 41$.

5. $a - b$

6. $a + c$

7. $c - b$

8. $a + b + c$

practice exercises

practice for example 1 (page 16)

Evaluate each expression for the given value of the variable.

1. $15 + x$, when $x = 12$
2. $m + 27$, when $m = 16$
3. $a - 27$, when $a = 89$
4. $63 - h$, when $h = 28$
5. $m + m$, when $m = 47$
6. $r - r$, when $r = 63$
7. $x + 24 + x$, when $x = 32$
8. $w + w + 79$, when $w = 57$
9. $r + r + 88$, when $r = 26$
10. $23 + p + 7$, when $p = 45$
11. $q + q + q$, when $q = 49$
12. $t + t + t + t$, when $t = 32$

practice for example 2 (page 16)

Evaluate each expression when $p = 40$, $q = 15$, and $r = 36$.

13. $p + q$
14. $p + r$
15. $q + r$
16. $p - q$
17. $r - q$
18. $p - r$
19. $p + r + q$
20. $q + p + r$
21. $p + r + p$
22. $p + r + r$
23. $q + r + q$
24. $r + r + r$

mixed practice (page 16)

Evaluate each expression when $w = 75$, $x = 112$, $y = 93$, and $z = 213$.

25. $w + 29$
26. $109 - w$
27. $97 - y$
28. $90 + z$
29. $x + 105 + x$
30. $w + w + 85$
31. $479 + z + 138$
32. $y + 618 + 29$
33. $z - x$
34. $z + y$
35. $z - w$
36. $x + y$
37. $w + x$
38. $y - w$
39. $w + y$
40. $x - w$
41. $x - y$
42. $w + w$
43. $w + z + x$
44. $z + w + x$
45. $z + w + y$
46. $x + x + w$
47. $x + z + z$
48. $z + y + z$

review exercises

Find each sum or difference.

1. $692 + 1049$
2. $12{,}146 - 9017$
3. $\$6000 - \$422$
4. $\$4328 + \$5924$
5. $14 + 9 + 6 + 3 + 1$
6. $50{,}040 - 16{,}791$

7. A blouse costs $29, a sweater costs $38, and a skirt costs $49. Which two items together cost about $70?

8. Attendance at the school play was 493 on Friday, 524 on Saturday, and 387 on Sunday. What was the total attendance for these three days?

Adding and Subtracting Whole Numbers **17**

SKILL REVIEW

Give the value of the underlined digit in each number.

1. 23,791
2. 144,802
3. 2,644,873
4. 49,999,733,112

1-1

Match the word form of each number with its numeral form.

5. four hundred thousand, two hundred
6. forty thousand, twenty
7. four thousand, twenty
8. forty-two thousand

- **A.** 4020
- **B.** 40,020
- **C.** 42,000
- **D.** 400,200

Find each sum.

9. $52 + 26 + 73$
10. $91 + 21 + 44$
11. $4831 + 1449$
12. $52,903 + 24,877$
13. $2381 + 174 + 3613$
14. $45,167 + 392$

1-2

15. A company produced 1883 passenger cars, 124 station wagons, and 97 trucks in one month. What was the total number of vehicles produced?

Estimate each sum.

16. $414 + 589 + 201$
17. $9342 + 3366 + 2491$
18. $34,912 + 39,923 + 36,278$
19. $702 + 556 + 49$

1-3

Find each difference.

20. $572 - 344$
21. $1717 - 532$
22. $4809 - 1443$
23. $6006 - 2442$
24. $30,024 - 2372$
25. $84,000 - 257$

1-4

26. There were 64,000 tickets available for the playoff game. So far, 36,907 tickets have been sold. How many tickets are still available?

Match each phrase with the correct variable expression.
Each expression may be used more than once.

27. a number x subtracted from twenty-four
28. twenty-four less than a number x
29. twenty-four more than a number x
30. a number x reduced by twenty-four

- **A.** $x + 24$
- **B.** $x - 24$
- **C.** $24 - x$

1-5

Evaluate each expression when $x = 35$, $y = 97$, and $z = 114$.

31. $x + 318$
32. $911 - x$
33. $z - 85$
34. $936 + y$
35. $x + y$
36. $z - y$
37. $x + y + z$
38. $z + x + z$

1-6

1-7 READING DISTANCES ON A MAP

The map shows air distances in miles (mi) between some major cities in the United States. To find the distance between two cities, you read the number on the connecting line.

example

a. Find the distance from Seattle to St. Louis through Denver.

b. How much farther is it from Atlanta to Washington than from Washington to Boston?

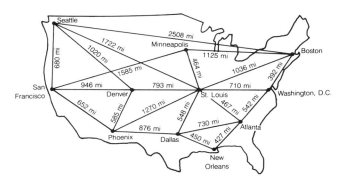

Air Distance in Miles

solution

a. Seattle to Denver: 1020 mi
Denver to St. Louis: + 793 mi
Add the distances: 1813 mi

b. Atlanta to Washington: 542 mi
Washington to Boston: −392 mi
Subtract the distances: 150 mi

exercises

Find the distance:

1. from San Francisco to Boston through Minneapolis
2. from Denver to Atlanta through St. Louis
3. from Minneapolis to Washington, D.C., through Boston

4. How much farther is it from Phoenix to St. Louis than from Phoenix to San Francisco?
5. How much farther is it from Seattle to Boston than from Seattle to Denver?
6. How much farther is it from St. Louis to Dallas than from St. Louis to Minneapolis?

Many airlines give one bonus point for each mile flown by frequent passengers.

7. If you wanted to earn 1000 points, how would you plan your trip to Atlanta from Dallas?
8. If you wanted to earn 3000 points, how would you plan your trip from San Francisco to New Orleans?

Adding and Subtracting Whole Numbers   19

1-8 READING DISTANCES ON A CHART

The chart shows distances in miles (mi) between some major cities. To find the distance between two cities, you find the point at which the row and column meet.

Mileage Chart

	Buenos Aires	Chicago	Honolulu	Los Angeles	Mexico City
Buenos Aires	. . .	5598	7653	6148	4609
Chicago	5598	. . .	4315	1714	1690
Honolulu	7653	4315	. . .	2620	3846
Los Angeles	6148	1714	2620	. . .	1445
Mexico City	4609	1690	3846	1445	. . .

example

Find the distance from Honolulu to Los Angeles.

solution

Find Honolulu in the left column. Find Los Angeles along the top. The distance is 2620 mi.

exercises

Find the distance:

1. from Honolulu to Mexico City
2. from Los Angeles to Buenos Aires
3. from Chicago to Honolulu
4. from Buenos Aires to Chicago
5. from Buenos Aires to Honolulu through Chicago
6. from Mexico City to Honolulu through Los Angeles
7. from Los Angeles to Chicago through Mexico City
8. from Mexico City to Los Angeles through Buenos Aires

9. Larry flew from Chicago to Mexico City and then from Mexico City to Los Angeles. He then returned to Chicago from Los Angeles. He told his friends that he flew about 5000 mi. Was he right? Explain.

10. Joanne flew from Honolulu to Los Angeles. Gus flew from Honolulu to Mexico City. Who flew farther? How much farther?

1-9 TIME ZONES

In general, the world is divided into 24 time zones that are one hour apart. As you move east, add one hour for each time zone through which you pass. As you move west, subtract one hour.

example

a. It is 8:00 A.M. in Seattle. What time is it in New Orleans?

b. It is 3:00 P.M. in Halifax. What time is it in Los Angeles?

solution

a. You are traveling *east* through 2 time zones, so *add* 2 hours. It is 10:00 A.M. in New Orleans.

b. You are traveling *west* through 4 time zones, so *subtract* 4 hours. It is 11:00 A.M. in Los Angeles.

exercises

Find the time:

1. in Chicago when it is 7:00 P.M. in Seattle

2. in San Francisco when it is 4:00 A.M. in Boston

3. in Atlanta when it is 6:00 A.M. in Dallas

4. in Montreal when it is 5:00 P.M. in Honolulu

5. in Honolulu when it is 4:30 A.M. in New York

6. in Edmonton when it is 11:15 P.M. in Winnipeg

7. A World Series game starts at 8:25 P.M. in Boston. At what time is the game seen in Dallas?

8. A Super Bowl game is broadcast at 2:30 P.M. from New Orleans. At what time is the game seen in Denver?

Adding and Subtracting Whole Numbers 21

FITNESS TECHNICIAN

Mike Drake designs and directs physical fitness programs. Before a person starts an exercise program, Mike must measure the person's level of fitness. He uses the following **step test** to measure *heart rate recovery*.

Fitness Score	Fitness Category
0 or less	excellent
1–2	good
3–4	fair
5–6	poor
7 or more	very poor

1. Take the pulse for one minute while the person is sitting. (This is the **starting rate**.)
2. Have the person step up and down a bench about one foot high for one minute at a comfortable rate of speed.
3. Wait one minute and again take the pulse for one minute. (This is the **recovery rate**.)

After administering the step test, Mike uses the following formula to get a **fitness score**. He then checks the chart to find a **fitness category**.

fitness score = recovery rate − starting rate

example

Emily O'Brien took the step test before starting a swimming program. Emily had a starting rate of 74. Her recovery rate was 77. What is her fitness category?

solution

First use the formula:

fitness score = recovery rate − starting rate

= 77 − 74 = 3

Emily's fitness score is 3, which gives her a fitness category of *fair*.

exercises

1. Peter took the step test. His starting rate was 68. His recovery rate was 71. What is his fitness score? What is his fitness category?
2. Shalma's rate at the start of the test was 71. Her rate at the end of the test was 72. Find her fitness score.
3. Gianna wants to start a running program. Her starting rate is 68. Her recovery rate is 68. What is her fitness category?

CHAPTER REVIEW

vocabulary   vo·cab·u·lar·y

Choose the correct word to complete each sentence.

1. When you subtract two numbers the answer is called the (*sum, difference*).
2. You know that $3 + 5 = 5 + 3$ by the (*associative, commutative*) property of addition.

skills

Match the numeral form of each number with its short word form.

3. 70,001
4. 71,000
5. 7,001,000
6. 7,010,000,000

   A. 71 thousand
   B. 70 thousand, 1
   C. 7 billion, 10 million
   D. 7 million, 1 thousand

Find each sum or difference.

7. $591 - 492$
8. $6420 + 3680$
9. $\$12,234 - \$8456$
10. $\$763 + \$152 + \$930$
11. $34 + 61 + 26 + 89$
12. $40,006 - 28,287$

Estimate each sum.

13. $24,831 + 34,402 + 12,090$
14. $4192 + 956 + 2223 + 7840$

Write each phrase as a variable expression. Use z as the variable.

15. a number decreased by 42
16. twenty-three more than a number

Evaluate each expression when $a = 72$, $b = 89$, and $c = 124$.

17. $c - b$
18. $a + c$
19. $a + b + c$
20. $c + c + 109$

21. Use the map on page 19. Find the distance from Atlanta to Seattle through St. Louis.
22. Use the map on page 19. How much farther is it from Phoenix to St. Louis than from Phoenix to Denver?
23. Use the chart on page 20. Find the distance from Chicago to Honolulu through Los Angeles.
24. Use the map on page 21. Find the time in Edmonton when it is 2:20 P.M. in New York.

Adding and Subtracting Whole Numbers   23

CHAPTER TEST

Write the word form of each number.

1. 45,224   2. 960,972   3. 14,378,413   4. 21,748,002,366

1-1

Write the numeral form of each number.

5. two hundred three thousand, eight hundred seventy-one
6. one billion, fifty-nine million, two hundred twenty thousand, four

Find each sum.

7. $792 + 819 + 203$ 8. $45,612 + 3407 + 249$ 9. $\$53,882 + \$79,408$

1-2

10. Ella has 1482 baseball cards. Her brother Steve has 1907 baseball cards. What is the total number of cards that they have together?

Estimate each sum.

11. $52,812 + 47,729$ 12. $4120 + 3970 + 982$ 13. $\$53,304 + \$6890$

1-3

14. A television set costs $339, a VCR is $469, and a video camera is $889. About how much would it cost to buy all three?

Find each difference.

15. $48,913 - 3924$ 16. $4006 - 2974$ 17. $\$63,048 - \$47,662$

1-4

18. The Emersons had $4000 in their vacation fund. They spent $1127 of this money on airline tickets. How much money was left in the fund?

Write each phrase as a variable expression. Use *m* as the variable.

19. a number fewer than 153   20. 46 increased by a number

1-5

Evaluate each expression when $a = 67$, $b = 205$, and $c = 73$.

21. $136 - a$ 22. $b + 348$ 23. $a + 49 + c$ 24. $a + b + c$

1-6

25. Use the map on page 19. Find the distance from Dallas to Washington, D.C., through Atlanta.

1-7

26. Use the map on page 19. How much farther is it from Minneapolis to San Francisco than from Minneapolis to St. Louis?

27. Use the chart on page 20. Find the distance from Buenos Aires to Chicago through Mexico City.

1-8

28. Use the map on page 21. Find the time in Atlanta when it is 7:00 P.M. in Seattle.

1-9

Rounded numbers are often used to state the size of large groups such as this one and to compare the sizes of several groups.

CHAPTER 2

ROUNDING AND COMPARING WHOLE NUMBERS

2-1 ROUNDING WHOLE NUMBERS

Often we use **rounded numbers** instead of *exact* numbers. For instance, a newscaster might report that 27,000 people attended a concert. The actual number was 26,531. The newscaster reported the number rounded *to the nearest thousand*.

To round a whole number to a given place, use the following method.

1. Circle the digit in the place to which you are rounding.
2. If the digit to the right of the circle is *less than 5,* copy the circled digit.
   If the digit to the right of the circle is *5 or more,* add 1 to the circled digit.
3. Replace all digits to the right of the circle with zeros.

2 ⑥, 5 3 1 ◀── The digit to the right of the circle is 5, so add 1 to the circled digit.

2 7 , 0 0 0

example 1

Round to the given place.

a. 2793; nearest hundred

b. $53,284; nearest ten dollars

solution

a. 2 ⑦ 9 3 ◀── 9 is more than 5, so add 1 to the circled digit.

2 8 0 0

b. $ 5 3 , 2 ⑧ 4 ◀── 4 is less than 5, so copy the circled digit.

$ 5 3 , 2 8 0

your turn

Round to the given place.

1. 5284; nearest hundred
2. 815; nearest ten
3. $16,349; nearest thousand dollars
4. $63; nearest hundred dollars

example 2

Round 4961 to the nearest hundred.

solution

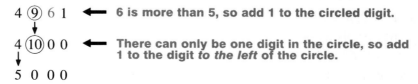

4 ⑨ 6 1 ◀── 6 is more than 5, so add 1 to the circled digit.

4 ⑩ 0 0 ◀── There can only be one digit in the circle, so add 1 to the digit *to the left* of the circle.

5 0 0 0

your turn

Round to the given place.

5. 1976; nearest hundred

6. $39,560; nearest thousand dollars

7. 3997; nearest ten

8. $79,962; nearest hundred dollars

The first nonzero digit of a whole number is called its **leading digit.**

example 3

Round to the place of the leading digit.

a. 381

b. $9704

solution

a. ③ 8 1 ⬅ **3 is in the hundreds' place. Round to the nearest hundred.**
      ↓
   4 0 0

b. $ ⑨ 7 0 4 ⬅ **9 is in the thousands' place. Round to the nearest thousand dollars.**
        ↓
   $ 10 , 0 0 0

your turn

Round to the place of the leading digit.

9. 47

10. $3052

11. $950

12. 9181

practice exercises

practice for example 1 *(page 26)*

Round to the given place.

1. 24; nearest ten

2. 755; nearest ten

3. $452; nearest hundred dollars

4. $8275; nearest thousand dollars

5. 28,349; nearest thousand

6. 14,484; nearest hundred

7. $4620; nearest thousand dollars

8. $7082; nearest hundred dollars

practice for example 2 *(pages 26–27)*

Round to the given place.

9. 2972; nearest hundred

10. 961; nearest hundred

11. $19,999; nearest thousand dollars

12. $296; nearest ten dollars

13. 3099; nearest ten

14. 59,521; nearest thousand

15. 4997; nearest ten

16. 69,981; nearest hundred

practice for example 3 (page 27)

Round to the place of the leading digit.

17. 25 **18.** 62 **19.** 953 **20.** 433

21. $8878 **22.** $4563 **23.** $29,513 **24.** $99,742

mixed practice (pages 26–27)

Round to the place of the underlined digit.

25. 3̲6 **26.** 9̲2 **27.** 3̲94 **28.** 32̲84

29. 429̲5 **30.** 45̲63 **31.** 99̲5 **32.** 5̲64

33. $399̲7 **34.** $12̲56 **35.** $4̲4,214 **36.** $3,9̲66,024

37. Write four numbers that round to 1000.

38. Write three amounts that round to $23,000.

39. The Bike-Away Company manufactured 9746 bicycles last year. Write this number rounded to the nearest hundred.

40. Brookview High received $136,984 for computer equipment. Write this amount rounded to the nearest thousand dollars.

review exercises

Estimate by adjusting the sum of the front-end digits.

1. 238 + 389 + 458

2. 4326 + 2389 + 1355

3. 356 + 129 + 259 + 278

4. 41,257 + 85,926 + 32,108

5. 342 + 517 + 59 + 175

6. 2289 + 258 + 3276 + 2339

mental math

You need to recognize whether a number is likely to be an *exact* or a *rounded* number. Suppose that you heard this report on television.

> The city council is reviewing bids from two companies for the construction of an apartment complex on 10 acres at Cottage Farm. Part of the 10 acres is now a 75-space parking lot. The two bids are about $700,000 apart. However, the higher bid includes a proposal for 22 more units. The council met for nearly three hours today but did not reach a final decision.

1. Write all the exact numbers that appear in the report.

2. Write all the rounded numbers that appear in the report.

2-2 ROUNDING TO ESTIMATE SUMS AND DIFFERENCES

On Friday, 6981 people attended the tennis match. On Saturday, 8127 people attended. About how many people attended altogether? About how many more were there on Saturday?

To estimate the answers to these questions, you can round to the place of the leading digit.

$$6981 \rightarrow 7{,}000$$
$$\underline{+8127} \rightarrow \underline{+8{,}000}$$
$$\text{about } 15{,}000$$

$$8127 \rightarrow 8000$$
$$\underline{-6981} \rightarrow \underline{-7000}$$
$$\text{about } 1000$$

About 15,000 people attended altogether. There were about 1000 more people on Saturday than on Friday.

example 1

Estimate by rounding to the place of the leading digit.

a. $450 + $576 + $238 + $84

b.
$$9624$$
$$\underline{- \quad 873}$$

solution

a.
$$\begin{array}{rcl} \$450 & \rightarrow & \$500 \\ 576 & \rightarrow & 600 \\ 238 & \rightarrow & 200 \\ \underline{+ \quad 84} & \rightarrow & \underline{+ \quad 100} \\ & & \text{about } \$1400 \end{array}$$

Round 84 to the same place as the other addends.

b.
$$\begin{array}{rcl} 9624 & \rightarrow & 10{,}000 \\ \underline{- \quad 873} & \rightarrow & \underline{- \quad 1{,}000} \\ & & \text{about } 9{,}000 \end{array}$$

Round 873 to the same place as 9624.

your turn

Estimate by rounding to the place of the leading digit.

1. 5503 + 2457   **2.** 4668 − 1709   **3.** $98,982 − $7699   **4.** $3962 + $1499 + $729

Rounding to the place of the leading digit often yields as good an estimate for a sum or difference as is needed. However, sometimes you need to round to a place that is more appropriate to get a good estimate for a difference.

example 2

Estimate by rounding to appropriate digits.

a. 7489 − 6526   b. $65,172 − $4872

solution

a. If you round to the place of the leading digit, the estimate is 0. Round to
the hundreds' place instead.

$$\begin{array}{rcr} 7489 & \rightarrow & 7500 \\ -6526 & \rightarrow & -6500 \\ \hline & & \text{about } 1000 \end{array}$$

b. If you round to the place of the leading digit, the estimate is $70,000.
Round to the thousands' place instead.

$$\begin{array}{rcr} \$65,172 & \rightarrow & \$65,000 \\ - \quad 4,872 & \rightarrow & - \quad 5,000 \\ \hline & & \text{about } \$60,000 \end{array}$$

your turn

Estimate by rounding to appropriate digits.

5. 849 − 754   6. 9507 − 492   7. $24,444 − $15,555   8. $857,216 − $39,347

practice exercises

practice for example 1 (page 29)

Estimate by rounding to the place of the leading digit.

1. 28 + 77   2. 879 − 283   3. 46,287 − 18,421   4. 735 + 852 + 281

5. $779 − $95   6. $493 − $77   7. $824 + $419 + $79   8. $647 + $582 + $12

9. 4,692,861 − 1,826,419   10. 72,520,000 − 28,690,000

11. $264 + $169 + $387 + $56   12. $4821 + $864 + $1591 + $3222

practice for example 2 (page 30)

Estimate by rounding to appropriate digits.

13. 6415 − 5517   14. 8889 − 8507   15. $3523 − $486   16. $28,812 − $4495

17. $\begin{array}{r} 247,692 \\ -183,519 \end{array}$ 18. $\begin{array}{r} 178,217 \\ - \quad 42,519 \end{array}$ 19. $\begin{array}{r} \$1,627,514 \\ - \quad 494,936 \end{array}$ 20. $\begin{array}{r} \$6,389,426 \\ - \quad 5,509,968 \end{array}$

mixed practice (pages 29–30)

Estimate by rounding.

21. 4587 + 8473   22. 8614 − 3861   23. 74,802 − 12,093

24. 8308 − 972   25. $8575 − $458   26. $892 + $359 + $37

27. six hundred sixty-two minus ninety-four   28. the total of $428, $860, $233, and $85

Choose the letter of the best estimate.

29. $6039 - 3783$ **a.** 1000   **b.** 2000   **c.** 3000   **d.** 10,000

30. $6491 + 512$ **a.** 5000   **b.** 6000   **c.** 7000   **d.** 11,000

31. List the letters of *all* the differences for which 1000 is a good estimate.
   a. $3489 - 2506$ **b.** $3506 - 2489$ **c.** $1549 - 495$ **d.** $6487 - 4502$

32. List the letters of *all* the differences for which 300 is a good estimate.
   a. $649 - 34$ **b.** $652 - 350$ **c.** $650 - 349$ **d.** $649 - 350$

33. This year, Juan Lopez got a raise of $3750. His salary is now $36,660. About how much did he earn last year?

34. The Hayley Company sold $16,219,000 worth of goods last year and $22,316,000 worth this year. Estimate the increase in sales.

review *exercises*

Give the value of the underlined digit in each number.

1. 48<u>1</u>2   **2.** <u>5</u>6,482   **3.** 9,4<u>3</u>6,014   **4.** 1<u>1</u>,248,768

Find each sum or difference.

5. $61,902 - 5208$ **6.** $46 + 971 + 400$ **7.** $\$36 + \$74 + \$2$ **8.** $\$6075 - \$3429$

Evaluate each expression when $x = 7$, $y = 43$, and $z = 502$.

9. $75 + x + y$ **10.** $x + y + z + y$ **11.** $z - 117$ **12.** $y - x$

calculator corner

Sometimes you might make a mistake in entering an addition or a subtraction on a calculator. For example, you might enter a wrong number, or you might press the button for the wrong operation. For this reason, it is a good practice to estimate to check the *reasonableness* of an answer.

example   Use a calculator to find the difference: $73,186 - 8476$

solution $73186 - 8476 = 64710$ Estimate: $70,000 - 10,000 = 60,000$
                                              The calculator answer is reasonable.

Use a calculator to find each sum or difference. Estimate to check the answer.

1. $78,196 + 5976$ **2.** $4786 + 987$ **3.** $393,186 + 286,143$

4. $9787 - 8146$ **5.** $76,276 - 13,976$ **6.** $3,786,140 - 2,896,180$

7. $5,890,143 + 4,465,000$ **8.** $708,945 - 380,802$ **9.** $8505 + 7200 + 5825$

2-3 COMPARING WHOLE NUMBERS

To **compare** two whole numbers, use the following method.

1. If one number has more digits, then it is the greater number.

2. If both numbers have the same number of digits, compare from left to right. Find the first place in which the digits are different. The number with the greater digit in that place is the greater number.

3. Insert the correct symbol between the numbers.

> *is greater than*   < *is less than*   = *is equal to*

same

↓

1,$\boxed{2}$0 3, 0 0 0

1,$\boxed{0}$2 3, 0 0 0

2 > 0

So 1,203,000 > 1,023,000.

example 1

Compare. Replace each __?__ with >, <, or =.

a. 23,040 __?__ 230,040   **b.** 8254 __?__ 8213

solution

a.   23,040 ← 5 digits
       230,040 ← 6 digits   So 23,040 < 230,040.

b.   8 2 $\boxed{5}$ 4   5 > 1
        8 2 $\boxed{1}$ 3   So 8254 > 8213.

your turn

Compare. Replace each __?__ with >, <, or =.

1. 3150 __?__ 3105   **2.** 8045 __?__ 80,450   **3.** $29,781 __?__ $29,781

example 2

Write the numbers in order from least to greatest: 3809; 2965; 3780

solution

$\boxed{3}$ 8 0 9   2 < 3, so
$\boxed{2}$ 9 6 5   2965 is the
$\boxed{3}$ 7 8 0   *least* number.

3 $\boxed{8}$ 0 9   8 > 7, so
3 $\boxed{7}$ 8 0   3809 is the
            greatest number.

The numbers in order from least to greatest:
2965; 3780; 3809

your turn

Write each set of numbers in order from least to greatest.

4. 891; 749; 873   **5.** $4739; $4654; $473   **6.** 61,428; 60,322; 61,824

practice exercises

practice for example 1 (page 32)

Compare. Replace each __?__ with >, <, or =.

1. 4700 __?__ 4070
2. 5820 __?__ 5820
3. 991 __?__ 9170
4. 2763 __?__ 3767
5. $80,716 __?__ $80,761
6. $2136 __?__ $21,345

practice for example 2 (page 32)

Write each set of numbers in order from least to greatest.

7. 160; 284; 177
8. 8300; 8030; 830
9. 122,654; 122,550; 122,585
10. 364,181; 36,418; 360,181
11. $4151; $4157; $417
12. $5003; $5030; $50,003

mixed practice (page 32)

Tell whether each statement is *true* or *false*.

13. 1783 > 1873
14. 10,405 = 10,045
15. 987 < 1002
16. 4020 = 4002
17. $3,207,006 > $32,706
18. $56,329 < $53,629

Write each set of numbers in order from least to greatest.

19. 326; 362; 302; 300
20. 4179; 1749; 9471; 1471
21. $5674; $764; $50,677; $5921
22. $1565; $1556; $1506; $1550

Estimate each sum. Tell whether each estimate will be *less than* or *greater than* the actual sum.

23. 82,162 + 71,294
24. $78,624 + $67,859
25. Naima collected 467 seashells. Kenan collected 457, and Judy collected 576. Who collected the most seashells?
26. Arthur's income is $37,500 per year, Roger's is $29,400, and Miguel's is $38,400. Is Arthur's income greater than Roger's income or greater than Miguel's?

review exercises

Round to the place of the underlined digit.

1. 104,549
2. 2,165,043
3. 12,349,999
4. 7851
5. 2375
6. 45,298
7. 85,459
8. 12,993,456

2-4 BAR GRAPHS

A **graph** is a picture that displays and compares numerical facts. To compare facts about different things at a given time, you can use a **bar graph.** In a bar graph, you display facts along a **horizontal axis** (—) and a **vertical axis** (|). You use the **scale** along one of these *axes* either to determine or to estimate a numerical fact.

example 1

Use the bar graph at the right. How many students chose baseball?

solution

Each space on the scale represents 1 student. The bar for baseball ends at the mark between 8 and 10. *Nine* students chose baseball.

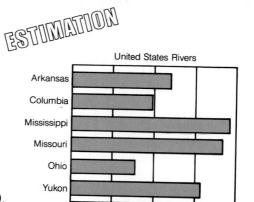

Homeroom Poll: Favorite Sports

your turn

Use the bar graph at the right.

1. How many students chose football as their favorite sport?
2. Which sports were the favorite of fewer than eight students?

example 2

ESTIMATION

Use the bar graph at the right. Estimate the length of each river.

a. Yukon   b. Ohio

solution

United States Rivers

a. The bar ends between 3000 and 4000, but closer to 3000.
   The length of the Yukon is about 3000 km.
b. The bar ends midway between 1000 and 2000.
   The length of the Ohio is about 1500 km.

your turn

Use the bar graph at the right. Estimate the length of each river.

3. Mississippi   4. Arkansas   5. Columbia   6. Missouri

example 3

Draw a bar graph to display the given information.

United States Dams

Name of Dam	Gatun	Grand Coulee	Hoover	Oroville	Shasta
Height in Feet (ft)	115	550	726	770	602

solution

- Draw the axes.
- The greatest number is 770, so draw a scale from 0 to 800. Let each space represent 100 ft.
- Draw one bar to represent the height of each dam. Estimate the length of the bar when necessary.
- Label each bar and the numerical axis.
- Title the graph.

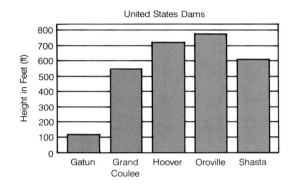

your turn

7. Draw a bar graph to display the given information.

Planets of the Solar System

Name of Planet	Mercury	Venus	Earth	Mars	Pluto
Diameter in Miles (mi)	3030	7517	7921	4215	2173

practice exercises

practice for example 1 (page 34)

Use the bar graph at the right. Determine the number of championships for each team.

1. Bears
2. Jets
3. Lions
4. Rockets
5. Which teams have more championships than the Rockets?
6. Which teams have fewer than ten championships?

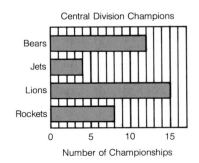

practice for example 2 (page 34)

Use the bar graph at the right. Estimate the height of each mountain.

7. Aconcagua   8. Everest

9. Kilimanjaro   10. McKinley

11. Which mountains are shorter than Mount Aconcagua?

12. Which mountains have heights greater than 6000 m?

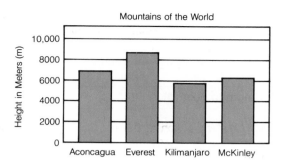

Mountains of the World

practice for example 3 (page 35)

13. Draw a bar graph to display the given information.

Mountains of the United States

Name of Mountain	Mauna Kea	McKinley	Pikes Peak	Rainier	Whitney
Height in Feet (ft)	13,825	20,320	14,110	14,408	14,495

mixed practice (pages 34–35)

14. Draw a bar graph to display the given information.

Known Depths of Oceans and Seas

Ocean or Sea	Arctic	Atlantic	Indian	Mediterranean	Pacific
Depth in Meters (m)	5625	9219	7455	4632	10,918

Use the bar graph that you drew for Exercise 14.

15. Which ocean or sea has the greatest known depth?

16. List the oceans and seas in order from least to greatest known depth.

17. Choose a topic such as sports, TV shows, or movies. Poll the students in your math class about their favorites. Make a bar graph that displays the results of your poll.

review exercises

Write the short word form of each number.

1. 32,427,018   2. 27,592   3. 1,000,791   4. 42,000,013

5. 7869   6. 82,000   7. 14,000,460   8. 19,000,000,000

2-5 LINE GRAPHS

To compare facts about one thing over a period of time, you can use a
line graph. A line graph shows both an *amount* and a *direction* of
change. The direction of change may be an **increase** or a **decrease.**

example 1

Use the line graph at the right. What was the
enrollment in 1985?

solution

Locate 1985 on the horizontal axis.
Move up to the point, then left to the vertical
axis. Each space on the scale represents 1 million.
The enrollment was about 44 million.

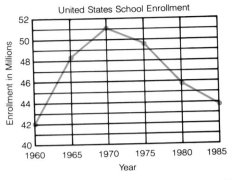

your turn

Use the line graph at the right.

1. What was the enrollment in 1970?
2. Between which two given years was there
   the greatest decrease?

example 2

Draw a line graph to display the given information.

United States National Parks

Year	1955	1960	1965	1970	1975	1980	1985
Number of Parks	28	29	32	35	38	48	48

solution

- Mark a scale from 20 to 50 on the vertical axis.
  Let each space represent 2 parks.
- Draw 7 vertical lines on the horizontal axis.
  Label them with the given years.
- Place a point on the graph for each year and the
  corresponding number of parks. Estimate the
  position of the point when necessary.
- Connect the points from left to right.
- Label the axes and title the graph.

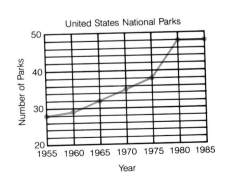

Rounding and Comparing Whole Numbers 37

your turn

3. Draw a line graph to display the given information.

Average Life Expectancy in the United States

Year of Birth	1920	1930	1940	1950	1960	1970	1980
Life Expectancy in Years	54	60	63	68	70	71	74

practice exercises

practice for example 1 (page 37)

Use the line graph at the right. Find the number of active volcanos in the given year.

1. 1930   2. 1950   3. 1920

4. 1940   5. 1960   6. 1980

Use the line graph at the right. Tell whether there was an *increase* or *decrease* between the given years.

7. 1930 and 1940   8. 1960 and 1970

9. Between which two given years was there the greatest increase in the number of active volcanos?

10. Between which two given years was there the greatest decrease in the number of active volcanos?

practice for example 2 (pages 37–38)

Draw a line graph to display the given information.

11. ### Average Temperatures for St. Louis, Missouri

Month	J	F	M	A	M	J	J	A	S	O	N	D
Temperature in Degrees Celsius (°C)	0	2	6	14	19	24	26	25	21	15	7	1

12. ### United States Passenger Railroads

Year	1955	1960	1965	1970	1975	1980	1985
Number of Cars in Service in Thousands	32	26	20	11	7	4	3

mixed practice (pages 37–38)

13. Draw a line graph to display the given information.

Price of Gasoline in the United States

Year	1974	1976	1978	1980	1982	1984	1986
Average Price in Cents per Gallon	53	59	63	119	122	113	81

14. Use the line graph that you drew for Exercise 13. Between which two given years was there the greatest increase in the price of gasoline?

Tell whether it would be more appropriate to draw a *bar graph* or a *line graph* to display the given information. Then draw the graph.

15. United States Population

Year	Population
1920	105,710,620
1930	122,775,046
1940	131,669,275
1950	150,697,361
1960	179,323,175
1970	203,302,031
1980	226,545,805

16. Continents of the World

Continent	Area in Square Miles (mi²)
Africa	11,694,000
Antarctica	5,100,000
Asia	16,968,000
Australia	2,966,000
Europe	4,066,000
North America	9,363,000
South America	6,886,000

review exercises

Estimate each sum or difference.

1. $98,500 - 81,488$

2. $5490 - 4781$

3. $4591 + 3322$

4. $981 + 8955$

5. $45,495 - 3996$

6. $29,880 + 56,003$

7. $699 + 145 + 208 + 69$

8. $451 + 302 + 93 + 248$

Find the next letter in this pattern: O, T, T, F, F, S, S, ___?___

2-6 UNDERSTANDING THE PROBLEM

In order to solve a problem, you must first understand it. Part of understanding a problem is identifying the facts that you need to know in order to answer the question.

example 1

Determine the missing fact that is needed to answer the question.

a. Robert bought three shirts. How much did he pay for them?

b. Tickets worth a total of $88,870 were sold. What was the profit?

solution

a. Given: three shirts
   Find: total cost
   Missing: the amount paid
            for each shirt

b. Given: total worth of tickets
   Find: profit
   Missing: the expenses

your turn

Determine the missing fact that is needed to answer the question.

1. Leslie paid $48 for dinner plates. How much did each plate cost?

2. If you buy a shirt and shorts for $52, how much do the shorts cost?

    Once you have solved a problem, you should check to see if the answer is reasonable. One way to do this is to estimate the answer.

example 2

Tell whether the given answer is *reasonable* or *not reasonable*.

Problem: Find 843 decreased by 247.   Answer: 1090

ESTIMATION

solution

Decreased by means to subtract. An estimate of $843 - 247$ is about 600. So the answer, 1090, is *not reasonable*.

your turn

Tell whether the given answer is *reasonable* or *not reasonable*.

3. Problem: Find the total of 337, 119, 225, and 208.

         Answer: 889

4. Problem: Joe paid $400 for his VCR. Jason paid $299 for his. How much more did Joe pay than Jason?

         Answer: $201

problems

practice for example 1 (page 40)

Determine the missing fact that is needed to answer the question.

1. One pen costs $2. How many pens can you buy?
2. Jesse and Diane each worked half the time. How long did each work?

practice for example 2 (page 40)

Tell whether the given answer is *reasonable* or *not reasonable*.

3. Joe jogs for 30 min (minutes), then spends 90 min walking. How much time does he spend on these two activities?   Answer: 60 min
4. Find the total of 349, 79, 722, and 447.   Answer: 1597

mixed practice (page 40)

Answer the question in red.

5. Stephanie made a $30 down payment on a coat. She then made weekly payments of $18. How much did she pay for the coat? What missing fact is needed before you can solve?

6. If you buy four posters, how much change will you receive? What missing facts are needed before you can solve?

7. Kim paid $89 each way to fly round-trip from Boston to Cleveland. Mary paid $119 for the round-trip fare. Who paid more? How much more? Is it reasonable to answer that Mary paid $30 more than Kim?

8. It takes John 40 min to deliver newspapers on his route. It takes his brother 70 min when he substitutes for John. How long would it take for them to deliver the papers together? Is the answer 55 min reasonable?

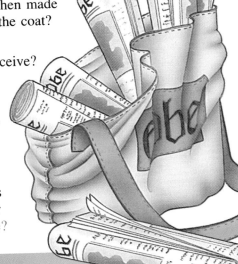

review exercises

Write the numeral form of each number.

1. two hundred twenty-six million
2. seven hundred eight
3. thirty billion, four thousand
4. seventy million, four hundred five
5. 447 million, 86 thousand, 973
6. 174 million, 223 thousand, 95
7. 92 billion, 7 thousand, 421
8. 4 million, 300 thousand, 17

SKILL REVIEW

Round to the place of the underlined digit.

1. 6̲3
2. 1̲79

3. $59̲6
4. $12̲,634

2-1

Estimate by rounding.

5. 387 + 426 + 85
6. $8199 − $2849
7. 9415 − 8760 2-2

Compare. Replace each __?__ with >, <, or =.

8. 5207 __?__ 5702
9. 74,321 __?__ 47,231
10. 9068 __?__ 9068 2-3

Write each set of numbers in order from least to greatest.

11. 487; 462; 591
12. $16,032; $10,632; $16,302
13. 50,216; 49,216; 57,489
14. $2398; $1367; $2309

15. Draw a bar graph to display the given information.

2-4

Cost of Compact Disc Players

Name of Model	XJ-6	Tonie	Super-M	X-cel
Cost in Dollars	530	460	260	310

16. Use the bar graph that you drew for Exercise 15. Which models cost more than $400?

17. Draw a line graph to display the given information.

2-5

Cable Television Subscribers

Year	1970	1975	1980	1985
Number of Subscribers	5,100,000	9,800,000	17,500,000	38,000,000

18. Use the graph that you drew for Exercise 17. Between which two given years was there the greatest increase?

Answer the question in red.

19. Kathie earns $2 per hour babysitting. How much did she earn? 2-6
    What missing fact is needed before you can solve?

20. Find the result when 1759 is increased by 730.
    Is the answer 1832 reasonable?

2-7 ELAPSED TIME

The amount of time that passes between the start and end of an event is the **elapsed time.** For instance, Danielle worked at the library from 9:45 A.M. until 4:15 P.M. If you compute the elapsed time, you find that she worked 6 h (hours) 30 min (minutes).

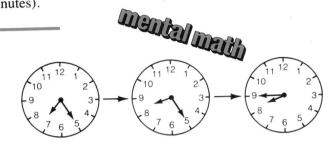

example

Aaron boarded the bus at 7:25 A.M. He arrived at his destination at 8:45 A.M. Find the elapsed time.

solution

Think of a clock and count forward:

7:25 to 8:25 → one hour
8:25 to 8:45 → 20 min

The elapsed time is 1 h 20 min.

exercises

Find the elapsed time.

1. 2:42 A.M. to 12:00 noon
2. 5:55 P.M. to 9:58 P.M.
3. 8:40 A.M. to 3:40 P.M.
4. 11:36 A.M. to 4:39 P.M.
5. 1:55 A.M. to 8:36 P.M.
6. 7:05 A.M. to 3:25 P.M.
7. 12:30 A.M. to 12:30 P.M.
8. 2:45 P.M. to 11:15 A.M.

9. Joel began rewinding a film at 8:12 P.M. He completed the rewind at 8:17 P.M. Find the elapsed time.

10. Dawn began working on the computer at 12:47 P.M. She finished at 2:35 P.M. Find the elapsed time.

11. Malcolm's class schedule is shown at the right. Find the elapsed time from the start of one activity to the start of the next. Then find the total elapsed time for the school day.

12. Make a schedule for your school day. Find the elapsed time between each activity and the total elapsed time for the day.

morning assembly	8:30 A.M.
math class	8:50 A.M.
English class	9:35 A.M.
gym class	10:23 A.M.
computer lab	11:25 A.M.
lunch	12:30 P.M.
Spanish class	1:15 P.M.
art class	1:58 P.M.
dismissal	2:45 P.M.

2-8 PLANNING A MEAL

Ms. Mach is planning a family dinner. She decided on a menu and then estimated the preparation and cooking times for each course.

example

Use the menu shown at the right.

a. About how long will it take to prepare and cook the squash?

b. Ms. Mach wants dinner to be ready at 6:00 P.M. When should she start cooking the potatoes?

Menu	Preparation Time	Cooking Time
roast turkey	30 min	4 h
mashed potatoes	30 min	20 min
squash	10 min	30 min
green beans	5 min	15 min
rolls	5 min	40 min

solution

a. It takes 10 min to prepare and 30 min to cook the squash.
Think: 10 + 30 = 40
It will take 40 min to prepare and cook the squash.

b. The potatoes take 20 min to cook.
Think of a clock set at 6:00.
Count back 20 min.
She should start cooking the potatoes at 5:40 P.M.

exercises

Use the menu shown above.

1. About how long will it take to prepare the rolls?

2. Which takes longer to prepare, squash or rolls?

3. About how long will it take to prepare and cook the beans?

4. About how much longer does the squash take to cook than the beans?

5. Which should Ms. Mach start cooking first, the squash or the rolls?

6. Which should Ms. Mach start cooking first, the potatoes or the beans?

7. Ms. Mach wants dinner to start at 6:00 P.M. The turkey should cool 30 min before serving. At what time should she start to prepare the turkey?

CHAPTER REVIEW

vocabulary vo·cab·u·lar·y

Choose the correct phrase to complete each sentence.

1. The symbol > means (*is less than, is greater than*).
2. When part of a line graph rises from left to right, the direction of change is (*an increase, a decrease*).

skills

Round to the place of the underlined digit.

3. 4<u>7</u>6

4. <u>8</u>9,670

5. $104,9<u>8</u>2

6. $60<u>9</u>7

Choose the letter of the best estimate.

7. 27,389 + 58,426 + 5291
   a. 70,000   **b.** 100,000   **c.** 140,000

8. $85,419 − $4889
   a. $40,000   **b.** $80,000   **c.** $90,000

Tell whether each statement is *true* or *false*.

9. 4020 > 4002

10. $11,716 = $1716

11. 92,503 < 92,501

12. $29,165 > $2916

Use the bar graph at the right.

13. Estimate the number of people who favor canoeing.

14. Name the sports in order from the most favorite to the least favorite.

15. Draw a line graph to display the given information.

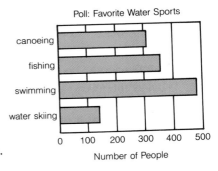

Poll: Favorite Water Sports

Video Club Membership

Year	1980	1981	1982	1983	1984
Number of Members	28	40	65	62	31

16. A skirt and blouse cost $120. You are asked to find the cost of the blouse. What missing fact is needed?

17. Find the elapsed time from 8:30 A.M. to 4:25 P.M.

18. Veal stew takes 40 min to prepare and 2 h 30 min to cook. When will the stew be ready if you begin to prepare it at 4:00 P.M.?

CHAPTER TEST

Round to the given place.

2-1

1. $46,952; nearest hundred dollars
2. 7430; nearest thousand
3. $87,096; nearest ten dollars
4. 18,211; nearest ten thousand

Estimate by rounding.

2-2

5. $85,391 − $26,499
6. $482 + $910 + $80
7. 25,674 − 4967
8. Tower Records sold $67,890,000 worth of records last year and $123,420,000 worth this year. Estimate the increase in sales.

Compare. Replace each __?__ with >, <, or =.

2-3

9. $317 __?__ $872
10. 21,087 __?__ 21,087
11. 9017 __?__ 1079
12. BookEnds has 76 maps, 36 novels, and 15 cookbooks in stock. List the stock in order from the least quantity to the greatest.

13. Draw a bar graph to display the given information.

2-4

Student Council Election: President

Candidate	Margie	Alex	Jared	Becky	Gladys
Number of Votes	123	79	137	220	84

Use the line graph at the right.

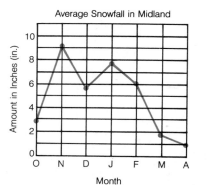

Average Snowfall in Midland

14. In which month is there the greatest average snowfall?

2-5

15. What is the average snowfall in October?

Answer the question in red.

16. The total cost of the tickets was $48. Find the cost of one ticket. What missing fact is needed?

2-6

17. Find the total of 4260 and 7811. Is the answer 12,071 reasonable?

Find the elapsed time.

18. 8:15 A.M. to 1:30 P.M.

2-7

19. 4:50 P.M. to 11:03 P.M.

20. Chicken wings take 20 min to prepare and 45 min to cook. If you want to eat at 6:00 P.M., at what time should you begin to prepare?

2-8

When objects such as these decoys are arranged
in rows and columns, you can find the total
number easily by using multiplication.

CHAPTER 3

MULTIPLYING WHOLE NUMBERS

3-1 MULTIPLYING BY MULTIPLES OF 10, 100, AND 1000

An addition in which all the addends are the same can be written as a multiplication.

$$\underbrace{7 + 7 + 7 + 7}_{\textbf{addends}} = \underset{\textbf{sum}}{28} \qquad \underbrace{4 \times 7}_{\textbf{factors}} = \underset{\textbf{product}}{28}$$

example 1

Write the corresponding addition. Then find the sum.

a. 3×80 **b.** 3×700 **c.** 2×9000

solution

a. $80 + 80 + 80 = 240$ **b.** $700 + 700 + 700 = 2100$ **c.** $9000 + 9000 = 18,000$

your turn

Write the corresponding addition. Then find the sum.

1. 7×60 **2.** 6×900 **3.** 8×8000 **4.** 4×5000

Now consider the multiplications in Example 1 in a different way.

$3 \times 8 \ \ = 24$ $\qquad 3 \times 7 \ \ \ = 21$ $\qquad 2 \times 9 \ \ \ = 18$

$3 \times 80 = 240$ $\qquad 3 \times 700 = 2100$ $\qquad 2 \times 9000 = 18,000$

To multiply by *multiples* of 10, 100, or 1000, use the following method.

1. Multiply the nonzero digits.

2. To this product, annex the total number of zeros in the factors.

example 2

Find each product.

a. 40×600 **b.** 500×8000

mental math

solution

a. $4 \ \ \times 6 \ \ \ = 24$
$40 \times 600 = 24,000$ ← **Annex 3 zeros.**

b. $5 \ \ \ \times 8 \ \ \ = 40$
$500 \times 8000 = 4,000,000$ ← **Annex 5 zeros.**

your turn

Find each product.

5. 2×30 **6.** 50×90 **7.** 400×200 **8.** 600×5000

practice exercises

practice for example 1 (page 48)

Write the corresponding addition. Then find the sum.

1. 4×20
2. 3×90
3. 2×800
4. 3×500
5. 6×800
6. 8×900
7. 5×400
8. 6×500
9. 4×3000
10. 7×6000
11. 2×5000
12. 5×6000

practice for example 2 (page 48)

Find each product.

13. 6×30
14. 9×40
15. 80×50
16. 70×30
17. 80×700
18. 90×400
19. 60×6000
20. 30×8000
21. 600×200
22. 800×400
23. 500×600
24. 400×500
25. 500×9000
26. 700×3000
27. $200 \times 12,000$
28. $400 \times 12,000$

mixed practice (page 48)

Find each answer.

29. $30 + 30 + 30 + 30 + 30$
30. 8×1100
31. $700 + 700 + 700$
32. $9000 + 9000 + 9000 + 9000$
33. 9×4000
34. 500×7000
35. $60 + 60 + 60 + 60 + 60 + 60$
36. 1200×400
37. $8 \times 90,000$
38. 2000×5000
39. $700 \times 40,000$
40. $6000 \times 10,000$

41. A total of 12,000 people paid $20 each to attend a concert. How much money was collected from the sale of these tickets?

42. A construction company needs to order 5000 steel beams for a new building. If each beam weighs 200 lb (pounds), what will be the total weight of the shipment of steel beams?

review exercises

Find each product.

1. 8×9
2. 7×6
3. 4×7
4. 9×6
5. 7×8
6. 3×8
7. 6×4
8. 7×9
9. 12×5
10. 9×4
11. 6×12
12. 8×6
13. 4×8
14. 12×7
15. 9×9
16. 12×8
17. 9×5
18. 7×7
19. 8×8
20. 5×12

3-2 MULTIPLYING BY A ONE-DIGIT NUMBER

To buy new uniforms, Kim's basketball team sold 175 boxes of greeting cards last week and three times as many boxes this week. You can multiply 175 by 3 to find that the team sold 525 boxes this week.

To multiply by a one-digit number, use the following method.

1. Multiply the ones' digit. Rename, if necessary.

$$\begin{array}{r} {\scriptstyle 1} \\ 1\,7\,5 \\ \times 3 \\ \hline 5 \end{array}$$

2. Multiply the tens' digit. Add and rename, if necessary.

$$\begin{array}{r} {\scriptstyle 2\;1} \\ 1\,7\,5 \\ \times 3 \\ \hline 2\,5 \end{array}$$

3. Continue column-by-column from right to left.

$$\begin{array}{r} {\scriptstyle 2\;1} \\ 1\,7\,5 \\ \times 3 \\ \hline 5\,2\,5 \end{array}$$

example 1

Find each product.

a.
$$\begin{array}{r} 2\,1 \\ \times 5 \\ \hline 1\,0\,5 \end{array}$$

b.
$$\begin{array}{r} {\scriptstyle 1\;4} \\ \$\,4\,2\,7 \\ \times 6 \\ \hline \$\,2\,5\,6\,2 \end{array}$$

c.
$$\begin{array}{r} {\scriptstyle 3\;3} \\ 2\,8\,0\,9 \\ \times 4 \\ \hline 1\,1{,}2\,3\,6 \end{array}$$

d.
$$\begin{array}{r} {\scriptstyle 4\;3\;1} \\ 1\,5{,}4\,2\,0 \\ \times 9 \\ \hline 1\,3\,8{,}7\,8\,0 \end{array}$$

your turn

Find each product.

1.
$$\begin{array}{r} \$43 \\ \times 2 \end{array}$$

2.
$$\begin{array}{r} 78 \\ \times 5 \end{array}$$

3.
$$\begin{array}{r} 824 \\ \times 7 \end{array}$$

4.
$$\begin{array}{r} \$53{,}044 \\ \times 8 \end{array}$$

example 2

Find each product: **a.** 9×5228 **b.** $3 \times \$21{,}029$

solution

a.
$$\begin{array}{r} {\scriptstyle 2\;2\;7} \\ 5\,2\,2\,8 \\ \times 9 \\ \hline 4\,7{,}0\,5\,2 \end{array}$$
← **Rewrite the multiplication in vertical form.**

b.
$$\begin{array}{r} {\scriptstyle 2} \\ \$2\,1{,}0\,2\,9 \\ \times 3 \\ \hline \$6\,3{,}0\,8\,7 \end{array}$$

your turn

Find each product.

5. 7×355 **6.** 8×5923 **7.** $6 \times \$90{,}843$ **8.** $2 \times \$77{,}542$

Estimating a product before you multiply helps
you tell if your answer is reasonable.

example 3

Estimate each product.

a. 9×87 **b.** $7 \times \$243$

ESTIMATION

solution

a.
$$\begin{array}{r} 87 \\ \times 9 \end{array} \rightarrow \begin{array}{r} 90 \\ \times 9 \\ \hline \text{about } 810 \end{array}$$

← Round
multi-digit
factors to
the place of
the leading
digit.

b.
$$\begin{array}{r} \$243 \\ \times 7 \end{array} \rightarrow \begin{array}{r} \$200 \\ \times 7 \\ \hline \text{about } \$1400 \end{array}$$

your turn

Estimate each product.

9. 8×64 **10.** 9×506

11. $6 \times \$4750$ **12.** $7 \times \$38,499$

practice exercises

practice for example 1 (page 50)

Find each product.

1. $\begin{array}{r} 24 \\ \times 2 \end{array}$
2. $\begin{array}{r} 18 \\ \times 4 \end{array}$
3. $\begin{array}{r} \$869 \\ \times 3 \end{array}$
4. $\begin{array}{r} \$557 \\ \times 6 \end{array}$

5. $\begin{array}{r} \$1239 \\ \times 3 \end{array}$
6. $\begin{array}{r} \$4162 \\ \times 9 \end{array}$
7. $\begin{array}{r} 38,006 \\ \times 7 \end{array}$
8. $\begin{array}{r} 64,783 \\ \times 5 \end{array}$

practice for example 2 (page 50)

Find each product.

9. $2 \times \$347$ **10.** $8 \times \$913$ **11.** 4×3701

12. 3×6832 **13.** $6 \times \$88,912$ **14.** $7 \times \$47,276$

practice for example 3 (page 51)

Estimate each product.

15. 6×47 **16.** 8×77

17. $5 \times \$122$ **18.** $6 \times \$318$

19. $5 \times \$99,512$ **20.** $8 \times \$45,448$

mixed practice (pages 50–51)

Find each product.

21. 73
    ×5

22. 94
    ×3

23. $49
    ×6

24. $36
    ×3

25. 563
    ×9

26. 327
    ×8

27. $8035
    ×5

28. $6172
    ×9

29. 2345
    ×4

30. 6419
    ×5

31. 52,158
    ×8

32. 63,409
    ×2

33. 5 × 44

34. 9 × 95

35. 8 × $87

36. 2 × $73

37. 4 × 212

38. 6 × 501

39. 7 × $499

40. 4 × $305

41. 8 × 790

42. 3 × 446

43. 5 × 1987

44. 7 × 1899

45. 9 × 4008

46. 3 × 7127

47. 6 × 30,446

48. 8 × 48,522

49. Mario plans to swim 9 laps of the pool every day to practice for the swim meet. About how many laps will he swim in 48 days?

50. There are six families living in an apartment building. If each family pays $425 rent each month, how much rent does the owner of the building collect each month?

Estimate to tell if each answer is reasonable. Then correct each unreasonable answer by finding the product.

51. $6 \times 42 \stackrel{?}{=} 252$

52. $9 \times 38 \stackrel{?}{=} 542$

53. $4 \times 79 \stackrel{?}{=} 2836$

54. $7 \times 29 \stackrel{?}{=} 203$

55. $3 \times 289 \stackrel{?}{=} 647$

56. $2 \times 895 \stackrel{?}{=} 17,810$

review exercises

Find each sum or difference.

1. 1422 + 896

2. 106 − 48

3. $24 + $178 + $19

4. $803 − $9

5. 4005 − 697

6. 30 + 9 + 498

7. 316 + 447 + 907

8. 10,418 − 1036

puzzle corner

In your dresser drawer there are ten blue socks and sixteen red socks. What is the least number of socks you must take out (without looking) to get two socks that match?

3-3 MULTIPLYING BY A TWO-DIGIT NUMBER

To multiply by a two-digit number, you can extend
the method you used to multiply by a one-digit number.

1. Multiply by the ones' digit.
2. Multiply by the tens' digit.
3. Add the partial products.

$$\begin{array}{r} 78 \\ \times 26 \\ \hline 468 \\ 1560 \\ \hline 2028 \end{array}$$

← Multiply by 6.
← Multiply by 20.

example 1

Find each product: **a.** 19×84 **b.** 37×145 **c.** 52×604

solution

a.
$$\begin{array}{r} 84 \\ \times 19 \\ \hline 756 \\ 840 \\ \hline 1596 \end{array}$$

b.
$$\begin{array}{r} 145 \\ \times 37 \\ \hline 1015 \\ 435 \\ \hline 5365 \end{array}$$

You don't need to
write the zero.
You can just
leave a space.

c.
$$\begin{array}{r} 604 \\ \times 52 \\ \hline 1208 \\ 3020 \\ \hline 31,408 \end{array}$$

your turn

Find each product.

1. 12×27 **2.** 43×69 **3.** 62×581 **4.** 55×1074

A good habit to form is to check the reasonableness of your answer
by estimating.

example 2

ESTIMATION

Find the product 72×235. Check the reasonableness of your answer.

solution

$$\begin{array}{r} 235 \\ \times 72 \\ \hline 470 \\ 1645 \\ \hline 16,920 \end{array}$$

Estimate: 72×235
$\downarrow$ $\downarrow$ } about 14,000
70×200

Round each factor
to the place of the
leading digit.

← reasonable answer

your turn

Find each product. Check the reasonableness of your answer.

5. 38×76 **6.** 19×54 **7.** 23×207 **8.** 87×979

Knowing some information about an estimate gives you more help in deciding whether an answer is reasonable.

ESTIMATION

example 3

Estimate each product. Write whether the estimate is an *overestimate*, an *underestimate*, or if you *can't tell*.

a. 27 × 89   **b.** 34 × 845   **c.** 65 × 128

solution

a. 27 × 89
↓   ↓   Both factors are rounded *up*.
30 × 90   2700 is *greater than* the actual product.
about 2700 ←2700 is an *overestimate*.

b. 34 × 845
↓   ↓   Both factors are rounded *down*.
30 × 800   24,000 is *less than* the actual product.
about 24,000 ←24,000 is an *underestimate*.

c. 65 × 128
↓   ↓   One factor is rounded *up*,
70 × 100   and the other is rounded *down*.
about 7000 ←You *can't tell* if 7000 is an overestimate or an underestimate.

your turn

Estimate each product. Write whether the estimate is an *overestimate*, an *underestimate*, or if you *can't tell*.

9. 35 × 76   **10.** 28 × 449   **11.** 34 × 567   **12.** 6 × 829

practice exercises

practice for example 1 (page 53)

Find each product.

1. 25 × 53   **2.** 32 × 11   **3.** 28 × 92   **4.** 63 × 40   **5.** 89 × 17
6. 29 × 94   **7.** 43 × 362   **8.** 16 × 179   **9.** 64 × 299   **10.** 83 × 708

practice for example 2 (page 53)

Find each product. Check the reasonableness of your answer.

11. 81 × 93   **12.** 27 × 45   **13.** 26 × 79   **14.** 63 × 84   **15.** 15 × 28
16. 74 × 91   **17.** 51 × 239   **18.** 17 × 653   **19.** 64 × 305   **20.** 36 × 678

Estimate. Write whether the estimate is an *overestimate*, an *underestimate*, or if you *can't tell*.

21. 84 × 86   **22.** 32 × 11   **23.** 92 × 28   **24.** 95 × 65   **25.** 77 × 46

26. 53 × 24   **27.** 59 × 287   **28.** 64 × 849   **29.** 52 × 163   **30.** 17 × 335

Find each product. Check the reasonableness of your answer.

31. 19 × 67   **32.** 42 × 82   **33.** 99 × 34   **34.** 57 × 12   **35.** 24 × 89

36. 25 × 78   **37.** 74 × 56   **38.** 81 × 63   **39.** 39 × 21   **40.** 50 × 72

41. 39 × 987   **42.** 52 × 846   **43.** 74 × 531   **44.** 65 × 905   **45.** 63 × 724

46. 91 × 408   **47.** 23 × 417   **48.** 68 × 764   **49.** 57 × 349   **50.** 82 × 698

Choose the letter of the best estimate for each product.

51. 47 × 59   **a.** 3000   **b.** 2400   **c.** 2000

52. 24 × 73   **a.** 1400   **b.** 14,000   **c.** 140,000

53. 97 × 57   **a.** 600   **b.** 6000   **c.** 60,000

54. 78 × 295   **a.** 14,000   **b.** 21,000   **c.** 24,000

55. 32 × 412   **a.** 20,000   **b.** 12,000   **c.** 16,000

56. 92 × 902   **a.** 81,000   **b.** 92,000   **c.** 90,000

57. If you earn $12 each time you cut the neighbors' lawn, about how much money would you have after cutting it 39 times?

58. Greta bought a stereo system by paying $126 a month for 36 months. How much did the stereo system cost her?

review exercises

Find each answer.

1. 3006 − 1579   **2.** 3 × 59

3. 4098 + 697   **4.** 7 × 84

5. 80,365 + 2608   **6.** 3017 − 892

Estimate each answer.

7. 54,815 + 76,987   **8.** 756 − 49

9. 9 × 374   **10.** 6 × 8399

3-4 MULTIPLYING BY A THREE-DIGIT NUMBER

In one year, Bob did 152 sit-ups every day. Since there are 365 days in a year, you multiply 152 by 365 to find that Bob did 55,480 sit-ups in all.

To multiply by a three-digit number, you can again extend the method you used to multiply by a two-digit number.

1. Multiply by the ones' digit.
2. Multiply by the tens' digit.
3. Multiply by the hundreds' digit.
4. Add the partial products.

$$
\begin{array}{r}
1\,5\,2 \\
\times 3\,6\,5 \\
\hline
7\,6\,0 \\
9\,1\,2\,0 \\
4\,5\,6\,0\,0 \\
\hline
5\,5{,}4\,8\,0
\end{array}
$$

← **Multiply by 5.**
← **Multiply by 60.**
← **Multiply by 300.**

example 1

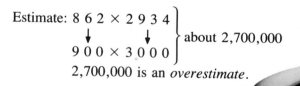

Find each product. Check the reasonableness of your answer.

a. 137 × 328   **b.** 862 × 2934

solution

a.

$$
\begin{array}{r}
3\,2\,8 \\
\times 1\,3\,7 \\
\hline
2\,2\,9\,6 \\
9\,8\,4 \\
3\,2\,8 \\
\hline
4\,4{,}9\,3\,6
\end{array}
$$

Estimate: 1 3 7 × 3 2 8
              ↓   ↓   } about 30,000
              1 0 0 × 3 0 0

30,000 is an *underestimate*.

← **reasonable answer**

b.

$$
\begin{array}{r}
2\,9\,3\,4 \\
\times 8\,6\,2 \\
\hline
5\,8\,6\,8 \\
1\,7\,6\,0\,4 \\
2\,3\,4\,7\,2 \\
\hline
2{,}5\,2\,9{,}1\,0\,8
\end{array}
$$

Estimate: 8 6 2 × 2 9 3 4
              ↓   ↓   } about 2,700,000
              9 0 0 × 3 0 0 0

2,700,000 is an *overestimate*.

← **reasonable answer**

your turn

Find each product. Check the reasonableness of your answer.

1. 366 × 472
2. 143 × 725
3. 434 × 5018
4. 277 × 9561

example 2

Find each product. Check the reasonableness of your answer.

a. 394×208 **b.** 924×1577

solution

a.
```
      2 0 8
    ×3 9 4
      8 3 2
    1 8 7 2
    6 2 4
  8 1,9 5 2
```
◄ **reasonable answer**

Estimate: 3 9 4 × 2 0 8 ↓   ↓ } about 80,000
         4 0 0 × 2 0 0

You can't tell if the estimate is *over* or *under*.

b.
```
    1 5 7 7
    ×9 2 4
    6 3 0 8
    3 1 5 4
  1 4 1 9 3
  1,4 5 7,1 4 8
```
◄ **reasonable answer**

Estimate: 9 2 4 × 1 5 7 7 ↓   ↓ } about 1,800,000
         9 0 0 × 2 0 0 0

You can't tell if the estimate is *over* or *under*.

The estimate 1,800,000 tells you that an answer such as 14,234,448 or 179,778 would not be reasonable.

your turn

Find each product. Check the reasonableness of your answer.

5. 690×912 **6.** 225×1865 **7.** 831×567

practice exercises

---

practice for example 1 (page 56)

Find each product. Check the reasonableness of your answer.

1. 123×665 **2.** 469×215 **3.** 812×522 **4.** 912×417 **5.** 785×467

6. 541×819 **7.** 134×4107 **8.** 795×4038 **9.** 264×8659 **10.** 261×6357

---

practice for example 2 (page 57)

Find each product. Check the reasonableness of your answer.

11. 221×387 **12.** 572×714 **13.** 861×133

14. 492×609 **15.** 375×501 **16.** 913×913

17. 732×4894 **18.** 924×1705 **19.** 658×5084

20. 415×7798 **21.** 298×6116 **22.** 747×2005

Multiplying Whole Numbers 57

mixed practice (pages 56–57)

Find each product. **Check the reasonableness of your answer.**

23. 375 × 684   24. 219 × 436   25. 873 × 941   26. 526 × 925
27. 680 × 432   28. 190 × 576   29. 178 × 2531   30. 195 × 4726
31. 746 × 1983   32. 634 × 7285   33. 228 × 3905   34. 617 × 5038

Choose the letter of the best estimate for each product.

35. 406 × 317   **a.** 1200   **b.** 12,000   **c.** 120,000
36. 696 × 120   **a.** 7000   **b.** 70,000   **c.** 700,000
37. 111 × 5024   **a.** 5000   **b.** 50,000   **c.** 500,000
38. 986 × 7803   **a.** 800,000   **b.** 8,000,000   **c.** 80,000,000

39. Mrs. Lee, an airplane pilot, flew the Chicago to Honolulu flight 148 times during this year. If the distance between Chicago and Honolulu is 4315 mi, how many miles did she fly in all?

40. The Theatrical Curtain Company uses 105 yards of material to make a stage curtain. If the company made 982 curtains last year, about how many yards of material did it use?

review *exercises*

Estimate each sum or difference.

1. 239 + 465   2. 385 + 592   3. 815 − 327   4. 67,742 − 18,495
5. 8355 − 7619   6. 2516 − 469   7. 396 + 246 + 452 8. 234 + 427 + 355

calculator corner

You can use a calculator to solve a multiplication problem by *trial and error*.

example Find the missing digits.   2■6 × ■4 = 8704

solution First use estimation.   200 × 40 = 8000
              Then try different digits.   206 × 44 = 9064 ⬅ **too high**
                                                 206 × 34 = 7004 ⬅ **too low**
              Keep trying until you discover that 256 × 34 = 8704.

Use your calculator to find the missing digits by trial and error.

1. 5■ × ■5 = 2475   2. 3■ × ■8 = 2244   3. 8■ × 2■ = 2376
4. ■6 × 5■ = 4992   5. 2■7 × ■9 = 8073   6. ■50 × ■1 = 7350

3-5 MULTIPLICATION SHORT CUTS

You may multiply two numbers in any order. This is called the **commutative property of multiplication.**

$$3 \times 4 = 12 \quad \text{and} \quad 4 \times 3 = 12$$

When you multiply three numbers, you may group them as shown below. This is called the **associative property of multiplication.**

$$(2 \times 4) \times 9 = 8 \times 9 = 72 \quad \text{and} \quad 2 \times (4 \times 9) = 2 \times 36 = 72$$

You can use these properties to multiply numbers *in any order* and *in any groups of two*.

example 1

Find the product: **a.** 905×268 **b.** 617×373

solution

a.
```
      9 0 5
    ×2 6 8
    7 2 4 0
    5 4 3 0
    1 8 1 0
  2 4 2,5 4 0
```
← **Changing the order to put 905 on top may be easier. Renaming is simpler because 905 has a zero.**

b.
```
      6 1 7
    ×3 7 3
    1 8 5 1
    4 3 1 9
    1 8 5 1
  2 3 0,1 4 1
```
← **Changing the order to multiply by 373 may be easier because 373 has repeated digits.**

your turn

Find each product.

1. 738×929 **2.** 507×824 **3.** 804×514 **4.** 351×662

example 2

Use the properties of multiplication to help you find each product.

a. $8 \times 62 \times 50$ **b.** $9 \times 5 \times 9 \times 2$

solution

a. $8 \times 62 \times 50$ ⟮400⟯
     $62 \times 400 = 24,800$ ← **Group numbers whose product is easy to find.**

b. $9 \times 5 \times 9 \times 2$ ⟮81⟯ ⟮10⟯
     $81 \times 10 = 810$

your turn

Use the properties of multiplication to help you find each product.

5. $60 \times 28 \times 5$ **6.** $33 \times 2 \times 15$ **7.** $4 \times 2 \times 7 \times 50$ **8.** $3 \times 5 \times 20 \times 3$

Multiplying Whole Numbers   59

The **distributive property** allows you to multiply numbers inside parentheses by a factor outside the parentheses as shown below.

$$8 \times (3 + 4) = 8 \times 7 = 56 \quad \text{and} \quad (8 \times 3) + (8 \times 4) = 24 + 32 = 56$$

example 3

Use the distributive property to find each product: **a.** 6×58 **b.** 7×98

solution

a. $6 \times 58 = 6 \times (50 + 8)$ ⟵ **Write 58 as 50 + 8.**
$ = (6 \times 50) + (6 \times 8)$
$ = 300 + 48$
$ = 348$

b. $7 \times 98 = 7 \times (100 - 2)$ ⟵ **Write 98 as 100 − 2.**
$ = (7 \times 100) - (7 \times 2)$
$ = 700 - 14$
$ = 686$

your turn

Use the distributive property to find each product.

9. 5×73	**10.** 4×69	**11.** 4×99	**12.** 6×98
13. 12×32	**14.** 3×97	**15.** 7×208	**16.** 2×996

practice exercises

practice for example 1 *(page 59)*

Find each product.

1. 806×329	**2.** 403×654	**3.** 938×515	**4.** 187×722
5. 508×894	**6.** 902×421	**7.** 827×336	**8.** 216×404

practice for example 2 *(page 59)*

Use the properties of multiplication to help you find each product.

9. $6 \times 43 \times 10$	**10.** $45 \times 15 \times 20$
11. $2 \times 16 \times 35$	**12.** $80 \times 27 \times 5$
13. $5 \times 16 \times 20$	**14.** $8 \times 25 \times 50$
15. $34 \times 45 \times 2$	**16.** $23 \times 5 \times 40$
17. $5 \times 7 \times 2 \times 7$	**18.** $8 \times 3 \times 3 \times 5$
19. $4 \times 3 \times 7 \times 5$	**20.** $9 \times 2 \times 15 \times 9$

Use the distributive property to find each product.

21. 4×33 **22.** 5×74 **23.** 3×99 **24.** 5×97 **25.** 4×998

26. 6×812 **27.** 7×305 **28.** 12×996 **29.** 2×9999 **30.** 8×9997

mixed practice (pages 59–60)

Use the properties of multiplication to help you find each product.

31. 6×78 **32.** 9×98 **33.** $5 \times 15 \times 2$ **34.** $6 \times 8 \times 5$

35. 7×19 **36.** 12×45 **37.** 7×903 **38.** 3×996

39. 4×1012 **40.** 8×999 **41.** $5 \times 4 \times 4 \times 2$ **42.** $7 \times 4 \times 6 \times 25$

43. 9×997 **44.** 8×102 **45.** 185×644 **46.** 12×995

47. Mrs. Fisher had three storm windows installed in her home at the cost of $198 each. How much did she pay for all three windows?

48. Last year on his farm, Mr. Gomez planted 50 rows of 26 tomato plants each. He wants to plant twice as many rows this year. How many plants should he buy?

review *exercises*

Evaluate each expression when $a = 84$, $b = 172$, and $c = 4207$.

1. $a + b$ **2.** $c - a$ **3.** $a + b + c$

Find each answer.

4. $755 + 876$ **5.** $6 \times 75,587$ **6.** $271 - 139$

7. $51,236 + 59$ **8.** $32 \times 14,903$ **9.** $47,275 - 502$

mental math

Properties often help you multiply mentally.

$(5 \times 43) \times 20$

$100 \times 43 = 4300$

$7 \times 99 = 7 \times (100 - 1)$
$= (7 \times 100) - (7 \times 1)$
$= 700 - 7 = 693$

$4 \times 16 = 4 \times (10 + 6)$
$= (4 \times 10) + (4 \times 6)$
$= 40 + 24 = 64$

Multiply mentally.

1. $(5 \times 16) \times 20$ **2.** $(2 \times 156) \times 5$ **3.** $(4 \times 34) \times 25$ **4.** $(2 \times 25) \times (4 \times 50)$

5. 6×99 **6.** 50×99 **7.** 3×199 **8.** 2×299

9. 4×23 **10.** 6×31 **11.** 2×78 **12.** 7×15

3-6 VARIABLE EXPRESSIONS AND MULTIPLICATION

There are a number of different symbols that indicate multiplication.

times sign 3×8 *raised dot* $3 \cdot 8$ *parentheses* $3(8)$ or $(3)8$

example 1

Write each multiplication in two other ways.

a. $12 \cdot 5$ **b.** $5(9)$

solution

a. $12 \cdot 5 \longrightarrow 12 \times 5$ $12(5)$ or $(12)5$
b. $5(9) \longrightarrow 5 \times 9$ $5 \cdot 9$

your turn

Write each multiplication in two other ways.

1. 7×2 **2.** $35 \cdot 4$
3. $9(11)$ **4.** $(28)6$

When a product contains a variable, we usually omit the multiplication symbol.

example 2

Evaluate each expression when $x = 24$, $y = 1$, and $z = 0$.

a. $9x$ **b.** $3xy$ **c.** $65xyz$

solution

a. $\left.\begin{array}{l} 9 \cdot x \\ 9 \cdot 24 \end{array}\right\}$ $\begin{array}{r} 24 \\ \times 9 \\ \hline 216 \end{array}$

b. $3 \cdot x \cdot y$
   $3 \cdot 24 \cdot 1 = 72$ ◀━━ **The product of a number and 1 is the number itself.**

c. $65 \cdot x \cdot y \cdot z$
   $65 \cdot 24 \cdot 1 \cdot 0 = 0$ ◀━━ **If any one of the factors is 0, the product is 0.**

your turn

Evaluate each expression when $a = 0$, $b = 32$, and $c = 1$.

5. $6a$ **6.** $25b$ **7.** $7bc$ **8.** abc

practice exercises

practice for example 1 *(page 62)*

Write each multiplication in two other ways.

1. 3×7
2. 8×51
3. $18 \cdot 42$
4. $36 \cdot 67$
5. $28(97)$
6. $(105)4$
7. $43 \cdot 139$
8. $9(522)$

practice for example 2 *(page 62)*

Evaluate each expression when $x = 5$, $y = 0$, and $z = 1$.

9. $5x$
10. $7y$
11. $18z$
12. $13yz$
13. $9xz$
14. $24xy$
15. $8zy$
16. $12xz$
17. $26xyz$
18. $45xyz$

mixed practice *(page 62)*

Write each multiplication in *three* other ways.

19. $3x$
20. $45g$
21. rs
22. $l \cdot m$
23. $p(q)$
24. $(18)z$
25. $x \cdot y$
26. $4a$

Evaluate each expression for the given values of the variables.

27. $8x$, when $x = 19$
28. $1000w$, when $w = 15$
29. $12y$, when $y = 21$
30. $10z$, when $z = 32$
31. xy, when $x = 0$ and $y = 9$
32. wz, when $w = 4$ and $z = 7$
33. $6mn$, when $m = 1$ and $n = 8$
34. $5rt$, when $r = 0$ and $t = 6$
35. $12xz$, when $x = 14$ and $z = 22$
36. $18pq$, when $p = 5$ and $q = 27$
37. xyz, when $x = 10$, $y = 11$, and $z = 4$
38. $9abc$, when $a = 9$, $b = 7$, and $c = 12$

review exercises

Compare. Replace each __?__ with >, <, or =.

1. $98{,}472 \underline{\ ?\ } 988{,}472$
2. $7253 \underline{\ ?\ } 7653$
3. $654{,}456 \underline{\ ?\ } 654{,}056$
4. $777{,}766 \underline{\ ?\ } 77{,}766$
5. $8249 \underline{\ ?\ } 8429$
6. $438{,}642 \underline{\ ?\ } 438{,}742$

7. Tony James is editing a reel of film that has 992 ft (feet) of film. There are 32 frames in each foot of film. How many frames in all will Tony see?

8. Light bulbs are delivered to stores in boxes of 150 bulbs. If Mrs. Cox orders 580 boxes for her store, what will be the total number of light bulbs ordered?

SKILL REVIEW

Write the corresponding addition. Then find the sum.

1. 3×60 **2.** 7×200 **3.** 4×4000 **4.** $8 \cdot 3000$ *3-1*

Find each product.

5. 4×50 **6.** 20×80 **7.** 900×400 **8.** 300×7000

Find each product.

9. 3×36 **10.** $5 \times \$72$ **11.** $9 \times \$281$ **12.** $4 \times 42,715$ *3-2*

Estimate each product.

13. 3×73 **14.** 8×52

15. 5×3944 **16.** $6 \times 26,671$

17. Each of five students received a $1275 scholarship from their school's scholarship fund. How much money in all was received?

Find each product. Check the reasonableness of your answer.

18. 17×34 **19.** 48×63 **20.** 97×525 **21.** 89×247 *3-3*

Estimate each product. Write whether each estimate is an *overestimate*, an *underestimate*, or if you *can't tell*.

22. 42×91 **23.** 78×55

24. 27×432 **25.** 86×678

26. Each student in a class of 379 students sold 25 calendars to raise money for their class trip. About how many calendars did they sell?

Find each product. Check the reasonableness of your answer.

27. 612×347 **28.** 251×463 **29.** 552×7256 **30.** 854×2997 *3-4*

Use the properties of multiplication to find each product.

31. $50 \times 36 \times 4$ **32.** 302×895 **33.** 8×76 *3-5*

34. $3 \times 25 \times 3 \times 2$ **35.** 7×98 **36.** 12×53

Write each multiplication in two other ways.

37. $3 \cdot 42$ **38.** $75(a)$ **39.** 9×28 **40.** $m \cdot n$ *3-6*

Evaluate each expression when $a = 35$, $b = 0$, and $c = 1$.

41. $8a$ **42.** ac **43.** $25bc$ **44.** abc

3-7 PHYSICAL FITNESS

The energy the body uses during physical activity is measured in **Calories.** You can use the following formula to calculate the approximate number of Calories used during one of these activities.

total Calories = Calories × number of
used   used in one   minutes
minute

Activity	Number of Calories Used in One Minute
sleeping	1
walking slowly	3
walking quickly	5
jogging	7
tennis	7
bicycling	11
cross-country skiing	16
swimming	9

example

Find the approximate number of Calories you would use in 4 min (minutes) of walking quickly followed by 30 min of jogging.

solution

Find the approximate number of Calories for each activity.

4 min walking quickly: $5 \times 4 = 20$
30 min jogging: $7 \times 30 = 210$

Find the total. $20 + 210 = 230$

You would use about 230 Calories.

exercises

Find the total number of Calories used.

1. 40 min bicycling
   20 min tennis

2. 30 min swimming
   45 min sleeping

3. It took Jenny 10 min to jog to the store. It took her 15 min to walk quickly home. About how many Calories did Jenny use altogether?

4. Amanda went cross-country skiing for 40 min, then walked slowly for another 45 min. About how many Calories did she use?

5. It took Marcia 20 min, walking quickly, to get to the tennis court. She played tennis for one hour. She then spent 30 min walking home slowly. About how many Calories did she use?

DIETITIAN

Ann Hanson is a dietitian for the Somerville School system. She plans meals for the school cafeterias. Ann also helps students plan sensible diets that meet their caloric and nutritional needs.

Ann uses the following formula to find out about how many Calories a student should consume each day.

Calories needed = activity rating × weight in pounds

Activity Level	Daily Activity Rating

Very light:
  reading, eating,
  sleeping, watching TV
	13

Light:
  golfing, bowling,
  slow walking
	14

Moderate:
  walking quickly,
  gardening, light chores
	15

Strenuous: physical labor, dancing	16

Very strenuous:
  swimming, tennis,
  football, bicycling
	17

example

Jed Barnes weighs 150 lb (pounds). His daily activity rating is 17. About how many Calories does Jed need each day?

solution

Use the formula: Calories needed = activity rating × weight in pounds
$$= 17 \times 150$$
$$= 2550$$
Jed needs about 2550 Calories per day.

exercises

1. Joan weighs 117 lb. She has a daily activity rating of 17. About how many Calories does she need every day?

2. Dennis has a daily activity rating of 15. He weighs 121 lb. About how many Calories should he consume each day?

3. Christian is on the swimming team. He weighs 135 lb. About how many Calories should he consume each day?

4. a. About how many Calories should you consume on a daily basis? To answer, think about your activities and assign an activity rating for yourself. Then multiply by your weight.

   b. How many Calories do you actually consume each day? Keep a log of what and how much you eat for several days. Then use a Calorie chart to add up your daily Calories.

CHAPTER REVIEW

vocabulary vo·cab·u·lar·y

Choose the correct word to complete each sentence.

1. When you multiply two numbers, the answer is called the *(sum, product)*.
2. You know that $(3 \times 4) \times 2 = 3 \times (4 \times 2)$ by the *(associative, commutative)* property of multiplication.

skills

Find each answer.

3. $20 + 20 + 20 + 20$
4. 7×400
5. $500 + 500 + 500$
6. 60×300
7. 900×700
8. 400×8000

Estimate each product.

9. 6×48
10. 7×22
11. 5×993
12. $3 \times 83,721$

Find each product. Check the reasonableness of your answer.

13. 9×84
14. 25×68
15. 97×359
16. 216×823
17. 971×1265
18. 436×6564

Choose the letter of the best estimate for each product.

19. 78×582 **a.** 35,000   **b.** 40,000   **c.** 48,000
20. 826×914 **a.** 72,000   **b.** 720,000   **c.** 7,200,000

Use the properties of multiplication to find each product.

21. $4 \times 3 \times 50 \times 9$
22. 6×99
23. 401×765
24. 5×64

Evaluate each expression when $x = 1$, $y = 72$, and $z = 339$.

25. $8y$
26. xy
27. $15z$
28. $3xz$

29. Use the table on page 65. Kim went swimming for 30 min. About how many Calories did she use?
30. Use the table on page 65. It took Greg 15 min to jog to the park. He played tennis for 45 min, then walked slowly for 25 min. About how many Calories did Greg use?

CHAPTER TEST

Find each answer.

1. $700 + 700 + 700 + 700$ 2. 90×90 3. 50×80 **3-1**
4. 200×3000 5. $50 + 50 + 50$ 6. $300 \times 70{,}000$

Find each product.

7. 7×34 8. $5 \times \$654$ 9. $2 \times 18{,}993$ 10. 8×607 **3-2**

Estimate each product.

11. 9×93 12. 8×686 13. $4 \times \$4235$

14. Each student in a sophomore class of 208 students wrote three letters to pen pals. About how many letters did they write in all?

Find each product. Check the reasonableness of your answer.

15. 38×77 16. 52×625 17. 94×2804 **3-3**

18. Sam earned $159 a week from his temporary job. How much money did he earn in 38 weeks?

Estimate each product. Write whether it is an *overestimate*, an *underestimate*, or if you *can't tell*.

19. 92×43 20. 79×26 21. 45×512

22. A printing company can print 1850 concert tickets in one hour. About how many tickets can be printed in a 36-hour period?

Find each product. Check the reasonableness of your answer.

23. 324×417 24. 885×6097 **3-4**

Use the properties of multiplication to find each product.

25. 4×73 26. 9×998 27. $45 \times 5 \times 4 \times 2$ **3-5**

Evaluate each expression when $s = 0$, $t = 54$, and $r = 390$.

28. $17s$ 29. $24r$ 30. $2st$ **3-6**

31. Use the table on page 65. Kathy went jogging for 50 min, then she slept for 30 min. About how many Calories did she use?   **3-7**

32. Use the table on page 65. It took Dave 15 min, riding his bike, to get to the swimming pool. He swam for 45 min. About how many Calories did he use?

To help us keep track of time, our days are divided into smaller units. Many kinds of instruments are used to show the correct time.

CHAPTER 4

DIVIDING WHOLE NUMBERS

4-1 DIVIDING BY A ONE-DIGIT NUMBER

Sue, Juan, Bob, and Maria formed the Odd Jobs Company to earn money during the summer. They earned $592 in July. To share the $592 equally, they divided by 4. Each person received $148.

To divide by a one-digit number, use the following method.

Start at the left.

1. *Divide* the dividend by the divisor in the greatest place value position possible.
2. *Multiply*.
3. *Subtract*.
4. *Bring down* the next digit or digits.

Repeat steps 1 to 4 until the remainder is less than the divisor.

```
                    $148   ← quotient
divisor →      4)$592      ← dividend
               − 4↓|
                 19|
               − 16↓
                  32
               − 32
                   0   ← remainder
```

Like addition and subtraction, multiplication and division are *inverse operations*. To check a quotient, multiply it by the divisor and add the remainder.

```
Check:     $148
            ×4
           592
         +   0
         $592 √
```

example 1

Find each quotient.

```
        $58
a.  6)$348      ← 6 > 3, so divide 6)34.
       30↓
       48          Check:     $58
       48                      ×6
        0                     348
                            +   0
                            $348 √
```

```
       158 R3
b.  5)793                   Check:     158
       5↓|                              ×5
       29|                             790
       25↓                           +   3
       43                             793 √
       40
        3   ← remainder
```

your turn

Find each quotient.

1. 3)846
2. 4)$2044
3. 6)6754
4. 8)12,379

You can also show a division by using the division symbol ÷.

example 2

Find each quotient.

a. $\$364 \div 7$ **b.** $526 \div 6$

solution

a.
$$
\begin{array}{r}
\$\ 52 \\
7\overline{)\$364} \\
35\downarrow \\
\hline
14 \\
14 \\
\hline
0
\end{array}
$$

Check:
$$
\begin{array}{r}
\$52 \\
\times 7 \\
\hline
364 \\
+\ \ 0 \\
\hline
\$364\ \checkmark
\end{array}
$$

b.
$$
\begin{array}{r}
87\ \text{R4} \\
6\overline{)526} \\
48\downarrow \\
\hline
46 \\
42 \\
\hline
4
\end{array}
$$

Check:
$$
\begin{array}{r}
87 \\
\times 6 \\
\hline
522 \\
+\ \ 4 \\
\hline
526\ \checkmark
\end{array}
$$

your turn

Find each quotient.

5. $\$312 \div 8$ **6.** $3578 \div 4$

7. $\$4239 \div 9$ **8.** $12{,}837 \div 5$

Quotients may have zeros in some place value positions.

example 3

Find each quotient.

a.
$$
\begin{array}{r}
208 \\
6\overline{)1248} \\
12\downarrow\downarrow \\
\hline
48 \\
48 \\
\hline
0
\end{array}
$$

6 > 4. Place a 0 in the quotient. Bring down the 8. ⬅

Check:
$$
\begin{array}{r}
208 \\
\times 6 \\
\hline
1248 \\
+\ \ 0 \\
\hline
1248\ \checkmark
\end{array}
$$

b.
$$
\begin{array}{r}
3\ 008\ \text{R2} \\
4\overline{)12{,}034} \\
12\downarrow\downarrow\downarrow \\
\hline
034 \\
32 \\
\hline
2
\end{array}
$$

Check:
$$
\begin{array}{r}
3008 \\
\times 4 \\
\hline
12{,}032 \\
+\ \ 2 \\
\hline
12{,}034\ \checkmark
\end{array}
$$

your turn

Find each quotient.

9. $8\overline{)4832}$ **10.** $\$1890 \div 9$ **11.** $35{,}284 \div 7$ **12.** $3\overline{)27{,}020}$

practice exercises

practice for example 1 (page 70)

Find each quotient.

1. $3\overline{)369}$ **2.** $7\overline{)\$1484}$ **3.** $5\overline{)\$2145}$ **4.** $4\overline{)32{,}484}$

5. $2\overline{)5245}$ **6.** $9\overline{)4019}$ **7.** $8\overline{)18{,}120}$ **8.** $6\overline{)22{,}454}$

Find each quotient.

9. $93 \div 3$
13. $6245 \div 2$

10. $\$658 \div 7$
14. $4029 \div 6$

11. $\$728 \div 8$
15. $18,120 \div 5$

12. $8496 \div 4$
16. $\$12,484 \div 4$

Find each quotient.

17. $2\overline{)204}$
21. $4\overline{)8147}$

18. $742 \div 7$
22. $34,260 \div 9$

19. $\$810 \div 3$
23. $16,043 \div 8$

20. $6\overline{)\$5436}$
24. $7\overline{)28,634}$

Find each quotient.

25. $462 \div 7$
29. $591 \div 6$
33. $9\overline{)15,555}$

26. $335 \div 5$
30. $4\overline{)532}$
34. $3\overline{)31,200}$

27. $8\overline{)176}$
31. $9\overline{)307}$
35. $3\overline{)50,040}$

28. $4\overline{)1212}$
32. $6314 \div 7$
36. $612,000 \div 6$

37. There are 68 people who want to play bridge. If four players are seated at each table, how many bridge tables are needed?

38. The athletics department has $125 for new baseballs. How many $6 baseballs can they buy? How much money will be left?

review exercises

Estimate each product.

1. 83×17
5. 202×53

2. 61×29
6. 95×107

3. 56×35
7. 179×47

4. 88×42
8. 311×96

mental math

You can use **short division** to divide 603 by 8. Divide, multiply, and subtract in your head. Repeat as often as needed.

$$8\overline{)603}_{4} \quad \longrightarrow \quad \overset{7\quad 5\ R3}{8\overline{)603}_{4}}$$

Divide using short division.

1. $8\overline{)462}$
6. $274 \div 3$

2. $5\overline{)873}$
7. $7851 \div 4$

3. $9\overline{)4368}$
8. $869 \div 5$

4. $7\overline{)4459}$
9. $8592 \div 6$

5. $2\overline{)34,679}$
10. $8492 \div 9$

4-2 ESTIMATING QUOTIENTS

Jerry drove 27,431 mi (miles) in 7 months. To estimate that he drove about 4000 mi each month, he used numbers that divide easily, or **compatible numbers.**

example 1

Use compatible numbers to estimate.

a. $7\overline{)27{,}431}$ **b.** $2791 \div 5$

solution

a. $7\overline{)27{,}431}$

$\dfrac{\text{about } 4000}{7\overline{)28{,}000}}$ ⬅ **28,000 is a number close to 27,431 that is easily divided by 7.**

b. $5\overline{)2791}$

$\dfrac{\text{about } 600}{5\overline{)3000}}$ ⬅ **5 divides both 2500 and 3000 easily, but 3000 will give a closer estimate.**

your turn

Use compatible numbers to estimate.

1. $6\overline{)4185}$ **2.** $7\overline{)6317}$ **3.** $4971 \div 8$ **4.** $82{,}175 \div 9$

Often you need to estimate a quotient when the divisor is greater than 10. You could change the dividend to a number that is compatible with the divisor, as shown at the right. However, it may be simpler to first round the divisor to the place of its leading digit.

$15\overline{)447}$

$\dfrac{\text{about } 30}{15\overline{)450}}$ ⬅ **15 and 45 are compatible.**

example 2

Round the divisor and then use compatible numbers to estimate.

a. $821 \div 42$ **b.** $73{,}421 \div 683$

solution

a. $42\overline{)821}$

$\dfrac{\text{about } 20}{40\overline{)800}}$ ⬅ **800 ÷ 40 and 80 ÷ 4 have the same quotient.**

b. $683\overline{)73{,}421}$

$\dfrac{\text{about } 100}{700\overline{)70{,}000}}$

your turn

Round the divisor and then use compatible numbers to estimate.

5. $82\overline{)6317}$ **6.** $51{,}589 \div 87$ **7.** $428\overline{)81{,}927}$ **8.** $668\overline{)35{,}824}$

practice exercises

practice for example 1 (page 73)

Use compatible numbers to estimate.

1. $1753 \div 6$
2. $4379 \div 7$
3. $9\overline{)8027}$
4. $8\overline{)33,196}$
5. $32,985 \div 5$
6. $22,712 \div 4$
7. $8\overline{)17,566}$
8. $3\overline{)73,015}$

practice for example 2 (page 73)

Round the divisor and then use compatible numbers to estimate.

9. $6512 \div 83$
10. $2016 \div 27$
11. $42\overline{)28,939}$
12. $67\overline{)43,104}$
13. $9327 \div 79$
14. $73,800 \div 58$
15. $579\overline{)17,955}$
16. $791\overline{)32,766}$
17. $906\overline{)77,210}$
18. $830\overline{)496,060}$
19. $4680\overline{)26,195}$
20. $6172\overline{)739,047}$

mixed practice (page 73)

Estimate.

21. $2284 \div 7$
22. $69,819 \div 9$
23. $93\overline{)53,018}$
24. $67\overline{)32,766}$
25. $562\overline{)40,219}$
26. $319\overline{)75,297}$
27. $819\overline{)64,209}$
28. $891\overline{)64,209}$

The exact answer for each exercise is one of those given at the right. **a.** 39 **b.** 384
Estimate to determine the letter of the exact answer. **c.** 68 **d.** 691

29. $84\overline{)3276}$
30. $59\overline{)4012}$
31. $33\overline{)22,803}$
32. $67\overline{)25,728}$
33. $481\overline{)184,704}$
34. $784\overline{)53,312}$
35. $489\overline{)337,899}$
36. $2371\overline{)92,469}$

Choose the division that will give you the best estimate.

37. $15\overline{)7566}$
   a. $10\overline{)8000}$
   b. $15\overline{)7500}$
   c. $20\overline{)8000}$

38. $22\overline{)88,798}$
   a. $20\overline{)88,000}$
   b. $20\overline{)90,000}$
   c. $22\overline{)88,000}$

39. Eight friends earned $254 doing odd jobs for neighbors. If the money is shared equally, about how much money will each friend get?

40. Rosa Lopez will earn $36,225 this year. There are 52 weeks in a year. About how much will she earn each week?

review exercises

Round to the place of the underlined digit.

1. $77\underline{7},888$
2. $69\underline{8},222$
3. $4,0\underline{9}0,091$
4. $8,7\underline{5}2,387$
5. $\underline{9}908$
6. $7,\underline{2}46,800$
7. $9,\underline{4}21,111$
8. $\underline{6}399$

4-3 DIVIDING BY A TWO-DIGIT NUMBER

To divide by a two-digit number, use the following method.
1. Round the divisor to the nearest ten. This is your **trial divisor.**
2. *Divide*. Estimate the first digit of the quotient using the trial divisor.
3. *Multiply* and *subtract*. Revise the estimate if necessary.
4. *Bring down* the next digit or digits.

Repeat steps 1 to 4 until the remainder is less than the divisor.

example 1

Find each quotient.

a. **Round to 30.** →

```
        84        Check:
32)2688             84
   256↓            ×32
   128             168
   128             252
     0            2688
                +   0
                  2688 ✓
```

b. **Round to 70.** →

```
        116 R54    Check:
68)7942             116
   68↓             ×68
   114             928
    68↓            696
   462            7888
   408          +   54
    54            7942 ✓
```

your turn

Find each quotient.

1. 41)779

2. 62)$5642

3. 63,157 ÷ 82

4. 59,112 ÷ 69

example 2

Find each quotient.

a.
```
      7      ← Try 7.
85)7011
   595       106 > 85, so
   106       7 is not enough.
          ← Revise up.
```
```
     82 R41  ← Try 8.
85)7011
   680↓
   211
   170
    41
```

b.
```
      8      ← Try 8.
64)4938
   512       493 < 512, so
          ← 8 is too much.
             Revise down.
```
```
     77 R10  ← Try 7.
64)4938
   448↓
   458
   448
    10
```

your turn

Find each quotient.

5. 64)1869

6. 54)3137

7. 2337 ÷ 36

8. 1639 ÷ 25

Dividing Whole Numbers 75

example 3

Find the quotient 40,492 ÷ 67. Check the reasonableness of your answer.

solution

$$\begin{array}{r} 604 \text{ R}24 \\ 67\overline{)40,492} \\ \underline{40\ 2}\downarrow\downarrow \\ 292 \\ \underline{268} \\ 24 \end{array}$$

Estimate: $\begin{array}{ccc} 40,492 & \div & 67 \\ \downarrow & & \downarrow \\ 42,000 & \div & 70 \end{array}$ $\left.\rule{0pt}{2.5em}\right\}$ about 600 $70\overline{)42,000}$ ⟵ **Use compatible numbers.**

604 R24 is a reasonable answer.

your turn

Find each quotient. Check the reasonableness of your answer.

9. $78\overline{)7942}$ 10. $23\overline{)9796}$ 11. $29,001 \div 27$ 12. $55,087 \div 83$

practice *exercises*

practice for example 1 (page 75)

Find each quotient.

1. $21\overline{)1743}$ 2. $6627 \div 81$ 3. $\$8496 \div 72$ 4. $18\overline{)8422}$
5. $26,939 \div 42$ 6. $47\overline{)36,911}$ 7. $\$68,442 \div 61$ 8. $72\overline{)22,680}$

practice for example 2 (page 75)

Find each quotient.

9. $27\overline{)2484}$ 10. $83\overline{)6512}$
11. $23\overline{)6372}$ 12. $49\overline{)4806}$
13. $57\overline{)17,955}$ 14. $55\overline{)74,302}$
15. $34\overline{)92,714}$ 16. $36\overline{)88,107}$

practice for example 3 (page 76)

Find each quotient. Check the reasonableness of your answer.

17. $23\overline{)8196}$ 18. $3655 \div 91$
19. $4126 \div 38$ 20. $67\overline{)21,146}$
21. $32,766 \div 79$ 22. $76\overline{)16,002}$
23. $87\overline{)43,104}$ 24. $53,018 \div 93$

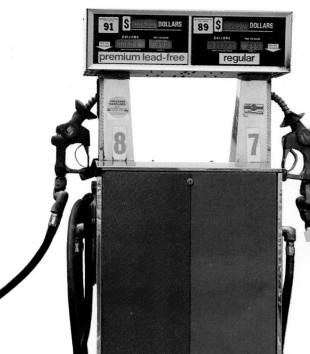

Find each quotient. Check the reasonableness of your answer.

25. $23\overline{)4922}$ 26. $17\overline{)3794}$ 27. $8641 \div 36$ 28. $8568 \div 42$

29. $52\overline{)10,567}$ 30. $34,524 \div 84$ 31. $78,389 \div 77$ 32. $68\overline{)136,068}$

33. $76,304 \div 38$ 34. $110,068 \div 56$ 35. $75\overline{)263,700}$ 36. $83\overline{)325,164}$

Choose the letter that corresponds to the best estimate of each quotient.

37. $33\overline{)18,471}$ 38. $51\overline{)19,284}$ a. 300   b. 400

39. $84\overline{)42,377}$ 40. $68\overline{)50,210}$ c. 500   d. 600

41. $77\overline{)23,876}$ 42. $92\overline{)76,500}$ e. 700   f. 800

Choose the letter that corresponds to the best way to estimate each division.

43. $82\overline{)4667}$ a. $80\overline{)4800}$ b. $80\overline{)4000}$ c. $90\overline{)4500}$

44. $11\overline{)4823}$ a. $10\overline{)4000}$ b. $10\overline{)5000}$ c. $10\overline{)4800}$

45. $27\overline{)6024}$ a. $30\overline{)6000}$ b. $25\overline{)5000}$ c. $24\overline{)7500}$

46. $68\overline{)5712}$ a. $70\overline{)5600}$ b. $60\overline{)5400}$ c. $68\overline{)6800}$

47. $15\overline{)4526}$ a. $10\overline{)4500}$ b. $20\overline{)4600}$ c. $15\overline{)4500}$

48. $44\overline{)8753}$ a. $40\overline{)8800}$ b. $44\overline{)8800}$ c. $40\overline{)8000}$

49. In twelve months, Mr. Lockard spent $852 for gasoline for his car. About how much did he spend each month?

50. Geraldine bought shares of stock. If each share of stock cost $25, how many shares did she buy with the $435 in her savings account? How much money is left in her account?

review exercises

Find each answer.

1. $659 + 327$ 2. $713 + 548$ 3. $536 + 491$ 4. $824 + 787$

5. $653 - 241$ 6. $7657 - 379$ 7. $8031 - 4763$ 8. $10,050 - 8493$

9. 73×45 10. 85×63 11. 361×47 12. 782×89

13. $5058 \div 4$ 14. $7\overline{)3843}$ 15. $8\overline{)6452}$ 16. $14,009 \div 3$

Compare. Replace each __?__ with >, <, or =.

17. $42 \underline{\ ?\ } 109$ 18. $75 \underline{\ ?\ } 57$ 19. $241 \underline{\ ?\ } 307$ 20. $489 \underline{\ ?\ } 389$

21. $541 \underline{\ ?\ } 561$ 22. $427 \underline{\ ?\ } 427$ 23. $358 \underline{\ ?\ } 355$ 24. $3465 \underline{\ ?\ } 3456$

4-4 DIVIDING BY A THREE-DIGIT NUMBER

Last year Linda Gomez worked 213 days. The amount of money she earned for the year was $26,625. Linda divided $26,625 by 213 to find that she earned $125 for each day that she worked.

　　　To divide by a three-digit number, you use a method similar to the one you used to divide by a two-digit number.

1. Round the divisor to the nearest hundred. This is your trial divisor.
2. *Divide*. Estimate the first digit of the quotient using the trial divisor.
3. *Multiply* and *subtract*. Revise the estimate if necessary.
4. *Bring down* the next digit or digits.

Repeat steps 1 to 4 until the remainder is less than the divisor.

Round to 200. ➡

```
          $125
213)$26,625
     21 3↓|
      5 32|
      4 26↓
      1 065
      1 065
          0
```

Check:
```
    $125
   ×213
    375
    125
    250
 26,625
+     0
 $26,625 √
```

example 1

Find each quotient.

a. **Round to 300.** ➡
```
              223
283)63,109
    56 6↓|
     6 50|
     5 66↓
      849
      849
        0
```

Check: 223 × 283 + 0
　　　　 63,109 + 0
　　　　　 63,109 √

b. **Round to 300.** ➡
```
            4              ← Try 4.
324)123,251
    129 6                  ← 1232 < 1296, so
                             4 is too much.
                             Revise down.

          380 R131         ← Try 3.
324)123,251
    97 2↓|
    26 05|
    25 92↓
       131
```

Check: 380 × 324 + 131
　　　　 123,120 + 131
　　　　　 123,251 √

your turn

Find each quotient.

1. 427)78,995
2. $36,072 ÷ 668
3. 329)648,750
4. $54,696 ÷ 159
5. 84,206 ÷ 248
6. 645)374,910

example 2

Find the quotient 13,194 ÷ 209. Check the reasonableness of your answer.

ESTIMATION

solution

$$
\begin{array}{r}
63\ \text{R27} \\
209\overline{)13,194} \\
\underline{12\ 54}\downarrow \\
654 \\
\underline{627} \\
27
\end{array}
$$

Estimate: $13{,}194 \div 209$

$\downarrow \qquad \downarrow$

$13{,}000 \div 200$

$\left.\begin{array}{}\ \\ \ \end{array}\right\}$ about 65
$200\overline{)13{,}000}$

63 R27 is a reasonable answer.

your turn

Find each quotient. Check the reasonableness of your answer.

7. $109\overline{)54{,}696}$ 8. $84{,}206 \div 298$ 9. $685\overline{)37{,}491}$

practice exercises

practice for example 1 (page 78)

Find each quotient.

1. $810\overline{)1620}$
2. $31{,}022 \div 872$
3. $\$3432 \div 312$
4. $12{,}543 \div 311$
5. $304\overline{)99{,}104}$
6. $552\overline{)\$30{,}360}$

practice for example 2 (page 79)

Find each quotient. Check the reasonableness of your answer.

7. $605\overline{)5413}$
8. $31{,}022 \div 759$
9. $\$90{,}288 \div 342$
10. $482\overline{)\$246{,}302}$
11. $830\overline{)496{,}060}$
12. $115{,}000 \div 575$

mixed practice (pages 78–79)

Find each quotient.

13. $468\overline{)2619}$
14. $9272 \div 872$
15. $99{,}122 \div 304$
16. $300\overline{)24{,}060}$
17. $46{,}070 \div 502$
18. $906\overline{)77{,}210}$

Choose the letter that corresponds to the first digit in the quotient.

19. $852\overline{)64{,}571}$
20. $265\overline{)159{,}530}$
21. $892\overline{)536{,}092}$
22. $403\overline{)3226}$

a. 6   b. 7
c. 8   d. 9

Estimate to tell if each answer is reasonable. Then correct
each unreasonable answer by finding the quotient.

23. $103\overline{)8305}$ 80 R65

24. $869\overline{)64,310}$ 744

25. $901\overline{)96,020}$ 16 R514

26. $492\overline{)50,120}$ 11 R428

27. $330\overline{)65,900}$ 299 R220

28. $570\overline{)75,006}$ 131 R336

29. A factory packages 144 pencils to a box. How many boxes will be
needed for 13,824 pencils?

30. Each section at State College Stadium holds 456 people. If the
stadium holds 67,488 people, how many sections are there?

review exercises

Write each multiplication in two other ways.

1. 6×36
2. $5(11)$
3. $42 \cdot 31$
4. $64 \cdot 49$
5. 54×107
6. $36(145)$
7. 59×241
8. $36(887)$

Evaluate each expression when $x = 64$, $y = 41$, and $z = 19$.

9. $x + 81$
10. $68 + y$
11. $x + 37 + z$
12. $x + y + z$
13. $103 - x$
14. $x - 27$
15. $87 - z$
16. $y - 7$

calculator corner

It is possible to make a mistake in entering a multiplication or a division
on a calculator. For this reason, it is good practice to estimate to check
the reasonableness of a calculator answer.

example   Use a calculator to find the quotient: $476,914 \div 389$

solution   476914 ÷ 389 = 1226
      Estimate: $480,000 \div 400 = 1200$ ⬅ **The calculator answer is reasonable.**

Use a calculator to find each product or quotient. Estimate to check
the reasonableness of the answer.

1. 869×78
2. 387×405
3. 3493×217
4. 578×2861
5. 3729×4178
6. 7069×2258
7. $517,731 \div 879$
8. $860,890 \div 985$
9. $134,649 \div 4987$
10. $948,177 \div 411$
11. $1,467,344 \div 293$
12. $2,889,675 \div 675$

4-5 VARIABLE EXPRESSIONS AND DIVISION

There are a number of different symbols that indicate division.

$18 \div 3$ $\qquad$ $3\overline{)18}$ $\qquad$ $\dfrac{18}{3}$ ← fraction bar

example 1

Write each division in two other ways.

a. $42 \div 6$ $\qquad\qquad$ **b.** $7\overline{)56}$

solution

a. $42 \div 6 \rightarrow 6\overline{)42}$; $\quad \dfrac{42}{6}$ $\qquad$ **b.** $7\overline{)56} \rightarrow 56 \div 7$; $\quad \dfrac{56}{7}$

your turn

Write each division in two other ways.

1. $84 \div 4$ $\qquad\qquad$ **2.** $9\overline{)108}$

3. $\dfrac{145}{5}$ $\qquad\qquad$ **4.** $512 \div 16$

example 2

Evaluate each expression when $w = 12$, $x = 3$, and $y = 0$.

a. $\dfrac{36}{w}$ $\qquad$ **b.** $\dfrac{w}{x}$ $\qquad$ **c.** $\dfrac{0}{x}$ $\qquad$ **d.** $\dfrac{42}{y}$

solution

a. $\dfrac{36}{w} \rightarrow \dfrac{36}{12} = 3$

b. $\dfrac{w}{x} \rightarrow \dfrac{12}{3} = 4$

c. $\dfrac{0}{x} \rightarrow \dfrac{0}{3} = 0$ ← **If you divide 0 by a nonzero number, the quotient is 0.**

d. $\dfrac{42}{y} \rightarrow \dfrac{42}{0}$; *undefined* ← **You cannot divide by 0.**

your turn

Evaluate each expression when $a = 4$, $b = 5$, $c = 12$, and $d = 60$.

5. $\dfrac{45}{b}$ $\qquad$ **6.** $\dfrac{56}{a}$ $\qquad$ **7.** $\dfrac{c}{2}$ $\qquad$ **8.** $\dfrac{c}{a}$ $\qquad$ **9.** $\dfrac{d}{c}$

practice exercises

practice for example 1 (page 81)

Write each division in two other ways.

1. $\dfrac{54}{6}$

2. $88 \div 11$

3. $7\overline{)140}$

4. $\dfrac{108}{12}$

5. $36\overline{)756}$

6. $1000 \div 25$

7. $1665 \div 15$

8. $42\overline{)8442}$

practice for example 2 (page 81)

Evaluate each expression when $w = 5$, $x = 6$, $y = 30$, and $z = 120$.

9. $\dfrac{66}{x}$

10. $\dfrac{40}{w}$

11. $\dfrac{y}{2}$

12. $\dfrac{z}{15}$

13. $\dfrac{z}{24}$

14. $\dfrac{0}{x}$

15. $\dfrac{z}{0}$

16. $\dfrac{y}{w}$

17. $\dfrac{z}{x}$

18. $\dfrac{z}{w}$

19. $\dfrac{y}{x}$

20. $\dfrac{z}{y}$

mixed practice (page 81)

Evaluate each expression when $x = 8$.

21. $\dfrac{x}{1}$

22. $\dfrac{0}{x}$

23. $\dfrac{x}{x}$

24. $\dfrac{x}{0}$

Evaluate each expression when $x = 4$, $y = 6$, and $z = 36$.

25. $\dfrac{x}{2}$

26. $\dfrac{y}{3}$

27. $\dfrac{z}{9}$

28. $\dfrac{24}{x}$

29. $\dfrac{60}{y}$

30. $\dfrac{16}{x}$

31. $\dfrac{0}{x}$

32. $\dfrac{y}{0}$

33. $\dfrac{z}{1}$

34. $\dfrac{z}{x}$

35. $\dfrac{z}{y}$

36. $\dfrac{z}{z}$

Write each division in two other ways.

37. $\dfrac{24}{x}$

38. $115 \div y$ $y\overline{)115};$

39. $a \div 9$

40. $\dfrac{c}{a}$

41. $16\overline{)y}$

42. $b \div n$

43. $m\overline{)x}$

44. $\dfrac{z}{12}$

review exercises

Sid weighs w lb (pounds). Write a variable expression for each person's weight.

1. Ann weighs 38 lb less than Sid.

2. Hector weighs 16 lb more than Sid.

3. Jim's weight exceeds Sid's by 29 lb.

4. Pearl weighs 47 lb less than Sid.

5. Tran's weight is 7 lb more than Sid's.

6. Lisa's weight is 11 lb less than Sid's.

4-6 MULTIPLICATION AND DIVISION PHRASES

Some English words and phrases suggest multiplication. Others suggest division. The chart lists some examples.

Multiplication		Division	
multiply	doubled (×2)	divide	quartered (÷4)
product	tripled (×3)	quotient	shared equally
times	quadrupled (×4)	divided by	equal parts
twice (×2)		halved (÷2)	

example 1

Find each number.

a. one hundred nine, doubled

b. 150 shared equally by 6

solution

a. *doubled* suggests multiplication by 2 $109 \times 2 = 218$

b. *shared equally* by suggests division $150 \div 6 = 25$

your turn

Find each number.

1. fifty-nine times sixteen

2. 228 divided by 4

3. sixty-seven, tripled

4. 144, halved

Multiplication and division phrases often involve variables. Division phrases involving variables are usually written with a fraction bar.

example 2

Write each phrase as a variable expression. Use *n* as the variable.

a. nine times a number

$9 \quad \times \quad n$

$9n$ ← Omit the × symbol.

b. a number divided by twelve

$n \quad \div \quad 12$

$\dfrac{n}{12}$ ← Use a fraction bar.

your turn

Write each phrase as a variable expression. Use *y* as the variable.

5. eleven multiplied by a number

6. 84 divided by a number

7. a number, quadrupled

8. a number divided by 10

Phrases may involve addition, subtraction, multiplication, or division.

example 3

Write each phrase as a variable expression. Use y as the variable.

a. seven more than a number

$$7 \quad + \quad y$$
$$7 + y$$

b. seven times a number

$$7 \quad \times \quad y$$
$$7y$$

your turn

Write each phrase as a variable expression. Use y as the variable.

9. a number decreased by fourteen

10. a number divided by fourteen

11. the sum of a number and twenty

12. the product of a number and twenty

practice exercises

practice for example 1 (page 83)

Find each number.

1. seventy-two, doubled

2. the product of nine and ninety

3. nineteen, tripled

4. eighty-one divided by three

5. divide sixty by twelve

6. nine multiplied by forty-seven

7. 3636 divided by 18

8. forty-four times fifteen

practice for example 2 (page 83)

Write each phrase as a variable expression. Use x as the variable.

9. a number times 11

10. a number divided by 4

11. divide 84 by a number

12. multiply 15 times a number

13. twice a number

14. a number, halved

15. a number, tripled

16. the product of a number and 17

practice for example 3 (page 84)

Write each phrase as a variable expression. Use b as the variable.

17. sixty-four fewer than a number

18. sixty-four divided by a number

19. a number added to eighty

20. a number times eighty

21. fifty-two divided by a number

22. fifty-two decreased by a number

23. a number times thirty-one

24. a number minus thirty-one

Match each phrase to the correct variable expression. Some expressions will be used more than once.

25. twenty-five minus a number z

26. twenty-five divided by a number z

27. the product of twenty-five and a number z

28. a number z plus twenty-five

29. a number z divided by twenty-five

30. twenty-five less than a number z

31. twenty-five times a number z

32. the sum of a number z and twenty-five

33. twenty-five decreased by a number z

34. twenty-five more than a number z

A. $z + 25$ **E.** $\frac{z}{25}$

B. $25z$

C. $z - 25$ **F.** $\frac{25}{z}$

D. $25 - z$

Mary is twenty years old.
Find the age of each person.

35. Eric is twice as old as Mary.

36. Grandmother's age is equal to Mary's age tripled.

37. Tom is half as old as Mary.

38. Martin's age is equal to one quarter of Mary's age.

39. Mr. Chou is four times as old as Mary.

review *exercises*

Find each answer.

1. $187 + 39$	**2.** $2009 + 368$	**3.** $92 + 3749$	**4.** $309 + 4907$
5. $368 - 146$	**6.** $3602 - 549$	**7.** $6051 - 4693$	**8.** $7411 - 5986$
9. 36×43	**10.** 82×246	**11.** 387×492	**12.** 294×657
13. $432 \div 18$	**14.** $38\overline{)1786}$	**15.** $327\overline{)28{,}122}$	**16.** $15{,}238 \div 401$

Find the least number that has a remainder of 1 when it is divided by 2, 3, 4, 5, or 6 and no remainder when it is divided by 7.

4-7 CHOOSING THE CORRECT OPERATION

To be a successful problem solver, you need to carry out these four steps.

Four-Step Method

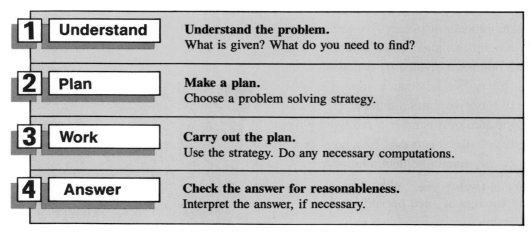

1	**Understand**	**Understand the problem.** What is given? What do you need to find?
2	**Plan**	**Make a plan.** Choose a problem solving strategy.
3	**Work**	**Carry out the plan.** Use the strategy. Do any necessary computations.
4	**Answer**	**Check the answer for reasonableness.** Interpret the answer, if necessary.

An important part of making a plan is choosing the correct operation to use.

example

Paying $12 a week on a layaway plan, how long
will it take for Wilma to pay for a $180 radio?

solution

Step 1 Given: weekly payments of $12
                    total cost of $180
           Find: the number of payments
                    needed to total $180

Step 2 *Divide* 180 by 12.

Step 3
$$\begin{array}{r} 15 \\ 12\overline{)180} \\ \underline{12}\!\downarrow \\ 60 \\ \underline{60} \\ 0 \end{array}$$

Step 4 *Multiply to check:*
           $15 \times \$12 = \$180$

It will take Wilma 15 weeks
to pay for the radio.

problems

Solve.

1. Karen is 65 in. (inches) tall. David is 73 in. tall. How much taller is David than Karen?

2. Bob weighs 135 lb (pounds) and Ken weighs 147 lb. What is their combined weight?

3. $133 is to be shared equally by 7 students. How much does each student get?

4. An employer pays each worker $135 a week. There are 14 workers. What is the total amount paid to the workers each week?

5. Pearl earns $26,500 a year and Don earns $25,750 a year. What is their total income?

6. A color television set costs $379 and a stereo costs $289. Which costs more? How much more?

7. Tickets to a concert cost $26 each. Find the cost of 8 tickets.

8. Twenty-three pairs of jeans cost $368. How much does each pair cost?

9. The book room has 47 reams of paper. Each ream contains 500 sheets of paper. How many sheets of paper are in the book room?

10. After spending $38, Carlos had $45 left. How much money did he begin with?

11. A company budgeted $94,000 for new desks. How many $229 desks could be bought? How much money would be left?

12. A farmer divided his land equally among his six children. Each son or daughter received 259 acres. How many acres did the farmer begin with?

review exercises

Find each sum or difference.

1. 39 + 87 + 41
2. 261 + 53 + 109
3. 63 + 215 + 39
4. 43 + 91 + 83 + 36
5. 107 + 46 + 249 + 81
6. 74 + 514 + 317 + 92
7. 398 − 143
8. 675 − 432
9. 523 − 357
10. 805 − 649
11. 1046 − 873
12. 1204 − 769

Find each product.

13. 93 × 10
14. 87 × 100
15. 149 × 4
16. 73 × 12
17. 419 × 7
18. 249 × 60
19. 543 × 52
20. 269 × 365

SKILL REVIEW

Find each quotient.

1. $4)\overline{2484}$
2. $6)\overline{\$7452}$
3. $16,168 \div 8$
4. $54,862 \div 3$
5. $5)\overline{\$30,105}$
6. $9)\overline{52,317}$

4-1

Use compatible numbers to estimate.

7. $6)\overline{23,751}$
8. $41,912 \div 5$
9. $\$13,531 \div 7$
10. $52)\overline{32,050}$
11. $28)\overline{\$89,768}$
12. $39,980 \div 19$

4-2

Find each quotient.

13. $7524 \div 15$
14. $37)\overline{9472}$
15. $64)\overline{37,747}$
16. $42,042 \div 21$
17. $78,920 \div 89$
18. $51)\overline{64,413}$

4-3

Find each quotient.

19. $621)\overline{1863}$
20. $\$5754 \div 274$
21. $398)\overline{37,946}$
22. $98,717 \div 487$
23. $525)\overline{\$588,000}$
24. $415,665 \div 403$

4-4

Write each division in two other ways.

25. $\dfrac{62}{4}$
26. $5)\overline{890}$
27. $72 \div 9$
28. $\dfrac{452}{24}$

4-5

Evaluate each expression when $a = 6$ and $b = 72$.

29. $\dfrac{48}{a}$
30. $\dfrac{246}{a}$
31. $\dfrac{b}{9}$
32. $\dfrac{b}{a}$

Find each number.

33. 363 divided by 11
34. seventy-four, doubled
35. the product of 24 and 16
36. 6416, quartered

4-6

Write each phrase as a variable expression. Use x as the variable.

37. 37 times a number
38. a number divided by 18
39. a number, tripled
40. a number, halved

Solve.

41. Sue earned $33,744 last year. There are twelve months in a year. How much money did Sue earn in a month?

4-7

42. Ramon had $3108 in his checking account. He wrote a check for $469. How much money was left in his account?

4-8 UNITS OF TIME

The table at the right shows
how some common units of time
are related. To change from
one unit of time to another,
use the following method.

To change to a *smaller* unit, *multiply*.
To change to a *larger* unit, *divide*.

60 seconds (s)	=	1 minute (min)
60 min	=	1 hour (h)
24 h	=	1 day
7 days	=	1 week
4 weeks (approximately)	=	1 month
365 days	=	1 year
52 weeks (approximately)	=	1 year
12 months	=	1 year
10 years	=	1 decade
100 years	=	1 century

example

Complete.

a. 1380 s = __?__ min

b. 26 decades = __?__ years

solution

a. A minute is a larger unit
than a second, so *divide*.

$$60 \text{ s} = 1 \text{ min}$$
$$\div 60$$
$$1380 \text{ s} = 23 \text{ min}$$
$$\div 60$$

A calculator may be helpful.

b. A year is a smaller unit
than a decade, so *multiply*.

$$1 \text{ decade} = 10 \text{ years}$$
$$\times 10$$
$$26 \text{ decades} = 260 \text{ years}$$
$$\times 10$$

Use mental math.

exercises

Complete. Use mental math, or use a calculator if you have one.

1. 1920 s = __?__ min

2. 5 weeks = __?__ days

3. 8 h = __?__ min

4. 700 years = __?__ centuries

5. 6 decades = __?__ years

6. 204 months = __?__ years

7. Lewis and Clark spent 2 years, 4 months, and 9 days
exploring the American Northwest. About how many
weeks was this?

8. The explorer Magellan circled the world in 1126 days.
About how many years was this?

9. The modern revival of the Olympic games occurred
in 1896. About how many centuries ago was this?

10. Calculate how many days you have been alive.
How many hours is this? How many minutes?
How many seconds?

Dividing Whole Numbers 89

4-9 AVERAGES

Rosie Rosello earns $1417 per month. She wants to estimate the amount she spends each month. She has kept track of her spending for several months to find the **average** amount she spends.

	Jan	Feb	Mar	Apr	Four Month Total
Food	$ 75	$ 63	$ 79	$ 75	
Transportation	40	42	37	45	
Clothes	39	0	43	18	
Gifts	0	12	0	20	
Entertainment	25	33	27	23	
Phone	6	10	4	8	
Rent	167	167	167	167	
Charity	6	9	10	7	
Club dues	6	6	6	6	
Other	15	12	18	23	
Monthly Total					

example

Find the average amount Rosie spends on food for the four months.

solution

Add to find the total spent on food for the four months.

$75 + $63 + $79 + $75 = $292

Rosie spends about $73 per month on food.

Divide the sum by the number of months to find the average.

$292 ÷ 4 = $73

exercises

Find the average amount spent for the four months for the given purpose. Use a calculator if you have one.

1. transportation
2. clothes
3. entertainment
4. gifts
5. telephone
6. rent
7. charity
8. other

9. a. Find the total amount spent for each month. Use a calculator if you have one.
   b. Use your answer from (a) to find the average amount spent in a month.

10. Keep track of your own expenses for at least three months. Find the average amount you spend in a month.

CHAPTER REVIEW

vocabulary vo·cab·u·lar·y

1. The answer to a division problem is called the *(dividend, quotient)*.
2. In a division, the number you divide by is the *(dividend, divisor)*.
3. When you double a number, you *(multiply, divide)* it by 2.
4. When a number is multiplied by 4, it is *(quartered, quadrupled)*.

skills

Find the quotient.

5. $3\overline{)9425}$
6. $\$17{,}480 \div 4$
7. $87{,}056 \div 9$
8. $6\overline{)\$48{,}726}$
9. $72\overline{)5793}$
10. $72{,}061 \div 45$
11. $23\overline{)\$193{,}246}$
12. $253{,}737 \div 99$
13. $8414 \div 127$
14. $\$72{,}520 \div 392$
15. $441\overline{)289{,}296}$
16. $975\overline{)136{,}503}$

Use compatible numbers to estimate.

17. $\$3534 \div 6$
18. $5\overline{)9975}$
19. $39\overline{)81{,}280}$
20. $\$35{,}892 \div 93$

Evaluate each expression when $a = 3$, $b = 4$, $c = 12$, and $d = 48$.

21. $\dfrac{c}{a}$
22. $\dfrac{144}{c}$
23. $\dfrac{d}{8}$
24. $\dfrac{d}{b}$

Find each number.

25. sixteen, quadrupled
26. one hundred divided by five
27. 832, halved
28. the product of 22 and 33

Write each phrase as a variable expression. Use y as the variable.

29. divide 82 by a number
30. a number, doubled
31. the product of 12 and a number
32. a number divided by 45

Solve.

33. A doll costs $14. How much will it cost if Mr. Sanchez buys a doll for each of his three children?
34. It takes Jeremy about 9 min to run one mile. How many seconds is this?
35. For the four weeks in February, Elinore spent $77, $63, $60, and $84 for food. Find the average amount Elinore spent for food in these four weeks.

CHAPTER TEST

Find each quotient.

1. $4\overline{)2763}$ 2. $7\overline{)\$11,970}$ 3. $81,291 \div 5$ **4-1**

Use compatible numbers to estimate.

4. $7\overline{)27,570}$ 5. $45,113 \div 52$ 6. $64\overline{)\$423,168}$ **4-2**

Find each quotient.

7. $45,063 \div 24$ 8. $92\overline{)75,616}$ 9. $\$157,916 \div 37$ **4-3**

Find each quotient.

10. $216\overline{)\$46,656}$ 11. $734,084 \div 352$ 12. $266,943 \div 627$ **4-4**

Write each division in two other ways.

13. $412 \div 4$ 14. $\dfrac{36}{9}$ 15. $11\overline{)121}$ **4-5**

Evaluate each expression when $x = 7$, $y = 8$, and $z = 56$.

16. $\dfrac{z}{x}$ 17. $\dfrac{120}{y}$ 18. $\dfrac{z}{y}$ 19. $\dfrac{z}{4}$ 20. $\dfrac{168}{z}$ 21. $\dfrac{0}{x}$

Find each number.

22. divide 189 by 9   23. the product of 8 and 14   **4-6**

24. 34 times 7   25. 256 divided by 16

Write each phrase as a variable expression. Use c as the variable.

26. 205 times a number

27. a number divided by 12

28. 310 divided by a number

29. a number multiplied by 11

Solve.

30. Paul weighs 163 lb (pounds). Andrea weighs 117 lb. How much more does Paul weigh than Andrea?   **4-7**

31. On Mehgan's fourteenth birthday, approximately how many days old was she?   **4-8**

32. Lisa Chou received six water bills last year. The amounts of the bills were $43, $37, $61, $56, $44, and $47. Find the average amount of Lisa's six water bills.   **4-9**

To keep her program running smoothly, this disc jockey has to think of many separate operations and perform them in the right order.

CHAPTER 5

ORDER OF OPERATIONS AND NUMBER THEORY

5-1 ORDER OF OPERATIONS

To unlock a door, you must proceed in a certain order. First you identify the correct key for the lock. Then you insert the key to release the lock. Similarly, the operations of multiplication, division, addition, and subtraction must be performed in a specific order.

Order of Operations

1. First do all work inside any parentheses.
2. Then do all multiplications and divisions, working from left to right.
3. Then do all additions and subtractions, working from left to right.

example 1

Find each answer: **a.** $21 + 28 \div 7$ **b.** $3 \times 4 + 10 - 18 \div 3$

solution

a. $21 + 28 \div 7$ ← Divide first, then add.
$\quad\ 21 + 4$
$\qquad 25$

b. $3 \times 4 + 10 - 18 \div 3$ ← Do the multiplication and division in order.
$\quad\ 12 + 10 - 18 \div 3$
$\quad\ 12 + 10 - 6$ ← Do the addition and subtraction in order.
$\qquad 22 - 6$
$\qquad\ 16$

your turn

Find each answer.

1. $50 - 4 \times 9$ **2.** $24 \div 2 + 10$ **3.** $6 \div 3 - 1 + 8 \times 2$ **4.** $3 + 9 \times 2 - 4 \times 4$

example 2

Find each answer: **a.** $50 \div (2 + 3)$ **b.** $5 + 8(7 - 4)$

solution

a. $50 \div (2 + 3)$ ← Work inside the parentheses first.
$\quad\ 50 \div 5$
$\qquad 10$

b. $5 + 8(7 - 4)$
$\quad\ 5 + 8(3)$ ← 8(3) means 8 × 3.
$\quad\ 5 + 24$
$\qquad 29$

your turn

Find each answer.

5. $(24 + 16) \div 8$ **6.** $49(15 - 5)$ **7.** $(5 + 21) \div (7 - 5)$ **8.** $4 + 3(9 - 2) - 5$

To evaluate variable expressions, follow the same order of operations.

example 3

Evaluate each expression when $x = 5$, $y = 10$, and $z = 2$.

a. $2x + 3$ **b.** $y - 4z$ **c.** $6 + \frac{y}{x}$

solution

a. $2 \cdot x + 3$
$2 \cdot 5 + 3$
$10 + 3$
13

b. $y - 4 \cdot z$
$10 - 4 \cdot 2$
$10 - 8$
2

c. $6 + y \div x$
$6 + 10 \div 5$
$6 + 2$
8

your turn

Evaluate each expression when $a = 4$, $b = 20$, and $c = 36$.

9. $3a - 2$ **10.** $56 + 2c$ **11.** $\frac{b}{5} + c$ **12.** $10 - \frac{b}{a}$

practice exercises

practice for example 1 (page 94)

Find each answer.

1. $15 - 8 + 9$

2. $17 + 9 - 21$

3. $12 \div 6 \times 2$

4. $3 \times 10 \div 5$

5. $8 + 2 \times 9$

6. $7 \times 8 - 7$

7. $18 \div 9 - 2 \div 2$

8. $6 \times 4 + 3 \times 2$

9. $6 + 7 \times 3 - 2$

10. $10 - 4 \times 2 + 50$

11. $36 \div 4 + 12 \div 3 - 3$

12. $2 \times 8 - 2 \times 7 - 1$

practice for example 2 (page 94)

Find each answer.

13. $24 \div (12 \div 3)$

14. $(24 + 36) \div 4$

15. $6(14 - 4)$

16. $5(2 + 9)$

17. $(2 + 6) \div (2 + 2)$

18. $(21 - 3) \div (1 + 5)$

19. $6 + 4(28 - 6)$

20. $75 - 3(12 - 2)$

21. $5(14 + 11) + 7$

22. $100(25 \div 5) - 3$

23. $13 + (6 \times 3) \div (5 + 4)$

24. $90 - (2 \times 10) \div (7 - 3)$

practice for example 3 (page 95)

Evaluate each expression when $p = 6$, $q = 12$, and $r = 30$.

25. $5p - 3$

26. $2q + 4$

27. $p + 2q$

28. $r + 3p$

29. $\frac{p}{3} + 8$

30. $\frac{r}{6} - 3$

31. $20 - \frac{q}{p}$

32. $\frac{24}{q} + p$

mixed practice (pages 94–95)

Find each answer.

33. $110 \div 10 \times 5$

34. $6 + 7 \times 11 + 30$

35. $20 - 18 \div 9 + 2$

36. $4(3 + 4)$

37. $18 \div (9 - 3)$

38. $6 \times 2(18 - 5) - 8$

Evaluate each expression for the given values of the variables.

39. $6x - 4$, when $x = 15$

40. $18 + 7m$, when $m = 16$

41. $2c + 3d$, when $c = 2$ and $d = 9$

42. $y - 40z$, when $y = 41$ and $z = 1$

43. $\frac{7}{s} + 15$, when $s = 7$

44. $\frac{x}{10} - 4$, when $x = 200$

45. $\frac{c}{d} + 55$, when $c = 0$ and $d = 2$

46. $77 - \frac{a}{b}$, when $a = 14$ and $b = 2$

47. Mark had $50 before he bought two cassettes at $12 each. Then his father gave him $10. How much money does Mark have now?

48. Five days a week Sarah drives 17 mi (miles) round trip to work. Twice a week she also drives 4 mi round trip to school. How many miles does she drive each week because of her work and classes?

review exercises

Find each quotient.

1. $75 \div 5$

2. $21 \div 3$

3. $54 \div 6$

4. $98 \div 7$

5. $84 \div 4$

6. $60 \div 12$

7. $30 \div 15$

8. $81 \div 27$

calculator corner

Many calculators have the order of operations built into them.

example Experiment with your calculator to find the answer: $5 + 7 \times 3$

solution Enter $5 + 7 \times 3$.
If the answer is 26, your calculator follows the order of operations.
If the answer is not 26, you must enter the problem in the correct order.
Enter $7 \times 3 + 5$ to get 26.

Use a calculator to find each answer.

1. $7 + 8 \times 9$

2. $36 + 4 \times 5$

3. $14 + 6 \div 2$

4. $15 + 15 \times 4$

5. $2(20 - 5)$

6. $3 + 3(4 - 2)$

7. $(29 - 5) \div 6$

8. $(12 + 144) \div 6$

5-2 DIVISIBILITY TESTS

A number is **divisible** by a second number if the remainder is zero when the first number is divided by the second.

$$\begin{array}{r} 6 \\ 8\overline{)48} \\ 48 \\ \hline 0 \end{array}$$ 48 is divisible by 8.

$$\begin{array}{r} 5 \\ 8\overline{)46} \\ 40 \\ \hline 6 \end{array}$$ 46 is *not* divisible by 8.

You can use special *divisibility tests* to determine if a whole number is divisible by certain numbers.

Divisibility Tests

Divisible by	Test
2 5 10	The last digit is 0, 2, 4, 6, or 8. The last digit is 0 or 5. The last digit is 0.
4 8	The number named by the last two digits is divisible by 4. The number named by the last three digits is divisible by 8.
3 9	The sum of the digits is divisible by 3. The sum of the digits is divisible by 9.

example 1

Is each number divisible by 5? by 10? by 2? Write *Yes* or *No*.

a. 285   **b.** 3506   **c.** 410   **d.** 7903

solution

a. 285
    Divisible:
        by 5? *Yes*
        by 10? *No*
        by 2? *No*

b. 3506
    Divisible:
        by 5? *No*
        by 10? *No*
        by 2? *Yes*

c. 410
    Divisible:
        by 5? *Yes*
        by 10? *Yes*
        by 2? *Yes*

d. 7903
    Divisible:
        by 5? *No*
        by 10? *No*
        by 2? *No*

your turn

Is each number divisible by 5? by 10? by 2? Write *Yes* or *No*.

1. 1295   **2.** 778   **3.** 380

4. 5063   **5.** 4728   **6.** 9225

example 2

Is each number divisible by 4? by 8? Write *Yes* or *No*.

a. 316

b. 4728

solution

a. $\overline{316}$ divisible by 4? *Yes*
        divisible by 8? *No*

b. $4\overline{728}$ divisible by 4? *Yes*
        divisible by 8? *Yes*

your turn

Is each number divisible by 4? by 8? Write *Yes* or *No*.

7. 128   **8.** 1440   **9.** 3330   **10.** 2002   **11.** 8124

example 3

Is each number divisible by 3? by 9? Write *Yes* or *No*.

a. 264

b. 189

solution

a. $2 + 6 + 4 = 12$
        divisible by 3? *Yes*
        divisible by 9? *No*

b. $1 + 8 + 9 = 18$
        divisible by 3? *Yes*
        divisible by 9? *Yes*

your turn

Is each number divisible by 3? by 9? Write *Yes* or *No*.

12. 723   **13.** 984   **14.** 3263   **15.** 8217   **16.** 12,726

practice exercises

practice for example 1 (page 97)

Is each number divisible by 5? by 10? by 2? Write *Yes* or *No*.

1. 83	**2.** 6010	**3.** 86	**4.** 5715	**5.** 445
6. 202	**7.** 2001	**8.** 970	**9.** 6543	**10.** 2134

practice for example 2 (page 98)

Is each number divisible by 4? by 8? Write *Yes* or *No*.

11. 9012	**12.** 444	**13.** 7752	**14.** 932	**15.** 5136
16. 3200	**17.** 3356	**18.** 7893	**19.** 8750	**20.** 81,464

Is each number divisible by 3? by 9? Write *Yes* or *No*.

21. 920 **22.** 5495 **23.** 2205 **24.** 2253 **25.** 6796

26. 8883 **27.** 41,679 **28.** 48,312 **29.** 63,578 **30.** 61,674

mixed practice *(pages 97-98)*

Is the first number divisible by the second number? Write *Yes* or *No*.

31. 1465; 5 **32.** 1111; 10 **33.** 3207; 2 **34.** 8520; 4

35. 65,644; 8 **36.** 37,932; 3 **37.** 274,789; 2 **38.** 754,308; 9

Any number that is divisible by 2 is an *even number*. Any number that is not divisible by 2 is an *odd number*. Tell whether the following numbers are *even* or *odd*.

39. 318 **40.** 95 **41.** 71 **42.** 530 **43.** 869 **44.** 1066

45. Any year whose number is divisible by 4 is a leap year, except the years with numbers that end in 00. The numbers of these years must be divisible by 400. Are the following years leap years: 1762, 1828, 1900, and 2000?

46. In the United States, presidential elections are held every four years, in years with numbers divisible by 4. How many presidential elections were there between 1930 and 1986?

review *exercises*

Find each answer.

1. 95 × 603 **2.** 1923 + 4587 **3.** 2020 ÷ 20 **4.** 27 × 313

5. 6522 − 396 **6.** 4250 ÷ 85 **7.** 5302 + 898 **8.** 3071 − 2684

mental math

Here are some mental math problems to sharpen your skills.

Add, subtract, or multiply mentally.

1. 5 × 99 **2.** (5 × 37) × 20 **3.** 36 + 14 **4.** 54 + 28

5. 63 + 99 **6.** 124 + 115 **7.** 574 − 299 **8.** 20 × (19 × 5)

9. 125 + 225 **10.** 285 − 99 **11.** 3 × 499 **12.** 1458 + 2999

5-3 FACTORS AND PRIMES

When one number is divisible by a second number, the second number is a **factor** of the first.

> 12 is *divisible* by 3.   3 is a *factor* of 12.

A **prime number** is a whole number greater than 1 that has exactly two factors, 1 and the number itself. A **composite number** has more than two factors.

> 3 is *prime* because its only factors are 1 and 3.
> 12 is *composite* because its factors are 1, 2, 3, 4, 6, and 12.

When you write a whole number as the product of numbers that are prime, you are finding the **prime factorization** of the number.

example 1

Write the prime factorization of 28.

solution

◄— **This is called a *factor tree*.**

The prime factorization of 28 is 2 × 2 × 7.

your turn

Write the prime factorization of each number.

1. 10   **2.** 20   **3.** 30   **4.** 16   **5.** 38   **6.** 45

The **common factors** of 12 and 28 are 1, 2, and 4. The **greatest common factor (GCF)** of 12 and 28 is 4. Two methods of finding the GCF are shown in Example 2.

example 2

Find the GCF: **a.** 24 and 36   **b.** 56 and 84

solution

a. List the factors of each number and look for the GCF.

24: 1, 2, 3, 4, 6, 8, 12, 24
36: 1, 2, 3, 4, 6, 9, 12, 18, 36

12 is the GCF of 24 and 36.

b. Multiply all the prime factors that are common to both numbers.

56 = 2 × 2 × 2 × 7
84 = 2 × 2 × 3 × 7

◄— **The GCF is 2 × 2 × 7.**

28 is the GCF of 56 and 84.

Find the GCF.

7. 36 and 60   **8.** 12 and 20   **9.** 18 and 27   **10.** 12, 15, and 18

practice exercises

practice for example 1 (page 100)

Write the prime factorization of each number.

1. 21   **2.** 50   **3.** 40   **4.** 66   **5.** 81   **6.** 77

7. 225   **8.** 108   **9.** 110   **10.** 144   **11.** 360   **12.** 500

practice for example 2 (pages 100–101)

Find the GCF.

13. 9 and 12   **14.** 6 and 18   **15.** 12 and 15   **16.** 20 and 28

17. 4 and 15   **18.** 8 and 9   **19.** 40 and 48   **20.** 24 and 90

21. 8, 12, and 18   **22.** 10, 25, and 30   **23.** 12, 16, and 20   **24.** 60, 90, and 150

mixed practice (pages 100–101)

Tell whether each number is *prime* or *composite*.

25. 2   **26.** 7   **27.** 9   **28.** 6   **29.** 15   **30.** 17

31. 29   **32.** 31   **33.** 51   **34.** 77   **35.** 87   **36.** 91

37. List all the prime numbers between 0 and 20.

38. Find the greatest prime number that is less than 100.

review exercises

Find each product.

1. 60 × 80   **2.** 30 × 600   **3.** 4000 × 70   **4.** 6000 × 500

5. 800 × 400   **6.** 70 × 9000   **7.** 800 × 500   **8.** 1200 × 3000

9. Hannah and her three sisters are renting a beach house for the month of July. The rent is $792. How much will each person pay?

10. Kathryn received 137 votes for class president. Charlie received 173 votes, and George received 107 votes. Who won the election?

5-4 MULTIPLES

When a number is multiplied by a nonzero whole number, the product is a **multiple** of the given number.

$8 \times 1 = 8$, $8 \times 2 = 16$, $8 \times 3 = 24$, $8 \times 4 = 32$,   and so on.

Multiples of 8: 8, 16, 24, 32, 40, ...

example 1

List six multiples of each number: **a.** 6   **b.** 9

solution

a. $6 \times 1 = 6, 6 \times 2 = 12, 6 \times 3 = 18, 6 \times 4 = 24, 6 \times 5 = 30, 6 \times 6 = 36$

b. 9, 18, 27, 36, 45, 54

your turn

List six multiples of each number.

1. 4   **2.** 5   **3.** 10   **4.** 2

The numbers 18 and 36 are called **common multiples** of 6 and 9. The **least common multiple (LCM)** of 6 and 9 is 18. Two methods of finding the LCM are shown in Example 2.

example 2

Find the LCM: **a.** 6 and 8   **b.** 90 and 150

solution

a. List the nonzero multiples of each number and look for the LCM.

6:   6, 12, 18, 24, 30, . . .
8:   8, 16, 24, 32, . . .

24 is the LCM of 6 and 8.

b. Multiply the prime factors that are common to both numbers by the prime factors that are not common to both.

$90 = 2 \times 3 \times 3 \times 5$
$150 = 2 \times 3 \times 5 \times 5$

$2 \times 3 \times 3 \times 5 \times 5 = 450$
450 is the LCM of 90 and 150.

your turn

Find the LCM.

5. 8 and 10   **6.** 12 and 16   **7.** 18 and 21   **8.** 4, 6, and 9

practice exercises

practice for example 1 (page 102)

List six multiples of each number.

1. 3   2. 7   3. 11   4. 12   5. 18   6. 45

practice for example 2 (page 102)

Find the LCM.

7. 10 and 25   8. 4 and 6   9. 4 and 12   10. 9 and 18

11. 6 and 16   12. 9 and 15   13. 3 and 5   14. 9 and 10

15. 3, 5, and 10   16. 27, 36, and 54   17. 10, 15, and 18   18. 12, 20, and 30

mixed practice (page 102)

19. List all the multiples of 6 between 40 and 100.
20. List all the multiples of 7 between 50 and 120.
21. Find the least multiple of 4 that is greater than 725.
22. Name two multiples of 16 and 24 that are also multiples of 40.
23. Sheets of writing paper come in boxes of 100, and envelopes come in boxes of 75. What is the least number of envelopes and sheets of paper that you can buy to get an equal number of each?
24. Suppose that plastic spoons come in packages of 6, plastic forks in packages of 8, and plastic knives in packages of 12. What is the least number of spoons, forks, and knives that you can buy to get an equal number of each?

review exercises

Find each product.

1. $4 \times 4 \times 4$ 2. $6 \cdot 6$ 3. $5 \cdot 5 \cdot 5$ 4. $10 \cdot 10 \cdot 10 \cdot 10$

5. $1 \times 8 \times 8$ 6. $1 \times 1 \times 1 \times 1 \times 1$ 7. $3 \cdot 3 \cdot 4 \cdot 4$ 8. $2 \cdot 2 \cdot 2 \cdot 2 \cdot 2 \cdot 1$

5-5 EXPONENTS AND WHOLE NUMBERS

Suppose you were offered a job that would pay you the salary shown at the right. What amount do you think you would receive on the tenth day? If you compute the tenth *power* of 2, you find that you would receive $1024.

Day 1	$2
Day 2	$2 × 2
Day 3	$2 × 2 × 2
Day 4	$2 × 2 × 2 × 2
Day 5	$2 × 2 × 2 × 2 × 2
and so on	

A multiplication in which all the factors are the same can be written in a shortened form called **exponential form.**

$$2 \times 2 \times 2 \times 2 \times 2 \times 2 \times 2 \times 2 \times 2 \times 2 = 2^{10} \leftarrow \textbf{exponent}$$

10 **factors**   base

The **exponent** 10 indicates the number of times that the **base** 2 is used as a factor. We read the expression 2^{10} as *two to the tenth power*.

$$2^{10} = 2 \times 2 \times 2 \times 2 \times 2 \times 2 \times 2 \times 2 \times 2 \times 2 = 1024$$

The number 1024 is called the tenth **power** of 2.

example 1

Find each product.

a. 5^3 **b.** 8^4 **c.** $2^2 \times 3^2$

solution

a. $5^3 = 5 \times 5 \times 5$
$= 125$

b. $8^4 = 8 \times 8 \times 8 \times 8$
$= 4096$

c. $2^2 \times 3^2 = 2 \times 2 \times 3 \times 3$
$= 36$

your turn

Find each product.

1. 9^2 **2.** 6^3 **3.** 2^5 **4.** 3^4 **5.** $5^2 \times 10^3$

When any base has the exponent 1, the power is equal to the base. When any *nonzero* base has the exponent 0, the power is equal to 1.

example 2

Find each answer: **a.** 4^0 **b.** 5^1 **c.** $6^1 \times 2^3$ **d.** $10^2 \times 8^0$

solution

a. $4^0 = 1$ **b.** $5^1 = 5$ **c.** $6^1 \times 2^3 = 6 \times 8 = 48$ **d.** $10^2 \times 8^0 = 100 \times 1 = 100$

your turn

Find each answer.

6. 9^0 **7.** 12^1 **8.** $5^0 \times 7^1$ **9.** $3^2 \times 15^0$ **10.** $4^1 \times 2^3$

practice exercises

practice for example 1 *(page 104)*

Find each product.

1. 7^2 **2.** 3^3 **3.** 2^4 **4.** 10^5 **5.** 3^6
6. 5^4 **7.** 9^3 **8.** 12^2 **9.** $8^2 \times 10^4$ **10.** $4^3 \times 5^2$

practice for example 2 *(pages 104–105)*

Find each answer.

11. 12^0 **12.** 9^0 **13.** 8^1 **14.** 10^1 **15.** 34^1
16. 28^0 **17.** $4^1 \times 7^0$ **18.** $6^0 \times 9^1$ **19.** $2^1 \times 3^2$ **20.** $2^0 \times 5^2$

mixed practice *(pages 104–105)*

Write each multiplication in exponential form.

21. $7 \times 7 \times 7 \times 7$ **22.** 3×3
23. $10 \times 10 \times 10$ **24.** $1 \times 1 \times 1 \times 1 \times 1$
25. $9 \times 9 \times 9$ **26.** 100×100
27. $4 \times 4 \times 4 \times 4$ **28.** $2 \times 2 \times 2 \times 2 \times 2$

Find each answer.

29. 2^6 **30.** 5^3 **31.** 4^0 **32.** 1^9 **33.** $3^1 \times 3^0$
34. $5^2 \times 3^1$ **35.** $2^2 \times 7^2$ **36.** $3^4 \times 10^3$ **37.** $5^3 \times 10^4$ **38.** $2^6 \times 6^2$

39. The population of the United States is about 2×10^8. Find this product. Write the short word form of this number.

40. Earth is about 9×10^7 mi (miles) from the sun. Find this product. Write the short word form of this number.

review exercises

Find each answer.

1. $5 + 3 \times 9$ **2.** $18 - 6 \div 2$ **3.** $20 + 12 \div 4$ **4.** $63 - 8 \times 5$
5. $4 \times 7 + 15 \div 3$ **6.** $16 \div 2 - 2 \times 3$ **7.** $8 + 2(9 - 5)$ **8.** $45 - 5(3 + 6)$

5-6 EXPONENTS AND VARIABLES

Sometimes a power can have a variable for its base. We write variable
powers in factored form by repeating the variables as factors.

$$a^3 = \underbrace{a \cdot a \cdot a}_{} \qquad b^2 = b \cdot b \qquad 5c^3 = 5 \cdot c \cdot c \cdot c$$

↑   ↑

exponential form   **factored form**

example 1

Write each expression in factored form: **a.** y^4 **b.** $4x^2$ **c.** $3c^2d^3$

solution

a. $y^4 = y \cdot y \cdot y \cdot y$ **b.** $4x^2 = 4 \cdot x \cdot x$ **c.** $3c^2d^3 = 3 \cdot c \cdot c \cdot d \cdot d \cdot d$

your turn

Write each expression in factored form.

   1. z^5 **2.** $9m^3$ **3.** $7rs^2$ **4.** $4x^2y^2$

       When you evaluate a variable expression
that contains exponents, write the expression
in factored form before you evaluate it.

example 2

**Evaluate each expression when
$m = 2$ and $n = 3$.**

a. m^4 **b.** $6mn^2$

solution

a. m^4 **b.** $6mn^2$

    $m \cdot m \cdot m \cdot m$ $6 \cdot m \cdot n \cdot n$

    $2 \cdot 2 \cdot 2 \cdot 2$ $6 \cdot 2 \cdot 3 \cdot 3$

       16   108

your turn

**Evaluate each expression when
$a = 5$, $b = 2$, and $c = 10$.**

   5. a^3 **6.** c^2

   7. bc^3 **8.** $5a^2b^2$

practice exercises

practice for example 1 (page 106)

Write each expression in factored form.

1. b^4
2. c^5
3. $3a^2$
4. $8b^3$
5. b^2c^4
6. a^2b^2
7. b^3c
8. ac^4
9. $6a^2b^2$
10. $14b^3c^3$

practice for example 2 (page 106)

Evaluate each expression when $k = 3$, $y = 5$, and $w = 10$.

11. w^3
12. y^2
13. k^4
14. yk^2
15. ky^2
16. y^2w
17. k^2w^2
18. k^2y^2
19. $4y^2w^2$
20. $2k^2w^3$

mixed practice (page 106)

Write each expression in its corresponding factored or exponential form.

21. $y \cdot y \cdot y \cdot y \cdot y$
22. $a \cdot a \cdot a$
23. $5a^2b$
24. $16x^3y^3$

Evaluate each expression for the given values of the variables.

25. a^4, when $a = 3$
26. y^3, when $y = 10$
27. c^2d, when $c = 4$ and $d = 5$
28. $4bc^2$, when $b = 4$ and $c = 2$
29. $10r^2s^2$, when $r = 3$ and $s = 1$
30. $2q^3r^2$, when $q = 10$ and $r = 2$

review exercises

Estimate each quotient.

1. $993 \div 21$
2. $1297 \div 43$
3. $3627 \div 52$
4. $23,219 \div 39$
5. $41,592 \div 585$
6. $34,268 \div 872$

7. Stanley earns $3 per page typing. How much does he earn typing a 276-page document?

8. Your rent is $674 a month. How much rent have you paid after 17 months?

puzzle corner

Name a nonzero whole number that has 2, 3, 5, and 7 as factors.

SKILL REVIEW

Find each answer.

1. $38 - 8 \times 2$ 2. $5 \times 2 + 2 \div 2$ 3. $15 + 60 \div (10 + 5)$ 4. $7(3 + 5)$ **5-1**

Evaluate each expression when $a = 5$, $b = 45$, and $c = 20$.

5. $3b - 35$ 6. $8 + 2a$ 7. $\frac{c}{2} + a$ 8. $14 - \frac{b}{a}$

9. $17 + \frac{c}{a}$ 10. $\frac{b}{9} + c$ 11. $11a + b$ 12. $\frac{b}{a} + 10$

Is the first number divisible by the second number? Write *Yes* or *No*.

13. $535; 5$ 14. $200; 10$ 15. $667; 2$ **5-2**
16. $792; 8$ 17. $5887; 3$ 18. $9119; 9$

19. The Olympics are held every four years, in years with numbers divisible by 4. How many Olympics have been held from the year 1950 to the year 1985?

Write the prime factorization of each number.

20. 63 21. 72 22. 150 **5-3**

Find the GCF.

23. 18 and 27 24. 20 and 30 25. $26, 39$, and 52

Find the LCM.

26. 14 and 21 27. 40 and 70 28. $4, 10$, and 18 **5-4**

29. A box of pencils contains 12 pencils, and a box of erasers contains 10 erasers. What is the least number of pencils and erasers that must be ordered to get an equal number?

Find each answer.

30. 10^4 31. 11^2 32. 9^0 33. 6^1 **5-5**
34. $5^2 \times 10^1$ 35. $2^3 \times 3^0$ 36. $3^3 \times 10^3$ 37. $2^3 \times 3^2$

Evaluate each expression when $x = 2$, $y = 3$, and $z = 10$.

38. y^2 39. x^3 **5-6**
40. $4z^3$ 41. xy^2
42. x^2y 43. x^2z^2
44. $2x^2y^2$ 45. $3y^3z^2$

5-7 WHOLESALE QUANTITIES

When Estelle Perez buys eggs from farmers for her supermarket, she buys dozens of dozens! Large amounts are often counted in **gross** and **great gross**.

1 dozen	$= 12$
1 gross	$= 12$ dozen $= 12^2 = 144$
1 great gross	$= 12$ gross $= 12^3 = 1728$

example

a. How many heads of lettuce will Estelle receive if she orders 15 dozen?

b. Estelle needs 7000 oranges. How many gross should she order?

solution

a. 1 dozen = 12
Multiply by 12.

$$\begin{array}{r} 15 \\ \times 12 \\ \hline 30 \\ 15 \\ \hline 180 \end{array}$$

Estelle will receive 180 heads of lettuce.

b. 1 gross = 144
Divide by 144.

$$\begin{array}{r} 48 \text{ R}88 \\ 144\overline{)7000} \\ 576 \\ \hline 1240 \\ 1152 \\ \hline 88 \end{array}$$

Because there is a remainder, she must round up to the next whole gross.

Estelle should order 49 gross of oranges.

exercises

Determine the number of items ordered. Use a calculator if you have one.

1. 2 great gross napkins
2. 5 gross corn
3. 6 dozen daffodils
4. 7 dozen watermelons
5. 9 great gross eggs
6. 3 gross carnations

Use the unit of measure given. How many are needed to fill each order?

7. 108 pencils; *dozen*
8. 600 peaches; *dozen*
9. 5000 potatoes; *great gross*
10. 550 pens; *gross*
11. 780 grapefruit; *gross*
12. 4500 cans of tuna; *great gross*

13. Estelle orders 3 gross of daisies and 2 gross of roses. How many flowers will she receive altogether?

14. Last year the Salem School District used 3855 tablets of paper. They expect to use the same amount this year. How many gross should they order for the coming year?

5-8 USING EXPRESSIONS OF TIME

There are many ways to express periods of time. Some of the most common expressions and their meanings are given at the right.

Times per Year		
	weekly (52)	biweekly (26)
semimonthly (24)	monthly (12)	bimonthly (6)
	quarterly (4)	
semiannually (2)	annually (1)	

example

a. Ed Baker took out a 3-year car loan. Find the number of monthly payments Ed makes.

b. Marisa Linehan owns stock in Boyd Motor Company. She receives quarterly dividend checks for $78. Find the total dividend she receives each year.

solution

a. monthly → 12 times per year
   3-year loan → 12 × 3 = 36
   Ed must make 36 monthly payments.

b. quarterly → 4 times per year
   $78 per quarter → $78 × 4 = $312
   Marisa's total dividend for one year is $312.

exercises

Find the total number of times.

1. quarterly for 4 years
2. weekly for 2 years
3. semiannually for 5 years
4. bimonthly for 20 years
5. biweekly for 10 years
6. monthly for 25 years

7. The Acorn Valley PTA publishes a semiannual newsletter. How many issues do they publish each year?

8. Stockholders in most companies receive quarterly reports. How many reports do they receive each year?

9. Lysandra Cooper owns a condominium. She makes monthly mortgage payments of $760. Find the total amount Lysandra pays in 30 years.

10. Larry Starbuck makes bimonthly payments for life insurance. Each payment is $154. Find the amount Larry pays in one year.

CHAPTER REVIEW

vocabulary vo·cab·u·lar·y

Choose the correct word to complete each sentence.

1. A (*prime, composite*) number has exactly two factors, 1 and the number itself.

2. A (*factor, multiple*) of a number is any product of that number and a nonzero whole number.

skills

Find each answer.

3. $18 \div 2 + 27 \div 9$ 4. $5 + 4 \times 3 - 2$ 5. $(24 + 16) \div 4$ 6. $50 \div (2 \times 5) - 2$

Is the first number divisible by the second number? Write *Yes* or *No*.

7. 675; 5   8. 321; 3   9. 4008; 10   10. 3600; 4   11. 5761; 2

Write the prime factorization of each number.

12. 12   13. 18   14. 98   15. 70   16. 24   17. 54

Find the GCF.

18. 6 and 8   19. 10 and 50   20. 36 and 60   21. 12, 18, and 72

Find the LCM.

22. 6 and 42   23. 16 and 24   24. 36 and 60   25. 12, 18, and 72

Find each product.

26. 2^5 27. 4^2 28. $3^2 \times 7^1$ 29. $9^0 \times 2^4$ 30. $5^3 \times 10^2$

Evaluate each expression when $x = 5$, $y = 2$, and $z = 10$.

31. x^4 32. xy^2
33. $3x^2z$ 34. y^2z^3

35. Cheryl ordered 6 gross of forks and 7 gross of spoons. How many items did she order in all?

36. Isaac is making bimonthly deposits of $130 in his savings account. How much money will he save in one year?

37. Describe the order in which arithmetic operations are performed.

Order of Operations and Number Theory 111

CHAPTER TEST

Find each answer.

1. $6 \times 5 - 4 \div 2$
2. $40 \div 2 + 3 \times 3 - 2$
3. $50(14 \div 7) + (6 \times 3)$

5-1

Evaluate each expression when $a = 3$, $b = 9$, and $c = 7$.

4. $3c - 20$
5. $34 + \dfrac{b}{3}$
6. $93 + \dfrac{27}{b}$
7. $12 - \dfrac{b}{a}$

8. Morgan poured two bags of 23 green marbles each into a jar. He then put in three bags of 17 red marbles each, plus 8 blue marbles. How many marbles are now in the jar?

Is the first number divisible by the second number? Write *Yes* or *No*.

9. 970; 5
10. 956; 8

5-2

11. 768; 2
12. 359; 9
13. 3318; 3
14. 8954; 4
15. 6945; 10
16. 86,709; 9

Find the GCF.

17. 30 and 4
18. 20 and 35

5-3

19. 36 and 42
20. 21, 35, and 49

Find the LCM.

21. 18 and 24
22. 8 and 40
23. 27 and 30
24. 20, 50, and 125

5-4

25. List all the multiples of 9 between 70 and 110.
26. Tulips come in bunches of 4, and daffodils come in bunches of 6. What is the least number of each kind of flower that you can buy in order to get an equal number?

Find each answer.

27. 9^2
28. 4^3
29. 11^0
30. 10^4

5-5

31. 26^1
32. $7^2 \times 15^0$
33. $6^1 \times 2^3$
34. $4^2 \times 10^3$

Evaluate each expression when $a = 2$, $b = 3$, and $c = 5$.

35. a^3
36. b^4
37. $a^2 b$

5-6

38. bc^2
39. $a^3 b^2$
40. $2ac^2$

41. Marie needs 100 eggs. How many dozen eggs should she buy? **5-7**
42. Shashi earns \$28,800 a year. Find Shashi's monthly income. **5-8**

The Parts of a Computer

Computers are changing the way we live, play, and work. Originally only highly trained specialists used computers to handle very complex calculations. Today the use of computers is widespread. Without computers, items such as digital watches, video games, word processors, and hand-held calculators would not exist.

Many schools, businesses, and individuals own one or more *personal computer systems*. A system such as this consists of the following equipment, or **hardware.**

monitor

disk drive

printer

computer with keyboard

All computers take the information you provide, or **input,** and process it. The result is called **output.** If you have access to a personal computer, you can use many different programs, or **software,** to tell the computer what to do. Many of these come on disks to be inserted into a disk drive. Most personal computers also allow you to write your own programs in a language such as BASIC.

exercises

1. What is another name for the information that you provide a computer to process?
2. Name the hardware that makes up a personal computer system.
3. Name two computer-related careers. You may consult professionals in the field or check with your school librarian.

COMPETENCY TEST

Choose the letter of the correct answer.

1. **Add.**

   7259
   +2834

   A. 1093
   B. 10,093
   C. 9083
   D. 90,083

2. **Subtract.**   2836 − 785

   A. 2511
   B. 2151
   C. 3621
   D. 2051

3. **Multiply.**

   656
   × 29

   A. 19,024
   B. 18,024
   C. 190,124
   D. 180,124

4. **What is the numeral form of seven hundred three million, sixty-eight thousand, five hundred twelve?**

   A. 73,068,512
   B. 730,680,512
   C. 703,068,512
   D. 703,608,512

5. **Name the digit in the millions' place in 427,615,890.**

   A. 4
   B. 7
   C. 5
   D. 2

6. **Multiply.**   125 × 3024

   A. 75,600
   B. 756,000
   C. 378,000
   D. 37,800

7. **Round 2,417,801 to the nearest thousand.**

   A. 2,418,000
   B. 2,417,000
   C. 2,417,800
   D. 2,420,000

8. **In 12 months, Ed earns $31,200. What does he earn each month?**

   A. $600
   B. $374,400
   C. $2500
   D. $2600

9. **The museum sold 274 adult tickets and 418 student tickets. How many more student tickets were sold?**

   A. 682
   B. 692
   C. 144
   D. 244

10. **Brian scored 14 points. Julie scored p more points than Brian. How many points did Julie score?**

    A. $14p$
    B. $p + 14$
    C. $p - 14$
    D. $14 - p$

11. Evaluate $2a^3b^2$ when $a = 2$ and $b = 3$.

  A. 72   B. 144
  C. 576   D. 216

12. Find the GCF of 18 and 24.

  A. 9   B. 6
  C. 12   D. 4

13. 4218 is divisible by which number?

  A. 3   B. 4
  C. 5   D. 9

14. Choose the best estimate.

72×792

  A. about 4900
  B. about 49,000
  C. about 5600
  D. about 56,000

15.

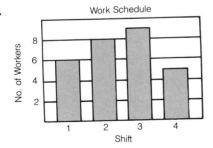

About how many workers work the first two shifts?

  A. 12   B. 14
  C. 5   D. 9

16. Find the LCM of 12 and 10.

  A. 60   B. 120
  C. 2   D. 30

17. Evaluate. $48 \div 6 - 3 \times 2$

  A. 10   B. 32
  C. 2   D. 8

18. Divide. $32\overline{)8866}$

  A. 27 R2   B. 23
  C. 277 R2   D. 273

19. Choose the best estimate.

$92\overline{)841,825}$

  A. about 90
  B. about 90,000
  C. about 900
  D. about 9000

20.

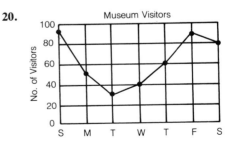

About how many people visited the museum on Thursday?

  A. 40   B. 50
  C. 60   D. 80

CUMULATIVE REVIEW CHAPTERS 1-5

Find each answer.

1. $4738 - 625$
2. $225 + 1278$
3. $36\overline{)2880}$
4. $8 + 6 \div 2$
5. 88×612
6. $24\overline{)728}$
7. $4(12 - 7) - 5$
8. $10^2 \times 9^0$
9. $3^3 \times 4^1$
10. 315×231
11. $812 + 1255 + 719$
12. $3 + 8 \times 4 - 6$

13. Round 718,927 to the nearest thousand.

14. Write the word form of 3,000,025,701.

15. Write in order from least to greatest: 1101; 1001; 1011.

Estimate each answer.

16. $5928 \div 28$
17. 62×81
18. $253 + 144$
19. $3209 + 4172 + 625$
20. $585 - 411$
21. 11×96
22. $62\overline{)49,715}$
23. 717×462
24. $94,895 - 86,697$

Evaluate each expression when $a = 5$, $b = 2$, and $c = 24$.

25. $c + b - a$
26. $2c + 3$
27. $\dfrac{0}{a}$
28. $\dfrac{c}{6} - 1$
29. b^3

Give the value of the underlined digit in each number.

30. $\underline{4}75,118$
31. $7\underline{2},615$
32. $628,\underline{4}15,703$

Write each phrase as a variable expression. Use n as the variable.

33. 17 less than a number
34. twice a number
35. a number increased by 21

Is the first number divisible by the second? Write *Yes* or *No*.

36. 2142; 4
37. 2005; 5
38. 32,310; 9

Find the GCF and the LCM.

39. 24 and 64
40. 9 and 21
41. 30, 12, and 18

42. A teacher divided 144 pencils equally among 23 students. How many pencils did each student get? How many pencils were left?

43. A sweater is on sale for $26. You are asked how much you will save by buying it on sale. What missing fact is needed?

44. Thursday, 105 people came to the school play. Friday, 210 people were in the audience, and 243 people came to the Saturday matinee. Find the average attendance for the 3 performances.

Music and mathematics have a very close relationship. In this chapter you will see how fractions are involved in musical notation.

CHAPTER 6

FRACTION CONCEPTS

6-1 WRITING FRACTIONS

The track in Glendale Park is divided into eight equal sections. For a race the runners use only the part of the track that is shaded in the figure at the right. The fraction $\frac{5}{8}$ represents the part of the track they use.

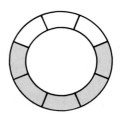

$$\frac{\text{number of shaded sections in the track} \rightarrow 5 \leftarrow \textbf{numerator}}{\text{total number of sections in the track} \rightarrow 8 \leftarrow \textbf{denominator}}$$

example 1

Write a fraction that names the shaded part of each region.

a.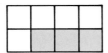

b.

solution

a. $\dfrac{\text{number shaded} \rightarrow 3}{\text{total number} \rightarrow 8}$

b. $\dfrac{\text{number shaded} \rightarrow 3}{\text{total number} \rightarrow 4}$

your turn

Write a fraction that names the shaded part of each region.

1.

2.

3.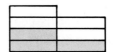

In Example 1 we used a fraction to describe a part of a single object. We can also use a fraction to describe a part of a *set* of objects.

example 2

Write a fraction that names the shaded part of each set.

a.

b.

solution

a. $\dfrac{\text{number shaded} \rightarrow 6}{\text{total number} \rightarrow 7}$

b. $\dfrac{\text{number shaded} \rightarrow 7}{\text{total number} \rightarrow 10}$

your turn

Write a fraction that names the shaded part of each set.

4.  5.   6.

You do not always need to look at a diagram in order to write a fraction.

---

example 3

Write a fraction that answers the question.

a. What part of a day is five hours?

b. What part of a week is three days?

solution

a. $\dfrac{\text{part}}{\text{total}} \rightarrow \dfrac{5}{24}$ ⬅ **There are twenty-four hours in a day.**

b. $\dfrac{\text{part}}{\text{total}} \rightarrow \dfrac{3}{7}$ ⬅ **There are seven days in a week.**

your turn

Write a fraction that answers the question.

7. What part of a week is two days?
8. What part of a minute is nineteen seconds?
9. What part of a year is one month?
10. What part of an hour is eleven minutes?

practice exercises

---

practice for example 1 (page 118)

Write a fraction that names the shaded part of each region.

1.  2. 3. 4.

---

practice for example 2 (pages 118–119)

Write a fraction that names the shaded part of each set.

5.   6.  7.  8.

practice for example 3 (page 119)

Write a fraction that answers the question.

9. What part of a year is seven months?
10. What part of an hour is nine minutes?
11. What part of a week is five days?
12. What part of a minute is thirty seconds?

mixed practice (pages 118–119)

Write a fraction that names the shaded part of each region or set.

13.
14.
15.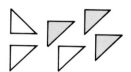
16.

Write a fraction that names the part of each region or set that is *not* shaded.

17.
18.
19.
20.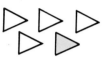

21. Of the letters in "Mississippi", what part are *i*'s?
22. Of the letters in "mathematics", what part are *t*'s?
23. What part of the given set of numbers is odd?   {1, 2, 5, 6, 8, 9, 10}
24. What part of the given set of numbers is prime?   {2, 3, 4, 5, 8, 10, 11}
25. Draw a circle and shade two sixths of it.
26. Draw a square and shade seven eighths of it.

review exercises

Find each product or quotient.

1. $48 \div 3$
2. 15×5
3. 18×2
4. $64 \div 4$
5. $108 \div 12$
6. 11×14
7. 15×16
8. $212 \div 4$
9. $180 \div 15$
10. 13×12

If today is Monday, what day will it be 274 days from now?

6-2 EQUIVALENT FRACTIONS

The rectangular region below has been divided first into 4 equal parts, then 8 equal parts, and then 16 equal parts.

 $\frac{3}{4}$ of the region is shaded.

$\frac{6}{8}$ of the region is shaded.

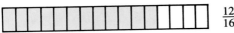 $\frac{12}{16}$ of the region is shaded.

The figures show that $\frac{3}{4}$, $\frac{6}{8}$, and $\frac{12}{16}$ name the same number. Fractions that name the same number are called **equivalent fractions.**
    To determine whether two given fractions are equivalent, multiply to find the **cross products.**

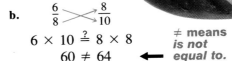

example 1

Tell whether the fractions are *equivalent* or *not equivalent*.

a. $\frac{3}{4}$ and $\frac{12}{16}$ **b.** $\frac{6}{8}$ and $\frac{8}{10}$

solution

a. $\frac{3}{4} \times \frac{12}{16}$ ← **cross products**

$3 \times 16 \overset{?}{=} 4 \times 12$

$48 = 48$

$\frac{3}{4}$ and $\frac{12}{16}$ are *equivalent*.

b. $\frac{6}{8} \times \frac{8}{10}$

$6 \times 10 \overset{?}{=} 8 \times 8$

$60 \neq 64$ ← $\neq$ **means *is not* equal to.**

$\frac{6}{8}$ and $\frac{8}{10}$ are *not equivalent*.

your turn

Tell whether the fractions are *equivalent* or *not equivalent*.

1. $\frac{2}{4}$ and $\frac{1}{2}$ **2.** $\frac{9}{6}$ and $\frac{3}{2}$ **3.** $\frac{3}{5}$ and $\frac{0}{3}$ **4.** $\frac{4}{5}$ and $\frac{5}{7}$

Sometimes you may be asked to find a fraction that is equivalent to a given fraction. One way to do this is to *multiply* both the numerator and the denominator by the same nonzero whole number. Another way is to *divide* by the same nonzero whole number.

example 2

Replace each __?__ with the number that will make the fractions equivalent.

a. $\dfrac{4}{5} = \dfrac{?}{15}$ **b.** $\dfrac{8}{9} = \dfrac{40}{?}$

solution

a. $\dfrac{4}{5} = \dfrac{4 \times 3}{5 \times 3} = \dfrac{12}{15}$ ← You see that $5 \times 3 = 15$, so multiply both the numerator and the denominator by 3.

b. $\dfrac{8}{9} = \dfrac{8 \times 5}{9 \times 5} = \dfrac{40}{45}$ ← You see that $8 \times 5 = 40$, so multiply both the numerator and the denominator by 5.

your turn

Replace each __?__ with the number that will make the fractions equivalent.

5. $\dfrac{3}{10} = \dfrac{12}{?}$ **6.** $\dfrac{7}{21} = \dfrac{?}{63}$ **7.** $\dfrac{11}{23} = \dfrac{?}{46}$ **8.** $\dfrac{2}{9} = \dfrac{10}{?}$

example 3

Replace each __?__ with the number that will make the fractions equivalent.

a. $\dfrac{25}{50} = \dfrac{?}{10}$ **b.** $\dfrac{12}{28} = \dfrac{6}{?}$

solution

a. $\dfrac{25}{50} = \dfrac{25 \div 5}{50 \div 5} = \dfrac{5}{10}$ ← You see that $50 \div 5 = 10$, so divide both the numerator and the denominator by 5.

b. $\dfrac{12}{28} = \dfrac{12 \div 2}{28 \div 2} = \dfrac{6}{14}$ ← You see that $12 \div 2 = 6$, so divide both the numerator and the denominator by 2.

your turn

Replace each __?__ with the number that will make the fractions equivalent.

9. $\dfrac{18}{38} = \dfrac{?}{19}$ **10.** $\dfrac{42}{56} = \dfrac{?}{8}$ **11.** $\dfrac{90}{100} = \dfrac{45}{?}$ **12.** $\dfrac{65}{85} = \dfrac{?}{17}$

practice exercises

practice for example 1 (page 121)

Tell whether the fractions are *equivalent* or *not equivalent*.

1. $\dfrac{1}{3}$ and $\dfrac{3}{5}$ **2.** $\dfrac{8}{11}$ and $\dfrac{16}{22}$ **3.** $\dfrac{12}{1}$ and $\dfrac{10}{1}$ **4.** $\dfrac{0}{6}$ and $\dfrac{6}{1}$

5. $\dfrac{1}{2}$ and $\dfrac{50}{100}$ **6.** $\dfrac{9}{4}$ and $\dfrac{8}{3}$ **7.** $\dfrac{0}{8}$ and $\dfrac{0}{28}$ **8.** $\dfrac{1}{5}$ and $\dfrac{1}{4}$

Replace each __?__ with the number that will make the fractions equivalent.

9. $\dfrac{2}{8} = \dfrac{?}{24}$ 10. $\dfrac{10}{11} = \dfrac{?}{22}$ 11. $\dfrac{7}{9} = \dfrac{49}{?}$ 12. $\dfrac{8}{13} = \dfrac{32}{?}$

13. $\dfrac{12}{27} = \dfrac{36}{?}$ 14. $\dfrac{17}{21} = \dfrac{51}{?}$ 15. $\dfrac{7}{22} = \dfrac{35}{?}$ 16. $\dfrac{6}{19} = \dfrac{24}{?}$

Replace each __?__ with the number that will make the fractions equivalent.

17. $\dfrac{18}{24} = \dfrac{6}{?}$ 18. $\dfrac{13}{26} = \dfrac{1}{?}$ 19. $\dfrac{27}{81} = \dfrac{?}{9}$ 20. $\dfrac{3}{30} = \dfrac{?}{10}$

21. $\dfrac{48}{36} = \dfrac{?}{6}$ 22. $\dfrac{52}{48} = \dfrac{?}{12}$ 23. $\dfrac{33}{55} = \dfrac{3}{?}$ 24. $\dfrac{28}{56} = \dfrac{14}{?}$

Replace each __?__ with the number that will make the fractions equivalent.

25. $\dfrac{1}{3} = \dfrac{?}{12}$ 26. $\dfrac{5}{6} = \dfrac{?}{30}$ 27. $\dfrac{4}{8} = \dfrac{?}{2}$ 28. $\dfrac{10}{14} = \dfrac{?}{98}$

29. $\dfrac{16}{20} = \dfrac{4}{?}$ 30. $\dfrac{18}{90} = \dfrac{2}{?}$ 31. $\dfrac{2}{9} = \dfrac{?}{108}$ 32. $\dfrac{12}{13} = \dfrac{?}{169}$

33. $\dfrac{16}{32} = \dfrac{8}{?} = \dfrac{?}{8} = \dfrac{?}{4}$ 34. $\dfrac{24}{36} = \dfrac{?}{9} = \dfrac{4}{?} = \dfrac{2}{?}$

35. Write four fractions that are equivalent to $\frac{1}{3}$.

36. Write four fractions that are equivalent to $\frac{18}{24}$.

review exercises

Is the first number divisible by the second? Write *Yes* or *No*.

1. 132; 4   2. 122; 5   3. 718; 8   4. 120; 3

5. 100; 10   6. 145; 9   7. 333; 3   8. 124; 4

Find the GCF of each pair of numbers.

9. 21 and 35   10. 54 and 18

11. 55 and 121   12. 75 and 150

13. Tickets to a play cost $40 each. Find the cost of 5 tickets.

14. The committee sold 862 tickets at $2 each. Did they reach their sales goal of $1650?

6-3 LOWEST TERMS

A fraction is in **lowest terms** if the greatest common factor (GCF) of the numerator and the denominator is 1.

example 1

Is the fraction in lowest terms? Write *Yes* or *No*: **a.** $\frac{7}{8}$ **b.** $\frac{3}{9}$

solution

a. Yes, $\frac{7}{8}$ is in lowest terms because the GCF of 7 and 8 is 1.

b. No, $\frac{3}{9}$ is not in lowest terms because the GCF of 3 and 9 is 3.

your turn

Is the fraction in lowest terms? Write *Yes* or *No*.

1. $\frac{6}{12}$ **2.** $\frac{3}{7}$ **3.** $\frac{5}{15}$ **4.** $\frac{4}{10}$

You can write a fraction in lowest terms by dividing both the numerator and the denominator by a common factor. You may have to divide more than once.

example 2

Write each fraction in lowest terms: **a.** $\frac{12}{20}$ **b.** $\frac{18}{24}$

solution

a. $\frac{12}{20} = \frac{12 \div 2}{20 \div 2} = \frac{6}{10}$ → $\frac{6}{10} = \frac{6 \div 2}{10 \div 2} = \frac{3}{5}$

b. $\frac{18}{24} = \frac{18 \div 6}{24 \div 6} = \frac{3}{4}$ ← **6 is the GCF of 18 and 24. If you use the GCF, you only have to divide once.**

your turn

Write each fraction in lowest terms.

5. $\frac{10}{15}$ **6.** $\frac{27}{36}$

7. $\frac{14}{49}$ **8.** $\frac{16}{36}$

practice exercises

practice for example 1 (page 124)

Is the fraction in lowest terms? Write *Yes* or *No*.

1. $\frac{2}{3}$ 2. $\frac{4}{8}$ 3. $\frac{2}{6}$ 4. $\frac{4}{12}$ 5. $\frac{1}{20}$ 6. $\frac{6}{26}$

7. $\frac{7}{17}$ 8. $\frac{17}{19}$ 9. $\frac{20}{24}$ 10. $\frac{3}{100}$ 11. $\frac{22}{33}$ 12. $\frac{29}{33}$

practice for example 2 (page 124)

Write each fraction in lowest terms.

13. $\frac{7}{28}$ 14. $\frac{10}{12}$ 15. $\frac{4}{22}$ 16. $\frac{14}{16}$ 17. $\frac{21}{28}$ 18. $\frac{16}{40}$

19. $\frac{70}{100}$ 20. $\frac{49}{63}$ 21. $\frac{19}{95}$ 22. $\frac{60}{81}$ 23. $\frac{72}{84}$ 24. $\frac{88}{99}$

mixed practice (page 124)

Write each fraction in lowest terms.

25. $\frac{2}{50}$ 26. $\frac{32}{80}$ 27. $\frac{9}{90}$ 28. $\frac{18}{48}$ 29. $\frac{125}{175}$ 30. $\frac{115}{220}$

31. $\frac{12}{144}$ 32. $\frac{18}{190}$ 33. $\frac{160}{200}$ 34. $\frac{222}{342}$ 35. $\frac{90}{1000}$ 36. $\frac{225}{400}$

37. Of the 35 students in Mr. Young's homeroom, 20 have after-school jobs. The part of the class with after-school jobs is $\frac{20}{35}$. Write the fraction in lowest terms.

38. An office building consists of 36 floors. The Graphics Company occupies 8 floors. The Graphics Company occupies $\frac{8}{36}$ of the building. Write the fraction in lowest terms.

review exercises

Complete. Replace each __?__ with >, <, or =.

1. 144 __?__ 1004   2. 915 __?__ 876   3. 1090 __?__ 1009   4. 63 __?__ 107

5. 86 __?__ 86   6. 111 __?__ 121   7. 9103 __?__ 9003   8. 1189 __?__ 1198

Find the LCM of each pair of numbers.

9. 6 and 7   10. 12 and 10   11. 4 and 18   12. 3 and 25

6-4 COMPARING FRACTIONS

To compare fractions with a common denominator, compare the numerators.

example 1

Compare. Replace each __?__ with >, <, or =.

a. $\frac{5}{9}$ __?__ $\frac{4}{9}$

b. $\frac{19}{21}$ __?__ $\frac{19}{21}$

c. $\frac{6}{11}$ __?__ $\frac{10}{11}$

solution

a. $5 > 4$, so $\frac{5}{9} > \frac{4}{9}$

b. $19 = 19$, so $\frac{19}{21} = \frac{19}{21}$

c. $6 < 10$, so $\frac{6}{11} < \frac{10}{11}$

your turn

Compare. Replace each __?__ with >, <, or =.

1. $\frac{17}{20}$ __?__ $\frac{7}{20}$

2. $\frac{19}{32}$ __?__ $\frac{19}{32}$

3. $\frac{11}{17}$ __?__ $\frac{15}{17}$

To compare fractions with different denominators, rename the fractions as equivalent fractions with a common denominator. Use the **least common denominator (LCD)**, which is the least common multiple (LCM) of the denominators.

example 2

Compare. Replace each __?__ with >, <, or =.

a. $\frac{5}{6}$ __?__ $\frac{2}{3}$

b. $\frac{2}{3}$ __?__ $\frac{3}{4}$

solution

a. $\frac{5}{6}$ __?__ $\frac{2}{3}$ ⬅ The LCM of 6 and 3 is 6, so the LCD is 6.

$\frac{5}{6}$ __?__ $\frac{4}{6}$ → $\frac{5}{6} > \frac{4}{6}$ → $\frac{5}{6} > \frac{2}{3}$

b. $\frac{2}{3}$ __?__ $\frac{3}{4}$ ⬅ The LCM of 3 and 4 is 12, so the LCD is 12.

$\frac{8}{12}$ __?__ $\frac{9}{12}$ → $\frac{8}{12} < \frac{9}{12}$ → $\frac{2}{3} < \frac{3}{4}$

your turn

Compare. Replace each __?__ with >, <, or =.

4. $\frac{1}{2}$ __?__ $\frac{5}{10}$

5. $\frac{3}{4}$ __?__ $\frac{5}{6}$

6. $\frac{3}{8}$ __?__ $\frac{1}{7}$

example 3

Write the fractions in order from least to greatest: $\frac{1}{2}, \frac{3}{5}, \frac{1}{10}$

solution

$\frac{1}{2} = \frac{5}{10}$ ⟵ **The LCM of 2, 5, and 10 is 10, so the LCD is 10.**

$\frac{3}{5} = \frac{6}{10}$

$\frac{1}{10} = \frac{1}{10}$

least to greatest: $\frac{1}{10}, \frac{5}{10}, \frac{6}{10}$

$\downarrow \quad \downarrow \quad \downarrow$

$\frac{1}{10}, \frac{1}{2}, \frac{3}{5}$

your turn

Write each set of fractions in order from least to greatest.

7. $\frac{3}{7}, \frac{1}{4}, \frac{1}{2}$

8. $\frac{7}{5}, \frac{3}{4}, \frac{5}{2}$

9. $\frac{6}{11}, \frac{3}{2}, \frac{5}{22}$

practice exercises

practice for example 1 (page 126)

Compare. Replace each __?__ with >, <, or =.

1. $\frac{3}{4}$ __?__ $\frac{1}{4}$

2. $\frac{2}{6}$ __?__ $\frac{2}{6}$

3. $\frac{1}{20}$ __?__ $\frac{9}{20}$

4. $\frac{1}{10}$ __?__ $\frac{7}{10}$

5. $\frac{17}{36}$ __?__ $\frac{13}{36}$

6. $\frac{21}{34}$ __?__ $\frac{19}{34}$

7. $\frac{10}{41}$ __?__ $\frac{20}{41}$

8. $\frac{10}{13}$ __?__ $\frac{9}{13}$

practice for example 2 (page 126)

Compare. Replace each __?__ with >, <, or =.

9. $\frac{1}{3}$ __?__ $\frac{3}{9}$

10. $\frac{1}{7}$ __?__ $\frac{1}{6}$

11. $\frac{3}{7}$ __?__ $\frac{24}{56}$

12. $\frac{5}{6}$ __?__ $\frac{9}{10}$

13. $\frac{2}{9}$ __?__ $\frac{4}{18}$

14. $\frac{3}{2}$ __?__ $\frac{4}{3}$

15. $\frac{1}{9}$ __?__ $\frac{1}{10}$

16. $\frac{1}{2}$ __?__ $\frac{5}{11}$

practice for example 3 (page 127)

Write each set of fractions in order from least to greatest.

17. $\frac{1}{5}, \frac{2}{5}, \frac{1}{2}$

18. $\frac{3}{4}, \frac{3}{8}, \frac{1}{2}$

19. $\frac{7}{10}, \frac{4}{5}, \frac{1}{2}$

20. $\frac{5}{6}, \frac{7}{12}, \frac{7}{8}$

21. $\frac{1}{10}, \frac{2}{25}, \frac{7}{50}, \frac{11}{20}$

22. $\frac{9}{10}, \frac{5}{8}, \frac{7}{10}, \frac{3}{8}$

Compare. Replace each __?__ with >, <, or =.

23. $\frac{5}{8}$ __?__ $\frac{3}{20}$

24. $\frac{29}{30}$ __?__ $\frac{19}{30}$

25. $\frac{8}{9}$ __?__ $\frac{11}{12}$

26. $\frac{6}{100}$ __?__ $\frac{6}{10}$

27. $\frac{81}{99}$ __?__ $\frac{81}{99}$

28. $\frac{5}{7}$ __?__ $\frac{10}{14}$

29. $\frac{43}{99}$ __?__ $\frac{43}{100}$

30. $\frac{101}{200}$ __?__ $\frac{110}{200}$

Tell whether each statement is *true* or *false*.

31. $\frac{6}{7} > \frac{2}{3}$

32. $\frac{4}{9} = \frac{2}{7}$

33. $\frac{2}{3} < \frac{5}{8}$

34. $\frac{5}{7} < \frac{3}{5}$

35. $\frac{13}{26} = \frac{26}{52}$

36. $\frac{7}{10} < \frac{13}{15}$

37. $\frac{21}{23} > \frac{2}{3}$

38. $\frac{21}{22} > \frac{31}{33}$

39. During a practice session, the Offsiders spend $\frac{1}{20}$ of the time jogging, $\frac{2}{15}$ lifting weights, $\frac{2}{5}$ looking at game films, and $\frac{5}{12}$ practicing plays. Order the activities from greatest to least amount of time spent.

40. Jim spent $\frac{7}{8}$ of an hour doing homework and $\frac{2}{3}$ of an hour bicycling. On which activity did he spend more time?

review *exercises*

Estimate.

1. $731 \div 9$

2. $237 \div 4$

3. $13{,}091 \div 6$

4. $33{,}978 \div 7$

5. $2045 \div 48$

6. $3872 \div 64$

7. $4997 \div 69$

8. $76{,}219 \div 28$

calculator corner

You can use your calculator to compare fractions by finding cross products. The cross products will show the order of the fractions.

example Compare: $\frac{7}{15}$ __?__ $\frac{9}{21}$

solution $\frac{7}{15}$ __?__ $\frac{9}{21}$ → 7×21 __?__ 15×9 → $\frac{7}{15} > \frac{9}{21}$
$\phantom{\frac{7}{15}} \phantom{\frac{9}{21}} \quad 147 \;>\; 135$

Use a calculator to compare. Replace each __?__ with >, <, or =.

1. $\frac{9}{23}$ __?__ $\frac{11}{30}$

2. $\frac{14}{48}$ __?__ $\frac{21}{72}$

3. $\frac{18}{25}$ __?__ $\frac{11}{18}$

4. $\frac{7}{10}$ __?__ $\frac{9}{16}$

5. $\frac{7}{10}$ __?__ $\frac{13}{18}$

6. $\frac{11}{42}$ __?__ $\frac{7}{29}$

6-5 ESTIMATING FRACTIONS

During a recent January, Chicago had ten days of snow. Minneapolis had twenty-one days of snow. You could write the part of the month that it snowed in these cities as $\frac{10}{31}$ and $\frac{21}{31}$. You could also use the following method to write the simpler fractions $\frac{1}{3}$ and $\frac{2}{3}$ as estimates for these fractions.

example 1

Write a simpler fraction as an estimate of each fraction.

a. $\frac{10}{31}$ **b.** $\frac{21}{31}$

solution

a. The denominator is about 3 times the numerator. ➡ $\frac{10}{31}$ ➡ about $\frac{1}{3}$

b. $\frac{21}{31}$ ➡ $\frac{20}{30}$, or about $\frac{2}{3}$

your turn

Write a simpler fraction as an estimate of each fraction.

1. $\frac{5}{26}$ **2.** $\frac{12}{35}$ **3.** $\frac{99}{402}$ **4.** $\frac{9}{61}$ **5.** $\frac{20}{51}$ **6.** $\frac{50}{73}$

A fraction is close to: 0 when the numerator is very small compared to the denominator.
                   $\frac{1}{2}$ when the denominator is about twice the numerator.
                   1 when the numerator and denominator are about the same.

example 2

Tell whether each fraction is closest to 0, $\frac{1}{2}$, or 1:   **a.** $\frac{1}{9}$ **b.** $\frac{7}{12}$ **c.** $\frac{4}{5}$

solution

a. 0   **b.** $\frac{1}{2}$ **c.** 1

your turn

Tell whether each fraction is closest to 0, $\frac{1}{2}$, or 1.

7. $\frac{39}{41}$ **8.** $\frac{2}{99}$ **9.** $\frac{14}{15}$ **10.** $\frac{17}{33}$

practice exercises

practice for example 1 (page 129)

Write a simpler fraction as an estimate of each fraction.

1. $\frac{45}{89}$ 2. $\frac{11}{87}$ 3. $\frac{9}{55}$ 4. $\frac{21}{59}$ 5. $\frac{39}{122}$ 6. $\frac{68}{139}$

7. $\frac{40}{59}$ 8. $\frac{81}{119}$ 9. $\frac{74}{99}$ 10. $\frac{29}{39}$ 11. $\frac{15}{121}$ 12. $\frac{12}{118}$

practice for example 2 (page 129)

Tell whether each fraction is closest to 0, $\frac{1}{2}$, or 1.

13. $\frac{19}{20}$ 14. $\frac{8}{17}$ 15. $\frac{2}{29}$ 16. $\frac{3}{17}$ 17. $\frac{58}{61}$ 18. $\frac{1}{11}$

19. $\frac{5}{11}$ 20. $\frac{17}{30}$ 21. $\frac{7}{200}$ 22. $\frac{26}{29}$ 23. $\frac{13}{30}$ 24. $\frac{9}{11}$

mixed practice (page 129)

Choose the best estimate from: a. 0 b. $\frac{1}{4}$ c. $\frac{1}{2}$ d. $\frac{3}{4}$ e. 1

25. $\frac{1}{20}$ 26. $\frac{9}{20}$ 27. $\frac{19}{21}$ 28. $\frac{12}{50}$ 29. $\frac{14}{20}$ 30. $\frac{21}{79}$

31. $\frac{40}{43}$ 32. $\frac{31}{61}$ 33. $\frac{27}{102}$ 34. $\frac{87}{95}$ 35. $\frac{34}{71}$ 36. $\frac{296}{405}$

37. About what part of an hour is sixteen minutes?

38. About what part of a day is five hours?

39. Carmen got 147 votes out of the 289 votes for class president. About what part of the total vote did she get?

40. The distance from Houston to San Antonio is approximately 180 mi (miles). About what part of the trip have you completed after traveling 118 mi?

review exercises

Write each fraction in lowest terms.

1. $\frac{6}{16}$ 2. $\frac{14}{35}$ 3. $\frac{42}{48}$

4. $\frac{75}{100}$ 5. $\frac{64}{96}$ 6. $\frac{108}{132}$

6-6 FRACTIONS AND MIXED NUMBERS

A number that consists of both a whole number and a fraction is called a **mixed number.**

$2\frac{7}{8} = \frac{23}{8}$

example 1

Write $2\frac{7}{8}$ as a fraction.

solution

1. Multiply the whole number by the denominator.

$$2\frac{7}{8}$$

$$8 \times 2 = 16$$

2. Add the numerator to this product.

$$2\frac{7}{8}$$

$$16 + 7 = 23$$

3. Write this sum over the denominator.

$$\frac{23}{8}$$

your turn

Write as a fraction in lowest terms.

1. $3\frac{1}{2}$ 2. $1\frac{7}{12}$ 3. $5\frac{11}{20}$ 4. $13\frac{1}{3}$ 5. $4\frac{2}{4}$ 6. $8\frac{3}{9}$

When the numerator of a fraction is greater than or equal to the denominator, you can write the fraction as either a mixed number or a whole number. To do this, remember that the fraction bar represents a division.

example 2

Write as a whole number or a mixed number in lowest terms: a. $\frac{16}{3}$ b. $\frac{24}{6}$

solution

a.
$$\begin{array}{r} 5 \\ 3\overline{)16} \\ 15 \\ \hline 1 \end{array}$$
$5\frac{1}{3}$ So $\frac{16}{3} = 5\frac{1}{3}$.

b.
$$\begin{array}{r} 4 \\ 6\overline{)24} \\ 24 \\ \hline 0 \end{array}$$
So $\frac{24}{6} = 4$.

your turn

Write as a whole number or a mixed number in lowest terms.

7. $\frac{12}{7}$ 8. $\frac{200}{100}$ 9. $\frac{34}{5}$ 10. $\frac{17}{2}$ 11. $\frac{15}{15}$ 12. $\frac{39}{6}$

Fraction Concepts 131

example 3

Compare. Replace each __?__ with >, <, or =.

a. $\frac{22}{9}$ __?__ $2\frac{5}{9}$

b. $1\frac{8}{11}$ __?__ $\frac{14}{11}$

solution

a. $\frac{22}{9}$ __?__ $2\frac{5}{9}$ ← **Write the fraction as a mixed number.**

$2\frac{4}{9}$ < $2\frac{5}{9}$ So $\frac{22}{9} < 2\frac{5}{9}$.

b. $1\frac{8}{11}$ __?__ $\frac{14}{11}$ ← **Write the mixed number as a fraction.**

$\frac{19}{11}$ > $\frac{14}{11}$ So $1\frac{8}{11} > \frac{14}{11}$.

your turn

Compare. Replace each __?__ with >, <, or =.

13. $4\frac{5}{7}$ __?__ $\frac{30}{7}$

14. $\frac{8}{5}$ __?__ $1\frac{3}{5}$

15. $\frac{14}{5}$ __?__ $2\frac{4}{7}$

16. $9\frac{7}{8}$ __?__ $\frac{79}{9}$

practice exercises

practice for example 1 (page 131)

Write as a fraction in lowest terms.

1. $10\frac{1}{5}$

2. $9\frac{3}{10}$

3. $1\frac{1}{7}$

4. $6\frac{4}{5}$

5. $11\frac{7}{10}$

6. $13\frac{4}{7}$

7. $15\frac{4}{9}$

8. $20\frac{8}{9}$

9. $33\frac{2}{6}$

10. $24\frac{2}{12}$

11. $41\frac{4}{8}$

12. $53\frac{3}{21}$

practice for example 2 (page 131)

Write as a whole number or a mixed number in lowest terms.

13. $\frac{21}{5}$

14. $\frac{29}{7}$

15. $\frac{43}{8}$

16. $\frac{38}{9}$

17. $\frac{63}{5}$

18. $\frac{75}{4}$

19. $\frac{512}{4}$

20. $\frac{663}{221}$

21. $\frac{134}{17}$

22. $\frac{488}{24}$

23. $\frac{846}{35}$

24. $\frac{973}{74}$

practice for example 3 (page 132)

Compare. Replace each __?__ with >, <, or =.

25. $1\frac{4}{9}$ __?__ $\frac{11}{9}$

26. $5\frac{3}{4}$ __?__ $\frac{27}{4}$

27. $\frac{32}{5}$ __?__ $4\frac{2}{5}$

28. $\frac{38}{3}$ __?__ $12\frac{2}{3}$

29. $\frac{67}{11}$ __?__ $8\frac{10}{11}$

30. $3\frac{5}{6}$ __?__ $\frac{46}{12}$

31. $1\frac{2}{3}$ __?__ $\frac{8}{9}$

32. $\frac{9}{4}$ __?__ $2\frac{5}{8}$

Complete.

33. $1\frac{3}{20} = \frac{?}{20}$

34. $\frac{79}{8} = 9\frac{?}{8}$

35. $14\frac{?}{10} = \frac{141}{10}$

36. $3\frac{5}{8} = \frac{?}{8}$

37. $\frac{102}{9} = 11\frac{?}{3}$

38. $6\frac{?}{5} = \frac{64}{10}$

39. $2\frac{?}{6} = \frac{34}{12}$

40. $1\frac{?}{4} = \frac{28}{16}$

Write each set of numbers in order from least to greatest.

41. $5\frac{6}{7}, 2\frac{1}{5}, 2\frac{5}{6}, 5\frac{2}{6}$

42. $3\frac{16}{20}, 1\frac{8}{12}, 1\frac{1}{3}, 3\frac{3}{4}$

43. $8\frac{6}{11}, 8\frac{6}{10}, 8\frac{1}{2}, 8\frac{2}{5}$

44. $11\frac{4}{7}, 11\frac{3}{7}, 11\frac{5}{9}, 11\frac{2}{3}$

45. $1\frac{1}{2}, \frac{5}{2}, 2\frac{4}{6}, \frac{16}{3}$

46. $\frac{19}{4}, 4\frac{1}{2}, \frac{15}{4}, 4\frac{1}{4}$

47. A handkerchief company uses $\frac{1}{4}$ yard of material to make a handkerchief. How many handkerchiefs can be made from a bolt of cloth that has $8\frac{1}{4}$ yards of material?

48. It took Theodore 57 h to build 4 bookcases. Each bookcase took the same amount of time. How many hours did it take him to make each bookcase?

review *exercises*

Find each answer.

1. 9×713

2. $10{,}885 \div 7$

3. $4005 - 129$

4. 225×46

5. $2314 \div 26$

6. $86{,}607 + 4893$

7. $9(42 - 18)$

8. $5 + 3 \times 9 - 2$

9. $8 \times 4 + 4 \div 2$

10. $18 \div (6 - 4)$

mental math

You can multiply or divide by 5, 50, and 500 mentally.

628×50 ← **Multiply by 100, then divide by 2.**

$628 \times 100 = 62{,}800$
$62{,}800 \div 2 = 31{,}400$

$3410 \div 5$ ← **Divide by 10, then multiply by 2.**

$3410 \div 10 = 341$
$341 \times 2 = 682$

Multiply or divide mentally.

1. 24×5

2. 48×500

3. 5×2680

4. 50×320

5. $8200 \div 50$

6. $6840 \div 5$

7. $9400 \div 50$

8. $7240 \div 5$

9. 5×4861

10. $39{,}000 \div 500$

6-7 USING MORE THAN ONE OPERATION

Sometimes it takes more than one operation to solve a problem. Not only must you decide which operations are needed, you must also determine the order in which to perform them.

example

a. Carlos bought three shirts costing $14 each. He gave the cashier a $50 bill. How much change did he receive?

b. The cash price of a certain refrigerator is $549. Since Mrs. Davis did not have that much money, she made a down payment of $70 and arranged to make twelve monthly payments of $52. How much more did it cost her to buy the refrigerator this way?

solution

a. Step 1 Given: Bought 3 shirts for $14 each.
　　　　　　　　　Gave cashier $50.
　　　　　　　Find: How much of the $50 is left?

Step 2 First: Multiply to find total cost. (3 × $14)
　　　　　Second: Subtract the total cost from $50.

Step 3 3 × $14 = $42　　　$50 − $42 = $8

Step 4 *Check:* $8 + (3 × $14) = $8 + $42 = $50

Carlos received $8 change.

b. Step 1 Given: Cash price is $549.
　　　　　　　　　Paid $70 plus 12 payments of $52 each.

Step 2 First: Multiply $52 by 12 to get total
　　　　　　　　monthly payments.
　　　　　Second: Add $70 to total monthly payments.
　　　　　Third: Subtract $549 from total payments.

Step 3

$$
\begin{array}{r} \$52 \\ \times 12 \\ \hline 104 \\ 52 \\ \hline \$624 \end{array}
\qquad
\begin{array}{r} \$624 \\ + \ 70 \\ \hline \$694 \end{array}
\qquad
\begin{array}{r} \$694 \\ - \ 549 \\ \hline \$145 \end{array}
$$

Step 4 *Check:* $70 + ($52 × 12) = $694
　　　　　$145 + $549 = $694

It cost Mrs. Davis $145 more to make monthly payments.

problems

Solve.

1. Mr. Jahn spent $28, $57, and $98 in three visits to the supermarket. His food budget is $200. How much money does he have left to spend for food?

2. Mary read 252 pages of a 591-page book. It took her three days to read the remaining pages. If she read the same number of pages each day, how many pages did she read each day?

3. In three rounds of golf Joanne shot 74, 81, and 76. Her total for four rounds was 306. What did she shoot in her fourth round?

4. Larry bought four T-shirts for $8 each and a pair of sneakers for $39. How much of his $100 clothing budget did he have left?

5. Mrs. Nelson sold 846 notebooks for $2 each and 128 notebooks for $5 each. If they cost her $1710 wholesale, what was her profit?

6. Fifteen hundred tickets costing $3 each were sold for a fund-raising event. Prizes of $1000, $500, and $300 were given away. What was the amount raised?

7. The temperature in a greenhouse is 72°F at 11:00 A.M. If it increases 3°F every hour, what will the temperature be at 5:00 P.M.?

8. Peter saved $193. After he earned an additional $89, he spent $119 for a small television, $28 for a jersey, and $59 for a skateboard. How much money did he have left?

review exercises

1. Lea bowled 432 in three games. What was her average per game?

2. Richard lifts weights for 120 min a week. How many hours does he spend each week lifting weights?

3. In one basketball game Pat made 8 two-point field goals, 2 three-point field goals, and 5 one-point free throws. How many points did Pat score in the game?

4. In twenty basketball games Eddie scored 377 points in field goals. He made 163 two-point field goals. How many three-point field goals did he make?

SKILL REVIEW

Write a fraction that names the shaded part of each region or set.

1. 2. 3. 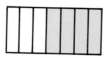 4.

6-1

Write a fraction that answers the question.

5. What part of a year is 3 months?

6. What part of an hour is 7 min?

Replace each __?__ with the number that will make the fractions equivalent.

7. $\frac{3}{4} = \frac{9}{?}$

8. $\frac{5}{7} = \frac{?}{28}$

9. $\frac{20}{22} = \frac{10}{?}$

10. $\frac{18}{36} = \frac{?}{2}$

6-2

Write the fraction in lowest terms.

11. $\frac{3}{12}$

12. $\frac{6}{15}$

13. $\frac{18}{42}$

14. $\frac{20}{36}$

15. $\frac{7}{63}$

16. $\frac{52}{100}$

6-3

Compare. Replace each __?__ with >, <, or =.

17. $\frac{5}{23}$ __?__ $\frac{7}{23}$

18. $\frac{8}{32}$ __?__ $\frac{4}{32}$

19. $\frac{1}{3}$ __?__ $\frac{2}{5}$

20. $\frac{6}{12}$ __?__ $\frac{4}{8}$

6-4

Write a simpler fraction as an estimate of each fraction.

21. $\frac{6}{37}$

22. $\frac{11}{111}$

23. $\frac{12}{35}$

24. $\frac{20}{29}$

25. $\frac{15}{61}$

26. $\frac{59}{79}$

6-5

Write each mixed number as a fraction in lowest terms.

27. $3\frac{3}{4}$

28. $2\frac{1}{5}$

29. $9\frac{7}{10}$

30. $7\frac{13}{18}$

31. $12\frac{2}{8}$

32. $4\frac{4}{6}$

6-6

Write as a whole number or a mixed number in lowest terms.

33. $\frac{27}{5}$

34. $\frac{100}{11}$

35. $\frac{65}{13}$

36. $\frac{59}{20}$

37. $\frac{53}{7}$

38. $\frac{108}{9}$

Solve.

39. Marcus earned $5 an hour for 38 hours. If he spent $92 of his earnings, how much did he have left?

6-7

40. On each of three nights Kim read 72 pages. On the fourth night she read 95 pages. How many pages did she read in all on the four nights?

136 Chapter 6

6-8 FRACTIONS OF A DAY

One Monday Mark kept track of the time he spent on various activities. He organized the information in a chart.

Activity	Approximate Time Spent
School	6h 55min
Homework	2h 10 min
Practicing Piano	1h
Basketball	2h 50 min
Eating	1h 15 min
Talking On Phone	30 min
Reading	1h
Sleeping	8h 20 min

example

a. Estimate the fraction of the day Mark spent sleeping.

b. On Tuesday Mark spent about $\frac{1}{6}$ of his day working in the library. About how many hours did Mark work?

solution

a. There are 24 h in a day.
Mark rounded 8 h 20 min to 8 h.

$$\frac{\text{hours sleeping}}{\text{total hours}} \rightarrow \frac{8}{24} = \frac{8 \div 8}{24 \div 8} = \frac{1}{3}$$

Mark spent about $\frac{1}{3}$ of his day sleeping.

b. There are 24 h in a day.
You know that $6 \times 4 = 24$.

$$\frac{1}{6} = \frac{1 \times 4}{6 \times 4} = \frac{4}{24} \leftarrow \frac{\text{hours in the library}}{\text{total hours}}$$

Mark worked about 4 h in the library.

exercises

Use the chart above.

1. Estimate the fraction of the day Mark spent playing basketball.
2. Did Mark spend a greater fraction of his time playing basketball or doing homework?
3. Estimate the fraction of the day Mark spent in school and reading.
4. On Saturday, Mark spent about $\frac{1}{8}$ of his day helping his mother. About how many hours did Mark help his mother?
5. On Saturday Mark spent about $\frac{1}{12}$ of the day playing soccer. About how many hours did Mark play soccer?
6. Keep track of the time you spend on your own activities for a day. Estimate the fraction of the day you spend sleeping. Estimate the fraction of the day you spend on schoolwork.

Fraction Concepts 137

6-9 MUSIC

Music is written so that musicians know how long to hold **notes.** The standard notation for some notes is shown at the right.

o whole note   ♩ quarter note

♪ half note   ♪ eighth note

The diagram at the right shows how a whole note can be divided.

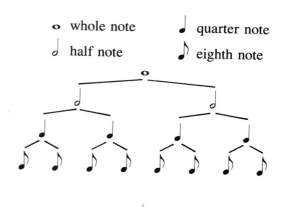

example 1

How many eighth notes make up a half note?

solution

Look at one of the half notes on the diagram. Two quarter notes make up a half note. Two eighth notes make up each quarter note. So four eighth notes are the same as one half note.

your turn

1. How many half notes make up a whole note?

2. What note is the same as two quarter notes?

Musical compositions are written in **measures.** Each measure consists of a number of **beats.** A fraction is written in the first measure to show the rhythm of the music. For example, $\frac{3}{4}$ means there are three beats to a measure and a quarter note gets one beat.

$\dfrac{3}{4}$ ← three beats to a measure
← quarter note gets one beat

example 2

Find one note to complete each measure.

a. 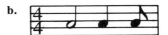 b.

solution

a. The fraction means there are three beats in the measure and a quarter note gets one beat. Since a quarter note gets one beat, the half note gets two beats. You need to find the number of quarter notes to complete the measure.

$$\text{♩} \quad + \quad \underline{\ ?\ } \ = 3 \text{ beats}$$
$$2 \text{ beats} + 1 \text{ beat} = 3 \text{ beats}$$

The measure needs one beat. The measure needs one quarter note.

b. The fraction means there are four beats in a measure and a quarter note gets one beat. The half note gets two beats and the quarter note gets one beat.

$$\text{♩} \quad + \quad \text{♩} \quad + \quad \underbrace{\text{♪} + \underline{\ ?\ }}_{1 \text{ beat}} = 4 \text{ beats}$$
$$2 \text{ beats} + 1 \text{ beat} + \qquad\qquad = 4 \text{ beats}$$

The measure needs another half beat. The measure needs one eighth note.

your turn

Find one note to complete each measure.

3.  4.

practice exercises

practice for example 1 (page 138)

Use the diagram on page 138.

1. How many eighth notes make up one quarter note?
2. How many quarter notes make up one half note?
3. How many quarter notes make up one whole note?
4. What note is the same as two eighth notes?

Find one note to complete each measure.

5.
6.

7.
8.

9. What note is the same as four eighth notes?

10. How many eighth notes are needed to make a whole note?

Find one note to complete each measure.

11.
12.

For each measure, write *Yes* if it is correct. If it is not correct, find one note to make it correct.

13.
14.

15.
16.

17. Try tapping the measure in Exercise 16, using the notes to space your taps. Repeat the measure over and over to make a rhythm. Try making up a rhythm and writing it using these notes. Trade your music with a friend's and see if the rhythm sounds the same.

CHAPTER REVIEW

vocabulary vo·cab·u·lar·y

Choose the correct word to complete each sentence.

1. In the fraction $\frac{4}{5}$, the number 4 is the *(numerator, denominator)*.

2. Two fractions that name the same number are *(equivalent, not equivalent)*.

skills

Write a fraction that answers the question.

3. What part of an hour is 27 min?

4. What part of a year is 5 months?

Tell whether the fractions are *equivalent* or *not equivalent*.

5. $\frac{5}{7}$ and $\frac{4}{5}$

6. $\frac{2}{4}$ and $\frac{26}{32}$

7. $\frac{8}{64}$ and $\frac{6}{48}$

8. $\frac{8}{15}$ and $\frac{120}{225}$

Write each set of fractions in order from least to greatest.

9. $\frac{5}{7}, \frac{3}{4}, \frac{19}{28}, \frac{6}{7}$

10. $\frac{41}{50}, \frac{21}{25}, \frac{4}{5}, \frac{19}{25}$

Write each mixed number as a fraction in lowest terms.

11. $6\frac{2}{3}$

12. $9\frac{4}{8}$

13. $12\frac{1}{4}$

14. $14\frac{4}{6}$

15. $11\frac{3}{7}$

16. $25\frac{1}{5}$

Is each fraction closest to 0, $\frac{1}{2}$, or 1?

17. $\frac{13}{15}$

18. $\frac{3}{7}$

19. $\frac{7}{16}$

20. $\frac{4}{21}$

21. $\frac{12}{25}$

22. $\frac{17}{19}$

Write as a whole number or a mixed number in lowest terms.

23. $\frac{29}{4}$

24. $\frac{36}{13}$

25. $\frac{56}{8}$

26. $\frac{12}{7}$

27. $\frac{40}{5}$

28. $\frac{77}{11}$

29. Describe a method to use to change a mixed number to a fraction.

30. Mike earned $275 a week for 5 weeks and $285 a week for 8 weeks. How much money did he earn?

31. On Saturday, Maureen spent about $\frac{1}{6}$ of the day ice skating. About how many hours did Maureen skate?

32. Use the diagram on page 138. How many quarter notes make up one whole note?

Fraction Concepts 141

CHAPTER TEST

Write a fraction that names the shaded part of each region or set.

1.   2. [three pairs of rectangles, some shaded]   3. [grid with some cells shaded]   4. [square with diagonal, half shaded]   **6-1**

Replace each __?__ with the number that will make the fractions equivalent.

5. $\frac{4}{6} = \frac{2}{?}$

6. $\frac{14}{35} = \frac{?}{5}$

7. $\frac{6}{7} = \frac{72}{?}$

8. $\frac{11}{13} = \frac{?}{52}$ **6-2**

Write each fraction in lowest terms.

9. $\frac{10}{15}$

10. $\frac{6}{48}$

11. $\frac{20}{70}$

12. $\frac{9}{36}$

13. $\frac{16}{96}$

14. $\frac{42}{160}$ **6-3**

Compare. Replace each __?__ with >, <, or =.

15. $\frac{15}{16}$ __?__ $\frac{13}{16}$

16. $\frac{4}{9}$ __?__ $\frac{13}{27}$

17. $\frac{8}{32}$ __?__ $\frac{2}{8}$

18. $\frac{13}{14}$ __?__ $\frac{5}{7}$ **6-4**

Write a simpler fraction as an estimate of each fraction.

19. $\frac{33}{100}$

20. $\frac{25}{49}$

21. $\frac{15}{73}$

22. $\frac{19}{81}$

23. $\frac{75}{101}$

24. $\frac{65}{99}$ **6-5**

Write each mixed number as a fraction in lowest terms.

25. $3\frac{1}{3}$

26. $9\frac{2}{5}$

27. $15\frac{2}{4}$

28. $14\frac{6}{7}$

29. $10\frac{11}{12}$

30. $18\frac{2}{6}$ **6-6**

Write as a whole number or a mixed number in lowest terms.

31. $\frac{17}{3}$

32. $\frac{49}{7}$

33. $\frac{25}{4}$

34. $\frac{60}{3}$

35. $\frac{120}{10}$

36. $\frac{85}{15}$

Solve.

37. Nicole wants to buy a car for $6795. If she saves $250 a month for 20 months, how much more money does she need?   **6-7**

38. Maria ran 6 mi (miles). The first three miles took her 8 min each. The last three took her 9 min each. How many minutes did Maria run?

39. Carol spent 5 h 45 min painting her house. Estimate the fraction of the day that Carol spent painting.   **6-8**

40. Use the diagram on page 138. Find how many eighth notes make up one whole note.   **6-9**

In cooking, a recipe indicates how much of each ingredient is needed. To adjust a recipe, you may need to multiply or divide fractions.

CHAPTER 7

MULTIPLYING AND DIVIDING FRACTIONS

7-1 MULTIPLYING WITH FRACTIONS

To multiply fractions, use the following method.

1. Multiply the numerators.
2. Multiply the denominators.

$$\frac{1}{3} \times \frac{3}{4} = \frac{1 \times 3}{3 \times 4} = \frac{3}{12} = \frac{1}{4}$$

3. Write the product in lowest terms.

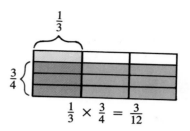

$$\frac{1}{3} \times \frac{3}{4} = \frac{3}{12}$$

example 1

Write each product in lowest terms: **a.** $\frac{1}{2} \times \frac{3}{5}$ **b.** $15 \times \frac{1}{5}$

solution

a. $\frac{1}{2} \times \frac{3}{5} = \frac{1 \times 3}{2 \times 5} = \frac{3}{10}$

b. $15 \times \frac{1}{5} = \frac{15}{1} \times \frac{1}{5} = \frac{15 \times 1}{1 \times 5} = \frac{15}{5} = 3$

your turn

Write each product in lowest terms.

1. $\frac{1}{2} \times \frac{1}{3}$ 2. $\frac{1}{4} \times \frac{8}{9}$ 3. $2 \times \frac{2}{7}$ 4. $\frac{3}{4} \times 8$

To simplify some multiplications, you can first divide the numerator of one fraction and the denominator of another by a common factor.

example 2

Write each product in lowest terms: **a.** $\frac{4}{5} \times \frac{5}{6}$ **b.** $8 \times \frac{11}{28}$

solution

a. $\frac{4}{5} \times \frac{5}{6} = \frac{\overset{2}{\cancel{4}} \times \overset{1}{\cancel{5}}}{\underset{1}{\cancel{5}} \times \underset{3}{\cancel{6}}} = \frac{2}{3}$ ⬅ **Divide 4 and 6 by 2. Divide the 5's by 5.**

b. $8 \times \frac{11}{28} = \frac{8 \times 11}{1 \times \underset{7}{\cancel{28}}} = \frac{22}{7} = 3\frac{1}{7}$

your turn

Write each product in lowest terms.

5. $\frac{9}{10} \times \frac{5}{8}$ 6. $\frac{4}{5} \times \frac{15}{16}$ 7. $\frac{3}{8} \times \frac{8}{15}$ 8. $8 \times \frac{1}{6}$

To estimate a product, you can use numbers that multiply easily, or **compatible numbers.**

example 3

Estimate using compatible numbers: **a.** $100 \times \frac{5}{19}$ **b.** $\frac{8}{17} \times 205$

ESTIMATION

solution

a. $100 \times \frac{5}{19}$

$\downarrow \qquad \downarrow$

$100 \times \frac{1}{4}$ ⟵ $\frac{1}{4}$ is an estimate for $\frac{5}{19}$ that is compatible with 100.

about 25

b. $\frac{8}{17} \times 205$

$\downarrow \qquad \downarrow$

$\frac{1}{2} \times 200$ ⟵ Replace $\frac{8}{17}$ and 205 with compatible estimates.

about 100

your turn

Estimate using compatible numbers.

9. $\frac{5}{31} \times 180$ **10.** $\frac{4}{13} \times 286$ **11.** $246 \times \frac{5}{26}$ **12.** $\frac{19}{30} \times 61$

practice exercises

practice for example 1 (page 144)

Write each product in lowest terms.

1. $\frac{1}{4} \times \frac{1}{5}$ **2.** $\frac{1}{2} \times \frac{1}{8}$ **3.** $\frac{1}{2} \times \frac{6}{7}$ **4.** $\frac{5}{6} \times \frac{3}{4}$ **5.** $17 \times \frac{1}{8}$

6. $\frac{1}{6} \times 11$ **7.** $\frac{2}{7} \times 14$ **8.** $\frac{2}{5} \times 20$ **9.** $\frac{6}{13} \times \frac{3}{5}$ **10.** $\frac{1}{4} \times \frac{5}{14}$

practice for example 2 (page 144)

Write each product in lowest terms.

11. $\frac{5}{8} \times \frac{7}{10}$ **12.** $\frac{1}{6} \times \frac{12}{13}$ **13.** $\frac{3}{4} \times \frac{4}{21}$ **14.** $\frac{8}{25} \times \frac{5}{16}$ **15.** $\frac{25}{36} \times \frac{24}{35}$

16. $\frac{11}{24} \times \frac{16}{33}$ **17.** $8 \times \frac{3}{16}$ **18.** $3 \times \frac{5}{6}$ **19.** $\frac{2}{3} \times 51$ **20.** $\frac{4}{9} \times 135$

practice for example 3 (page 145)

Estimate using compatible numbers.

21. $90 \times \frac{6}{17}$ **22.** $\frac{11}{40} \times 80$ **23.** $\frac{4}{17} \times 58$ **24.** $\frac{13}{24} \times 403$

25. $\frac{29}{92} \times 29$ **26.** $101 \times \frac{1}{19}$ **27.** $\frac{198}{302} \times 6$ **28.** $\frac{152}{197} \times 388$

Multiplying and Dividing Fractions   145

Write each product in lowest terms.

29. $\frac{2}{9} \times \frac{4}{9}$ **30.** $\frac{1}{3} \times \frac{5}{6}$ **31.** $\frac{2}{9} \times \frac{27}{10}$ **32.** $\frac{5}{9} \times \frac{18}{25}$ **33.** $\frac{3}{5} \times 15$

34. $40 \times \frac{7}{2}$ **35.** $\frac{0}{8} \times \frac{7}{3}$ **36.** $\frac{1}{5} \times \frac{10}{11}$ **37.** $\frac{8}{21} \times \frac{7}{10} \times \frac{5}{16}$ **38.** $24 \times \frac{3}{8} \times \frac{2}{3}$

Estimate using compatible numbers.

39. $\frac{21}{22} \times 100$ **40.** $\frac{99}{100} \times 13$ **41.** $\frac{1}{4} \times 202$ **42.** $\frac{7}{20} \times 611$

43. $498 \times \frac{8}{17}$ **44.** $247 \times \frac{10}{51}$ **45.** $91 \times \frac{19}{29}$ **46.** $805 \times \frac{75}{99}$

47. A calculator regularly priced at $30 is advertised on sale at four fifths of its regular price. What is the sale price?

48. Two thirds of the teams in the NBA have at least one seven-foot player. Five sixths of these teams have winning records. What fraction of the teams in the NBA have both a seven-foot player and a winning record?

review *exercises*

Round to the place of the underlined digit.

1. 23<u>5</u>6   **2.** 5<u>3</u>87   **3.** 10,<u>9</u>57   **4.** <u>3</u>6,552

5. 312,2<u>6</u>1   **6.** 483,<u>0</u>59   **7.** 200,0<u>9</u>9   **8.** 998,5<u>1</u>1

9. 2,<u>5</u>36,708   **10.** 8,7<u>7</u>4,732   **11.** 14,<u>3</u>67,874   **12.** 9<u>1</u>,555,438

mental math

You can use patterns to help you multiply mentally.

$$\frac{1}{3} \times \$90 = \$30, \quad \text{so} \quad \frac{2}{3} \times \$90 = \$60.$$

$$\frac{1}{5} \times 60 = 12, \quad \text{so} \quad \frac{2}{5} \times 60 = 24, \quad \frac{3}{5} \times 60 = 36, \quad \frac{4}{5} \times 60 = 48.$$

Multiply mentally.

1. $\frac{1}{4} \times 80$ **2.** $\frac{2}{4} \times 80$ **3.** $\frac{3}{4} \times 80$ **4.** $\frac{1}{8} \times 64$ **5.** $\frac{3}{8} \times 64$ **6.** $\frac{5}{8} \times 64$

7. $\frac{1}{2} \times 30$ **8.** $\frac{3}{2} \times 30$ **9.** $\frac{3}{10} \times 20$ **10.** $\frac{5}{6} \times 120$ **11.** $\frac{3}{4} \times 16$ **12.** $\frac{10}{9} \times 18$

7-2 ESTIMATING PRODUCTS OF MIXED NUMBERS

One gallon of water weighs about $8\frac{1}{3}$ lb (pounds). So $4\frac{1}{2}$ gal weighs about $4\frac{1}{2} \times 8\frac{1}{3}$ lb. You can use *rounding to the nearest whole number* to determine that this is about 40 lb.

example 1

Estimate $4\frac{1}{2} \times 8\frac{1}{3}$ by rounding.

solution

$4\frac{1}{2} \times 8\frac{1}{3} \rightarrow \underbrace{5 \times 8}_{\text{about 40}}$

◄── If the fractional part of a mixed number is greater than or equal to $\frac{1}{2}$, round up. Otherwise, round down.

your turn

Estimate by rounding.

1. $2\frac{7}{8} \times 4\frac{5}{6}$
2. $1\frac{1}{9} \times 3\frac{3}{17}$
3. $5\frac{1}{3} \times 6\frac{5}{7}$
4. $9\frac{1}{2} \times 10\frac{1}{4}$

If one factor is a fraction less than 1, you can often use compatible numbers to estimate the product.

example 2

Estimate using compatible numbers.

a. $\frac{1}{3} \times 8\frac{2}{7}$ **◄── Change $8\frac{2}{7}$ to a whole number close to it that is compatible with $\frac{1}{3}$.**

$\downarrow \quad \downarrow$

$\underbrace{\frac{1}{3} \times 9}_{\text{about 3}}$

b. $\frac{4}{7} \times 11\frac{2}{5}$ **◄── Choose compatible numbers that are close to the given factors.**

$\downarrow \quad \downarrow$

$\underbrace{\frac{1}{2} \times 12}_{\text{about 6}}$

your turn

Estimate using compatible numbers.

5. $\frac{1}{4} \times 11\frac{1}{3}$
6. $18\frac{1}{3} \times \frac{1}{5}$
7. $\frac{7}{15} \times 31\frac{1}{5}$
8. $\frac{4}{13} \times 58\frac{1}{7}$

Multiplying and Dividing Fractions 147

practice exercises

practice for example 1 (page 147)

Estimate by rounding.

1. $1\frac{4}{5} \times 2\frac{1}{3}$

2. $2\frac{1}{2} \times 2\frac{1}{4}$

3. $3\frac{2}{3} \times 6\frac{1}{2}$

4. $7\frac{1}{8} \times 9\frac{3}{14}$

5. $4\frac{1}{6} \times 8\frac{6}{7}$

6. $15\frac{4}{17} \times 9\frac{9}{10}$

7. $21\frac{14}{19} \times 4\frac{4}{21}$

8. $50\frac{2}{9} \times 99\frac{8}{9}$

practice for example 2 (page 147)

Estimate using compatible numbers.

9. $\frac{1}{2} \times 6\frac{3}{5}$

10. $\frac{1}{3} \times 17\frac{1}{4}$

11. $9\frac{1}{3} \times \frac{1}{5}$

12. $23\frac{1}{2} \times \frac{6}{19}$

13. $\frac{3}{4} \times 41\frac{1}{8}$

14. $\frac{2}{3} \times 12\frac{4}{5}$

15. $\frac{19}{61} \times 75\frac{1}{2}$

16. $\frac{26}{99} \times 58\frac{4}{7}$

mixed practice (page 147)

Estimate.

17. $6\frac{3}{4} \times 2\frac{1}{7}$

18. $14\frac{1}{3} \times \frac{1}{5}$

19. $\frac{1}{7} \times 33\frac{5}{9}$

20. $8\frac{3}{20} \times 5\frac{2}{7}$

21. $\frac{19}{40} \times 10\frac{1}{2}$

22. $\frac{17}{35} \times 17\frac{1}{4}$

23. $\frac{3}{11} \times 17\frac{1}{4}$

24. $\frac{33}{100} \times 14\frac{2}{7}$

25. $\frac{21}{100} \times 31\frac{1}{2}$

26. $\frac{67}{100} \times 9\frac{1}{2}$

27. $1\frac{1}{5} \times 1\frac{9}{11}$

28. $11\frac{1}{9} \times 8\frac{1}{2}$

29. Harry averages about $7\frac{1}{2}$ mi/h (miles per hour) while bicycling. About how far will he go in $2\frac{1}{3}$ h?

30. Jane has about $5\frac{3}{4}$ gal of paint but will use only about $\frac{1}{3}$ of that amount. Estimate how much paint Jane will use.

review exercises

Write each mixed number as a fraction in lowest terms.

1. $3\frac{1}{4}$

2. $6\frac{2}{7}$

3. $12\frac{2}{3}$

4. $1\frac{9}{99}$

5. $2\frac{8}{12}$

6. $11\frac{18}{27}$

Find each product.

7. 24×3

8. 81×6

9. 10×17

10. 64×32

11. 36×25

12. 72×211

13. 253×124

14. 707×698

7-3 MULTIPLYING WITH MIXED NUMBERS

A photograph that is 2 in. (inches) wide and $2\frac{3}{4}$ in. long is to be enlarged $1\frac{1}{2}$ times. If you multiply $1\frac{1}{2}$ times the width and $1\frac{1}{2}$ times the length, you find that the enlarged photograph will be 3 in. wide and $4\frac{1}{8}$ in. long.

To multiply with mixed numbers, use this method.

1. Write each number as a fraction.
2. Multiply the numerators.
3. Multiply the denominators.
4. Write the product in lowest terms.

$$1\frac{1}{2} \times 2$$
$$\downarrow \quad \downarrow$$
$$\frac{3}{2} \times \frac{2}{1} = \frac{3 \times \cancel{2}^{1}}{\cancel{2}_{1} \times 1} = \frac{3}{1} = 3$$

$$1\frac{1}{2} \times 2\frac{3}{4}$$
$$\downarrow \quad \downarrow$$
$$\frac{3}{2} \times \frac{11}{4} = \frac{3 \times 11}{2 \times 4} = \frac{33}{8} = 4\frac{1}{8}$$

example 1

Write each product in lowest terms.

a. $2\frac{1}{6} \times 3$ **b.** $5 \times 1\frac{3}{4}$

solution

a. $2\frac{1}{6} \times 3$
$$\downarrow \quad \downarrow$$
$$\frac{13}{6} \times \frac{3}{1} = \frac{13 \times \cancel{3}^{1}}{\cancel{6}_{2} \times 1} = \frac{13}{2} = 6\frac{1}{2}$$

b. $5 \times 1\frac{3}{4}$
$$\downarrow \quad \downarrow$$
$$\frac{5}{1} \times \frac{7}{4} = \frac{5 \times 7}{1 \times 4} = \frac{35}{4} = 8\frac{3}{4}$$

your turn

Write each product in lowest terms.

1. $7\frac{1}{5} \times 10$ **2.** $2\frac{1}{3} \times 9$ **3.** $4 \times 2\frac{7}{8}$ **4.** $3 \times 12\frac{1}{2}$

example 2

Write each product in lowest terms:　　a. $3\frac{1}{2} \times 2\frac{2}{3}$　　b. $\frac{4}{5} \times 1\frac{1}{2}$

solution

a. $3\frac{1}{2} \times 2\frac{2}{3}$

$$\frac{7}{2} \times \frac{\overset{4}{\cancel{8}}}{3} = \frac{7 \times \cancel{8}}{\underset{1}{\cancel{2}} \times 3} = \frac{28}{3} = 9\frac{1}{3}$$

b. $\frac{4}{5} \times 1\frac{1}{2}$

$$\frac{4}{5} \times \frac{\overset{2}{\cancel{3}}}{2} = \frac{\cancel{4} \times 3}{5 \times \underset{1}{\cancel{2}}} = \frac{6}{5} = 1\frac{1}{5}$$

your turn

Write each product in lowest terms.

5. $4\frac{1}{11} \times 2\frac{1}{5}$　　　6. $1\frac{1}{3} \times 2\frac{1}{4}$　　　7. $5\frac{3}{4} \times \frac{2}{3}$　　　8. $5\frac{1}{3} \times \frac{7}{8}$

practice exercises

practice for example 1 (page 149)

Write each product in lowest terms.

1. $1\frac{3}{5} \times 15$　　　　2. $2\frac{1}{2} \times 30$　　　　3. $2\frac{1}{4} \times 16$　　　　4. $3\frac{1}{3} \times 9$

5. $10 \times 2\frac{4}{5}$　　　　6. $16 \times 5\frac{1}{8}$　　　　7. $2 \times 3\frac{1}{4}$　　　　8. $3 \times 5\frac{1}{9}$

9. $1\frac{2}{5} \times 4$　　　　10. $3\frac{2}{7} \times 3$　　　　11. $6 \times 4\frac{1}{8}$　　　　12. $6 \times 2\frac{4}{9}$

13. $5\frac{2}{5} \times 3$　　　　14. $3\frac{1}{7} \times 9$　　　　15. $7\frac{1}{11} \times 22$　　　　16. $12\frac{1}{2} \times 30$

practice for example 2 (page 150)

Write each product in lowest terms.

17. $\frac{4}{7} \times 1\frac{3}{8}$　　　　18. $\frac{8}{9} \times 2\frac{1}{4}$　　　　19. $2\frac{3}{7} \times 1\frac{1}{34}$　　　　20. $3\frac{2}{3} \times \frac{3}{5}$

21. $2\frac{1}{3} \times \frac{1}{2}$　　　　22. $\frac{5}{14} \times 3\frac{1}{2}$　　　　23. $1\frac{1}{10} \times \frac{5}{9}$　　　　24. $\frac{7}{9} \times 1\frac{2}{7}$

25. $7\frac{1}{7} \times 3\frac{11}{15}$　　　26. $2\frac{3}{7} \times 2\frac{4}{5}$　　　27. $6\frac{2}{3} \times \frac{17}{25}$　　　28. $11\frac{1}{9} \times 8\frac{1}{10}$

29. $\frac{7}{8} \times 2\frac{2}{11}$　　　　30. $7\frac{1}{3} \times 6\frac{1}{2}$　　　　31. $6\frac{1}{9} \times 3\frac{3}{5}$　　　　32. $13\frac{3}{4} \times 5\frac{1}{11}$

Write each product in lowest terms.

33. $1\frac{7}{9} \times \frac{3}{4}$ 34. $2\frac{2}{9} \times 6$ 35. $8\frac{4}{7} \times 2\frac{1}{3}$ 36. $2\frac{2}{5} \times 3\frac{1}{3}$

37. $9 \times 3\frac{2}{3}$ 38. $\frac{1}{15} \times 2\frac{1}{7}$ 39. $4\frac{4}{5} \times \frac{7}{12}$ 40. $21 \times 4\frac{5}{7}$

41. $6\frac{2}{3} \times 1\frac{1}{5}$ 42. $5\frac{4}{5} \times 10$ 43. $\frac{2}{13} \times 8\frac{2}{3}$ 44. $1\frac{9}{11} \times 1\frac{1}{10}$

45. $9\frac{1}{3} \times \frac{5}{14}$ 46. $7\frac{1}{3} \times \frac{9}{13}$ 47. $18 \times 2\frac{8}{9}$ 48. $9\frac{1}{2} \times \frac{1}{38}$

49. $\frac{1}{5} \times 2\frac{1}{2}$ 50. $\frac{2}{3} \times 5\frac{1}{4}$ 51. $3 \times 12\frac{1}{2}$ 52. $4 \times 2\frac{7}{8}$

53. $1\frac{2}{3} \times 1\frac{2}{3}$ 54. $2\frac{6}{7} \times \frac{3}{4}$ 55. $3\frac{1}{6} \times 2\frac{3}{4}$ 56. $14\frac{1}{3} \times 4\frac{1}{2}$

57. $2\frac{2}{5} \times \frac{5}{6}$ 58. $5\frac{1}{4} \times \frac{2}{3}$ 59. $\frac{4}{7} \times 9 \times 2\frac{1}{3}$ 60. $\frac{2}{3} \times 6 \times 1\frac{1}{4}$

61. Mr. Washington earns $6 per hour. If he gets time and a half for overtime, what is his hourly rate for overtime work?

62. The scale on a map is one inch = $5\frac{1}{4}$ mi (miles). How many miles do three and one third inches represent?

review exercises

Find each difference.

1. $5000 - 2491$ 2. $402 - 178$ 3. $80 - 18$ 4. $200 - 179$
5. $324 - 298$ 6. $802 - 347$ 7. $10{,}200 - 8902$ 8. $765 - 648$

Estimate each product.

9. 59×23 10. 78×31 11. 6×935 12. 377×8
13. 49×797 14. 38×450 15. 431×689 16. 247×734

The numerator and denominator of a fraction are two-digit numbers. The denominator is formed by reversing the order of the digits in the numerator. The fraction is equivalent to $\frac{4}{7}$. One possible solution is $\frac{12}{21}$. Find all other solutions.

7-4 DIVIDING WITH FRACTIONS

Two numbers whose product is 1 are called **reciprocals.**

$$9 \times \frac{1}{9} = 1 \qquad\qquad \frac{2}{3} \times \frac{3}{2} = 1 \qquad\qquad \frac{4}{5} \times 1\frac{1}{4} = 1$$

9 and $\frac{1}{9}$ are reciprocals. $\quad \frac{2}{3}$ and $\frac{3}{2}$ are reciprocals. $\quad \frac{4}{5}$ and $1\frac{1}{4}$ are reciprocals.

You find the reciprocal of a fraction by interchanging the numerator and the denominator. With the exception of zero, every number has exactly one reciprocal. Zero has no reciprocal.

example 1

Write the reciprocal of each number: **a.** $\frac{4}{13}$ **b.** 15 **c.** $1\frac{8}{9}$

solution

a. $\frac{4}{13} \diagdown \frac{13}{4}$

$\frac{13}{4}$ is the reciprocal.

b. $15 = \frac{15}{1} \diagdown \frac{1}{15}$

$\frac{1}{15}$ is the reciprocal.

c. $1\frac{8}{9} = \frac{17}{9} \diagdown \frac{9}{17}$

$\frac{9}{17}$ is the reciprocal.

your turn

Write the reciprocal of each number, if possible.

1. $\frac{3}{8}$ **2.** $\frac{4}{7}$ **3.** 10 **4.** 0 **5.** $\frac{9}{4}$ **6.** $2\frac{11}{13}$

To divide by a fraction, use the following method.
1. Multiply by the reciprocal of the divisor.
2. Write the product in lowest terms.

example 2

Write each quotient in lowest terms: **a.** $\frac{2}{3} \div \frac{17}{9}$ **b.** $\frac{7}{8} \div \frac{14}{19}$

solution

a. $\frac{2}{3} \div \frac{17}{9} = \frac{2}{3} \times \frac{9}{17}$ ⟵ **The reciprocal of $\frac{17}{9}$ is $\frac{9}{17}$.**

$= \frac{2}{\overset{}{\underset{1}{3}}} \times \frac{\overset{3}{\cancel{9}}}{17}$

$= \frac{6}{17}$

b. $\frac{7}{8} \div \frac{14}{19} = \frac{7}{8} \times \frac{19}{14}$ ⟵ **The reciprocal of $\frac{14}{19}$ is $\frac{19}{14}$.**

$= \frac{\overset{1}{\cancel{7}}}{8} \times \frac{19}{\underset{2}{\cancel{14}}}$

$= \frac{19}{16} = 1\frac{3}{16}$

your turn

Write each quotient in lowest terms.

7. $\frac{3}{4} \div \frac{9}{10}$ 8. $\frac{9}{5} \div \frac{11}{10}$ 9. $\frac{3}{14} \div \frac{12}{7}$ 10. $\frac{3}{5} \div \frac{7}{12}$

example 3

Write each quotient in lowest terms.

a. $15 \div \frac{1}{2}$ b. $\frac{4}{5} \div 12$

solution

a. $15 \div \frac{1}{2} = \frac{15}{1} \times \frac{2}{1}$ ⬅ **The reciprocal of $\frac{1}{2}$ is 2.**

$= 30$

b. $\frac{4}{5} \div 12 = \frac{4}{5} \times \frac{1}{12}$ ⬅ **The reciprocal of 12 is $\frac{1}{12}$.**

$= \frac{1}{15}$

your turn

Write each quotient in lowest terms.

11. $6 \div \frac{2}{3}$ 12. $10 \div \frac{1}{4}$ 13. $\frac{3}{7} \div 5$ 14. $\frac{3}{4} \div 9$

practice exercises

practice for example 1 *(page 152)*

Write the reciprocal of each number.

1. $\frac{1}{2}$ 2. $\frac{7}{5}$ 3. 13 4. 1 5. $\frac{16}{19}$ 6. $\frac{8}{21}$

7. $1\frac{1}{8}$ 8. $7\frac{3}{4}$ 9. $\frac{71}{33}$ 10. $\frac{101}{100}$ 11. $3\frac{3}{4}$ 12. $2\frac{5}{9}$

practice for example 2 *(pages 152–153)*

Write each quotient in lowest terms.

13. $\frac{15}{17} \div \frac{5}{2}$ 14. $\frac{6}{11} \div \frac{7}{22}$ 15. $\frac{5}{9} \div \frac{1}{3}$ 16. $\frac{2}{5} \div \frac{11}{5}$

17. $\frac{12}{25} \div \frac{4}{5}$ 18. $\frac{8}{9} \div \frac{2}{9}$ 19. $\frac{3}{4} \div \frac{3}{4}$ 20. $\frac{5}{6} \div \frac{5}{6}$

21. $\frac{6}{7} \div \frac{2}{3}$ 22. $\frac{13}{14} \div \frac{7}{26}$ 23. $\frac{9}{11} \div \frac{27}{33}$ 24. $\frac{13}{20} \div \frac{52}{55}$

practice for example 3 (page 153)

Write each quotient in lowest terms.

25. $1 \div \frac{1}{10}$ 26. $5 \div \frac{1}{7}$ 27. $\frac{7}{12} \div 8$ 28. $\frac{10}{13} \div 20$ 29. $\frac{12}{13} \div 72$

30. $\frac{11}{12} \div 66$ 31. $2 \div \frac{8}{3}$ 32. $2 \div \frac{5}{7}$ 33. $\frac{7}{2} \div 3$ 34. $\frac{27}{28} \div 18$

mixed practice (pages 152–153)

Write each quotient in lowest terms.

35. $\frac{9}{21} \div \frac{3}{7}$ 36. $\frac{9}{100} \div \frac{11}{10}$ 37. $1 \div \frac{5}{9}$ 38. $0 \div \frac{12}{7}$ 39. $\frac{3}{4} \div \frac{1}{2}$

40. $\frac{5}{3} \div \frac{2}{3}$ 41. $\frac{7}{8} \div \frac{8}{7}$ 42. $\frac{5}{6} \div \frac{15}{16}$ 43. $\frac{2}{3} \div 16$ 44. $\frac{1}{7} \div 14$

Tell whether each quotient is greater than, less than, or equal to 1.

45. $5 \div \frac{3}{4}$ 46. $\frac{3}{4} \div \frac{4}{5}$ 47. $\frac{9}{7} \div \frac{9}{7}$ 48. $\frac{2}{3} \div \frac{1}{4}$

49. If 9 people drink $\frac{3}{4}$ gal (gallon) of milk, how much milk does each person drink?

50. How many $\frac{1}{4}$-lb (pound) servings of raisins can you get from a 10 lb box of raisins?

review exercises

Write each mixed number as a fraction.

1. $4\frac{8}{21}$ 2. $10\frac{5}{9}$ 3. $5\frac{11}{12}$ 4. $2\frac{3}{14}$ 5. $3\frac{5}{7}$ 6. $11\frac{14}{15}$

Write each fraction as a mixed number in lowest terms.

7. $\frac{19}{4}$ 8. $\frac{27}{5}$ 9. $\frac{39}{6}$ 10. $\frac{59}{8}$ 11. $\frac{123}{2}$ 12. $\frac{247}{6}$

mental math

You can use mental math to divide by a *unit fraction*, a fraction whose numerator is 1.

$6 \div \frac{1}{3} = 18$ ◄── Think: **6 × 3 = 18**

Divide mentally.

1. $9 \div \frac{1}{2}$ 2. $12 \div \frac{1}{2}$ 3. $12 \div \frac{1}{4}$ 4. $7 \div \frac{1}{5}$ 5. $3 \div \frac{1}{3}$ 6. $2 \div \frac{1}{6}$

7-5 DIVIDING WITH MIXED NUMBERS

Ben has a piece of fabric that is $7\frac{1}{2}$ yd (yards) long. Each costume for the play requires $1\frac{1}{4}$ yd of fabric. Ben found the quotient $7\frac{1}{2} \div 1\frac{1}{4}$ to report that he could make 6 costumes from the piece of fabric.

To divide with mixed numbers, use the following method.

1. Write each mixed number as a fraction.

$$7\frac{1}{2} \div 1\frac{1}{4} = \frac{15}{2} \div \frac{5}{4}$$

2. Divide the fractions.

$$= \frac{\overset{3}{\cancel{15}}}{2} \times \frac{\overset{2}{\cancel{4}}}{\underset{1}{\cancel{5}}}$$

3. Write the quotient in lowest terms.

$$= \frac{6}{1} = 6$$

example 1

a. $1\frac{1}{3} \div 2\frac{1}{2} = \frac{4}{3} \div \frac{5}{2}$

$= \frac{4}{3} \times \frac{2}{5}$

$= \frac{8}{15}$

b. $2\frac{1}{4} \div 1\frac{1}{4} = \frac{9}{4} \div \frac{5}{4}$

$= \frac{9}{\underset{1}{\cancel{4}}} \times \frac{\overset{1}{\cancel{4}}}{5}$

$= \frac{9}{5} = 1\frac{4}{5}$

your turn

Write each quotient in lowest terms.

1. $7\frac{1}{2} \div 3\frac{1}{2}$

2. $3\frac{3}{7} \div 1\frac{1}{7}$

3. $1\frac{3}{4} \div 7\frac{7}{8}$

4. $5\frac{1}{2} \div 1\frac{1}{3}$

example 2

a. $10 \div 2\frac{1}{2} = \frac{10}{1} \div \frac{5}{2}$

$= \frac{\overset{2}{\cancel{10}}}{1} \times \frac{2}{\underset{1}{\cancel{5}}}$

$= \frac{4}{1} = 4$

b. $8\frac{1}{2} \div \frac{3}{4} = \frac{17}{2} \div \frac{3}{4}$

$= \frac{17}{\underset{1}{\cancel{2}}} \times \frac{\overset{2}{\cancel{4}}}{3}$

$= \frac{34}{3} = 11\frac{1}{3}$

your turn

Write each quotient in lowest terms.

5. $4 \div 5\frac{1}{2}$

6. $8\frac{1}{3} \div 15$

7. $6\frac{2}{9} \div \frac{1}{6}$

8. $\frac{4}{7} \div 11\frac{1}{2}$

Multiplying and Dividing Fractions 155

You can estimate a quotient of mixed numbers by changing the given numbers to compatible numbers that are close to the given numbers.

example 3

Estimate using compatible numbers.

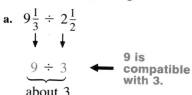

a. $9\frac{1}{3} \div 2\frac{1}{2}$

$9 \div 3$ ← **9 is compatible with 3.**

about 3

b. $11\frac{3}{7} \div 2\frac{1}{2}$

$12 \div 3$

about 4

c. $4\frac{3}{4} \div \frac{4}{9}$

$5 \div \frac{1}{2}$, or 5×2

about 10

your turn

Estimate using compatible numbers.

9. $8\frac{2}{3} \div 2\frac{1}{4}$ **10.** $16\frac{2}{3} \div 2\frac{5}{6}$ **11.** $21\frac{1}{2} \div \frac{1}{5}$ **12.** $10\frac{3}{4} \div \frac{6}{11}$

practice exercises

practice for example 1 *(page 155)*

Write each quotient in lowest terms.

1. $3\frac{1}{4} \div 1\frac{3}{8}$ **2.** $2\frac{1}{6} \div 1\frac{2}{3}$ **3.** $2\frac{3}{4} \div 1\frac{1}{8}$ **4.** $2\frac{1}{10} \div 1\frac{4}{5}$ **5.** $5\frac{1}{6} \div 3\frac{1}{10}$

6. $1\frac{3}{8} \div 2\frac{3}{4}$ **7.** $4\frac{3}{4} \div 4\frac{3}{4}$ **8.** $1\frac{7}{9} \div 1\frac{7}{9}$ **9.** $1\frac{1}{5} \div 1\frac{3}{4}$ **10.** $2\frac{1}{2} \div 3\frac{2}{5}$

practice for example 2 *(page 155)*

Write each quotient in lowest terms.

11. $3 \div 1\frac{1}{2}$ **12.** $3\frac{1}{4} \div \frac{1}{8}$ **13.** $3\frac{1}{3} \div 1$ **14.** $5 \div 5\frac{1}{3}$ **15.** $\frac{5}{8} \div 3\frac{3}{4}$

16. $\frac{3}{10} \div 7\frac{1}{2}$ **17.** $8\frac{1}{2} \div 17$ **18.** $6\frac{3}{4} \div 12$ **19.** $9\frac{7}{11} \div \frac{1}{3}$ **20.** $3\frac{4}{13} \div \frac{5}{11}$

practice for example 3 *(page 156)*

Estimate using compatible numbers.

21. $1\frac{1}{5} \div 1\frac{1}{6}$ **22.** $2\frac{9}{10} \div 1\frac{1}{5}$ **23.** $7\frac{1}{4} \div 3\frac{3}{4}$ **24.** $26\frac{3}{4} \div 5\frac{1}{3}$ **25.** $15\frac{3}{4} \div 3\frac{1}{3}$

26. $13\frac{1}{3} \div 4\frac{1}{4}$ **27.** $1\frac{1}{5} \div \frac{1}{3}$ **28.** $2\frac{6}{7} \div \frac{1}{4}$ **29.** $4\frac{4}{5} \div \frac{10}{31}$ **30.** $8\frac{1}{6} \div \frac{9}{19}$

Write each quotient in lowest terms.

31. $2 \div 1\frac{1}{10}$ 32. $3 \div 5\frac{1}{2}$ 33. $3\frac{1}{4} \div 1\frac{1}{8}$ 34. $2\frac{1}{6} \div 1\frac{2}{3}$ 35. $\frac{3}{4} \div 3\frac{1}{2}$

36. $\frac{9}{5} \div 1\frac{1}{3}$ 37. $9\frac{1}{2} \div 19$ 38. $7\frac{1}{8} \div 5$ 39. $\frac{22}{17} \div 1\frac{4}{51}$ 40. $\frac{6}{7} \div 2\frac{5}{14}$

Estimate using compatible numbers.

41. $10\frac{1}{3} \div 4\frac{2}{3}$ 42. $16\frac{3}{8} \div 5\frac{5}{7}$ 43. $19\frac{1}{5} \div \frac{9}{10}$ 44. $3\frac{1}{9} \div \frac{8}{15}$

45. $1\frac{7}{8} \div \frac{6}{17}$ 46. $1\frac{1}{6} \div \frac{5}{19}$ 47. $97\frac{1}{5} \div 51\frac{1}{10}$ 48. $4\frac{2}{3} \div \frac{6}{59}$

49. Kim Wong tutors English. In April she worked $7\frac{1}{2}$ h and was paid $60. How much was she paid per hour?

50. If a mechanic needs about $1\frac{3}{4}$ h to inspect an automobile, about how many automobiles can be inspected in $7\frac{1}{2}$ h?

review *exercises*

Estimate.

1. $498 + 429$ 2. $541 + 965$ 3. $2374 + 4629$ 4. $267 + 196 + 132$
5. $487 + 193$ 6. $1896 + 5931$ 7. $8926 + 6841$ 8. $429 + 326 + 57$

calculator corner

You can multiply fractions easily on a calculator because multiplication and division are done in the order in which they occur. The answers will be in decimal form, however, and some will not be exact.

example   **a.** $\frac{1}{2} \times \frac{1}{4}$ **b.** $\frac{5}{6} \times \frac{6}{5}$

solution   Enter 1 ÷ 2 ✕ 1 ÷ 4 =.   Enter 5 ÷ 6 ✕ 6 ÷ 5 =.
The answer is 0.125.   The answer is 1 or 0.9999999.

Multiply using a calculator.

1. $\frac{9}{13} \times \frac{5}{12}$ 2. $\frac{7}{10} \times \frac{1}{4}$ 3. $\frac{3}{8} \times \frac{7}{12}$ 4. $\frac{1}{3} \times 3$

5. $\frac{2}{3} \times \frac{6}{5}$ 6. $\frac{9}{10} \times \frac{1}{4}$ 7. $5 \times \frac{2}{3}$ 8. $\frac{7}{11} \times \frac{1}{4}$

SKILL REVIEW

Write each product in lowest terms.

1. $\frac{1}{3} \times \frac{1}{5}$ 2. $\frac{3}{7} \times \frac{1}{4}$ 3. $\frac{2}{9} \times \frac{3}{11}$ **7-1**

4. $5 \times \frac{4}{13}$ 5. $\frac{14}{15} \times \frac{5}{6}$ 6. $\frac{0}{22} \times \frac{9}{17}$

7. $\frac{17}{20} \times \frac{50}{51}$ 8. $\frac{21}{33} \times \frac{11}{28}$ 9. $\frac{7}{9} \times \frac{2}{3}$

10. $\frac{7}{12} \times \frac{6}{49}$ 11. $\frac{3}{11} \times \frac{6}{11}$ 12. $\frac{3}{4} \times \frac{3}{5}$

13. One fifth of a class of 200 students were absent because of illness. How many students were absent?

Estimate.

14. $2\frac{3}{4} \times 3\frac{1}{3}$ 15. $4\frac{2}{7} \times 5\frac{3}{7}$ 16. $7\frac{7}{10} \times 1\frac{1}{2}$ 17. $3\frac{1}{6} \times 9\frac{2}{11}$ **7-2**

18. $4\frac{14}{15} \times 10\frac{6}{7}$ 19. $3\frac{3}{8} \times 11\frac{1}{5}$ 20. $9\frac{8}{9} \times 2\frac{2}{11}$ 21. $2\frac{2}{17} \times 5\frac{1}{4}$

Write each product in lowest terms.

22. $3\frac{1}{2} \times 6$ 23. $5 \times 7\frac{1}{5}$ 24. $6\frac{2}{7} \times \frac{14}{15}$ 25. $9\frac{1}{3} \times 2\frac{3}{4}$ **7-3**

26. $1\frac{3}{5} \times 5\frac{7}{8}$ 27. $7 \times 3\frac{3}{7}$ 28. $\frac{7}{8} \times 4\frac{4}{11}$ 29. $11\frac{2}{3} \times 8\frac{4}{7}$

30. Last summer Joe earned $1500. This summer he earned $1\frac{1}{3}$ times that amount. How much did he earn this summer?

Write each quotient in lowest terms.

31. $14 \div \frac{7}{9}$ 32. $\frac{5}{6} \div 10$ 33. $\frac{1}{2} \div 4$ 34. $\frac{3}{8} \div 6$ **7-4**

35. $\frac{3}{4} \div \frac{5}{8}$ 36. $\frac{2}{5} \div \frac{14}{15}$ 37. $\frac{10}{11} \div \frac{10}{11}$ 38. $\frac{12}{13} \div \frac{6}{7}$

39. $2\frac{1}{7} \div 1\frac{1}{6}$ 40. $1\frac{5}{8} \div 6\frac{1}{7}$ 41. $3\frac{5}{8} \div 1\frac{5}{6}$ 42. $6\frac{2}{3} \div 5\frac{1}{3}$ **7-5**

43. $8\frac{1}{6} \div 1\frac{19}{30}$ 44. $7\frac{1}{2} \div 2\frac{1}{2}$ 45. $3\frac{3}{4} \div 5\frac{1}{3}$ 46. $3\frac{5}{8} \div 4\frac{1}{3}$

Estimate using compatible numbers.

47. $3\frac{4}{5} \div 2\frac{1}{3}$ 48. $14\frac{2}{7} \div 5\frac{1}{4}$ 49. $7\frac{2}{5} \div 6\frac{1}{2}$ 50. $2\frac{4}{5} \div \frac{3}{10}$

METALLURGIST

Joe Samuels is a physical metallurgist. He makes metal compounds by melting and combining certain metals. In the laboratory he uses an electron microscope and X-rays to help him with his work.

example

Joe has an order for 20 lb (pounds) of pewter. Pewter is $\frac{17}{20}$ tin, $\frac{7}{100}$ copper, and $\frac{2}{25}$ bismuth. Find the amount of each metal Joe needs.

solution

Since Joe needs 20 lb of pewter, he multiplies each fraction by 20.

tin: $\quad \frac{17}{20} \times \frac{20}{1} = \frac{17 \times \overset{1}{\cancel{20}}}{\underset{1}{\cancel{20}} \times 1} = \frac{17}{1} = 17$

copper: $\quad \frac{7}{100} \times \frac{20}{1} = \frac{7 \times \overset{1}{\cancel{20}}}{\underset{5}{\cancel{100}} \times 1} = \frac{7}{5} = 1\frac{2}{5}$

bismuth: $\quad \frac{2}{25} \times \frac{20}{1} = \frac{2 \times \overset{4}{\cancel{20}}}{\underset{5}{\cancel{25}} \times 1} = \frac{8}{5} = 1\frac{3}{5}$

Joe needs 17 lb of tin, $1\frac{2}{5}$ lb of copper, and $1\frac{3}{5}$ lb of bismuth.

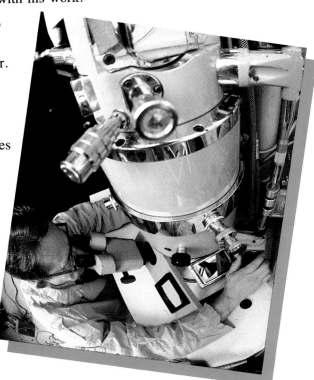

exercises

1. A manufacturing company needs 150 lb of yellow brass to make pliers. Yellow brass is $\frac{2}{3}$ nickel and $\frac{1}{3}$ zinc. Find the amount of each metal needed to make 150 lb of yellow brass.

2. Tony Bachus needs 5 lb of sterling silver for a set of candlesticks. Sterling silver is $\frac{9}{10}$ silver and $\frac{1}{10}$ copper. Find the amount of each metal needed to make 5 lb of sterling silver.

3. Dr. Julia Heath needs $12\frac{1}{2}$ lb of dental silver for fillings. Dental silver is $\frac{7}{10}$ silver, $\frac{1}{4}$ lead, $\frac{3}{100}$ copper, and $\frac{1}{50}$ mercury.
   a. Is there more copper or mercury in dental silver?
   b. Find the amount of each metal needed to make $12\frac{1}{2}$ lb of dental silver.

4. A manufacturer needs $16\frac{2}{3}$ lb of stainless steel. Stainless steel is $\frac{8}{10}$ iron, $\frac{19}{100}$ chromium, and $\frac{1}{100}$ nickel. Find the amount of each metal needed to make $16\frac{2}{3}$ lb of stainless steel.

7-6 ADJUSTING RECIPES

Recipes usually specify the number of servings that can be made. You may need to adjust a recipe to *increase* the number of servings. For instance, the recipe at the right makes 12 muffins, but you can change it to make more if you increase the amount of each ingredient.

To read a recipe, you should be familiar with these abbreviations.

c (cup)
tsp (teaspoon)
tbsp (tablespoon)
lb (pound)
oz (ounce)

Marvin's Muffins   Makes 12

1 c grated carrots   2 tsp baking powder
1¼ c whole-wheat flour   1 tsp baking soda
2 eggs   ¼ c lemon juice
½ c honey   ½ c chopped nuts
½ c melted butter
½ tsp cinnamon

---

example 1

Use the muffin recipe above. Find the amount of honey needed to make 18 muffins.

solution

$$\frac{\text{number of muffins needed}}{\text{number of muffins in recipe}} \quad \rightarrow \quad \frac{18}{12} = 1\frac{1}{2}$$

You need $\frac{1}{2}$ c of honey to make the recipe. You want to make $1\frac{1}{2}$ times the recipe, so you need $1\frac{1}{2}$ times the amount of honey.

$$1\frac{1}{2} \times \frac{1}{2} = \frac{3}{2} \times \frac{1}{2} = \frac{3 \times 1}{2 \times 2} = \frac{3}{4}$$

You need $\frac{3}{4}$ c of honey.

your turn

Use the muffin recipe above. Find the amount of each ingredient needed to make 15 muffins.

1. carrots   2. butter
3. baking powder   4. cinnamon

Sometimes you will want to adjust a recipe to *decrease* the number of servings. To do this, you decrease the amount of each ingredient used.

example 2

Use the chili recipe at the right. Find the amount of canned tomatoes needed to make chili for 4 people.

solution

$$\frac{\text{number to be served}}{\text{number served by recipe}} \longrightarrow \frac{4}{8} = \frac{1}{2}$$

You need 5 c of tomatoes to make the recipe. You want to make $\frac{1}{2}$ the recipe, so you need $\frac{1}{2}$ the amount of canned tomatoes.

$$\frac{1}{2} \times 5 = \frac{1}{2} \times \frac{5}{1} = \frac{1 \times 5}{2 \times 1} = \frac{5}{2} = 2\frac{1}{2}$$

You need $2\frac{1}{2}$ c of canned tomatoes.

your turn

Use the chili recipe above. Find the amount of each ingredient needed to serve 2 people.

5. pinto beans

6. lean ground chuck

7. chili powder

8. pepper

> Texas Chili   Serves 8
> $\frac{1}{2}$ lb pinto beans $\frac{1}{2}$ c butter
> 5 c canned tomatoes   2 cloves garlic
> 1 lb green peppers   1 tsp salt
> 3 $\frac{1}{2}$ lb lean ground chuck $\frac{1}{3}$ c chili powder
> 1 $\frac{1}{2}$ tbsp salad oil   1 $\frac{1}{2}$ tsp pepper
> $\frac{1}{2}$ c chopped parsley

practice *exercises*

practice for example 1 (page 160)

Use the recipe at the right. Find the amount of each ingredient needed to serve 16 people.

1. sweet potatoes

2. eggs

3. cinnamon

4. cardamom

5. evaporated milk

6. butter

Use the recipe at the right. Find the amount of each ingredient needed to serve 20 people.

7. butter

8. eggs

9. sugar

10. cinnamon

> Sweet Potato Casserole   Serves 8
> 24 oz canned sweet   5 tbsp butter
>   potatoes
> 2$\frac{1}{2}$ c evaporated $\frac{3}{4}$ tsp cinnamon
>   milk
> 4 eggs   1 $\frac{1}{4}$ tsp cardamom
> $\frac{1}{2}$ c sugar

Multiplying and Dividing Fractions **161**

Use the recipe at the right. Find the amount of each ingredient needed to make 2 c.

11. lemon juice
12. dry mustard
13. minced onion
14. tomato juice
15. sugar
16. pepper

Salad Dressing	Makes 4c
5 tbsp lemon juice	2½ tsp dry mustard
5 tbsp salad oil	2 tsp salt
3½ c tomato juice	½ tsp pepper
3 tsp cornstarch	1 tbsp minced onion
3 tsp sugar	

Use the recipe above. Find the amount of each ingredient needed to make 3 c.

17. salad oil   18. pepper   19. tomato juice   20. salt

Use the recipe at the right. Find the amount of each ingredient needed to serve the given number of people.

21. boiled rice; 3
22. vanilla; 12
23. brown sugar; 15
24. eggs; 4
25. lemon juice; 24
26. raisins; 2
27. milk; 18
28. lemon rind; 3

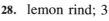

Rice Pudding	Serves 6
2 c boiled rice	1 tsp vanilla
1⅓ c milk	½ c brown sugar
⅛ tsp salt	½ tsp grated lemon rind
3 eggs	
1 tsp lemon juice	
	½ c raisins

CHAPTER REVIEW

vocabulary vo·cab·u·lar·y

Choose the correct word to complete each sentence.

1. (Factors, reciprocals) are two numbers whose product is 1.
2. Numbers chosen for estimation because they multiply or divide easily are called (rounded numbers, compatible numbers).

skills

Write each product in lowest terms.

3. $\frac{2}{7} \times \frac{3}{4}$

4. $\frac{9}{10} \times \frac{1}{3}$

5. $\frac{4}{5} \times \frac{7}{9}$

6. $\frac{1}{4} \times \frac{3}{10}$

7. $3\frac{1}{3} \times \frac{2}{5}$

8. $\frac{1}{6} \times 4\frac{1}{2}$

9. $7 \times \frac{5}{6}$

10. $\frac{11}{12} \times 4$

11. $7 \times 4\frac{1}{7}$

12. $5\frac{9}{10} \times 20$

13. $10\frac{1}{2} \times \frac{3}{7}$

14. $\frac{7}{9} \times 3\frac{3}{5}$

15. $1\frac{1}{6} \times 2\frac{2}{3}$

16. $9\frac{1}{4} \times 1\frac{1}{3}$

17. $\frac{14}{15} \times 1\frac{1}{3}$

18. $\frac{1}{11} \times \frac{22}{25}$

Estimate using compatible numbers.

19. $5\frac{2}{5} \times \frac{1}{3}$

20. $\frac{5}{21} \times 12$

21. $4\frac{5}{9} \times \frac{5}{26}$

22. $8\frac{2}{3} \times \frac{3}{10}$

23. $4\frac{1}{8} \div 2\frac{1}{5}$

24. $9\frac{2}{7} \div 5\frac{3}{8}$

25. $7\frac{3}{11} \div \frac{4}{9}$

26. $5\frac{6}{7} \div \frac{20}{21}$

Write the reciprocal of each number.

27. 12

28. $\frac{7}{9}$

29. $\frac{24}{5}$

30. 34

31. $1\frac{2}{3}$

32. $3\frac{11}{12}$

Write each quotient in lowest terms.

33. $\frac{3}{20} \div \frac{1}{5}$

34. $\frac{7}{12} \div \frac{3}{4}$

35. $\frac{2}{5} \div 3$

36. $4 \div \frac{3}{10}$

37. $6\frac{1}{2} \div 1\frac{2}{3}$

38. $10\frac{3}{8} \div 2\frac{2}{3}$

39. $5\frac{6}{7} \div \frac{1}{14}$

40. $\frac{3}{8} \div 4\frac{3}{4}$

41. A pudding recipe that serves 6 people requires $1\frac{1}{3}$ c of milk. How much milk is needed to make enough pudding to serve 9 people?

42. Harry averages around $6\frac{1}{2}$ mi/h (miles per hour) while bicycling. About how far has he biked after $3\frac{1}{3}$ h?

Multiplying and Dividing Fractions 163

CHAPTER TEST

Write each product in lowest terms.

1. $\frac{4}{9} \times \frac{5}{8}$ 2. $\frac{3}{4} \times \frac{7}{12}$ 3. $\frac{21}{22} \times \frac{33}{35}$ 4. $\frac{2}{11} \times \frac{2}{9}$ 5. $\frac{2}{3} \times \frac{4}{5}$ **7-1**

Estimate by rounding.

6. $2\frac{3}{10} \times 9\frac{9}{10}$ 7. $4\frac{5}{12} \times 5\frac{1}{7}$ 8. $1\frac{4}{9} \times 13\frac{7}{13}$ 9. $6\frac{12}{17} \times 3\frac{2}{9}$ **7-2**

Estimate using compatible numbers.

10. $\frac{1}{5} \times 4\frac{2}{3}$ 11. $7\frac{3}{10} \times \frac{1}{4}$ 12. $3\frac{6}{7} \times \frac{9}{20}$ 13. $\frac{7}{8} \times 10\frac{1}{3}$

Write each product in lowest terms.

14. $3\frac{1}{4} \times 4$ 15. $\frac{5}{6} \times 2\frac{1}{2}$ 16. $4\frac{5}{7} \times 5\frac{1}{11}$ 17. $9\frac{2}{3} \times 3\frac{1}{6}$ 18. $8\frac{4}{7} \times \frac{9}{20}$ **7-3**

Write the reciprocal of each number.

19. $\frac{17}{24}$ 20. $\frac{45}{11}$ 21. 15 22. $1\frac{3}{7}$ 23. 92 **7-4**

Write each quotient in lowest terms.

24. $\frac{1}{8} \div 3$ 25. $\frac{2}{9} \div \frac{2}{3}$ 26. $7 \div \frac{14}{15}$ 27. $\frac{4}{11} \div \frac{6}{13}$ 28. $\frac{7}{10} \div \frac{4}{15}$

29. Each bag of peanuts weighs $\frac{1}{2}$ lb (pound). How many bags can be filled from 8 lb of peanuts?

Write each quotient in lowest terms.

30. $8 \div 2\frac{1}{4}$ 31. $4\frac{1}{6} \div 3\frac{2}{3}$ 32. $5\frac{3}{8} \div \frac{1}{2}$ 33. $\frac{11}{12} \div 1\frac{1}{3}$ **7-5**

34. $3\frac{1}{8} \div 15$ 35. $1\frac{5}{12} \div \frac{2}{3}$ 36. $3\frac{3}{4} \div 2\frac{5}{8}$ 37. $\frac{5}{6} \div 1\frac{3}{8}$

38. If $12\frac{3}{4}$ lb of fruit is divided among 3 people, how much does each person get?

39. One box of spaghetti serves 6 people. How many boxes are needed to serve 10 people?   **7-6**

40. A recipe for 24 rolls requires 2 c of flour. How much flour is needed if you want to make only 18 rolls?

Many types of yarn are used in manufacturing rugs, clothing, and other articles. In adjusting sizes, you often add or subtract fractions.

CHAPTER 8

ADDING AND SUBTRACTING FRACTIONS

8-1 ADDING AND SUBTRACTING FRACTIONS WITH COMMON DENOMINATORS

To add or subtract fractions with a common denominator, use the following method.

1. Add or subtract the numerators.
2. Write the sum or difference over the common denominator.
3. Write the answer in lowest terms.

example 1

Write each sum or difference in lowest terms.

a. $\frac{3}{8} + \frac{2}{8}$

b. $\frac{8}{9} - \frac{2}{9}$

solution

a. $\frac{3}{8} + \frac{2}{8} = \frac{3+2}{8} = \frac{5}{8}$

b. $\frac{8}{9} - \frac{2}{9} = \frac{8-2}{9} = \frac{6}{9} = \frac{2}{3}$

your turn

Write each sum or difference in lowest terms.

1. $\frac{6}{19} + \frac{10}{19}$

2. $\frac{7}{11} - \frac{5}{11}$

3. $\frac{3}{14} + \frac{9}{14}$

4. $\frac{23}{24} - \frac{7}{24}$

When you add fractions, the sum may be a whole number or a mixed number.

example 2

Write each sum in lowest terms: a. $\frac{3}{6} + \frac{5}{6}$ b. $\frac{1}{5} + \frac{4}{5}$

solution

a. $\frac{3}{6} + \frac{5}{6} = \frac{3+5}{6} = \frac{8}{6} = 1\frac{2}{6} = 1\frac{1}{3}$

b. $\frac{1}{5} + \frac{4}{5} = \frac{1+4}{5} = \frac{5}{5} = 1$

your turn

Write each sum in lowest terms.

5. $\frac{2}{3} + \frac{1}{3}$

6. $\frac{5}{9} + \frac{5}{9}$

7. $\frac{5}{11} + \frac{10}{11}$

8. $\frac{5}{8} + \frac{7}{8}$

practice exercises

practice for example 1 (page 166)

Write each sum or difference in lowest terms.

1. $\frac{4}{9} + \frac{3}{9}$

2. $\frac{1}{3} + \frac{1}{3}$

3. $\frac{1}{6} - \frac{0}{6}$

4. $\frac{14}{17} - \frac{7}{17}$

5. $\frac{9}{10} + \frac{0}{10}$

6. $\frac{7}{18} + \frac{8}{18}$

7. $\frac{3}{4} - \frac{1}{4}$

8. $\frac{7}{8} - \frac{3}{8}$

9. $\frac{2}{9} + \frac{1}{9}$

10. $\frac{13}{40} + \frac{11}{40}$

practice for example 2 (page 166)

Write each sum in lowest terms.

11. $\frac{5}{7} + \frac{2}{7}$

12. $\frac{20}{23} + \frac{3}{23}$

13. $\frac{11}{17} + \frac{12}{17}$

14. $\frac{3}{14} + \frac{13}{14}$

15. $\frac{6}{7} + \frac{5}{7}$

16. $\frac{18}{19} + \frac{8}{19}$

17. $\frac{7}{8} + \frac{7}{8}$

18. $\frac{3}{4} + \frac{3}{4}$

19. $\frac{17}{18} + \frac{1}{18}$

20. $\frac{21}{26} + \frac{5}{26}$

mixed practice (page 166)

Write each sum or difference in lowest terms.

21. $\frac{41}{50} - \frac{39}{50}$

22. $\frac{15}{16} - \frac{1}{16}$

23. $\frac{9}{16} + \frac{3}{16}$

24. $\frac{2}{21} + \frac{5}{21}$

25. $\frac{12}{19} + \frac{17}{19}$

26. $\frac{14}{17} + \frac{9}{17}$

27. $\frac{5}{21} + \frac{16}{21}$

28. $\frac{19}{24} + \frac{5}{24}$

29. $\frac{11}{27} - \frac{8}{27}$

30. $\frac{16}{21} - \frac{7}{21}$

31. $\frac{3}{7} + \frac{3}{7} + \frac{1}{7}$

32. $\frac{7}{9} + \frac{4}{9} + \frac{7}{9}$

33. Naomi caught one fish that weighs $\frac{13}{16}$ lb (pound) and a second that weighs $\frac{3}{16}$ lb. What is the difference between the weights of the two fish?

34. On Saturday Angela rode her bicycle a distance of $\frac{7}{8}$ mi (mile), and on Sunday she rode $\frac{5}{8}$ mi. How many miles did she ride altogether?

review exercises

Replace each ? with the number that will make the fractions equivalent.

1. $\frac{1}{2} = \frac{4}{?}$

2. $\frac{3}{9} = \frac{?}{18}$

3. $\frac{45}{50} = \frac{?}{10}$

4. $\frac{26}{65} = \frac{2}{?}$

5. $\frac{39}{52} = \frac{?}{4}$

6. $\frac{16}{21} = \frac{64}{?}$

Find the LCD of each pair of fractions.

7. $\frac{2}{3}, \frac{1}{2}$

8. $\frac{4}{7}, \frac{11}{14}$

9. $\frac{3}{10}, \frac{1}{4}$

10. $\frac{11}{12}, \frac{5}{8}$

11. $\frac{7}{21}, \frac{8}{9}$

12. $\frac{13}{24}, \frac{83}{120}$

8-2 ADDING AND SUBTRACTING FRACTIONS WITH DIFFERENT DENOMINATORS

George bought $\frac{1}{2}$ lb (pound) of peppers and $\frac{2}{3}$ lb of carrots. If you add $\frac{1}{2} + \frac{2}{3}$, you find that George bought $1\frac{1}{6}$ lb of vegetables.

To add or subtract fractions with different denominators, use the following method.

1. Rewrite each fraction as an equivalent fraction using the least common denominator (LCD).
2. Add or subtract the numerators as appropriate.
3. Write this sum or difference over the LCD.
4. Write the answer in lowest terms.

$$\begin{aligned} \frac{1}{2} &= \frac{3}{6} \quad \longleftarrow \text{ The LCD is 6.} \\ +\frac{2}{3} &= +\frac{4}{6} \\ \hline \frac{7}{6} &= 1\frac{1}{6} \end{aligned}$$

example 1

Write each sum in lowest terms.

a. $\dfrac{3}{4} + \dfrac{3}{8}$ **b.** $\dfrac{5}{6} + \dfrac{1}{8}$

solution

a.
$$\begin{aligned} \frac{3}{4} &= \frac{6}{8} \quad \longleftarrow \text{ The LCD is 8.} \\ +\frac{3}{8} &= +\frac{3}{8} \\ \hline \frac{9}{8} &= 1\frac{1}{8} \end{aligned}$$

b.
$$\begin{aligned} \frac{5}{6} &= \frac{20}{24} \quad \longleftarrow \text{ The LCD is 24.} \\ +\frac{1}{8} &= +\frac{3}{24} \\ \hline \frac{23}{24} \end{aligned}$$

your turn

Write each sum in lowest terms.

1.
$$\begin{aligned} &\frac{1}{2} \\ &+\frac{1}{4} \\ \hline \end{aligned}$$

2.
$$\begin{aligned} &\frac{3}{7} \\ &+\frac{2}{5} \\ \hline \end{aligned}$$

3. $\dfrac{5}{6} + \dfrac{7}{10}$

4. $\dfrac{9}{11} + \dfrac{5}{22}$

example 2

Write each difference in lowest terms: a. $\dfrac{11}{12} - \dfrac{1}{4}$ b. $\dfrac{5}{6} - \dfrac{2}{9}$

solution

a.
$$\begin{array}{r}
\dfrac{11}{12} = \dfrac{11}{12} \\[6pt]
-\dfrac{1}{4} = -\dfrac{3}{12} \\[6pt]
\hline
\dfrac{8}{12} = \dfrac{2}{3}
\end{array}$$ ← **The LCD is 12.**

b.
$$\begin{array}{r}
\dfrac{5}{6} = \dfrac{15}{18} \\[6pt]
-\dfrac{2}{9} = -\dfrac{4}{18} \\[6pt]
\hline
\dfrac{11}{18}
\end{array}$$ ← **The LCD is 18.**

your turn

Write each difference in lowest terms.

5.
$$\begin{array}{r} \dfrac{9}{10} \\[6pt] -\dfrac{1}{5} \\ \hline \end{array}$$

6.
$$\begin{array}{r} \dfrac{5}{18} \\[6pt] -\dfrac{1}{4} \\ \hline \end{array}$$

7. $\dfrac{5}{7} - \dfrac{1}{3}$

8. $\dfrac{4}{11} - \dfrac{1}{3}$

practice exercises

practice for example 1 (page 168)

Write each sum in lowest terms.

1.
$$\begin{array}{r} \dfrac{2}{7} \\[6pt] +\dfrac{1}{2} \\ \hline \end{array}$$

2.
$$\begin{array}{r} \dfrac{2}{5} \\[6pt] +\dfrac{1}{6} \\ \hline \end{array}$$

3.
$$\begin{array}{r} \dfrac{1}{2} \\[6pt] +\dfrac{1}{10} \\ \hline \end{array}$$

4.
$$\begin{array}{r} \dfrac{1}{4} \\[6pt] +\dfrac{3}{20} \\ \hline \end{array}$$

5.
$$\begin{array}{r} \dfrac{5}{9} \\[6pt] +\dfrac{11}{12} \\ \hline \end{array}$$

6.
$$\begin{array}{r} \dfrac{7}{8} \\[6pt] +\dfrac{1}{6} \\ \hline \end{array}$$

7. $\dfrac{4}{7} + \dfrac{7}{8}$

8. $\dfrac{8}{9} + \dfrac{8}{11}$

9. $\dfrac{5}{6} + \dfrac{7}{30}$

10. $\dfrac{11}{15} + \dfrac{3}{5}$

practice for example 2 (page 169)

Write each difference in lowest terms.

11.
$$\begin{array}{r} \dfrac{1}{2} \\[6pt] -\dfrac{1}{3} \\ \hline \end{array}$$

12.
$$\begin{array}{r} \dfrac{8}{9} \\[6pt] -\dfrac{3}{4} \\ \hline \end{array}$$

13.
$$\begin{array}{r} \dfrac{9}{10} \\[6pt] -\dfrac{2}{5} \\ \hline \end{array}$$

14.
$$\begin{array}{r} \dfrac{7}{9} \\[6pt] -\dfrac{5}{18} \\ \hline \end{array}$$

15.
$$\begin{array}{r} \dfrac{7}{8} \\[6pt] -\dfrac{5}{12} \\ \hline \end{array}$$

16.
$$\begin{array}{r} \dfrac{5}{12} \\[6pt] -\dfrac{3}{10} \\ \hline \end{array}$$

17. $\dfrac{13}{21} - \dfrac{3}{14}$

18. $\dfrac{7}{18} - \dfrac{1}{4}$

19. $\dfrac{33}{34} - \dfrac{9}{17}$

20. $\dfrac{11}{15} - \dfrac{17}{45}$

Adding and Subtracting Fractions   169

Write each sum or difference in lowest terms.

21. $\dfrac{1}{5}$
$+\dfrac{3}{4}$

22. $\dfrac{1}{12}$
$+\dfrac{1}{7}$

23. $\dfrac{3}{5}$
$-\dfrac{7}{12}$

24. $\dfrac{4}{5}$
$-\dfrac{1}{2}$

25. $\dfrac{4}{5}$
$+\dfrac{7}{15}$

26. $\dfrac{5}{18}$
$+\dfrac{5}{6}$

27. $\dfrac{9}{10} - \dfrac{3}{100}$

28. $\dfrac{17}{22} - \dfrac{5}{11}$

29. $\dfrac{8}{9} - \dfrac{5}{6}$

30. $\dfrac{11}{12} - \dfrac{4}{9}$

31. $\dfrac{7}{10} - \dfrac{9}{20}$

32. $\dfrac{6}{13} - \dfrac{5}{39}$

33. $\dfrac{1}{2} + \dfrac{1}{3} + \dfrac{1}{6}$

34. $\dfrac{3}{10} + \dfrac{19}{30} + \dfrac{1}{3}$

35. Kirk pitched $\frac{1}{2}$ of the games this season and Shawn pitched $\frac{1}{4}$ of the games. What fractional part of the games did they pitch altogether?

36. Sally jogged $\frac{8}{9}$ mi (mile), then walked $\frac{7}{8}$ mi to school. Did she travel farther walking or jogging? How much farther?

review exercises

Write a simpler fraction as an estimate of each fraction.

1. $\dfrac{8}{25}$
2. $\dfrac{11}{45}$
3. $\dfrac{8}{17}$
4. $\dfrac{6}{17}$
5. $\dfrac{11}{29}$
6. $\dfrac{19}{31}$

Estimate by rounding.

7. $3\frac{5}{6} \times 2\frac{3}{4}$
8. $4\frac{1}{6} \times 5\frac{3}{7}$
9. $2\frac{4}{7} \times 5\frac{1}{8}$
10. $9\frac{5}{9} \times 12\frac{3}{8}$

calculator corner

If you have a calculator, a quick way to find the LCD of fractions is to multiply the denominators, then divide by the GCF of the denominators.

example Find the LCD of $\dfrac{9}{24}$ and $\dfrac{7}{36}$.

solution The GCF of 24 and 36 is 12.
Enter 24 × 36 ÷ 12 =. The LCD is 72.

Find the LCD of each pair of fractions using a calculator.

1. $\dfrac{7}{12}, \dfrac{4}{15}$
2. $\dfrac{9}{20}, \dfrac{1}{15}$
3. $\dfrac{6}{16}, \dfrac{9}{20}$
4. $\dfrac{7}{15}, \dfrac{2}{21}$
5. $\dfrac{1}{16}, \dfrac{7}{12}$
6. $\dfrac{7}{9}, \dfrac{7}{8}$

8-3 ESTIMATING SUMS AND DIFFERENCES OF FRACTIONS AND MIXED NUMBERS

You can use rounding to the nearest whole number to estimate a sum or difference of mixed numbers.

example 1

Estimate by rounding.

a. $21\frac{1}{2} + 24\frac{2}{3}$ ← **If the fractional part of a mixed number is greater than or equal to $\frac{1}{2}$, round up.**

$\underbrace{22 + 25}_{\text{about } 47}$

b. $11\frac{3}{5} - 8\frac{1}{4}$

$\underbrace{12 - 8}_{\text{about } 4}$

your turn

Estimate by rounding.

1. $1\frac{2}{3} + 3\frac{1}{6}$ **2.** $6\frac{1}{2} + 3\frac{3}{4}$ **3.** $15\frac{1}{4} - 4\frac{1}{3}$ **4.** $8\frac{2}{7} - 2\frac{5}{6}$

Sometimes you can get a better estimate by first adding the whole numbers and then adjusting.

example 2

Estimate by adding the whole numbers, and then adjusting.

a. $3\frac{1}{3} + 5\frac{5}{14} + \frac{1}{3}$ **Add the whole numbers. Add the fractions, estimating if necessary.**

$\underbrace{3\frac{1}{3} + 5\frac{1}{3} + \frac{1}{3}}_{\text{about } 8 + 1, \text{ or } 9}$

b. $4\frac{7}{8} + 6\frac{1}{10} + 1\frac{5}{9} + 1\frac{4}{7}$

$\underbrace{4 + 1 + 6 + 0 + 1\frac{1}{2} + 1\frac{1}{2}}_{\text{about } 12 + 2, \text{ or } 14}$

your turn

Estimate by adding the whole numbers, and then adjusting.

5. $1\frac{1}{2} + \frac{6}{11} + 3\frac{1}{20}$ **6.** $2\frac{1}{3} + \frac{2}{7} + 1\frac{6}{17}$ **7.** $2\frac{3}{4} + 5\frac{5}{19} + 3\frac{9}{10}$

Adding and Subtracting Fractions **171**

practice exercises

Estimate by rounding.

1. $1\frac{1}{3} + 1\frac{5}{8}$

2. $2\frac{5}{6} + 1\frac{3}{10}$

3. $4\frac{2}{3} - 1\frac{3}{5}$

4. $3\frac{6}{7} - 1\frac{5}{7}$

5. $4\frac{1}{3} + 5\frac{5}{6}$

6. $9\frac{7}{8} + 8\frac{10}{11}$

7. $14\frac{1}{2} - 11\frac{3}{4}$

8. $18\frac{1}{5} - 6\frac{2}{7}$

Estimate by adding the whole numbers, and then adjusting.

9. $2 + \frac{1}{2} + 3\frac{5}{11}$

10. $\frac{12}{13} + 3\frac{1}{2} + 9\frac{5}{8}$

11. $4\frac{7}{8} + \frac{1}{3} + 5\frac{6}{17} + 1\frac{1}{3}$

12. $\frac{1}{3} + \frac{7}{8} + 2\frac{20}{61} + 1\frac{4}{15}$

13. $\frac{10}{11} + 2\frac{7}{8} + 8 + 9\frac{5}{36}$

14. $7\frac{30}{59} + 3\frac{1}{10} + 1\frac{25}{47}$

Estimate.

15. $8\frac{9}{10} + 2\frac{5}{6}$

16. $4\frac{3}{4} - 1\frac{3}{7}$

17. $3\frac{5}{11} + 1\frac{1}{2} + 4\frac{7}{8}$

18. $7\frac{1}{3} + 5\frac{4}{13} + 11\frac{9}{26}$

19. Is the sum $2\frac{1}{5} + 3\frac{1}{4}$ more or less than 6?

20. Is the sum $6\frac{1}{2} + 4 + \frac{8}{17} + \frac{17}{20}$ more or less than 11?

Estimate the following, using Danny's record of the amount of gas he put in his car weekly.

Week	Number of Gallons
1	$6\frac{9}{10}$
2	3
3	$8\frac{1}{2}$
4	$10\frac{4}{10}$

21. the total amount of gas bought in weeks 1 and 2

22. the total amount of gas bought in weeks 3 and 4

23. the difference between the amounts of gas bought in weeks 1 and 3

24. the amount of gas bought in all four weeks

review exercises

Find each answer.

1. $4 + 3 \times 5 - 8$

2. $52 - 6 \times 7 - 2$

3. $50 \div 5 + 2 \times 6$

4. $2 \times 16 + 5 \times 7$

5. $2 \times (9 + 7) - 7$

6. $20 + (30 \div 10) + 4$

8-4 ADDING MIXED NUMBERS

Vic decided to make a suit. He needed $1\frac{1}{4}$ yd (yards) of fabric for the pants and $2\frac{3}{8}$ yd of fabric for the jacket. When he added $1\frac{1}{4} + 2\frac{3}{8}$, he found that he needed $3\frac{5}{8}$ yd of fabric.

To add mixed numbers, use the following method.

1. If necessary, rewrite each fraction as an equivalent fraction using the LCD.

$$\begin{array}{r} 1\frac{1}{4} = 1\frac{2}{8} \\ +2\frac{3}{8} = +2\frac{3}{8} \\ \hline 3\frac{5}{8} \end{array}$$

2. Add the fractions.
   Add the whole numbers.

3. Write the answer in lowest terms.

example 1

Write each sum in lowest terms.

a. $7\frac{2}{9} + 11\frac{5}{9}$

b. $8\frac{2}{3} + 4$

c. $3\frac{2}{5} + 1\frac{1}{4}$

solution

a.
$$\begin{array}{r} 7\frac{2}{9} \\ +11\frac{5}{9} \\ \hline 18\frac{7}{9} \end{array}$$

b.
$$\begin{array}{r} 8\frac{2}{3} \\ +4 \\ \hline 12\frac{2}{3} \end{array}$$

c.
$$\begin{array}{r} 3\frac{2}{5} = 3\frac{8}{20} \\ +1\frac{1}{4} = +1\frac{5}{20} \\ \hline 4\frac{13}{20} \end{array}$$

your turn

Write each sum in lowest terms.

1.
$$\begin{array}{r} 3\frac{3}{8} \\ +2\frac{1}{2} \\ \hline \end{array}$$

2.
$$\begin{array}{r} 1\frac{1}{2} \\ +1\frac{1}{3} \\ \hline \end{array}$$

3. $8\frac{1}{2} + 9$

4. $7\frac{1}{6} + 1\frac{1}{6}$

A sum of mixed numbers is in lowest terms if the fraction part is in lowest terms *and* is less than 1.

example 2

Write each sum in lowest terms: **a.** $5\frac{4}{5} + 3\frac{3}{4}$ **b.** $5\frac{1}{6} + 7\frac{5}{6}$

solution

a. $5\frac{4}{5} = 5\frac{16}{20}$

$+3\frac{3}{4} = +3\frac{15}{20}$

$8\frac{31}{20} = 8 + 1\frac{11}{20} = 9\frac{11}{20}$

b. $5\frac{1}{6}$

$+7\frac{5}{6}$

$12\frac{6}{6} = 12 + 1 = 13$

your turn

Write each sum in lowest terms.

5. $6\frac{7}{10}$

$+9\frac{3}{10}$

6. $4\frac{3}{8}$

$+5\frac{3}{4}$

7. $3\frac{8}{9}$

$+1\frac{1}{2}$

8. $11\frac{3}{10}$

$+ 5\frac{5}{6}$

practice exercises

practice for example 1 (page 173)

Write each sum in lowest terms.

1. $2\frac{1}{3}$

$+ \frac{1}{3}$

2. $1\frac{1}{5}$

$+6\frac{3}{5}$

3. $1\frac{2}{13}$

$+3\frac{4}{13}$

4. $1\frac{1}{10}$

$+2\frac{3}{4}$

5. $9\frac{1}{6}$

$+3\frac{1}{9}$

6. $7\frac{4}{11} + 9\frac{6}{11}$

7. $8\frac{1}{11} + 1\frac{1}{2}$

8. $6\frac{5}{6} + 4\frac{1}{7}$

9. $13\frac{2}{7} + 2\frac{1}{2}$

practice for example 2 (page 174)

Write each sum in lowest terms.

10. $3\frac{4}{5}$

$+1\frac{1}{2}$

11. $3\frac{4}{5}$

$+1\frac{5}{6}$

12. $12\frac{1}{9}$

$+4\frac{8}{9}$

13. $3\frac{6}{11}$

$+2\frac{5}{11}$

14. $6\frac{7}{9}$

$+2\frac{1}{3}$

15. $3\frac{7}{8} + 1\frac{1}{2}$

16. $3\frac{2}{3} + 4\frac{4}{5}$

17. $7\frac{3}{5} + 2\frac{6}{11}$

18. $1\frac{11}{12} + 6\frac{3}{8}$

Write each sum in lowest terms.

19. $4\frac{2}{9}$
    $+6\frac{5}{9}$

20. $4\frac{2}{13}$
    $+7\frac{10}{13}$

21. $1\frac{2}{3}$
    $+3\frac{1}{2}$

22. $8\frac{1}{7}$
    $+4\frac{2}{3}$

23. $4 + 7\frac{1}{6}$

24. $1 + 5\frac{4}{7}$

25. $3\frac{5}{6} + 2\frac{1}{4}$

26. $8\frac{1}{6} + 4\frac{13}{21}$

27. $\frac{3}{7} + 3\frac{4}{7}$

28. $1\frac{1}{8} + \frac{7}{8}$

29. $5\frac{1}{6} + 4\frac{1}{8}$

30. $7\frac{5}{6} + 3\frac{1}{9}$

31. $25\frac{17}{32} + 15\frac{3}{16}$

32. $22\frac{5}{24} + 35\frac{11}{12}$

33. $7\frac{13}{15} + 9\frac{11}{18}$

34. $5\frac{9}{14} + 3\frac{11}{18}$

35. Kathy practiced dancing $6\frac{1}{4}$ h on Sunday, $4\frac{1}{2}$ h on Monday, and $2\frac{2}{3}$ h on Tuesday. How many hours did she practice in all?

36. A car's cooling system requires $3\frac{1}{2}$ gal (gallons) of antifreeze, $5\frac{3}{4}$ gal of water, and $\frac{1}{3}$ gal of rust preventive. How much fluid is in the cooling system?

review *exercises*

Is the first number divisible by the second number? Write *Yes* or *No*.

1. 897; 3

2. 5289; 9

3. 24,838; 4

4. 173,490; 5

Write the numeral form of each number.

5. 17 million, 5 thousand, 149

6. 1 million, 789 thousand

7. nine thousand, forty-six

8. eighty thousand, one

mental math

The commutative and associative properties for addition enable you to group fractions so they are easy to add mentally.

$\frac{1}{4} + \frac{1}{8} + \frac{3}{4} = 1\frac{1}{8}$

Add mentally.

1. $\frac{1}{2} + \frac{1}{3} + \frac{1}{2}$

2. $\frac{1}{4} + \frac{3}{8} + \frac{3}{4}$

3. $\frac{1}{4} + \frac{6}{7} + \frac{3}{4} + \frac{1}{7}$

4. $\frac{7}{9} + \frac{2}{5} + \frac{3}{5} + \frac{2}{9}$

5. $\frac{2}{5} + \frac{3}{8} + \frac{2}{5} + \frac{1}{5}$

6. $\frac{3}{8} + \frac{1}{4} + \frac{1}{4} + \frac{1}{8}$

7. $3\frac{1}{2} + 2\frac{1}{3} + 1\frac{1}{2}$

8. $2\frac{3}{8} + 1\frac{1}{7} + \frac{5}{8}$

9. $1\frac{2}{5} + 2\frac{5}{9} + 1\frac{1}{5} + \frac{2}{5}$

8-5 SUBTRACTING MIXED NUMBERS WITHOUT RENAMING

To subtract mixed numbers, use this method.

1. If necessary, rewrite each fraction as an equivalent fraction using the LCD.
2. Subtract the fractions.
   Subtract the whole numbers.
3. Write the answer in lowest terms.

example 1

Write each difference in lowest terms.

a. $2\frac{4}{5} - 1\frac{1}{5}$ b. $5\frac{9}{10} - 3\frac{3}{10}$

solution

a.
$$2\frac{4}{5}$$
$$-1\frac{1}{5}$$
$$\overline{1\frac{3}{5}}$$

b.
$$5\frac{9}{10}$$
$$-3\frac{3}{10}$$
$$\overline{2\frac{6}{10}} = 2\frac{3}{5}$$

Sam and Ken work in a warehouse. Sam's fork lift carries $2\frac{4}{5}$ tons. Ken's fork lift carries $1\frac{1}{5}$ tons. Sam's fork lift carries $1\frac{3}{5}$ tons more than Ken's.

your turn

Write each difference in lowest terms.

1.
$$5\frac{4}{5}$$
$$-3\frac{1}{5}$$

2.
$$6\frac{3}{4}$$
$$-4\frac{3}{4}$$

3. $2\frac{9}{10} - 1\frac{7}{10}$

4. $103\frac{5}{9} - 48\frac{2}{9}$

example 2

Write each difference in lowest terms: a. $6\frac{1}{2} - 3\frac{1}{4}$ b. $1\frac{3}{5} - 1\frac{1}{3}$

solution

a.
$$6\frac{1}{2} = 6\frac{2}{4}$$
$$-3\frac{1}{4} = -3\frac{1}{4}$$
$$\overline{\phantom{-3\frac{1}{4} = } 3\frac{1}{4}}$$

b.
$$1\frac{3}{5} = 1\frac{9}{15}$$
$$-1\frac{1}{3} = -1\frac{5}{15}$$
$$\overline{\phantom{-1\frac{1}{3} = } \frac{4}{15}}$$

your turn

Write each difference in lowest terms.

5. $12\frac{4}{9}$
    $-\ 8\frac{1}{4}$

6. $15\frac{5}{6}$
    $-\ 9\frac{3}{4}$

7. $103\frac{2}{3} - 101\frac{1}{2}$ 8. $114\frac{1}{2} - 114\frac{3}{10}$

practice exercises

practice for example 1 (page 176)

Write each difference in lowest terms.

1. $4\frac{2}{3}$
    $-1\frac{1}{3}$

2. $5\frac{8}{9}$
    $-2\frac{1}{9}$

3. $5\frac{1}{3}$
    $-\ \frac{1}{3}$

4. $7\frac{3}{5}$
    $-2\frac{3}{5}$

5. $4\frac{3}{4} - 4\frac{1}{4}$

6. $6\frac{9}{10} - 6\frac{1}{10}$

7. $8\frac{7}{8} - 6\frac{3}{8}$

8. $8\frac{11}{12} - 2\frac{5}{12}$

9. $9\frac{14}{27} - 5\frac{5}{27}$

10. $76\frac{15}{16} - 38\frac{9}{16}$

practice for example 2 (pages 176–177)

Write each difference in lowest terms.

11. $3\frac{5}{8}$
     $-2\frac{1}{4}$

12. $4\frac{4}{7}$
     $-1\frac{1}{3}$

13. $2\frac{3}{4}$
     $-2\frac{1}{2}$

14. $100\frac{5}{9}$
     $-100\frac{1}{6}$

15. $4\frac{2}{3} - \frac{1}{5}$

16. $3\frac{1}{2} - \frac{2}{5}$

17. $1\frac{5}{9} - 1\frac{7}{18}$

18. $4\frac{5}{6} - 2\frac{1}{12}$

19. $9\frac{1}{4} - 3\frac{1}{7}$

20. $13\frac{4}{5} - 7\frac{5}{8}$

21. $15\frac{5}{6} - 10\frac{3}{4}$

22. $45\frac{7}{9} - 21\frac{3}{4}$

Adding and Subtracting Fractions 177

Write each difference in lowest terms.

23. $8\frac{8}{9}$
    $-6\frac{8}{9}$

24. $3\frac{1}{2}$
    $-3\frac{1}{2}$

25. $19\frac{5}{6}$
    $-16\frac{2}{9}$

26. $6\frac{5}{6}$
    $-3\frac{3}{8}$

27. $9\frac{7}{8} - 3\frac{1}{4}$

28. $3\frac{5}{12} - 1\frac{1}{3}$

29. $6\frac{4}{7} - 3\frac{3}{14}$

30. $12\frac{7}{10} - 8\frac{1}{2}$

31. $65\frac{17}{100} - 59\frac{5}{100}$

32. $82\frac{11}{12} - 63\frac{1}{12}$

33. $23\frac{9}{10} - 16\frac{3}{7}$

34. $37\frac{9}{16} - 13\frac{9}{20}$

35. $7\frac{1}{4} - 3\frac{1}{4}$

36. $19\frac{1}{6} - \frac{1}{6}$

37. $5\frac{5}{18} - 2\frac{1}{9}$

38. $106\frac{19}{20} - 88\frac{1}{5}$

39. Jerome is saving trading stamps. He needs $1\frac{1}{4}$ books for a can of tennis balls and $3\frac{3}{4}$ books for a tennis racket. How many more books does he need for the tennis racket than for the tennis balls?

40. Mrs. Lewis bought a crate of oranges. The total weight was $39\frac{1}{2}$ lb (pounds). If the crate alone weighed $2\frac{1}{3}$ lb, what was the weight of the oranges?

review *exercises*

Estimate.

1. $657 + $235
2. $8267 - 2195$
3. 27×684
4. $26,419 \div 7$
5. $61,893 \div 87$
6. 350×547
7. $23,845 - 16,249$
8. $50,842 \div 687$
9. $4\frac{7}{8} \times 2\frac{1}{2}$
10. $\frac{1}{5} \times 14\frac{2}{7}$
11. $10\frac{4}{9} \times \frac{1}{4}$
12. $5\frac{1}{2} \times 3\frac{3}{8}$
13. $8\frac{1}{5} - 2\frac{7}{8}$
14. $\frac{3}{17} \times 12\frac{1}{2}$
15. $13\frac{4}{5} \times \frac{7}{15}$
16. $1\frac{9}{10} + 2\frac{1}{2} + 3\frac{3}{7}$
17. $632 + $289 + $37 + $255
18. $2896 + 3460 + 2097 + 1589$

Puzzle corner

Four friends eat regularly at the same restaurant. The first eats there every day. The second eats there every 2 days, the third every 3 days, and the fourth every 4 days. Suppose they all eat together on July 1. What is the next day that they will all eat together again?

8-6 SUBTRACTING MIXED NUMBERS WITH RENAMING

Steve owns stock in EZ Credit Company. The newspaper listed the opening price of a share of his stock as $9\frac{1}{4}$ and the closing price as $7\frac{1}{2}$. When he subtracted $9\frac{1}{4} - 7\frac{1}{2}$, he found that the stock was down $1\frac{3}{4}$.

To subtract mixed numbers when renaming is necessary, use the following method.

1. Rewrite each fraction as an equivalent fraction using the LCD.

2. Rename the whole number or mixed number.

3. Subtract the fractions.
   Subtract the whole numbers.

4. Write the answer in lowest terms.

$$9\frac{1}{4} = \quad 9\frac{1}{4} = \quad 8\frac{5}{4} \quad \longleftarrow \quad 9\frac{1}{4} = 8 + 1\frac{1}{4}$$
$$= 8\frac{5}{4}$$
$$-7\frac{1}{2} = -7\frac{2}{4} = -7\frac{2}{4}$$
$$1\frac{3}{4}$$

example 1

Write each difference in lowest terms.

a. $4\frac{1}{8} - 3\frac{5}{8}$

b. $9\frac{3}{4} - 5\frac{5}{6}$

solution

a.
$$4\frac{1}{8} = \quad 3\frac{9}{8} \quad \longleftarrow \quad 4\frac{1}{8} = 3 + 1\frac{1}{8}$$
$$= 3\frac{9}{8}$$
$$-3\frac{5}{8} = -3\frac{5}{8}$$
$$\frac{4}{8} = \frac{1}{2}$$

b.
$$9\frac{3}{4} = \quad 9\frac{9}{12} = \quad 8\frac{21}{12} \quad \longleftarrow \quad 9\frac{9}{12} = 8 + 1\frac{9}{12}$$
$$= 8\frac{21}{12}$$
$$-5\frac{5}{6} = -5\frac{10}{12} = -5\frac{10}{12}$$
$$3\frac{11}{12}$$

your turn

Write each difference in lowest terms.

1. $\quad 3\frac{7}{12}$
$$-2\frac{11}{12}$$

2. $\quad 7\frac{1}{8}$
$$-2\frac{1}{2}$$

3. $2\frac{1}{4} - 1\frac{2}{5}$

4. $11\frac{5}{18} - 2\frac{5}{6}$

To subtract a mixed number from a whole number, you must first rename the whole number as a mixed number.

example 2

Write each difference in lowest terms: **a.** $49 - 48\frac{3}{4}$ **b.** $16 - 13\frac{1}{2}$

solution

a.

$$\begin{array}{r} 49 = 48\frac{4}{4} \\ -48\frac{3}{4} = -48\frac{3}{4} \\ \hline \frac{1}{4} \end{array}$$ ← $49 = 48 + 1$
$= 48 + \frac{4}{4}$

b.

$$\begin{array}{r} 16 = 15\frac{2}{2} \\ -13\frac{1}{2} = -13\frac{1}{2} \\ \hline 2\frac{1}{2} \end{array}$$ ← $16 = 15 + 1$
$= 15 + \frac{2}{2}$

your turn

Write each difference in lowest terms.

5.
$$\begin{array}{r} 9 \\ -8\frac{1}{6} \\ \hline \end{array}$$

6.
$$\begin{array}{r} 7 \\ -6\frac{2}{3} \\ \hline \end{array}$$

7. $3 - 1\frac{4}{7}$

8. $10 - 4\frac{3}{8}$

practice exercises

practice for example 1 (page 179)

Write each difference in lowest terms.

1.
$$\begin{array}{r} 16\frac{1}{4} \\ -3\frac{3}{4} \\ \hline \end{array}$$

2.
$$\begin{array}{r} 13\frac{1}{18} \\ -2\frac{7}{18} \\ \hline \end{array}$$

3.
$$\begin{array}{r} 8\frac{1}{3} \\ -3\frac{4}{9} \\ \hline \end{array}$$

4.
$$\begin{array}{r} 3\frac{1}{2} \\ -1\frac{5}{8} \\ \hline \end{array}$$

5.
$$\begin{array}{r} 7\frac{1}{6} \\ -3\frac{5}{9} \\ \hline \end{array}$$

6.
$$\begin{array}{r} 7\frac{2}{7} \\ -1\frac{3}{5} \\ \hline \end{array}$$

7. $6\frac{1}{6} - 3\frac{5}{6}$

8. $22\frac{1}{15} - 3\frac{11}{15}$

9. $3\frac{1}{12} - 1\frac{7}{8}$

10. $21\frac{4}{9} - 4\frac{7}{12}$

11. $9\frac{2}{7} - 7\frac{1}{2}$

12. $14\frac{3}{11} - 10\frac{2}{7}$

13. $10\frac{5}{6} - 9\frac{17}{18}$

14. $16\frac{9}{13} - 15\frac{31}{39}$

practice for example 2 (page 180)

Write each difference in lowest terms.

15.
$$\begin{array}{r} 1 \\ -\frac{3}{5} \\ \hline \end{array}$$

16.
$$\begin{array}{r} 1 \\ -\frac{6}{7} \\ \hline \end{array}$$

17.
$$\begin{array}{r} 5 \\ -4\frac{1}{8} \\ \hline \end{array}$$

18.
$$\begin{array}{r} 7 \\ -6\frac{3}{4} \\ \hline \end{array}$$

19.
$$\begin{array}{r} 15 \\ -3\frac{2}{3} \\ \hline \end{array}$$

20.
$$\begin{array}{r} 17 \\ -6\frac{1}{2} \\ \hline \end{array}$$

21. $20 - 10\frac{2}{5}$

22. $42 - 23\frac{7}{8}$

23. $34 - 21\frac{1}{3}$

24. $35 - 19\frac{5}{16}$

Write each difference in lowest terms.

25. $10 - \frac{2}{3}$

26. $15 - \frac{1}{2}$

27. $4\frac{2}{5} - 2\frac{4}{5}$

28. $8\frac{1}{5} - 2\frac{3}{5}$

29. $8\frac{1}{2} - 2\frac{2}{3}$

30. $8\frac{2}{5} - 6\frac{1}{2}$

31. $12 - 9\frac{3}{4}$

32. $7 - 5\frac{19}{20}$

33. $7\frac{1}{3} - 5\frac{2}{3}$

34. $5\frac{2}{5} - 1\frac{4}{5}$

35. $66\frac{3}{14} - 59\frac{10}{21}$

36. $148\frac{17}{50} - 146\frac{3}{4}$

37. During the baseball season, the Astros were 8 games out of first place, and the Dodgers were $4\frac{1}{2}$ games out of first place. How many games behind the Dodgers were the Astros?

38. One of the world's largest species of birds is the wandering albatross. Its average wing-span is $10\frac{1}{3}$ ft (feet). One albatross had a recorded wingspan of $11\frac{1}{6}$ ft. How much wider than average is this?

review *exercises*

Find each answer.

1. $11{,}461 \div 73$

2. $60{,}090 - 4328$

3. 696×53

4. $49 + 135 + 7$

5. 40×2200

6. $6345 + 9349$

7. $21{,}624 \div 8$

8. $5822 - 4946$

9. $\frac{1}{4} \times \frac{8}{9}$

10. $\frac{1}{5} + \frac{2}{3}$

11. $\frac{3}{4} - \frac{1}{6}$

12. $\frac{2}{5} \div \frac{1}{2}$

13. $2\frac{1}{3} + 1\frac{1}{4}$

14. $6 \div \frac{1}{3}$

15. $4\frac{1}{2} \times 3\frac{1}{3}$

16. $8 - \frac{3}{4}$

mental math

To subtract $5 - 1\frac{1}{2}$ mentally, *add on* from $1\frac{1}{2}$ to 5.

$$1\frac{1}{2} + \frac{1}{2} = 2 \qquad 2 + 3 = 5 \qquad \frac{1}{2} + 3 = 3\frac{1}{2} \qquad \text{So } 5 - 1\frac{1}{2} = 3\frac{1}{2}.$$

Subtract mentally.

1. $7 - 5\frac{1}{3}$

2. $5 - \frac{4}{5}$

3. $6 - 1\frac{9}{10}$

4. $5\frac{1}{3} - 4\frac{2}{3}$

5. $3\frac{2}{5} - 1\frac{3}{5}$

Adding and Subtracting Fractions 181

8-7 IDENTIFYING PATTERNS

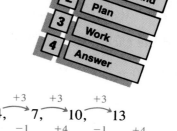

You can solve some problems by identifying a pattern. Several ways number patterns can be formed are shown below.

Perform the same operation consistently.

$$1, \overset{+3}{\longrightarrow} 4, \overset{+3}{\longrightarrow} 7, \overset{+3}{\longrightarrow} 10, \overset{+3}{\longrightarrow} 13$$

Alternately perform different operations.

$$1, \overset{+4}{\longrightarrow} 5, \overset{-1}{\longrightarrow} 4, \overset{+4}{\longrightarrow} 8, \overset{-1}{\longrightarrow} 7, \overset{+4}{\longrightarrow} 11$$

Use one operation, but change the number involved.

$$1, \overset{+2}{\longrightarrow} 3, \overset{+4}{\longrightarrow} 7, \overset{+6}{\longrightarrow} 13, \overset{+8}{\longrightarrow} 21$$

example

Look for a pattern. Then write the next three numbers.

a. 2, 6, 18, 54, _?_, _?_, _?_

b. 6, 12, 20, 30, _?_, _?_, _?_

c. $\frac{1}{5}, \frac{4}{5}, \frac{7}{5}, 2, \frac{13}{5}$, _?_, _?_, _?_

d. 10, 11, 9, 12, 8, _?_, _?_, _?_

solution

a. Pattern: Multiply by 3.
2, 6, 18, 54, 162, 486, 1458

b. Pattern: Add 6, add 8, add 10, and so on.
6, 12, 20, 30, 42, 56, 72

c. Pattern: Add $\frac{3}{5}$.
$\frac{1}{5}, \frac{4}{5}, \frac{7}{5}, 2, \frac{13}{5}, \frac{16}{5}, \frac{19}{5}, \frac{22}{5}$

d. Pattern: Alternately add and subtract 1, 2, 3, 4, and so on.
10, 11, 9, 12, 8, 13, 7, 14

problems

Look for a pattern. Then write the next three numbers.

1. 16, 22, 28, 34, _?_, _?_, _?_

2. 84, 77, 70, 63, _?_, _?_, _?_

3. $\frac{1}{8}, \frac{1}{2}, 2, 8$, _?_, _?_, _?_

4. $1, \frac{1}{2}, \frac{1}{4}, \frac{1}{8}, \frac{1}{16}$, _?_, _?_, _?_

5. 1, 2, 5, 10, 17, _?_, _?_, _?_

6. 2, 9, 23, 44, _?_, _?_, _?_

7. 1, 7, 5, 11, 9, _?_, _?_, _?_

8. 1, 2, 4, 5, 7, 8, 10, _?_, _?_, _?_

9. $\frac{1}{2}, \frac{3}{4}, 1, \frac{5}{4}$, _?_, _?_, _?_

10. $1, \frac{5}{2}, 4, \frac{11}{2}$, _?_, _?_, _?_

11. $4, 6, 9, \frac{27}{2}$, _?_, _?_, _?_

12. $1, \frac{5}{6}, \frac{2}{3}, \frac{1}{2}$, _?_, _?_, _?_

13. 1, 6, 3, 18, 9, 54, _?_, _?_, _?_

14. 1, 10, 5, 50, 25, _?_, _?_, _?_

15. 5, 5, 10, 30, 120, _?_, _?_, _?_

16. 1, 3, 5, 9, 13, 19, _?_, _?_, _?_

17. $2, \frac{9}{5}, \frac{11}{5}, \frac{8}{5}, \frac{12}{5}$, _?_, _?_, _?_

18. $\frac{1}{2}, \frac{3}{4}, \frac{7}{8}, \frac{15}{16}$, _?_, _?_, _?_

Look for a pattern. Then answer the question.

19. How many dots are in the twelfth *oblong number?*

Oblong Numbers				
No. of Rows/ No. of Columns	1/2	2/3	3/4	4/5
No. of Dots	2	6	12	20

20. How many dots are in the tenth *triangular number?*

Triangular Numbers				
No. of Rows	1	2	3	4
No. of Dots	1	3	6	10

Solve.

21. At 8 A.M. there were 12 students in the computer room. At 8:30 A.M. two students left, and at 9 A.M. one student arrived. Thereafter two students left at half past each hour and one student arrived as the clock struck each hour. When did the computer room first become empty?

22. One week Doris mowed half the lawn. The next week she mowed two thirds as much as she had the first week. The third week she mowed three fourths as much as she had the second week, and so on. The tenth week she mowed ten elevenths as much as she mowed the ninth week. How much of the lawn did she mow the tenth week?

review exercises

1. Fifteen hundred people were asked if they plan to buy a car in the next year. Eight hundred sixty-one said they do not. Two thirds of those planning to buy a car plan to buy a new car. How many people polled plan to buy a new car?

2. Theresa Mendoza bought 200 shares of stock. She paid $16\frac{1}{8}$ dollars for each share. A year later she sold the 200 shares for $20\frac{3}{4}$ dollars per share. How much profit did she make?

3. Look for a pattern. Then write the next three numbers:
1, 1, 2, 3, 5, 8, 13, 21, __?__, __?__, __?__

Adding and Subtracting Fractions   183

SKILL REVIEW

Write each sum or difference in lowest terms.

1. $\frac{3}{7} + \frac{2}{7}$ 2. $\frac{4}{5} + \frac{4}{5}$ 3. $\frac{8}{9} - \frac{5}{9}$ 4. $\frac{7}{12} - \frac{5}{12}$ 5. $\frac{15}{41} + \frac{30}{41}$ **8-1**

6. $\frac{7}{8} - \frac{2}{3}$ 7. $\frac{4}{7} + \frac{11}{14}$ 8. $\frac{7}{10} + \frac{2}{5}$ 9. $\frac{14}{15} + \frac{1}{6}$ 10. $\frac{3}{4} - \frac{5}{7}$ **8-2**

11. Jill studied $\frac{3}{4}$ h on Saturday and $\frac{4}{5}$ h on Sunday. How many hours in all did she study on these two days?

Estimate by rounding.

12. $2\frac{1}{4} + 3\frac{4}{5}$ 13. $7\frac{3}{8} + 5\frac{5}{11}$ 14. $6\frac{1}{3} - 4\frac{7}{10}$ 15. $12\frac{1}{2} - 3\frac{2}{3}$ **8-3**

Estimate by adding the whole numbers, and then adjusting.

16. $4\frac{1}{3} + \frac{5}{14} + 6\frac{4}{15}$ 17. $3\frac{4}{9} + 7\frac{9}{10} + 1\frac{8}{15}$ 18. $\frac{4}{7} + 2\frac{1}{2} + \frac{2}{19} + \frac{1}{10}$

Write each sum in lowest terms.

19. $2\frac{1}{2} + 4\frac{1}{3}$ 20. $4\frac{5}{9} + 12\frac{4}{9}$ 21. $13\frac{3}{4} + 1\frac{3}{5}$ **8-4**

22. $15\frac{2}{3} + 8\frac{11}{12}$ 23. $2\frac{1}{6} + 7\frac{9}{10}$ 24. $20\frac{6}{13} + 9\frac{1}{2}$

25. Matt rode his bicycle for $2\frac{3}{4}$ h on Monday, $1\frac{1}{2}$ h on Tuesday, and $3\frac{1}{3}$ h on Friday. How many hours in all did he ride his bicycle?

Write each difference in lowest terms.

26. $10\frac{8}{9} - 9\frac{8}{9}$ 27. $3\frac{3}{4} - 1\frac{1}{8}$ 28. $7\frac{3}{5} - 2\frac{2}{25}$ **8-5**

29. $3\frac{5}{6} - \frac{4}{9}$ 30. $24\frac{41}{50} - 24\frac{7}{10}$ 31. $56\frac{3}{5} - 52\frac{1}{8}$

32. $15\frac{5}{6} - 14\frac{10}{11}$ 33. $8\frac{3}{13} - 7\frac{14}{39}$ 34. $24\frac{1}{4} - 19\frac{5}{6}$ **8-6**

35. Rita had $2\frac{1}{2}$ gal (gallons) of milk in the refrigerator. Her family used $1\frac{3}{4}$ gal of milk. How many gallons of milk were left?

Look for a pattern. Then write the next three numbers.

8-7

36. 1, 4, 2, 5, 3, 6, __?__, __?__, __?__

37. 1, 1, 2, 6, 24, 120, __?__, __?__, __?__

8-8 TIME CARDS

In many occupations, workers are paid on an hourly basis. To compute an employee's wages, the employer must first know how many hours the person worked. Workers often punch a time clock. A **time card** indicates the time of arrival and the time of departure.

example

To compute the number of hours worked on Monday, round the times to the nearest quarter hour.

In: 8:01 rounds to 8:00
Out: 11:59 rounds to 12:00
In: 1:00 = 1:00
Out: 4:08 rounds to 4:15

TIME CARD					
Name: Sam Shapiro					
Day	In	Out	In	Out	Hours
M	8:01	11:59	1:00	4:08	?
T	7:35	11:47	12:50	5:00	?
W	8:00	12:10	1:05	5:14	?
TH	8:37	12:15	1:00	4:58	?
F	7:49	11:50	12:50	5:17	?

Find the elapsed time between each *In* and *Out* time.

From 8:00 to 12:00 is 4 h.   From 1:00 to 4:15 is 3 h 15 min, or $3\frac{1}{4}$ h.

Add to find the total time. $4 \text{ h} + 3\frac{1}{4} \text{ h} = 7\frac{1}{4} \text{ h}$

exercises

Use the time card above. Round each time to the nearest quarter hour. Find the total hours worked for the given day.

1. Tuesday   2. Wednesday   3. Thursday   4. Friday

5. On Monday, Merril Hayes worked from 7:47 A.M. until 12:00 noon and from 1:05 P.M. until 5:37 P.M. Find the total hours she worked for the day.

6. On Thursday, Josh Garver worked from 8:55 A.M. until 11:45 A.M. and from 12:50 P.M. until 5:03 P.M. Find the total hours Josh worked on Thursday.

7. Jesse Rojas worked $7\frac{1}{2}$ h on Monday, on Tuesday, and on Wednesday. Find the number of hours worked for the three days.

8. Marilyn Hennesey worked four nights one week from 7:00 P.M. to 9:30 P.M. Find the number of hours worked for the week.

Adding and Subtracting Fractions 185

CARPENTER

Beth Holmes is a carpenter. In her work she uses many kinds and sizes of lumber. Lumber is sold by **nominal** size. Each board is actually smaller than its nominal size due to shrinkage during processing. The actual size is called the **dressed** size.

example

Beth buys lumber with a nominal thickness of $1\frac{1}{4}$ in. Find the amount lost in processing.

solution

The table shows that the dressed size of the wood is $1\frac{1}{8}$ in.
Subtract the dressed size from the nominal size.

$1\frac{1}{4} - 1\frac{1}{8} = 1\frac{2}{8} - 1\frac{1}{8} = \frac{1}{8}$

The amount lost in processing is $\frac{1}{8}$ in.

Thickness in Inches		Width in Inches	
Nominal	Dressed	Nominal	Dressed
1	$\frac{3}{4}$	2	$1\frac{1}{2}$
$1\frac{1}{4}$	$1\frac{1}{8}$	3	$2\frac{1}{2}$
$1\frac{1}{2}$	$1\frac{3}{8}$	4	$3\frac{1}{2}$
2	$1\frac{1}{2}$	5	$4\frac{1}{2}$
$2\frac{1}{2}$	2	6	$5\frac{1}{2}$
3	$2\frac{1}{2}$	8	$7\frac{1}{4}$

exercises

Find the amount lost in processing for the given nominal size.

1. 3 in. thick
2. $1\frac{1}{2}$ in. thick
3. 5 in. wide
4. 4 in. wide
5. 1 in. thick
6. 8 in. wide

7. Graham Muldari is building a deck. He plans to use 24 boards that each have a nominal width of 8 in. Find the total width of the dressed boards.

8. Eliza Jacobs is building a picnic table. For the table top, she plans to use 16 boards with a nominal width of 5 in. and lay them side-by-side. She also plans to leave $\frac{1}{2}$ in. of space between the boards. Find the finished width of the table top.

CHAPTER REVIEW

vocabulary vo·cab·u·lar·y

Choose the correct word to complete each sentence.

1. The LCD of two or more fractions is the *(greatest common factor, least common multiple)* of their denominators.

2. The number $5\frac{7}{8}$ is an example of a *(whole number, mixed number)*.

skills

Write each sum or difference in lowest terms.

3.
$$\begin{array}{r} \frac{3}{8} \\ +\frac{1}{8} \\ \hline \end{array}$$

4.
$$\begin{array}{r} \frac{11}{12} \\ -\frac{5}{12} \\ \hline \end{array}$$

5.
$$\begin{array}{r} \frac{5}{9} \\ +\frac{3}{4} \\ \hline \end{array}$$

6.
$$\begin{array}{r} 4\frac{9}{14} \\ -1\frac{5}{14} \\ \hline \end{array}$$

7.
$$\begin{array}{r} 16\frac{5}{9} \\ -\ 8\frac{4}{9} \\ \hline \end{array}$$

8.
$$\begin{array}{r} 7\frac{3}{8} \\ +4\frac{5}{8} \\ \hline \end{array}$$

9. $\frac{9}{13} - \frac{17}{26}$

10. $\frac{2}{7} + \frac{9}{42}$

11. $\frac{3}{4} - \frac{2}{5}$

12. $\frac{6}{7} + \frac{3}{5}$

13. $3\frac{4}{5} + 1\frac{1}{3}$

14. $9\frac{2}{7} + 6\frac{5}{11}$

15. $12 - 6\frac{1}{3}$

16. $8 - 4\frac{2}{7}$

17. $9\frac{3}{10} + 10\frac{1}{4}$

18. $16\frac{3}{8} + 5\frac{1}{3}$

19. $5\frac{4}{13} - 2\frac{1}{3}$

20. $7\frac{1}{9} - 5\frac{2}{5}$

21. $1\frac{8}{9} + 5\frac{5}{7}$

22. $3\frac{2}{3} - 3\frac{1}{4}$

23. $16\frac{1}{3} - 15\frac{7}{8}$

24. $14\frac{7}{12} - 6\frac{3}{4}$

Estimate.

25. $19\frac{2}{9} - 16\frac{5}{6}$

26. $23\frac{1}{4} - 8\frac{1}{3}$

27. $4\frac{1}{2} + 6\frac{5}{11}$

28. $2\frac{1}{8} + 3\frac{3}{7} + 1\frac{8}{9} + 2\frac{6}{11}$

29. Rich can repair his car in $4\frac{1}{2}$ h. A mechanic can do the same job in $3\frac{7}{8}$ h. How much longer does it take Rich to do the job?

30. Vic worked $6\frac{1}{4}$ h on Thursday, $9\frac{2}{3}$ h on Friday, and $9\frac{1}{2}$ h on Saturday. How many hours in all did he work on these three days?

31. Look for a pattern. Then write the next three numbers:

$$\frac{1}{12}, \frac{1}{6}, \frac{1}{3}, \frac{2}{3}, \frac{4}{3}, \underline{\ ?\ }, \underline{\ ?\ }, \underline{\ ?\ }$$

32. Claudia works four afternoons a week from 2:30 P.M. to 5:00 P.M. How many hours a week does she work?

CHAPTER TEST

Write each sum or difference in lowest terms.

8-1

1. $\dfrac{5}{16} + \dfrac{9}{16}$ 2. $\dfrac{3}{4} + \dfrac{3}{4}$ 3. $\dfrac{5}{6} - \dfrac{1}{6}$ 4. $\dfrac{10}{21} - \dfrac{4}{21}$ 5. $\dfrac{13}{36} - \dfrac{7}{36}$ **8-1**

6. $\dfrac{1}{6} + \dfrac{1}{9}$ 7. $\dfrac{5}{6} + \dfrac{1}{4}$ 8. $\dfrac{7}{12} - \dfrac{1}{6}$ 9. $\dfrac{15}{16} - \dfrac{5}{8}$ 10. $\dfrac{11}{13} + \dfrac{1}{3}$ **8-2**

11. Laura drove $\frac{1}{3}$ of the way from Boston to Newark. Martha drove $\frac{1}{4}$ of the way. How much of the way did they drive altogether?

Estimate by rounding.

12. $4\dfrac{3}{5} - 1\dfrac{1}{6}$ 13. $15\dfrac{2}{7} + 5\dfrac{1}{2}$ 14. $9\dfrac{4}{9} + 7\dfrac{6}{11}$ **8-3**

15. Mike bought $35\frac{1}{2}$ ft (feet) of wire molding on Tuesday and $24\frac{3}{4}$ ft on Friday. About how many feet of wire molding did he buy in all?

Estimate by adding the whole numbers, and then adjusting.

16. $2\dfrac{1}{3} + 7\dfrac{2}{9} + 1\dfrac{9}{28}$ 17. $\dfrac{5}{9} + 3\dfrac{1}{2} + 1\dfrac{11}{12}$ 18. $3\dfrac{4}{7} + 2\dfrac{1}{9} + \dfrac{5}{11}$

Write each sum or difference in lowest terms.

19. $2\dfrac{1}{4} + 3\dfrac{3}{4}$ 20. $9\dfrac{7}{12} + 1\dfrac{1}{3}$ 21. $4\dfrac{7}{10} + 3\dfrac{2}{5}$ **8-4**

22. $6\dfrac{4}{5} + 11\dfrac{1}{4}$ 23. $20\dfrac{7}{16} + 7\dfrac{1}{5}$ 24. $19\dfrac{7}{10} + 3\dfrac{5}{7}$

25. $11\dfrac{4}{5} - 2\dfrac{1}{5}$ 26. $9\dfrac{11}{20} - 7\dfrac{7}{20}$ 27. $16\dfrac{3}{11} - 7\dfrac{1}{22}$ **8-5**

28. $19\dfrac{11}{15} - 2\dfrac{2}{3}$ 29. $29\dfrac{7}{8} - 23\dfrac{3}{7}$ 30. $41\dfrac{4}{9} - 22\dfrac{1}{6}$

31. $6\dfrac{3}{8} - 5\dfrac{4}{5}$ 32. $3\dfrac{15}{16} - 2\dfrac{31}{32}$ 33. $9\dfrac{1}{2} - 4\dfrac{12}{21}$ **8-6**

34. Lou caught an $8\frac{1}{3}$-in. fish and Ron caught a $9\frac{1}{4}$-in. fish. Who caught the bigger fish? How much bigger?

35. Look for a pattern. Then write the next three numbers: **8-7**
    3, 9, 7, 13, 11, 17, __?__, __?__, __?__

36. Erica worked $4\frac{1}{2}$ h on Monday, 5 h on Wednesday, and   **8-8**
    $6\frac{1}{2}$ h on Friday. How many hours in all did she work on these three days?

Paint and many of the other materials used in building and home repair are generally measured in U.S. Customary units.

CHAPTER 9

U.S. CUSTOMARY MEASUREMENT

9-1 U.S. CUSTOMARY UNITS OF LENGTH

In the United States Customary system of measurement, the commonly used units of length are the **inch, foot, yard,** and **mile.** The chart at the right shows how these units are related.

U.S. Customary Measures
12 inches (in.) = 1 foot (ft)
3 feet = 1 yard (yd)
36 inches = 1 yard
5280 feet = 1 mile (mi)
1760 yards = 1 mile

To change from one unit of length to another, use the following rules.

To change from a larger unit to a smaller unit, you *multiply*.

To change from a smaller unit to a larger unit, you *divide*.

example 1

Complete: a. 48 in. = __?__ ft   b. 7 ft = __?__ in.

solution

a. 12 in. = 1 ft, so 48 in. = 4 ft ◄── *Think:* **smaller to larger, so *divide.***
   ↳ ÷ 12 ↗   ↳ ÷ 12 ↗

b. 1 ft = 12 in., so 7 ft = 84 in. ◄── *Think:* **larger to smaller, so *multiply.***
   ↳ × 12 ↗   ↳ × 12 ↗

your turn

Complete.

1. 10 yd = __?__ in.   2. 72 ft = __?__ in.   3. 108 in. = __?__ ft

example 2

Complete: a. 5 yd 2 ft = __?__ ft   b. 68 in. = __?__ ft __?__ in.

solution

a.
```
    3
   ×5   ◄── Think:
   ──       larger to smaller,
   15       so multiply.
  + 2
  ──       1 yd = 3 ft
   17         ↳ × 3 ↗
```
5 yd 2 ft = 17 ft

b.
```
       5
   12)68   ◄── Think:
      60       smaller to larger,
      ──       so divide.
       8
           12 in. = 1 ft
              ↳ ÷ 12 ↗
```
68 in. = 5 ft 8 in.

your turn

Complete.

4. 93 in. = __?__ yd __?__ in.   5. 25 ft 11 in. = __?__ in.   6. 6000 yd = __?__ mi __?__ yd

practice exercises

practice for example 1 (page 190)

Complete.

1. $10 \text{ ft} = \underline{} \text{ in.}$
2. $7 \text{ mi} = \underline{} \text{ yd}$
3. $211 \text{ yd} = \underline{} \text{ ft}$
4. $27 \text{ mi} = \underline{} \text{ ft}$
5. $180 \text{ in.} = \underline{} \text{ ft}$
6. $15,840 \text{ ft} = \underline{} \text{ mi}$

practice for example 2 (page 190)

Complete.

7. $4 \text{ yd } 2 \text{ ft} = \underline{} \text{ ft}$
8. $3 \text{ yd } 23 \text{ in.} = \underline{} \text{ in.}$
9. $63 \text{ in.} = \underline{} \text{ ft } \underline{} \text{ in.}$
10. $1510 \text{ ft} = \underline{} \text{ yd } \underline{} \text{ ft}$
11. $6000 \text{ ft} = \underline{} \text{ mi } \underline{} \text{ ft}$
12. $400 \text{ in.} = \underline{} \text{ yd } \underline{} \text{ in.}$

mixed practice (page 190)

Complete.

13. $120 \text{ ft} = \underline{} \text{ yd}$
14. $7040 \text{ yd} = \underline{} \text{ mi}$
15. $327 \text{ in.} = \underline{} \text{ yd } \underline{} \text{ in.}$
16. $21,120 \text{ ft} = \underline{} \text{ in.}$
17. $5 \text{ mi } 2 \text{ yd } 1 \text{ ft} = \underline{} \text{ ft}$
18. $4 \text{ mi } 70 \text{ yd } 2 \text{ ft} = \underline{} \text{ ft}$
19. $5 \text{ mi} = \underline{} \text{ yd} = \underline{} \text{ ft} = \underline{} \text{ in.}$
20. $\underline{} \text{ mi} = 15,840 \text{ yd} = \underline{} \text{ ft} = \underline{} \text{ in.}$

Select the most reasonable measure.

21. distance of a marathon
    26 yd   26 ft   26 mi
22. length of a football field
    100 ft   100 yd   100 mi
23. height of a door
    7 yd   7 in.   7 ft

24. width of a street
    10 ft   10 yd   10 mi
25. length of a car
    15 yd   15 in.   15 ft
26. length of a book
    9 ft   9 yd   9 in.

27. Sam Spiral passed the football for a total of $9\frac{1}{4}$ mi during his career. Write this total in yards.
28. Mount McKinley is 20,320 ft high. About how many miles is this?

review exercises

Evaluate each expression when $x = 4$, $y = 2$, and $z = 5$.

1. $2x$
2. $3y$
3. $6z - 6$
4. $9x - 5$
5. $18 + 3z$
6. $4z + 6$
7. $12y - 20$
8. $36 - 7x$

Give the value of the underlined digit in each number.

9. $112,89\underline{6},371$
10. $9,\underline{6}27,119$
11. $2,7\underline{3}1,891,435$
12. $9\underline{9},712,849$

9-2 USING A CUSTOMARY RULER

In the United States Customary system, small lengths are measured in inches. To measure the length of an object, use the following method.

1. Place a ruler so that the leftmost mark lines up with one end of the object.
2. Read the mark nearest the other end of the object.

example 1

Measure the length of each ribbon to the nearest inch.

a.  ← **Nearer to 3 in. than to 4 in.** To the nearest inch, the length is 3 in.

b.  ← **Halfway between 1 in. and 2 in. Round up.** To the nearest inch, the length is 2 in.

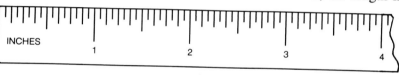

your turn

Measure the length of each ribbon to the nearest inch.

1.

2.

When a more precise measurement is needed, you can measure lengths in fractions of an inch. Many customary rulers separate the inch into sixteen equal parts. Each part represents $\frac{1}{16}$ inch.

example 2

Measure the length of each nail to the nearest $\frac{1}{16}$ inch.

a.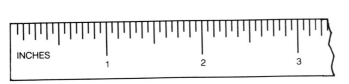

b.

To the nearest $\frac{1}{16}$ inch,
the length is $3\frac{1}{16}$ in.

To the nearest $\frac{1}{16}$ inch,
the length is $1\frac{14}{16}$ in. $= 1\frac{7}{8}$ in.

your turn

Measure the length of each nail to the nearest $\frac{1}{16}$ inch.

3.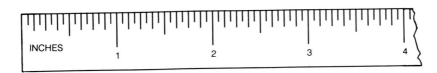

4.

practice exercises

practice for example 1 (page 192)

Measure the length of each pencil to the nearest inch.

1.

2.

3.

U.S. Customary Measurement 193

Measure the length of each screw to the nearest $\frac{1}{16}$ inch.

4.

5.

6.

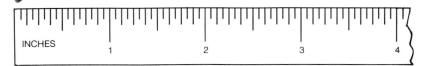

Use an inch ruler. Measure the length of each object to the nearest $\frac{1}{16}$ inch.

7.    **8.**    **9.**

10.

Draw a line segment of the given length.

11. 6 in.   **12.** $3\frac{3}{16}$ in.   **13.** $2\frac{5}{8}$ in.   **14.** $1\frac{3}{4}$ in.   **15.** $5\frac{1}{2}$ in.   **16.** 1 ft

Estimate, then measure the length of each object to the nearest inch.

17. length of this page   **18.** width of this page
19. width of your classroom window   **20.** height of your classroom door

review exercises

Estimate.

1. $\frac{33}{100} \times 61\frac{1}{9}$ **2.** $77\frac{1}{3} \times \frac{10}{21}$ **3.** $\frac{9}{10} + \frac{15}{16}$ **4.** $1\frac{1}{2} + 2\frac{4}{9} + 2\frac{1}{10}$

5. $4\frac{1}{9} - 1\frac{10}{11}$ **6.** $6\frac{1}{5} \times 2\frac{6}{7}$ **7.** $\frac{19}{80} \times 15\frac{1}{3}$ **8.** $15\frac{1}{2} \times \frac{61}{90}$

9-3 U.S. CUSTOMARY UNITS OF WEIGHT

In the United States Customary system of measurement, the commonly used units of weight are the **ounce, pound,** and **ton.** The chart at the right shows how these units are related.

U.S. Customary Measures
16 ounces (oz) = 1 pound (lb)
2000 pounds = 1 ton (t)

   To change from one unit of weight to another, use the same rules that you used for units of length.

   To change from a larger unit to a smaller unit, you *multiply*.
   To change from a smaller unit to a larger unit, you *divide*.

example 1

Complete: **a.** 48 oz = __?__ lb   **b.** 4 lb = __?__ oz

solution

a. 16 oz = 1 lb, so 48 oz = 3 lb ← *Think:* smaller to larger, so *divide.*
         ⌣ ÷ 16 ↗   ⌣ ÷ 16 ↗

b. 1 lb = 16 oz, so 4 lb = 64 oz ← *Think:* larger to smaller, so *multiply.*
         ⌣ × 16 ↗   ⌣ × 16 ↗

your turn

Complete.

   1. 7 t = __?__ lb   **2.** 6 lb = __?__ oz   **3.** 6000 lb = __?__ t

example 2

Complete: **a.** 7 lb 6 oz = __?__ oz   **b.** 3800 lb = __?__ t __?__ lb

solution

a.   16
          ×7   ← *Think:* larger to smaller, so *multiply.*
         ─────
          112
         + 6   1 lb = 16 oz
         ─────   ⌣ × 16 ↗
          118
         7 lb 6 oz = 118 oz

b.   1
         2000)3800   ← *Think:* smaller to larger, so *divide.*
              2000
              ─────
              1800   2000 lb = 1 t
                         ⌣ ÷ 2000 ↗

         3800 lb = 1 t 1800 lb

your turn

Complete.

   4. 3 t 900 lb = __?__ lb   **5.** 8 lb 13 oz = __?__ oz   **6.** 180 oz = __?__ lb __?__ oz

practice exercises

practice for example 1 (page 195)

Complete.

1. 2 lb = __?__ oz
2. 4 t = __?__ lb
3. 80 oz = __?__ lb
4. 128 oz = __?__ lb
5. 12,000 lb = __?__ t
6. 36,000 lb = __?__ t

practice for example 2 (page 195)

Complete.

7. 2 t 800 lb = __?__ lb
8. 3 lb 14 oz = __?__ oz
9. 12 lb 15 oz = __?__ oz
10. 11 t 1990 lb = __?__ lb
11. 1630 oz = __?__ lb __?__ oz
12. 5580 lb = __?__ t __?__ lb

mixed practice (page 195)

Complete.

13. 11 t = __?__ lb
14. 38 lb = __?__ oz
15. 216 oz = __?__ lb __?__ oz
16. 325 oz = __?__ lb __?__ oz
17. 4308 lb = __?__ t __?__ lb
18. 7692 lb = __?__ t __?__ lb

Compare. Replace each __?__ with >, <, or =.

19. 32 oz __?__ 2 lb
20. 6 lb __?__ 106 oz
21. 3 t __?__ 600 lb
22. 34,000 lb __?__ 16 t
23. 2 t 30 lb __?__ 23,000 lb
24. 15 lb 15 oz __?__ 255 oz

25. An elephant weighs $5\frac{1}{2}$ t. What is its weight in pounds?
26. An elephant eats 48,000 lb of peanuts a year. How many tons is this?

review exercises

Find each answer.

1. 18×973
2. $60,005 - 4329$
3. $3942 \div 27$
4. $16 + 9 + 472$
5. $4410 \div 35$
6. $82,399 + 5417$
7. 148×202
8. $9354 - 8628$

mental math

Add, subtract, multiply, or divide mentally.

1. $8 \div \frac{1}{2}$
2. $\frac{1}{2} + \frac{1}{5} + \frac{1}{2}$
3. $\frac{4}{5} \times \$30$
4. $4 - 2\frac{1}{5}$
5. $\frac{2}{3} \times 18$
6. $4 \div \frac{1}{3}$
7. $\frac{3}{5} + \frac{1}{4} + \frac{2}{5}$
8. $7\frac{1}{7} - 4\frac{3}{7}$

9-4 U.S. CUSTOMARY UNITS OF CAPACITY

In the United States Customary system of measurement, the commonly used units of liquid capacity are the **fluid ounce, cup, pint, quart,** and **gallon.** The chart at the right shows how these units are related.

U.S. Customary Measures
8 fluid ounces (fl oz) = 1 cup (c)
2 cups = 1 pint (pt)
2 pints = 1 quart (qt)
4 quarts = 1 gallon (gal)
8 pints = 1 gallon

To change from one unit of liquid capacity to another, use these rules.

To change from a larger unit to a smaller unit, you *multiply*.
To change from a smaller unit to a larger unit, you *divide*.

example 1

Complete: a. 6 c = __?__ pt   b. 7 pt = __?__ c

solution

a. 2 c = 1 pt, so 6 c = 3 pt ◄── *Think:* smaller to larger, so *divide.*
     ╰÷ 2 ╯   ╰÷ 2 ╯

b. 1 pt = 2 c, so 7 pt = 14 c ◄── *Think:* larger to smaller, so *multiply.*
     ╰× 2 ╯   ╰× 2 ╯

your turn

Complete.

1. 6 gal = __?__ pt   2. 3 qt = __?__ pt   3. 24 qt = __?__ gal

example 2

Complete: a. 6 c 3 fl oz = __?__ fl oz   b. 11 qt = __?__ gal __?__ qt

solution

a.
$$\begin{array}{r} 8 \\ \times 6 \\ \hline 48 \\ + 3 \\ \hline 51 \end{array}$$

Think: larger to smaller, so *multiply.*

1 c = 8 fl oz
╰× 8 ╯

6 c 3 fl oz = 51 fl oz

b.
$$\begin{array}{r} 2 \\ 4\overline{)11} \\ 8 \\ \hline 3 \end{array}$$

Think: smaller to larger, so *divide.*

4 qt = 1 gal
╰÷ 4 ╯

11 qt = 2 gal 3 qt

your turn

Complete.

4. 9 gal 1 qt = __?__ qt   5. 3 pt 1 c = __?__ c   6. 17 pt = __?__ qt __?__ pt

practice exercises

practice for example 1 (page 197)

Complete.

1. 16 fl oz = __?__ c
2. 12 qt = __?__ gal
3. 7 gal = __?__ qt
4. 5 qt = __?__ pt
5. 20 c = __?__ pt
6. 64 pt = __?__ gal

practice for example 2 (page 197)

Complete.

7. 15 qt = __?__ gal __?__ qt
8. 20 fl oz = __?__ c __?__ fl oz
9. 5 pt 1 c = __?__ c
10. 7 gal 2 qt = __?__ qt
11. 25 qt = __?__ gal __?__ qt
12. 37 pt = __?__ gal __?__ pt

mixed practice (page 197)

Complete.

13. 11 pt = __?__ c
14. 9 gal = __?__ pt
15. 15 qt 1 pt = __?__ pt
16. 13 c 5 fl oz = __?__ fl oz
17. 2 gal 2 pt = __?__ qt
18. 9 qt 2 c = __?__ pt

Choose the letter of the appropriate unit for measuring the given quantity.

19. weight of a truck   **a.** t   **b.** gal   **c.** mi
20. capacity of a glass of milk   **a.** ft   **b.** lb   **c.** fl oz
21. length of a sofa   **a.** c   **b.** ft   **c.** mi
22. capacity of a swimming pool   **a.** yd   **b.** gal   **c.** t

23. Fred put 9 gal of water in his fish tank. How many quarts is this?
24. Many doctors suggest that a person should drink six 8-oz glasses of water each day. How many pints of water is this each week?

review exercises

Write the prime factorization of each number.

1. 10
2. 91
3. 125
4. 45
5. 100
6. 54

PUZZLE CORNER

Eight of nine baseballs weigh exactly the same. The ninth is heavier. Describe how you could use a balance scale to find the heaviest ball with just two weighings.

9-5 COMPUTING WITH CUSTOMARY UNITS

To add or subtract with customary units, use the following method.

1. Line up the units vertically. Numbers with the same units should be in the same column.
2. Add or subtract each column as appropriate.
3. Write the sum or difference in simplest form.

example 1

Write each sum or difference in simplest form.

a. 6 mi 9 yd + 8 mi 12 yd

b. 11 lb 12 oz − 5 lb 10 oz

solution

a.
```
   6 mi  9 yd
 +8 mi 12 yd
  14 mi 21 yd
```

b.
```
   11 lb 12 oz
 −  5 lb 10 oz
    6 lb  2 oz
```

your turn

Write each sum or difference in simplest form.

1. 16 yd 4 in. + 8 yd 3 in.   **2.** 9 gal 2 qt − 3 gal 1 qt   **3.** 143 t + 29 t 37 lb

example 2

Write each sum in simplest form.

a. 148 lb 5 oz + 9 lb 12 oz

b. 5 qt 1 pt + 3 qt 1 pt

solution

a.
```
   148 lb  5 oz
 +   9 lb 12 oz
   157 lb 17 oz  =  157 lb + 1 lb 1 oz
                      158 lb 1 oz
```

b.
```
    5 qt 1 pt
  +3 qt 1 pt
    8 qt 2 pt  =  9 qt
```

your turn

Write each sum in simplest form.

4. 9 ft 5 in. + 4 ft 8 in.   **5.** 20 gal 3 qt + 11 gal 1 qt   **6.** 7 t 1643 lb + 500 lb

You may need to rename some measurements before subtracting.

example 3

Write each difference in simplest form.

a. 12 ft − 2 ft 3 in.

b. 6 gal 2 qt − 4 gal 3 qt

solution

a.

$$
\begin{array}{rcl}
12 \text{ ft} & = & 11 \text{ ft } 12 \text{ in.} \\
- 2 \text{ ft } 3 \text{ in.} & = & - 2 \text{ ft } 3 \text{ in.} \\
\hline
 & & 9 \text{ ft } 9 \text{ in.}
\end{array}
$$

b.

$$
\begin{array}{rcl}
6 \text{ gal } 2 \text{ qt} & = & 5 \text{ gal } 6 \text{ qt} \\
-4 \text{ gal } 3 \text{ qt} & = & -4 \text{ gal } 3 \text{ qt} \\
\hline
 & & 1 \text{ gal } 3 \text{ qt}
\end{array}
$$

your turn

Write each difference in simplest form.

7. 3 pt − 1 pt 1 c   **8.** 103 lb 3 oz − 19 lb 14 oz   **9.** 6 mi 24 yd − 2 mi 56 yd

practice exercises

practice for example 1 (page 199)

Write each sum or difference in simplest form.

1.
$$\begin{array}{r} 4 \text{ ft } 6 \text{ in.} \\ +2 \text{ ft } 5 \text{ in.} \\ \hline \end{array}$$

2.
$$\begin{array}{r} 9 \text{ gal } 2 \text{ qt} \\ +5 \text{ gal } 1 \text{ qt} \\ \hline \end{array}$$

3.
$$\begin{array}{r} 3 \text{ ft } 8 \text{ in.} \\ -1 \text{ ft } 4 \text{ in.} \\ \hline \end{array}$$

4.
$$\begin{array}{r} 9 \text{ gal } 3 \text{ qt} \\ -2 \text{ gal } 1 \text{ qt} \\ \hline \end{array}$$

5. 17 gal 2 qt + 11 gal

6. 17 mi 400 yd − 287 yd

7. 123 mi 643 ft − 37 mi 234 ft

8. 4 t 700 lb + 3 t 450 lb

practice for example 2 (page 199)

Write each sum in simplest form.

9.
$$\begin{array}{r} 14 \text{ yd } 2 \text{ ft} \\ +24 \text{ yd } 2 \text{ ft} \\ \hline \end{array}$$

10.
$$\begin{array}{r} 10 \text{ lb } 12 \text{ oz} \\ + 8 \text{ lb } 14 \text{ oz} \\ \hline \end{array}$$

11.
$$\begin{array}{r} 33 \text{ gal } 2 \text{ qt} \\ +43 \text{ gal } 2 \text{ qt} \\ \hline \end{array}$$

12.
$$\begin{array}{r} 12 \text{ qt } 1 \text{ pt} \\ + 9 \text{ qt } 1 \text{ pt} \\ \hline \end{array}$$

13. 27 yd 29 in. + 30 in.

14. 37 lb 14 oz + 15 oz

15. 14 t 1674 lb + 3 t 436 lb

16. 20 mi 1470 yd + 3 mi 822 yd

practice for example 3 (page 200)

Write each difference in simplest form.

17.
$$\begin{array}{r} 9 \text{ ft } 7 \text{ in.} \\ -6 \text{ ft } 10 \text{ in.} \\ \hline \end{array}$$

18.
$$\begin{array}{r} 6 \text{ gal } 1 \text{ qt} \\ -4 \text{ gal } 3 \text{ qt} \\ \hline \end{array}$$

19.
$$\begin{array}{r} 16 \text{ gal } 1 \text{ qt} \\ - 7 \text{ gal } 3 \text{ qt} \\ \hline \end{array}$$

20.
$$\begin{array}{r} 13 \text{ lb } 7 \text{ oz} \\ - 9 \text{ lb } 15 \text{ oz} \\ \hline \end{array}$$

21. 43 mi 24 yd − 21 mi 33 yd

22. 54 lb 3 oz − 27 lb 13 oz

23. 11 qt − 8 qt 1 pt

24. 19 yd − 2 yd 2 ft

mixed practice *(pages 199–200)*

Write each sum or difference in simplest form.

25.   5 lb 3 oz
    +3 lb 8 oz

26.   23 mi 7 yd
    +15 mi 3 yd

27.   12 yd 2 ft
    − 9 yd 1 ft

28.   16 c 6 fl oz
    −13 c 2 fl oz

29. 6 gal 3 qt + 6 gal 1 qt

30. 4 t 1500 lb + 3 t 800 lb

31. 57 lb 3 oz − 8 oz

32. 72 gal 1 qt − 3 qt

33. 7 in. + 10 ft 8 in.

34. 397 lb + 3 t 1875 lb

35. 25 gal 2 qt 1 pt − 18 gal 3 qt 1 pt

36. 32 mi 63 yd 2 ft − 23 mi 90 yd 1 ft

37. During lunch period, the sophomores consumed 22 gal 3 pt of milk, and the seniors consumed 168 pt. How much more did the sophomores consume?

38. The winner of the long-jump competition jumped 24 ft 9 in. The closest competitor jumped 7 yd 2 ft. How much farther did the winner jump?

review *exercises*

Round to the place of the underlined digit.

1. 6<u>3</u>5

2. 237<u>1</u>

3. 6<u>5</u>89

4. <u>3</u>3,784

5. 396,<u>2</u>15

6. 2<u>9</u>0,843

7. 7<u>8</u>6,451

8. 1,<u>8</u>92,903

9. 1<u>0</u>,900,300

10. <u>8</u>1,927,541

11. 112,289,<u>0</u>58

12. <u>9</u>,482,188,336

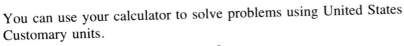

calculator corner

You can use your calculator to solve problems using United States Customary units.

example   Complete: 5 mi = _?_ in.

solution   1 mi = 5280 ft, and 1 ft = 12 in.
           Enter 5 × 5280 × 12 =. The result is 316800.
           So 5 mi = 316,800 in.

Use a calculator to complete.

1. 8 mi = _?_ in.   2. 8 gal = _?_ fl oz   3. 7 t = _?_ oz   4. 29 mi = _?_ in.

SKILL REVIEW

Complete.

1. 17 mi = __?__ yd   **2.** 86 in. = __?__ ft __?__ in.   **3.** 6 mi 68 yd 2 ft = __?__ ft   **9-1**

Select the most reasonable measure.

4. width of a soccer field
 80 in. 80 yd 80 ft

5. length of a pencil
 7 ft   7 mi   7 in.

6. height of an adult
 6 ft   6 mi   6 yd

Measure the length of each object to the nearest $\frac{1}{16}$ inch.

7.

9-2

8.

Complete.

9. 176 oz = __?__ lb   **10.** 7375 lb = __?__ t __?__ lb   **11.** 8 lb 5 oz = __?__ oz   **9-3**

Complete. Replace each __?__ with >, <, or =.

12. 8200 lb __?__ 41 t   **13.** 17 lb __?__ 27 oz   **14.** 4 lb 14 oz __?__ 76 oz

15. A cargo shipment weighs $1\frac{1}{2}$ t. How many pounds is this?

Complete.

16. 18 c = __?__ fl oz   **17.** 17 pt = __?__ gal __?__ pt   **18.** 32 gal 3 qt = __?__ qt   **9-4**

19. During the game the football team consumed 12 gal of water. How
many fluid ounces did they consume?

Write each sum in simplest form.

20. 8 lb 3 oz + 14 lb 11 oz

22. 6 t 1300 lb + 5 t 1200 lb

21. 2 ft 8 in. + 3 ft 9 in.

23. 4 gal 3 qt + 5 gal 3 qt

9-5

Write each difference in simplest form.

24. 3 c 5 fl oz − 1 c 2 fl oz

26. 19 lb − 16 lb 5 oz

25. 27 mi 9 yd − 21 mi 13 yd

27. 36 gal 3 qt 1 pt − 28 gal 3 qt 1 pt

28. Tom and Sue were asked for their heights. Tom said he is 5 ft 9 in. tall.
Sue said she is 68 in. tall. Who is taller? How much taller?

9-6 SPORTS RECORDS

Sports records are frequently given in a combination of units. Sometimes a measure must be changed from one unit to another in order to compare it to a record.

example

In 1981, Ben Plucknett threw the discus 79 yd 4 in. Did he break the U.S. record of 232 ft 10 in.?

solution

Change the yards to feet.

Think: larger to smaller, so *multiply.*

1 yard = 3 ft, so 79 yards = 237 ft

Because 237 ft 4 in. is greater than 232 ft 10 in., Ben did break the record.

exercises

Solve. Use a calculator if you have one.

1. The record for the longest field goal in college basketball is 89 ft 3 in., set by Les Henson. How many inches is this?

2. Wesley Paul ran the New York City marathon when he was eight years old. He ran 26 mi 385 yd in 3 h 39 s, setting a new record for his age group. How many yards did he run?

3. Mildred (Babe) Didrikson was a championship golfer and a world-record breaker in track and field. She held the women's record for the longest baseball throw, 296 ft. A competitor threw the ball 91 yd. Did Babe have to give up her title? Explain.

4. The record for the longest ski jump was 593 ft 10 in. Toni Innauer jumped 6929 in. Did he break the record?

5. In 1977 John York tried to swim the 21-mi round trip from the California coast to Catalina Island. He collapsed 200 yd from the end. How many yards did he swim?

U.S. Customary Measurement 203

TERMINAL MANAGER

Charles Taylor is the terminal manager for a trucking company. He calculates the amount of material that can be loaded onto each tractor-trailer.

example

Mr. Taylor has a contract to move sections of pipe. Each section of pipe weighs 980 lb. Each truck can carry a maximum load of 10 t. How many sections of pipe can each truck carry?

solution

When you work with two quantities, first change them to the same unit.

Change tons to pounds: 1 t = 2000 lb, so 10 t = 20,000 lb
$$\underset{\times\ 2000}{} \qquad \underset{\times\ 2000}{}$$

Divide the maximum load of the truck by the weight of each section:

$$20{,}000 \div 980 = 20\frac{20}{49}$$

A truck cannot carry a fraction of a section of pipe, so the quotient must be rounded down. Each truck can carry 20 sections of pipe.

exercises

1. Martin Down's pickup truck can carry a maximum load of 1500 lb. How many 80-lb bags of sand can he place onto his truck?

2. A ferry can carry a maximum load of 30,000 lb. The average weight of a passenger is 130 lb. About how many passengers can the ferry carry?

3. Medical supplies are being flown to the victims of an earthquake. The plane can carry 4 t. Each crate of supplies weighs 120 lb. Can the plane carry 70 crates of supplies?

4. Jane is loading a truck with building supplies. She loads 4 pallets of bricks. Each pallet weighs 450 lb. She plans to load the rest of the truck with cement bags. The maximum load of the truck is 5 t. How many 100-lb bags of cement can she load?

CHAPTER REVIEW

vocabulary vo·cab·u·lar·y

Choose the correct word to complete each sentence.

1. The most commonly used customary units of *(length, weight)* are the ounce, pound, and ton.

2. The pint, quart, and gallon are commonly used customary units of *(liquid capacity, weight)*.

skills

Select the most reasonable measure.

3. length of a basketball court
   90 ft   90 yd   9 mi

4. length of your leg
   1 ft   1 yd   2 yd

5. weight of a rhinoceros
   4 t   400 t   80 lb

6. capacity of a can of soup
   8 pt   8 fl oz   8 qt

Draw a line segment of the given length.

7. 4 in.

8. $6\frac{1}{2}$ in.

9. $2\frac{5}{16}$ in.

10. $4\frac{3}{8}$ in.

11. $1\frac{11}{16}$ in.

Complete.

12. 32 fl oz = __?__ c

13. 4000 lb = __?__ t

14. 8 ft 2 in. = __?__ in.

15. 2 mi 100 yd = __?__ yd

16. 8 lb 5 oz = __?__ oz

17. 6 t 40 lb = __?__ lb

18. 40 in. = __?__ yd __?__ in.

19. 5 gal 3 pt = __?__ pt

20. 21 lb 13 oz = __?__ oz

Write each sum or difference in simplest form.

21.   4 ft 3 in.
     +6 ft 7 in.

22.   10 gal 1 qt
    +11 gal 3 qt

23.   25 t 1700 lb
    +18 t 800 lb

24.   16 qt 1 pt
    + 3 qt 1 pt

25.   11 lb 9 oz
    − 4 lb 3 oz

26. 5 pt 6 fl oz
    −2 pt 3 fl oz

27.   12 qt
    − 1 qt 1 pt

28.   14 ft
    − 3 ft 9 in.

29. 9 gal 3 qt 1 pt + 4 gal 1 qt 1 pt

30. 12 mi 1346 yd 2 ft + 23 mi 523 yd 1 ft

31. A football player carries the ball 45 ft. How many yards is this?

32. A truck can carry a maximum load of 2 t. How many 75-lb bags of sand can be loaded onto the truck?

33. Many midsized cars weigh $1\frac{1}{4}$ t. How many pounds is this?

34. To change from a larger to a smaller unit of measure, you __?__.

CHAPTER TEST

Complete.

1. 5 yd = _?_ in.

2. 36,400 ft = _?_ mi _?_ ft

9-1

Select the most reasonable measure.

3. length of the Ohio River
   981 ft   981 yd   981 mi

4. length of a baseball bat
   3 ft   3 yd   3 in.

5. Roy won the Running High Jump event with a jump of 5 ft 11 in. Write this length in inches.

Measure the length of each object to the nearest $\frac{1}{16}$ inch.

6.

7.

9-2

Complete.

8. 6 t = _?_ lb

9. 172 oz = _?_ lb _?_ oz

9-3

10. A baby's weight at birth was $7\frac{1}{4}$ lb. Change the baby's weight to ounces.

Complete.

11. 18 pt = _?_ c

12. 13 gal 3 qt = _?_ qt

9-4

Complete. Replace each _?_ with <, >, or =.

13. 34 fl oz _?_ 17 c

14. 4 gal _?_ 3 gal 3 qt

15. How many quarts of grapefruit juice are in a can marked 64 fl oz?

Write each sum or difference in simplest form.

16.   2 ft 5 in.
      +6 ft 2 in.

17.   26 t 350 lb
      +17 t   85 lb

18.   12 c 7 fl oz
      +11 c 6 fl oz

19.   20 yd 2 ft
      +17 yd 2 ft

9-5

20. 3 mi 280 ft − 360 ft

21. 75 lb 3 oz − 19 lb 14 oz

22. 34 gal 2 pt − 18 gal 7 pt

23. 75 mi 65 ft − 58 mi 77 ft

24. Mr. Nelson had 2 t of building materials in his truck. He removed 1 t 712 lb. How much did the remaining material weigh?

25. Amy had 120 yd of string on a ball of string. After 59 yd 1 ft were unwound, how much string remained on the ball?

26. Glen Gorbaus holds the men's record for the longest baseball throw, 445 ft 10 in. How many inches is this?

9-6

COMPUTER

→ BASIC

BASIC is only one of several computer programming languages. Because it is similar to English, many people find the BASIC language easy to learn. It is the most popular language used in personal computers today.

In BASIC, the following symbols represent the operations of arithmetic.

+   addition   −   subtraction

*   multiplication   /   division

To compute $3 \div 4 + (1 \div 2) \times 8 + 1 \div 4$ in BASIC, you need to input the expression using the correct symbols.

$$3/4 + (1/2) * 8 + 1/4$$

Since BASIC follows the same rules for order of operations that you learned in Chapter 5, the output for the expression above will be 5.

exercises

Rewrite each expression using correct BASIC symbols.

1. $3 \div 5 \times 1 \div 2$

2. $3 \div 4 + 5 \div 6$

3. $1 \div 2 + 3 \times 4 + 3 \div 8$

4. $12 \times (1 \div 5) - 7 \times (8 \div 9)$

Write the correct output.

5. $20 + 6 * (8 * 11 - 11 + 3)$

6. $8/4 + 10/2 - 2/1$

7. $7 * (3 + 8) - 14 + 5 * 6$

8. $(8/8 + 4/4 + 2/2) * 8 + 9 * 7 - 3$

9. BASIC is one programming language. Find the names of three other computer languages.

10. The word "BASIC" is called an *acronym*. This means that the letters in the word represent the initial letters of a *series* of words. Find out what the letters in BASIC represent.

COMPETENCY TEST

Choose the letter of the correct answer.

1. **Add.** $\frac{3}{5} + \frac{5}{12}$

   A. $\frac{8}{17}$ B. $\frac{2}{3}$

   C. $1\frac{1}{60}$ D. $1\frac{1}{4}$

2. **Divide.** $12 \div \frac{2}{3}$

   A. 8   B. 18

   C. $\frac{1}{8}$ D. $\frac{1}{18}$

3. **Complete the pattern.**

   2, 4, 5, 10, 11, 22, 23, _?_, _?_, _?_

   A. 24, 48, 49
   B. 24, 25, 50
   C. 46, 47, 94
   D. 46, 92, 184

4. **To tile the floor, Maria needs 180 tiles. She has put 135 tiles in place. What fraction of the job is done?**

   A. $\frac{1}{4}$ B. $\frac{3}{4}$

   C. $\frac{9}{13}$ D. $\frac{2}{3}$

5. **Subtract.** $\frac{11}{12} - \frac{3}{4}$

   A. 2   B. $\frac{1}{6}$

   C. $\frac{7}{8}$ D. $\frac{2}{3}$

6. **Add.** $\frac{1}{8} + \frac{3}{5} + \frac{1}{4}$

   A. $\frac{39}{40}$ B. $\frac{5}{17}$

   C. $\frac{23}{40}$ D. $\frac{17}{20}$

7. **Divide.** $\frac{4}{9} \div \frac{5}{12}$

   A. $\frac{5}{27}$ B. $5\frac{2}{15}$

   C. $\frac{15}{16}$ D. $1\frac{1}{15}$

8. **Choose the best estimate.**

   $\frac{3}{14} \times 21\frac{3}{7}$

   A. about 10
   B. about 4
   C. about 20
   D. about 40

9. **Ken has $\frac{7}{8}$ yd of fabric. A vest requires $\frac{3}{4}$ yd. What part of a yard will be left?**

   A. $\frac{1}{8}$ B. $\frac{5}{6}$

   C. $1\frac{5}{8}$ D. $\frac{1}{2}$

10. **Multiply.** $\frac{14}{25} \times \frac{5}{7}$

    A. $\frac{3}{7}$ B. $\frac{19}{32}$

    C. $\frac{2}{5}$ D. $\frac{98}{125}$

11. **Which fraction is greatest?**

 A. $\frac{2}{3}$ B. $\frac{4}{15}$

 C. $\frac{4}{5}$ D. $\frac{7}{15}$

12. **Compute.** $\frac{1}{4} + \frac{7}{8} - \frac{5}{8}$

 A. $\frac{1}{4}$ B. $\frac{3}{4}$

 C. $\frac{13}{20}$ D. $\frac{1}{2}$

13. **What part is shaded?**

 A. $\frac{3}{5}$

 B. $\frac{5}{8}$

 C. $\frac{1}{4}$

 D. $\frac{3}{8}$

14. **Choose the best estimate for** $\frac{8}{71}$.

 A. about $\frac{1}{9}$ B. about $\frac{8}{9}$

 C. about $\frac{1}{2}$ D. about $\frac{1}{5}$

15. **Complete.** 724 in. = __?__ ft __?__ in.

 A. 20 ft 4 in.
 B. 60 ft 4 in.
 C. 741 ft 1 in.
 D. 8688 ft 0 in.

16. **Multiply.** $4\frac{1}{2} \times 1\frac{1}{3}$

 A. $4\frac{1}{6}$ B. $3\frac{3}{8}$

 C. $\frac{8}{27}$ D. 6

17. **Subtract.** $8\frac{3}{8} - 5\frac{3}{4}$

 A. $3\frac{3}{4}$ B. $3\frac{5}{8}$

 C. $2\frac{5}{8}$ D. $2\frac{3}{8}$

18. **Subtract.**
$$67 \text{ ft } 3 \text{ in.}$$
$$-14 \text{ ft } 8 \text{ in.}$$

 A. 81 ft 11 in.
 B. 53 ft 5 in.
 C. 52 ft 5 in.
 D. 52 ft 7 in.

19. **Choose the best estimate.**

$$3\frac{5}{9} + 2\frac{1}{15} + 5\frac{7}{8} + 6\frac{3}{8}$$

 A. about 16   B. about 18
 C. about 20   D. about 22

20. **One loaf of oatmeal bread requires** $\frac{3}{4}$c **of oatmeal. How many loaves can be made with** $4\frac{1}{2}$c**?**

 A. 6   B. 3   C. $3\frac{3}{8}$ D. $2\frac{1}{6}$

CUMULATIVE REVIEW CHAPTERS 1–9

Find each answer. Write your answer in lowest terms.

1. $1214 + 3588$

2. $9123 - 4567$

3. $42\overline{)9682}$

4. $\dfrac{3}{10} + \dfrac{1}{10}$

5. $\dfrac{7}{15} - \dfrac{2}{15}$

6. $3\dfrac{9}{16} - 1\dfrac{1}{4}$

7. $3\dfrac{1}{2} \times 2\dfrac{3}{4}$

8. $7 \times 5 - 3 \times 2$

9. $\dfrac{5}{9} + 8\dfrac{2}{5}$

10. $16 - 5\dfrac{3}{5}$

11. $\dfrac{3}{5} \div \dfrac{2}{3}$

12. $3\dfrac{4}{7} + 5\dfrac{2}{3}$

13. $\$196 + \$612 + \$553$

14. 405×27

15. $5^2 \times 2^3 \times 7^0$

16. $\dfrac{3}{11} \times \dfrac{5}{6}$

17. $\dfrac{5}{6} - \dfrac{3}{4}$

18. $8\dfrac{2}{5} \div \dfrac{1}{5}$

19. Write $\dfrac{42}{15}$ as a mixed number in lowest terms.

20. Given 24 and 60, find the GCF and the LCM.

21. Write the word form of 42,070,023.

22. Complete the pattern: 1, 2, 4, 7, 11, __?__, __?__, __?__

23. Write an expression for the product of 11 and a number n.

Estimate.

24. $\dfrac{5}{19} \times 811$

25. $27\overline{)876,541}$

26. $8\dfrac{9}{11} \div \dfrac{4}{11}$

27. $57,812 - 39,619$

28. $2\dfrac{1}{12} + 8\dfrac{9}{16} + 3\dfrac{7}{15}$

29. $24\dfrac{1}{7} - 14\dfrac{7}{8}$

Complete.

30. 5 ft = __?__ in.

31. 10,000 lb = __?__ t

32. 82 in. = __?__ ft __?__ in.

Write the numbers in order from least to greatest.

33. 2412, 2214, 2421, 2142

34. $\dfrac{10}{21}, \dfrac{3}{7}, \dfrac{2}{3}, \dfrac{5}{9}$

Evaluate each expression when $a = 3$, $b = 4$, and $c = 9$.

35. a^2b

36. $2c - a$

37. $\dfrac{c}{a}$

38. $b + c - a$

39. The price of a car is $7622. The Sandlers made a down payment of $550 and arranged to make 48 monthly payments of $159. How much more did it cost them to buy the car this way?

The world record for the women's one-mile race is 4 min 16.71 s. In sports, times are often recorded to the nearest hundredth of a second.

CHAPTER 10

DECIMAL CONCEPTS

10-1 DECIMALS AND PLACE VALUE

Many numbers have **decimal** places to the right of the ones' place. Digits in these places have values less than one. A **decimal point** separates the whole-number places from the decimal places.

We can extend the place value chart to show decimal places.

millions 1,000,000	hundred thousands 100,000	ten thousands 10,000	thousands 1000	hundreds 100	tens 10	ones 1	tenths 0.1	hundredths 0.01	thousandths 0.001	ten-thousandths 0.0001	hundred-thousandths 0.00001	millionths 0.000001
						5	1	7	3	0	9	2

example 1

Give the value of each of the following digits in the chart above.

a. 7   **b.** 9

solution

a. 7 is in the hundredths' place. Its value is 0.07.

b. 9 is in the hundred-thousandths' place. Its value is 0.00009.

your turn

Give the value of the underlined digit in each decimal.

1. 8.1<u>4</u>36
2. 16.2<u>4</u>9
3. 0.039<u>1</u>28
4. 32.5<u>0</u>9
5. 3451.27<u>4</u>
6. 0.46127<u>8</u>

When you read a decimal, read the place of the last digit last. If the whole-number part of the number is greater than zero, read the decimal point as "and."

$$\boxed{0.912}$$

nine hundred twelve
thousandths

$$\boxed{147.53}$$

one hundred forty-seven *and*
fifty-three *hundredths*

You can write a decimal either in *words* or as a *numeral*.

example 2

Write 42.0813 in words.

solution

word form: forty-two *and* eight hundred thirteen *ten-thousandths*
short word form: 42 *and* 813 *ten-thousandths*

your turn

Write the word form of each decimal.

7. 176.95   8. 9.7317   9. 0.305

Write the short word form of each decimal.

10. 385.9   11. 49.631   12. 0.0071

example 3

Write the numeral form of the following decimal:

two thousand, three hundred nine and fifteen ten-thousandths

solution

Write the whole-number part and the decimal point.   2309.
Determine the number of decimal places.   2309. _ _ _ _
Write the decimal part with the last digit in the last place. 2309. _ _ 1 5
Fill in the empty places with zeros.   2309. 0 0 1 5
The numeral form is 2309.0015.

your turn

Write the numeral form of each decimal.

13. 5321 ten-thousandths   14. twenty-two and seven ten-thousandths
15. 392 and 46 hundredths   16. three and forty-one thousandths

practice exercises

practice for example 1 (page 212)

Give the value of the underlined digit in each decimal.

1. 0.5<u>4</u>8   2. 332.<u>7</u>6   3. 30.19<u>8</u>57   4. 9.44210<u>8</u>
5. 12.47<u>1</u>   6. 8.0319<u>6</u>   7. 149.8<u>0</u>7   8. 3348.2<u>9</u>

Write the word form of each decimal.

9. 1.6
10. 23.54
11. 8.05
12. 317.002
13. 0.98
14. 0.1675
15. 415.502
16. 1922.0406

Write the short word form of each decimal.

17. 7.3
18. 59.148
19. 10.0002
20. 768.05
21. 0.907
22. 0.2
23. 761.25
24. 88.032

Write the numeral form of each decimal.

25. 64 hundredths
26. 82 thousandths
27. 192 and 3 hundredths
28. 14 and 6 ten-thousandths
29. fourteen and one tenth
30. two hundred and six tenths
31. six hundred three and thirty-six thousandths
32. three thousand, eight hundred and ninety-five ten-thousandths

Name the digit in the given place in 0.713825.

33. thousandths
34. tenths
35. hundred-thousandths
36. millionths
37. hundredths
38. ten-thousandths

Give the value of each of the following digits in 36.045178.

39. 7
40. 4
41. 0
42. 8
43. 5
44. 1

45. The world's longest bridging is the Second Lake Pontchartrain Causeway near New Orleans. Its length is 38.44 km (kilometers). Write the word form of this decimal.

46. The normal annual precipitation in Phoenix is seven and fifty-three thousandths inches. Write the numeral form of this decimal.

review exercises

Round to the place of the underlined digit.

1. 4<u>9</u>5
2. 2006
3. 87<u>3</u>1
4. 10,<u>4</u>22
5. 349<u>7</u>
6. <u>6</u>8
7. <u>1</u>25
8. 2<u>3</u>94
9. <u>6</u>533
10. 9<u>9</u>,421

10-2 ROUNDING DECIMALS

At the 1948 Summer Olympic Games, Wally Ris's winning time in the Men's 100-Meter Freestyle was clocked at 57.25 s. However, the record books often report this time as 57.3 s. The time has been rounded *to the nearest tenth* of a second.

To round a decimal to a given place, use the following method.

1. Circle the digit in the place to which you are rounding.

2. If the digit to the right of the circle is *less than 5*, copy the circled digit. If the digit to the right of the circle is *5 or more*, add 1 to the circled digit.

3. Drop the digits to the right of the circle.

5 7 . ②5 ← The digit to the right of the circle is 5, so add 1 to the circled digit.

5 7 . 3

example 1

a. Round 1.398 to the nearest hundredth.
b. Round 0.0736 to the place of the leading digit.

solution

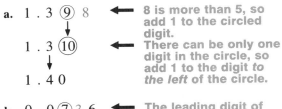

a. 1 . 3 ⑨ 8 ← 8 is more than 5, so add 1 to the circled digit.

1 . 3 ⑩ ← There can be only one digit in the circle, so add 1 to the digit *to the left* of the circle.

1 . 4 0

b. 0 . 0 ⑦ 3 6 ← The leading digit of a decimal is its first nonzero digit.

0 . 0 7

your turn

Round to the indicated place.

1. 12.07; nearest tenth
2. 0.4195; nearest thousandth
3. 0.0819; nearest hundredth
4. 24.81; nearest whole number

Round to the place of the leading digit.

5. 0.028
6. 1.405
7. 0.962
8. 0.0053

Rounding an amount of money *to the nearest dollar* is the same as rounding to the nearest whole number. Rounding *to the nearest cent* is the same as rounding to the nearest hundredth.

example 2

a. Round $17.50 to the nearest dollar.

b. Round $.0743 to the nearest cent.

solution

a. $ 1⑦ . 5 0 ⟵ **The digit to the right of the circle is 5, so add 1 to the circled digit.**

$ 1 8

b. $. 0 ⑦ 4 3 ⟵ **4 is less than 5, so copy the circled digit.**

$. 0 7

your turn

Round to the indicated place.

9. $19.98; nearest dollar

10. $14.49; nearest dollar

11. $1.098; nearest cent

12. $7.666; nearest cent

practice *exercises*

practice for example 1 (page 215)

Round to the indicated place.

1. 0.251; nearest tenth

2. 0.7983; nearest thousandth

3. 8.146; nearest tenth

4. 9.1999; nearest whole number

5. 2.7961; nearest hundredth

6. 0.0015; nearest thousandth

Round to the place of the leading digit.

7. 27.4

8. 60.5

9. 0.837

10. 0.461

11. 0.0925

12. 0.0883

13. 0.0019

14. 0.0096

practice for example 2 (page 216)

Round to the nearest dollar.

15. $1.16

16. $8.49

17. $319.94

18. $5999.50

19. $29.75

20. $356.49

21. $27.092

22. $67.77

Round to the nearest cent.

23. $.365

24. $2.848

25. $4.998

26. $62.1648

27. $5.555

28. $6.097

29. $3.3339

30. $1.7909

Round to the place of the underlined digit.

31. 1.0̲5

32. 83.57̲19

33. 0.009̲6

34. 23.306̲4

35. 9.70̲86

36. 0.99̲52

37. 351.16̲7

38. 41.4̲5

39. 0.3̲445

40. 0.161̲1

41. 4.579̲7

42. 7.0̲20

43. 6.99̲5

44. 12.509̲7

45. $.46̲5

46. $3.247̲9

47. List the letters of *all* the numbers that round to 2.8.
   a. 2.75   **b.** 2.85   **c.** 2.709   **d.** 2.809

48. Write four numbers that round to 0.03.

49. In 1976 an Olympic downhill ski champion averaged 102.889 km/h (kilometers per hour) skiing in Innsbruck, Austria. Round this number to the nearest tenth.

50. Jim and Sue bought milk, peanut butter, and bread for $4.77. Round this total to the nearest dollar.

review *exercises*

Compare. Replace each ___?___ with >, <, or =.

1. 14,239 __?__ 114,139

2. 3650 __?__ 3605

3. $5724 __?__ $5699

4. $7266 __?__ $7266

5. 6247 __?__ 6244

6. 10,001 __?__ 10,010

Write each product in lowest terms.

7. $\frac{14}{15} \times \frac{5}{7}$

8. $\frac{2}{9} \times \frac{3}{5}$

9. $\frac{5}{8} \times 400$

10. $\frac{1}{4} \times 300$

11. $\frac{2}{3} \times 144$

12. $\frac{3}{5} \times 135$

13. $\frac{2}{3} \times \frac{1}{2}$

14. $\frac{7}{10} \times \frac{5}{42}$

puzzle corner

What is the total number of squares in the figure?

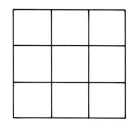

10-3 COMPARING DECIMALS

The length of the Golden Gate Bridge is 1.28 km (kilometers). The length of the Mackinac Bridge is 1.158 km. If you compare 1.28 and 1.158, you find that the Golden Gate Bridge is longer.

   To compare two decimals, use the following method.

1. If one decimal has a greater whole-number part, then it is the greater decimal.

2. If the whole-number parts are the same, compare the decimal part from left to right. Find the first place in which the digits are different. The decimal with the greater digit in that place is the greater decimal.

3. Insert the correct symbol (>, <, or =) between the numbers.

same
↓
1.$\boxed{2}$8
1.$\boxed{1}$5 8
2 > 1
So 1.28 > 1.158.

---

example 1

Compare. Replace each __?__ with >, <, or =.

a. 4.6298 __?__ 4.6307

b. 0.6340 __?__ 0.634

solution

a. 4 . 6 $\boxed{2}$ 9 8   2 < 3
4 . 6 $\boxed{3}$ 0 7   So 4.6298 < 4.6307.

b. 0 . 6 3 4 $\boxed{0}$ ⟵ A zero at the end of a decimal does not change the value of the decimal.
0 . 6 3 4 $\boxed{}$
So 0.6340 = 0.634.

your turn

Compare. Replace each __?__ with >, <, or =.

1. 2.776 __?__ 2.856   **2.** 1.07 __?__ 1.032   **3.** 2.93 __?__ 2.930

---

example 2

Write the numbers in order from least to greatest: 0.47; 0.407; 0.047

solution

0 . $\boxed{4}$ 7   0 < 4, so
0 . $\boxed{4}$ 0 7   0.047 is the
0 . $\boxed{0}$ 4 7   *least* number.

0 . 4 $\boxed{7}$ 7 > 0, so
0 . 4 $\boxed{0}$ 7   0.47 is the
                      greatest number.

The numbers in order from least to greatest: 0.047; 0.407; 0.47

your turn

Write each set of numbers in order from least to greatest.

4. 2.54; 2.09; 2.89   **5.** 0.203; 0.31; 0.312

6. 0.33; 0.333; 0.033   **7.** 9.801; 9.981; 9.81

practice exercises

practice for example 1 (page 218)

Compare. Replace each __?__ with >, <, or =.

1. 1.1 __?__ 1.09
2. 0.50 __?__ 0.059
3. 1.6 __?__ 1.60
4. 4 __?__ 4.00
5. 6.38 __?__ 6.4
6. 9.873 __?__ 9.875
7. 0.76 __?__ 0.077
8. 5.462 __?__ 5.459
9. 6.2 __?__ 6.247
10. 2.01 __?__ 2.1
11. 0.065 __?__ 0.075
12. 3.95 __?__ 3.949

practice for example 2 (page 218)

Write each set of numbers in order from least to greatest.

13. 2.25; 0.52; 1.95
14. 5.04; 4.44; 0.4
15. 4.05; 4.51; 4.5
16. 16.75; 16.7; 16.07
17. 1.023; 3.201; 3.102
18. 2.762; 6.762; 6.862
19. 0.566; 0.506; 0.56
20. 7.35; 7.355; 3.759

mixed practice (page 218)

Tell whether each statement is _true_ or _false_.

21. 55.6 > 56.5
22. 6.75 > 6.8
23. 30 = 30.0
24. 44.3 = 44.30
25. 51.2 < 52.2
26. 18.99 < 18.09
27. 0.3 > 0.33
28. 0.29 > 0.26
29. 7.967 < 7.977
30. 4.329 < 4.3
31. 122.49 < 122.59
32. 65.03 > 65.35

Write each set of numbers in order from least to greatest.

33. 1.38; 3.18; 8.13; 11.13
34. 10.1; 10.11; 11.1; 11.01
35. 6.36; 3.66; 6.30; 3.63
36. 0.965; 0.956; 0.444; 0.404

37. The Laker family is trying to obtain the least mortgage loan rate that is available. They found these available rates.

11.05;   11.15;   12.25;   12.55;   11.5;   11.75;   12.1;   12.5

List these rates in order from least to greatest.

38. Baseball batting champions often have batting averages that are extremely close. List these ten recent champion batting averages in order from least to greatest.

0.332 0.318 0.350 0.364 0.359
0.388 0.333 0.361 0.368 0.357

review *exercises*

Write the word form of each number.

1. 3.57
2. 0.17
3. 103.436
4. 0.1025
5. 4.069
6. 182.09
7. 9.0231
8. 5.002

Find each difference.

9. 92 − 78
10. 55 − 46
11. 307 − 218
12. 966 − 47
13. 9853 − 2043
14. 1235 − 146
15. 7680 − 924
16. 7809 − 3075

calculator corner

A calculator does not always display a number exactly as you enter it. A whole number may be displayed with a decimal point, and certain zeros will be omitted.

example Enter the number 8.50. Then press ⊟.

solution The calculator will not display the last zero. It will display 8.50 as "**8.5**".

Enter each number or expression into a calculator. Then press ⊟. Write the number that appears in the calculator display.

1. 7
2. 00800
3. 40.00
4. 0.03
5. 40.03
6. 40.00300
7. 2.5 + 2.5
8. 2.5 + 2.50
9. 2.500 + 2.500

10-4 WRITING DECIMALS AS FRACTIONS

The region at the right is divided into one hundred equal parts. Sixty-three parts are shaded. You can use either a decimal or a fraction to represent the shaded part of the region.

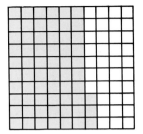

63 hundredths = $0.63 = \dfrac{63}{100}$ ← number of shaded parts
← total number of parts

You can often write a decimal less than one as a fraction whose denominator is a power of ten.

example 1

Write each decimal as a fraction in lowest terms.

a. 0.103   **b.** 0.6

solution

a. $0.103 = \dfrac{103}{1000}$ ← **103 thousandths**   **b.** $0.6 = \dfrac{6}{10} = \dfrac{3}{5}$ ← **Write in lowest terms.**

your turn

Write each decimal as a fraction in lowest terms.

1. 0.9	**2.** 0.221	**3.** 0.4
4. 0.24	**5.** 0.825	**6.** 0.307

If a decimal is greater than one, you can write it as a mixed number in lowest terms.

example 2

Write each decimal as a mixed number in lowest terms.

a. 21.09   **b.** 7.125

solution

a. $21.09 = 21\dfrac{9}{100}$ ← **21 and 9 hundredths**   **b.** $7.125 = 7\dfrac{125}{1000} = 7\dfrac{1}{8}$

your turn

Write each decimal as a mixed number in lowest terms.

7. 9.7	**8.** 44.08	**9.** 293.8
10. 90.63	**11.** 5.022	**12.** 15.713

practice *exercises*

practice for example 1 (page 221)

Write each decimal as a fraction in lowest terms.

1. 0.3   **2.** 0.401   **3.** 0.5   **4.** 0.675   **5.** 0.62

6. 0.082   **7.** 0.07   **8.** 0.999   **9.** 0.168   **10.** 0.755

practice for example 2 (page 221)

Write each decimal as a mixed number in lowest terms.

11. 5.21   **12.** 3.9   **13.** 1.034   **14.** 4.6   **15.** 46.897

16. 127.07   **17.** 17.85   **18.** 8.248   **19.** 55.63   **20.** 2.02

mixed practice (page 221)

Write each decimal as a fraction or mixed number in lowest terms.

21. 0.77   **22.** 0.025   **23.** 8.505   **24.** 33.2   **25.** 16.941

26. 0.64   **27.** 0.86   **28.** 287.4   **29.** 0.009   **30.** 49.36

Write both a decimal and a fraction in lowest terms to represent the shaded part of each region.

31. 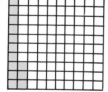   **32.** 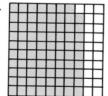   **33.** 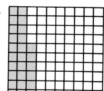   **34.**

review *exercises*

Write a simpler fraction as an estimate of each fraction.

1. $\frac{51}{100}$ **2.** $\frac{26}{101}$ **3.** $\frac{31}{90}$ **4.** $\frac{44}{65}$ **5.** $\frac{59}{99}$

6. $\frac{32}{41}$ **7.** $\frac{5}{51}$ **8.** $\frac{79}{101}$ **9.** $\frac{34}{70}$ **10.** $\frac{12}{37}$

11. How many bunches of six flowers each can Mr. Jones make with 474 flowers?

12. If Joan rides her bicycle for 25 min a day, how many minutes does she ride in six days?

10-5 WRITING FRACTIONS AS DECIMALS

Pete has 3 hits in 8 times at bat. You could say that he has hit safely $\frac{3}{8}$ of the times that he was at bat. His coach writes the fraction as a decimal and records his batting average as 0.375.

To write a fraction as a decimal, use the following method.

1. Write the fraction as a division.
2. Place a decimal point after the dividend. Place a decimal point directly above in the quotient.
3. Annex zeros as needed to divide.

$$\frac{3}{8} \rightarrow 8\overline{)3} \rightarrow 8\overline{)3.} \rightarrow 8\overline{)3.000}$$

$$\begin{array}{r} 0.375 \\ 8\overline{)3.000} \\ \underline{2\ 4} \\ 60 \\ \underline{56} \\ 40 \\ \underline{40} \\ 0 \end{array}$$

example 1

a. $\frac{2}{5} \rightarrow$
$$\begin{array}{r} 0.4 \\ 5\overline{)2.0} \\ \underline{2\ 0} \\ 0 \end{array}$$

So $\frac{2}{5} = 0.4$.

Divide until the remainder is zero.

b. $6\frac{2}{5} = 6 + \frac{2}{5} = 6 + 0.4 = 6.4$

your turn

Write each fraction or mixed number as a decimal.

1. $\frac{4}{5}$

2. $\frac{6}{25}$

3. $\frac{7}{40}$

4. $2\frac{1}{2}$

example 2

$\frac{2}{3} \rightarrow$
$$\begin{array}{r} 0.666\ldots \\ 3\overline{)2.000} \\ \underline{1\ 8} \\ 20 \\ \underline{18} \\ 20 \\ \underline{18} \\ 2 \end{array}$$

← **The digit 6 will always repeat.**

← **The remainder will always be 2.**

You can round a *repeating decimal* like 0.666... to the nearest hundredth.

$0.666\ldots \approx 0.67$ ← **$\approx$ means *is approximately equal to.***

So $\frac{2}{3} \approx 0.67$.

your turn

Write each fraction as a decimal rounded to the nearest hundredth.

5. $\frac{1}{3}$

6. $\frac{4}{9}$

7. $\frac{5}{18}$

8. $\frac{9}{11}$

Some simple fractions can be estimates for decimals. For example, you could say that $\frac{1}{2}$ is an estimate for 0.49, 0.52, or 0.514.

example 3

Estimate each decimal as a simple fraction.

a. 0.092 **b.** 0.27 **c.** 0.6597 **d.** 0.7613

solution

a. $\frac{1}{10}$ **b.** $\frac{1}{4}$ **c.** $\frac{2}{3}$ **d.** $\frac{3}{4}$

your turn

Estimate each decimal as a simple fraction.

9. 0.512 **10.** 0.897 **11.** 0.345 **12.** 0.413

practice exercises

practice for example 1 (page 223)

Write each fraction or mixed number as a decimal.

1. $\frac{9}{10}$ **2.** $\frac{3}{20}$ **3.** $\frac{1}{8}$ **4.** $\frac{1}{20}$

5. $\frac{1}{4}$ **6.** $\frac{3}{5}$ **7.** $\frac{7}{8}$ **8.** $\frac{3}{40}$

9. $4\frac{2}{5}$ **10.** $2\frac{3}{8}$ **11.** $3\frac{1}{25}$ **12.** $9\frac{9}{50}$

practice for example 2 (page 223)

Write each fraction as a decimal rounded to the nearest hundredth.

13. $\frac{1}{9}$ **14.** $\frac{1}{6}$ **15.** $\frac{5}{6}$ **16.** $\frac{2}{9}$ **17.** $\frac{8}{11}$

18. $\frac{2}{15}$ **19.** $\frac{7}{18}$ **20.** $\frac{13}{15}$ **21.** $\frac{11}{18}$ **22.** $\frac{10}{11}$

practice for example 3 (page 224)

Estimate each decimal as a simple fraction.

23. 0.498 **24.** 0.3296 **25.** 0.2503 **26.** 0.118 **27.** 0.7338

28. 0.589 **29.** 0.67 **30.** 0.198 **31.** 0.533 **32.** 0.0966

mixed practice (pages 223–224)

Write each fraction as a decimal. If the decimal is a repeating decimal, round it to the nearest hundredth.

33. $\frac{1}{2}$ 34. $\frac{2}{25}$ 35. $\frac{1}{3}$ 36. $\frac{3}{250}$ 37. $\frac{17}{30}$

38. $6\frac{2}{3}$ 39. $3\frac{5}{9}$ 40. $\frac{7}{9}$ 41. $\frac{13}{18}$ 42. $\frac{7}{11}$

Match each decimal with its estimated simple fraction.

43. 0.6633 44. 0.799 45. 0.26 46. 0.8002 A. $\frac{1}{3}$ B. $\frac{4}{5}$ C. $\frac{2}{3}$ D. $\frac{1}{4}$

47. 0.3297 48. 0.2612 49. 0.34 50. 0.248

review exercises

Round to the indicated place.

1. $2.7\underline{5}$ 2. $0.6\underline{3}85$ 3. $0.43\underline{4}3$
4. $19.9\underline{9}5$ 5. $0.67\underline{1}3$ 6. $3.0\underline{9}8$

7. Tickets for rides at the fair cost $1 each. Lou had $25. He bought 10 tickets, used all 10, and bought 5 more. How much money did he have left?

8. Jill needs 50 oz of beans to make chili. She has three 12-oz cans and one 8-oz can of beans. How many more ounces does she need?

mental math

You should be able to mentally interchange certain simple fractions and their decimal equivalents.

Write the equivalent fraction in lowest terms.

1. 0.1 2. 0.3 3. 0.5 4. 0.25 5. 0.75 6. 0.4
7. 0.6 8. 0.8 9. 0.01 10. 0.001 11. $0.333\ldots$ 12. $0.666\ldots$

Write the equivalent decimal.

13. $\frac{1}{2}$ 14. $\frac{1}{10}$ 15. $\frac{1}{4}$ 16. $\frac{7}{10}$ 17. $\frac{3}{4}$ 18. $\frac{1}{5}$

19. $\frac{1}{3}$ 20. $\frac{1}{100}$ 21. $\frac{2}{5}$ 22. $\frac{3}{5}$ 23. $\frac{4}{5}$ 24. $\frac{2}{3}$

10-6 IDENTIFYING TOO MUCH OR TOO LITTLE INFORMATION

Some problems supply more information than you need to solve them. Other problems may not supply enough information.

example

If possible, solve. If it is not possible to solve, tell what additional information is needed.

a. Find the cost of three tablecloths, each 68 in. long and 52 in. wide. Each tablecloth costs $18.

b. Sarah paid for some compact discs with $40. Each compact disc costs the same. She received $3 in change. What did each disc cost?

solution

a. **Step 1** Given: Cost of each tablecloth is $18.
  Each tablecloth is 68 in. long and 52 in. wide. ◄— **This information is not needed.**
  Find: Cost of three tablecloths.

Step 2 Multiply $18 × 3.

Step 3 $18 × 3 = $54

Step 4 Estimate to check: $20 × 3 = $60 ◄— **$54 is a reasonable answer.**

Three tablecloths cost $54.

b. **Step 1** Given: Sarah received $3 change from $40.
  Find: Cost of each compact disc.

Step 2 You can determine that Sarah paid $40 − $3 = $37.

You cannot solve the problem. To find the cost of each disc, you need to know *how many discs* Sarah bought.

problems

If possible, solve. If it is not possible to solve, tell what additional information is needed.

1. Alan is 68 in. tall and weighs 150 lb. He grew 4 in. in the past year. How tall was he one year ago?

2. Four thirteen-inch tires weigh a total of 88 lb and cost $324 altogether. Find the cost of one thirteen-inch tire.

3. A bat and 2 balls cost a total of $22. What is the cost of the bat?

4. Food for the party cost $28, and party supplies cost $8. Renee and her friends have agreed to share the total cost of food and supplies equally. How much will each pay?

5. Darryl sells magazine subscriptions and receives a weekly salary of $138. He also receives a $2 bonus for each subscription that he sells. Last week he sold 29 subscriptions. What was the amount of his bonus?

6. Mrs. Malik grows strawberries, packs them in pints, and sells them to the local market for 80¢/pt. How many packing crates does she need in order to ship 160 pt of strawberries to the market?

7. In shopping for a popular recording, Marcy found that the cost of the compact disc is $9 more than the cost of the album, and the cost of the cassette is $3 less than the cost of the album. How much less than the cost of the compact disc is the cost of the cassette?

8. Dan is 13 years old and is 5 years older than Tom. How old will Harry be in 8 years, if Tom is two years older than Harry is now?

review exercises

If possible, solve. If it is not possible to solve, tell what additional information is needed.

1. Lynette drove her 1987 car to Midville, which was 192 mi from her home. On the trip she used 6 gal of gasoline costing $92\frac{1}{2}$¢/gal. How many miles did her car average per gallon of gasoline?

2. Marjorie finished 26 of the 30 math problems on the test. She had 8 min left to finish the test. What is the average number of minutes she could spend on each of the remaining problems?

3. Myron bought 4 shirts for $20 apiece. He also bought 12 pairs of socks. How much did Myron pay for the shirts and the socks?

SKILL REVIEW

Write the word form of each decimal.

1. 0.79
2. 0.3
3. 4.259
4. 16.03
5. 295.95
6. 2.007
7. 4677.1
8. 0.6081

10-1

Round to the place of the underlined digit.

9. 0.7502
10. 9.8504
11. 0.1387
12. 52.97

10-2

13. Talia bought sweaters and a blouse for $35.52. Round this amount to the nearest dollar.

Compare. Replace each __?__ with >, <, or =.

14. 3.35 __?__ 3.277
15. 56.2 __?__ 56.20
16. 7.06 __?__ 7.6
17. 0.4365 __?__ 0.4344

10-3

18. Three of the world's volcanoes are similar in height. The height of Mauna Kea is 4.205 km (kilometers). The height of Mauna Loa is 4.170 km, and the height of Mount Wrangell is 4.317 km. List the heights in order from least to greatest.

Write each decimal as a fraction or mixed number in lowest terms.

19. 0.17
20. 0.9
21. 7.25
22. 0.84
23. 36.111
24. 0.557
25. 94.208
26. 0.442

10-4

Write each fraction or mixed number as a decimal. If the decimal is a repeating decimal, round it to the nearest hundredth.

27. $\frac{1}{5}$
28. $\frac{5}{8}$
29. $7\frac{1}{6}$
30. $\frac{8}{9}$
31. $\frac{2}{11}$
32. $6\frac{13}{20}$
33. $\frac{7}{8}$
34. $\frac{4}{15}$

10-5

Estimate each decimal as a simple fraction.

35. 0.6712
36. 0.248
37. 0.51
38. 0.7406
39. 0.21
40. 0.098
41. 0.342
42. 0.61

If possible, solve. If it is not possible to solve, tell what additional information is needed.

43. Sue's score on a test was 72. Joe's score was 75, and the class average was 79. How much lower was Sue's score than Joe's?

10-6

44. Carl paid $4 for his books. How much did each book cost?

10-7 WRITING CHECKS

A checking account is a safe, easy way to manage your money. You can pay for an item by writing a check. Most checks are similar to the one below.

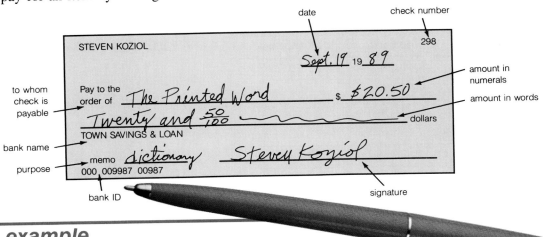

example

Use the check above.

a. Who wrote the check?

c. To whom is the check payable?

b. On what date was the check written?

d. What is the amount of the check?

solution

a. Steven Koziol

c. The Printed Word

b. September 19, 1989

d. $20.50

exercises

Write the amount in words as if on a check.

1. $28.43   2. $5.25   3. $127.98

4. $63.35   5. $577.09   6. $1707.60

Use the check at the right.

7. Who wrote the check?

8. To whom is the check payable?

9. For what purpose was the check written?

10. What is the name of the bank?

11. Write the amount in numeral form.

12. Why do you think it is important to number each check?

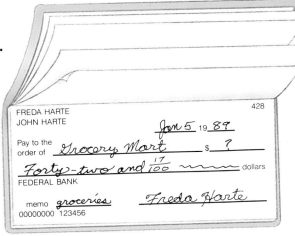

10-8 READ AND WRITE GREATER NUMBERS

The chart shows the value of exports and imports for several countries in 1984. The amounts are given in a short word form that includes decimals.

Value of Exports and Imports for 1984

Country	Exports	Imports
Burma	$310.0 million	$239.0 million
Italy	73.3 billion	84.2 billion
Pakistan	2.6 billion	5.9 billion
Somalia	45.1 million	109.2 million
United States	217.9 billion	341.2 billion

example

Write the value of Italy's exports in numeral form.

solution

The value is given as $73.3 billion.
You know that 1 billion = 1,000,000,000.
So move the decimal point 9 places to the right. Annex zeros as needed.

$73.3 billion → $73.300000000 → $73,300,000,000

exercises

Write each number in numeral form.

1. 3.5 million
2. 17.6 billion
3. 219.3 billion
4. 5.4 million
5. 75.9 million
6. 100.8 billion

Use the chart above. Write each amount in numeral form.

7. the value of Pakistan's imports
8. the value of the United States' exports
9. the value of Somalia's exports
10. the value of Italy's imports

Complete each __?__ with *million* or *billion*.

11. 7,600,000 = 7.6 __?__
12. 11,500,000,000 = 11.5 __?__
13. 132,800,000 = 132.8 __?__
14. 909,900,000,000 = 909.9 __?__

Compare. Replace each __?__ with > or <.

15. 14.4 billion __?__ 98.5 million
16. 234.5 million __?__ 90.6 billion
17. 1.1 billion __?__ 833.2 million
18. 330.6 million __?__ 36.0 billion

CHAPTER REVIEW

vocabulary vo·cab·u·lar·y

Choose the correct word to complete each sentence.

1. A decimal such as 0.333... is called a *(repeating, rounded)* decimal.
2. The symbol ≈ means "is *(exactly, approximately)* equal to."

skills

Give the value of the underlined digit in each decimal.

3. 77.0<u>7</u>   4. 6.10<u>6</u>   5. 2.59348<u>2</u>   6. 0.412<u>9</u>6

Round to the nearest cent.

7. $4.1163   8. $.955   9. $9.2345   10. $7.496

Tell whether each statement is *true* or *false*.

11. 0.07 = 0.070   12. 6.213 < 6.123   13. 0.64 > 0.74   14. 0.9892 < 0.9884

Write each decimal or mixed number as a fraction in lowest terms.

15. 0.1   16. 0.888   17. 3.48   18. 40.997

Write each fraction as a decimal. If the decimal is a repeating decimal, round it to the nearest hundredth.

19. $\frac{7}{10}$ 20. $\frac{9}{25}$ 21. $\frac{2}{9}$ 22. $\frac{4}{11}$ 23. $\frac{5}{6}$

24. $\frac{17}{20}$ 25. $\frac{3}{8}$ 26. $\frac{37}{40}$ 27. $\frac{8}{15}$ 28. $\frac{1}{18}$

29. Describe a method to round a decimal to a given place.
30. Sue, Fran, and Jill each bought a new record album. Sue paid $6.98 and Fran paid $7.50. Who of the three paid the least? If possible, solve. If it is not possible to solve, tell what additional information is needed.

Write the amount in words as if on a check.

31. $4.87   32. $422.60   33. $60.01   34. $72.09

Complete.

35. 7,900,000 = __?__ million

36. 846,700,000,000 = __?__ billion

CHAPTER TEST

Write the short word form of each decimal.

1. 0.6
2. 21.21
3. 0.005
4. 457.07
5. 0.0009
6. 0.8043
7. 5476.3
8. 0.869

10-1

Round to the place of the underlined digit.

9. 22.6<u>0</u>7
10. $3.<u>9</u>4
11. 0.50<u>9</u>5
12. 1.8<u>9</u>5
13. 0.443<u>3</u>5
14. $12.<u>9</u>7
15. 8.5<u>6</u>2
16. 76.00<u>8</u>1

10-2

17. The average depth of the Indian Ocean is 3.963 km (kilometers). Round this number to the nearest tenth.

Tell whether each statement is *true* or *false*.

18. $47.9953 > 47.9553$
19. $0.325 < 0.308$
20. $6.238 < 6.23$
21. $5.702 > 5.7008$

10-3

22. For the last four seasons, the town hockey team averaged the following number of goals per game: 3.3, 3.03, 3.23, and 3.31. List these averages in order from least to greatest.

Write each decimal as a fraction or mixed number in lowest terms.

23. 0.7
24. 0.88
25. 0.4
26. 0.14
27. 6.222
28. 40.003
29. 89.17
30. 6.275

10-4

Write each fraction or mixed number as a decimal. If the decimal is a repeating decimal, round it to the nearest hundredth.

31. $\frac{9}{40}$
32. $7\frac{7}{8}$
33. $250\frac{7}{20}$
34. $\frac{3}{10}$
35. $\frac{3}{5}$
36. $\frac{11}{15}$
37. $\frac{1}{6}$
38. $\frac{7}{9}$

10-5

39. Mrs. Carr bought one container of yogurt for 75¢. How much change did she receive? If possible, solve. If it is not possible to solve, tell what additional information is needed.

10-6

Write each amount in numeral form.

40. Thirty-five dollars and twelve cents
41. One hundred sixty-nine dollars and five cents

10-7

Write each number in numeral form.

42. 84.3 billion
43. 179.2 million
44. 10.1 million

10-8

The United States uses a decimal system of currency. Skill in adding and subtracting decimals is helpful when you work with money.

CHAPTER 11

ADDING AND SUBTRACTING DECIMALS

11-1 ADDING DECIMALS

Members of a Drama Club sold tickets to the club's play. The top four sellers were Julia, with $65.00 worth of ticket sales; Nathan, with $52.25; Jesse, with $40.75; and Pam, with $33.50. When you add, you find that the total amount of their ticket sales was $191.50.

To add two or more decimals, use the following method.

1. Line up the decimal points.
2. Add the digits in each place-value column. If the sum is 10 or more, rename.
3. Continue column-by-column from right to left.
4. Place the decimal point in the sum directly under the decimal points in the addends.

$$
\begin{array}{r}
\overset{1\ \ 1\ \ \downarrow\ 1}{\$6\ 5\ .\ 0\ 0} \\
5\ 2\ .\ 2\ 5 \\
4\ 0\ .\ 7\ 5 \\
+\ 3\ 3\ .\ 5\ 0 \\
\hline
\$1\ 9\ 1\ .\ 5\ 0
\end{array}
$$

example 1

a.
$$
\begin{array}{r}
11.3 \\
+\ 7.5 \\
\hline
18.8
\end{array}
$$

b.
$$
\begin{array}{r}
\$6.92 \\
+\ \ .48 \\
\hline
\$7.40
\end{array}
$$

c.
$$
\begin{array}{r}
320.938 \\
600.082 \\
+\ 81.007 \\
\hline
1002.027
\end{array}
$$

your turn

Find each sum.

1.
$$
\begin{array}{r}
4.2 \\
+0.9
\end{array}
$$

2.
$$
\begin{array}{r}
56.80 \\
+16.12
\end{array}
$$

3.
$$
\begin{array}{r}
\$176.09 \\
+\ \ 23.95
\end{array}
$$

4.
$$
\begin{array}{r}
34.476 \\
8.032 \\
+\ 0.905
\end{array}
$$

example 2

Find each sum.

a. $24.25 + $5.98

b. 7.63 + 8.4

c. 0.635 + 1.2 + 4.79

solution

a.
$$
\begin{array}{r}
\$24.25 \\
+\ \ 5.98 \\
\hline
\$30.23
\end{array}
$$
← **Rewrite the addition in vertical form. Line up the decimal points.**

b.
$$
\begin{array}{r}
7.63 \\
+8.40 \\
\hline
16.03
\end{array}
$$
← **Annex zeros so there are the same number of decimal places.**

c.
$$
\begin{array}{r}
0.635 \\
1.200 \\
+4.790 \\
\hline
6.625
\end{array}
$$

your turn

Find each sum.

5. $26.25 + $7.64

6. 5.8 + 0.31

7. 3.907 + 1.11 + 40.6

example 3

Find each sum.

a. 7.99 + 0.01   **b.** 4 + 2.76   **c.** 8.1 + 0.052 + 20

solution

a. $\begin{array}{r} 7.99 \\ +0.01 \\ \hline 8.00 \end{array}$ ← You can write the sum as 8.

b. $\begin{array}{r} 4.00 \\ +2.76 \\ \hline 6.76 \end{array}$ ← Write 4 as 4.00.

c. $\begin{array}{r} 8.100 \\ 0.052 \\ +20.000 \\ \hline 28.152 \end{array}$

your turn

Find each sum.

8. 5.1 + 10.9

9. 3.37 + 2

10. 6 + 1.4 + 0.6

11. $7 + $.42 + $.05

12. 0.09 + 8 + 14.5

13. 47.008 + 2.32 + 590

practice exercises

practice for example 1 (page 234)

Find each sum.

1. $\begin{array}{r} 0.3 \\ +0.6 \end{array}$

2. $\begin{array}{r} 34.2 \\ +\ 8.1 \end{array}$

3. $\begin{array}{r} $9.64 \\ +\ 8.56 \end{array}$

4. $\begin{array}{r} $.75 \\ +\ .28 \end{array}$

5. $\begin{array}{r} 86.338 \\ +17.209 \end{array}$

6. $\begin{array}{r} 152.764 \\ +391.024 \end{array}$

7. $\begin{array}{r} 2.120 \\ 4.506 \\ +6.875 \end{array}$

8. $\begin{array}{r} 11.981 \\ 0.026 \\ +\ 3.071 \end{array}$

practice for example 2 (page 234)

Find each sum.

9. 7.4 + 6.74

10. 35.69 + 0.5

11. 8.21 + 0.933

12. 95.5 + 2.864

13. $46.58 + $23.07 + $1.92

14. 40.969 + 0.22 + 4.9

practice for example 3 (page 235)

Find each sum.

15. $.37 + $.63

16. 91.22 + 9.78

17. 8 + 3.5

18. 0.003 + 6

19. $6.56 + $30 + $.45

20. 4.2 + 11.675 + 93

Adding and Subtracting Decimals 235

Find each sum.

21.	4.5 5.4 +7.0	**22.**	1.6 3.2 +6.4	**23.**	$ 8.05 .85 + 14.10	**24.**	$52.19 48.78 + 3.52
25.	16.562 + 8.083	**26.**	102.854 + 60.307	**27.**	0.1090 +0.0042	**28.**	0.6666 +5.3334

29. $49.06 + $5 + $.32   **30.** $8 + $28 + $6.97   **31.** 50.46 + 2.54

32. 442.88 + 1057.12   **33.** 16.048 + 1.943   **34.** 0.7571 + 0.4352

35. 9.04 + 3.6 + 5.78   **36.** 95.5 + 21.06 + 12.9   **37.** 3 + 1.008 + 0.4

38. 23.03 + 7.117 + 10   **39.** 0.0053 + 3.42 + 9.706   **40.** 48.291 + 24.4 + 71.0093

Write the fraction as a decimal. Then find the sum.

41. $2 + \frac{1}{4}$ **42.** $1\frac{1}{2} + 0.6$ **43.** $6\frac{3}{4} + 2.52$ **44.** $3.375 + \frac{5}{8}$

45. In a recent year Iowa received 30.85 in. of rain and North Dakota received 16.16 in. of rain. What is the total amount of rain that fell on these states in that year?

46. At the end of each month, Sally pays $243.08 for her federal income tax and $73.94 for her state income tax. What is the total amount of federal and state income tax that Sally pays each month?

review *exercises*

Estimate by adjusting the sum of the front-end digits.

1. 206 + 347 + 459

2. 135 + 239 + 287 + 437

3. 42,569 + 22,618 + 15,989

4. 1497 + 2289 + 527 + 2754

Estimate by rounding.

5. 2484 + 6721

6. 18,216 + 49,421

7. $847 + $219 + $86

8. 367 + 418 + 295

9. $40,922 + $56,419

10. 2153 + 3500 + 942

puzzle corner

What is the next symbol in the following sequence?

    ?

11-2 ESTIMATING DECIMAL SUMS

It is useful to be able to estimate the total cost of items you buy.

$ 3.69
1.19
1.32
.79
.98
.49

example 1

Estimate by adjusting the sum of the front-end digits.

a. $3.69 + $1.19 + $1.32 + $.79 + $.98 + $.49

b. 329.5 + 255.2 + 127.6 + 118.4 + 80.8

solution

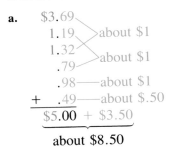

a.
$3.69
1.19 } about $1
1.32
.79 } about $1
.98 —— about $1
+ .49 —— about $.50
$5.00 + $3.50
about $8.50

TOTAL $8.46

b.
329.5
255.2 } about 100
127.6
118.4
+ 80.8 } about 100
700 + 200
about 900

your turn

Estimate by adjusting the sum of the front-end digits.

1. 631.9 + 288.6 + 158.4

2. 14.65 + 9.83 + 23.75 + 13.27

3. $2.16 + $1.49 + $.55 + $.89 + $2.49

example 2

Estimate $0.085 + 0.0629 + 0.0077$ by rounding.

solution

0.085 → 0.09 ← **Round to the place of the leading digit.**

0.0629 → 0.06

+0.0077 → +0.01 ← **0.0077 is rounded to the same place as the other addends.**

about 0.16

your turn

Estimate by rounding.

4. $47.69 + $58.35

5. 0.3418 + 0.7805

6. $84.98 + $47.69 + $7.49

7. 0.082 + 0.0399 + 0.0048

Adding and Subtracting Decimals 237

practice exercises

practice for example 1 (page 237)

Estimate by adjusting the sum of the front-end digits.

1. 58.4 + 33.5   **2.** 6.39 + 8.73   **3.** 145.96 + 961.25   **4.** 0.1109 + 0.0897

5. 314.76 + 163.51 + 119.28   **6.** $42.69 + $12.95 + $32.49 + $2.39

7. 10.26 + 9.42 + 5.43   **8.** $814.52 + $197.26 + $35.09

practice for example 2 (page 237)

Estimate by rounding.

9. 52.666 + 39.35   **10.** 345.26 + 377.4   **11.** 0.6671 + 0.4198

12. 8.45 + 3.509   **13.** 178.6 + 73.8 + 306.4   **14.** 0.6493 + 0.2955 + 0.0098

mixed practice (page 237)

Estimate.

15. $11.09 + $8.97   **16.** $16.39 + $22.57   **17.** 159.3 + 428.1 + 222.7

18. 1.68 + 3.44 + 0.89   **19.** 12.86 + 5.37 + 21.19   **20.** 176.2 + 231.9 + 47.45

Choose the letter of the best estimate.

21. 0.2468 + 0.6791   **a.** 0.8   **b.** 0.9   **c.** 1.0   **d.** 1.2

22. 0.01 + 0.001 + 0.00009   **a.** 0.01   **b.** 0.1   **c.** 1   **d.** 11

23. 46.83 + 9.3 + 4.6   **a.** 17   **b.** 50   **c.** 60   **d.** 150

24. 247 + 648.1 + 2.345   **a.** 800   **b.** 900   **c.** 1000   **d.** 1100

25. On the first three days of their vacation the Stein family drove 436.9 mi, 362.3 mi, and 87.5 mi. About how far did they drive?

26. Tom's grocery cart contains chicken costing $3.49, milk for $1.89, bananas for $1.18, a pineapple for $2.38, and two heads of lettuce for $.49 each. Estimate to determine if $9 is enough to pay for this food.

review exercises

Find each difference.

1. 502 − 288   **2.** 4090 − 1366   **3.** $1600 − $970   **4.** $2003 − $1910

5. $40,274 − $6198   **6.** $80,000 − $805   **7.** 3723 − 3687   **8.** 12,010 − 91

11-3 SUBTRACTING DECIMALS

At the beginning of the Schultzes' ski trip, their car's odometer read
9752.6 (mi). At the end of the trip, the odometer read 11043.1 (mi).
You can subtract to find that they traveled 1290.5 mi.

    To subtract two decimals, use the following method.

1. Line up the decimal points.
2. Subtract the digits in each place-value column. Rename when necessary.
3. Continue column-by-column from right to left.
4. Place the decimal point in the difference directly under the decimal points in the two numbers above.

$$
\begin{array}{r}
\text{0 10 9 14 2 | 11} \\
\cancel{1}\,\cancel{1}\,\cancel{0}\,\cancel{4}\,\cancel{3}\,.\,\cancel{1} \\
-\ \ 9\,7\,5\,2\,.\,6 \\
\hline
1\,2\,9\,0\,.\,5
\end{array}
$$

Check:
$$
\begin{array}{r}
1290.5 \\
+9752.6 \\
\hline
11043.1 \ \checkmark
\end{array}
$$

example 1

a.
$$
\begin{array}{r}
3.9 \\
-1.5 \\
\hline
2.4
\end{array}
$$

b.
$$
\begin{array}{r}
\$17.45 \\
-\ \ 6.08 \\
\hline
\$11.37
\end{array}
$$

c.
$$
\begin{array}{r}
152.374 \\
-\ \ 9.026 \\
\hline
143.348
\end{array}
$$

your turn

Find each difference.

1.
$$
\begin{array}{r}
5.3 \\
-4.1
\end{array}
$$

2.
$$
\begin{array}{r}
18.14 \\
-\ 9.60
\end{array}
$$

3.
$$
\begin{array}{r}
\$5.87 \\
-3.92
\end{array}
$$

4.
$$
\begin{array}{r}
0.647 \\
-0.583
\end{array}
$$

example 2

Find each difference.

a. $1.6 - 1.38$

b. $5.007 - 0.94$

c. $20.43 - 9.8211$

solution

a.
$$
\begin{array}{r}
1.60 \\
-1.38 \\
\hline
0.22
\end{array}
$$
← **Annex zeros so there are the same number of decimal places.**

b.
$$
\begin{array}{r}
5.007 \\
-0.940 \\
\hline
4.067
\end{array}
$$

c.
$$
\begin{array}{r}
20.4300 \\
-\ 9.8211 \\
\hline
10.6089
\end{array}
$$

your turn

Find each difference.

5. $7.8 - 3.89$

6. $4.581 - 2.3$

7. $0.512 - 0.3$

8. $61.4 - 1.4065$

example 3

Find each difference.

a. $6 - 2.47$ **b.** $10.449 - 3$ **c.** $\$8 - \$5.28$

solution

a.
$$\begin{array}{r} 6.00 \\ -2.47 \\ \hline 3.53 \end{array}$$
← Write 6 as 6.00.

b.
$$\begin{array}{r} 10.449 \\ -\ 3.000 \\ \hline 7.449 \end{array}$$

c.
$$\begin{array}{r} \$8.00 \\ -\ 5.28 \\ \hline \$2.72 \end{array}$$

your turn

Find each difference.

9. $35 - 8.2$ **10.** $7.75 - 4$ **11.** $\$17 - \$3.10$ **12.** $1 - 0.003$

practice exercises

practice for example 1 (page 239)

Find each difference.

1.
$$\begin{array}{r} 0.9 \\ -0.3 \end{array}$$

2.
$$\begin{array}{r} 6.2 \\ -2.8 \end{array}$$

3.
$$\begin{array}{r} 711.5 \\ -709.1 \end{array}$$

4.
$$\begin{array}{r} 54.0 \\ -29.9 \end{array}$$

5.
$$\begin{array}{r} 0.47 \\ -0.07 \end{array}$$

6.
$$\begin{array}{r} 8.06 \\ -0.18 \end{array}$$

7.
$$\begin{array}{r} \$5.14 \\ -\ 0.65 \end{array}$$

8.
$$\begin{array}{r} \$132.73 \\ -\ 49.16 \end{array}$$

9.
$$\begin{array}{r} 0.835 \\ -0.197 \end{array}$$

10.
$$\begin{array}{r} 33.781 \\ -\ 5.482 \end{array}$$

11.
$$\begin{array}{r} 10.1094 \\ -\ 7.0088 \end{array}$$

12.
$$\begin{array}{r} 345.0231 \\ -299.0234 \end{array}$$

practice for example 2 (page 239)

Find each difference.

13. $0.5 - 0.11$ **14.** $8.4 - 8.31$ **15.** $3.2 - 0.85$ **16.** $74.3 - 59.33$

17. $8.01 - 3.7$ **18.** $290.68 - 176.6$ **19.** $11.4 - 1.406$ **20.** $5.1 - 2.029$

21. $6.27 - 0.099$ **22.** $0.7 - 0.3262$ **23.** $4.506 - 3.5$ **24.** $25.9108 - 6.9$

practice for example 3 (page 240)

Find each difference.

25. $9 - 7.4$ **26.** $15 - 14.5$ **27.** $7.8 - 3$ **28.** $44.1 - 22$

29. $5 - 1.08$ **30.** $1000.7 - 82$ **31.** $\$23 - \$8.59$ **32.** $\$4 - \$1.34$

33. $62.075 - 58$ **34.** $15.7036 - 12$ **35.** $8 - 6.181$ **36.** $9 - 2.3008$

Find each answer.

37.
$$\begin{array}{r} \$3.58 \\ -\ 2.49 \\ \hline \end{array}$$

38.
$$\begin{array}{r} \$309.17 \\ -\ \ \ 3.09 \\ \hline \end{array}$$

39.
$$\begin{array}{r} 0.0526 \\ -0.0256 \\ \hline \end{array}$$

40.
$$\begin{array}{r} 8.0460 \\ -5.0771 \\ \hline \end{array}$$

41. $25.8 - 7.5$

42. $0.0014 - 0.0003$

43. $\$1 - \$0.02$

44. $15.09 - 13.3$

45. $\$6.96 - \$4.99$

46. $4.685 - 1.6$

47. $197 - 102.808$

48. $7.381 - 2.5$

49. $89.03 - 61.074$

50. $4.4 - 1.1122$

51. $3.96 + 1.4 - 2.559$

52. $6 - 5.8 + 7.062$

Write the fraction as a decimal. Then find the difference.

53. $8 - \dfrac{1}{5}$

54. $5\dfrac{1}{5} - 3.2$

55. $9.16 - 2\dfrac{3}{4}$

56. $7\dfrac{7}{8} - 1.95$

57. The highest reading on the barometric pressure scale was 32 in Siberia, USSR. The lowest reading was 25.69 in Guam. How much higher was the reading in Siberia than the reading in Guam?

58. Sophia had $5.50. She received her allowance of $4 and spent $7.42 for an umbrella. How much money did she have left?

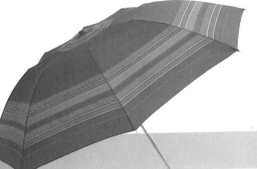

review exercises

Estimate by rounding.

1. $669 - 384$

2. $8269 - 2482$

3. $5829 - 3167$

4. $81,926 - 27,264$

5. $\$649 - \$552$

6. $3389 - 2557$

7. $5528 - 482$

8. $46,852 - 4783$

calculator corner

If you understand place value, you can use addition and subtraction on a calculator to correct an incorrect decimal entry in one step.

example Enter 7.208. Correct it to 7.258 in one step.

solution 7.208 + 0.05 = 7.258 ◄— Increase the hundredths' place by 0.05.

Enter the first number. Correct it to the second number in one step.

1. $36.02 \rightarrow 36.22$

2. $0.084 \rightarrow 0.004$

3. $9.5 \rightarrow 49.5$

4. $18.77 \rightarrow 18.07$

5. $2.316 \rightarrow 2.318$

6. $0.5291 \rightarrow 0.5231$

11-4 ESTIMATING DECIMAL DIFFERENCES

The ninth grade at the Bayside High School Fair raised $467.50 at its booth. The tenth grade raised $271.75 at its booth. You could estimate as shown in part (a) of the following example to find that the ninth grade raised about $200 more.

example 1

Estimate by rounding to the place of the leading digit.

a. $467.50 - $271.75   **b.** 55.9 - 8.4

solution

a.
$$
\begin{array}{rcr}
\$467.50 & \rightarrow & \$500 \\
-\ 271.75 & \rightarrow & -\ 300 \\
\hline
& & \text{about } \$200
\end{array}
$$

b.
$$
\begin{array}{rcr}
55.9 & \rightarrow & 60 \\
-\ 8.4 & \rightarrow & -10 \\
\hline
& & \text{about } 50
\end{array}
$$
⬅ **Round 8.4 to the same place as 55.9.**

your turn

Estimate by rounding to the place of the leading digit.

1. 956.37 - 332.09   **2.** $87.47 - $16.69   **3.** 3292.6 - 926.8

Sometimes you need to round to a place other than that of the leading digit in order to get a good estimate.

example 2

Estimate by rounding to appropriate digits.

a. $347.50 - $271.75   **b.** 56.75 - 4.98

solution

a. Round to the tens' place to avoid an estimate of $0.
$$
\begin{array}{rcr}
\$347.50 & \rightarrow & \$350 \\
-\ 271.75 & \rightarrow & -\ 270 \\
\hline
& & \text{about } \$80
\end{array}
$$

b. Round to the ones' place to avoid an estimate greater than 56.75.
$$
\begin{array}{rcr}
56.75 & \rightarrow & 57 \\
-\ 4.98 & \rightarrow & -\ 5 \\
\hline
& & \text{about } 52
\end{array}
$$

your turn

Estimate by rounding to appropriate digits.

4. 44.54 - 35.35   **5.** 4.637 - 0.4237   **6.** 7.387 - 6.629

practice *exercises*

practice for example 1 (page 242)

Estimate by rounding to the place of the leading digit.

1. $88.63 − $15.07　　　　**2.** 9.5 − 2.6784　　　　**3.** 0.463 − 0.1237

4. 0.996 − 0.613　　　　　**5.** $21.95 − $8.79　　　**6.** 8.694 − 0.758

practice for example 2 (page 242)

Estimate by rounding to appropriate digits.

7. 3345.1 − 2961.2　　　　**8.** 107.6 − 63.9　　　**9.** $85.21 − $4.75

10. $272.49 − $43.89　　　**11.** $112.53 − $78.05　　**12.** 0.5674 − 0.0427

mixed practice (page 242)

Estimate.

13. $46.08 − $17.37　　　　**14.** 0.805 − 0.6902　　　**15.** $21.37 − $15.13

16. 1.576 − 0.481　　　　　**17.** 0.556 − 0.2196　　　**18.** $1456.06 − $743.39

19. Ken earned $21,865.75 this year and $18,789.98 last year. Estimate the increase in his pay.

20. Kathy earned $24.75 and $35.95 last month. She spent $18.98 for a sweater. About how much money does she have left?

review *exercises*

Find each product.

1. 6 × 400　　　　**2.** 50 × 900　　　**3.** 800 × 300　　　**4.** 9000 × 9000

5. 2 × 73,859　　**6.** 28 × 837　　　**7.** 92 × 516　　　**8.** 304 × 2903

mental math

To subtract 1.99 from 8.75 mentally, first subtract 2, then add 0.01.

　　8.75 − 2 = 6.75　　　6.75 + 0.01 = 6.76　　　So 8.75 − 1.99 = 6.76.

Add or subtract mentally.

1. 9.86 − 5.99　　　**2.** $2.67 + $3.99　　　**3.** $9.32 + $1.99　　　**4.** 8.22 − 2.99

5. 28.3 − 7.9　　　**6.** 15.4 + 7.9　　　　**7.** $13.99 + $4.99　　**8.** $5.99 + $3.98

SKILL REVIEW

Find each sum.

1. 32.4
   +15.2

2. 47.9
   + 6.1

3. $21.04
   + 73.56

4. 2.783
   0.495
   +6.570 **11-1**

5. $59.45 + $1.55

6. 13.22 + 8.3

7. 71.325 + 14.92

8. 2.796 + 15.9

9. $4 + $2.65 + $.78

10. 9.45 + 6 + 0.003

Estimate by adjusting the sum of the front-end digits.

11. $4.95 + $2.30 + $.68

12. 312.7 + 473.2 + 484.5 + 122.1 **11-2**

13. 0.343 + 0.904 + 0.263

14. 45.39 + 5.23 + 12.17 + 3.40

Estimate by rounding.

15. $42.95 + $24.36

16. 14.3 + 24.9 + 6.2

17. 0.7593 + 0.0921

18. 0.3421 + 0.762 + 0.0593

19. Four performances of the senior play raised $297.25, $356.50, $324.75, and $329.50. About how much was raised altogether?

Find each difference.

20. $3.25
    − 1.06

21. 24.2
    −16.3

22. 3.500
    −0.402

23. 48.30
    −36.29 **11-3**

24. 300.7 − 85.9

25. $69.29 − $4.75

26. 0.9263 − 0.0875

27. 1.032 − 0.52

28. 63.8 − 12.87

29. 7 − 3.1614

30. Joe went to the grocery store with $10 and spent $6.20. How much money did he have left?

Estimate by rounding to the place of the leading digit.

31. 32.971 − 19.347

32. 0.7456 − 0.2499 **11-4**

Estimate by rounding to appropriate digits.

33. 916.3 − 880.4

34. $17.62 − $4.95

Estimate.

35. $495.21 − $109.15

36. 84.2 − 36.9

37. 3654.5 − 299.3

38. 4.292 − 3.871

11-5 CHECKBOOK REGISTERS

Every checkbook has a place for keeping records. In some cases, each check has a stub. In others, the checkbook has a **register** like the one below. Any deposit is added to the previous **balance**. Checks, service charges, or electronic withdrawals are subtracted.

example

Find the balance after the last deposit.

		RECORD ALL CHARGES OR CREDITS THAT AFFECT YOUR ACCOUNT			BALANCE	
NUMBER	DATE	DESCRIPTION OF TRANSACTION	PAYMENT	DEPOSIT	763	40
107	8/30	Top Value Foods	96 14		667	26
108	8/30	Heart Fund	25 00		642	26
	9/1	Deposit		414 09	1056	35
	9/5	Electronic withdrawal	125 00			
	9/8	Deposit		350 89		

solution

Find the most recent balance. $1056.35
Subtract the electronic withdrawal. − 125.00

  $ 931.35

Add the deposit dated 9/8. + 350.89
New balance: $1282.24

exercises

1. Marta Velez had a balance of $1824.50. She wrote a check for $61.24. Find her new balance.

2. Richard Baum deposited $375.00. His previous balance was $1215.73. Find his new balance.

3. Alex Deforge opened a new account with a deposit of $500.00. The first check he wrote was for $16.95. Find the new balance.

4. Tracy Swajian wrote a check for $81.95. She also made a deposit for $115.00. Her previous balance was $612.23. Find the new balance.

5. Marge and Terry Finnerty had a balance of $1664.28. They wrote a check for $72.48 and made an electronic withdrawal of $315.00. They also made a deposit of $625.00. Find the new balance.

11-6 MAKING CHANGE

When you pay for a purchase, the change you receive is usually given with the fewest coins and bills possible. Many cash registers compute the change when the amount offered is entered.

example 1

Sally Ling paid a restaurant bill of $41.98 with $50.00. The cash register indicated change due of $8.02. The cashier counted the change starting with the greatest amount.

Change:	one $5 bill	→	$5.00
	three $1 bills	→	$3.00
	two pennies	→	$ .02
			$8.02

your turn

Describe how to make the given amount of change using the fewest coins and bills.

1. $10.50
2. $4.98
3. $.78
4. $21.76

If the cash register does not compute the change, a cashier may *count on* from the amount owed to the amount offered in payment.

example 2

Bud Lee bought fish for $12.45. He offered a $20 bill. The cashier counted on, beginning with the least amount.

Amount given			Cashier said
one nickel	→	$ .05	$12.50
two quarters	→	$ .50	$13.00
two $1 bills	→	$2.00	$15.00
one $5 bill	→	$5.00	$20.00
		$7.55	

your turn

Describe how to make the change due using the fewest coins and bills.

5. amount owed: $6.75
   amount offered: $7.00

6. amount owed: $.69
   amount offered: $5 bill

practice exercises

practice for example 1 *(page 246)*

Describe how to make the given amount of change using the fewest coins and bills.

1. $7.25
2. $14.37
3. $25.15
4. $.88

practice for example 2 *(page 246)*

Describe the change due using the fewest coins and bills.

5. amount owed: $4.39
   amount offered: $5 bill

6. amount owed: $7.75
   amount offered: $10 bill

7. amount owed: $21.50
   amount offered: $25.50

8. amount owed: $12.35
   amount offered: $13.00

mixed practice *(page 246)*

Write *Correct* if the indicated change is correct. If not, describe how to make the correct change using the fewest coins and bills.

9. amount owed: $9.50
   amount offered: $10.00
   change: two quarters

10. amount owed: $13.88
    amount offered: $15.03
    change: one $1 bill; one quarter

11. amount owed: $32.40
    amount offered: $40.40
    change: one $5 bill; three $1 bills;
          four dimes

12. amount owed: $6.12
    amount offered: $7.00
    change: three pennies; one
          dime; two quarters

Describe two ways to make each amount of change without using quarters.

13. $4.50
14. $2.39
15. $10.76
16. $20.29

17. Assume you can spend a maximum of $10.00. Choose three items from the menu at the right. Find the cost of your meal and describe your change using the fewest coins and bills.

MENU			
green salad	$3.50	apple	$.65
fruit salad	$4.95	milk sm	$.75
soup	$1.40	lg	$1.25
tuna sandwich	$2.95	juice sm	$.95
quiche	$4.25	lg	$1.35

Adding and Subtracting Decimals   247

BOOKKEEPER

Yolanda Moore is a bookkeeper for Wholesale Heat Company. She uses a **T-account** to keep track of the firm's accounts.

example

On Monday, the cash account had a balance of $13,328.06. Ms. Moore made payments of $440.00 for rent, $84.27 for the electric bill, and $3750.00 for salaries. She received payments of $850.75 for water heaters, $668.18 for air conditioners, and $1482.58 for work on an apartment complex. Prepare a T-account and find the new balance.

solution

1. Draw a large T.
2. Write "Cash" at the top of the T.
3. List increases at the left and decreases at the right.
4. Find the total of each side.
5. Subtract the decreases from the increases.

Cash

(Increases)		(Decreases)	
beg. balance	13,328.06	rent	440.00
water heaters	850.75	electric bill	84.27
air conditioners	668.18	salaries	3750.00
payments	1 492.58		
	16,329.57		4 274.27
New balance	12,055.30		

exercises

Prepare a T-account and find the new balance. Use a calculator if you have one.

1. Peter Hess's clothing store received $1348.27 for merchandise on Friday. His balance Friday morning was $847.32.
2. Toni Hu's ice cream store account started with $2365.14 on Saturday. By the end of the day she had received $845.09 for ice cream orders and had paid $795.00 for store rent.
3. Daniel Mendez is the accountant for a private airline. One day he paid $130.45 for fuel, paid $340.25 for hangar rent, received $750.81 for a flight to Orlando, and paid $256.32 for plane repairs. The beginning balance was $556.32.

CHAPTER REVIEW

vocabulary vo·cab·u·lar·y

Choose the correct word to complete each sentence.

1. When you add two decimals, the answer is called the *(sum, difference)*.

2. When you use rounded numbers in a problem, you are finding an *(exact, estimated)* answer.

skills

Find each sum or difference.

3. $73.9 - 16.3$

4. $10.7 + 8.9$

5. $\$6.99 + \$22.49$

6. $\$74.75 - \$33.80$

7. $5.0945 + 2.1364$

8. $127.2 + 304.96$

9. $62.5 + 8.1085$

10. $9701.24 - 8550.3$

11. $1.3 - 0.237$

12. $95.6 - 50$

13. $1.95 + 12 + 0.8$

14. $18.72 - 16.7222$

Estimate each sum.

15. $\$56.27 + \$73.79$

16. $236.54 + 122.89 + 51.89$

17. $39.43 + 14.6 + 25.95$

18. $0.845 + 0.312 + 0.487 + 0.269$

Estimate each difference.

19. $931.3 - 670.1$

20. $0.9564 - 0.3221$

21. $\$47.62 - \$3.49$

22. $\$24.95 - \$18.17$

23. Karen bought items costing $2.09, $2.89, $1.34, $3.38, and $.49. About how much did she spend?

24. Nancy had a balance of $220.64. She wrote a check for $37.21 and then deposited $25.00. Find her new balance.

25. Eric made an electronic withdrawal of $50.00 and wrote a check for $42.25. His previous balance was $1573.34. Find his new balance.

Write *Correct* if the indicated change is correct. If not, describe how to make the correct change using the fewest coins and bills.

26. amount owed: $7.35
amount offered: $10.00
change: two $1 bills; one quarter; one dime; one nickel

27. amount owed: $22.52
amount offered: $23.00
change: three pennies; one quarter; one dime

Adding and Subtracting Decimals 249

CHAPTER TEST

Find each sum.

11-1

1. $25.4 + 6.9$
2. $\$3.34 + \$1.86 + \$5.13$
3. $43.99 + 8.01$
4. $\$12.27 + \$8 + \$.64$
5. $1.009 + 3.25 + 0.2$
6. $1934.5 + 781.7109$

7. Carlos, Marie, and Robert went to their favorite restaurant for lunch. Carlos spent $6.53, Marie spent $5.20, and Robert spent $7.14. How much did they spend altogether?

8. Pat walked 2.3 mi to the park, 0.4 mi to the store, and 2.1 mi home. How far did Pat walk in all?

Choose the letter of the best estimate.

11-2

9. $\$44.97 + \$35.57$ a. $9   b. $70   c. $80
10. $127.3 + 351.4 + 732.1$ a. 1100   b. 1200   c. 1300
11. $0.376 + 0.124 + 0.098$ a. 0.6   b. 1.4   c. 15
12. $0.1 + 0.004 + 0.0005$ a. 0.1   b. 0.2   c. 10

Find each difference.

11-3

13. $\$7.35 - \$5.91$
14. $34.2 - 6.6$
15. $2.9 - 2.45$
16. $121.37 - 72.014$
17. $0.89 - 0.216$
18. $43 - 1.979$

19. Brian had $736.24 saved and spent $505.85 on his vacation. How much money did Brian have left in his savings?

Estimate each difference.

11-4

20. $95.45 - 26.79$
21. $125.2 - 98.9$
22. $\$17.27 - \$8.49$

Choose the letter of the best estimate.

23. $237.08 - 165.39$ a. 0   b. 70   c. 100   d. 400
24. $48.06 - 2.816$ a. 0   b. 40   c. 45   d. 50

11-5

25. Drew had a balance of $95.94. He wrote a check for $26.49. Find his new balance.

26. Anna Norton deposited $156.20 and made an electronic withdrawal of $60.00. Her previous balance was $203.05. Find the new balance.

Describe how to make the change due using the fewest coins and bills.

11-6

27. amount owed: $64.29
    amount offered: $80.00

28. amount owed: $11.07
    amount offered: $12.10

Truck drivers must monitor amounts of time, money, fuel, and cargo very carefully. In doing this, they often need to multiply decimals.

CHAPTER 12

MULTIPLYING DECIMALS

12-1 MULTIPLYING A DECIMAL BY A WHOLE NUMBER

A tourist boat travels 2.9 km (kilometers) on a round trip of Lake Serene. The boat makes six round trips each day. You can multiply 2.9 by 6 to find that the boat travels 17.4 km each day.

To multiply a decimal by a whole number, use the following method.

1. Multiply as with whole numbers.
2. Count the number of decimal places in the decimal factor.
3. Counting from the right, insert a decimal point in the product so that it has the same number of decimal places.

$$
\begin{array}{r}
^{5}\ \ \ \\
2.9 \leftarrow \textbf{1 place} \\
\times 6 \ \ \ \\
\hline
17.4 \leftarrow \textbf{1 place}
\end{array}
$$

example 1

Find each product.

a.
$$
\begin{array}{r}
1.124 \leftarrow \textbf{3 places} \\
\times 4 \ \ \ \\
\hline
4.496 \leftarrow \textbf{3 places}
\end{array}
$$

b.
$$
\begin{array}{r}
\$3.85 \leftarrow \textbf{2 places} \\
\times 5 \ \ \ \\
\hline
\$19.25 \leftarrow \textbf{2 places}
\end{array}
$$

your turn

Find each product.

1.
$$
\begin{array}{r}
2.647 \\
\times 3 \\
\hline
\end{array}
$$

2.
$$
\begin{array}{r}
6.2 \\
\times 18 \\
\hline
\end{array}
$$

3.
$$
\begin{array}{r}
\$7.89 \\
\times 24 \\
\hline
\end{array}
$$

4.
$$
\begin{array}{r}
\$15.25 \\
\times 7 \\
\hline
\end{array}
$$

example 2

Find each product.

a. 4×0.659

b. $8 \times \$5.26$

solution

a.
$$
\begin{array}{r}
0.659 \\
\times 4 \\
\hline
2.636
\end{array}
$$
Rewrite the multiplication in vertical form.

b.
$$
\begin{array}{r}
\$5.26 \\
\times 8 \\
\hline
\$42.08
\end{array}
$$

your turn

Find each product.

5. 7×0.19 **6.** 6.3×46 **7.** 1.29×15 **8.** $\$4.52 \times 73$

example 3

Find each product.

a. 6×0.003 **b.** 0.38×225 **c.** $25 \times \$24.70$

solution

a.
$$
\begin{array}{r} 0.003 \\ \times 6 \\ \hline 0.018 \end{array}
$$
Insert a zero so there are 3 places.

b.
$$
\begin{array}{r} 225 \\ \times 0.38 \\ \hline 1800 \\ 675 \\ \hline 85.50 \end{array}
$$
You can write the product as 85.5.

c.
$$
\begin{array}{r} \$24.70 \\ \times 25 \\ \hline 12350 \\ 4940 \\ \hline \$617.50 \end{array}
$$
Keep the zero in the product to show the number of cents.

your turn

Find each product.

9. 3×0.009 **10.** 25×1.8 **11.** 6.2×20 **12.** $275 \times \$5.50$

practice exercises

practice for example 1 *(page 252)*

Find each product.

1.
$$
\begin{array}{r} 1.2 \\ \times 8 \end{array}
$$
2.
$$
\begin{array}{r} 0.6 \\ \times 7 \end{array}
$$
3.
$$
\begin{array}{r} 0.276 \\ \times 13 \end{array}
$$
4.
$$
\begin{array}{r} 2.149 \\ \times 18 \end{array}
$$

5.
$$
\begin{array}{r} \$1.45 \\ \times 19 \end{array}
$$
6.
$$
\begin{array}{r} \$6.39 \\ \times 43 \end{array}
$$
7.
$$
\begin{array}{r} \$18.63 \\ \times 201 \end{array}
$$
8.
$$
\begin{array}{r} \$16.71 \\ \times 403 \end{array}
$$

practice for example 2 *(pages 252–253)*

Find each product.

9. 6×8.2 **10.** 4×9.7 **11.** 1.93×26 **12.** 1.33×48

13. 67×6.23 **14.** 18×6.51 **15.** $4 \times \$6.89$ **16.** $2 \times \$15.27$

practice for example 3 *(page 253)*

Find each product.

17. 5×0.007 **18.** 0.003×3 **19.** 2.4×25 **20.** 12×4.5

21. 300×0.34 **22.** 40×0.019 **23.** $\$1.14 \times 155$ **24.** $\$.05 \times 516$

Find each product.

25. 5.982
    ×6

26. 6.329
    ×3

27. $8.63
    ×19

28. $6.71
    ×22

29. 1.427 × 3

30. 2 × 78.663

31. 317 × 0.95

32. 53 × 0.95

33. 6 × 0.02

34. 208 × 1.5

35. $3.55 × 6

36. 4 × 97.14

37. 26 × 5.61

38. 45 × 0.24

39. 38 × $6.52

40. 171.95 × 2

41. 74 × $1.29

42. 8.3 × 406

43. 2 × 0.03

44. 5.741 × 6

45. A local restaurant uses a 1.2-oz slice of cheese to make its cheese sandwiches. How many ounces of cheese must be ordered for 400 cheese sandwiches?

46. Joan bought two blouses for $12.95 each and two skirts for $34.99 each. How much money did she spend?

review *exercises*

Give the value of the underlined digit in each decimal.

1. 2.00<u>3</u>

2. 125.0<u>7</u>1

3. 0.1<u>7</u>2

4. 4.6<u>3</u>1

5. 0.<u>2</u>356

6. 1002.99<u>6</u>

7. 4.444<u>6</u>

8. 202.300<u>5</u>

Find each product.

9. 70 × 40

10. 200 × 10

11. 14,000 × 300

12. 60 × 800

13. 30 × 7000

14. 41,000 × 200

15. 50 × 90

16. 900 × 70

mental math

The following addends are all close to 0.7:

$$0.631 + 0.71 + 0.702 + 0.69 + 0.685$$

We say that the addends *cluster* around the number 0.7. To estimate their sum, you could multiply 0.7 by 5, the number of addends. The sum is about 5 × 0.7, or 3.5.

Mentally estimate the sum.

1. 3.2 + 2.95 + 3.047 + 2.99

2. 0.52 + 0.49 + 0.53 + 0.519

3. 79 + 76 + 83 + 81 + 82

4. 90.1 + 88.7 + 90.5 + 89 + 90 + 88

5. 73 + 76 + 75 + 77 + 72 + 73

6. 0.43 + 0.38 + 0.41 + 0.35 + 0.329

12-2 MULTIPLYING A DECIMAL BY 10, 100, OR 1000

How many pennies are there in $7.74? There are 100 pennies in a dollar, so multiply 100 × 7.74 to find that there are 774 pennies.

To multiply a decimal by 10, 100, or 1000, use the following method.

1. Count the number of zeros in 10, 100, or 1000.
2. Move the decimal point to the right the same number of places as there are zeros.
3. Annex zeros *if necessary* in order to move the decimal point the correct number of places.

$$\begin{array}{r} 7.74 \\ \times 100 \\ \hline 774.00 \end{array}$$

example 1

Find each product.

a. 10 × 0.487

b. 100 × 0.555

c. 1000 × 0.6293

solution

a. Move the decimal point *one* place to the right.
10 × 0.487 = 4.87

b. Move the decimal point *two* places to the right.
100 × 0.555 = 55.5

c. Move the decimal point *three* places to the right.
1000 × 0.6293 = 629.3

your turn

Find each product.

1. 10 × 0.752

2. 100 × 7.234

3. 14.75 × 100

4. 0.1496 × 1000

example 2

Find each product.

a. 100 × 29.8

b. 1000 × 4.6

solution

a. Move the decimal point *two* places to the right.   **Annex one zero.**
100 × 29.8 = 2980

b. Move the decimal point *three* places to the right.   **Annex two zeros.**
1000 × 4.6 = 4600

your turn

Find each product.

5. 100 × 40.1

6. 888.8 × 100

7. 3.1 × 1000

8. 6.55 × 1000

practice exercises

practice for example 1 (page 255)

Find each product.

1. 10×0.125
2. 100×0.883
3. 100×21.75
4. 1000×0.245
5. 8.877×100
6. 4.159×100
7. 7.4471×1000
8. 2.341×1000

practice for example 2 (page 255)

Find each product.

9. 100×8.2
10. 100×333.6
11. 100×6.9
12. 100×9.8
13. 19.1×1000
14. 3.4×1000
15. 3.09×1000
16. 15.3×1000

mixed practice (page 255)

Find each product.

17. 10×885.36
18. 100×0.224
19. 0.2199×1000
20. 10×0.449
21. 100×48.22
22. 0.4561×1000
23. 1000×6.6
24. 9.237×100
25. 0.586×1000
26. 0.26×1000
27. 9.5×100
28. 1000×3.7
29. 100×67.5
30. 88.89×100
31. 1.2×100
32. 100×44.3

33. What is the cost of 1000 ft of wire selling at $.29 per foot?
34. Dennis has $42.30 in dimes. How many dimes is this?

review exercises

Find each product.

1. 25×678
2. 420×19
3. 37×562
4. 704×63
5. 992×105
6. 437×456
7. 881×946
8. 531×807

Round each decimal to the nearest tenth.

9. 6.718
10. 14.96
11. 295.98
12. 987.72
13. 3.45
14. 2.1522
15. 68.734
16. 6.017

puzzle corner

Fill in the boxes with two different numbers to make this a true statement.

$$\frac{\blacksquare}{3} \times \frac{6}{\blacksquare} = \frac{4}{5}$$

12-3 MULTIPLYING A DECIMAL BY A DECIMAL

The method for multiplying a decimal by a decimal is similar to the one used for multiplying a decimal by a whole number.

1. Multiply as with whole numbers.
2. Count the number of decimal places in each factor.
3. Insert a decimal point in the product so that it has the same number of decimal places as the *total* number of places in the factors.

$$
\begin{array}{r}
3.27 \leftarrow \textbf{2 places} \\
\times 1.5 \leftarrow \textbf{+1 place} \\
\hline
1635 \\
327 \\
\hline
4.905 \leftarrow \textbf{3 places}
\end{array}
$$

example 1

Find each product.

a. 2.9×8.4

b. 0.71×12.65

solution

a.
$$
\begin{array}{r}
8.4 \leftarrow \textbf{1 place} \\
\times 2.9 \leftarrow \textbf{1 place} \\
\hline
756 \\
168 \\
\hline
24.36 \leftarrow \textbf{2 places}
\end{array}
$$

b.
$$
\begin{array}{r}
12.65 \leftarrow \textbf{2 places} \\
\times 0.71 \leftarrow \textbf{2 places} \\
\hline
1265 \\
8855 \\
\hline
8.9815 \leftarrow \textbf{4 places}
\end{array}
$$

your turn

Find each product.

1. 0.8×3.3 **2.** 0.26×3.4 **3.** 0.33×5.48 **4.** 6.24×5.3

example 2

Find each product.

a. 0.8×0.002

b. 0.4×0.05

solution

a.
$$
\begin{array}{r}
0.002 \\
\times 0.8 \\
\hline
0.0016
\end{array}
$$
Insert zeros as placeholders.

b.
$$
\begin{array}{r}
0.05 \\
\times 0.4 \\
\hline
0.020
\end{array}
$$
You can write the product as 0.02.

your turn

Find each product.

5. 0.006×0.4 **6.** 0.03×0.01 **7.** 0.05×0.6 **8.** 0.5×0.08

In problems involving money, you may need to round the product to the nearest cent.

example 3

Find each product. Round to the nearest cent.

a. 1.8 × $4.55   **b.** 7.3 × $9.25

solution

a.
$$\begin{array}{r} \$4.55 \\ \times 1.8 \\ \hline 3640 \\ 455 \\ \hline \$8.190 = \$8.19 \end{array}$$

b.
$$\begin{array}{r} \$9.25 \\ \times 7.3 \\ \hline 2775 \\ 6475 \\ \hline \$67.525 \approx \$67.53 \end{array}$$

your turn

Find each product. If necessary, round to the nearest cent.

9. 0.5 × $7.50   **10.** 2.8 × $9.45   **11.** 3.9 × $14.75   **12.** $8.92 × 1.98

practice exercises

practice for example 1 (page 257)

Find each product.

1. 0.9 × 7.6	**2.** 0.9 × 2.5	**3.** 2.2 × 0.63	**4.** 0.65 × 0.71
5. 1.81 × 0.79	**6.** 0.037 × 12.3	**7.** 0.423 × 22.2	**8.** 0.5 × 1.999
9. 0.4 × 8.518	**10.** 0.7 × 0.257	**11.** 3.44 × 0.72	**12.** 6.7 × 3.46

practice for example 2 (page 257)

Find each product.

13. 0.08 × 0.06	**14.** 0.6 × 0.04	**15.** 0.7 × 0.006	**16.** 0.07 × 0.05
17. 0.06 × 0.5	**18.** 0.05 × 0.8	**19.** 0.005 × 0.6	**20.** 0.005 × 0.4
21. 0.08 × 0.05	**22.** 0.04 × 0.5	**23.** 0.03 × 1.06	**24.** 0.09 × 0.2

practice for example 3 (page 258)

Find each product. If necessary, round to the nearest cent.

25. $7.50 × 6.5	**26.** $4.05 × 19.4	**27.** $23.86 × 0.01	**28.** 0.4 × $7.35
29. 0.88 × $2.95	**30.** 1.04 × $49.08	**31.** 0.076 × $3.54	**32.** $24.29 × 2.4

mixed practice (pages 257–258)

Find each product. If necessary, round to the nearest cent.

33. 0.4×0.4
34. 1.06×6.29
35. 0.02×0.3
36. 0.1415×0.2

37. 0.14×3.13
38. 0.08×0.02
39. 2.25×43.1
40. 4.72×65.5

41. $\$9.25 \times 7.3$
42. $6.5 \times \$27.40$
43. $11.6 \times \$4.53$
44. $\$1.50 \times 7.38$

45. 0.3×0.004
46. 34.4×6.5
47. $\$3.99 \times 22.24$
48. 1.2×4.68

Write the fraction as a decimal. Then find the product.

49. $\frac{1}{2} \times 150$
50. $300 \times \frac{3}{4}$
51. $\frac{2}{5} \times 10.6$
52. $0.06 \times 2\frac{3}{10}$

53. Andy earns \$5.50 per hour. On Thursday he worked 3.75 h and on Friday he worked 4.5 h. How much money did he earn on Thursday?

54. If linen costs \$5.99 per yard, how much does 0.5 yd of linen cost?

review *exercises*

Estimate by rounding.

1. 247×58
2. 67×359
3. $\$214 \times 82$
4. $55 \times \$625$

Round to the place of the leading digit.

5. 47.5
6. 6.95
7. 0.45
8. $\$2.59$

Estimate each decimal as a simple fraction.

9. 0.525
10. 0.245
11. 0.67
12. 0.73

calculator corner

Find each product using a calculator.

1. a. 972×0.1
b. 972×0.01
c. 972×0.001

2. a. 0.53×0.1
b. 0.53×0.01
c. 0.53×0.001

Use your answers in Exercises 1 and 2 to find a pattern. Use the pattern to find the following products mentally.

3. 102×0.1
4. 8.4×0.01
5. 14.2×0.001

6. 6.1×0.001
7. 0.18×0.1
8. 70.3×0.01

12-4 ESTIMATING DECIMAL PRODUCTS

Steve's Superette advertised cheese for
$3.79 per pound. You can estimate
the cost of 6.5 lb of cheese by rounding
both $3.79 and 6.5 to the place of the
leading digit. Then multiply to find
that the cost is *about* $28.

example 1

Estimate by rounding.

a. $6.5 \times \$3.79$ **b.** 0.63×52.7

solution

a.
$$\begin{array}{r} \$3.79 \rightarrow \$\ 4 \\ \times 6.5 \rightarrow \times 7 \\ \hline \text{about } \$28 \end{array}$$
Since both factors were rounded up, $28 is an overestimate.

b.
$$\begin{array}{r} 52.7 \rightarrow 50 \\ \times 0.63 \rightarrow \times 0.6 \\ \hline \text{about } 30 \end{array}$$
Since both factors were rounded down, 30 is an underestimate.

your turn

Estimate by rounding.

1.
$$\begin{array}{r} 8.902 \\ \times 37 \\ \hline \end{array}$$

2.
$$\begin{array}{r} 629.7 \\ \times 48.3 \\ \hline \end{array}$$

3.
$$\begin{array}{r} 13.6 \\ \times 0.437 \\ \hline \end{array}$$

4.
$$\begin{array}{r} 0.45 \\ \times 0.35 \\ \hline \end{array}$$

When one of the factors is a decimal less than 1, you can sometimes
use compatible numbers to estimate.

example 2

Estimate using compatible numbers.

a. 0.352×592 ← *First* **choose an appropriate fraction.**

$$\underbrace{\frac{1}{3} \times 600}_{\text{about } 200}$$

b. 264×0.732

$$\underbrace{280 \times \frac{3}{4}}_{\text{about } 210}$$

your turn

Estimate using compatible numbers.

5. 0.49×365 **6.** 3725×0.261 **7.** 0.65×1523 **8.** 0.1077×351

practice exercises

practice for example 1 (page 260)

Estimate by rounding.

1. $5.85 × 2.4
2. $1.95 × 3.46
3. 18.03 × 0.89
4. 102.9 × 39.48
5. 88.75 × 28.4
6. 5394 × 0.011
7. 298.4 × 0.029
8. 47,895 × 0.0098

practice for example 2 (page 260)

Estimate using compatible numbers.

9. 417 × 0.241
10. 0.339 × 8876
11. 3098 × 0.6588
12. 0.4815 × 18,039
13. 823 × 0.773
14. 0.19 × 24.89
15. 0.098 × 4500
16. 2997 × 0.115

mixed practice (page 260)

Estimate.

17. $68.23 × 12.75
18. 8.59 × 6.5
19. 0.33306 × 452.9
20. 0.103 × 0.0062
21. 348.5 × 0.2705
22. 0.756 × 31,612

Estimate to choose the exact product.

23. 3.3 × 2.2   **a.** 0.726   **b.** 7.26   **c.** 72.6
24. 18 × 4.73   **a.** 85.14   **b.** 851.4   **c.** 8514
25. 0.85 × 1.04   **a.** 0.0884   **b.** 0.884   **c.** 8.84
26. 0.65 × 880   **a.** 5.72   **b.** 57.2   **c.** 572

Estimate to place the decimal point in the product.

27. 396.4 × 0.25 = $\boxed{9\ 9\ 1\ 0}$
28. 2.5 × 3.02 = $\boxed{7\ 5\ 5}$
29. 0.08 × 1.04 = $\boxed{0\ 0\ 0\ 8\ 3\ 2\ 0}$
30. 425 × 5.2 = $\boxed{2\ 2\ 1\ 0\ 0\ 0}$
31. 177.8 × 0.35 = $\boxed{6\ 2\ 2\ 3}$
32. 986.5 × 13.4 = $\boxed{1\ 3\ 2\ 1\ 9\ 1}$

33. Estimate the cost of a lunch for 37 people at $8.25 per person.
34. Estimate the cost of 2.85 lb of bananas at $.39 per pound.

review exercises

Write the prime factorization of each number.

1. 6
2. 35
3. 55
4. 39
5. 8
6. 12
7. 50
8. 30
9. 24
10. 60
11. 120
12. 108

12-5 USING ESTIMATION

1 Understand
2 Plan
3 Work
4 Answer

You can often use estimation to check the reasonableness of your solution to a problem. Other times an estimated answer is the only solution that is required.

example

A craft project requires $6\frac{1}{8}$ yd of ribbon at 63¢ per yard and $3\frac{1}{4}$ yd of ribbon at 81¢ per yard. Choose the letter of the best estimate of the total cost.

a. between $2 and $4

b. between $4 and $6

c. between $6 and $8

d. between $8 and $10

solution

Step 1 Given: $6\frac{1}{8}$ yd at 63¢ per yard
$3\frac{1}{4}$ yd at 81¢ per yard
Find: an estimate of the total cost

Step 2 Round the number of yards and the cost per yard. Multiply to estimate the cost of each ribbon. Add to estimate the total cost. Choose the best estimate.

Step 3

$6\frac{1}{8} \times 63¢$ $3\frac{1}{4} \times 81¢$

↓   ↓   ↓   ↓

$6 \times 60¢$ $3 \times 80¢$

about $3.60   +   about $2.40 = about $6.00

Since all factors were rounded down, both $3.60 and $2.40 are underestimates. So $6 is also an underestimate.

Step 4 The best estimate is (c).

problems

Choose the letter of the best estimate.

1. The population of Brownsville is 28,293. The population of Elmira is 61,296. About how many more people does Elmira have?

    a. 3000   b. 20,000   c. 30,000   d. 90,000

2. Karen Johnson earned $287.75 per week for $1\frac{1}{2}$ years. About how much did she earn altogether?

   a. $450   b. $5400   c. $15,000   d. $22,500

3. Laurie bought items costing $1.49, $2.89, $.67, $.48, and $1.39. About how much was the total?

   a. between $4 and $5   b. between $6 and $7
   c. between $8 and $9   d. between $10 and $11

4. A suit pattern requires $6\frac{7}{8}$ yd of wool at $9.50 per yard and $4\frac{3}{4}$ yd of lining at $5.59 per yard. About how much will the fabric for the suit cost?

   a. between $60 and $70   b. between $70 and $80
   c. between $90 and $100   d. between $100 and $110

Solve.

5. A new car costs $18,769. About how much do six new cars cost?

6. The distance around the track is 895 ft. How many times must you run around the track to run about 1 mi?

7. A bricklayer has 234 bricks to lay. How many bricks will have been laid when the job is about three-quarters finished?

8. Greta bought 187 shares of stock for $50\frac{1}{4}$ dollars a share. One year later she sold all the shares for $69\frac{3}{8}$ dollars a share. About how much was Greta's profit?

9. If three apples cost 89¢, four oranges cost 82¢, and eight bananas cost 79¢, about how much will it cost to buy two of each?

10. The fruit baskets on sale this week for $1.98 contain six apples, four oranges, and two grapefruit. If there are 178 apples, 129 oranges, and 73 grapefruit available, about how many fruit baskets can be made?

review exercises

Estimate to tell whether the given answer is reasonable.

1. Mr. Linn bought items costing $2.98, $1.48, $.49, $1.36, $3.89, $1.45 and $.38. How much change did he get from a $20 bill?

   Answer: $12.03

2. What is the cost of 3.17 lb of chicken at 89¢ per pound?

   Answer: $3.71

3. How many software disks for $48 each can the Buckingham School buy with $260?

   Answer: 5

4. Dr. Martinez earned $47,273 last year and paid $19,269 in taxes. How much was left after taxes?

   Answer: $66,542

SKILL REVIEW

Find each product.

1. 0.6×6
2. 3×0.003
3. 0.9×3 **12-1**
4. 4×0.007
5. 54×1.22
6. 68×0.633
7. $\$28.50 \times 3$
8. $\$94.15 \times 4$
9. $57 \times \$1.99$
10. 182×4.5
11. 6.7×784
12. $\$2.41 \times 36$

Find each product.

13. 10×0.644
14. 0.28×1000
15. 10×0.68 **12-2**
16. 1000×0.25
17. 100×0.17
18. 0.495×100

19. If a blouse weighs 0.8 lb, how many pounds does a store's order of 100 blouses weigh?

Find each product. If necessary, round to the nearest cent.

20. 6.8×0.4
21. $\$3.46 \times 3.7$
22. $7.6 \times \$4.05$ **12-3**
23. 3.2×0.6
24. $\$2.81 \times 4.9$
25. $0.8 \times \$4.75$
26. 0.003×0.8
27. 0.4×0.002
28. 0.004×0.3
29. 2.94×0.75
30. 1.14×1.82
31. 0.007×0.5

32. Sarah purchased 1.8 kg (kilograms) of cherries that sold for $1.10 per kilogram. How much did she pay for the cherries?

Estimate by rounding.

33. $\$4.95 \times 2.1$
34. 41.2×0.955
35. 6.221×85.3 **12-4**
36. 6182×0.039
37. 479.8×18.2
38. 8453×0.0012

Estimate using compatible numbers.

39. 0.52×6029
40. 0.334×8771
41. 0.266×478.2
42. 49.6×0.098
43. 411×0.73
44. 0.64×597.4

45. Betsy bought $5\frac{3}{4}$ lb of chicken at 98¢ per pound and $2\frac{7}{8}$ lb of steak at **12-5**
$3.95 per pound. Choose the letter of the best estimate of the total cost.

    a. between $12 and $15
    b. between $15 and $18
    c. between $18 and $21
    d. between $21 and $24

46. David bought items costing $2.37, $1.98, $2.43, $.87, and $3.39.
About how much was the total?

12-6 WEEKLY PAY

Some workers are paid an hourly rate. To find weekly pay, you multiply the hourly rate by the number of hours worked in a week.

If more than 40 h are worked in a week, the job may pay **overtime.** The sum of regular and overtime earnings is called **gross pay.**

example

Anita Hadden earns $8.30/h (per hour) as a construction worker. She earns time-and-a-half, or 1.5 times her regular rate, for overtime. Find Anita's gross pay if she works 44 h in one week.

solution

regular earnings

$$\begin{aligned}
&= \text{regular hourly rate} \times \text{number of hours} \\
&= \quad\quad \$8.30 \quad\quad \times \quad\quad 40 \\
&= \quad\quad\quad\quad \$332.00
\end{aligned}$$

overtime earnings

$$\begin{aligned}
&= \text{ overtime rate } \times \text{ number of hours} \\
&= (\$8.30 \times 1.5) \times \quad (44 - 40) \\
&= \quad \$12.45 \quad \times \quad\quad 4 \\
&= \quad\quad\quad\quad \$49.80
\end{aligned}$$

gross pay

$$\begin{aligned}
&= \text{regular earnings} + \text{overtime earnings} \\
&= \quad \$332.00 \quad + \quad\quad \$49.80 \\
&= \quad\quad\quad\quad \$381.80
\end{aligned}$$

Anita's gross pay is $381.80.

exercises

Find the gross pay. Assume time-and-a-half for any hours over 40.

1. 40 h at $10.12/h
2. 21 h at $9.15/h
3. 32.5 h at $6.00/h
4. 18.25 h at $3.60/h
5. 43 h at $7.00/h
6. 50 h at $11.20/h

Some workers receive a higher rate for working on holidays. It is usually double time, or twice the regular rate. Find the gross pay.

7. 40 h at $9.00/h, 8 h at double time
8. 40 h at $7.50/h, 3 h at double time
9. 40 h at $6.50/h, 5 h at time-and-a-half, 4 h at double time
10. 40 h at $12.50/h, 6 h at time-and-a-half, 4 h at double time

12-7 PAYROLL DEDUCTIONS

Employers issue a statement to help employees keep track of their earnings. The statement itemizes gross earnings and any **deductions,** such as taxes and insurance. It also shows the earnings after deductions, or **net pay.**

example

YEAR-TO-DATE		CURRENT PAY PERIOD			
		EARNINGS		DEDUCTIONS	
TAXABLE EARNINGS	7200.00	GROSS EARN.	360.00	UNION DUES	2.50
FED. INC. TAX	2016.00			CREDIT UNION	10.00
STATE TAX	360.00			INSURANCE	13.67
UNION DUES	50.00			FED. INC. TAX	100.80
F.I.C.A.	514.80			STATE TAX	18.00
MISC.	473.40			F.I.C.A.	25.74
NET PAY	3785.80	NET PAY	?	TOTAL DED.	?
O'BRIAN, MARK	week of 5/18				

Use the CURRENT PAY PERIOD information.
Find the following.

a. total deductions   **b.** net pay   **c.** annual amount for F.I.C.A.

solution

a. Add the deductions shown on the statement.
$2.50 + $10.00 + $13.67 + $100.80 + $18.00 + $25.74 = $170.71
The total deductions are $170.71.

b. Subtract the deductions from the gross earnings.
$360.00 − $170.71 = $189.29
The net pay is $189.29.

c. F.I.C.A. stands for Federal Insurance Contributions Act. It is usually referred to as *social security tax*. The statement shows that $25.74 is paid for F.I.C.A. There are 52 weeks in a year, so multiply by 52.
$25.74 × 52 = $1338.48
Mark pays $1338.48 annually for F.I.C.A.

exercises

Find the total deductions and net pay. Use a calculator if you have one.

	GROSS PAY	FED. TAX	F.I.C.A.	STATE TAX	INS.
1.	$788.90	$105.25	$56.41	$41.00	$3.99
2.	$367.00	$45.88	$26.24	$25.00	$5.75
3.	$480.77	$72.12	$34.38	$16.83	$12.13
4.	$375.00	$33.75	$26.81	—	$15.39

Use the statement of weekly earnings at the right. Find the annual amount deducted for the given purpose.

5. insurance
6. F.I.C.A.
7. pension
8. state tax
9. federal income tax

10. Ron Evans earns $487.74 per week. His weekly deductions are: Fed. Tax, $72.00; state tax, $22.05; F.I.C.A., $34.87. Find Ron's total weekly deductions and net pay.

11. Jothi Murali has $37.88 deducted from her weekly pay for a car payment. Find the annual amount deducted for car payments.

12. Elaine Biden earns $675.00 per week. Her earnings statement shows the following deductions for each pay period: Fed. Inc. Tax, $105.67; F.I.C.A., $48.26; State Tax, $38.90; Ins., $11.15. Find Elaine's total deductions and net pay.

CURRENT PAY PERIOD	WEEK OF 6/7	
EARNINGS	**DEDUCTIONS**	
REG. EARN. 538.46	INSURANCE	15.38
	FED. INC. TAX	150.77
	F.I.C.A.	38.50
	STATE TAX	26.92
	PENSION	15.65
	TOTAL DED.	247.22
	NET PAY	291.24

12-8 CATALOGUE BUYING

Sok Muong shops at home using catalogues. Once he chooses items, he must fill out the order form. Often shipping charges are added at the end of an order.

example

Sok decides to buy 4 shirts and 3 ties. Complete the order form.

Cotton Shirts
100% cotton. Dramatic plaid shirt with no-wrinkle collar. Machine wash. Two styles.
326M   Short sleeve cotton shirt $17.95
327M   Long sleeve cotton shirt $19.95

100% Silk Ties
Multicolored on silk.
Dry clean only.
463J   Regular $15.95
464J   Long $16.95

solution

Item No.	Size	How many	Price each	Total price
327M	M	4	$19.95	$79.80
463J	–	3	$15.95	$47.85

SHIPPING & HANDLING
Up to $10.00 add $1.50
$10.01 to $20.00 add $2.50
$20.01 to $30.00 add $3.50
$30.01 to $40.00 add $4.00
$40.01 to $60.00 add $5.00
$60.01 to $80.00 add $7.00
$80.01 and over add $9.00

Item total	$127.65
Shipping	$9.00
Total due	$136.65

← Multiply 4 × $19.95 to find the total cost of the shirts.

← Multiply 3 × $15.95 to find the total cost of the ties.

← Add the costs.

← Use the chart to find shipping charges.

← Add the shipping to the item total.

exercises

Copy and complete the order forms. Use the shipping chart at the bottom of the page.

1.

Item No.	How many	Description	Price each	Total price
0403	12	Tulip bulbs	$2.50	?
5671	7	Tomato seeds	$ .75	?
			Item total	?
			Shipping	?
			Total due	?

2.

Item No.	How many	Description	Price each	Total price
0167	3	Basketballs	$25.84	?
0154	4	Volleyballs	$18.65	?
			Item total	?
			Shipping	?
			Total due	?

Use the shipping chart below.

3. Marion orders 3 skirts that cost $34.50 each. Find the total due. Include shipping charges.

4. Bill orders 5 T-shirts costing $12.95 each. Find the total due. Include shipping charges.

5. Suppose you can spend no more than $300. Look at the catalogue page at the right and pick out items you would like. Make up and complete an order form, including shipping charges, but keep the total due under $300.

Orders up to	$ 30	add $3
Orders from $30.01 to	$ 60	add $4
Orders from $60.01 to	$100	add $5
Orders over	$100	add $6

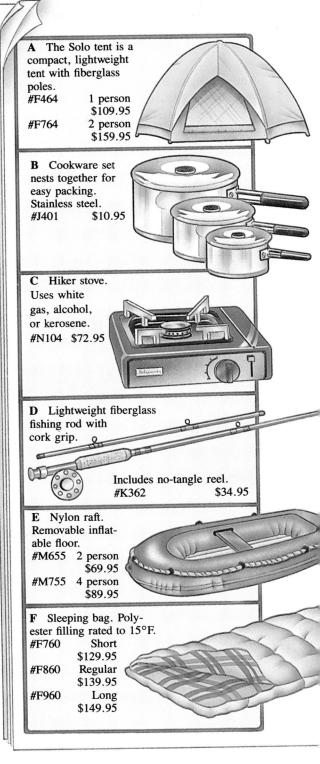

A The Solo tent is a compact, lightweight tent with fiberglass poles.
#F464   1 person $109.95
#F764   2 person $159.95

B Cookware set nests together for easy packing. Stainless steel.
#J401 $10.95

C Hiker stove. Uses white gas, alcohol, or kerosene.
#N104 $72.95

D Lightweight fiberglass fishing rod with cork grip.
Includes no-tangle reel.
#K362 $34.95

E Nylon raft. Removable inflatable floor.
#M655   2 person $69.95
#M755   4 person $89.95

F Sleeping bag. Polyester filling rated to 15°F.
#F760   Short $129.95
#F860   Regular $139.95
#F960   Long $149.95

ELECTRONICS TECHNICIAN

Andy Boughton is building a stereo system. The system must take a very small electrical signal and increase it so that you can hear the sound from the speakers. Andy uses an *amplifier* to increase the electrical signal. An amplifier multiplies the **input voltage** by a factor called the **amplifier gain** to produce the **output voltage.**

example

Find the output voltage for the amplifier shown.

The input voltage is 0.25 V (volts).
The amplifier gain is 20.4.

$$
\begin{aligned}
\text{output voltage} &= \text{input voltage} \times \text{amplifier gain} \\
&= \quad 0.25 \text{ V} \quad \times \quad 20.4 \\
&= \quad\quad\quad 5.1 \text{ V}
\end{aligned}
$$

The output voltage will be 5.1 V.

exercises

Find the output voltage for each amplifier.

1.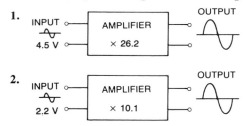

2. INPUT 2.2 V AMPLIFIER × 10.1 OUTPUT

3. Sandy's stereo has an input voltage of 1.4 V. The stereo uses an amplifier with an amplifier gain of 12.2. Find the output voltage.

4. Two connecting amplifiers are shown below. The output voltage of the first amplifier becomes the input voltage for the second amplifier. Find the output voltage from the second amplifier.

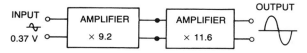

CHAPTER REVIEW

vocabulary vo·cab·u·lar·y

Choose the correct word to complete each sentence.

1. When you multiply two decimals the answer is called the (*factor*, *product*).

2. Earnings after deductions are called (*gross pay*, *net pay*).

skills

Find each product. If necessary, round to the nearest cent.

3. 33×1.1	4. 1.5×1.05	5. 0.003×4
6. $9 \times \$3.50$	7. 3.06×10	8. 10×0.871
9. 0.05×1000	10. 1000×52.3	11. 0.125×100
12. 1000×42.1	13. 1.4×1000	14. 4.4×42.8
15. 0.57×0.36	16. 0.2×0.528	17. $0.6 \times \$14.15$
18. $0.4 \times \$10.45$	19. $\$89.60 \times 0.31$	20. $\$1.44 \times 6.2$

Estimate by rounding.

21. 50.4×19.95	22. 634×0.294	23. 67.7×3.39
24. 925×0.029	25. $\$4.89 \times 3.9$	26. 45.45×8.51

Estimate using compatible numbers.

27. 422.6×0.264	28. 0.52×3951.6	29. 0.74×804
30. 912.1×0.348	31. 402×0.106	32. 0.65×9.11

33. Last week Mrs. Phelps sold 40 albums costing $9.99 each and 102 cassettes costing $7.89 each. After paying expenses of $125, about how much money did she make that week?
    a. between $800 and $900
    b. between $900 and $1000
    c. between $1000 and $2000
    d. between $2000 and $3000

34. Describe a method for multiplying a decimal by a decimal.

35. Find Joe's weekly pay for 40 h at $8.30/h and 5 h at double time.

36. George Stillman worked 40 h at $9.50/h. His deductions are: F.I.C.A., $27.17; federal income tax, $106.40; union dues, $7.49. Find his net pay.

37. Find the cost of ordering three shirts that cost $19.95 each. Include a shipping charge of $1.50.

CHAPTER TEST

Find each product.

1. 5×2.669
2. 29×4.45
3. 0.006×2

4. 4×0.002
5. 2.05×14
6. $\$3.45 \times 4$

12-1

7. If a book is 4.3 cm (centimeters) thick, how tall is a stack of 15 books?

Find each product. If necessary, round to the nearest cent.

8. 100×28.48
9. 1000×17.17
10. 10×0.009

11. 17.4×100
12. 1000×0.03
13. 4.666×10

12-2

14. 0.03×0.01
15. $\$20.57 \times 0.05$
16. 6.5×4.9

12-3

17. What is the cost of 2.7 kg (kilograms) of tomatoes at $2.59 per kg?

Estimate by rounding.

18. 52.5×27.6
19. 86.17×6.4
20. 1249×0.013

12-4

Estimate using compatible numbers.

21. 1215×0.257
22. 0.66×883
23. $0.104 \times 35,022$

Solve.

24. If the school year is 184 days long, after how many school days is the school year about one-third finished?

25. One ticket costs $3. Dave sold 102 tickets and Irene sold 197 tickets. About how much more money did Irene raise than Dave?

12-5

Find the gross pay.

26. 40 h at $10.50/h

27. 40 h at $9.50/h, 5 h at time-and-a-half

12-6

28. Henry Ortega's weekly gross pay is $540. His deductions are: F.I.C.A., $38.61; federal income tax, $110.08; state income tax, $8.10; life insurance, $3.50; pension, $20. Find his net pay.

12-7

Suppose a shipping charge of $2.50 is added to all orders over $50. Find the cost of each order.

29. three lamps at $12.50 each

30. two shirts at $19.95 each and three belts at $8.85 each

12-8

Scientific notation is often used to express the very large and very small numbers involved in constructing vehicles for space travel.

CHAPTER 13

DIVIDING DECIMALS

13-1 DIVIDING A DECIMAL BY A WHOLE NUMBER

Joni bought six cartons of juice for $1.74. You can divide $1.74 by six to find that each carton cost $.29.

To divide a decimal by a nonzero whole number, use the following method.

1. Place the decimal point in the quotient directly above the decimal point in the dividend.
2. Divide as with whole numbers.

```
   $ .29          Check:    $ .29
6)$1.74                      ×6
   1 2                     $1.74
   54                      +  0
   54                      $1.74 √
    0
```

---

example 1

Find each quotient: **a.** $3.748 \div 4$ **b.** $24.4 \div 5$ **c.** $27 \div 12$

solution

```
      0.937                    4.88                         2.25
a.  4)3.748        b.  5)24.40  ◄── Annex zeros     c.  12)27.00  ◄── Write the
      3 6                20         as needed                24          decimal point in
      ───                ──         in the                   ──          the dividend.
      14                 4 4        dividend.                3 0         Annex zeros
      12                 4 0                                 2 4         as needed.
      ──                 ──                                  ──
      28                  40                                 60
      28                  40                                 60
      ──                  ──                                 ──
       0                   0                                  0
```

your turn

Find each quotient.

1. $2)\overline{3.8}$ **2.** $5)\overline{4.68}$ **3.** $8.92 \div 4$ **4.** $93 \div 12$

---

example 2

Find each quotient: **a.** $8.72 \div 8$ **b.** $15.03 \div 15$ **c.** $\$11.20 \div 16$

solution

```
      1.09  ◄── Insert one               1.002                   $  .70  ◄── Keep the zero
a.  8)8.72      zero as a     b.  15)15.030      c.  16)$11.20        in the quotient
      8         placeholder.          15                 11 2         to show the
      ─                               ──                 ────         number of cents.
      72                              030                  00
      72                               30                   0
      ──                               ──                   ─
       0                                0                   0
```

your turn

Find each quotient.

5. $7\overline{)0.56}$ **6.** $24\overline{)48.144}$ **7.** $\$72.81 \div 9$ **8.** $\$34.10 \div 11$

Sometimes it is not possible to find an *exact* quotient. In cases like these, you *round* the quotient to an appropriate place. To round a quotient to a given place, you carry out the division to one additional decimal place.

example 3

Find each quotient to the indicated place.

a. $3\overline{)0.41}$; nearest tenth   **b.** $6.7 \div 11$; nearest hundredth

solution

a.
$$\begin{array}{r} 0.13 \\ 3\overline{)0.41} \\ \underline{3} \\ 11 \\ \underline{9} \\ 2 \end{array}$$

◄ Divide to *hundredths*. Round to *tenths*.

$0.13 \approx 0.1$

b.
$$\begin{array}{r} 0.609 \\ 11\overline{)6.700} \\ \underline{6\ 6} \\ 100 \\ \underline{99} \\ 1 \end{array}$$

◄ Divide to *thousandths*. Round to *hundredths*.

$0.609 \approx 0.61$

your turn

Find each quotient to the indicated place.

9. $3\overline{)17.84}$; nearest tenth   **10.** $7\overline{)56.664}$; nearest hundredth

11. $5 \div 18$; nearest thousandth   **12.** $13.99 \div 3$; nearest thousandth

practice exercises

practice for example 1 (page 274)

Find each quotient.

1. $5\overline{)255.95}$ **2.** $7\overline{)44.324}$ **3.** $76\overline{)190}$ **4.** $12\overline{)43.8}$

5. $1.32 \div 5$ **6.** $55 \div 44$ **7.** $\$5.68 \div 8$ **8.** $\$12.96 \div 9$

practice for example 2 (pages 274–275)

Find each quotient.

9. $4\overline{)12.28}$ **10.** $26\overline{)0.182}$ **11.** $151 \div 25$ **12.** $203 \div 50$

13. $\$22.50 \div 3$ **14.** $\$29.60 \div 8$ **15.** $1.035 \div 5$ **16.** $96.4 \div 8$

Find each quotient to the indicated place.

17. $7\overline{)4.61}$; nearest tenth
18. $9\overline{)38.53}$; nearest tenth
19. $13\overline{)77.7}$; nearest hundredth
20. $41\overline{)8.97}$; nearest hundredth
21. $1.132 \div 6$; nearest thousandth
22. $7.29 \div 7$; nearest thousandth
23. $7 \div 15$; nearest thousandth
24. $73 \div 30$; nearest thousandth

Find each quotient. If necessary, round to the nearest thousandth.

25. $2\overline{)9.02}$
26. $25\overline{)12.9}$
27. $16\overline{)80.8}$
28. $4\overline{)612.88}$
29. $8\overline{)100}$
30. $24\overline{)33}$
31. $6\overline{)56}$
32. $17\overline{)27.1}$
33. $0.108 \div 12$
34. $8.42 \div 4$
35. $4.5 \div 11$
36. $40 \div 9$
37. $\$144.60 \div 6$
38. $\$20.40 \div 17$
39. $83.1 \div 2$
40. $66.4 \div 5$

41. If a dozen pencils cost $2.04, how much does one pencil cost?
42. Ivan earned $22 for working four hours. How much did he earn per hour?

review exercises

Find each answer.

1. 1000×0.4422
2. 1000×5.9
3. 41.5×100
4. 97.1×100
5. 1000×3.8
6. 0.6413×1000
7. 0.66×10
8. 10×3.498

Write each fraction as a decimal.

9. $\frac{3}{4}$
10. $\frac{7}{10}$
11. $\frac{3}{8}$
12. $\frac{7}{20}$
13. $\frac{7}{100}$
14. $\frac{3}{50}$
15. $\frac{1}{16}$
16. $\frac{1}{40}$

puzzle corner

This arrangement of pennies forms a triangle that points upward. By moving only three pennies, make the triangle point downward.

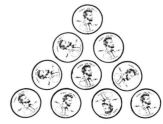

13-2 DIVIDING BY 10, 100, OR 1000

A ten-pound bag of onions costs $2.80. You can divide by ten to find that the cost of one pound is $.28.

To divide a number by 10, 100, or 1000, use the following method.

1. Count the number of zeros in 10, 100, or 1000.
2. Move the decimal point in the dividend to the *left* the same number of places as there are zeros.
3. Insert zeros *if necessary* in order to have the correct number of decimal places.

$$
\begin{array}{r}
\$\ .28 \\
10\overline{)\$2.80} \\
\underline{2\ 0} \\
80 \\
\underline{80} \\
0
\end{array}
$$

example 1

Find each quotient.

a. 14.28 ÷ 10

b. 2531.6 ÷ 100

c. 1794 ÷ 1000

solution

a. Move the decimal point *one* place to the left.

14.28 ÷ 10 = 1.428

b. Move the decimal point *two* places to the left.

2531.6 ÷ 100 = 25.316

c. Move the decimal point *three* places to the left.

1794 ÷ 1000 = 1.794

your turn

Find each quotient.

1. 198.2 ÷ 10

2. 57.03 ÷ 100

3. 185.2 ÷ 1000

4. 4229 ÷ 1000

example 2

Find each quotient.

a. 0.39 ÷ 10

b. 5.2 ÷ 1000

solution

a. Move the decimal point *one* place to the left.

0.39 ÷ 10 = 0.039   ◄── **Insert one zero as a placeholder.**

b. Move the decimal point *three* places to the left.

5.2 ÷ 1000 = 0.0052

your turn

Find each quotient.

5. 0.46 ÷ 10

6. 0.75 ÷ 100

7. 38.7 ÷ 1000

8. 41 ÷ 1000

practice exercises

practice for example 1 (page 277)

Find each quotient.

1. $603.4 \div 10$
2. $424.93 \div 10$
3. $1956.4 \div 1000$
4. $240.3 \div 1000$
5. $164.03 \div 100$
6. $732.9 \div 100$
7. $1825 \div 100$
8. $151 \div 100$
9. $215 \div 1000$
10. $986 \div 1000$
11. $\$6.50 \div 10$
12. $\$3.90 \div 10$

practice for example 2 (page 277)

Find each quotient.

13. $0.139 \div 10$
14. $0.047 \div 10$
15. $7.9 \div 100$
16. $6.12 \div 100$
17. $0.2 \div 1000$
18. $0.4 \div 1000$
19. $26 \div 1000$
20. $78 \div 1000$
21. $4 \div 100$
22. $85 \div 1000$
23. $0.78 \div 100$
24. $0.12 \div 100$

mixed practice (page 277)

Find each quotient.

25. $4.3 \div 10$
26. $6.84 \div 100$
27. $3 \div 100$
28. $0.203 \div 10$
29. $103.6 \div 1000$
30. $196.24 \div 100$
31. $0.225 \div 10$
32. $7 \div 1000$
33. $2845.6 \div 100$
34. $14.7 \div 10$
35. $4951 \div 1000$
36. $0.3 \div 100$
37. $0.66 \div 10$
38. $349.77 \div 100$
39. $3.24 \div 10$
40. $9.8 \div 100$

41. Ten roses cost $\$11.50$. How much does one rose cost?

42. A bank teller counted $\$50,000$ in $\$10$ bills. How many $\$10$ bills is this?

review exercises

Find each quotient.

1. $6084 \div 18$
2. $4893 \div 21$
3. $246 \div 123$
4. $625 \div 125$
5. $3380 \div 52$
6. $2623 \div 43$
7. $5000 \div 10$
8. $250 \div 10$

13-3 DIVIDING BY A DECIMAL

To divide by a decimal, use the following method.

1. Multiply the divisor by a *power* of 10 (10, 100, 1000, and so on) to make the divisor a whole number.
2. Multiply the dividend by the same power of 10.
3. Divide as when dividing by a whole number.

example 1

Find each quotient: **a.** $0.11\overline{)0.143}$ **b.** $0.042 \div 0.006$

solution

a.
$$\begin{array}{r} 1.3 \\ 0.11\overline{)0.14\ 3} \\ \underline{11} \\ 3\ 3 \\ \underline{3\ 3} \\ 0 \end{array}$$
← $0.11 \times 100 = 11$, so move *both* decimal points *two* places to the right.

b.
$$\begin{array}{r} 7 \\ 0.006\overline{)0.042} \\ \underline{42} \\ 0 \end{array}$$
← $0.006 \times 1000 = 6$, so move *both* decimal points *three* places to the right.

your turn

Find each quotient.

1. $0.5\overline{)2.5}$ **2.** $0.4\overline{)2.852}$ **3.** $2.684 \div 0.61$ **4.** $0.065 \div 0.013$

example 2

Find each quotient.

a. $0.5\overline{)6}$ **b.** $0.8 \div 0.25$ **c.** $0.01 \div 0.004$

solution

a.
$$\begin{array}{r} 1\ 2 \\ 0.5\overline{)6.0} \\ \underline{5} \\ 1\ 0 \\ \underline{1\ 0} \\ 0 \end{array}$$
← Annex zeros as needed in the dividend.

b.
$$\begin{array}{r} 3.2 \\ 0.25\overline{)0.80\ 0} \\ \underline{75} \\ 5\ 0 \\ \underline{5\ 0} \\ 0 \end{array}$$

c.
$$\begin{array}{r} 2.5 \\ 0.004\overline{)0.010\ 0} \\ \underline{8} \\ 2\ 0 \\ \underline{2\ 0} \\ 0 \end{array}$$

your turn

Find each quotient.

5. $0.2\overline{)42}$ **6.** $0.16\overline{)8.6}$ **7.** $9.2 \div 0.04$ **8.** $3.25 \div 0.025$

example 3

Find each quotient to the indicated place.

a. $0.6\overline{)2.8}$; nearest tenth

b. $0.012 \div 0.09$; nearest hundredth

solution

a.
$$
\begin{array}{r}
4.66 \\
0.6\overline{)2.8\ 00} \\
\underline{2\ 4} \\
4\ 0 \\
\underline{3\ 6} \\
40 \\
\underline{36} \\
4
\end{array}
$$

← **Divide to hundredths. Round to *tenths*.**

$4.66 \approx 4.7$

b.
$$
\begin{array}{r}
0.133 \\
0.09\overline{)0.01\ 200} \\
\underline{9} \\
30 \\
\underline{27} \\
30 \\
\underline{27} \\
3
\end{array}
$$

← **Divide to thousandths. Round to *hundredths*.**

$0.133 \approx 0.13$

your turn

Find each quotient to the indicated place.

9. $0.6\overline{)1.472}$; nearest tenth

10. $2.4\overline{)1.16}$; nearest hundredth

11. $2 \div 1.4$; nearest hundredth

12. $0.17 \div 0.009$; nearest thousandth

practice exercises

practice for example 1 (page 279)

Find each quotient.

1. $1.3\overline{)2.6}$

2. $0.6\overline{)0.84}$

3. $1.5\overline{)7.95}$

4. $4.3\overline{)7.138}$

5. $40.32 \div 0.36$

6. $1.71 \div 0.57$

7. $2.499 \div 4.9$

8. $0.006 \div 0.012$

practice for example 2 (page 279)

Find each quotient.

9. $0.8\overline{)30}$

10. $2.5\overline{)14}$

11. $0.05\overline{)2.2}$

12. $0.44\overline{)19.8}$

13. $1.5 \div 0.16$

14. $36.3 \div 0.44$

15. $0.6 \div 0.003$

16. $1.5 \div 0.004$

practice for example 3 (page 280)

Find each quotient to the indicated place.

17. $7.2\overline{)8.591}$; nearest tenth

18. $3.1\overline{)7.326}$; nearest tenth

19. $11 \div 0.07$; nearest hundredth

20. $9.3 \div 0.18$; nearest hundredth

21. $0.008 \div 0.007$; nearest thousandth

22. $0.03 \div 0.011$; nearest thousandth

mixed practice (pages 279–280)

Find each quotient. If necessary, round to the nearest thousandth.

23. $1.5\overline{)0.42}$ **24.** $0.5\overline{)0.19}$ **25.** $0.16\overline{)0.3}$ **26.** $0.12\overline{)0.267}$

27. $0.12\overline{)0.492}$ **28.** $0.002\overline{)1.8}$ **29.** $0.75\overline{)3.5}$ **30.** $0.03\overline{)0.1}$

31. $0.7\overline{)7}$ **32.** $0.41\overline{)0.287}$ **33.** $1.5\overline{)3.8}$ **34.** $5.5\overline{)21.45}$

35. $0.5 \div 0.7$ **36.** $0.7 \div 0.09$ **37.** $1.608 \div 0.24$ **38.** $0.3 \div 0.07$

39. $0.252 \div 1.2$ **40.** $4.2 \div 0.24$ **41.** $2.5 \div 0.04$ **42.** $0.0921 \div 0.03$

43. A baseball weighs about 155.9 g (grams). A golf ball weighs about 45.9 g. To the nearest tenth, about how many times heavier is a baseball than a golf ball?

44. Sarah has a board 2.5 m (meters) long. She needs to cut it into pieces. How many pieces that are 0.8 m long can she cut?

review *exercises*

Estimate.

1. $3648 \div 5$ **2.** $4823 \div 7$

3. $4669 \div 63$ **4.** $30{,}597 \div 39$

5. $5252 \div 88$ **6.** $614{,}962 \div 33$

7. $65{,}219 \div 829$ **8.** $41{,}216 \div 675$

mental math

Mentally divide to check whether the decimal point in the quotient is in the right place. If it is, write *correct*. Otherwise, write the correct quotient.

1. $4\overline{)3.6}$ (0.9)   **2.** $4\overline{)0.36}$ (0.9)   **3.** $0.4\overline{)0.36}$ (0.09)   **4.** $11\overline{)5.5}$ (5.0)   **5.** $1.1\overline{)5.5}$ (0.5)

6. $15\overline{)0.30}$ (0.02)   **7.** $1.5\overline{)0.30}$ (0.02)   **8.** $0.15\overline{)0.30}$ (0.02)   **9.** $0.1\overline{)500}$ (5000)   **10.** $0.2\overline{)400}$ (200)

Mentally find the quotient.

11. $0.7\overline{)5.6}$ **12.** $0.5\overline{)\$3.50}$ **13.** $0.3\overline{)0.09}$ **14.** $0.08\overline{)64}$ **15.** $0.09\overline{)5.4}$

13-4 ESTIMATING DECIMAL QUOTIENTS

Roller Rama sold skates for $48.99 a pair, for a
total of $3478.29. You can use compatible
numbers to estimate that about 70 pairs of skates
were sold.

example 1

Estimate.

a. $3478.29 ÷ $48.99

b. $8.95\overline{)4636.1}$

solution

a. $48.99\overline{)3478.29}$

b. $8.95\overline{)4636.1}$

**Round the
divisor and
use compatible
numbers.**

$\underset{50\overline{)3500}}{\text{about } 70}$

$\underset{9\overline{)4500}}{\text{about } 500}$

your turn

Estimate.

1. 8.7 ÷ 3.1
2. 42.5 ÷ 6.6
3. $1643 ÷ 7.5
4. $493.92 ÷ $10.29
5. 444.6 ÷ 29.2
6. $3197.02 ÷ 53.6

example 2

Estimate.

a. 185.7 ÷ 0.03

b. 2618 ÷ 0.53

solution

a. $0.03\overline{)185.7}$

b. $0.53\overline{)2618}$

$\underset{0.03\overline{)180.00}}{\text{about } 6000}$

$\underset{0.5\overline{)2500.0}}{\text{about } 5000}$

your turn

Estimate.

7. 44.27 ÷ 0.05
8. 2.675 ÷ 0.004
9. 46.75 ÷ 0.069
10. 0.0624 ÷ 0.31
11. 0.7859 ÷ 0.21
12. 45.06 ÷ 0.98

practice exercises

practice for example 1 (page 282)

Estimate.

1. $41.7 \div 3.8$
2. $16.2 \div 5.3$
3. $\$12.39 \div \$1.96$
4. $\$61.95 \div \$7.75$
5. $52\overline{)\$263.75}$
6. $18\overline{)\$5729.50}$
7. $38.65\overline{)777.93}$
8. $32.07\overline{)2935}$
9. $4.05 \div 1.786$
10. $35.03 \div 4.297$
11. $65.85 \div 8.72$
12. $4459.5 \div 61.95$

practice for example 2 (page 282)

Estimate.

13. $58.59 \div 0.4$
14. $61.9 \div 0.07$
15. $0.456 \div 0.887$
16. $91.36 \div 0.289$
17. $25.18 \div 0.099$
18. $0.0328 \div 0.044$
19. $573.6 \div 0.583$
20. $4.12 \div 0.058$

mixed practice (page 282)

Estimate.

21. $21.5 \div 6.5$
22. $3068.9 \div 1.138$
23. $402.5 \div 0.961$
24. $15.77 \div 2.81$
25. $97.2 \div 0.92$
26. $16.9 \div 0.28$
27. $347.03 \div 81.59$
28. $1.05 \div 4.79$
29. $41.87 \div 78.5$
30. $0.077 \div 1.92$
31. $35.54 \div 0.071$
32. $4.64 \div 0.077$

33. Last month Carmen earned $490.88 for working 82.5 h. About how much did she earn per hour?

34. Roger earns $4.90 per hour. If he earned $340.55 last month, about how many hours did he work?

35. Each sheet of a certain kind of paper is about 0.068 mm (millimeters) thick. About how many sheets of paper are in a stack that is 5 mm high?

36. A restaurant owner paid $156.62 for shrimp at $7.95 per pound and $59.68 for turkey at $.98 per pound. About how many total pounds of shrimp and turkey did the owner buy?

review exercises

Find each product or quotient.

1. 10^2
2. 10^5
3. 2.468×1000
4. 8.95×100
5. 6.5×100
6. 4.9×1000
7. 8×10^3
8. 5×10^4
9. $18.5 \div 10$
10. $295 \div 100$
11. $594.6 \div 100$
12. $3697 \div 1000$

13-5 SCIENTIFIC NOTATION

Earth is approximately 150,000,000 km (kilometers) from the sun. If you use a simpler form called **scientific notation**, you can write this distance as 1.5×10^8 km. Scientific notation involves two factors.

at least 1, but less than 10 ➜ 1.5×10^8 ⬅ a power of 10

To write a number in scientific notation, use the following method.

1. Write the first factor by moving the decimal point to get a number that is at least 1, but less than 10.
2. The second factor is a power of 10 (10^1, 10^2, 10^3 and so on). Use the number of places that the decimal point was moved as the exponent for the power of 10.

example 1

Write in scientific notation: **a.** 2,500,000   **b.** 426.5   **c.** 12

solution

a. 2,500,000. ⬅ **Move the decimal point six places to the left.**
   2.5×10^6

b. 426.5
   4.265×10^2

c. 12.
   1.2×10^1

your turn

Write in scientific notation.

1. 33,500   **2.** 25,000,000   **3.** 374.9   **4.** 76

example 2

Write the numeral form of each number.

a. 6.82×10^5 **b.** 3.018×10^9

solution

a. Move the decimal point *five* places to the right.
   $6.82 \times 10^5 = 682,000$ ⬅ **Annex zeros as necessary.**

b. Move the decimal point *nine* places to the right.
   $3.018 \times 10^9 = 3,018,000,000$

your turn

Write the numeral form of each number.

5. 3.59×10^2 **6.** 1.285×10^{10} **7.** 7×10^3 **8.** 2×10^9

practice exercises

practice for example 1 *(page 284)*

Write in scientific notation.

1. 890,000
2. 85,000,000
3. 300,000,000
4. 91,000
5. 412.6
6. 68.79
7. 51
8. 2020

practice for example 2 *(page 284)*

Write the numeral form of each number.

9. 1.6×10^6
10. 2.02×10^5
11. 8×10^7
12. 3×10^{11}
13. 4.608×10^3
14. 7.7×10^1
15. 3.263×10^1
16. 6.8395×10^2

mixed practice *(page 284)*

Is each number written in scientific notation? Write *Yes* or *No*.

17. 15.8×10^5
18. 1.2×10^2
19. 3.571×8^{10}
20. 31.8×10^3

21. At times the planet Venus is 40,200,000 km away from Earth. Write this distance in scientific notation.
22. Light travels at a speed of about 3×10^5 km/s (kilometers per second). Write this speed in numeral form.

review exercises

Write each fraction in lowest terms.

1. $\dfrac{4}{16}$
2. $\dfrac{15}{5}$
3. $\dfrac{40}{48}$
4. $\dfrac{45}{50}$
5. $\dfrac{33}{42}$
6. $\dfrac{48}{54}$

calculator corner

Most calculators can display a maximum of eight or ten digits. If you enter 6000000 × 20000000 =, your calculator may show 1.2 14 . This answer represents 1.2×10^{14}, or 120,000,000,000,000.

Find each answer using a calculator.

1. 75,000,000 + 45,000,000
2. 90,000,000 + 60,000,000
3. 50,000 × 500,000
4. 800,000 × 40,000
5. 600 × 70 × 25 × 35 × 500
6. 57,896 × 5,000,000

SKILL REVIEW

Find each quotient. If necessary, round to the nearest thousandth.

1. $5\overline{)18.145}$ 2. $7\overline{)27.71}$ 3. $8\overline{)\$20}$ 4. $4\overline{)142}$ **13-1**
5. $6\overline{)17}$ 6. $14\overline{)295.1}$ 7. $15\overline{)100.8}$ 8. $20\overline{)107}$
9. $54.36 \div 9$ 10. $68.068 \div 34$ 11. $2.046 \div 2$ 12. $0.229 \div 9$
13. $8.056 \div 8$ 14. $\$49.20 \div 41$ 15. $256 \div 13$ 16. $54 \div 24$

Find each quotient.

17. $260.8 \div 10$ 18. $931.43 \div 100$ 19. $1826.7 \div 1000$ **13-2**
20. $0.05 \div 10$ 21. $2 \div 100$ 22. $6 \div 1000$
23. $0.892 \div 10$ 24. $42 \div 1000$ 25. $67.1 \div 100$
26. $3.5 \div 1000$ 27. $86 \div 100$ 28. $1157 \div 10$

29. Ten cheerleaders rented a van and traveled 100 mi. If the rental cost was $40, what was each cheerleader's share?

Find each quotient. If necessary, round to the nearest thousandth.

30. $1.6\overline{)11.84}$ 31. $0.004\overline{)0.124}$ 32. $6.11\overline{)3.7}$ **13-3**
33. $0.008\overline{)0.512}$ 34. $0.3\overline{)13.23}$ 35. $0.06\overline{)6.74}$
36. $196.92 \div 0.4$ 37. $1 \div 0.09$ 38. $57.82 \div 6.8$
39. $2 \div 1.4$ 40. $0.18 \div 0.6$ 41. $1.63 \div 0.008$

42. Lean hamburger costs $1.69 per pound. Sharon bought some hamburger for $6.76. How many pounds of hamburger did she buy?

Estimate.

43. $7.2\overline{)715.44}$ 44. $6.9\overline{)62.41}$ 45. $53.5\overline{)2721.9}$ 46. $9.7\overline{)348.44}$ **13-4**
47. $121.79 \div 0.04$ 48. $591.64 \div 0.31$ 49. $40.25 \div 0.058$ 50. $655.75 \div 0.83$

Write the numeral form of each number.

51. 2.48×10^3 52. 6.3×10^5 53. 3.115×10^1 54. 4.007×10^2 **13-5**
55. 4.02×10^4 56. 6.901×10^6 57. 7.14×10^7 58. 3.056×10^8
59. 5×10^5 60. 9.27×10^1 61. 4.523×10^4 62. 2.06×10^3

Write in scientific notation.

63. $19,170,000,000$ 64. $2,700,000$ 65. 3651
66. $26,030,000,000$ 67. 508.9 68. 45.88
69. $4,000,000,000$ 70. $308,000$ 71. $65,940$

13-6 ANNUAL SALARY

Many people look for jobs in the classified section of the newspaper. Help-wanted ads describe the job. They also include job requirements such as education, training, and experience. Some ads list an **annual salary.**

example

In the ad at the right, the annual salary is $25,000.

a. Find the monthly salary.

b. Find the weekly salary.

solution

a. To find the monthly salary, divide by 12.

$25,000 ÷ 12 ≈ $2083.333

To the nearest cent, the monthly salary is $2083.33.

b. To find the weekly salary, divide by 52.

$25,000 ÷ 52 ≈ $480.769

To the nearest cent, the weekly salary is $480.77.

ACCOUNT CORRESPONDENT

A major magazine publisher has opportunities available in its International Division. The successful candidate will maintain all customer accounts, fill customer orders, perform data entry and process various transactions on a computer terminal. Previous customer service experience and fluent Spanish are desirable. Excellent bookkeeping and communication skills and previous computer terminal use are required. Salary $25,000. Call 555-0000.

exercises

Find the monthly salary for the given annual salary.

1. $15,750
2. $22,500
3. $32,500
4. $43,925

Find the weekly salary for the given annual salary.

5. $11,700
6. $16,420
7. $27,340
8. $33,900

9. John Banks saw a job advertised with an annual salary of $17,500. Find the weekly salary.

10. Diana Cartwright saw an ad for a job with a weekly salary of $459.00. Find the annual salary.

11. Duane Hodges earns $31,700 per year. Find his weekly salary.

12. Find job listings in your local newspaper that include annual salaries. Choose a job you would like to have. Find the weekly and monthly salaries.

Dividing Decimals 287

13-7 HOUSING COSTS

A **mortgage loan** is secured by property. When you buy a house, you usually make a **down payment.** You borrow the balance and repay it with interest in equal monthly installments for a specific number of years.

example 1

Karen is getting a $120,000 mortgage loan for 30 years at a 10.5% *(ten and five-tenths per-cent)* interest rate. Find her monthly payment.

solution

Read down the rate column to 10.5%. Read across to the column headed by 30 yr. The monthly payment per $1000 is $9.15. Multiply by 120 since the loan is for $120,000 and the payment is given as an amount per thousand.

$$120 \times \$9.15 = \$1098$$

The monthly payment is $1098.

Monthly Payment per $1000

Rate (%)	15 yr	20 yr	30 yr
8.5	$9.85	$8.68	$7.69
9.0	10.14	9.00	8.00
9.5	10.44	9.32	8.41
10.0	10.75	9.65	8.78
10.5	11.05	9.98	9.15
11.0	11.37	10.32	9.53

your turn

Use the table to find the monthly payment.

1. loan amount: $185,000
   rate: 9.5%
   years: 15

2. loan amount: $63,000
   rate: 8.5%
   years: 20

Many mortgage lenders require that you pay money into an **escrow** account every month to pay property tax and insurance bills.

example 2

The Morgans' annual property tax is $2709.60 and annual property insurance bill is $732. Find the monthly escrow payment.

solution

Add the payments to find the total amount due.

Divide by 12 to find the monthly payment.

$2709.60 + $732.00 = $3441.60

$3441.60 ÷ 12 = $286.80

The monthly escrow payment is $286.80.

your turn

Find the monthly escrow payment for the given annual payments.

3. property tax: $3477.24
   insurance: $1296.00

4. property tax: $624.72
   insurance: $486.96

practice exercises

practice for example 1 (page 288)

Use the table on page 288. Find the monthly payment for the given mortgage loan.

	LOAN AMOUNT	RATE (%)	YEARS
1.	$100,000	9.0	20
2.	$70,000	11.0	30
3.	$125,000	9.5	15
4.	$165,000	10.0	30

practice for example 2 (pages 288–289)

Find the monthly escrow payment for the given annual payments.

5. property tax: $1359.36
   insurance: $756.00

6. property tax: $2590.56
   insurance: $504.96

7. property tax: $1052.04
   insurance: $684.00

8. property tax: $397.56
   insurance: $330.00

mixed practice (pages 288–289)

9. The O'Haras are taking out a mortgage loan for $148,000 at 8.5% for 30 years. Find their monthly payment.

10. Bob Tatung is buying a house for $153,000. He is making a down payment of $30,000. For the balance, he is taking out a mortgage loan at 9.0% for 20 years. Find the amount of the mortgage loan and the monthly payment.

11. The Carreras have a 30-year mortgage loan for $127,000 at 9.0%. They have annual property tax payments of $1191.72 and property insurance payments of $625.80. Find their monthly mortgage loan and escrow payments.

12. Joanna Blair makes monthly escrow payments of $187.00 for property taxes and $72.77 for property insurance. Find the annual amounts Joanna pays for property taxes and insurance.

TEACHER

Mark Osborne teaches social studies at Hayes High School. As part of his job, he must compute his students' quiz averages.

Quiz Scores					
Quiz	1	2	3	4	5
Jo Sims	80	75	63	72	68
Mike Stevens	70	72	78	85	90
Wayne Thiese	67	77	69	82	80
Sally Tan	89	91	98	88	91
Larry Tolin	86	79	84	87	80

example

Use the quiz scores at the right. Find Jo's quiz average.

solution

Add the grades for each quiz. Then divide the sum by the number of grades. Round the quotient to the nearest whole number.

$$80 + 75 + 63 + 72 + 68 = 358$$

$$358 \div 5 = 71.6 \approx 72 \quad \longleftarrow \quad \text{A calculator may be helpful.}$$

Jo's quiz average is 72.

exercises

Find each student's quiz average.

1. Mike
2. Wayne
3. Sally
4. Larry

Find the average. Then use the grading scale below to find the letter grade.

5. Lupita's history quiz grades were 92, 87, 85, and 78.

6. Frank's math quiz grades were 75, 79, 82, 77, 82, and 90.

7. Harry's English quiz grades were 90, 92, 95, 88, and 90.

8. Ruth's French quiz grades were 100, 87, 86, 96, 92, and 93.

Grading Scale

A^+ = 97–100	A = 94–96	A^- = 90–93
B^+ = 87–89	B = 84–86	B^- = 80–83
C^+ = 77–79	C = 74–76	C^- = 70–73
D^+ = 68–69	D = 65–67	F = 0–64

CHAPTER REVIEW

vocabulary vo·cab·u·lar·y

Choose the correct word to complete each sentence.

1. When you divide two decimals, the answer is called the (*dividend, quotient*).

2. The number 1.4×2^{10} (*is, is not*) written in scientific notation.

skills

Find each quotient. If necessary, round to the nearest thousandth.

3. $6\overline{)2.1}$
4. $5\overline{)0.875}$
5. $16\overline{)100}$

6. $0.064 \div 8$
7. $\$159.50 \div 11$
8. $\$92.16 \div 32$

9. $0.9 \div 100$
10. $0.12 \div 10$
11. $113.62 \div 10$

12. $248.91 \div 10$
13. $42.26 \div 100$
14. $7.92 \div 10$

15. $0.3\overline{)156.63}$
16. $0.5\overline{)0.009}$
17. $0.002\overline{)1.554}$

18. $3 \div 1.332$
19. $0.504 \div 0.008$
20. $4.8 \div 0.12$

Estimate.

21. $5.9\overline{)34.9}$
22. $27.8\overline{)245.5}$
23. $74.1\overline{)369.85}$
24. $87.9\overline{)7925.5}$

25. $578.9 \div 0.08$
26. $436.9 \div 0.047$
27. $64.97 \div 0.099$
28. $2.65 \div 0.38$

Match the scientific notation with the correct numeral form.

29. 1.208×10^4
30. 1.208×10^5

31. 1.208×10^7
32. 1.208×10^2

33. 1.208×10^1
34. 1.208×10^8

A. 12,080,000
B. 12.08
C. 1,208,000
D. 12,080
E. 120,800
F. 120.8
G. 120,800,000
H. 1208

35. Fifteen students contributed equally to a class gift costing $127.50. How much money did each student contribute?

36. Robert Shapiro saw an ad for a job with an annual salary of $23,000. Find the weekly salary.

37. Use the table on page 288. The Johnsons are taking out a $100,000 mortgage loan at 9.0% for 15 years. Find their monthly payment.

38. Concert tickets cost $19.50 each. If $3861 was collected from the sale of tickets, about how many tickets were sold?

39. The Gilberts' annual property tax is $2138.88. Their annual property insurance bill is $456. Find the monthly escrow payment.

CHAPTER TEST

Find each quotient. If necessary, round to the nearest thousandth.

1. $5\overline{)22.1}$ 2. $5\overline{)\$7.25}$ 3. $6\overline{)0.036}$ 4. $7\overline{)16.5}$ **13-1**

5. $6.21 \div 30$ 6. $10 \div 80$ 7. $\$5333.44 \div 14$ 8. $3.33 \div 11$

9. Four friends contributed equally to buy a gift for $46. What was each friend's share of the total cost?

Find each quotient.

10. $16.28 \div 100$ 11. $74 \div 100$ 12. $0.355 \div 10$ 13. $0.42 \div 10$ **13-2**

14. $1498 \div 1000$ 15. $1515 \div 1000$ 16. $0.16 \div 100$ 17. $32.3 \div 10$

18. If one kilowatt equals 1000 watts, how many kilowatts are in 18,400 watts?

Find each quotient. If necessary, round to the nearest thousandth.

19. $8.1\overline{)33.3}$ 20. $4.1\overline{)5.33}$ 21. $0.4\overline{)22.6}$ 22. $0.83\overline{)0.84}$ **13-3**

23. $12 \div 0.04$ 24. $4.4 \div 0.11$ 25. $17.98 \div 2.9$ 26. $0.141 \div 0.003$

27. Joshua paid $1.80 for 1.44 kg (kilograms) of grapes. How much did the grapes cost per kilogram?

Estimate.

28. $7.95\overline{)62.95}$ 29. $53.1\overline{)458.9}$ 30. $307.7 \div 0.08$ 31. $3418 \div 0.72$ **13-4**

32. Frank earns $5.10 per hour. If he earned $198.90 last month, about how many hours did he work?

Write in scientific notation.

33. 68,000   34. 4,900,000   35. 3067   **13-5**

36. 515   37. 16.2   38. 933.8

Write in numeral form.

39. 4.27×10^9 40. 7.655×10^8 41. 1.3×10^1

42. 1.424×10^2 43. 5.9×10^4 44. 8.93×10^5

45. Susan saw a job advertised with an annual salary of $13,350. Find the monthly salary.   **13-6**

46. Use the table on page 288. Find the monthly payment on a $120,000 mortgage loan for 15 years at a 10.0% interest rate.   **13-7**

The precise measurements needed in the design and construction of this automobile engine were specified in metric units.

CHAPTER 14

METRIC MEASUREMENT

14-1 METRIC UNITS OF LENGTH

The **meter** is the basic unit of length in the metric system. The measure of one long step is about one meter (m).

The chart below shows how other metric units of length are related to the meter.

Unit	Symbol	Relationship to Meter
*kilometer	km	1 km = 1000 m
hectometer	hm	1 hm = 100 m
dekameter	dam	1 dam = 10 m
*meter	m	1 m = 1 m
decimeter	dm	1 dm = 0.1 m
*centimeter	cm	1 cm = 0.01 m
*millimeter	mm	1 mm = 0.001 m

*most commonly used units

The **kilometer** is used to measure long distances. The length of twelve city blocks is about one kilometer (km). A marathon runner can cover a distance of one kilometer in about three minutes.

example 1

Select the more reasonable unit. Choose m or km.

a. The distance from New York to Chicago is about 1144 ___?___.
b. The length of a compact car is about 4.5 ___?___.

solution

a. km

Chicago ● 1144 km ● New York

b. m

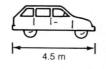

4.5 m

your turn

Select the more reasonable unit. Choose m or km.

1. The height of a flagpole is about 10 ___?___.
2. The length of the Mississippi River is about 3760 ___?___.
3. The length of a marathon run is about 42.2 ___?___.

294 Chapter 14

Short lengths are measured in **centimeters** (cm) or **millimeters** (mm).

The width of a large paper clip is about one centimeter (cm).

The thickness of a large paper clip is about one millimeter (mm).

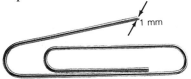

example 2

Select the more reasonable unit. Choose cm or mm.

a. The length of a house key is about 50 __?__.
b. The thickness of a textbook is about 2.5 __?__.

solution

a. mm

b. cm

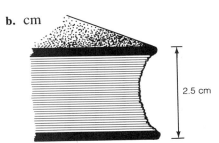

your turn

Select the more reasonable unit. Choose cm or mm.

4. The length of a new pencil is about 19 __?__.
5. The length of a large paper clip is about 47 __?__.
6. The width of a sheet of notebook paper is about 21.6 __?__.

practice exercises

practice for example 1 (page 294)

Select the more reasonable unit. Choose m or km.

1. The length of an airport runway is about 1700 __?__.
2. The length of a swimming pool is about 50 __?__.
3. The height of a refrigerator is about 1.6 __?__.
4. The distance from Dallas to Houston is about 387.2 __?__.

Select the more reasonable unit. Choose cm or mm.

5. The length of a hammer is about 26 __?__.
6. The width of a thumbnail is about 15 __?__.
7. The thickness of a sheet of notebook paper is about 0.1 __?__.
8. The length of a sheet of notebook paper is about 27.8 __?__.

mixed practice (pages 294–295)

Select the most reasonable unit. Choose mm, cm, m, or km.

9. thickness of a button: 2 __?__
10. thickness of a wire: 2 __?__
11. length of a hiking trail: 24 __?__
12. height of a mountain: 5800 __?__
13. width of a dollar bill: 6.6 __?__
14. height of a ceiling: 2.4 __?__
15. distance across a lake: 3.2 __?__
16. height of a vase: 25.5 __?__

Select the most reasonable measure.

17. height of a door:
    2 cm   2 m   2 km

18. length of a baseball bat:
    85 mm   85 cm   85 m

19. thickness of a nickel:
    2 mm   2 cm   2 m

20. distance around a track:
    4 cm   4 m   4 km

21. height of a person:
    150 mm   150 cm   150 m

22. height of a tall building:
    21 cm   21 m   21 km

23. length of a table:
    1.4 cm   1.4 m   1.4 km

24. distance of a paper route:
    0.6 cm   0.6 m   0.6 km

25. thickness of cardboard:
    0.2 mm   0.2 cm   0.2 m

26. length of a ball-point pen:
    15.1 mm   15.1 cm   15.1 m

review *exercises*

Evaluate each expression when $a = 16$, $b = 8$, and $c = 2$.

1. $a + b$
2. $b - c$
3. ac
4. abc
5. $12a$
6. $14c + 3a$
7. $\frac{a}{b}$
8. $\frac{b}{a}$

Compare. Replace each __?__ with <, >, or =.

9. 0.7519 __?__ 0.7591
10. 12.39 __?__ 12.309
11. 1.3 __?__ 1.27
12. 0.4 __?__ 0.40

14-2 USING A METRIC RULER

You can use a metric ruler to measure lengths in centimeters or millimeters.

example 1

To measure the pencil to the nearest centimeter, place the ruler along the pencil so that the leftmost mark on the ruler lines up with one end of the pencil.

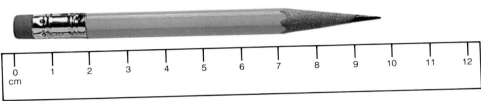

On the ruler, read the mark nearest the other end of the pencil.
The end of the pencil is nearer 10 cm than 9 cm.

To the nearest centimeter, the length of the pencil is 10 cm.

your turn

Measure each object to the nearest centimeter.

1.

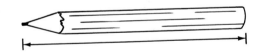

2.

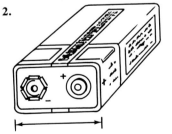

   On a metric ruler, each centimeter can be divided into ten equal parts. Each of these parts is one millimeter long. You can express a measurement in both centimeters and millimeters.

One centimeter equals ten millimeters.   1 cm = 10 mm
One millimeter equals one tenth of a centimeter.   1 mm = 0.1 cm

example 2

To measure the height of the stamp in centimeters and millimeters, place the ruler along the stamp so the bottom mark on the ruler lines up with the base of the stamp. Read the mark nearest the top of the stamp.

a. The height of the stamp in millimeters is 19 mm.

b. Since 1 mm = 0.1 cm, 19 mm = 1.9 cm.
   The height of the stamp in centimeters is 1.9 cm.

your turn

Measure the height of each stamp in:

a. millimeters   **b. centimeters**

3.

4.

practice *exercises*

practice for example 1 (page 297)

Measure the length of each object to the nearest centimeter.

1.

2.

3.

4.

practice for example 2 (page 298)

Measure the length of each object in:
a. millimeters   b. centimeters

5.

6.

7.

8.

mixed practice (pages 297–298)

Measure each distance in: a. millimeters   b. centimeters

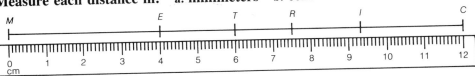

9. *ME*   **10.** *MT*   **11.** *MR*   **12.** *MI*   **13.** *MC*   **14.** *TI*

Draw a line segment of the given length.

15. 9 cm   **16.** 4 cm   **17.** 3.2 cm   **18.** 11.5 cm   **19.** 60 mm   **20.** 115 mm

Guess which distance is longer. Measure to check your guess.

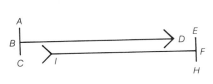

21. *AC* or *EH*   **22.** *BD* or *IF*   **23.** *MO* or *OP*   **24.** *WY* or *XZ*

review *exercises*

Find each product or quotient.

1. 17.6×10 **2.** $450 \div 100$ **3.** $24 \div 1000$ **4.** 32.5×100

Replace each __?__ with <, >, or =.

5. $\frac{3}{4}$ __?__ $\frac{17}{20}$ **6.** $\frac{2}{5}$ __?__ $\frac{3}{4}$ **7.** $\frac{5}{9}$ __?__ $\frac{2}{9}$ **8.** $\frac{7}{9}$ __?__ $\frac{7}{10}$

calculator corner

The average distance from Earth to the moon is 384,000 km. Use this fact to solve the problems below.

1. Suppose you drive a car to the moon at a speed of 88 km/h. About how many hours will it take to reach the moon? how many days?
2. Suppose you ride a bicycle to the moon at a speed of 20 km/h.
   a. About how many hours will it take to reach the moon?
   b. If you leave for the moon by bicycle on your next birthday, about how old will you be when you reach the moon? when you return?

14-3 CHANGING UNITS OF LENGTH IN THE METRIC SYSTEM

You can think of metric units of length as steps on a ladder. The smallest unit shown, the millimeter, is on the bottom step. The largest unit shown, the kilometer, is on the top step. Each unit is ten times as large as the unit on the step directly below.

You *multiply* to change from a larger unit to a smaller unit.

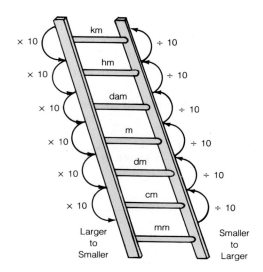

From cm to mm is *one* step down the ladder.

$$1 \text{ cm} = 10 \text{ mm}$$
$$\times 10$$

From m to cm is *two* steps down the ladder.

$$1 \text{ m} = 100 \text{ cm}$$
$$\times 10 \times 10$$

From m to mm is *three* steps down the ladder.

$$1 \text{ m} = 1000 \text{ mm}$$
$$\times 10 \times 10 \times 10$$

From km to m is *three* steps down the ladder.

$$1 \text{ km} = 1000 \text{ m}$$
$$\times 10 \times 10 \times 10$$

example 1

Complete.

a. 9 km = _?_ m

b. 3.2 cm = _?_ mm

solution

a. From km to m is 3 steps down the ladder. So multiply by 1000.

9 km = 9000 m ⟵ **Move the decimal point three places to the right.**
$$\times 1000$$

b. From cm to mm is 1 step down the ladder. So multiply by 10.

3.2 cm = 32 mm ⟵ **Move the decimal point one place to the right.**
$$\times 10$$

your turn

Complete.

1. 5 cm = _?_ mm

2. 4 m = _?_ mm

3. 30 km = _?_ m

4. 8.2 m = _?_ cm

5. 3.4 km = _?_ m

6. 12.9 m = _?_ cm

You *divide* to change from a smaller unit to a larger unit.

example 2

Complete.

a. 4000 mm = __?__ m   **b.** 485 cm = __?__ m

solution

a. From mm to m is 3 steps up the ladder. So divide by 1000.

4000 mm = 4 m ← **Move the decimal point three places to the left.**

↳ ÷ 1000 ↗

b. From cm to m is 2 steps up the ladder. So divide by 100.

485 cm = 4.85 m ← **Move the decimal point two places to the left.**

↳ ÷ 100 ↗

your turn

Complete.

7. 8000 m = __?__ km   **8.** 2000 cm = __?__ m   **9.** 420 mm = __?__ cm

10. 3700 mm = __?__ m   **11.** 3700 mm = __?__ cm   **12.** 298 cm = __?__ m

practice *exercises*

practice for example 1 *(page 300)*

Complete.

1. 4 km = __?__ m   **2.** 8.4 m = __?__ cm   **3.** 4.9 km = __?__ m

4. 15.2 m = __?__ cm   **5.** 2.3 m = __?__ mm   **6.** 45 cm = __?__ mm

practice for example 2 *(page 301)*

Complete.

7. 4000 m = __?__ km   **8.** 350 cm = __?__ m   **9.** 380 mm = __?__ cm

10. 629 cm = __?__ m   **11.** 58 m = __?__ km   **12.** 8500 mm = __?__ cm

mixed practice *(pages 300–301)*

Complete.

13. 5.8 m = __?__ cm   **14.** 280 mm = __?__ cm   **15.** 350 m = __?__ km

16. 4.32 km = __?__ m   **17.** 0.86 m = __?__ mm   **18.** 45.9 cm = __?__ m

Metric Measurement 301

Complete. Replace each __?__ with <, >, or =.

19. 0.5 m __?__ 50 cm

20. 360 mm __?__ 47 cm

21. 60 cm __?__ 6 m

22. 3.8 m __?__ 3800 mm

23. 32 cm __?__ 310 mm

24. 0.6 km __?__ 60 m

25. 420 mm __?__ 4.2 m

26. 8000 m __?__ 0.8 km

27. Toni rode 5.4 km on her bike. How many meters did she ride?

28. A math book is 30 mm thick. How many centimeters is this?

29. Tyrill walks 345 m to school. Express this distance in kilometers.

30. Arrange the following measures in order from largest to smallest: 369.4 cm, 3.6 m, 3750 mm

review *exercises*

Find each answer.

1. 8431 + 17,279

2. 68.9 × 1.4

3. 78 ÷ 0.2

4. 38,232 ÷ 81

5. 14 − 3.75

6. 198 × 403

7. 24,005 − 6739

8. 9.4 + 0.65 + 7

9. $12 \div \frac{1}{2}$

10. $\frac{1}{3} + \frac{1}{4}$

11. $\frac{7}{12} - \frac{1}{6}$

12. $\frac{2}{3} \times \frac{9}{10}$

mental math

To do mental math with money, it may help to think about the dollars and cents separately.

$1.75 + $4.30 = $5 + $1.05
               = $6.05

3 × $2.75 = (3 × $2) + (3 × $.75)
          = $6 + $2.25 = $8.25

Add, subtract, or multiply mentally.

1. $6.80 + $4.20

2. $9.25 − $3.15

3. $2.30 + $1.45 + $3.25

4. 8 × $1.25

5. 7 × $2.25

6. $1.25 + $3.75 + $6.15

14-4 METRIC UNITS OF CAPACITY

The **liter** is the basic unit of liquid capacity in the
metric system. A milk carton holds about one liter (L).
Milliliters are used to measure small amounts of liquid.

$$1 \text{ L} = 1000 \text{ mL}$$

about 1 L

about 1 mL

Unit	Symbol	Relationship to Liter		
kiloliter	kL	1 kL	=	1000 L
hectoliter	hL	1 hL	=	100 L
dekaliter	daL	1 daL	=	10 L
*Liter	L	1 L	=	1 L
deciliter	dL	1 dL	=	0.1 L
centiliter	cL	1 cL	=	0.01 L
*milliliter	mL	1 mL	=	0.001 L

*most commonly used units

example 1

Select the more reasonable unit. Choose L or mL.

a. A teaspoon holds about 5 __?__.

b. A water bucket holds about 6.2 __?__.

solution

a. mL

b. L

your turn

Select the more reasonable unit. Choose L or mL.

1. A mug holds about 250 __?__.

2. A vase has a capacity of about 0.89 __?__.

example 2

Complete.

a. 7000 mL = __?__ L

b. 2.5 L = __?__ mL

solution

a. 1000 mL = 1 L, so 7000 mL = 7 L
$\div 1000$ $\div 1000$

b. 1 L = 1000 mL, so 2.5 L = 2500 mL
$\times 1000$ $\times 1000$

your turn

Complete.

3. 9 L = __?__ mL **4.** 11,000 mL = __?__ L **5.** 3.2 L = __?__ mL **6.** 40 mL = __?__ L

practice exercises

practice for example 1 (page 303)

**Select the more reasonable unit.
Choose L or mL.**

1. A milk glass contains 300 __?__.
2. A fish tank has a capacity of 85.4 __?__.
3. A paint container holds 3.9 __?__.
4. A recipe calls for 5 __?__ of vanilla.

practice for example 2 (page 303)

Complete.

5. 8.2 L = __?__ mL   6. 3 L = __?__ mL   7. 4500 mL = __?__ L
8. 750 mL = __?__ L   9. 300 mL = __?__ L   10. 0.6 L = __?__ mL

mixed practice (page 303)

Complete. Replace each __?__ with >, <, or =.

11. 890 mL __?__ 1 L   12. 0.75 L __?__ 750 mL   13. 3.2 L __?__ 3000 mL
14. 500 mL __?__ 0.5 L   15. 12 L __?__ 15,000 mL   16. 5 L __?__ 500 mL

17. A carton contains 800 mL of grape juice. Express this in liters.
18. A pitcher has a capacity of 0.4 L. What is its capacity in milliliters?
19. A bowl is filled with punch. The capacity of the bowl is 5.4 L.
    About how many 250-mL glasses of punch can be served
    from the bowl?

review exercises

Write each fraction as a mixed number in lowest terms.

1. $\frac{28}{9}$ 2. $\frac{53}{6}$ 3. $\frac{100}{45}$ 4. $\frac{1010}{125}$

Write each fraction as a decimal.

5. $\frac{7}{20}$ 6. $\frac{5}{8}$ 7. $\frac{2}{9}$ 8. $\frac{5}{11}$

9. Cassie earns $8.25 per hour. How much does she earn in 40 h?
10. Ed worked 30 h and earned $195. What is his hourly rate of pay?

14-5 METRIC UNITS OF MASS

The **gram** is the basic unit of mass in the metric system. The mass of a large paper clip is about 1 gram (g).

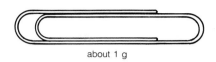

about 1 g

The chart below shows how other metric units of mass are related to the gram.

Unit	Symbol	Relationship to Gram
*kilogram	kg	1 kg = 1000 g
hectogram	hg	1 hg = 100 g
dekagram	dag	1 dag = 10 g
*gram	g	1 g = 1 g
decigram	dg	1 dg = 0.1 g
centigram	cg	1 cg = 0.01 g
*milligram	mg	1 mg = 0.001 g

*most commonly used units

Kilograms are used to measure the mass of heavy objects.

Milligrams are used to measure the mass of light objects.

about 1 kg

about 20 mg

example 1

Select the most reasonable unit. Choose mg, g, or kg.

a. A watch has a mass of about 85 _?_.

b. A maple leaf has a mass of about 10 _?_.

c. A lawn mower has a mass of about 52.5 _?_.

solution

a. g   b. mg   c. kg

your turn

Select the most reasonable unit. Choose mg, g, or kg.

1. A postage stamp has a mass of about 20 _?_.
2. A typewriter has a mass of about 10.5 _?_.
3. An alarm clock has a mass of about 35 _?_.
4. An envelope has a mass of about 84.2 _?_.
5. This textbook has a mass of about 1 _?_.

In changing from one metric unit of mass to another, you use these relationships most often:

$$1 \text{ kg} = 1000 \text{ g}$$
$$1 \text{ g} = 1000 \text{ mg}$$

Remember, you *multiply* to change from a larger unit to a smaller unit. You *divide* to change from a smaller unit to a larger unit.

example 2

Complete.

a. $32.5 \text{ kg} = \underline{\ ?\ } \text{ g}$ **b.** $400 \text{ mg} = \underline{\ ?\ } \text{ g}$

solution

a. *Think:* larger unit → smaller unit. Multiply.

$$1 \text{ kg} = 1000 \text{ g}, \quad \text{so} \quad 32.5 \text{ kg} = 32{,}500 \text{ g}$$
$$\underbrace{\qquad}_{\times\ 1000} \qquad\qquad\qquad \underbrace{\qquad}_{\times\ 1000}$$

b. *Think:* smaller unit → larger unit. Divide.

$$1000 \text{ mg} = 1 \text{ g}, \quad \text{so} \quad 400 \text{ mg} = 0.4 \text{ g}$$
$$\underbrace{\qquad}_{\div\ 1000} \qquad\qquad\qquad \underbrace{\qquad}_{\div\ 1000}$$

your turn

Complete.

6. $8 \text{ g} = \underline{\ ?\ } \text{ mg}$ **7.** $3000 \text{ g} = \underline{\ ?\ } \text{ kg}$ **8.** $60 \text{ kg} = \underline{\ ?\ } \text{ g}$

9. $76 \text{ mg} = \underline{\ ?\ } \text{ g}$ **10.** $5.93 \text{ kg} = \underline{\ ?\ } \text{ g}$ **11.** $4500 \text{ mg} = \underline{\ ?\ } \text{ g}$

practice exercises

practice for example 1 (page 305)

Select the most reasonable unit. Choose mg, g, or kg.

1. A box of cereal has a mass of 425 $\underline{\ ?\ }$.   **2.** A pencil has a mass of 25 $\underline{\ ?\ }$.

3. A camera has a mass of 0.5 $\underline{\ ?\ }$.   **4.** An apple has a mass of 300 $\underline{\ ?\ }$.

5. A person has a mass of 60.4 $\underline{\ ?\ }$.   **6.** A feather has a mass of 6 $\underline{\ ?\ }$.

practice for example 2 (page 306)

Complete.

7. $380 \text{ g} = \underline{\ ?\ } \text{ mg}$ **8.** $3 \text{ kg} = \underline{\ ?\ } \text{ g}$ **9.** $2500 \text{ mg} = \underline{\ ?\ } \text{ g}$

10. $5420 \text{ mg} = \underline{\ ?\ } \text{ g}$ **11.** $1.6 \text{ kg} = \underline{\ ?\ } \text{ g}$ **12.** $320 \text{ mg} = \underline{\ ?\ } \text{ g}$

mixed practice (pages 305–306)

Complete. Replace each $\underline{\ ?\ }$ with >, <, or =.

13. $0.2 \text{ kg} \underline{\ ?\ } 20 \text{ g}$ **14.** $1200 \text{ mg} \underline{\ ?\ } 1.2 \text{ g}$ **15.** $198 \text{ g} \underline{\ ?\ } 0.2 \text{ kg}$

16. $4.2 \text{ kg} \underline{\ ?\ } 4200 \text{ g}$ **17.** $750 \text{ mg} \underline{\ ?\ } 1 \text{ g}$ **18.** $450 \text{ g} \underline{\ ?\ } 30{,}000 \text{ mg}$

Choose the letter of the appropriate unit for measuring the given object.

19. the mass of a banana   **a.** L   **b.** cm   **c.** g
20. the length of your foot   **a.** cm   **b.** g   **c.** km
21. the capacity of a bathtub   **a.** mm   **b.** L   **c.** m
22. the distance between two cities   **a.** mL   **b.** km   **c.** kg

23. A lantern has a mass of 1.6 kg. How many grams is this?
24. A pair of tennis shoes has a mass of 635 g. How many kilograms is this?
25. A can of dog food has a mass of 120 g. Find the mass of 12 cans of dog food. Express your answer in grams and in kilograms.
26. Which has the greater mass: a 450-g box of cereal or a 0.5-kg box of cereal? How much greater?

review exercises

Complete.

1. 3.4 cm = __?__ m
2. 6 cm = __?__ mm
3. 480 mm = __?__ cm
4. 4.1 km = __?__ m
5. 0.5 m = __?__ cm
6. 3400 mm = __?__ cm
7. 8.3 L = __?__ mL
8. 74 mL = __?__ L
9. 220 mg = __?__ g
10. 19 kg = __?__ g
11. 34 g = __?__ mg
12. 7.8 g = __?__ kg

puzzle corner

Place a dime in the middle of an index card. Trace its outline. Carefully cut out a dime-size hole. Now figure out how to fit a nickel through the hole.

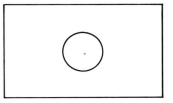

14-6 USING DRAWINGS

To solve some problems, you may find it helpful
to make a drawing that pictures the given facts.

example

Mia leaves her house and walks 4 blocks due south and 2 blocks due east
to Lori's house. Together they walk 1 block due north, 4 blocks due
east, then 3 blocks due north to the library. Where is the library located
in relation to Mia's house?

solution

Step 1 Given: Mia's house → Lori's house—4 blocks S, 2 blocks E
Lori's house → library—1 block N, 4 E, 3 N

Find: Mia's house → library—How many blocks? What direction?

Step 2 Draw a simple grid map of city streets. Identify the directions north,
south, east, and west. Trace the girls' route on the map.

Step 3

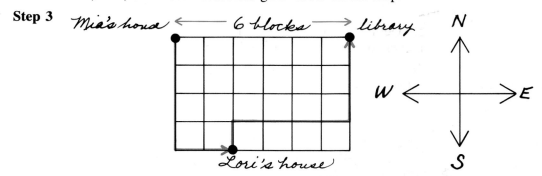

Step 4 The library is 6 blocks due east of Mia's house.

problems

Draw a simple grid map to picture the problem. Then solve.

1. Tom leaves his house and jogs 3 blocks due west, 2 blocks due
   north, 4 blocks due west, 5 blocks due south, and 7 blocks due east.
   At that point, where is Tom in relation to his house?

2. Ella leaves school and bicycles 8 blocks due north, then makes a left
   turn and bicycles 4 blocks to the dentist's office. When she leaves
   the dentist's office, she bicycles 4 blocks due north, then makes a
   right turn and bicycles 4 blocks to her house. Where is Ella's house
   in relation to her school?

3. Kim drives a school bus. She leaves school, drives 12 blocks due south, and picks up 8 students. She then makes a right turn, drives 4 blocks, and picks up 12 more students. She makes another right turn, drives 12 blocks, and picks up 6 more students. At that point, where is Kim in relation to school?

4. Luis delivers groceries for the Best Buy Market. To make his first delivery of the day, he leaves the market and drives 4 blocks due east. He then makes a right turn and drives 12 blocks to make his second delivery. To make his third delivery, he reverses direction and drives 4 blocks, then makes a left turn and drives 4 blocks. After the third delivery, where is Luis in relation to the market?

Make a drawing to picture the problem. Then solve.

5. Assuming that each corner must be tacked, what is the least number of tacks that you need to display six 8-in. by 10-in. photographs so that they can all be seen?

6. Making identical cuts, a lumberjack can saw a log into 5 pieces in 20 min. How long would it take to cut a log of the same size and shape into 10 pieces?

7. The lengths of three steel rods are 12 cm, 18 cm, and 22 cm. How could you use these rods to mark off a length of 28 cm?

8. The capacities of three containers are 3 L, 5 L, and 9 L. How could you use these containers to measure exactly 7 L of water?

review *exercises*

1. One week the Computer Center sold eight identical computers for a total of $15,118. What did each computer sell for?

2. The three volumes of a set of books are arranged in order on a bookshelf. The thickness of each cover is 0.18 cm. The total thickness of the pages of each book is 2.5 cm. What is the distance from the first page of Volume I to the last page of Volume III?

3. Look for a pattern. Then write the next three numbers:
   2, 6, 3, 9, 6, 18, 15, __?__, __?__, __?__

4. For the senior class play 287 tickets were sold for $6 each and 396 tickets were sold for $4.75 each. Choose the letter of the best estimate of the profit from the ticket sales.
   a. between $2600 and $3200
   b. between $3200 and $3800
   c. between $3800 and $4400
   d. between $4400 and $5000

SKILL REVIEW

Select the most reasonable measure.

14-1

1. length of a classroom
   20 mm   20 m   20 km
2. width of a paperback book
   11 cm   11 m   11 km
3. distance from Dallas to New Orleans
   600 cm   600 m   600 km
4. width of a watchband
   7 mm   7 cm   7 km

Measure the length of each object in: a. centimeters   b. millimeters

14-2

5.

6.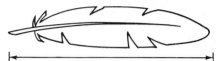

Complete.

14-3

7. 34 cm = _?_ mm
8. 65 mm = _?_ m
9. 40 km = _?_ m
10. 23 m = _?_ cm
11. 4780 m = _?_ km
12. 56 cm = _?_ m

Select the more reasonable unit.   Choose L or mL.

14-4

13. amount of water in a raindrop: 3 _?_
14. capacity of a saucepan: 2 _?_
15. capacity of an aquarium: 8.6 _?_
16. capacity of a bottle cap: 10 _?_

Arrange the measures in order from smallest to largest.

17. 4 L, 4200 mL, 420 mL, 4.5 L
18. 8800 mL, 7.8 L, 0.87 L, 860 mL

Select the most reasonable measure.

14-5

19. mass of a snowflake
    2 mg   2 g   2 kg
20. mass of a cafeteria tray
    156 mg   156 g   156 kg
21. mass of a pitcher of juice
    1.3 mg   1.3 g   1.3 kg
22. mass of a bicycle
    6.8 mg   6.8 g   6.8 kg

Complete.   Replace each _?_ with <, >, or =.

23. 5 mg _?_ 50 g
24. 4500 g _?_ 5 kg
25. 23 kg _?_ 23,000 g
26. 0.242 g _?_ 24.2 mg
27. 600 mg _?_ 0.6 g
28. 9.1 g _?_ 90 kg

Make a drawing to picture the problem.   Then solve.

14-6

29. Mary Sue leaves her house and walks 3 blocks due west, then turns right and walks 5 blocks to the post office. She reverses her direction, walks 7 blocks, then turns left and walks 3 blocks to the store. Where is the store in relation to Mary Sue's house?

14-7 ELECTRICITY COSTS

Appliance	Wattage Rating
clock	3
TV	150
60-watt light bulb	60
hair dryer	1250
computer	120
vacuum cleaner	960
clothes dryer	5600
toaster	1500

You pay for electricity by the kilowatt-hour (kW • h). One kilowatt-hour is used each time 1000 watts of energy are used for one hour. The table at the right shows wattage ratings for some appliances.

You can use a formula to compute the cost of operating an appliance.

$$\text{operating cost} = \frac{\text{wattage rating} \times \text{hours}}{1000 \text{ watt-hours}} \times \text{cost per kilowatt-hour}$$

example

Electricity costs $.11/kW • h (per kilowatt-hour). A toaster is used for about 8 h per month. Find the cost of operating the toaster for a month.

solution

From the table, the wattage rating is 1500.

$$\text{operating cost} = \frac{1500 \times 8}{1000} \times \$.11$$

$$= \frac{12,000}{1000} \times \$.11 = \$1.32$$

It costs about $1.32 per month to operate the toaster.

exercises

Assume that the cost of electricity is $.08/kW • h. Find the cost of operating each appliance for the given length of time.

1. computer; 25 h
2. vacuum cleaner; 25 h
3. TV; 120 h
4. clothes dryer; 20 h

5. A lamp with a 60-watt bulb is on for 100 h. Electricity costs $.10/kW • h. Find the cost of operating the lamp.

6. A hair dryer is used for 4 h. Electricity costs $.12/kW • h. Find the cost of operating the hair dryer.

7. A clock runs for 24 h a day. Assume that electricity costs $.09/kW • h. Find the cost of operating the clock for 125 days.

8. Check the wattage rating on an appliance in your home. Estimate the amount of time the appliance is used each month. Round your estimate to the nearest hour. Use the cost of electricity in your area to estimate the cost of operating the appliance for one month.

14-8 READING METERS

Electricity is measured in kilowatt-hours (kW • h). You read the dials on an electric meter from left to right. If a pointer is between two numbers, read the lesser number. If a pointer is between 9 and 0, think of 0 as 10 and read 9.

example 1

Read the meter.

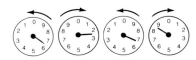

solution

The meter reading is 6268.

your turn

Read the meter.

1.

2.

example 2

Find the number of kilowatt-hours used during the month.

January 1   February 1

solution

The reading for January is 2169. The reading for February is 3288.
Subtract January's reading from February's reading.

$$3288 - 2169 = 1119$$

During the month, 1119 kW • h of electricity were used.

your turn

Find the number of kilowatt-hours used during the month.

3. May 1 / June 1

4. April 1 / May 1

practice exercises

practice for example 1 (page 312)

Read the meter.

1.    2.

3.    4.

practice for example 2 (page 312)

Find the number of kilowatt-hours used during the month.

5.    6.

7.    8.

mixed practice (page 312)

9. The Maguires' electric meter read 4589 on July 1 and 5681 on August 1. Find the amount of electricity used during the month.

10. Jessica Stone's electric meter read 4509 on December 1 and 5490 on January 1. Electricity in her area costs $.09 per kilowatt-hour. Find the cost of electricity for the month.

11. Your electric bill shows the date of the next scheduled meter reading. Read your own electric meter on the scheduled day. Use your reading and the current reading shown on your electric bill to determine how many kilowatt-hours you used. Calculate what your next electric bill should be.

14-9 UNIT PRICING

Many supermarkets display **unit prices** of grocery items. The unit price is the *cost per unit*. The unit price is given in terms of the unit in which the product is measured. You can use this formula to find unit price.

unit price = cost of an item ÷ number of units

example 1

A 5-kg box of laundry detergent costs $9.79.
Find the unit price to the nearest cent.

solution

Use the formula:

unit price = cost of item ÷ number of units
= $9.79 ÷ 5
= $1.958
≈ $1.96

The unit price is $1.96/kg (per kilogram).

your turn

**Find the unit price to the nearest cent.
Use a calculator if you have one.**

1. daisies: $1.89 for 12
2. lobster meat: $8.40 for 250 g

For some items, the unit price is less than $.01. The unit price is then shown as a three-place decimal, or to the nearest tenth of a cent.

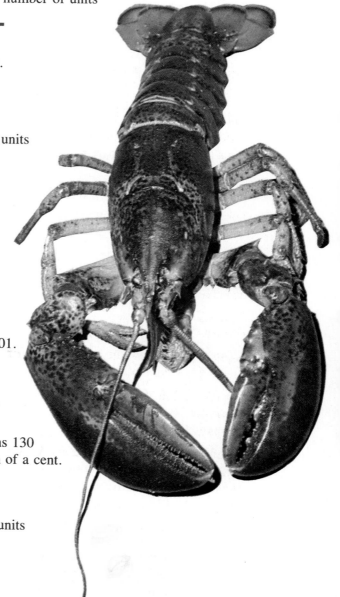

example 2

A roll of paper towels that costs $.99 contains 130 sheets. Find the unit price to the nearest tenth of a cent.

solution

Use the formula:

unit price = cost of item ÷ number of units
= $.99 ÷ 130
= $.007$\frac{80}{130}$
≈ $.008

The unit price is $.008/sheet, or 0.8¢/sheet.

Find the unit price to the nearest tenth of a cent. Use a calculator if you have one.

3. tuna: $1.39 for 185 g
4. yogurt: $.55 for 225 g

practice exercises

---

practice for example 1 (page 314)

Find the unit price to the nearest cent. Use a calculator if you have one.

1. milk: $1.79 for 3.8 L
2. dog food: $7.99 for 9 kg
3. light bulbs: $4.39 for 6 bulbs
4. sesame seed: $1.29 for 53 g
5. hand cream: $3.29 for 56 g
6. herb tea: $2.29 for 50 bags

---

practice for example 2 (pages 314–315)

Find the unit price to the nearest tenth of a cent. Use a calculator if you have one.

7. mustard: $.59 for 255 g
8. fruit juice: $.29 for 250 mL
9. cereal: $1.29 for 198 g
10. oatmeal: $1.19 for 510 g
11. canned milk: $.55 for 354 mL
12. salad oil: $2.19 for 500 mL

---

mixed practice (pages 314–315)

Find the unit price to the nearest cent or the nearest tenth of a cent. Use a calculator if you have one.

13. applesauce: $.59 for 425 g
14. peanut butter: $3.49 for 935 g
15. flour: $1.39 for 2.5 kg
16. juice: $1.29 for 6 boxes
17. soap: $2.25 for 6 bars
18. orange juice: $1.49 for 2 L

19. Shop for your favorite juice drink. Find the unit price for the smallest size available and for the largest. Compare and decide which size is least expensive.

14-10 COMPARISON SHOPPING

When you shop, your choice of items may be affected by many things. If you have a large family, you may prefer large packages. If your family is small, or if you have limited storage space, you may prefer small packages. However, if your choices depend only on price, you can use unit prices to help you choose the best buy.

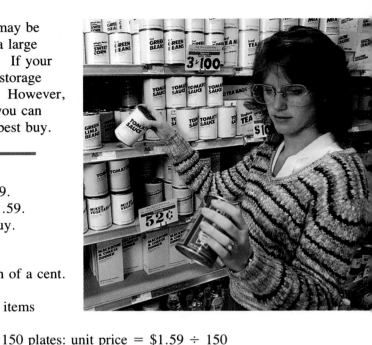

example

A package of 80 paper plates costs $.99.
A package of 150 paper plates costs $1.59.
Based on price alone, find the better buy.

solution

Find each unit price to the nearest tenth of a cent. Use the formula:
unit price = cost of item ÷ number of items
Then compare.

80 plates: unit price = $.99 ÷ 80   150 plates: unit price = $1.59 ÷ 150
                     = $.012375   = $.0106
unit price: $.012 per plate   unit price: $.011 per plate
Since $.011 < $.012, the package of 150 plates is the better buy.

exercises

Find the better buy.

1. flour: $1.51 for 2.5 kg or
                   $.73 for 0.9 kg

2. frozen dinner: $2.49 for 503 g or
                   $.99 for 174 g

3. cat food: $3.35 for 1.4 kg or
             $1.47 for 0.5 kg

4. rice: $1.29 for 1.36 kg or
                  $.79 for 0.9 kg

5. salad oil: $3.19 for 1.4 kg or
              $1.49 for 0.7 kg

6. ketchup: $1.39 for 175 mL or
                  $1.99 for 350 mL

7. Do you think the larger package is usually the better buy? There are eight products listed below. Choose one brand of each item. Find the unit prices of the smallest and largest sizes available. Then decide which size of each is the better buy.

| cornflakes | spaghetti | laundry detergent | paper napkins |
| hand lotion | peanut butter | canned peaches | toothpaste |

CHAPTER REVIEW

vocabulary vo·cab·u·lar·y

Choose the correct word to complete each sentence.

1. The basic metric unit of length is the *(milligram, meter)*.
2. The basic metric unit of mass is the *(gram, liter)*.

skills

Draw a line segment of the given length.

3. 24 mm

4. 6.7 cm

5. 0.8 cm

Complete.

6. 2.8 cm = _?_ mm

7. 470 mm = _?_ m

8. 8.9 km = _?_ m

9. 0.35 L = _?_ mL

10. 6.003 g = _?_ mg

11. 60 g = _?_ kg

Tell whether each statement is *true* or *false*. If it is false, change the unit to make it true.

12. The capacity of a flowerpot is about 2.2 cm.
13. The mass of a bumblebee is about 52 mg.
14. The height of a skyscraper is about 112 mm.
15. The length of this page is about 23.2 cm.

Find the unit price of each item. Choose the better buy in each exercise.

16. **a.** 480 mL shampoo; $1.79
    b. 730 mL shampoo; $2.39

17. **a.** 0.5 kg birdseed; $1.05
    b. 1.5 kg birdseed; $4.23

Solve.

18. The Poes' oven has a wattage rating of 900 W and was used 3 h on Tuesday. The Poes pay $.10/kW • h for electricity. Find the cost of operating the oven on Tuesday.

19. Maria's electric meter read 3619 on April 1 and 4967 on May 1. The electric company charges $.12/kW • h for electricity. Find the amount of Maria's electric bill for the month.

20. Nan leaves her house and jogs 3 blocks due north, 4 blocks due west, 3 blocks due north, 9 blocks due east, and 6 blocks due south. Where is Nan in relation to her house?

CHAPTER TEST

Select the most reasonable unit. Choose mm, cm, m, or km.

1. length of a fingernail: 17 __?__

2. height of a coffee cup: 9.5 __?__ **14-1**

Measure the length of each object in: a. millimeters b. centimeters

3.

4. **14-2**

Complete. Replace each __?__ with <, >, or =.

5. 7.2 cm __?__ 0.072 m

6. 2.6 km __?__ 260 m **14-3**

Select the more reasonable unit. Choose L or mL.

7. capacity of a bathtub: 96 __?__

8. capacity of a glass: 120 __?__ **14-4**

Select the most reasonable measure.

9. mass of a telephone
   1.2 mg   1.2 g   1.2 kg

10. mass of an ant
    35 mg   35 g   35 kg **14-5**

Complete.

11. 28 g = __?__ kg

12. 0.006 g = __?__ mg

13. 1.5 mg = __?__ g

14. Make a drawing to picture the problem. Joe leaves the market and drives 3 blocks due south. He then turns left and drives 4 blocks, turns left again and drives 8 blocks, and turns left again and drives 4 blocks. Where is Joe in relation to the market? **14-6**

15. A refrigerator has a wattage rating of 1020 W. Assume that the cost of electricity is $.11/kW · h. Find the cost of operating the refrigerator for 50 h. **14-7**

16. On May 1 the Engvalls' electric meter read 4982. On June 1 the meter read 6011. The electric company charges $.12/kW · h. Find the cost of electricity for the month. **14-8**

17. A 400-g box of raisins costs $3.49. Find the unit price. **14-9**

18. A 310-g can of peanuts costs $2.29. A 200-g can of peanuts costs $1.69. Find the better buy. **14-10**

COMPUTER

Programming in BASIC

A set of instructions that you give a computer is called a **program.** The following are examples of two simple programs in the BASIC language.

```
10   PRINT "15 + 25"
20   END
RUN
15 + 25
```
← **RUN is a** *command* **that tells the computer to carry out the program.**

```
10   PRINT  15 + 25
20   END
RUN
40
```

Notice that each program has two numbered lines. Each of these lines contains an instruction to the computer. The line numbers tell the computer the order in which to carry out these instructions. Line 20 of each program is the END statement, which instructs the computer to stop running the program.

In the program at the left above, the word PRINT is followed by an addition exercise *between* quotation marks. When you RUN the program, the computer simply prints the addition exercise. In the program at the right above, the word PRINT is followed by the same addition exercise *without* quotation marks. In this case the computer performs the addition and prints the sum, which is 40.

Sometimes after you type RUN the computer displays the message SYNTAX ERROR. This means that there is an error, or **bug,** in the program. Finding and correcting errors in a computer program is called **debugging** the program.

exercises

Write the output.

1. ```
   10   PRINT "THE ANSWER TO"
   20   PRINT "3 × 9 + 3 IS"
   30   PRINT 3 * 9 + 3
   40   END
   ```

2. ```
   10   PRINT "WHAT IS THE PRODUCT?"
   20   PRINT "20 × 40 ="
   30   PRINT 20 * 40
   40   END
   ```

Find the syntax error.

3. ```
   10   PIRNT "HOWDY!"
   20   END
   RUN
   SYNTAX ERROR IN 10
   ```

4. ```
   10   PRINT HOWDY!
   20   END
   RUN
   SYNTAX ERROR IN 10
   ```

5. Find out how the term *debugging* became associated with errors in computer programs.

COMPETENCY TEST

Choose the letter of the correct answer.

1. **Add.**   15.246 + 3.88

   A. 18.112
   B. 11.36
   C. 15.634
   D. 19.126

2. **Subtract.**   112.79 − 8.465

   A. 104.325
   B. 104.33
   C. 121.55
   D. 104.335

3. **Round 3672.4381 to the nearest thousandth.**

   A. 3672.44
   B. 3672.438
   C. 4000
   D. 3700

4. **Write 0.64 as a fraction.**

   A. $\frac{1}{64}$ B. $\frac{1}{640}$

   C. $\frac{16}{25}$ D. $\frac{8}{125}$

5. **Sheldon had a balance of $483.72. He wrote a check for $17.95 and made a deposit of $48.95. Find the new balance.**

   A. $550.62
   B. $514.72
   C. $452.72
   D. $416.82

6. **Multiply.**   32 × 0.003

   A. 32.003
   B. 0.323
   C. 0.96
   D. 0.096

7. **Divide.**   3.25 ÷ 2.6

   A. 0.125
   B. 1.25
   C. 12.5
   D. 125

8. **Divide and round to the nearest tenth.**

   $4.1\overline{)27.85}$

   A. 67.9
   B. 0.7
   C. 6.8
   D. 6.7

9. **Multiply.**   0.08 × 1000

   A. 80,000
   B. 8000
   C. 800
   D. 80

10. **Margo earns $34,820 per year. Find her weekly salary to the nearest cent.**

    A. $669.62
    B. $696.40
    C. $752.42
    D. $2901.67

11. **Which number is the least?**

    A. 5.1732
    B. 5.1273
    C. 5.2173
    D. 5.1237

12. **Choose the best estimate.**

    $9.76\overline{)408.6175}$

    A. about 40
    B. about 400
    C. about 50
    D. about 500

13. **Write $\frac{5}{8}$ as a decimal.**

    A. 0.58
    B. 0.0625
    C. 0.625
    D. 0.85

14. **Write the numeral form of forty-six and eleven ten-thousandths.**

    A. 46.11
    B. 46.011
    C. 46.0011
    D. 46.00011

15. **Multiply.**
    $\begin{array}{r} 9.04 \\ \times\ 2.5 \\ \hline \end{array}$

    A. 2.268
    B. 6.328
    C. 22.5
    D. 22.6

16. **Complete.**   4.5 m = __?__ cm

    A. 450
    B. 4500
    C. 0.45
    D. 0.045

17. **Choose the best estimate.**

    0.749×3852.61

    A. about 2000
    B. about 3000
    C. about 4000
    D. about 5000

18. **Write 1,280,000 in scientific notation.**

    A. 1.28×10^6
    B. 1.28×10^5
    C. 1.28×10^4
    D. 128×10^6

19. **Which unit should be used to measure the mass of a table?**

    A. L
    B. kg
    C. m
    D. km

20. **Order from least to greatest:**

    8250 mL; 8 L; 8.2 L

    A. 8250 mL, 8 L, 8.2 L
    B. 8250 mL, 8.2 L, 8L
    C. 8 L, 8.2 L, 8250 mL
    D. 8.2 L, 8 L, 8250 mL

CUMULATIVE REVIEW CHAPTERS 1–14

Find each answer.

1. $3.9 - 2.45$
2. $\$825 - \$714$
3. $0.38 \div 100$
4. 312×705
5. 6.24×3
6. $51\overline{)8721}$
7. 5.2×0.82
8. $7\overline{)29.75}$
9. $\frac{7}{8} - \frac{3}{5}$
10. $5^3 \times 10^0$
11. $2\frac{1}{3} + 5\frac{4}{5}$
12. $\frac{8}{15} \div \frac{4}{5}$
13. $389 + 41 + 1191$
14. $7.28 \div 0.4$
15. $0.281 + 6.5 + 0.09$
16. $3\frac{1}{2} \times 1\frac{3}{5}$
17. $6 \div 1\frac{1}{3}$
18. $9\frac{3}{4} \div 3$

19. Write 73,600,000 in scientific notation.
20. Write 0.56 as a fraction in lowest terms.
21. Write $\frac{3}{5}$ as a decimal.
22. Write $\frac{43}{8}$ as a mixed number.
23. Write the word form of 5.0021; give the value of the underlined digit.

Estimate.

24. $312.17 - 118.2$
25. $5\frac{5}{9} - 1\frac{7}{8}$
26. 0.34×2107
27. $\frac{11}{20} \times 403$
28. 7.64×5.81
29. $988,142 \div 51$
30. $7.96\overline{)62.876}$
31. $82,645 - 39,694$
32. $1.89 + 4.2 + 3.796$

Complete.

33. $9200 \text{ mL} = \underline{\ ?\ } \text{ L}$
34. $3.8 \text{ m} = \underline{\ ?\ } \text{ cm}$
35. $34 \text{ in.} = \underline{\ ?\ } \text{ ft } \underline{\ ?\ } \text{ in.}$

Select the most reasonable measure.

36. length of a calculator
    12 mm   12 cm   12 m
37. mass of a car
    1350 mg   1350 g   1350 kg

Evaluate each expression when $a = 100$, $b = 5$, and $c = 11$.

38. $ab + c$
39. $\frac{a}{b}$
40. $a(b + c)$

41. Alberto bought one student ticket and two adult tickets. He paid a total of $15.50. What missing fact is needed to find the cost of the student ticket?
42. Dawn bought 3 pairs of socks for $1.79 per pair. How much change will she receive from a $10 bill?

Architects use models to show how their projects will look when completed. Ratio and proportion are essential in making accurate models.

CHAPTER 15

RATIO AND PROPORTION

15-1 RATIOS

A **ratio** is a comparison of two numbers by division.

    The table at the right shows the numbers of different vehicles sold at Bargain Motors in December. You say that *the ratio of recreational vehicles to trucks is 9 to 25*. You can write this ratio in three ways.

$$9 \text{ to } 25 \qquad 9:25 \qquad \frac{9}{25}$$

December Sales Record

Type of Vehicle	Number Sold
vans	36
trucks	25
cars	45
recreational vehicles	9

In a ratio, the order of the numbers is very important.

        The ratio of recreational vehicles to trucks is 9 to 25.

        The ratio of trucks to recreational vehicles is 25 to 9.

When writing a ratio as a fraction, you write the fraction in lowest terms.

example 1

Use the table above. Write each ratio as a fraction in lowest terms.

a. cars to vans

b. vans to recreational vehicles

c. cars to total number of vehicles

solution

a. $\dfrac{\text{cars} \rightarrow 45}{\text{vans} \rightarrow 36} = \dfrac{45 \div 9}{36 \div 9} = \dfrac{5}{4}$ ⬅ **Do not rewrite as a mixed number.**

b. $\dfrac{\text{vans}}{\text{recreational vehicles}} \dfrac{\rightarrow 36}{\rightarrow 9} = \dfrac{36 \div 9}{9 \div 9} = \dfrac{4}{1}$ ⬅ **Keep the 1 in the denominator.**

c. $\dfrac{\text{cars} \rightarrow}{\text{total} \rightarrow} \dfrac{45}{36 + 25 + 45 + 9} = \dfrac{45}{115} = \dfrac{45 \div 5}{115 \div 5} = \dfrac{9}{23}$

your turn

Use the table above. Write each ratio as a fraction in lowest terms.

1. vans to cars

2. trucks to vans

3. cars to recreational vehicles

4. recreational vehicles to cars

5. cars to trucks

6. recreational vehicles to vans

7. trucks to cars

8. vans to trucks

9. vans to total number of vehicles

10. trucks to total number of vehicles

Sometimes the quantities you are comparing are expressed in different units. To write a ratio between these quantities, first change them to the same unit.

example 2

Write the ratio 8 in. to 2 ft as a fraction in lowest terms.

solution

Change 2 ft to inches.

1 ft = 12 in., so 2 ft = 24 in. $\frac{8}{24} = \frac{8 \div 8}{24 \div 8} = \frac{1}{3}$

your turn

Write each ratio as a fraction in lowest terms.

11. 4 ft to 6 yd

12. 5 cm to 25 mm

13. 25¢ to $2

14. 10 days to 3 weeks

practice exercises

practice for example 1 (page 324)

Use the table at the right. Write each ratio as a fraction in lowest terms.

1. red platys to catfish
2. neons to catfish
3. rasboras to black mollies
4. catfish to rasboras
5. black mollies to red platys
6. neons to total fish

Fish in an Aquarium

Fish Type	Number
red platy	6
black molly	4
catfish	10
rasbora	5
neon	15

practice for example 2 (page 325)

Write each ratio as a fraction in lowest terms.

7. 6 yd to 62 ft

8. 8 h to 1 day

9. 9 cm to 1 m

10. 10 in. to 3 ft

11. 40 mL to 4 L

12. 280 g to 7 kg

13. 12 oz to 3 lb

14. 1000 yd to 1 mi

Write each ratio in two different ways.

15. 5 to 7   **16.** 9:4   **17.** $\frac{8}{15}$ **18.** 18 to 5

19. 13:22   **20.** $\frac{5}{11}$ **21.** 50 to 1   **22.** 11:6

Write each ratio as a fraction in lowest terms.

23. 7:21   **24.** $\frac{18}{24}$ **25.** 75 to 25   **26.** $\frac{9}{15}$

27. $\frac{11}{44}$ **28.** 45 to 18   **29.** 30:15   **30.** $\frac{55}{50}$

31. $\frac{36}{12}$ **32.** 6:7   **33.** 75 to 5   **34.** $\frac{19}{57}$

35. A badminton court is 44 ft long and 20 ft wide. Write the ratio of length to width as a fraction in lowest terms.

36. A recipe for salad dressing calls for 3 fl oz of vinegar and 6 fl oz of oil. Write the ratio of vinegar to oil as a fraction in lowest terms.

review *exercises*

Write each fraction in lowest terms.

1. $\frac{3}{9}$ **2.** $\frac{12}{4}$ **3.** $\frac{75}{100}$ **4.** $\frac{25}{15}$ **5.** $\frac{17}{51}$ **6.** $\frac{16}{24}$

Complete.

7. 2 lb = __?__ oz   **8.** 50 mm = __?__ m   **9.** 21 ft = __?__ yd

10. 17 in. = __?__ ft __?__ in.   **11.** 3 L = __?__ mL   **12.** 3456 m = __?__ km

13. 4 gal = __?__ qt   **14.** 96 h = __?__ days   **15.** 3 quarters = __?__ nickels

Find each answer.

16. 1.5×0.4 **17.** $43.7 + 6.45$ **18.** $17 - 5.19$ **19.** $6.3 \div 5$

20. $14.31 - 0.9$ **21.** 0.4×0.02 **22.** $48 \div 0.06$ **23.** $0.05 + 9 + 1.6$

puzzle corner

A seamstress cut a 12-in.-long ribbon into two pieces. The resulting pieces were in the ratio $\frac{1}{2}$. Find the length of each piece.

15-2 RATES

A ratio that compares two unlike measures is called a **rate**.
A **unit rate** is a rate for one unit of a given quantity. *Miles per hour*
and *cents per pound* are some familiar unit rates.

example 1

Wendy jogs 12 mi in 2 h.
Write the unit rate.

solution

Write the rate as a fraction in lowest terms.

$$\frac{\text{miles} \rightarrow}{\text{hours} \rightarrow} \frac{12}{2} = \frac{12 \div 2}{2 \div 2} = \frac{6}{1}$$

Wendy's rate is 6 mi in 1 h, or
6 mi/h (miles per hour).

your turn

Write the unit rate.

1. $35 for 7 h
2. $280 for 10 shirts
3. 420 mi on 14 gal
4. 20 mi in 5 min

example 2

Sam earned $32 for 5 h work. Write the unit rate.

solution

Write the rate as a fraction. $\dfrac{\text{dollars} \rightarrow}{\text{hours} \rightarrow} \dfrac{32}{5}$

Divide the numerator $\dfrac{\text{dollars} \rightarrow}{\text{hours} \rightarrow} \dfrac{32 \div 5}{5 \div 5} = \dfrac{6.4}{1}$ ← **The numerator will be a decimal.**
and denominator by 5.

The rate is $6.40 for 1 h, or $6.40/h ($6.40 per hour).

your turn

Write the unit rate.

5. $55 in 4 h
6. $28 for 5 records
7. $45 for 2 lb
8. $11 for 50 stamps

practice exercises

practice for example 1 (page 327)

Write the unit rate.

1. 480 mi on 20 gal
2. $450 for 15 h
3. 160 words in 2 min
4. 240 km in 4 h
5. 32 cm in 8 days
6. $150 for 5 blouses

practice for example 2 (page 327)

Write the unit rate.

7. 125 km in 2 h
8. $15 for 2 ads
9. $24,986 in 52 weeks
10. $27 for 12 issues
11. 35 h for 10 classes
12. 23 m for 10 dresses

mixed practice (page 327)

Write the unit rate.

13. 750 mi in 2 days
14. $10.20 for 2 lb
15. 60 tokens for 12 rides
16. $125 for 20 days
17. $45 for 12 tickets
18. 800 flowers for 32 bouquets
19. 3 L for 15 children
20. 12 eggs for 4 omelets
21. 72 boxes of shoes in 6 cartons
22. $1150 for 2 weeks

23. Sonia rented a car at noon on Saturday. She paid $87 for three days. Find the rate per day.
24. Jerry bought 12 lb of peanuts for $5.88. Find the unit price.
25. Brian can type 390 words in 6 min. Sylvia can type 490 words in 7 min. Who is the faster typist?

review exercises

Tell whether the fractions are _equivalent_ or _not equivalent_.

1. $\frac{3}{5}$ and $\frac{5}{3}$
2. $\frac{18}{16}$ and $\frac{9}{8}$
3. $\frac{17}{21}$ and $\frac{34}{40}$
4. $\frac{10}{14}$ and $\frac{15}{21}$
5. $\frac{4}{12}$ and $\frac{5}{15}$
6. $\frac{21}{7}$ and $\frac{18}{6}$
7. $\frac{5}{11}$ and $\frac{22}{10}$
8. $\frac{25}{14}$ and $\frac{15}{7}$

Replace each ? with the number that will make the fractions equivalent.

9. $\frac{5}{6} = \frac{?}{12}$
10. $\frac{12}{30} = \frac{2}{?}$
11. $\frac{7}{?} = \frac{21}{3}$
12. $\frac{?}{8} = \frac{4}{32}$

15-3 PROPORTIONS

Andre made 12 free throws in 20 tries. Earl made 9 free throws in 15 tries. You can write a ratio to show each player's record. If you write each ratio in lowest terms, you find that they are equal.

Andre: $\dfrac{\text{free throws made} \rightarrow 12}{\text{free throws tried} \rightarrow 20} = \dfrac{12 \div 4}{20 \div 4} = \dfrac{3}{5}$

Earl: $\dfrac{\text{free throws made} \rightarrow 9}{\text{free throws tried} \rightarrow 15} = \dfrac{9 \div 3}{15 \div 3} = \dfrac{3}{5}$

A statement that two ratios are equal is called a **proportion.**

You write: $\dfrac{12}{20} = \dfrac{9}{15}$ or $12:20 = 9:15$

You read: *12 is to 20 as 9 is to 15.*

The numbers 12, 20, 9, and 15 are called the **terms** of the proportion. If a statement is a *true* proportion, the **cross products** of the terms are equal.

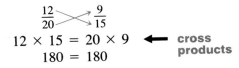

$12 \times 15 = 20 \times 9$ ← **cross products**

$180 = 180$

---

example 1

Tell whether each proportion is *true* or *false*.

a. $\dfrac{9}{12} = \dfrac{3}{4}$

b. $\dfrac{14}{20} = \dfrac{2}{3}$

solution

a. $\dfrac{9}{12} \times \dfrac{3}{4}$

$9 \times 4 \overset{?}{=} 12 \times 3$

$36 = 36 \quad true$

b. $\dfrac{14}{20} \times \dfrac{2}{3}$

$14 \times 3 \overset{?}{=} 20 \times 2$

$42 = 40 \quad false$

your turn

Tell whether each proportion is *true* or *false*.

1. $\dfrac{15}{20} = \dfrac{6}{8}$

2. $\dfrac{10}{16} = \dfrac{3}{5}$

3. $\dfrac{8}{12} = \dfrac{2}{3}$

4. $\dfrac{20}{8} = \dfrac{35}{14}$

Sometimes one term of a proportion is unknown and is represented by a variable. You can use cross products to find the value of this unknown term. This is called *solving* the proportion.

example 2

Solve each proportion.

a. $\dfrac{6}{8} = \dfrac{9}{n}$ b. $\dfrac{a}{10} = \dfrac{8}{5}$

solution

a.
$$\dfrac{6}{8} \diagdown\diagup \dfrac{9}{n}$$

$6 \times n = 8 \times 9$

$6n = 72$

$\dfrac{6n}{6} = \dfrac{72}{6}$ ⬅ **Divide by 6 on each side of the equals sign.**

$n = 12$

b.
$$\dfrac{a}{10} \diagdown\diagup \dfrac{8}{5}$$

$a \times 5 = 10 \times 8$

$5a = 80$

$\dfrac{5a}{5} = \dfrac{80}{5}$ ⬅ **Divide by 5 on each side of the equals sign.**

$a = 16$

your turn

Solve each proportion.

5. $\dfrac{4}{6} = \dfrac{10}{y}$

6. $\dfrac{8}{m} = \dfrac{6}{15}$

7. $\dfrac{x}{14} = \dfrac{2}{1}$

8. $\dfrac{30}{4} = \dfrac{c}{6}$

practice exercises

practice for example 1 *(page 329)*

Tell whether each proportion is *true* or *false*.

1. $\dfrac{8}{5} = \dfrac{24}{15}$

2. $\dfrac{4}{8} = \dfrac{5}{10}$

3. $\dfrac{15}{10} = \dfrac{4}{3}$

4. $\dfrac{9}{12} = \dfrac{4}{5}$

5. $\dfrac{21}{24} = \dfrac{7}{8}$

6. $\dfrac{15}{5} = \dfrac{9}{3}$

7. $\dfrac{6}{1} = \dfrac{1}{6}$

8. $\dfrac{4}{10} = \dfrac{2}{6}$

9. $\dfrac{15}{25} = \dfrac{6}{10}$

10. $\dfrac{25}{6} = \dfrac{20}{5}$

11. $\dfrac{25}{100} = \dfrac{2}{8}$

12. $\dfrac{35}{9} = \dfrac{15}{4}$

practice for example 2 *(page 330)*

Solve each proportion.

13. $\dfrac{6}{4} = \dfrac{15}{m}$

14. $\dfrac{14}{t} = \dfrac{4}{6}$

15. $\dfrac{5}{9} = \dfrac{n}{72}$

16. $\dfrac{20}{8} = \dfrac{5}{c}$

17. $\dfrac{z}{100} = \dfrac{4}{5}$

18. $\dfrac{7}{20} = \dfrac{a}{100}$

19. $\dfrac{15}{y} = \dfrac{10}{6}$

20. $\dfrac{35}{40} = \dfrac{r}{8}$

21. $\dfrac{64}{1} = \dfrac{k}{5}$

22. $\dfrac{18}{12} = \dfrac{d}{4}$

23. $\dfrac{6}{9} = \dfrac{z}{9}$

24. $\dfrac{s}{6} = \dfrac{6}{4}$

Write each proportion in a different way.

25. $12:7 = 24:14$ **26.** $3:6 = 11:22$ **27.** $k:9 = 1:3$ **28.** $6:27 = 9:n$

29. $\frac{6}{21} = \frac{2}{7}$ **30.** $\frac{40}{15} = \frac{16}{6}$ **31.** $\frac{10}{r} = \frac{15}{6}$ **32.** $\frac{7}{8} = \frac{t}{24}$

Solve each proportion.

33. $15:n = 10:8$ **34.** $45:40 = q:8$ **35.** $64:1 = j:4$ **36.** $x:4 = 20:16$

37. $\frac{m}{27} = \frac{2}{3}$ **38.** $\frac{6}{13} = \frac{z}{13}$ **39.** $\frac{12}{3} = \frac{8}{y}$ **40.** $\frac{14}{50} = \frac{k}{100}$

41. Joanne can keypunch 16 computer cards in 1 min. Yvette can keypunch 80 cards in 5 min. Who can keypunch faster?

42. Mike can keypunch 15 computer cards in 1 min. Steven can keypunch 20 cards in 80 s. Who can keypunch faster?

review *exercises*

Find each answer.

1. 16×0.02 **2.** $16{,}701 \div 879$ **3.** $16.08 \div 0.4$ **4.** $29 - 3.61$

5. $461 \div 4$ **6.** $80{,}040 - 1293$ **7.** 134×202 **8.** $0.8 + 14 + 3.95$

calculator corner

You can solve a proportion that involves greater numbers by using a calculator.

example   **Solve.** $\frac{a}{24} = \frac{105}{15}$

solution $15a = 24 \times 105$ ◄— Use a calculator to multiply.

$15a = 2520$

$a = 2520 \div 15$ ◄— Use a calculator to divide.

$a = 168$

Solve each proportion using a calculator.

1. $\frac{12}{17} = \frac{n}{85}$ **2.** $\frac{a}{13} = \frac{28}{91}$ **3.** $\frac{165}{b} = \frac{45}{63}$ **4.** $\frac{123}{15} = \frac{369}{y}$

5. $\frac{112}{q} = \frac{49}{28}$ **6.** $\frac{19}{38} = \frac{z}{114}$ **7.** $\frac{n}{51} = \frac{85}{255}$ **8.** $\frac{23}{31} = \frac{92}{w}$

15-4 USING PROPORTIONS

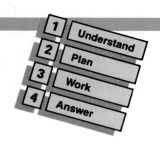

1 Understand
2 Plan
3 Work
4 Answer

You can solve some problems by using a proportion.
To set up the proportion, you use a variable to
represent the unknown amount.

example 1

At the Farmer's Market, 3 apples cost $.84. Find the cost of 5 apples.

solution

Step 1   Given: cost of 3 apples is $.84   Find: cost of 5 apples

Step 2   Write a proportion. $\dfrac{\text{number} \rightarrow}{\text{cost} \rightarrow} \dfrac{3}{\$.84} = \dfrac{5}{n}$ ◀— **Let *n* represent the cost of 5 apples.**

Step 3   Solve the proportion. $3 \times n = \$.84 \times 5$
$$3n = \$4.20$$
$$\frac{3n}{3} = \frac{\$4.20}{3}$$ ◀— **Divide by 3 on each side of the equals sign.**
$$n = \$1.40$$

Step 4   *Check:* $\dfrac{3}{\$.84} = \dfrac{5}{n}$

$\dfrac{3}{\$.84} \stackrel{?}{=} \dfrac{5}{\$1.40}$ ◀— **Replace *n* with $1.40.**

$3 \times \$1.40 \stackrel{?}{=} \$.84 \times 5$

$\$4.20 = \$4.20 \checkmark$

The cost of 5 apples is $1.40.

your turn

Solve using a proportion.

1. The cost of 3 notebooks is $.96.
   Find the cost of 10 notebooks.

2. At the art supply store, 5 poster
   boards cost $3.35. Find the cost
   of 2 poster boards.

example 2

In the school band, the ratio of boys to girls is $5:4$. There are 60 girls in the band. Find the number of boys.

solution

Step 1 Given: ratio of boys to girls is $5:4$
number of girls is 60
Find: number of boys

Step 2 Write a proportion. $\dfrac{\text{number of boys} \rightarrow 5}{\text{number of girls} \rightarrow 4} = \dfrac{n}{60}$ ← **Let *n* represent the number of boys.**

Step 3 Solve the proportion. $5 \times 60 = 4 \times n$
$$300 = 4n$$
$$\frac{300}{4} = \frac{4n}{4}$$ ← **Divide by 4 on each side of the equals sign.**
$$75 = n$$

Step 4 *Check:* $\dfrac{5}{4} = \dfrac{n}{60}$

$\dfrac{5}{4} \overset{?}{=} \dfrac{75}{60}$ ← **Replace *n* with 75.**

$5 \times 60 \overset{?}{=} 4 \times 75$
$300 = 300 \checkmark$ There are 75 boys in the school band.

your turn

Solve using a proportion.

3. The ratio of students to adults at a school dance was $25:3$. There were 12 adults at the dance. Find the number of students.

4. The ratio of irises to jonquils in a bouquet is 2 to 1. There are 6 jonquils in each bouquet. Find the number of irises.

practice exercises

practice for example 1 *(page 332)*

Solve using a proportion.

1. Tom bought 13 pencils for $1.04. Find the cost of 5 pencils.

2. A quality control inspector can inspect 50 bottles in 20 min. Find the number of bottles that can be inspected in 60 min.

3. A keypunch operator can process 54 cards in 6 min. Find the number of cards that can be processed in 15 min.

4. Three records cost $13.20. How many can you buy for $35.20?

Solve using a proportion.

5. The ratio of workers to supervisors in a factory is 45:2. There are 12 supervisors. Find the number of workers.

6. The ratio of teachers to students in a school is $\frac{1}{24}$. There are 360 students. Find the number of teachers.

7. For the Cougars, the ratio of games won to games lost was 1:2. The team lost 20 games. Find the number of games won.

8. The ratio of blue to red in a paint mixture is 3 to 2. Harold has 4 gal of red paint. How many gallons of blue paint does he need?

Solve using a proportion.

9. The ratio of boys to girls at a dance was 5:3. There were 42 girls at the dance. Find the number of boys.

10. A laser printer can print at the rate of 8 pages per minute. How long will it take to print 56 pages?

11. A standard alternating current has a frequency of 60 cycles per second. Find the number of cycles per minute.

12. The mass of 20 mL of water is 20 g. What is the mass of 450 mL of water? What is the mass of 2 L of water?

13. In Lee, the property tax is $4 per $1000 of assessed value. The Engs' home is assessed for $145,000. Find their property taxes.

14. Part of a recipe includes 2 tsp of water and 14 fl oz of condensed milk. To adjust the recipe for more people, you use 5 tsp of water. How many fluid ounces of condensed milk will you need?

review exercises

1. Find the cost of a dozen roses if one rose costs $2.75.

2. A certain telephone directory lists 148,153 phone numbers. About 484 numbers are listed on each page. About how many pages does the directory contain?

3. Kathryn bought two records for $6.98 each and three tapes for $7.98 each. She paid a sales tax of $1.90. What was the total cost?

4. The ratio of cars to trucks at a car dealership is 3 to 1. There are 60 cars. Find the number of trucks.

15-5 SCALE DRAWINGS AND MODELS

Scale drawings and **models** represent real objects. The **scale** is the ratio of the size of the drawing or model to the actual size of the object.

example 1

The scale of this floor plan is 1 in.: 10 ft. Find the actual length of the closet.

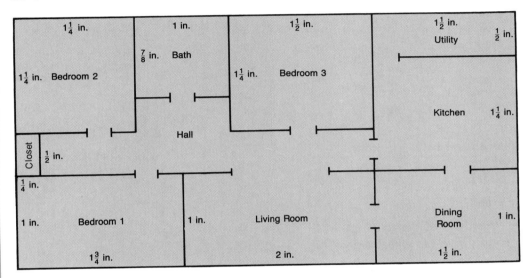

solution

Find the length of the closet in the drawing. It is $\frac{1}{2}$ in.
Use the scale 1 in.: 10 ft to write a proportion.

$$\frac{\text{plan length in inches}}{\text{actual length in feet}} \rightarrow \frac{1}{10} = \frac{\frac{1}{2}}{n} \longleftarrow \text{Let } n \text{ represent the actual}$$
length of the closet.

Solve the proportion.
$$1 \times n = 10 \times \frac{1}{2}$$

$$n = \frac{\overset{5}{\cancel{10}}}{1} \times \frac{1}{\underset{1}{\cancel{2}}}$$

$$n = 5 \qquad\qquad \text{The closet is 5 ft long.}$$

your turn

Use the scale drawing above. Find the length and width of each room.

1. Dining Room
2. Bedroom 1
3. Kitchen
4. Bath

example 2

An automobile designer is building a model of a car. The scale is 1:8. The actual car length will be 172 in. Find the length of the model.

solution

Use the scale 1:8 to write a proportion.

$$\frac{\text{model length in inches} \rightarrow 1}{\text{actual length in inches} \rightarrow 8} = \frac{n}{172}$$

← Let n represent the length of the car model.

Solve the proportion: $1 \times 172 = 8 \times n$

$$172 = 8n$$

$$\frac{172}{8} = \frac{8n}{8}$$

$$21\frac{4}{8} = n$$

$$21\frac{1}{2} = n$$

The model should be $21\frac{1}{2}$ in. long.

your turn

Use the scale 1:8.

5. The wheelbase of the actual car will be 96 in. Find the wheelbase of the model.

6. The overall height of the actual car will be 52 in. Find the height of the model.

practice exercises

practice for example 1 (page 335)

Esther Green made a scale drawing to plan her garden. Find the actual length and width of the area she set aside for each crop. In the drawing, the scale is 1 in.:4 ft.

1. tomatoes
2. peas
3. corn
4. peppers
5. lettuce
6. beans

	$1\frac{1}{2}$ in.		$\frac{1}{2}$ in.	$\frac{3}{4}$ in.
$\frac{3}{4}$ in.	Tomatoes		Peas	
				$1\frac{1}{4}$ in.
				Corn

Peppers / Lettuce / Beans section:

$\frac{1}{2}$ in. Peppers $\frac{1}{4}$ in. Lettuce
$\frac{3}{4}$ in. $\frac{1}{4}$ in. $1\frac{1}{4}$ in. Beans

A toy manufacturer is making models of cars. The scale is 1:32. For each actual length given, find the length of the model.

7. sedan: 176 in. long

8. hatchback: 160 in. long

9. luxury: 192 in. long

10. sports car: 144 in. long

11. A model train is built using the scale 1:80. The length of an actual sleeping car is 2400 cm. Find the length of the model.

12. In an architect's drawing of an office complex, the parking deck is 15 in. long. The scale is 1 in.:8 ft. Find the length of the actual parking deck.

13. The model of an airplane is built using the scale 1:48. The actual length of the plane is 96 ft. Find the length of the model.

14. Frank Sale is constructing a model of his bicycle. His bicycle is actually 210 cm long. The length of the drawing is 10.5 cm. Find the scale.

review exercises

Estimate.

1. $82.95 - 28.98$

2. 8.79×4.68

3. $439.27 + 275.98

4. $295.6 \div 7.24$

5. 394.7×0.039

6. $49.25 \div 0.061$

7. 68.98×8.95

8. $94.47 - 86.89

9. $64.95 + $28.78 + 15.69

Evaluate each expression when $a = 1$, $b = 3$, and $c = 4$.

10. c^2

11. b^4

12. a^{10}

13. b^3c

14. b^2c^2

15. $7b^4a$

mental math

Write the equivalent fraction in lowest terms.

1. 0.3

2. 0.5

3. 0.1

4. 0.25

5. 0.8

6. 0.01

7. 0.75

8. 0.2

9. $0.333 \ldots$

10. 0.6

11. $0.666 \ldots$

12. 0.4

Write the equivalent decimal.

13. $\frac{1}{2}$

14. $\frac{1}{4}$

15. $\frac{3}{4}$

16. $\frac{2}{5}$

17. $\frac{1}{3}$

18. $\frac{2}{3}$

SKILL REVIEW

Write each ratio as a fraction in lowest terms.

1. 30 to 18
2. 3 to 57
3. $\frac{15}{60}$
4. 63:12
5. 4 km:50 m
6. 30 min to 6 h
7. 30¢ to $1
8. 7 days:3 weeks

15-1

Write each ratio in two different ways.

9. 43:77
10. 71 to 84
11. $\frac{14}{33}$
12. $\frac{25}{7}$

Write the unit rate.

13. 62 km in 1 h
14. 144 mi in 3 h
15. $6.32 for 2 lb
16. $458 for 40 h
17. 240 words in 3 min
18. 364 km in 8 h

15-2

Tell whether each proportion is *true* or *false*.

19. $\frac{1}{3} = \frac{9}{26}$
20. $\frac{2}{5} = \frac{8}{20}$
21. $\frac{17}{3} = \frac{34}{6}$
22. $\frac{16}{2} = \frac{4}{1}$ 15-3

Solve each proportion.

23. $\frac{2}{3} = \frac{x}{24}$
24. $\frac{3}{4} = \frac{15}{s}$
25. $\frac{n}{2} = \frac{18}{12}$
26. $\frac{10}{y} = \frac{6}{9}$

Solve using a proportion.

27. Four dinner plates cost $10.98. Find the cost of 12 dinner plates.

15-4

28. The ratio of nurses to doctors in a hospital is $\frac{5}{2}$. There are 210 nurses. Find the number of doctors.
29. A person who weighs 160 lb on Earth would weigh 416 lb on Jupiter. Sara weighs 120 lb on Earth. Find her weight on Jupiter.
30. To make a certain shade of orange, red paint is mixed with yellow paint in the ratio 1:2. Donna has 6 gal of yellow paint. How many gallons of red paint does she need?

**A woodworker is making scale models of trains.
The scale is 1:32.**

31. The length of an actual caboose is 80 ft. Find the model length.

15-5

32. The height of the model smokestack is 2 in. Find the height of the actual smokestack in inches.

KITCHEN MANAGER

Jim Hastings manages a restaurant kitchen. He does *time and motion studies* to see if work is being done efficiently. He uses this formula to compute a worker's **efficiency rating.**

$$\text{efficiency rating} = \frac{\text{number of }\sqrt{}\text{'s}}{\text{number of observations}} \times 100$$

Jim made the following observations.

Name	Observations
Sam	√ √ √ √ 0 √ 0 0 √ √ √ √
Jordan	0 0 √ √ √ 0 0 √ √ √
Kim	0 √ √ √ √ 0 √ 0 √ √
Carol	0 0 √ 0 √ √ 0 √ √ √ 0 0

√ = work being done
0 = no work being done

example

To find Sam's efficiency rating, use the formula.

$$\text{efficiency rating} = \frac{\text{number of }\sqrt{}\text{'s}}{\text{number of observations}} \times 100$$

$$= \frac{9}{12} \times 100 \quad \longleftarrow \text{ Sam had 9 } \sqrt{}\text{'s.}$$
$$\longleftarrow \text{ Sam was observed 12 times.}$$

$$= 0.75 \times 100 = 75$$

Sam's efficiency rating is 75.

exercises

1. Find the efficiency rating for Kim, Jordan, and Carol.

2. For this kitchen, a 70 or higher efficiency rating is acceptable. Which workers have an acceptable rating?

3. Industrial engineers observe assembly procedures to see if an operation can be improved. Marsha Sims completed the observation table at the right. Find the efficiency rating for each worker.

Worker	Number of √'s	Number of Observations
Brent	28	35
Petra	22	25
Carmen	33	40

15-6 SCALE ON A MAP

Most maps contain a small ruler. This ruler illustrates the scale of the map. On a map, the scale is the ratio of the map distance to the actual distance. The map below shows part of southern California. On this map, 1 in. represents 21 mi. We write 1 in.:21 mi.

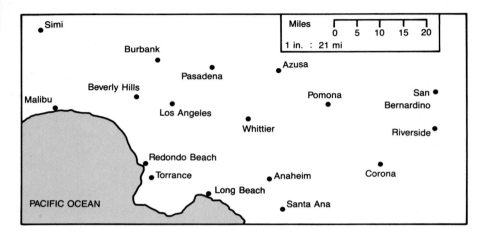

example 1

On the map, Torrance is about $1\frac{1}{4}$ in. from Anaheim.
Estimate the actual distance.

solution

Write a proportion.

$$\begin{array}{l}\text{map distance in inches} \rightarrow \\ \text{actual distance in miles} \rightarrow\end{array} \frac{1}{21} = \frac{1\frac{1}{4}}{d}$$ **Let d represent the actual distance in miles.**

Solve the proportion.

$$1 \times d = 21 \times 1\frac{1}{4}$$

$$d = \frac{21}{1} \times \frac{5}{4}$$

$$d = \frac{105}{4}$$

$$d = 26\frac{1}{4}$$

$$d \approx 26 \quad \longleftarrow \text{ Round to the nearest mile.}$$

The distance from Torrance to Anaheim is about 26 mi.

your turn

Estimate the actual distance for each map distance.

1. Malibu to Whittier; 2 in.

2. Simi to Azusa; $2\frac{1}{2}$ in.

You won't always have a ruler when you need to estimate a distance on a map. You can get an idea of the distance between places on a map using informal measurement.

example 2

Use the map on page 340. Estimate the distance from Whittier to Corona.

solution

Copy the map scale on a strip of paper and use the strip to find the map distance. Each map unit represents 5 mi. On the map, Whittier is about 6 units from Corona.

Think: 6×5 mi ≈ 30 mi

The distance from Whittier to Corona is about 30 mi.

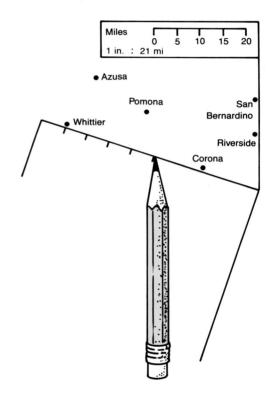

your turn

Without using a ruler, estimate the distance between the given cities.

3. Redondo Beach and Azusa

4. Beverly Hills and Redondo Beach

5. Los Angeles and Burbank

6. Torrance and Pomona

practice exercises

practice for example 1 *(pages 340–341)*

Use the map on page 340. Estimate the actual distance for each map distance.

1. Burbank to Long Beach; $1\frac{1}{2}$ in.

2. Simi to Malibu; $\frac{7}{8}$ in.

3. Torrance to Azusa; $1\frac{3}{4}$ in.

4. Redondo Beach to Long Beach; $\frac{3}{4}$ in.

5. Santa Ana to Corona; $1\frac{1}{8}$ in.

6. Anaheim to Malibu; $2\frac{3}{8}$ in.

7. Los Angeles to San Bernardino; $2\frac{3}{4}$ in.

8. Riverside to Beverly Hills; $3\frac{1}{8}$ in.

The map below shows part of Washington, D.C. Without using a ruler, estimate the distance between the given points.

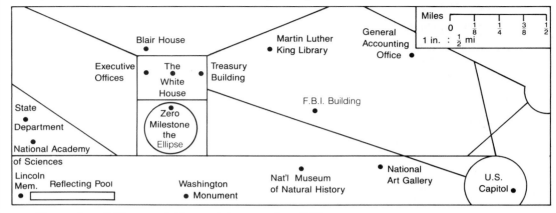

9. Executive Offices and General Accounting Office
10. Lincoln Memorial and Washington Monument
11. General Accounting Office and National Academy of Sciences
12. Lincoln Memorial and the Martin Luther King Library
13. Washington Monument and the White House
14. the U.S. Capitol and the F.B.I. building

Use the map at the right. Estimate the distance between the given cities without using a ruler.

15. Sioux City and Fort Dodge
16. Council Bluffs and Waterloo
17. Des Moines and Ottumwa
18. Fort Dodge and Dubuque

Estimate the distance between the given cities using a ruler and the scale 1 in. : 100 mi.

19. Cedar Rapids and Des Moines
20. Ottumwa and Council Bluffs
21. Waterloo and Mason City
22. Cedar Rapids and Fort Dodge

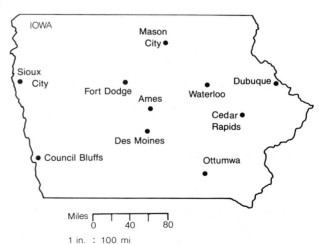

CHAPTER REVIEW

vocabulary vo·cab·u·lar·y

Choose the correct word to complete each sentence.

1. A (*ratio, proportion*) is a comparison of two numbers by division.
2. A ratio that compares two unlike measures is a (*proportion, rate*).

skills

Write each ratio as a fraction in lowest terms.

3. 32 to 100

4. 45:9

5. 8 m to 64 m

6. $\frac{24}{56}$

7. 7 mL:7 L

8. 4 yd to 14 ft

9. 6 mm:38 cm

10. 36:28

Write each ratio in two different ways.

11. 28:21

12. $\frac{52}{113}$

13. $\frac{7}{13}$

14. 7 to 2

Write the unit rate.

15. $1.38 for 6 oz

16. 32 L in 8 h

17. 64 m in 4 s

18. $42 for 24 disks

Solve each proportion.

19. $\frac{2}{5} = \frac{x}{20}$

20. $\frac{9}{6} = \frac{6}{c}$

21. $\frac{x}{4} = \frac{3}{12}$

22. $\frac{33}{w} = \frac{11}{1}$

23. $\frac{40}{14} = \frac{20}{i}$

24. $\frac{3}{v} = \frac{4}{28}$

25. $\frac{2}{x} = \frac{3}{12}$

26. $\frac{12}{8} = \frac{k}{6}$

Solve using a proportion.

27. The cost of 5 grapefruit is $1.40. Find the cost of 6 grapefruit.
28. In a survey, the ratio of men to women was 4 to 5. There were 100 women in the survey. How many men were there?
29. A biologist collected 15 frogs from a pond. Six of the frogs were males. The biologist estimates there are about 200 frogs in the pond. About how many of them are males?
30. A model of a house is being made using the scale 1 in.:3 ft. The kitchen in the model is 5 in. long and 4 in. wide. Find the actual length and width of the kitchen.
31. On a map, the distance between two cities is 5 cm. The map scale is 1 cm:5 km. Estimate the actual distance between the two cities.

CHAPTER TEST

Write each ratio as a fraction in lowest terms.

15-1

1. 45:25
2. 24 to 72
3. $\frac{55}{11}$
4. $\frac{6}{14}$

5. 4 mm to 6 cm
6. 780 mL:1 L
7. 2 min to 55 s
8. 3 kg:500 g

Write each ratio in two different ways.

9. 1 to 5
10. $\frac{4}{9}$
11. 46:13
12. 10 to 1

Write the unit rate.

13. 400 revolutions in 50 s
14. 15 m for 4 banners
15. 172 km in 2 h **15-2**
16. $12 for 10 gal
17. $75 for 5 tickets
18. $52 for 4 lb

Tell whether each proportion is *true* or *false*.

19. $\frac{1}{7} = \frac{3}{21}$
20. $\frac{4}{5} = \frac{18}{20}$
21. $\frac{8}{3} = \frac{17}{6}$
22. $\frac{5}{25} = \frac{1}{5}$ **15-3**

Solve each proportion.

23. $\frac{2}{8} = \frac{x}{12}$
24. $\frac{7}{6} = \frac{7}{b}$
25. $\frac{p}{5} = \frac{3}{15}$
26. $\frac{56}{w} = \frac{14}{1}$

Solve using a proportion.

27. The cost of 5 lb of carrots is $3.20. Find the cost of 3 lb of carrots. **15-4**
28. In pewter the ratio of tin to copper is 17:7. Find the amount of tin needed when 14 lb of copper are used to make pewter.
29. Joseph earns $520 for 40 h of work. How much will he earn for 100 h of work?

An architect is drawing plans for a new school. The scale is 1 in.:8 ft.

30. The length of a classroom in the plans is 3 in. Find the length of the actual classroom. **15-5**
31. The school will be 20 ft high. Find the height in the plans.

32. Use the map on page 340. Estimate the distance between Los Angeles and Pomona if the map distance is $1\frac{5}{8}$ in. **15-6**
33. Use the map of Iowa on page 342. Without using a ruler, estimate the distance between Ames and Fort Dodge.

Many complex calculations are involved in designing a lightweight aircraft. A number of these calculations call for the use of percent.

CHAPTER 16

PERCENTS

16-1 PERCENT CONCEPTS

A **percent** represents a ratio that compares a number to 100. Percent means *per hundred, hundredths,* or *out of every hundred*. The symbol % is read "percent."

The region at the right is divided into one hundred equal parts. The shaded square represents 1 hundredth, or 1%, of the region.

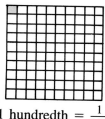

1 hundredth = $\frac{1}{100}$

= 1%

example 1

Write a percent to represent the shaded part of each region.

a.    **b.** 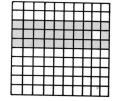   **c.**

solution

a. 5%   **b.** 29%   **c.** 99%

your turn

Write a percent to represent the shaded part of each region.

1.    **2.**    **3.**

example 2

Use the % symbol to write each as a percent.

a. 15 percent   **b.** 39 out of every 100   **c.** 27 hundredths   **d.** $\frac{19}{100}$

solution

a. 15%   **b.** 39%   **c.** 27%   **d.** 19%

your turn

Use the % symbol to write each as a percent.

4. 6 percent   **5.** 79 out of every 100   **6.** 94 hundredths   **7.** $\frac{23}{100}$

practice exercises

practice for example 1 (page 346)

Write a percent to represent the shaded part of each region.

1. 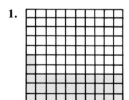 2. 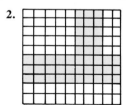 3. 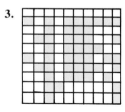 4.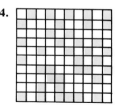

practice for example 2 (page 346)

Use the % symbol to write each as a percent.

5. 17 percent   6. 88 percent   7. 62 out of every 100   8. 58 out of every 100

9. 10 hundredths 10. 34 hundredths 11. 23.7 percent   12. 14.5 percent

13. $\frac{37}{100}$ 14. $\frac{89}{100}$ 15. $75\frac{3}{4}$ percent   16. $42\frac{1}{2}$ percent

mixed practice (page 346)

17. A factory found that 94 out of every 100 light bulbs it produced were good. What percent of the light bulbs were good?

18. A newspaper carrier earns 15 cents for every 100 cents ($1.00) collected. What percent of the money collected does the carrier earn?

19. At Vista High School, 65 out of every 100 students use calculators in mathematics. What percent of the students use calculators?

20. In an election, 85 out of 100 registered voters voted. What percent of the registered voters voted?

21. The chart at the right shows how a total of 100 votes were cast for the presidential candidate in the last ninth-grade election. Write the percent of the vote that each candidate received.

Candidate	Votes
Erica	26
Joel	35
Randall	17
Gena	22

review exercises

Find each product or quotient.

1. $504.2 \div 10$ 2. $373.43 \div 10$ 3. 9.75×10 4. 4.33×10

5. 1045×1000 6. 2395×1000 7. $163 \div 100$ 8. $2275 \div 100$

16-2 PERCENTS AND DECIMALS

Because percent means *hundredths*, you can write a percent as a decimal.
$$26\% = 26 \text{ hundredths} = 0.26$$
To write a percent as a decimal, use the following short-cut method.

1. Move the decimal point two places to the left. $7\% = 0.07$ ← **Insert zeros as placeholders if necessary.**
2. Remove the percent symbol.

example 1

Write each percent as a decimal.

a. 42%   b. 3%   c. 8.2%   d. 120%   e. $33\frac{1}{3}\%$

solution

a. 0.42   b. 0.03   c. 0.082   d. 1.2   e. $0.33\frac{1}{3}$

your turn

Write each percent as a decimal.

1. 67%   2. 5%   3. 2.3%   4. 230%   5. $66\frac{2}{3}\%$

You can use the fact that percent means hundredths to write a decimal as a percent.
$$0.63 = 63 \text{ hundredths} = 63\%$$
To write a decimal as a percent, use the following short-cut method.

1. Move the decimal point two places to the right. $0.5 = 50\%$ ← **Insert zeros as placeholders if necessary.**
2. Write the percent symbol.

example 2

Write each decimal as a percent.

a. 0.85   b. 0.09   c. 0.4   d. 0.265   e. 2.4

solution

a. 85%   b. 9%   c. 40%   d. 26.5%   e. 240%

your turn

Write each decimal as a percent.

6. 0.58   7. 0.055   8. 0.7   9. $0.14\frac{1}{8}$ 10. 3.75

practice exercises

practice for example 1 (page 348)

Write each percent as a decimal.

1. 27%
2. 39%
3. 26.5%
4. 54.9%
5. 7.32%
6. 9.65%

7. 141%
8. 237%
9. 0.3%
10. 0.8%
11. $8\frac{1}{2}\%$
12. $6\frac{3}{4}\%$

practice for example 2 (page 348)

Write each decimal as a percent.

13. 0.43
14. 0.97
15. 0.04
16. 0.06
17. 0.616
18. 0.749

19. 2.34
20. 1.61
21. 1.7
22. 2.6
23. $0.12\frac{1}{2}$
24. $0.87\frac{1}{2}$

mixed practice (page 348)

Write each percent as a decimal. Write each decimal as a percent.

25. 94%
26. 62%
27. 0.23
28. 0.47
29. 87.5%
30. 53.2%

31. 1.9
32. 3.41
33. 0.531
34. 0.499
35. $37\frac{1}{2}\%$
36. $62\frac{1}{2}\%$

37. In one month a clothing store's sales decreased 4%. Write this percent as a decimal.
38. The sale price of a radio was 0.75 of the original price. Write this decimal as a percent.

review exercises

Write each decimal as a fraction or mixed number in lowest terms.

1. 0.43
2. 0.90
3. 0.22
4. 0.86
5. 5.04
6. 10.06

7. Tell whether it would be more appropriate to draw a *bar graph* or a *line graph* to display the given information. Then draw the graph.

Use of Coal in the United States

Year	1880	1900	1920	1940	1960	1980
Percent of Total Energy Used	41	71	73	50	23	20

16-3 WRITING PERCENTS AS FRACTIONS

The reader survey at the right appeared in a local newspaper. If you write 60% as a fraction, you find that $\frac{3}{5}$ of the people who phoned in voted yes.

To write a percent as a fraction, use the following method.

1. Write the percent as a ratio of a number to 100.

2. Write the ratio in lowest terms.

Should our city construct a domed sports stadium?		
Vote	Phone Number	Results
YES	721-6341	60%
NO	721-6351	27%
UNDECIDED	721-6361	13%

$$60\% = \frac{60}{100} = \frac{60 \div 20}{100 \div 20} = \frac{3}{5}$$

example 1

Write each percent as a fraction or a mixed number in lowest terms.

a. 19%   **b.** 101%   **c.** 78%

solution

a. $19\% = \frac{19}{100}$ **b.** $101\% = \frac{101}{100} = 1\frac{1}{100}$ **c.** $78\% = \frac{78}{100} = \frac{78 \div 2}{100 \div 2} = \frac{39}{50}$

your turn

Write each percent as a fraction or a mixed number in lowest terms.

1. 31%   **2.** 45%   **3.** 72%   **4.** 27%   **5.** 120%

example 2

Write each percent as a fraction in lowest terms.

a. 1.7%   **b.** 0.25%

solution

a. $1.7\% = \frac{1.7}{100}$

$= \frac{1.7 \times 10}{100 \times 10} = \frac{17}{1000}$ ← **The numerator should be a whole number.**

b. $0.25\% = \frac{0.25}{100}$

$= \frac{0.25 \times 100}{100 \times 100} = \frac{25}{10,000} = \frac{1}{400}$

your turn

Write each percent as a fraction in lowest terms.

6. 16.3%   **7.** 22.5%   **8.** 12.5%   **9.** 0.8%   **10.** 0.05%

example 3

Write each percent as a fraction in lowest terms.

a. $\frac{1}{3}\%$

b. $8\frac{1}{2}\%$

solution

a. $\frac{1}{3}\% = \dfrac{\frac{1}{3}}{100} = \frac{1}{3} \div 100$

$= \frac{1}{3} \times \frac{1}{100} = \frac{1}{300}$

b. $8\frac{1}{2}\% = \dfrac{8\frac{1}{2}}{100} = 8\frac{1}{2} \div 100$

$= \frac{17}{2} \times \frac{1}{100} = \frac{17}{200}$

your turn

Write each percent as a fraction in lowest terms.

11. $\frac{1}{2}\%$　　　　**12.** $\frac{4}{5}\%$　　　　**13.** $16\frac{2}{3}\%$　　　　**14.** $21\frac{3}{4}\%$　　　　**15.** $23\frac{1}{5}\%$

practice exercises

---

practice for example 1 (page 350)

Write each percent as a fraction or a mixed number in lowest terms.

1. 49%　　　　**2.** 53%　　　　**3.** 80%　　　　**4.** 38%

5. 15%　　　　**6.** 95%　　　　**7.** 75%　　　　**8.** 60%

9. 99%　　　　**10.** 79%　　　　**11.** 110%　　　　**12.** 230%

---

practice for example 2 (page 350)

Write each percent as a fraction in lowest terms.

13. 1.3%　　　　**14.** 2.9%　　　　**15.** 31.6%　　　　**16.** 25.5%

17. 0.3%　　　　**18.** 0.7%　　　　**19.** 1.5%　　　　**20.** 2.2%

21. 0.07%　　　　**22.** 0.02%　　　　**23.** 2.75%　　　　**24.** 6.25%

---

practice for example 3 (page 351)

Write each percent as a fraction in lowest terms.

25. $\frac{7}{8}\%$　　　　**26.** $\frac{3}{7}\%$　　　　**27.** $\frac{6}{7}\%$　　　　**28.** $\frac{5}{9}\%$

29. $2\frac{3}{4}\%$　　　　**30.** $16\frac{1}{2}\%$　　　　**31.** $33\frac{1}{3}\%$　　　　**32.** $6\frac{2}{3}\%$

33. $37\frac{1}{2}\%$　　　　**34.** $66\frac{2}{3}\%$　　　　**35.** $99\frac{1}{2}\%$　　　　**36.** $87\frac{1}{2}\%$

Write each percent as a fraction or a mixed number in lowest terms.

37. 47%   **38.** 93%   **39.** 77%   **40.** 32%   **41.** 100%

42. 40%   **43.** 0.6%   **44.** 5.06%   **45.** 22.2%   **46.** 105%

47. 275%   **48.** $\frac{2}{3}$%   **49.** $\frac{2}{5}$%   **50.** $1\frac{7}{10}$%   **51.** $2\frac{1}{9}$%

Complete.

52. Fraction	$\frac{3}{4}$	?	?	?	?
53. Decimal	?	0.71	0.125	?	?
54. Percent	?	?	?	$33\frac{1}{3}$%	20%

55. Mr. Iuliano agrees to make a 25% down payment on a house. What fraction of the purchase price is his down payment?

56. Marla estimates that 15% of the incoming phone calls are long distance. What fraction of the incoming calls are long distance?

review exercises

Find each quotient.

1. $5\overline{)3}$ **2.** $8\overline{)4}$ **3.** $80\overline{)5}$ **4.** $40\overline{)1}$

5. 731 ÷ 4.3   **6.** 60.3 ÷ 0.4   **7.** 1.65 ÷ 33   **8.** 10.64 ÷ 14

puzzle corner

Find the percent that names the shaded part of each region.

1.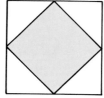

2.

3.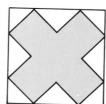

4.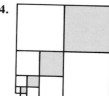

16-4 WRITING FRACTIONS AS PERCENTS

Since percent means hundredths, you can write a fraction as a percent by finding an equivalent fraction with a denominator of 100.

example 1

Write each fraction as a percent: **a.** $\frac{1}{2}$ **b.** $\frac{17}{25}$

solution

a. $\frac{1}{2} = \frac{1 \times 50}{2 \times 50} = \frac{50}{100} = 50\%$ **b.** $\frac{17}{25} = \frac{17 \times 4}{25 \times 4} = \frac{68}{100} = 68\%$

your turn

Write each fraction as a percent.

1. $\frac{4}{5}$ **2.** $\frac{9}{20}$ **3.** $\frac{3}{4}$ **4.** $\frac{7}{10}$

Sometimes it is not easy to find an equivalent fraction with a denominator of 100. In these cases, you can first write the fraction as a decimal. Then write the decimal as a percent.

example 2

Write each fraction as a percent: **a.** $\frac{3}{8}$ **b.** $\frac{1}{12}$

solution

a.
$$\frac{3}{8} \rightarrow 8\overline{)3.00}^{\,0.37\frac{4}{8}} \quad \longleftarrow \text{ } \textbf{Divide to the hundredths' place.}$$
$$\frac{2\ 4}{\ \ 60}$$
$$\frac{56}{4}$$

So $\frac{3}{8} = 0.37\frac{4}{8} = 37\frac{4}{8}\% = 37\frac{1}{2}\%$.

b.
$$\frac{1}{12} \rightarrow 12\overline{)1.00}^{\,0.08\frac{4}{12}}$$
$$\frac{96}{4}$$

So $\frac{1}{12} = 0.08\frac{4}{12} = 8\frac{4}{12}\% = 8\frac{1}{3}\%$.

your turn

Write each fraction as a percent.

5. $\frac{1}{6}$ **6.** $\frac{2}{9}$ **7.** $\frac{5}{8}$ **8.** $\frac{1}{3}$

practice exercises

practice for example 1 (page 353)

Write each fraction as a percent.

1. $\dfrac{2}{5}$ 2. $\dfrac{11}{50}$ 3. $\dfrac{13}{25}$ 4. $\dfrac{9}{10}$ 5. $\dfrac{19}{20}$ 6. $\dfrac{37}{50}$

practice for example 2 (page 353)

Write each fraction as a percent.

7. $\dfrac{5}{6}$ 8. $\dfrac{5}{16}$ 9. $\dfrac{1}{40}$ 10. $\dfrac{5}{7}$ 11. $\dfrac{11}{12}$ 12. $\dfrac{7}{8}$

mixed practice (page 353)

Write each fraction as a percent.

13. $\dfrac{3}{10}$ 14. $\dfrac{2}{25}$ 15. $\dfrac{17}{20}$ 16. $\dfrac{1}{8}$ 17. $\dfrac{11}{16}$ 18. $\dfrac{7}{15}$

19. A basketball team won 24 of its first 36 games. What percent of the games did the team win?

20. A recent study shows that 16 out of every 25 college students have part-time jobs. What percent of the students have part-time jobs?

review exercises

Evaluate each expression when $a = 12$, $b = 1$, and $c = 0$.

1. $7a$ 2. $3ab$ 3. abc 4. $\dfrac{a}{4}$ 5. $\dfrac{b}{1}$ 6. $\dfrac{7}{c}$

calculator corner

A calculator may be helpful when writing a fraction as a percent.

example Complete: $\dfrac{9}{16} = \underline{\ ?\ }\%$.

solution Enter 9 ÷ 16 [%] =. The result is 56.25.   So $\dfrac{9}{16} = 56.25\%$.

Complete, using a calculator.

1. $\dfrac{3}{5} = \underline{\ ?\ }\%$ 2. $\dfrac{7}{8} = \underline{\ ?\ }\%$ 3. $\dfrac{9}{10} = \underline{\ ?\ }\%$ 4. $\dfrac{2}{3} = \underline{\ ?\ }\%$ 5. $\dfrac{61}{50} = \underline{\ ?\ }\%$

16-5 FINDING A PERCENT OF A NUMBER

To find a percent of a number, use the following method.

1. Translate the question into a number sentence. Let n represent the unknown quantity.
2. Write the percent as a decimal or as a fraction.
3. Find the value of n.

example 1

Find each answer.

a. What number is 53% of 180?

$$n = 53\% \times 180$$
$$n = 0.53 \times 180$$
$$n = 95.4$$

So 95.4 is 53% of 180.

b. 3.5% of 72 is what number?

$$3.5\% \times 72 = n$$
$$0.035 \times 72 = n$$
$$2.52 = n$$

So 3.5% of 72 is 2.52.

your turn

Find each answer.

1. What number is 19% of 234?
2. 42.5% of 162 is what number?
3. 0.4% of 94.5 is what number?
4. What number is 18% of 264?

example 2

Find each answer.

a. What number is 40% of 205?

$$n = 40\% \times 205$$
$$n = \frac{2}{\cancel{5}_{1}} \times \frac{\cancel{205}^{41}}{1}$$
$$n = 82$$

So 82 is 40% of 205.

b. $66\frac{2}{3}\%$ of 147 is what number?

$$66\frac{2}{3}\% \times 147 = n$$
$$\frac{2}{\cancel{3}_{1}} \times \frac{\cancel{147}^{49}}{1} = n$$
$$98 = n$$

So $66\frac{2}{3}\%$ of 147 is 98.

your turn

Find each answer.

5. What number is 80% of 130?
6. What number is $12\frac{1}{2}\%$ of 168?
7. 25% of 154 is what number?
8. $33\frac{1}{3}\%$ of 234 is what number?

You should be able to memorize certain common percents and their decimal and fraction *equivalents*. The chart below lists some of these.

Equivalent Percents, Decimals, and Fractions				
$20\% = 0.2 = \frac{1}{5}$	$25\% = 0.25 = \frac{1}{4}$	$12\frac{1}{2}\% = 0.125 = \frac{1}{8}$	$33\frac{1}{3}\% = 0.333... = \frac{1}{3}$	
$40\% = 0.4 = \frac{2}{5}$	$50\% = 0.5 = \frac{1}{2}$	$37\frac{1}{2}\% = 0.375 = \frac{3}{8}$	$66\frac{2}{3}\% = 0.666... = \frac{2}{3}$	$100\% = 1$
$60\% = 0.6 = \frac{3}{5}$	$75\% = 0.75 = \frac{3}{4}$	$62\frac{1}{2}\% = 0.625 = \frac{5}{8}$		
$80\% = 0.8 = \frac{4}{5}$		$87\frac{1}{2}\% = 0.875 = \frac{7}{8}$		

example 3

mental math

Give the decimal and fraction equivalent of each percent.

a. 50%   **b.** 70%   **c.** $62\frac{1}{2}\%$

solution

a. $0.5; \frac{1}{2}$ **b.** $0.7; \frac{7}{10}$ **c.** $0.625; \frac{5}{8}$

your turn

Give the decimal and fraction equivalent of each percent.

9. 20%   **10.** 75%   **11.** $33\frac{1}{3}\%$ **12.** $37\frac{1}{2}\%$

practice exercises

practice for example 1 *(page 355)*

Find each answer.

1. 1% of 58 is what number?
2. 32% of 80 is what number?
3. What number is 50% of 9.28?
4. What number is 45% of 7.2?
5. 2.5% of 3000 is what number?
6. 8.7% of 860 is what number?

practice for example 2 *(page 355)*

Find each answer.

7. What number is 60% of 280?
8. 75% of 380 is what number?
9. What number is $62\frac{1}{2}\%$ of 384?
10. $66\frac{2}{3}\%$ of 615 is what number?
11. What number is 25% of 462?
12. What number is $12\frac{1}{2}\%$ of 473?

Give the decimal and fraction equivalent of each percent.

13. 10%   **14.** 25%   **15.** 60%   **16.** 90%   **17.** $12\frac{1}{2}\%$ **18.** $66\frac{2}{3}\%$

Find each answer.

19. 20% of 125 is what number?   **20.** 70% of 200 is what number?

21. What number is 50% of 42.8?   **22.** What number is 90% of 64.2?

23. $66\frac{2}{3}\%$ of 150 is what number?   **24.** $37\frac{1}{2}\%$ of 84 is what number?

Give the percent equivalent of each decimal or fraction.

25. 0.2   **26.** 0.625   **27.** $\frac{3}{4}$ **28.** $\frac{2}{5}$ **29.** $\frac{1}{3}$ **30.** $\frac{1}{8}$

31. A television station has 80 employees. 40% of the employees are women. How many women are employees of the station?

32. Inez took an 80-item test and received a score of 75%. How many items did she get correct?

review exercises

Estimate using compatible numbers.

1. $\frac{25}{99} \times 197$ **2.** $\frac{33}{100} \times 244$ **3.** $13\frac{1}{7} \times \frac{49}{100}$ **4.** $\frac{67}{100} \times 148$

5. 0.74×123 **6.** 0.103×651 **7.** 355×0.24 **8.** 0.34×86

mental math

Sometimes you can find a percent of a number mentally.

What is $33\frac{1}{3}\%$ of 90?   *Think:* $\frac{1}{3} \times 90 = 30$

What is 10% of 84?   *Think:* $0.1 \times 84 = 8.4$

Find each answer mentally.

1. 10% of 150   **2.** 50% of 60   **3.** 50% of 150   **4.** 1% of 200

5. 25% of 80   **6.** 50% of 42   **7.** 1% of $30   **8.** 10% of $28

9. $33\frac{1}{3}\%$ of 60   **10.** $33\frac{1}{3}\%$ of 150   **11.** $66\frac{2}{3}\%$ of 90   **12.** 75% of 40

16-6 ESTIMATING A PERCENT OF A NUMBER

You can use compatible numbers to estimate a percent of a number.

example 1

Estimate.

a. 26% of 406

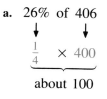

$\frac{1}{4} \times 400$

about 100

b. 33% of $743.89

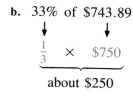

$\frac{1}{3} \times \$750$

about $250

c. 66% of 235

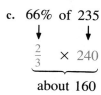

$\frac{2}{3} \times 240$

about 160

your turn

Estimate.

1. 52% of 600

2. 34% of $148.98

3. 75% of $807

4. 38% of 147

example 2

Estimate.

a. 89% of $6.85 ⟵ **89% is about 90%. You can use the decimal equivalent of 90%.**

$0.9 \times \$7$

about $6.30

b. 6.25% of $217

$0.06 \times \$200$

about $12

your turn

Estimate.

5. 61% of 68

6. 9.9% of 25

7. 7.2% of $487

8. $5\frac{7}{8}$% of $88,750

practice exercises

practice for example 1 (page 358)

Estimate.

1. 50% of $148.75 **2.** 25% of 157 **3.** 67% of 240 **4.** 74% of 80

5. 19% of 348 **6.** 33% of $275 **7.** 26.4% of $33 **8.** 41.5% of 246

9. 59% of 394 **10.** 46% of 308 **11.** 35% of $17.25 **12.** 65% of 351

practice for example 2 (page 358)

Estimate.

13. 82% of $8.98 **14.** 9.9% of $260.95 **15.** 5.2% of $289 **16.** 6.7% of $78,369

17. 5.9% of $61.95 **18.** 4.1% of $82.69 **19.** $6\frac{7}{8}$% of 187 **20.** $8\frac{1}{8}$% of 612

mixed practice (page 358)

Estimate.

21. 9.5% of $451 **22.** 11% of $694 **23.** 33% of $448 **24.** 26% of 123

25. 47% of 2086 **26.** 19% of 446 **27.** 1.2% of $609 **28.** 3.9% of $41

29. 67% of $215 **30.** 74% of $191 **31.** 29% of 789 **32.** 53% of 3086

33. A magazine mailed a survey to 3675 subscribers. Twenty-four percent of the subscribers answered the survey. About how many people answered the survey?

34. The Tennis Shop held a one-day sale. All merchandise was sold for 65% of the original prices. If the total of the original prices of the merchandise sold was $1462.95, about how much money did the Tennis Shop take in during the sale?

review *exercises*

Find the GCF and the LCM.

1. 2 and 3 **2.** 2 and 4 **3.** 4 and 6 **4.** 4 and 5

5. 6 and 9 **6.** 12 and 18 **7.** 10 and 15 **8.** 25 and 75

mental math

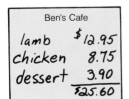

Ben's Cafe

lamb $12.95
chicken 8.75
dessert 3.90
   $25.60

You can use the fact that 15% = 10% + 5% to mentally estimate a 15% tip.

$25.60 is about $26.   10% of $26 = $2.60

5% of $26 ➔ $\frac{1}{2}$ of $2.60 = $1.30

about $3.90 ⬅ tip

Mentally estimate a 15% tip for the given amount.

1. $20 **2.** $12 **3.** $15 **4.** $30 **5.** $9.60

6. $8.05 **7.** $5.95 **8.** $8.85 **9.** $49.85 **10.** $24.50

16-7 USING LOGICAL REASONING

Using a chart to organize given facts often helps you to reason logically.

example

Barb, Dee, and Gina play bass, drums, and guitar. No one plays an instrument that begins with the same letter as her name. Dee and the guitar player are neighbors. Who plays drums?

solution

Make a chart showing all possibilities. Put an × in a space when you eliminate the possibility. Use a √ when you make a match.

	Bass	Drums	Guitar
Barb	×		
Dee		×	
Gina			×

No one's instrument begins with the same letter as her name.

	Bass	Drums	Guitar
Barb	×		
Dee		×	×
Gina			×

Dee and the guitar player are neighbors. So Dee is not the guitar player.

	Bass	Drums	Guitar
Barb	×		√
Dee	√	×	×
Gina			×

Barb must play guitar. Dee must play bass.

So Gina plays drums.

problems

1. Bev, Walt, and Sol went to a costume party dressed as a ghost, a clown, and a witch. Bev walked to the party with the ghost and the witch. Sol and the witch played guitars. Who was the ghost?

2. In 1847 three novels written by sisters Anne, Charlotte, and Emily Bronte were published. *Jane Eyre* was written after Anne's book. Emily was younger than the author of *Jane Eyre* and older than the author of *Agnes Grey*. The third book was *Wuthering Heights*. Who wrote which book?

3. Rita, Chris, and Lyn play right, center, and left field on a softball team. No one plays a position that begins with the same letter as her name. Rita and Chris do not play positions next to each other. Who plays which position?

4. Linda, Frank, and Victor play tennis, golf, and volleyball, but not necessarily in that order. Frank does not play volleyball. The golfer is the tennis player's aunt. Who plays what?

5. Anne, Barry, Carol, and David live in Denver, Chicago, Boston, and Anchorage, but not necessarily in that order. No one lives in a city that begins with the same letter as his or her name. Anne and Carol were born in Boston, but neither has been back there in the past five years. Carol has never been to Alaska. Who lives where?

6. The four class officers of the freshman class are Laura, Ben, Juan, and Jade. Juan is in the same mathematics class as Ben and the class secretary. Jade lives on the same block as the vice president and the same street as the secretary. The treasurer is in the same homeroom as Ben and Jade. Who holds each office?

review *exercises*

1. How many dots are in the twenty-fourth *square number*?

Square Numbers				
No. of Rows	1	2	3	4
No. of Dots	1	4	9	16

2. In the hot desert a camel drinks about 5 gal of water every 8 days. About how much water would a camel drink in 24 days?

3. Miguel, Jeff, and Renee are a doctor, a lawyer, and an engineer. The lawyer went to college with Jeff. Miguel is married to the engineer. Match each person with the correct occupation.

SKILL REVIEW

Use the percent symbol to write each as a percent.

1. 26 percent
2. 59.3 percent
3. 48 out of every 100
4. 100 out of every 100
5. 12 hundredths
6. $\frac{99}{100}$

16-1

Write each percent as a decimal. Write each decimal as a percent.

7. 16%
8. 164%
9. 0.86
10. 0.4
11. 0.014
12. 0.175
13. $53\frac{1}{2}\%$
14. $67\frac{2}{3}\%$
15. $0.06\frac{5}{8}$
16. $0.87\frac{3}{4}$

16-2

Write each percent as a fraction in lowest terms.

17. 65%
18. 18%
19. 1.5%
20. 6.06%
21. $6\frac{1}{2}\%$
22. $16\frac{2}{3}\%$
23. $\frac{2}{5}\%$
24. 21.4%
25. 225%
26. 455%

16-3

Write each fraction as a percent.

27. $\frac{7}{10}$
28. $\frac{1}{50}$
29. $\frac{14}{25}$
30. $\frac{19}{20}$
31. $\frac{1}{8}$
32. $\frac{3}{16}$
33. $\frac{2}{3}$
34. $\frac{7}{8}$
35. $\frac{5}{12}$
36. $\frac{37}{40}$

16-4

Find each answer.

37. 25% of 20 is what number?
38. 50% of 30 is what number?
39. What number is 9% of 85?
40. What number is 16% of 75?
41. What number is $33\frac{1}{3}\%$ of 66?
42. What number is $62\frac{1}{2}\%$ of 48?
43. 63% of 135 is what number?
44. 49% of 221 is what number?
45. 4.2% of 200 is what number?
46. 16.5% of 94 is what number?

16-5

Estimate.

47. 52% of $177
48. 33% of 145
49. 26.5% of $16.95
50. 67% of 74
51. 10.3% of $249.39
52. 3.9% of $68.89

16-6

53. Barbara, Tom, and Amy plan to vacation in Bermuda, Tahiti, and Aruba. Each person is going to only one island. No one is going to an island that begins with the same letter as his or her name. Amy is not going to Bermuda. Who is going where?

16-7

16-8 BORROWING MONEY

You must pay **interest** (*I*) when you borrow money. The **principal** (*P*) is the amount borrowed. When you repay the money borrowed, you must pay both principal and interest. The percent of interest is called the **rate** (*r*). The **time** (*t*) is the period for which the money is borrowed. To find *simple interest*, use this formula:

$$I = P \times r \times t$$

example

Find the interest if the principal is $800, the rate is 9% per year, and the time is 6 months.

solution

$P = \$800$ $r = 9\%$ $t = 6$ months
                     $= 0.09$ $= 0.5$ year ← **The formula requires time to be in years.**

Use the formula: $I = P \times r \times t$
                  $= 800 \times 0.09 \times 0.5$
                  $= 36$

The interest is $36.

exercises

Complete. Use a calculator if you have one.

	PRINCIPAL	RATE PER YEAR	TIME	INTEREST
1.	$710	13%	6 months	?
2.	$6000	1.2%	3 years	?
3.	$12,000	9%	3 months	?
4.	$12,000	9%	3 years	?

5. Running Deer borrowed $900 for 3 months. The interest rate was 12% per year. Find the interest owed at the end of 3 months. Find the total amount that must be repaid.

6. Suppose you borrow $200 for 9 months. The interest rate is 17% per year. Find the interest owed at the end of 9 months. Find the total amount that must be repaid.

16-9 SAVINGS ACCOUNTS

Savings accounts earn interest regularly on the amount of money in the account. If you leave the interest payments in the account you will receive interest on the interest. This is called **compound interest.** When the interest is *compounded* annually, interest is added to the account once a year. Interest also may be compounded semiannually, quarterly, monthly, or daily.

example

Neil put $1500 into a savings account for one year. No other deposits or withdrawals were made. The bank paid 6% interest per year, compounded semiannually (two times per year). How much money did Neil have in the account at the end of the year?

solution

First period interest
Find the present balance:

Find the interest using the interest formula:
$P = \$1500.00$
$r = 6\%$
$t = 0.5$ year

$$I = P \times r \times t$$
$$= \$1500.00 \times 0.06 \times 0.5$$

Add the interest to the present balance:

$1500.00 ◄── original balance

+ $45.00
$1545.00 ◄── new balance

Second period interest
Find the present balance:

Find the interest using the interest formula:
$P = \$1545$
$r = 6\%$
$t = 0.5$ year

$$I = P \times r \times t$$
$$= \$1545.00 \times 0.06 \times 0.5$$

Add the interest to the present balance:

$1545.00

+ $46.35
$1591.35 ◄── final balance

Neil had a balance of $1591.35 in his account at the end of the year.

exercises

Complete. If necessary, round your answer to the nearest cent.

	PRESENT BALANCE	INTEREST RATE PER YEAR	INTEREST PERIOD	FIRST PERIOD INTEREST	NEW BALANCE	SECOND PERIOD INTEREST	NEW BALANCE
1.	$200	5%	annually	?	?	?	?
2.	$900	6%	semiannually	?	?	?	?
3.	$2400	5.5%	quarterly	?	?	?	?
4.	$15,000	$11\frac{1}{2}$%	annually	?	?	?	?
5.	$12,840	10.25%	semiannually	?	?	?	?
6.	$4776	15%	quarterly	?	?	?	?

7. Taylor deposited $2950 in a new savings account that paid $7\frac{1}{2}$% interest per year, compounded semiannually. How much money did Taylor have in the account at the end of 6 months?

8. Suppose $785 is deposited at an interest rate of 8% per year, compounded quarterly. What will the balance be after 3 months?

9. Suppose $10,000 is deposited at an interest rate of 6% per year, compounded quarterly. What will the balance be after 3 months? after 6 months?

10. A money market account pays interest at an annual rate of 9% per year, compounded semiannually. If $5500 is deposited in the account, what will be the balance after the first interest period?

11. Jessica's savings account had a balance of $3864. The account earns interest at a rate of $5\frac{1}{4}$% per year, compounded annually. What is the amount in her account at the end of 2 years?

12. Suppose Rick deposited $1100 into a savings account at an interest rate of 8% per year, compounded semiannually. Suppose Robert deposited $1100 into a savings account at an interest rate of $7\frac{1}{2}$% per year, compounded annually. Who would have more money at the end of 1 year? How much more?

16-10 INCOME TAX

An **income tax** is a tax on earnings. Employers withhold a certain amount of each employee's gross income for income tax. Most employed persons pay a percent of their gross income to the federal government for income tax.

To determine the amount withheld, you use an employee's gross income, filing status, the number of withholding allowances, and tax tables supplied by the federal government.

example

Lenny's weekly gross income is $415.16. He is single and claims one withholding allowance. How much of his weekly gross income is withheld for federal income tax?

solution

Locate in the tax table for single persons the row that contains Lenny's wage.

$415.16 is "at least $410 but less than $420."

Next, read across to the column marked "1".

$59 of Lenny's weekly gross income is withheld for federal income tax.

SINGLE Persons—WEEKLY Payroll Period

And the wages are—		And the number of withholding allowances claimed is—				
At least	But less than	0	1	2	3	4
		The amount of income tax to be withheld shall be—				
$320	$330	$46	$40	$35	$29	$24
330	340	47	42	36	31	25
340	350	50	43	38	32	27
350	360	53	45	39	34	28
360	370	55	46	41	35	30
370	380	58	48	42	37	31
380	390	61	51	44	38	33
390	400	64	54	45	40	34
400	410	67	56	47	41	36
410	420	69	59	49	43	37
420	430	72	62	52	44	39
430	440	75	65	55	46	40
440	450	78	68	57	47	42
450	460	81	70	60	50	43
460	470	83	73	63	53	45
470	480	86	76	66	55	46
480	490	89	79	69	58	48
490	500	92	82	71	61	51

exercises

Complete using the appropriate table from pages 366–367.

	WEEKLY GROSS INCOME	FILING STATUS	NUMBER OF WITHHOLDING ALLOWANCES	AMOUNT WITHHELD FOR FEDERAL INCOME TAX
1.	$335.74	single	1	?
2.	$563.06	married	3	?
3.	$604.98	married	2	?
4.	$479.05	single	0	?

Find the amount withheld for federal income tax.

5. Jeffrey earned $521.73 this week. He is married and claims one withholding allowance.

6. Kerry worked 34 hours last week at $13.44 per hour. She is single and claims two withholding allowances.

7. Hal is married and claims two withholding allowances. If $63 is withheld from his paycheck this week for federal income tax, give the range that his salary could have been for this week.

8. Katy is single and claims zero withholding allowances. If $46 was withheld from her paycheck last week for federal income tax, give the range that her salary could have been for last week.

MARRIED Persons—WEEKLY Payroll Period

And the wages are—		And the number of withholding allowances claimed is—				
At least	But less than	0	1	2	3	4
		The amount of income tax to be withheld shall be—				
$440	$450	$59	$54	$48	$43	$37
450	460	61	55	50	44	39
460	470	62	57	51	46	40
470	480	64	58	53	47	42
480	490	65	60	54	49	43
490	500	67	61	56	50	45
500	510	68	63	57	52	46
510	520	70	64	59	53	48
520	530	71	66	60	55	49
530	540	73	67	62	56	51
540	550	74	69	63	58	52
550	560	76	70	65	59	54
560	570	77	72	66	61	55
570	580	79	73	68	62	57
580	590	81	75	69	64	58
590	600	84	76	71	65	60
600	610	87	78	72	67	61
610	620	90	80	74	68	63

16-11 SALES TAX

Many states collect a sales tax to help pay
the cost of running the state government.
The sales tax rate is given as a percent.
To find the sales tax and the total cost of an
item, you can use the following formulas.

sales tax = price × tax rate

total cost = price + sales tax

example

Eve plans to buy a coat priced at $159.99.
The sales tax rate is $5\frac{1}{4}\%$. Find the sales
tax and the total cost of the coat.

Use the formulas: sales tax = price × tax rate

= $159.99 × 0.0525   ⟵ $5\frac{1}{4}\% = 0.05\frac{1}{4} = 0.0525$

= $8.399475

≈ $8.40   ⟵ *Round up* to the next cent.

total cost = price + sales tax

= $159.99 + $8.40

= $168.39

The sales tax is $8.40. The total cost is $168.39.

exercises

**Find the sales tax and the total cost of each item. Round the sales
tax up to the next cent. Use a calculator if you have one.**

	ITEM	PRICE	SALES TAX RATE	SALES TAX	TOTAL COST
1.	radio	$12.95	4%	?	?
2.	sweater	$34.99	4.5%	?	?
3.	wallet	$15.75	5%	?	?
4.	shirt	$14.50	$6\frac{3}{4}\%$	?	?

5. Samantha bought three books at $15.99 each. The sales tax rate
   is 6.5%. Find the sales tax and the total cost.

6. Al bought three records at $9.95 each and one cassette for $16.00.
   The sales tax rate is 5%. Find the sales tax and the total cost.

7. Patty bought a suit for $99.99 and a blouse for $19.99. The sales
   tax rate is $5\frac{1}{4}\%$. About how much did Patty spend for both items?

CHAPTER REVIEW

vocabulary vo·cab·u·lar·y

Choose the correct word to complete each sentence.

1. A percent is a (*ratio, proportion*) that compares a number to 100.
2. When you borrow money, the amount of money that you borrow is called the (*principal, interest*).

skills

Write each percent as a decimal. Write each decimal as a percent.

3. 93%   4. 8%   5. 0.145   6. 2.1   7. 3.7%   8. 0.1%

Write each percent as a fraction or mixed number in lowest terms.

9. 67%   10. 52%   11. 400%   12. 6.25%   13. 42.7%   14. $37\frac{1}{2}\%$

Write each fraction as a percent.

15. $\frac{41}{50}$ 16. $\frac{23}{25}$ 17. $\frac{1}{6}$ 18. $\frac{3}{7}$ 19. $\frac{7}{16}$ 20. $\frac{4}{15}$

Find each answer.

21. What number is 40% of 873?
22. What number is 1.2% of 450?
23. $37\frac{1}{2}\%$ of 24.8 is what number?
24. 100% of 762 is what number?

Estimate.

25. 48% of 157
26. 9.9% of 65
27. 6.9% of $31.95

28. Spot, Fang, and Mickey are the names of a cat, a dog, and a parrot. Fang and the dog are the same age. Fang, Mickey, and the cat have different owners. Match each animal with its name.

29. Find the interest if the principal is $1200, the rate is 11% per year, and the time is 6 months.

30. Suppose $1000 is deposited at an interest rate of 6% per year, compounded semiannually. What will the balance be after 1 year?

31. Brendan earned $393.54 last week. He is single and claims one withholding allowance. Using the tax tables on pages 366 and 367, find the amount withheld that week for federal income tax.

32. Ed bought a new car priced at $18,895.99. The sales tax rate is 5%. Find the sales tax and the total cost.

CHAPTER TEST

Use the percent symbol to write each as a percent.

16-1

1. 7 hundredths   2. 84 out of every 100   3. $68\frac{1}{2}$ percent

Write each percent as a decimal. Write each decimal as a percent.

16-2

4. 2%   5. 0.08   6. 0.1   7. 10.8%   8. $0.86\frac{1}{5}$

Write each percent as a fraction or mixed number in lowest terms.

16-3

9. 1%   10. 210%   11. 28.8%   12. $62\frac{1}{2}$%   13. $\frac{1}{3}$%

Write each fraction as a percent.

16-4

14. $\frac{1}{10}$ 15. $\frac{3}{4}$ 16. $\frac{3}{5}$ 17. $\frac{1}{3}$ 18. $\frac{5}{8}$

Find each answer.

16-5

19. 7% of 210 is what number?   20. 36% of 95 is what number?

21. What number is $66\frac{2}{3}$% of 15?   22. What number is $87\frac{1}{2}$% of 16?

Estimate.

16-6

23. 26% of 123   24. 34% of 148   25. 5.8% of $689.95

16-7

26. The last names of Kathy, Joe, and Marie are Power, Petranic, and Carter. Marie's last name is not Carter. Power is Petranic's brother. What is each person's full name?

16-8

27. Find the interest if the principal is $13,256, the rate is 13% per year, and the time is 3 months.

16-9

28. Betty put $4000 into a savings account for one year. The bank paid 8% interest per year compounded quarterly. How much money did Betty have in the account at the end of six months?

16-10

29. Vicki earned $356.78 this week. She is single and claims zero withholding allowances. Using the tax tables from pages 366 and 367, find the amount withheld this week for federal income tax.

16-11

30. Pat purchased $36 worth of records. The sales tax rate was 5%. Find the sales tax and the total cost of the records.

An automobile purchase is often financed with a loan. The interest rate, usually expressed as a percent, affects the monthly payment.

CHAPTER 17

MORE PERCENTS

17-1 FINDING THE PERCENT ONE NUMBER IS OF ANOTHER

Mr. Simmons coached 250 basketball games during his career. His teams won 120 of those games. You can use a number sentence to find that his teams won 48% of the games played.

To find the percent one number is of another, use the following method.

1. Write a number sentence. Let n represent the unknown percent in fraction or decimal form.
2. Find the value of n.
3. Write n as a percent.

example 1

Find each answer.

a. 120 is what percent of 250?

b. What percent of 10 is 50?

solution

a. 120 is what percent of 250?

$$120 = n \times 250$$

$$120 = 250n$$

$$\frac{120}{250} = \frac{250n}{250}$$ ← **Divide by 250 on each side of the equals sign.**

$$\frac{120}{250} = n$$

$$\frac{120}{250} = \frac{12}{25} = \frac{12 \times 4}{25 \times 4} = \frac{48}{100} = 48\%$$

So 120 is 48% of 250.

b. What percent of 10 is 50?

$$n \times 10 = 50$$

$$10n = 50$$

$$\frac{10n}{10} = \frac{50}{10}$$ ← **Divide by 10 on each side of the equals sign.**

$$n = \frac{50}{10}$$

$$\frac{50}{10} = \frac{50 \times 10}{10 \times 10} = \frac{500}{100} = 500\%$$

So 50 is 500% of 10.

your turn

Find each answer.

1. 15 is what percent of 75?
2. What percent of 120 is 6?
3. What percent of 2 is 4?
4. 12 is what percent of 8?

example 2

Find each answer.

a. 7 is what percent of 8?　　　　**b.** What percent of 180 is 6?

solution

a.　7　is　what percent　of　8?

$$7 = n \times 8$$

$$7 = 8n$$

$$\frac{7}{8} = \frac{8n}{8} \quad \longleftarrow \quad \text{Divide by 8 on each side of the equals sign.}$$

$$\frac{7}{8} = n$$

$$\frac{7}{8} \to \quad 8\overline{)7.00}^{\,0.87\frac{4}{8}} \quad \longleftarrow \quad \text{Divide to the hundredths' place.}$$
$$\frac{6\,4}{60}$$
$$\frac{56}{4}$$

$$0.87\frac{4}{8} = 0.87\frac{1}{2} = 87\frac{1}{2}\%$$

So 7 is $87\frac{1}{2}\%$ of 8.

b.　What percent　of　180　is　6?

$$n \times 180 = 6$$

$$180n = 6$$

$$\frac{180n}{180} = \frac{6}{180} \quad \longleftarrow \quad \text{Divide by 180 on each side of the equals sign.}$$

$$n = \frac{6}{180} = \frac{1}{30}$$

$$\frac{1}{30} \to \quad 30\overline{)1.00}^{\,0.03\frac{10}{30}} \quad \longleftarrow \quad \text{Divide to the hundredths' place.}$$
$$\frac{90}{10}$$

$$0.03\frac{10}{30} = 0.03\frac{1}{3} = 3\frac{1}{3}\%$$

So 6 is $3\frac{1}{3}\%$ of 180.

your turn

Find each answer.

5. 21 is what percent of 80?
7. What percent of 33 is 22?
9. 21 is what percent of 200?

6. 9 is what percent of 120?
8. What percent of 12 is 7?
10. 15 is what percent of 80?

practice exercises

practice for example 1 (page 372)

Find each answer.

1. 36 is what percent of 60?
3. What percent of 20 is 1?
5. What percent of 10 is 20?
7. 90 is what percent of 60?

2. 12 is what percent of 25?
4. What percent of 5 is 1?
6. What percent of 4 is 16?
8. 30 is what percent of 24?

Find each answer.

9. 5 is what percent of 8?
10. 35 is what percent of 40?
11. 15 is what percent of 18?
12. 21 is what percent of 36?
13. What percent of 60 is 34?
14. What percent of 64 is 42?
15. What percent of 24 is 2?
16. What percent of 144 is 9?

mixed practice (pages 372–373)

Find each answer.

17. 11 is what percent of 25?
18. 1 is what percent of 10?
19. 2 is what percent of 6?
20. 25 is what percent of 5?
21. What percent of 50 is 75?
22. What percent of 2000 is 85?
23. What percent of 45 is 1.5?
24. What percent of 24 is 1.5?

25. Joyce correctly answered 15 out of 20 questions on a French test. What percent of the questions did she answer correctly?

26. The All Seasons Lawn Shop expected to sell 150 lawn mowers last year. They actually sold 180. What percent of the expected sales were the actual sales?

review *exercises*

Give the decimal and fraction equivalents of each percent.

1. 50%
2. $66\frac{2}{3}\%$
3. $37\frac{1}{2}\%$
4. 75%
5. 60%
6. $12\frac{1}{2}\%$
7. 25%
8. 30%
9. $87\frac{1}{2}\%$
10. $33\frac{1}{3}\%$

mental math

You can find percents like the following mentally.

What percent of 30 is 15?   *Think:* $\frac{15}{30} \rightarrow \frac{1}{2} \rightarrow 50\%$

2 is what percent of 200?   *Think:* $\frac{2}{200} \rightarrow \frac{1}{100} \rightarrow 1\%$

Find each percent mentally.

1. What percent of 60 is 6?
2. What percent of 26 is 13?
3. 8 is what percent of 800?
4. 12 is what percent of 12?
5. What percent of 30 is 10?
6. 20 is what percent of 80?

17-2 FINDING A NUMBER WHEN A PERCENT OF IT IS KNOWN

Judy's Store hired 24 teenagers. This was 6% of the employees. You can use a number sentence to find that the store had 400 employees.

To find a number when a percent of it is known, use the following method.

1. Write a number sentence. Let n represent the unknown number.
2. Write the percent as a decimal or as a fraction.
3. Find the value of n.

example 1

Find each answer.

a. 24 is 6% of what number?

b. 125% of what number is 375?

solution

a. 24 is 6% of what number?

$$24 = 6\% \times n$$

$$24 = 0.06n \quad \longleftarrow \text{ Write the percent as a decimal.}$$

$$\frac{24}{0.06} = \frac{0.06n}{0.06} \quad \longleftarrow \text{ Divide both sides by 0.06.}$$

$$\frac{24}{0.06} = n$$

$$\frac{24}{0.06} \rightarrow 0.06)\overline{24.00} \begin{array}{r} 4\ 00 \\ \underline{24} \\ 0\ 00 \\ \underline{0\ 00} \\ 0 \end{array}$$

So 24 is 6% of 400.

b. 125% of what number is 375?

$$125\% \times n = 375$$

$$1.25n = 375 \quad \longleftarrow \text{ Write the percent as a decimal.}$$

$$\frac{1.25n}{1.25} = \frac{375}{1.25} \quad \longleftarrow \text{ Divide both sides by 1.25.}$$

$$n = \frac{375}{1.25}$$

$$1.25)\overline{375.00} \begin{array}{r} 3\ 00 \\ \underline{375} \\ 0\ 00 \\ \underline{0\ 00} \\ 0 \end{array}$$

So 125% of 300 is 375.

your turn

Find each answer.

1. 30 is 40% of what number?
2. 27 is 9% of what number?
3. 30% of what number is 108?
4. 1.2% of what number is 36?

example 2

Find each answer.

a. 40 is 25% of what number?

b. $62\frac{1}{2}\%$ of what number is 30?

solution

a. 40 is 25% of $\underbrace{\text{what number}}$?
    ↓   ↓   ↓   ↓

$40 = 25\% \times \qquad n$

$40 = \frac{1}{4}n$ ← **Write the percent as a fraction.**

$\dfrac{40}{\frac{1}{4}} = \dfrac{\frac{1}{4}n}{\frac{1}{4}}$ ← **Divide both sides by $\frac{1}{4}$.**

$40 \div \frac{1}{4} = n$

$40 \times 4 = n$

$160 = n$

So 40 is 25% of 160.

b. $62\frac{1}{2}\%$ of $\underbrace{\text{what number}}$ is 30?
      ↓   ↓   ↓ ↓

$62\frac{1}{2}\% \times \qquad n \qquad = 30$

$\frac{5}{8}n = 30$ ← **Write the percent as a fraction.**

$\dfrac{\frac{5}{8}n}{\frac{5}{8}} = \dfrac{30}{\frac{5}{8}}$ ← **Divide both sides by $\frac{5}{8}$.**

$n = 30 \div \frac{5}{8}$

$n = 30 \times \frac{8}{5} = \overset{6}{\cancel{\frac{30}{1}}} \times \frac{8}{\underset{1}{\cancel{5}}}$

$n = 48$

So $62\frac{1}{2}\%$ of 48 is 30.

your turn

Find each answer.

5. 9 is 75% of what number?

6. 20 is 80% of what number?

7. $33\frac{1}{3}\%$ of what number is 45?

8. $37\frac{1}{2}\%$ of what number is 51?

practice exercises

practice for example 1 (page 375)

Find each answer.

1. 44 is 22% of what number?

2. 14 is 35% of what number?

3. 81 is 9% of what number?

4. 18 is 8% of what number?

5. 150% of what number is 204?

6. 125% of what number is 75?

7. 12.5% of what number is 343?

8. 9.3% of what number is 186?

9. 101 is 10.1% of what number?

10. 31 is 15.5% of what number?

11. 45% of what number is 135?

12. 88% of what number is 352?

Find each answer.

13. 40 is $62\frac{1}{2}\%$ of what number?

14. 50 is $66\frac{2}{3}\%$ of what number?

15. 24 is 50% of what number?

16. 9 is $37\frac{1}{2}\%$ of what number?

17. $87\frac{1}{2}\%$ of what number is 49?

18. 25% of what number is 68?

19. 20% of what number is 88?

20. 40% of what number is 90?

Find each answer.

21. 72 is 36% of what number?

22. 70 is 140% of what number?

23. 419 is 100% of what number?

24. 100 is $62\frac{1}{2}\%$ of what number?

25. 220% of what number is 770?

26. $33\frac{1}{3}\%$ of what number is 630?

27. 2.7% of what number is 189?

28. 7.5% of what number is 81?

29. Last year a life insurance company paid claims to 924 people. This represented 15% of its customers. How many customers did the company have?

30. In the last election $37\frac{1}{2}\%$ of the people voted for Dobbs. If Dobbs received 1665 votes, how many people voted in the election?

review exercises

Solve each proportion.

1. $\frac{b}{4} = \frac{3}{12}$

2. $\frac{5}{t} = \frac{1}{10}$

3. $\frac{2}{8} = \frac{z}{64}$

4. $\frac{15}{20} = \frac{60}{a}$

5. $\frac{y}{24} = \frac{5}{6}$

6. $\frac{7}{8} = \frac{p}{64}$

7. $\frac{10}{c} = \frac{5}{60}$

8. $\frac{1}{3} = \frac{50}{w}$

Estimate.

9. $17\frac{2}{3} - 10\frac{1}{4}$

10. $6\frac{7}{8} \div \frac{9}{17}$

11. $\frac{5}{19} \times 79$

12. $6\frac{5}{11} + 2\frac{3}{5} + 3\frac{9}{10}$

13. 453×0.328

14. $8.39 - 7.846$

15. $7.825 \div 0.99$

16. $\$4.47 + \$1.51$

17. $8\frac{3}{5} + 14\frac{9}{20}$

18. $91 \times \frac{5}{16}$

19. $5\frac{1}{9} \div \frac{10}{39}$

20. $20\frac{14}{15} - 14\frac{1}{8}$

17-3 PERCENT AND PROPORTIONS

Sometimes it is helpful to rewrite a percent question as a proportion.

example 1

What number is 75% of 160?

solution

Rewrite the question as a proportion:
An unknown number is to 160 as 75 is to 100. ◄── **You are looking for a percent of a number.**

$$\frac{unknown \text{ part} \rightarrow \quad n}{\text{whole} \quad \rightarrow \quad 160} = \frac{75 \leftarrow \text{ part}}{100 \leftarrow \text{ whole}}$$

Solve the proportion.

$$100n = 160 \times 75$$
$$100n = 12{,}000$$
$$n = 120 \qquad \text{So 120 is 75\% of 160.}$$

your turn

Find each answer using a proportion.

1. 55% of 300 is what number?
2. 200% of 25 is what number?
3. What number is 8% of 180?
4. What number is 3.5% of 500?

example 2

35 is what percent of 140?

solution

Rewrite the question as a proportion:
35 is to 140 as an unknown number is to 100. ◄── **You are looking for what percent one number is of another.**

$$\frac{\text{part} \rightarrow \quad 35}{\text{whole} \rightarrow 140} = \frac{n \leftarrow unknown \text{ part}}{100 \leftarrow \quad \text{whole}}$$

Solve the proportion. $35 \times 100 = 140n$

$$\frac{3500}{140} = \frac{140n}{140}$$
$$25 = n \qquad \text{So 35 is 25\% of 140.}$$

your turn

Find each answer using a proportion.

5. 15 is what percent of 25?
6. 55 is what percent of 25?
7. What percent of 40 is 3.6?
8. What percent of 240 is 6?

example 3

90 is 50% of what number?

solution

Rewrite the question as a proportion:
90 is to an unknown number as 50 is to 100. ◀ **You are looking for a number when a percent of it is known.**

$$\frac{\text{part}}{\text{unknown whole}} \rightarrow \frac{90}{n} = \frac{50}{100} \leftarrow \frac{\text{part}}{\text{whole}}$$

Solve the proportion.

$$90 \times 100 = 50n$$
$$\frac{9000}{50} = \frac{50n}{50}$$
$$180 = n \qquad \text{So 90 is 50\% of 180.}$$

your turn

Find each answer using a proportion.

9. 20 is 25% of what number?

10. 18 is 40% of what number?

11. 0.5% of what number is 12?

12. 230% of what number is 4.6?

practice exercises

practice for example 1 (page 378)

Find each answer using a proportion.

1. What number is 75% of 750?

2. What number is 65% of 3000?

3. What number is 120% of 440?

4. What number is 125% of 90?

5. 2% of 400 is what number?

6. 7% of 60 is what number?

7. 75% of 2.2 is what number?

8. 5% of 0.4 is what number?

9. What is 2.5% of 1800?

10. 4.8% of 500 is what number?

practice for example 2 (page 378)

Find each answer using a proportion.

11. 13 is what percent of 52?

12. 6 is what percent of 200?

13. 30 is what percent of 24?

14. 7 is what percent of 4?

15. What percent of 90 is 60?

16. What percent of 16 is 1?

17. What percent of 40 is 2.4?

18. What percent of 50 is 12.5?

19. 8 is what percent of 64?

20. What percent of 80 is 120?

Find each answer using a proportion.

21. 175 is 25% of what number?
22. 96 is 30% of what number?
23. 2 is 200% of what number?
24. 110 is 250% of what number?
25. 8.8% of what number is 220?
26. 1.4% of what number is 28?
27. 80% of what number is 5.6?
28. 4% of what number is 5.2?

Find each answer using a proportion.

29. 180% of 240 is what number?
30. What percent of 14 is 42?
31. 66 is 3.3% of what number?
32. What number is 80% of 12.5?
33. What percent of 104 is 260?
34. 400% of what number is 34?
35. What number is 65% of 20?
36. 56 is what percent of 280?

37. The Ashby Public Library has 450 science fiction books. They represent 5% of all the books in the library. How many books are in the library?

38. Last month United Motors sold 50 vehicles. Of the 50 vehicles sold, 38 were cars, 8 were vans, and 4 were trucks. What percent of the 50 vehicles sold were trucks?

39. Cable TV Company finds that 40% of all subscribers own video recorders. If 600 subscribers own recorders, how many people subscribe to the company?

review exercises

Find each answer.

1. $906 - 347$
2. $587 + 73$
3. $216.4 + 5.81$
4. $96.8 - 54.33$
5. $2\frac{1}{8} + 3\frac{5}{12}$
6. $14\frac{9}{20} - 6\frac{3}{5}$
7. $\frac{19}{25} - \frac{3}{10}$
8. $\frac{1}{15} + \frac{3}{4}$
9. $48 \div 0.06$
10. 822×37
11. 6.5×3.4
12. $32,812 \div 52$
13. $\frac{3}{4} \times \frac{10}{21}$
14. $\frac{2}{3} \div \frac{9}{10}$
15. $3\frac{1}{2} \div 2\frac{1}{3}$
16. $7\frac{1}{2} \times 3\frac{1}{3}$

puzzle corner

What amount is 10,000% of a dime?

17-4 PERCENT OF INCREASE OR DECREASE

In March, Galaxy Discount Records sold 600 classical music records. In April, they sold 750 classical music records. You can use a ratio to find that the **percent of increase** in records sold is 25%.

To find the percent of increase, use the following method.

1. Find the amount of increase.
$$750 - 600 = 150$$

2. Write a ratio comparing the amount of increase to the original amount.
$$\frac{150}{600} = \frac{1}{4}$$

3. Write the ratio as a percent.
$$\frac{1}{4} = 25\%$$

example 1

Find each percent of increase.

a. original weekly salary = $20
new weekly salary = $23

b. original weight = 64 kg
new weight = 120 kg

solution

a. amount of increase: $23 − $20 = $3

$$\frac{\text{amount of increase} \rightarrow \$3}{\text{original amount} \rightarrow \$20}$$

$$\frac{3}{20} = \frac{3 \times 5}{20 \times 5} = \frac{15}{100} = 15\%$$

The percent of increase is 15%.

b. amount of increase: 120 − 64 = 56

$$\frac{\text{amount of increase} \rightarrow 56}{\text{original amount} \rightarrow 64} = \frac{7}{8}$$

$$\frac{7}{8} = 87\frac{1}{2}\%$$

The percent of increase is $87\frac{1}{2}\%$.

your turn

Find each percent of increase.

1. original salary = $400
new salary = $520

2. original salary = $250
new salary = $270

3. original weight = 48 kg
new weight = 64 kg

4. original weight = 80 kg
new weight = 90 kg

To find the **percent of decrease,** use the following method.

1. Find the amount of decrease.
2. Write a ratio comparing the amount of decrease to the original amount.
3. Write the ratio as a percent.

example 2

Find each percent of decrease.

a. original amount = $1000
   new amount = $800

b. original price = $120
   new price = $80

solution

a. amount of decrease: $1000 - 800 = 200$

$$\frac{\text{amount of decrease}}{\text{original amount}} \rightarrow \frac{200}{1000} = \frac{1}{5}$$

$$\frac{1}{5} = 20\%$$

The percent of decrease is 20%.

b. amount of decrease: $120 - 80 = 40$

$$\frac{\text{amount of decrease}}{\text{original amount}} \rightarrow \frac{40}{120} = \frac{1}{3}$$

$$\frac{1}{3} = 33\frac{1}{3}\%$$

The percent of decrease is $33\frac{1}{3}\%$.

your turn

Find each percent of decrease.

5. original cost = $44
   new cost = $33

6. original price = $240
   new price = $228

7. original cost = $16
   new cost = $10

8. original length = 540 cm
   new length = 180 cm

practice exercises

practice for example 1 (page 381)

Find each percent of increase.

1. original weight = 50 kg
   new weight = 53 kg

2. original length = 150 m
   new length = 162 m

3. original fare = $85
   new fare = $102

4. original weight = 85 kg
   new weight = 119 kg

5. original cost = $40
   new cost = $66

6. original salary = $600
   new salary = $750

7. original weight = 120 g
   new weight = 200 g

8. original cost = $280
   new cost = $315

Find each percent of decrease.

9. original bill = $25
   new bill = $18

10. original weight = 38 g
    new weight = 19 g

11. original weight = 300 kg
    new weight = 250 kg

12. original price = $200
    new price = $175

13. original cost = $1250
    new cost = $1225

14. original cost = $280
    new cost = $266

15. original cost = $600
    new cost = $400

16. original weight = 18 g
    new weight = 6 g

Tell whether there is an *increase* or a *decrease*. Then find the percent of increase or decrease.

17. original weight = 36 g
    new weight = 45 g

18. original cost = $50
    new cost = $34

19. original length = 120 m
    new length = 105 m

20. original price = $120
    new price = $160

21. original cost = $600
    new cost = $558

22. original length = 320 m
    new length = 304 m

23. original length = 32 m
    new length = 12 m

24. original weight = 80 kg
    new weight = 50 kg

25. In June, Sunset Motors sold 12 vans. In July, they sold only two vans. Find the percent of decrease in sales of vans.

26. Last year Frank threw 32 touchdown passes. This year he threw 40 touchdown passes. Find the percent of increase.

review exercises

Write each decimal as a fraction or mixed number in lowest terms.

1. 0.27
2. 0.633
3. 3.74
4. 239.25
5. 77.8
6. 0.65
7. 0.96
8. 12.52

Compare. Replace each ___?___ with >, <, or =.

9. $\frac{2}{6}$ ___?___ $\frac{1}{3}$

10. $\frac{3}{5}$ ___?___ $\frac{6}{10}$

11. $\frac{7}{10}$ ___?___ $\frac{7}{12}$

12. $\frac{3}{4}$ ___?___ $\frac{3}{5}$

13. $\frac{3}{4}$ ___?___ $\frac{4}{5}$

14. $\frac{2}{5}$ ___?___ $\frac{3}{8}$

15. $\frac{2}{3}$ ___?___ $\frac{3}{4}$

16. $\frac{7}{10}$ ___?___ $\frac{1}{2}$

SKILL REVIEW

Find each answer.

17-1

1. 22 is what percent of 25?
2. What percent of 150 is 12?
3. What percent of 25 is 35?
4. What percent of 240 is 40?
5. 13 is what percent of 16?
6. What percent of 300 is 162?
7. 15 is what percent of 900?
8. 63 is what percent of 36?
9. What percent of 400 is 58?
10. 240 is what percent of 320?

17-2

11. 75% of what number is 102?
12. 18 is $33\frac{1}{3}$% of what number?
13. $37\frac{1}{2}$% of what number is 24?
14. 90% of what number is 2250?
15. 40 is 5% of what number?
16. 130% of what number is 312?
17. 84 is 7.5% of what number?
18. 19.5% of what number is 78?
19. 55% of what number is 33?
20. 48 is 40% of what number?

21. Systems Steel Company found that $62\frac{1}{2}$% of its employees own compact cars. If 4800 of its employees own compact cars, how many employees are there?

Find each answer using a proportion.

17-3

22. What percent of 200 is 4?
23. 170 is what percent of 680?
24. 2.5% of what number is 20?
25. 2.7 is 45% of what number?
26. What number is 75% of 24?
27. 2% of 310 is what number?
28. 12 is what percent of 144?
29. 90 is what percent of 45?
30. What number is 12% of 360?
31. What number is 30% of 600?

32. Savings Appliance Store sold 45 televisions last month. This amount represented 60% of all the televisions in their stock. How many televisions did they have in stock?

Tell whether there is an *increase* or a *decrease*. Then find each percent of increase or decrease.

17-4

33. original weight = 24 kg
    new weight = 15 kg
34. original length = 210 m
    new length = 140 m
35. original cost = $250
    new cost = $275
36. original salary = $300
    new salary = $375
37. original width = 250 cm
    new width = 270 cm
38. original amount = $300
    new amount = $294

17-5 COMMISSION

Many salespeople earn a *commission* for selling goods or services. A **commission** is an amount of money earned based on a percent of total sales. The percent is called the **commission rate.**

example

Maureen's commission rate on all sales is 7%. Last month her sales were $44,646. Find Maureen's commission.

solution

Use the formula:

commission = sales × commission rate
$$= \$44,646 \times \quad 0.07 \quad \longleftarrow \text{ Write the rate as a decimal.}$$
$$= \quad \$3125.22$$

Maureen earned a commission of $3125.22.

exercises

1. Ed Fogarty is a shoe salesman. His commission rate on all sales is 9%. Last month Ed had sales of $15,895. Find Ed's commission for the month.

2. Lois Holmes sells real estate. Her commission rate on all sales is 5%. She recently sold a house for $102,500. Find her commission.

3. Paul Richmond sells carpets. His monthly commission rate is $6\frac{1}{2}\%$. Last month his carpet sales were $7560. Find his commission.

4. Edgar Cannon's commission rate on furniture sales is 7.5%. He sold a bedroom set for $1242.50. Find Edgar's commission rounded to the nearest cent.

5. Nancy Franklin sells real estate. Her commission rate on all sales is 4%. She recently sold a condominium for $85,800. Find her commission.

17-6 DISCOUNTS

During a two-day sale, Sports Mart sold its merchandise at a *discount*. A **discount** is an amount of money subtracted from the regular price. The **rate of discount** is the percent the regular price is reduced. You use the regular price and the rate of discount to find the discount and the sale price.

example 1

Brian finds a tennis racket regularly priced at $120. It is discounted 25%. Find the discount and the sale price.

solution

Use the formula:

$$\text{discount} = \text{regular price} \times \text{rate of discount}$$
$$= \quad \$120 \quad \times \quad 0.25 \quad \longleftarrow \text{ Write the rate as a decimal.}$$
$$= \quad \$30$$

Subtract to find the sale price: $120 − $30 = $90

The discount is $30. The sale price is $90.

your turn

Find the discount and the sale price for each item.

1. baseball glove: regular price, $32; rate of discount, 25%
2. basketball: regular price, $20; rate of discount, 20%
3. swimsuit: regular price, $40; rate of discount, 30%
4. tennis shoes: regular price, $50; rate of discount, $12\frac{1}{2}$%

If you know the regular price and the sale price of an item, you can find the rate of discount.

example 2

A rowing machine regularly priced at $160 is on sale for $112. Find the rate of discount.

solution

Subtract to find the amount of the discount. $160 − $112 = $48

Use the formula:

$$\text{rate of discount} = \text{discount} \div \text{regular price}$$
$$= \quad \$48 \quad \div \quad \$160$$
$$= \quad 0.3 = 30\%$$

The rate of discount is 30%.

your turn

Find the rate of discount.

5. barbells: regular price, $50; sale price, $35
6. fishing-tackle kit: regular price, $12; sale price, $9
7. running shoes: regular price, $42; sale price, $27.30
8. binoculars: regular price, $40; sale price, $25

practice exercises

practice for example 1 (page 386)

Find the discount and the sale price for each item.

1. stereo: regular price, $210; rate of discount, 30%
2. electric mower: regular price, $490; rate of discount, 20%
3. sweater: regular price, $50; rate of discount, 15%
4. electronic keyboard: regular price, $159; rate of discount, $33\frac{1}{3}\%$

practice for example 2 (pages 386–387)

Find the rate of discount.

5. key chain: regular price, $4; sale price, $2
6. tent: regular price, $150; sale price, $117
7. sweater: regular price, $36; sale price, $23.40
8. table-tennis paddles: regular price, $12; sale price, $10

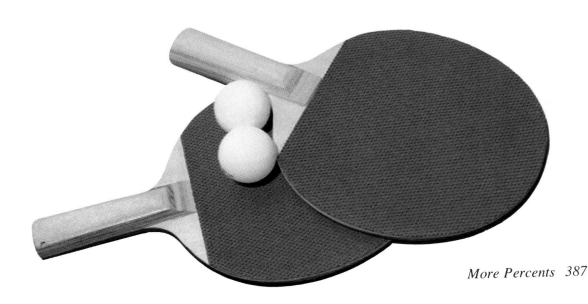

mixed practice (pages 386–387)

Complete the table.

	REGULAR PRICE	RATE OF DISCOUNT	DISCOUNT	SALE PRICE
9.	$34	25%	?	?
10.	$40	?	?	$24
11.	$16	10%	?	?
12.	$280	?	?	$140
13.	$72	?	?	$54
14.	$13	10%	?	?

15. A pair of running shoes with a regular price of $48 is on sale for $36. Find the rate of discount.

16. A TV that regularly sells for $350 is on sale at a 20% discount. Employees at the store receive an additional 15% discount on the sale price.
    a. Find the cost of the TV if bought by a customer.
    b. Find the cost of the TV if bought by an employee.

17. A lamp that regularly sells for $28 is on sale at a 15% discount. Find the sale price.

18. A radio that regularly sells for $50 is on sale for $44. Find the rate of discount.

calculator corner

You can use a calculator to compute a discount. If you do, it is usually helpful to estimate to check the reasonableness of your answer.

example Find the discount: regular price, $14.80; 20% discount

solution Enter: 14.80 × 20 % =.
The answer is 2.96.
The discount is $2.96.

Estimate: 20% of $14.80

$\frac{1}{5}$ × $15
about $3

The answer $2.96 is reasonable.

Find each discount using a calculator.

1. regular price, $14.50; 50% discount
2. regular price, $20.20; 25% discount
3. regular price, $24.50; 30% discount
4. regular price, $506.95; 40% discount

17-7 CREDIT CARDS

Using a credit card is like borrowing money. You agree to make monthly payments to repay the borrowed money. If you fail to pay the total amount each month, you must pay a **finance charge.** The finance charge is based on the rate of interest charged and the **unpaid balance.** The interest rates on some credit cards vary with the amount owed.

example

Leslie Putnam has a United Credit Card. She pays a monthly interest rate of 1.5% on the unpaid balance. Last month she had a balance of $264.50. She paid $75. Find her finance charge on the unpaid balance.

solution

Subtract to find the unpaid balance: $264.50 − $75 = $189.50

Use the formula:

finance charge = rate of interest × unpaid balance
$$= \quad 0.015 \quad × \quad \$189.50 \longleftarrow \textbf{Write the rate as a decimal.}$$
$$= \quad \$2.8425$$
$$≈ \quad \$2.84 \qquad \longleftarrow \textbf{Round to the nearest cent.}$$

The finance charge is $2.84.

exercises

Find the unpaid balance and the monthly finance charge. The monthly interest rate is 1.5% on the unpaid balance. Use a calculator if you have one.

1. balance: $215.04; payment = $200
2. balance: $179.47; payment = $79
3. balance: $100.44; payment = $45
4. balance: $2000.09; payment = $600
5. Sid Garden has a Federal Credit Card. He pays 1.7% monthly interest on the unpaid balance. Last month he bought a tractor for $1800. He made a payment of $400. Find his finance charge for the first month.
6. Furniture City charges its credit card holders 1.6% interest monthly on any unpaid balance. Last month the Mortons bought furniture for $650. They made a first payment of $320. Find their finance charge for the first month.

TRAVEL AGENT

Connie Taub is a travel agent. She makes travel arrangements for individuals or groups. She can book a single flight or a total vacation package. Connie receives a commission from hotels, airlines, or rental agencies for the sale of travel arrangements. The commission is based on a percent of her sales.

example

Jonathan Parker went to a travel agent to arrange his trip. The agent sold him a round-trip plane ticket for $249. The agent arranged a car rental that cost $79. Find the commission earned by the travel agent. The commission rate is 10%.

solution

Find the total amount of the sales.

$$\$249 + \$79 = \$328$$

Use the formula: commission = sales × commission rate

$$= \$328 \times \quad 0.10 \quad \longleftarrow \text{ Write the rate as a decimal.}$$
$$= \quad \$32.80$$

The commission earned by the travel agent was $32.80.

exercises

1. A travel agency booked Sarah Stabler's plane tickets and hotel reservations. The arrangements cost $657. The commission rate is 9%. Find the travel agent's commission.

2. A travel agent arranged air fare from Kansas City to New Orleans for the Sibleys. The total cost was $1440. The commission rate is 8.5%. Find the agent's commission.

3. Mark Flagler, his wife, and two children rented a car for one week at a rate of $79. The agent received a $6.32 commission. Find the agent's commission rate.

4. Light Travel Agency arranged a hotel stay for the Wallach family. The commission rate is 5%, and the agent received a commission of $35.50. Find the cost of the hotel stay.

CHAPTER REVIEW

vocabulary vo·cab·u·lar·y

Choose the correct word to complete each sentence.

1. If the original amount is $250 and the new amount is $200, then 20% is the percent of (*increase, decrease*).

2. The money a salesperson earns based on total sales is called the (*discount, commission*).

skills

Find each answer.

3. 105 is what percent of 60?

4. What percent of 300 is 280?

5. 50% of what number is 140?

6. 27 is $37\frac{1}{2}\%$ of what number?

7. What percent of 48 is 192?

8. What percent of 80 is 30?

9. 17 is 4% of what number?

10. 84 is 1.4% of what number?

11. 2 is what percent of 25?

12. 45 is what percent of 200?

13. $37\frac{1}{2}\%$ of what number is 24?

14. $66\frac{2}{3}\%$ of what number is 804?

Find each answer using a proportion.

15. What number is 20% of 440?

16. What number is 4.5% of 400?

17. 28% of what number is 23.8?

18. 19 is what percent of 25?

Tell whether there is an *increase* or a *decrease*. Then find each percent of increase or decrease.

19. original length = 20 m
    new length = 27 m

20. original cost = $12
    new cost = $10

21. Describe a method to find a percent of decrease.

22. Last week 60 young children, 120 teenagers, and 20 adults attended a new film. What percent of the people attending were young children?

23. Tony Mazzola sells office supplies. His commission rate on all sales is 8%. Last week he had sales of $5250. Find his commission.

24. Jo saw a dress regularly priced at $78. It was on sale at a discount of 30%. Find the amount of discount and the sale price.

25. Alex has a Global Credit Card. He pays a monthly interest rate of 1.8% on the unpaid balance. Last month he had a balance of $250. He paid $45. Find his finance charge on the unpaid balance.

CHAPTER TEST

Find each answer.

17-1

1. What percent of 24 is 6?
2. 14 is what percent of 175?
3. 750 is what percent of 150?
4. What percent of 200 is 450?
5. What percent of 189 is 63?
6. 11 is what percent of 16?
7. There were 300 students at a recent school dance. Of those, 40 were freshmen. What percent of students at the dance were freshmen?

Find each answer.

17-2

8. 25% of what number is 11?
9. 200 is 125% of what number?
10. 36 is 2.5% of what number?
11. $87\frac{1}{2}$% of what number is 14?
12. 525 is 175% of what number?
13. 65% of what number is 26?
14. The Boosters Club sold 600 raffle tickets. This was 80% of their goal. What was their goal?

Find each answer using a proportion.

17-3

15. 4% of what number is 166?
16. 150% of what number is 300?
17. What number is 9% of 250?
18. What percent of 64 is 56?
19. Joanne received 672 of the 1200 votes cast in the class election. What percent of the votes cast did she receive?

Tell whether there is an *increase* or a *decrease*. Then find each percent of increase or decrease.

17-4

20. original price = $160
    new price = $168
21. original weight = 6 g
    new weight = 4 g
22. original length = 1800 m
    new length = 675 m
23. original cost = $20
    new cost = $22

24. Sharon McNamara's commission rate on carpet sales is 4%. She sold a carpet for $1500. Find her commission.

17-5

25. A quartz watch regularly priced at $80 is on sale for $64. Find the rate of discount.

17-6

26. Carla Atwood has an Allied Credit Card. She pays 1.6% monthly interest on the unpaid balance. Last month Carla Atwood used her credit card to buy flowers worth $54. She made a payment of $9. Find her finance charge for the first month.

17-7

COMPUTER

Electronic Spreadsheets

A good way to organize information is to use an **electronic spreadsheet.** This type of software is particularly useful in making a budget. It can calculate total income, total expenses, and savings.

A spreadsheet is divided into columns and rows. Letters name the columns, and numbers name the rows. The place where a column meets a row is called a **cell.** Whenever you change a cell entry, the computer will adjust all other cells affected. For example, suppose that you change cell C5 to $5.00. The computer will adjust cells C6, C13, E5, E6, and E13.

	A	B	C	D	E
1		Week 1	Week 2	Week 3	TOTAL
2	INCOME				
3	Allowance	$15.00	$15.00	$15.00	$45.00
4	Paper Route	$ 7.50	$ 7.50	$ 7.50	$22.50
5	Misc. Jobs	$ 4.25	$ 0.00	$ 6.00	$10.25
6	Total Income	$26.75	$22.50	$28.50	$77.75
7	EXPENSES				
8	Bus Fare	$ 3.00	$ 3.00	$ 3.00	$ 9.00
9	Lunch	$11.70	$ 7.20	$10.00	$28.90
10	Clothes	$ 0.00	$ 6.50	$ 4.00	$10.50
11	Other	$ 9.00	$ 0.00	$ 5.00	$14.00
12	Total Expenses	$23.70	$16.70	$22.00	$62.40
13	SAVINGS	$ 3.05	$ 5.80	$ 6.50	$15.35

exercises

Name the entry in the given cell.

1. B9
2. D1
3. E11
4. C13
5. B12
6. A3

7. What is the total income for Week 1?
8. What are the total expenses for Week 2?
9. How much money is saved in Week 3?
10. What is the total savings at the end of the three weeks?

COMPETENCY TEST

Choose the letter of the correct answer.

1. **What percent of 180 is 81?**

   A. $22\frac{2}{9}\%$ B. $222\frac{2}{9}\%$

   C. 45%   D. 0.45%

2. **Choose the letter of the best estimate.**

   26% of 605

   A. about 200   B. about 300
   C. about 150   D. about 1200

3. **The Porters bought 6 chairs at $54 each. The sales tax rate is 6%. Find the total cost.**

   A. $518.40   B. $19.44
   C. $324   D. $343.44

4. **Choose the letter of the best estimate.**

   4.3% of $29,875

   A. about $120
   B. about $1200
   C. about $12,000
   D. about $120,000

5. **On a map, the distance between two cities is $1\frac{3}{4}$ in. The scale is 1 in.:280 mi. Find the actual distance.**

   A. about 490 mi
   B. about 160 mi
   C. about 210 mi
   D. about 600 mi

6. **What number is 35% of 140?**

   A. 4   B. 400
   C. 49   D. 4900

7. **The cost of 6 pads of paper is $5.52. Find the cost of 4 pads.**

   A. $8.28   B. $3.68
   C. $22.08   D. $33.12

8. **A video recorder is regularly priced at $385. It was discounted 20%. Find the sale price.**

   A. $308   B. $462
   C. $77   D. $365

9. **Find the percent of decrease.**

   original weight = 45 kg
   new weight = 36 kg

   A. 80%   B. 20%
   C. 9%   D. 25%

10. **A scale drawing of an airplane is 15 in. long. The scale is 1 in.:7 ft. Find the length of the actual airplane.**

    A. 105 ft
    B. 180 ft
    C. 1260 ft
    D. 1260 in.

RATIO, PROPORTION, AND PERCENT

11. 12% of what number is 75?

A. 9
B. 6.25
C. 625
D. 900

12. Solve the proportion. $\frac{36}{9} = \frac{x}{36}$

A. $x = 9$ B. $x = 4$
C. $x = 324$ D. $x = 144$

13. Write the ratio as a fraction in lowest terms. 8 in. to 6 ft

A. $\frac{4}{3}$ B. $\frac{8}{72}$
C. $\frac{8}{6}$ D. $\frac{1}{9}$

14. Find the interest if the principal is $1200, the rate is 8% per year, and the time is 9 months.

A. $72   B. $86.40
C. $96   D. $864

15. A savings account earns 8.5% interest per year, compounded semiannually. The account was opened with $2400. No deposit or withdrawals were made. How much was in the account at the end of one year?

A. $2610.59   B. $2825.34
C. $2604   D. $2608.34

16. Write 0.653 as a percent.

A. 0.653%
B. 6.53%
C. 65.3%
D. 653%

17. Write the unit rate. 156 mi in 3 h

A. 156 mi/3 h   B. 52 mi/3 h
C. 52 mi/h   D. 52/1

18. Write 3.5% as a fraction in lowest terms.

A. $\frac{7}{2}$ B. $\frac{7}{200}$
C. $\frac{7}{20}$ D. $\frac{7}{2000}$

19. Find the percent of increase.

original amount = $1200
new amount = $1500

A. 25%   B. 300%
C. 20%   D. 80%

20. Anne, Beverly, and Chad are an architect, a banker, and a chef. No one's job begins with the same letter as his or her name. The banker is the architect's uncle. Choose the correct conclusion.

A. Anne is a banker.
B. Beverly is an architect.
C. Chad is an architect.
D. Beverly is a chef.

CUMULATIVE REVIEW CHAPTERS 1–17

Find each answer.

1. $65\overline{)8421}$

2. $0.79 + 3.5$

3. $21{,}715 - 14{,}919$

4. 321×814

5. $5.2 - 3.721$

6. $3\frac{1}{4} \times 4\frac{2}{3}$

7. 6.5×30.9

8. $5\frac{3}{4} + 8\frac{5}{12}$

9. Write as a fraction in lowest terms: **a.** $\frac{72}{108}$ **b.** 82.5% **c.** $42:35$

10. Write as a decimal: **a.** 180% **b.** $4\frac{3}{4}\%$ **c.** $\frac{13}{25}$

11. Write as a percent: **a.** 0.315 **b.** 6.12 **c.** $\frac{21}{25}$

12. 18% of what number is 9?

13. 52% of 425 is what number?

14. What percent of 80 is 12?

15. Find the percent of increase: original cost = $20; new cost = $24

16. Find the GCF and the LCM: **a.** 24 and 32 **b.** 15 and 19

Estimate.

17. $5\frac{5}{6} - 2\frac{1}{8}$

18. 66% of 152

19. $21\overline{)612{,}745}$

20. 71% of 198

21. 3.1245×9.7584

22. $782{,}197 + 163{,}678$

Solve each proportion.

23. $\frac{5}{7} = \frac{x}{21}$

24. $\frac{y}{12} = \frac{6}{9}$

25. $\frac{15}{9} = \frac{n}{15}$

26. $\frac{11}{8} = \frac{33}{z}$

Complete.

27. $87 \text{ in.} = \underline{\ ?\ } \text{ ft } \underline{\ ?\ } \text{ in.}$

28. $16 \text{ lb} = \underline{\ ?\ } \text{ oz}$

29. $15.6 \text{ kg} = \underline{\ ?\ } \text{ g}$

30. A savings account earns 9% interest per year, compounded semi-annually. The account was opened with $3600. No deposits or withdrawals were made. How much was in the account at the end of one year?

31. Five video tapes cost $28.95. How many can you buy for $17.37?

32. Ed, Arlene, and Matt teach English, art, and mathematics. No one's subject begins with the same letter as his or her name. Ed is married to the mathematics teacher. Who teaches what subject?

33. Last month, 54 out of every 100 babies born at City General Hospital were girls. What percent of the babies were girls?

Many baseball fans keep track of the progress of
their favorite teams and players through
statistics such as batting averages.

CHAPTER 18

STATISTICS

18-1 ORGANIZING DATA

The branch of mathematics that deals with organizing and analyzing numerical facts is called **statistics.** The numerical facts are often called **data.**

In Chapter 2 you saw data presented in bar graphs and line graphs. Data can also be organized in a **frequency table** like the one at the right. A tally mark stands for 1. For every fifth tally, a mark is made diagonally across four (卌) to make counting easier.

Election Results

Person	Tally	Frequency
Brian	卌 III	8
Irma	卌 卌 II	12
Jason	卌 IIII	9

example 1

Make a frequency table for the data.

Ages of Students in Drama Club

16 15 15 17 17 16 18 15
16 17 18 18 17 15 16 17

solution

- Set up a table organized into columns.
- For the first column, find the different numbers in the data. Order them from least to greatest.
- Make appropriate tally marks.
- Count the frequency of each number.

Ages of Students in Drama Club

Age	Tally	Frequency
15	IIII	4
16	IIII	4
17	卌	5
18	III	3

your turn

Make a frequency table for the data.

1. **Scores on a Math Test (%)**

70	85	75	95	75	85	75
80	70	75	70	95	70	80
60	80	75	60	85	80	75
80	75	75	70	90	75	80

2. **Number of Games Attended**

5	7	6	0	3
5	4	7	7	1
7	6	2	5	4
6	0	5	4	7

The **range** of a set of data is the difference between the greatest and the least numbers. In Example 1 the range is $18 - 15$, or 3. When the range is great, or when few numbers in the data repeat, the data in a frequency table are often grouped in *intervals.*

example 2

Make a frequency table for the data.

Prices of Tennis Shoes ($)

19	24	39	29	45	32	30
20	24	30	27	29	24	35

solution

There are 10 different numbers in the data.
- Determine the least price, $19, and the greatest price, $45.
- For the first column, decide upon equal intervals.
- Complete the tally and count the frequency.

Prices of Tennis Shoes ($)

Price	Tally	Frequency
10–19	I	1
20–29	IHT II	7
30–39	IHT	5
40–49	I	1

your turn

Make a frequency table for the data.

3. **Scores on a Science Test (%)**

98	72	83	61	74	83	80
100	74	67	88	77	82	95
91	70	57	74	68	84	79
90	52	83	77	72	87	65

(Use intervals such as 91–100.)

4. **Heights of Buildings (ft)**

454	620	414	516	718
395	454	625	571	363
398	738	390	857	671
435	367	699	452	582

(Use intervals such as 600–699.)

practice exercises

practice for example 1 (page 398)

Make a frequency table for the data.

1. **Heights of Students (in.)**

60	64	62	66	63	65
65	61	64	63	63	64
66	64	62	63	64	66

2. **Prices of Movie Tickets ($)**

5.50	5.00	5.00	6.00	5.50
6.00	5.50	4.50	6.00	6.00
5.50	5.50	5.00	6.00	5.50

practice for example 2 (page 399)

Make a frequency table for the data.

3. **Number of Calories**

329	345	284	287	287
317	399	232	341	310
238	265	285	291	255
284	359	347	314	268

(Use intervals such as 300–349.)

4. **Ages of College Professors**

31	52	46	63	44	35	43
68	57	37	52	48	36	51
39	35	46	33	52	57	69
48	52	38	36	58	56	52

(Use intervals such as 40–44.)

Make a frequency table for the data.

5. Ages of Students

15	17	15	16	14	15
16	17	15	15	16	17
15	16	15	15	16	17
18	15	16	16	15	18

6. Batting Averages

.368	.295	.291	.333	.322
.288	.359	.367	.230	.207
.305	.355	.286	.314	.282
.321	.440	.267	.345	.285

Give the range of the data for the given exercise.

7. Ex. 5   **8.** Ex. 6   **9.** Ex. 3   **10.** Ex. 4

Find out the month and day of the month when each student in your mathematics class was born.

11. Make a frequency table for the months of birth.

12. Make a frequency table for the days of the month. Use intervals such as 6–10, with the last interval being 26–31.

review *exercises*

Use the bar graph at the right. Determine the maximum speed of each animal.

1. greyhound   **2.** racehorse

3. penguin   **4.** rabbit

5. Which is the fastest animal?

6. Which two animals have about the same maximum speed?

7. Which animals shown have a maximum speed faster than a racehorse?

8. The maximum speed of a human being is about 23 mi/h. Which animals have a maximum speed slower than this?

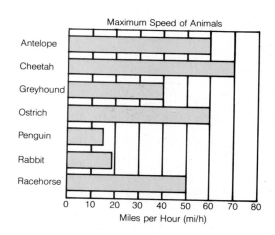

Maximum Speed of Animals

The product of the page numbers of this page and the facing page is 400 × 401, or 160,400. Where would you open a book so that the product of the page numbers on facing pages is 377,610?

18-2 ANALYZING DATA: MEAN, MEDIAN, AND MODE

Three *statistical measures* used to describe a set of data are the *mean, median,* and *mode*.

Data: 78   78   95   82   66   87

The **mean** is the sum of the items in a set of data divided by the number of items. The mean is often called the *average*.

- mean $= \dfrac{78 + 78 + 95 + 82 + 66 + 87}{6}$

  $= \dfrac{486}{6} = 81$

The **median** is the middle number when the data are arranged in numerical order. If the number of items is even, the median is the mean of the *two* middle numbers.

- 66   78   78   82   87   95

  $\dfrac{78 + 82}{2} = 80$

  median $= 80$

The **mode** is the number that appears most often. There could be more than one mode, or there could be no mode.

- 66   78   78   82   87   95

  mode $= 78$

example 1

Find the mean, median, and mode(s).

a. 70, 77, 95, 95, 70

b. 0.63, 0.49, 0.69, 0.71

solution

a. • There are 5 items.

mean $= \dfrac{70 + 77 + 95 + 95 + 70}{5}$

$= \dfrac{407}{5}$

$= 81.4$

• 70   70   77   95   95 ← List the numbers in order.

median $= 77$

• modes: 70 and 95
(Two numbers are repeated.)

b. • There are 4 items.

mean $= \dfrac{0.63 + 0.49 + 0.69 + 0.71}{4}$

$= \dfrac{2.52}{4}$

$= 0.63$

0.49   0.63   0.69   0.71

$= \dfrac{0.63 + 0.69}{2} = 0.66$

one
·ber is repeated.)

your turn

Find the mean, median, and mode(s).

1. 26, 32, 35, 26, 31
3. 12, 50, 12, 50, 20, 12

5
4.5, 3.7

Sometimes it is necessary to round when finding the mean.

example 2

Find the mean. Round to the nearest tenth or cent.

a. 1.6, 2.7, 3.9

b. $2.50, $1.75, $2.25

solution

a. mean $= \dfrac{1.6 + 2.7 + 3.9}{3}$

$= \dfrac{8.2}{3} \approx 2.73$

To the nearest tenth, mean = 2.7.

b. mean $= \dfrac{\$2.50 + \$1.75 + \$2.25}{3}$

$= \dfrac{\$6.50}{3} \approx \$2.166$

To the nearest cent, mean = $2.17.

your turn

Find the mean. Round to the nearest tenth or cent.

5. $2, $5, $4, $3, $7, $2

6. 2, 4, 6, 3, 9, 7, 3

practice *exercises*

practice for example 1 (page 401)

Find the mean, median, and mode(s).

1. 67, 80, 60, 77

2. 2, 7, 5, 9, 7, 0

3. 5, 7, 4, 5, 4, 8

4. 2.2, 3.6, 3.5

5. 2.5, 4.9, 4.5, 2.5

6. 75, 90, 75, 100

7. 12, 15, 10, 32, 63, 15

8. 4, 1, 5, 5, 8, 2, 3, 5

9. 7.3, 9.3, 8.8, 9.3, 7.3

10. 100, 75, 75, 65, 65, 55

practice for example 2 (page 402)

Find the mean. Round to the nearest tenth or cent.

11. $57, $59, $62

12. $29, $20, $41, $40, $10, $11

13. 8, 6, 5, 4, 9, 8

14. 0.5, 0.4, 0.8, 0.9, 0.3, 0.4, 0.6

mixed practice (pages 401

Find the mean, media **necessary, round the mean to the nearest tenth.**

15. 18, 10, 19, 23,

, 6, 3, 2

17. 70, 70, 63, 71, 63, 19

18. 55, 40, 56, 55,

, 102, 111, 128

20. 2.5, 7.2, 2.1, 5.5, 2.5

Use the data in the table at the right.

21. What is the range of the salaries?
22. What is the mode of the salaries?
23. What is the median salary?
24. What is the mean salary?
25. Which of the mode, median, and mean best describes the salaries?

Salary	No. of Employees	
$80,000	I	1
$25,000	I	1
$15,000	III	3
$10,000	IIII	5

In a bag of fifty potatoes, the mean weight of a potato is 7.0 oz, the median weight is 6.9 oz, and the mode weight is 6.8 oz.

26. What would you expect one dozen of the potatoes to weigh?
27. Suppose you want to bake six potatoes of the same size. What would be the best size to look for?
28. Suppose you took the twenty lightest potatoes from the bag. What would you expect to be true of the weight of each of them?

review exercises

Use the line graph at the right.
Determine the closing price at the end of the given day.

1. Thursday   2. Tuesday   3. Wednesday
4. On what day did the price of ABC Corporation stock decrease?
5. On what day did the price of ABC Corporation stock increase the most?
6. What was the increase in closing price between Monday and Tuesday?

mental math

Since 7.8, 8.4, 8.3, and 7.6 *cluster* around 8, their mean is about 8.

Mentally estimate the mean.

1. 6.2, 5.7, 5.5, 6.2, 6.1
2. 88, 86, 92, 94, 91, 88, 89
3. $3.65, $3.79, $4.37, $3.99
4. ⁻2194, 2082, 1896, 1987, 2032
5. $3\frac{1}{7}, 2\frac{8}{9}, 2\frac{7}{8}, 3\frac{1}{5}, 2\frac{2}{3}, 3\frac{1}{4}$
6. $16\frac{1}{4}, 15\frac{1}{9}, 16\frac{1}{3}, 15\frac{1}{4}, 16\frac{1}{3}$

18-3 PRESENTING DATA: PICTOGRAPHS

Newspapers often use *pictographs* to present data to their readers.
A **pictograph** uses a symbol to represent a specified number of items.
The **key** tells you how many items are represented by each symbol.

example 1

Use the pictograph to answer the questions.

a. How many bushels of corn did the United States produce in 1981?

b. How many bushels were produced in 1984?

c. How many more bushels were produced in 1978 than in 1975?

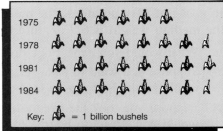
United States Corn Production

solution

a. Each symbol represents 1 billion bushels. 1981 has 8 symbols. Multiply 8 × 1 billion. In 1981 the United States produced about 8 billion bushels.

b. 1984 has $7\frac{1}{2}$, or 7.5, symbols. Multiply 7.5 × 1 billion. In 1984 the United States produced about 7.5 billion bushels.

c. There are $1\frac{1}{2}$ more symbols for 1978 than for 1975. Multiply 1.5 × 1 billion. About 1.5 billion bushels more were produced in 1978 than in 1975.

your turn

Use the pictograph to answer the questions.

1. How many hours of TV does an average 40-year-old man watch?

2. How many hours of TV does an average 25-year-old woman watch?

3. Who watches the most TV?

4. On average, how many more hours does a 60-year-old woman watch than a man the same age?

example 2

Draw a pictograph to display the number of eggs produced by the hens on the Edwards Farms.

Week 1: 9 gross   Week 2: 6 gross   Week 3: 12 gross   Week 4: 10 gross

solution

- Let each 2 gross of eggs be represented by ○.
- Determine the number of symbols needed for each numerical fact.
- Draw the pictograph. Include a title and the key.

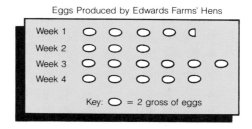

your turn

5. Draw a pictograph to display the number of basketball games won by each of these teams in the first half of the season.

Lakers: 32   Hawks: 24   Celtics: 30   Nets: 19

practice exercises

practice for example 1 *(page 404)*

Use the pictograph to answer the questions.

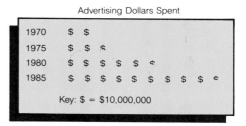

1. How many advertising dollars were spent in 1970?

2. How much was spent in 1980?

3. In what year was about half as much spent as in 1980?

4. How much more was spent for advertising in 1985 than in 1980?

practice for example 2 *(page 405)*

Draw a pictograph to display the given data.

5. Number of Containers of Milk Sold
   whole milk: 80   skim milk: 60   2% milk: 45   chocolate milk: 20

6. Number of Cars Registered
   California: 14,000,000   Florida: 8,000,000   Illinois: 6,000,000
   New Jersey: 4,000,000   Louisiana: 2,000,000   Texas: 9,000,000

Use the pictograph to answer the questions.

7. How many red balloons were sold?
8. How many green balloons were sold?
9. What color was about half as popular as red?
10. How many balloons in all were sold?
11. If there were 34 white balloons sold, how many symbols would you use?
12. If there were 22 purple balloons sold, draw the symbols you would use to represent them.

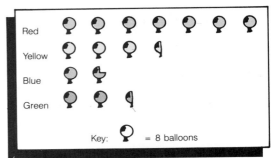

Number of Balloons Sold

Red
Yellow
Blue
Green

Key: = 8 balloons

13. Draw a pictograph to display the given data.

Electric Energy Production

Year	1965	1970	1975	1980	1985
Billions of kilowatt-hours (kW · h)	1000	1500	2000	2250	2500

review exercises

1. What is 25% of 280?
2. What is 20% of 160?
3. What is 8% of 350?
4. 15 is 30% of what number?
5. 65 is 25% of what number?
6. 27 is 6% of what number?

calculator corner

Find the mean using a calculator. Round to the nearest tenth or cent.

1. 3, 9, 27, 4, 18, 11, 16
2. 16, 2, 0, 14, 30, 17, 11
3. 91.3, 86.4, 90.9, 87.6, 52.8, 47.8
4. $33.76, $29.95, $17.50, $29.46

Sometimes an approximate value for the mean is all that is needed. For each of the following exercises, use clustering if possible to mentally estimate the mean. If that is not possible, use a calculator to find the mean to the nearest whole number.

5. 29, 28, 32, 30, 29, 26, 33
6. 396, 404, 407, 38.2, 41.5
7. 68, 63, 66, 62.5, 64, 67.5
8. 85.5, 76.4, 62, 89.7, 95.5, 82
9. 75, 70, 0, 80, 85, 82.5, 70
10. 253, 246, 242, 259, 258, 239

18-4 PRESENTING DATA: CIRCLE GRAPHS

A **circle graph** is often used to present data expressed as percents.

example 1

a. What fraction of the students prefer basketball?

b. There are 380 students. How many prefer baseball?

solution

a. $25\% = \frac{1}{4}$
One fourth of the students prefer basketball.

b. 35% of $380 = 0.35 \times 380 = 133$
133 students prefer baseball.

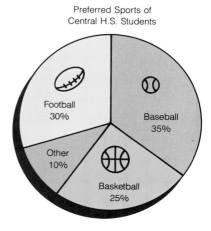

Preferred Sports of
Central H.S. Students

your turn

1. What fraction of the students prefer football?

2. How many of the 380 students prefer basketball?

example 2

The circle graph shows the part of each vacation dollar spent on each category.

a. If $740 was spent on the entire vacation, how much was spent on transportation?

b. If $200 was spent on meals, how much was spent on the entire vacation?

solution

a. $\frac{20¢}{100¢} = \frac{1}{5}$ $\frac{1}{5} \times \$740 = \$148$
$148 was spent on transportation.

b. $\frac{25¢}{100¢} = 25\%$ $\$200 = 25\% \times n \rightarrow n = \$800$
The total cost was $800.

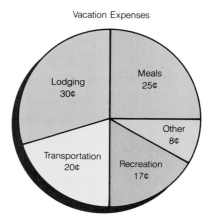

Vacation Expenses

your turn

3. What percent of the vacation money was spent for recreation?

4. If the total vacation cost was $640, how much was spent on meals?

5. If $180 was spent for lodging, what was the total vacation cost?

practice *exercises*

practice for example 1 (page 407)

Use the circle graph at the right.

1. What fraction of the books are science books?
2. What fraction of the books are fiction books?
3. What percent of the books are not fiction books?
4. What percent of the books are either history or science books?
5. If there are 430 books in the library, how many of them are science books?
6. If there are 350 books in the library, how many of them are reference books?
7. If there are 156 history books, how many books are in the library?
8. If there are 198 fiction books, how many books are in the library?

Books in the Library

practice for example 2 (page 407)

The circle graph shows the part of each dollar that the Chinn family has budgeted for each category.

9. What percent of the budget is for food?
10. What percent of the budget is not saved?
11. Which two items account for the greatest expenses?
12. What fractional part of the budget is for housing?
13. If the monthly income is $1575, how much do the Chinns plan to save each month?
14. If the Chinns spend $325 monthly for food, what is their monthly income?
15. If the family spends $375 monthly for housing, how much do they spend for clothing?
16. If the family spends $100 monthly for clothing, how much do they spend for food?

Chinn Family Budget

Use the circle graph at the right.

Earth's Land

17. Which is the largest continent?
18. Which two continents are together about the size of South America?
19. Which continent is about half the size of Africa?
20. Which continent is about three times as large as Europe?
21. Which two continents together make up about half of Earth's land?
22. What is the ratio of the size of South America to the size of North America?
23. If Africa contains about 11.7 million square miles of land, about how many square miles of land does Asia contain?
24. If Europe contains about 4.1 million square miles of land, about how many square miles of land are there on Earth?

review *exercises*

1. Draw a bar graph to display the given information.

Distance from the Sun

Planet	Earth	Mars	Mercury	Venus
Distance (in millions of miles)	93	142	36	67

2. Draw a line graph to display the given information.

Average Weekly Pay in Manufacturing Industries

Year	1970	1975	1980	1985
Weekly Pay	$190	$289	$371	$386

18-5 DISPLAYING INFORMATION

1	Understand
2	Plan
3	Work
4	Answer

Some problems can be solved more easily if you make an organized list. Sometimes a table can be used to organize the facts of the problem.

example

Barbara has a total of twenty dimes and quarters. The total value of the coins is $3.65. How many of each kind of coin does she have?

solution

Step 1 Given: 20 dimes and quarters
    total value of $3.65
Find: number of dimes and number of quarters

Step 2 Make a table that displays different combinations of dimes and quarters so that the total number is 20.
Find the total value for each combination. For example, the total value of 4 dimes and 16 quarters is 4($.10) + 16($.25), or $4.40.

Step 3

number of dimes	0	1	2	3	4
number of quarters	20	19	18	17	16
total value	$5	$4.85	$4.70	$4.55	$4.40

◀— **Look for a pattern.**

You could continue the table, but that is not necessary if you see the pattern. Each time you have 1 more dime and 1 fewer quarter, the total value decreases by $.15.

$$\$5 - \$3.65 = \$1.35 \qquad \$1.35 \div \$.15 = 9$$

So the number of dimes is 0 + 9, or 9. The number of quarters is 20 − 9, or 11.

Step 4 *Check:* The total value of 9 dimes and 11 quarters is
    9($.10) + 11($.25), or $3.65.

Barbara has 9 dimes and 11 quarters.

problems

Solve.

1. David has forty nickels and dimes altogether. Their total value is $2.80. How many dimes does David have?

2. If you have a total of fifty nickels and quarters, with a total value of $8.30, how many of each kind of coin do you have?

3. Carrie has twenty bills, each of which is either a one-dollar bill or a five-dollar bill. The total value is $40. How many of each kind of bill does she have?

4. The Drama Club sold 280 tickets. Some cost $5 and the others cost $8. If $1850 was raised, how many $5 tickets were sold?

5. Kareem changed two one-dollar bills and received 33 coins, each of which was a nickel or dime. How many of each kind of coin did he get?

6. A warehouse contains 60 tables. Some have three legs and the others have four legs. If there are 202 legs altogether, how many of the tables have only three legs?

7. You have three dimes and three quarters. List the amounts of all the exact-change telephone calls you can make using one or more of these coins.

8. Laurel has one $1 bill, two $5 bills, and one $10 bill. How many different amounts of money can she make using one or more of these bills?

9. How many different ways can you make change for a quarter?

10. You have exactly 20 pennies, 20 nickels, and 20 dimes. Find all the ways you can choose 22 coins whose total value is $1, if you must use at least one coin of each type.

review exercises

1. Sound travels through water at the rate of 5000 ft/s. The deepest part of the oceans on Earth is near Guam, where the ocean floor is 36,198 ft below the surface. About how long will it take for a sound wave to travel from the surface to the ocean floor there and then return to the surface?

2. There are twenty-five animals in the barnyard. Some are chickens and the others are cows. If there are eighty-four legs altogether, how many chickens are there?

SKILL REVIEW

Make a frequency table for the data.

18-1

1. **Weekly Hours of Homework**

7	8	5	8	5	7
9	8	5	7	8	8
4	7	6	5	9	5
8	9	10	9	5	6
5	6	9	8	5	10

2. **Used Car Prices (Dollars)**

4995	1795	2495	6996
895	1595	3595	2600
2995	3850	1795	1295
4999	3495	1595	3295
3295	1895	999	1745

(Use intervals such as 2000–2999.)

Find the mean, median, and mode(s). If necessary, round the mean to the nearest tenth or cent.

18-2

3. 85, 70, 60, 60, 75
4. 2.5, 4.0, 3.5, 2.4
5. 3, 5, 9, 7, 4, 7, 5
6. $17, $18, $24, $21
7. 8, 5, 0, 3, 0, 5
8. $5.50, $4.25, $4.25

Use the pictograph to answer the questions.

18-3

9. How many pairs were sold in May?
10. In which month were about twice as many pairs sold as in April?
11. How many more pairs were sold in June than in April?
12. If 275 pairs were sold in July, how many symbols would you use?

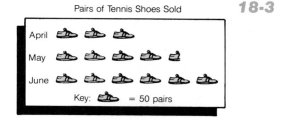

Pairs of Tennis Shoes Sold

April

May

June

Key: = 50 pairs

Use the circle graph at the right.

18-4

13. What fraction of the people surveyed use a computer more than 10 h per week?
14. If 240 people were surveyed, how many of them use a computer between 5 h and 10 h a week?
15. If 167 of the people surveyed use a computer less than 5 h a week, how many people were surveyed?

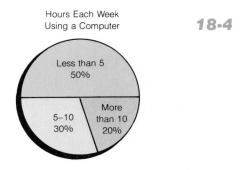

Hours Each Week
Using a Computer

Less than 5
50%

5–10
30%

More
than 10
20%

18-5

16. A certain cash register contains a total of 77 one-dollar bills and five-dollar bills. The total value of these bills is $205. How many five-dollar bills are there?

18-6 MISLEADING STATISTICS

Sometimes diagrams and statistics can give misleading impressions.
There are many choices on how to present data, and some people choose
a way that makes the data appear most favorable.

example

The sales data below were collected from
nearby stores to help Ms. Chan decide
which store to include in a new shopping
mall. She is interested in the store with
the most sales. Is the bar graph at the right
a reasonable picture of sales for both stores?

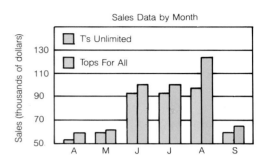

Sales Data by Month

Month	April	May	June	July	Aug.	Sept.
T's Unlimited	$53,300	$58,600	$91,000	$91,000	$96,500	$60,300
Tops For All	$58,700	$60,800	$99,000	$99,000	$125,000	$65,700

solution

The graph makes it look as though *Tops For All* has substantially greater
sales than *T's Unlimited*. However, the vertical axis on the graph starts at
$50,000, not $0. This makes the difference in sales between the two
stores *appear* greater than it is.

exercises

1. Draw a *double* bar graph like the one
   shown above that fairly represents total
   sales for the six months for the two stores.

Do you think the following are misleading? Explain.

2. A representative of *Tops For All* said, ''Our
   sales for the summer months averaged $107,700
   per month.''

3. A representative of *T's Unlimited* said, ''Most
   months we have $91,000 in sales. *Tops For
   All* averages $84,700.''

4. What is the best statistic to compare the sales of
   the two stores? Explain.

18-7 BUYING INSURANCE

Life insurance is purchased to provide financial protection for your family in the event of your death. Statistics about life expectancy at different ages help to set **premiums** for life insurance. **Whole life insurance** pays the full amount of coverage when the insured dies.

example

A 30-year-old nonsmoker wants to purchase a $50,000 policy. Use the table to find the annual premium.

solution

The premium per $1000 is $12.80. Since the policy is for $50,000, multiply by 50.

50 × $12.80 = $640.00

The annual premium is $640.00.

Annual Premiums per $1000 of Coverage

Age begun	25	30	35	40
Smoker	$12.55	$14.10	$15.50	$17.40
Nonsmoker	$11.10	$12.80	$14.25	$16.85

exercises

Use the table above. Find the annual premium.

1. 30-year-old nonsmoker; $10,000 policy

2. 35-year-old smoker; $80,000 policy

3. 25-year-old smoker; $25,000 policy

4. 40-year-old nonsmoker; $12,000 policy

5. Molly Russo, who is a nonsmoker, bought a $25,000 whole-life policy at age 35. Find the annual premium.

6. Jake Braun is a 40-year-old smoker. He plans to buy a $75,000 life insurance policy. Find the annual premium. Find the amount Jake could save over a ten-year period if he were a nonsmoker.

7. The Russells want to buy two life insurance policies for $20,000 each. Mr. Russell is a 30-year-old nonsmoker. Mrs. Russell is a 25-year-old nonsmoker. Find the total annual premium for the two policies.

8. Kate Ransom receives a life insurance policy from her employer. The coverage is equal to 1.5 times Kate's annual salary. Kate is a 35-year-old smoker and earns $38,000 per year. Find the annual premium that Kate's employer pays.

18-8 BUDGETS

A **budget** is a plan for allocating money. **Fixed expenses,** such as rent or insurance payments, are the same each month. **Variable expenses,** such as food and utilities, change each month. You can estimate variable expenses by computing the average amount spent per month.

example

a. In the last five months, James Barba spent $257.50, $308.68, $299.45, $268.72, and $335.00 on food. Estimate the amount he should budget monthly for food.

b. Last year Sarah Cone spent $675 on gifts. Estimate the amount she should budget monthly for gifts.

solution

a. Add to find the total spent on food for the five months.
$257.50 + $308.68 + $299.45 + $268.72 + $335.00 = $1469.35

Divide to find the average for one month.
$1469.35 ÷ 5 = $293.87
$293.87 rounds to $300.

James should budget about $300 per month for food.

b. Divide the total spent in one year by the number of months.
$675 ÷ 12 = $56.25
$56.25 rounds to $60.

Sarah should budget about $60 per month for gifts.

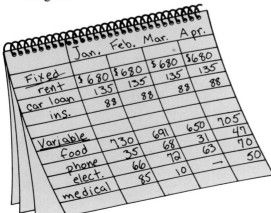

	Jan.	Feb.	Mar.	Apr.
Fixed				
rent	$680	$680	$680	$680
car loan	135	135	135	135
ins.	88	88	88	88
Variable				
food	730	691	650	705
phone	35	68	31	47
elect.	66	72	63	70
medical	85	10	—	50

exercises

Estimate the monthly amount that should be budgeted for the given budget item.

1. In the last four months, Lisa Morris spent $42.79, $75.98, $22.50, and $68.00 on clothes.

2. Carrie Hanson spent $25.00, $5.00, $45.00, $17.00 and $82.00 on entertainment in the last five months.

3. Last year, Carla Colizzi spent $1057.00 on car repairs.

4. Liam McDonald saved $1080 last year.

5. Izzy Searles spent $67, $38, and $54 for electricity in a 3-month period.

6. Ralph Pill spent the following amounts on entertainment from July through December: $42, $38, $86, $29, $33, $56.

7. Harriet Urso spent $12, $9, $35, $7, and $16 on school supplies in 5 months.

8. Donald Hughes spent $15, $55, $34, and $18 on home repairs in the last four months.

9. Ada Roe contributed $585 to charity last year.

10. Harry Tilson paid $1087 for medical expenses last year.

11. Rowena Parsons had home maintenance expenses of $1116 last year.

12. Baker Ross paid $577 for pet care last year.

13. Mark Howards paid $55, $42, $48, and $65 for gasoline in a four-month period.

14. Karen Gould paid $4, $12, $5, $7, and $17 for dry cleaning in the last five months.

15. Brad Scittano paid $485 for art supplies last year.

16. Clarke McNulty spent $388 on his record collection last year.

CHAPTER REVIEW

vocabulary vo·cab·u·lar·y

Choose the correct word to complete each sentence.

1. The sum of seven numbers divided by 7 is the *(mean, median, mode)* of the numbers.

2. The number in a set of data that appears most often is called the *(mean, median, mode)*.

skills

Make a frequency table for the data.

3. **Games Played**

6	4	3	6	7	5	7	5
5	7	6	5	2	6	7	7
6	5	7	6	7	4	6	7

4. **Points Scored**

11	7	14	4	8	12	8	7
14	5	2	9	6	14	21	10
9	28	12	9	17	13	3	18

(Use intervals such as 1–5.)

Find the mean, median, and mode(s).

5. 60, 75, 90, 95, 80, 75, 85

6. 3.8, 2.5, 3.0, 5.5, 2.5, 5.5

7. Draw a pictograph to display the median sale price of a new home in the given years.
1965: $20,000   1970: $25,000   1975: $40,000   1980: $65,000   1985: $85,000

The circle graph shows where each dollar earned by raising fruit in the United States comes from.

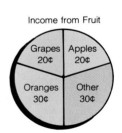

Income from Fruit

8. What percent comes from grapes and apples combined?

9. If the total value of fruit raised each year in the United States is $4,400,000,000, how much of that comes from oranges?

10. The total value of forty-two dimes and quarters is $8.10. Find the number of each type of coin.

11. Terry's mathematics test scores are 90, 85, 90, 90, 60, and 65. He tells his parents he usually gets 90. Is he misleading them? Explain.

12. Use the table on page 414. Find the annual premium for a $100,000 life insurance policy for a 25-year-old nonsmoker.

13. Bob Walters' telephone bills for the past five months were $27.50, $12.85, $20.75, $15.65, and $13.15. Estimate the amount he should budget monthly for his telephone bill.

CHAPTER TEST

1. Make a frequency table for the data.
   Use intervals such as $350–$399.

Prices of TV Sets (Dollars)   *18-1*

399	359	447	419	498	419
289	349	549	299	359	379
449	378	419	269	397	549

Find the mean, median, and mode(s). Round the mean to the nearest tenth.

2. 70, 70, 80, 65, 90, 100, 80   3. 6.0, 2.9, 0, 4.5, 3.5, 2.1   *18-2*

Use the pictograph at the right.

4. What was the median household
   income in 1980?

5. In what year was the median
   household income about twice
   that of 1975?

6. Draw a pictograph to display the number
   of cable TV subscribers in each year.
   1970: 5,000,000   1975: 10,000,000
   1980: 17,500,000   1985: 35,000,000

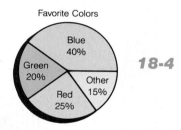

Median Household Income   *18-3*

1975	$ $ $
1980	$ $ $ $ ¢
1985	$ $ $ $ $ $

Key: $ = $4000

Use the circle graph at the right.

7. What percent chose green as their favorite color?
8. Which categories together total as much as blue?
9. If 344 people were surveyed, how many chose
   red as their favorite color?

Favorite Colors

Blue 40%
Green 20%
Other 15%
Red 25%

18-4

10. The Sterling Publishing Company bought thirty computers. Some
    cost $1200 each, and the others cost $1400 each. How many of
    each kind were bought if the total cost was $37,200?   *18-5*

11. In June, July, and August Ella's store sold a total of 3300 frozen
    yogurt bars. Is it reasonable for her to expect to sell 1100 frozen
    yogurt bars in December? Explain.   *18-6*

12. Use the table on page 414. Find the difference in annual premiums
    for $50,000 life insurance policies for a 30-year-old smoker and a
    30-year-old nonsmoker.   *18-7*

13. Dan Cooper spent $357 on pet supplies last year. Estimate the amount
    he should budget monthly for pet supplies.   *18-8*

Recent steps taken to protect the bald eagle, the national bird of the United States, have greatly increased its chances of survival.

CHAPTER 19

PROBABILITY

19-1 COUNTING OUTCOMES

When you toss a coin, you could toss either *heads* or *tails*. There are two possible results, or **outcomes**. When you toss a coin and spin a spinner, you can use either a **tree diagram** or the **counting principle** to find the number of possible outcomes.

example 1

Use a tree diagram to find the number of possible outcomes when tossing a quarter and spinning the spinner.

solution

Choices for quarter: heads (H) or tails (T)
Choices for spinner: 1, 2, or 3
The *tree diagram* is shown at the right.

quarter	spinner	outcomes
H	1	H1
	2	H2
	3	H3
T	1	T1
	2	T2
	3	T3

There are 6 possible outcomes.

your turn

Use a tree diagram to find the number of possible outcomes.

1. rolling a number cube and tossing a dime
2. tossing a nickel, a dime, and a quarter

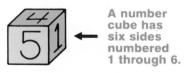

A number cube has six sides numbered 1 through 6.

example 2

Use the counting principle to find the number of possible outcomes when tossing a quarter and spinning the spinner above.

solution

Count the number of choices at each step, then multiply.

number of choices for quarter		number of choices for spinner	
2	×	3	= 6 possible outcomes

your turn

Use the counting principle to find the number of possible outcomes.

3. choosing an outfit from 4 pairs of pants, 5 shirts, and 2 belts

4. making a dentist appointment; dates: July 9, July 11, July 18; times: 9:00 A.M., 9:30 A.M.

practice *exercises*

practice for example 1 (page 420)

Use a tree diagram to find the number of possible outcomes.

1. tossing a penny and
   rolling a number cube

2. rolling a number cube and choosing
   a letter from A through C

3. choosing a skirt and a blouse;
   skirts: red, green, blue;
   blouses: gray, white, yellow

4. selecting the colors of a car;
   exterior: blue, silver, red, green;
   interior: cream, white

practice for example 2 (page 420)

Use the counting principle to find the number of possible outcomes.

5. choosing a letter from A
   through E and tossing a dime

6. rolling three number cubes

7. electing class officers;
   president: 4 candidates;
   secretary: 4 candidates;
   treasurer: 3 candidates

8. selecting a notepad;
   sizes: small, letter, legal;
   type: lined, unlined;
   colors: white, yellow

mixed practice (page 420)

**Use the cards and the spinner at the right.
Find the number of possible outcomes.**

9. spinning the spinner
10. drawing a card
11. drawing a card and spinning the spinner
12. spinning the spinner twice
13. spinning the spinner and tossing two nickels
14. rolling a number cube, drawing a card, and
    spinning the spinner

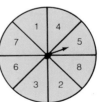

review *exercises*

Find each answer.

1. $3\frac{8}{9} + 1\frac{1}{2}$

2. $2.307 + 4.6$

3. $8 - 0.324$

4. $\frac{7}{8} - \frac{5}{12}$

5. 5.7×91

6. $7\frac{1}{3} \times \frac{9}{10}$

7. $\frac{13}{14} \div \frac{7}{26}$

8. $1.5 \div 0.004$

19-2 PERMUTATIONS

An arrangement of objects in a particular order is called a **permutation.**
You can use the counting principle to find the number of permutations of
any group of objects.

example 1

In how many different ways can 4 people be seated in 4 chairs?

solution

As each chair is occupied, the number of people available for the
next chair decreases by 1.

number of choices for 1st chair		number of choices for 2nd chair		number of choices for 3rd chair		number of choices for 4th chair		
4	×	3	×	2	×	1	=	24

You can write
4 × 3 × 2 × 1 as
4!, which you read
as "four factorial."

There are 24 ways for 4 people to sit in 4 chairs.

your turn

In how many different ways can each of the following be arranged?

1. 3 people in 3 places in line for the bus

2. 7 subjects in a 7-period daily schedule

Sometimes you need to find permutations that involve only *part* of a
group of objects.

example 2

In how many different ways can 2 out of 4 people be seated in 2 chairs?

solution

number of choices for 1st chair		number of choices for 2nd chair		
4	×	3	=	12 ways to seat 2 of 4 people in 2 chairs

your turn

In how many different ways can each of the following happen?

3. creating a 2-flag signal from 6 flags of different colors

4. awarding first, second, and third prizes in a contest among 8 people

practice exercises

practice for example 1 *(page 422)*

In how many different ways can each of the following be arranged?

1. 5 swimmers in 5 pool lanes

2. 8 students at 8 desks

3. 6 bands in 6 positions in a parade

4. the letters in the word MATH

practice for example 2 *(page 422)*

In how many different ways can each of the following happen?

5. filling the jobs of cook and assistant cook from 5 applicants

6. electing a president and a vice president from 7 candidates

7. awarding first, second, and third places in a track meet of 10 teams

8. creating a three-letter ''word'' from the letters in the word FRACTION

mixed practice *(page 422)*

In how many different ways can each of the following happen?

9. placing 7 cars in 7 parking spaces

10. showing 6 movies in 6 theaters

11. creating a 3-digit number from the digits 1 to 7 with no repeats

12. arranging 4 songs, chosen from 20 songs, to be played on the radio

Find the number represented by each factorial.

13. 2!   **14.** 7!   **15.** 10!   **16.** 5!

review exercises

Write each fraction in lowest terms.

1. $\frac{6}{8}$ **2.** $\frac{16}{40}$ **3.** $\frac{20}{24}$ **4.** $\frac{15}{21}$ **5.** $\frac{55}{100}$ **6.** $\frac{16}{36}$

7. $\frac{10}{15}$ **8.** $\frac{72}{99}$ **9.** $\frac{18}{51}$ **10.** $\frac{16}{88}$ **11.** $\frac{35}{42}$ **12.** $\frac{49}{84}$

puzzle corner

A *perfect* number is equal to the sum of its factors, excluding itself. For example, 6 = 1 + 2 + 3. What is the next perfect number after 6?

19-3 FINDING THE PROBABILITY OF AN EVENT

When you spin the spinner at the right, there are 8 possible outcomes. Each outcome is **equally likely** to occur. The **event** of spinning an odd number has 4 **favorable outcomes:** 1, 3, 5, or 7. You say that the **probability,** or chance, that this event will occur is $\frac{4}{8}$, or $\frac{1}{2}$.

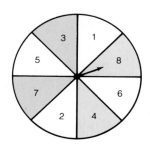

When all outcomes are equally likely, you can compute the probability of an event E, written $P(E)$, as follows.

$$P(E) = \frac{\text{number of favorable outcomes}}{\text{number of possible outcomes}}$$

example 1

Use the spinner above. Find each probability.

a. $P(6)$ **b.** $P(9)$ **c.** $P(\text{not red})$ **d.** $P(\text{number} > 0)$

solution

a. $P(6) = \frac{1}{8}$

b. $P(9) = \frac{0}{8} = 0$ $\longleftarrow$ The probability of an *impossible* event is 0.

c. $P(\text{not red}) = \frac{6}{8} = \frac{3}{4}$ $\longleftarrow$ Write the fraction in lowest terms.

d. $P(\text{number} > 0) = \frac{8}{8} = 1$ $\longleftarrow$ The probability of a *certain* event is 1.

your turn

Use the spinner above. Find each probability.

1. $P(7)$ **2.** $P(\text{not a 2})$ **3.** $P(\text{number} < 10)$ **4.** $P(\text{blue})$

example 2

Use the spinner above. Find $P(\text{red or even number})$.

solution

There are 2 outcomes that are red.
There are 4 *different* outcomes that are even numbers.
So there are 6 outcomes that are either red or even numbers.

$P(\text{red or even number}) = \frac{6}{8} = \frac{3}{4}$

your turn

Use the spinner on page 424. Find each probability.

5. P(red or blue) **6.** P(5 or not white) **7.** P(blue or prime number)

practice exercises

practice for example 1 (page 424)

A number cube is rolled. Find each probability.

1. $P(1)$ **2.** P(even number) **3.** $P(9)$
4. P(number < 4) **5.** P(not a 5) **6.** P(number > 0)

practice for example 2 (pages 424–425)

A card is chosen at random from those above. Find each probability.

7. P(o or T) **8.** P(M or red) **9.** P(red or blue)
10. P(a vowel or white) **11.** P(T or not a consonant) **12.** P(U or not blue)

mixed practice (pages 424–425)

The winner in a contest draws a ball from a jar to determine the prize. The chart at the right shows the number of balls of each color that are in the jar. Find each probability.

Color	Number	Prize
red	2	portable TV
green	6	dinner for 2
white	8	AM/FM radio
blue	10	sweatshirt
yellow	14	gold charm
purple	20	t-shirt
Total:	60	

13. P(purple ball) **14.** P(red ball)
15. P(blue or red ball) **16.** P(not blue ball)

17. P(not winning the dinner) **18.** P(winning the charm, dinner, or radio)
19. P(winning a cordless phone) **20.** P(brown ball)

21. The freshman class sold 500 raffle tickets at \$3 each to raise money for charity. The principal of the school bought 10 tickets. What is the probability that the principal wins the grand prize?

22. Jessica has 3 pennies, 4 nickels, 2 quarters, and 2 dollar bills in her purse. She needs a quarter for a pay phone. What is the probability that she picks a quarter or a nickel when she takes a coin at random from her purse?

23. A government official reports that the likelihood is "1 out of 10" that the price of gasoline will decrease this month. What is the probability that gasoline prices decrease? Write the probability as a percent.

24. A weather forecaster says that there is a 20% chance of rain tomorrow. What is the probability that it rains tomorrow? What is the probability that it does *not* rain?

review exercises

Write in scientific notation.

1. 375   2. 64,000   3. 800,000   4. 1009
5. 4,152,000   6. 77   7. 4891.3   8. 23.65

Complete.

9. 6.2 km = _?_ m   10. 4 mi = _?_ yd   11. 42 days = _?_ weeks
12. 112 oz = _?_ lb   13. 8 gal 3 qt = _?_ qt   14. 0.07 m = _?_ mm
15. 58 in. = _?_ ft _?_ in. 16. 810 mm = _?_ cm   17. 11.5 L = _?_ mL
18. 32 min = _?_ s   19. 6500 g = _?_ kg   20. 32 fl oz = _?_ c

Write each percent as a decimal.

21. 46%   22. 7%   23. 285%   24. 3.9%

calculator corner

Finding a factorial can be time-consuming. Using a calculator is usually helpful. Some calculators even have a factorial key, $\boxed{x!}$.

example   Use a calculator to find the number represented by 12!.

solution   Method 1: Enter the number and then press the $\boxed{x!}$ key.
12 $\boxed{x!}$ = 479001600
Method 2: If your calculator does not have this key, multiply the factors.
12 × 11 × 10 × 9 × 8 × 7 × 6 × 5 × 4 × 3 × 2 × 1 = 479001600

Use a calculator to find the number represented by each factorial or expression.

1. 9!   2. 11!   3. 14!
4. 15!   5. 3! × 6!   6. 4! × 8!

19-4 INDEPENDENT AND DEPENDENT EVENTS

At times you need to find the probability that two events occur either at the same time or consecutively. If the occurrence of one event does not affect the occurrence of the other event, the two events are **independent.**

example 1

A bag contains 4 red, 5 white, and 3 black marbles. Two marbles are drawn at random. The first marble is *replaced* before the second one is drawn. Find the probability of selecting a white and then a red marble.

solution

P(white, then red) $= P$(white) $\times P$(red)　　　　◄── **Multiply the probabilities of the events.**

$$= \quad \frac{5}{12} \quad \times \quad \frac{4}{12} \quad = \frac{5}{12} \times \frac{1}{3} = \frac{5}{36}$$

your turn

Use the set of marbles described above. The first marble is replaced before the second one is drawn. Find each probability.

1. P(black, then white)　　　　2. P(two red)

Two events are **dependent** if the occurrence of the first event affects the occurrence of the second event.

example 2

Use the set of marbles described above. Two marbles are drawn at random. The first marble is *not* replaced before the second one is drawn. Find the probability of selecting a white and then a red marble.

solution

P(white, then red) $= P$(white) $\times P$(red after white)

$$= \quad \frac{5}{12} \quad \times \quad \frac{4}{11} \quad = \frac{5}{33}$$　◄── **After the first marble is selected, only 11 marbles remain in the bag.**

your turn

Use the set of marbles described above. The first marble is *not* replaced before the second one is drawn. Find each probability.

3. P(red, then black)　　　　4. P(two white)

practice exercises

practice for example 1 *(page 427)*

Luis spins the spinner and rolls a number cube. Find each probability.

1. P(blue, then 6)
2. P(white, then 1)
3. P(red, then number > 2)
4. P(not blue, then even number)

practice for example 2 *(page 427)*

A purse contains 3 quarters, 4 dimes, and 3 nickels. Two coins are drawn at random. The first coin is *not* replaced before the second one is drawn. Find each probability.

5. P(quarter, then dime)
6. P(nickel, then quarter)
7. P(two nickels)
8. P(two dimes)

mixed practice *(page 427)*

Two cards are drawn at random from those shown at the right. The first card is replaced before the second one is drawn. Find each probability.

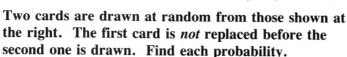

9. P(6, then 4)
10. P(white, then 3)
11. P(two blue)
12. P(blue, then not 10)

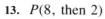

Two cards are drawn at random from those shown at the right. The first card is *not* replaced before the second one is drawn. Find each probability.

13. P(8, then 2)
14. P(9, then white)
15. P(two 5's)
16. P(white, then blue)

17. Doris chooses two socks at random from 14 brown, 10 black, and 16 blue socks. What is the probability she selects two black socks?

18. There are 10 seniors, 11 juniors, and 12 sophomores in the student council. Two representatives are selected at random. What is the probability that first a junior and then a sophomore is selected?

review exercises

Write each product in lowest terms.

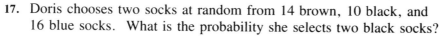

1. $\frac{3}{4} \times 200$
2. $\frac{5}{6} \times 180$
3. $\frac{14}{55} \times 400$
4. $\frac{8}{9} \times 100$

19-5 MAKING PREDICTIONS

You can use probability to make a **prediction** about the number of times an event is *expected* to occur.

example 1

A number cube is rolled 30 times. Find the number of times that a 4 is expected to occur.

solution

$P(4) \times$ number of tosses = expected number

$$\frac{1}{6} \quad \times \quad 30 \quad = \quad 5 \rightarrow \text{about 5 times}$$

your turn

A marble is selected from 5 red, 4 yellow, and 3 blue marbles and then replaced. If there are 36 selections, find the number of times that each event is expected to occur.

1. yellow marble
2. red marble

When you cannot assume that all outcomes are equally likely, you can perform an **experiment** to estimate the probability.

example 2

The frequency table shows the results when a tack is tossed 30 times. If the tack is tossed 100 times, how many times would you expect the point to be down?

Outcome	Tally	Frequency
point up	ⅢⅠ ⅠⅠⅠⅠ	9
point down	ⅢⅠ ⅢⅠ ⅢⅠ ⅢⅠ Ⅰ	21
		Total: 30

solution

$P(\text{down}) \times$ number of tosses = expected number

$$\frac{21}{30} \quad \times \quad 100 \quad = \frac{7}{10} \times 100 = 70 \rightarrow \text{about 70 times}$$

your turn

The table shows what 40 cars did after stopping at a stop sign. If 500 cars stop at the sign, how many would you expect to do the following?

Direction	Tally	Frequency
right turn	ⅢⅠ ⅢⅠ	10
straight	ⅢⅠ ⅢⅠ ⅢⅠ ⅢⅠ ⅠⅠⅠⅠ	24
left turn	ⅢⅠ Ⅰ	6
		Total: 40

3. turn right
4. go straight

practice *exercises*

practice for example 1 *(page 429)*

Use the spinner at the right. If the spinner is spun 40 times, find the number of times that each event is expected to occur.

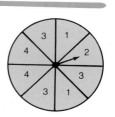

1. 3

2. 1

3. number > 2

4. even number

practice for example 2 *(page 429)*

The frequency table shows the results when a paper cup is tossed 20 times. If the cup is tossed 160 times, how many times would you expect each of the following outcomes?

Outcome	Tally	Frequency
up	I	1
down	⊞Ⅰ	5
side	⊞Ⅰ ⊞Ⅰ IIII	14
	Total:	20

5. side

6. down

7. not up

8. not side

mixed practice *(page 429)*

Keith's batting average is 0.250. Write the average as a fraction. Then use the fraction to estimate the number of hits Keith might expect to get in the given number of times at bat.

9. 120

10. 400

11. 88

12. 216

Maureen's free-throw average is 0.600. Write the average as a fraction. Then use the fraction to estimate the number of baskets Maureen might expect to get in the given number of shots.

13. 45

14. 65

15. 100

16. 150

17. A hair stylist gave haircuts to 6 blondes, 2 redheads, and 16 brunettes. Of the next 100 haircuts, how many would the stylist expect to give to redheads? Round the answer to the nearest whole number.

18. Out of 30 light bulbs tested at random from a carton, 3 were found to be defective. Find the expected number of defective bulbs if the carton contains 5000 bulbs.

19. A librarian recorded that, out of 50 items borrowed, 30 were fiction books, 16 were nonfiction books, and 4 were magazines. If the library loans 350 items in a day, how many would you expect to be nonfiction books?

20. An inspector found that 1 out of 45 shirts in a carton was labeled with an incorrect size. If the delivery carton contains 300 shirts, how many shirts with a correct label would you expect to find in the carton? Round the answer to the nearest whole number.

review exercises

Estimate.

1. $595 + 224 + 173$
2. $7245 - 6891$
3. 673×31
4. $79{,}843 \div 27$
5. $43.95 \div 0.062$
6. 4038×0.197
7. $33.95 - 18.12$
8. $0.511 + 0.8896$
9. $4\frac{1}{8} + 1\frac{3}{4}$
10. $\frac{1}{3} \times 14\frac{1}{5}$
11. $6\frac{5}{8} \div 3\frac{1}{6}$
12. $16\frac{3}{7} - 9\frac{8}{9}$

Evaluate each expression when $a = 5$, $b = 3$, and $c = 10$.

13. a^2
14. b^4
15. bc^3
16. a^3c^2
17. $4b^2c^2$
18. $10a^2b^3$

mental math

Write as a fraction in lowest terms.

1. 10%
2. 25%
3. 50%
4. 70%
5. 75%
6. 80%

Write as a decimal.

7. 10%
8. 25%
9. 40%
10. 80%
11. 1%
12. 100%

Write as a percent.

13. 0.01
14. 0.1
15. 1
16. $\frac{1}{2}$
17. $\frac{1}{4}$
18. $\frac{1}{3}$

Find each answer mentally.

19. What is 50% of 90?
20. What is 25% of $200?
21. What percent of 300 is 30?
22. 10 is what percent of 1000?
23. What is $33\frac{1}{3}\%$ of 600?
24. 5 is what percent of 20?
25. Estimate a 15% tip for a meal costing $5.
26. Estimate a 15% tip for a meal costing $19.75.

SKILL REVIEW

19-1

1. Use a tree diagram to find the number of possible outcomes when selecting a seat at a baseball stadium. Type: box seat, grandstand, bleachers; sections: 1, 2, 3, 4, 5

2. Use the counting principle to find the number of possible outcomes when choosing a main dish, a vegetable, and a drink from a menu listing 6 main dishes, 3 vegetables, and 4 drinks.

19-2

3. In how many different ways can 8 runners be placed in 8 lanes?
4. In how many different ways can a three-letter ''word'' be created from the letters in the word SILENT?
5. Find the number represented by 4!.
6. Find the number represented by 7!.

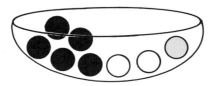

Use the spinner above. Find each probability.

7. $P(4)$ 8. $P(\text{not } 5)$

9. $P(1 \text{ or number} > 4)$ 10. $P(6 \text{ or odd})$

19-3

Use the marbles and the spinner above. A marble is drawn at random and the spinner is spun once. Find each probability.

11. $P(\text{red, then } 1)$ 12. $P(\text{black, then not prime})$

13. $P(\text{not white, then number} > 2)$ 14. $P(\text{not red, then even})$

19-4

Two marbles are drawn at random from those shown above. The first marble is not replaced before the second one is drawn. Find each probability.

15. $P(\text{red, then white})$ 16. $P(\text{two black})$

17. $P(\text{black, then red})$ 18. $P(\text{two white})$

19. If the spinner above is spun 50 times, find the number of times that an even number is expected to occur.

19-5

20. In a random test, 2 out of 70 radios in a crate were found to have broken antennas. If the crate holds a total of 210 radios, how many radios in the crate would you expect to have broken antennas?

19-6 TAKING A POLL

You can make predictions about a large group of people, or **population,** by taking a **poll.** A pollster questions a **sample,** a small group chosen at random from the population. The results are used to make predictions about the entire population.

example

The *Ellwood Banner* polled a sample of 150 registered voters before the mayoral election. 72 people supported Levy, 54 supported LoPresti, and 24 were undecided. There are 120,000 registered voters. From how many registered voters does LoPresti currently expect support?

solution

P(LoPresti) × number in population = expected number

$$\frac{54}{150} \quad \times \quad 120,000 \quad = \quad 43,200$$

LoPresti expects support from about 43,200 voters.

exercises

Refer to the information in the example above.

1. What fraction of those polled support Levy?
2. What percent of the population can you assume to be undecided?
3. From how many registered voters does Levy currently expect support?
4. About how many registered voters are currently undecided?

A marketing company polled residents of Waterburg. The results: 54 use soap A, 32 use soap B, 86 use soap C, and 28 use soap D.

5. How many residents were in the sample?
6. Has the manufacturer of soap C reached its goal of selling soap to 50% of the residents in Waterburg? Explain.
7. How many of the 55,000 Waterburg residents would be expected to use soap A?
8. How many of the 55,000 Waterburg residents would be expected to use a soap other than soap D?

19-7 DETERMINING ODDS

You often hear people speak of **odds:** the odds in favor of winning a contest, the odds against a team winning a championship, and so on. You calculate the odds in favor of an event E as follows.

$$\text{odds in favor of event } E = \frac{\text{number of favorable outcomes}}{\text{number of unfavorable outcomes}}$$

example

A bag contains 6 red, 3 blue, and 4 yellow marbles. Hal draws one marble at random. Find the odds in favor of each event.

a. drawing a red marble   **b.** drawing a red or a blue marble

solution

a. odds in favor of red $= \dfrac{6}{3+4} = \dfrac{6}{7}$ ⟵   3 blue and 4 yellow marbles are *unfavorable* outcomes for the event of drawing a red marble.

The odds are 6 to 7.

b. odds in favor of red or blue $= \dfrac{6+3}{4} = \dfrac{9}{4}$

The odds are 9 to 4.

exercises

Julie draws one card at random from a box of 6 green, 5 red, and 3 blue cards. Find the odds in favor of each event.

1. drawing a red card
2. drawing a green card
3. drawing a green or a blue card
4. drawing a blue or a red card

A number cube is rolled. Find the odds.

5. in favor of rolling a 5
6. in favor of rolling a number > 2
7. *against* rolling a 1
8. *against* rolling an odd number

9. Astronomers at Lookout Observatory calculate that the odds in favor of a visible meteor shower occurring in March are 2 to 13. Find the *probability* that a visible meteor shower occurs in March.

10. The *probability* of winning a contest is $\frac{4}{25}$. What are the odds in favor of winning the contest?

CHAPTER REVIEW

Choose the correct word to complete each sentence.

1. Rolling a number cube has 6 possible (*events, outcomes*).
2. The (*probability, odds*) of an event can be calculated by the ratio
   $$\frac{\text{number of favorable outcomes}}{\text{number of possible outcomes}}$$

skills

Find the number of possible outcomes.

3. rolling a number cube and tossing a nickel

4. choosing a shirt and tie; shirt: white, beige, blue; tie: black, blue

In how many different ways can each of the following happen?

5. arranging 6 people in 6 positions in line to buy movie tickets

6. awarding first, second, and third places in a race among 24 cars

7. Find the number represented by 4!.

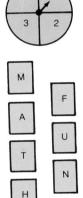

Use the spinner at the right. Find each probability.

8. $P(1)$

9. $P(2 \text{ or } 3)$

10. $P(4 \text{ or odd number})$

11. A card is drawn from those shown at the right and replaced. Another card is drawn. Find $P(\text{F, then T})$.

12. A card is drawn from those shown at the right and not replaced. Another card is drawn. Find $P(\text{U, then not a vowel})$.

13. A card is drawn from those shown at the right and replaced. In 35 selections, find the number of times that an M is expected to occur.

14. If the spinner at the right is spun 64 times, how many times would you expect an odd number to occur?

A marketing company polled 50 of the 32,000 residents in Mystic. 32 use shampoo *X*, 16 use shampoo *Y*, and 2 use shampoo Z.

15. What percent of Mystic residents are expected to use shampoo Z?

16. How many Mystic residents would be expected to use shampoo *Y*?

Use the cards above. Find the odds.

17. in favor of drawing the letter N

18. against drawing a vowel

Probability 435

CHAPTER TEST

19-1

1. Use a tree diagram to find the number of possible outcomes when electing a president and vice president. Candidates: Mary, Silvario, Charles for president; Lois, Doug for vice president

2. Use the counting principle to find the number of possible outcomes when choosing a telephone. Type: cordless, desk, wall; colors: white, red, black, beige

In how many different ways can each of the following happen?

19-2

3. arranging the letters in the word PRIME

4. awarding first, second, and third prizes in a pet show of 12 animals

5. Find the number represented by 6!.

A card is chosen at random from those above. Find each probability.

19-3

6. $P(\text{C})$

7. $P(\text{a letter before G in the alphabet})$

8. $P(\text{A or B})$

9. $P(\text{J or not a consonant})$

Use the cards and the number cube above. A card is drawn at random and the number cube is rolled once. Find each probability.

19-4

10. $P(\text{H, then 2})$

11. $P(\text{not a vowel, then odd})$

Two cards are drawn at random from those above. The first card is not replaced before the second one is drawn. Find each probability.

12. $P(\text{E, then J})$

13. $P(\text{vowel, then F})$

14. John tossed a thumbtack 20 times. It landed point up 7 times and point down 13 times. If John tosses the tack 80 times, how many times would he expect the point to be down?

19-5

15. The student council polled a sample of 30 students about the choice of school colors. 12 liked green and white, 8 liked blue and gold, and 10 liked neither choice. How many of the 1650 students in the school would be expected to like green and white?

19-6

Leon draws one card at random from a box of 5 yellow, 4 green, and 7 red cards. Find the odds.

16. in favor of drawing a red card

17. against drawing a green card

19-7

THE MANY USES OF COMPUTERS

Today we are using computers in many aspects of our lives. For instance, at home you can set a video cassette recorder days or hours ahead of time to tape a televison show. You can set a microwave oven to turn on at a specific time and at a specific oven temperature. Personal computers can help you keep track of household expenses and correspondence.

At school, computers frequently are used for instruction and recordkeeping. Software with geometric displays helps students visualize different shapes and figures. Student records, grades, and other information can be computerized. There are even desktop publishing programs students can use to create newspapers, flyers, and banners. At the school library, scanners may be used to check books in and out and to update inventory.

In business, computers have revolutionized the way we work. Graphic artists use computers in design work. In hospitals, computers provide doctors and nurses with vital information and list possible treatments. Computers can pinpoint automobile engine problems during a tune-up at the garage. Computerized traffic light systems monitor and manage rush-hour traffic jams.

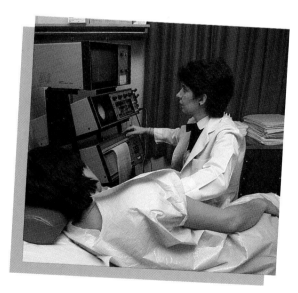

exercises

1. The Universal Product Code (UPC) has changed the way we shop in supermarkets. Find out how the UPC works.

2. Many banks now use automatic tellers to handle routine banking transactions. Find out how you use one of these machines to do your banking.

COMPETENCY TEST

Choose the letter of the correct answer.

1. **Find the median.**

   112, 79, 54, 85, 79, 125

   A. 79   B. 85
   C. 89   D. 82

5. **Find the mean.**

   74, 94, 82, 74, 91

   A. 83   B. 82
   C. 74   D. 20

2. **Luther has a total of 17 dimes and nickels. The total value of the coins is $1.25. How many of each kind of coin does he have?**

   A. 6 dimes, 11 nickels
   B. 10 dimes, 7 nickels
   C. 7 dimes, 11 nickels
   D. 8 dimes, 9 nickels

6. **An inspector rejected 3 out of 80 model kits due to missing or defective parts. How many kits would you expect the inspector to *pass* in a shipment of 2400?**

   A. about 90   B. about 900
   C. about 2310   D. about 2397

3.

Muffin Sales

Blueberry, Corn, Bran

Key: = 10,000 muffins

   How many muffins were sold in all?

   A. 97,500   B. 100,000
   C. 110,000   D. 165,000

7. **Find the annual premium for a $120,000 life insurance policy for a 25-year-old nonsmoker.**

   ### Annual Premium per $1000

Age Begun	25	35
Smoker	$12.55	$14.10
Nonsmoker	$11.10	$12.80

   A. $133.20   B. $1332
   C. $150.60   D. $1506

4. **Refer to Exercise 3. How many more blueberry muffins were sold than corn muffins?**

   A. 7500
   B. 1750
   C. 17,500
   D. 22,500

8. **Find the number of possible lunches (sandwich, salad, drink) when choosing from 3 sandwiches, 2 salads, and 4 drinks.**

   A. 9   B. 11
   C. 20   D. 24

9. Stacey has 3 quarters, 2 dimes, and 3 nickels in her purse. She draws a coin at random, replaces it, and draws another at random. Find P(quarter, then nickel).

A. $\frac{9}{64}$ B. $\frac{1}{4}$ C. $\frac{9}{56}$ D. $\frac{3}{4}$

10. Refer to Exercise 9. Find P(quarter, then dime) if Stacey does *not* replace the first coin before drawing the second.

A. $\frac{5}{56}$ B. $\frac{37}{56}$ C. $\frac{3}{28}$ D. $\frac{3}{32}$

11. If car expenses totaled $422, how much was spent on gasoline?

A. $20
B. $21.10
C. $84.40
D. $211

Car Costs per Dollar

Repair 16¢
20¢ Gasoline   14¢ Insurance
Loan Payment 50¢

12. Last year Alice spent $978 on gas. Find the amount she should budget monthly for gas.

A. about $20   B. about $33
C. about $82   D. about $11,736

13. Find the mode.

7, 27, 36, 15, 7, 27, 7

A. 29   B. 18   C. 15   D. 7

14. A bag contains 3 red, 4 blue, and 2 yellow marbles. One marble is drawn at random. Find the *odds* in favor of drawing a red or a yellow marble.

A. 5 to 9   B. 5 to 4
C. 5 to 24   D. 1 to 4

15. Refer to Exercise 14. Find the probability of *not* drawing a blue marble.

A. $\frac{4}{9}$ B. $\frac{5}{4}$ C. $\frac{5}{24}$ D. $\frac{5}{9}$

16. The number cube is rolled 150 times. Find the number of times that a number greater than 2 is expected to appear.

A. about 100
B. about 125
C. about 25
D. about 50

17. Each of the letters A, B, C, D, E, F is written on a card. A card is chosen at random. Find P(vowel).

A. $\frac{1}{6}$ B. $\frac{1}{2}$ C. $\frac{1}{3}$ D. $\frac{2}{3}$

18. Ana rolls a number cube and tosses a penny. Find P(5, then heads).

A. $\frac{1}{6}$ B. $\frac{1}{12}$ C. $\frac{5}{12}$ D. $\frac{5}{36}$

CUMULATIVE REVIEW CHAPTERS 1–19

Find each answer.

1. 614×1052

2. $2532.7 - 856.449$

3. $96\overline{)84,591}$

4. $\$8702 + \$4496$

5. 0.68×1.52

6. $5\frac{3}{8} - 2\frac{2}{3}$

7. $8.2\overline{)9635}$

8. $7\frac{5}{12} + 3\frac{7}{8}$

9. In how many ways can a president, vice-president, secretary, and treasurer be chosen from among ten candidates?

10. Find the mean, median, and mode(s): 63, 112, 104, 72, 63

11. Write as a fraction in lowest terms: **a.** $\frac{36}{96}$ **b.** 92% **c.** 0.45

12. Write as a decimal: **a.** 225% **b.** $\frac{2}{5}$ **c.** $15\frac{1}{2}\%$

13. Write as a percent: **a.** $\frac{23}{25}$ **b.** 0.724 **c.** 6.5

14. Find the GCF and the LCM: **a.** 25 and 70 **b.** 16, 24, and 30

15. Write in order from least to greatest: $\frac{3}{5}, \frac{5}{12}, \frac{3}{4}$

16. Evaluate $3a^3b$ when $a = 2$ and $b = 3$.

Estimate.

17. 33% of 1472

18. $489,394 - 295,704$

19. $183\overline{)379,615}$

20. $29\frac{7}{8} + 79\frac{9}{11}$

21. $\frac{7}{22} \times 887$

22. 32.67×11.0096

A number cube is rolled. Find each probability.

23. $P(\text{multiple of } 3)$

24. $P(\text{number} > 2)$

25. $P(8)$

26. Draw a pictograph to display the number of hits.
    Flanders: 170   Enriquez: 150   McGuire: 90   Moreland: 65   Dunn: 49

27. A box contains 38 nickels and dimes worth a total of $2.75. How many of each kind of coin are in the box?

28. Eight apples cost $1.76. How much will 5 apples cost?

29. A number cube is rolled, and a quarter and a dime are tossed. Find the number of possible outcomes.

30. An account earns 8.5% interest compounded semiannually. Find the balance at the end of one year if the principal is $5000. Round your answer to the nearest cent.

31. A box contains 5 green, 2 red, and 3 white marbles. Two marbles are drawn at random. Find $P(\text{green, then red})$ if the first marble is not replaced before the second is drawn.

Negative numbers are used to record temperatures below zero. On the Celsius scale, zero marks the point at which water will freeze.

CHAPTER 20

INTEGERS

20-1 WRITING AND COMPARING INTEGERS

Numbers greater than zero are **positive numbers.**
Numbers less than zero are **negative numbers.**
Zero is neither positive nor negative.

Record U.S. Temperatures in Degrees Fahrenheit	
High	Low
134°F above 0	80°F below 0

example 1

Write a positive or negative number to represent each phrase.

a. 80°F below zero

b. 134°F above zero

solution

a. ⁻80 ◄── Read as "negative 80."

b. 134 ◄── No sign indicates a positive number.

your turn

Write a positive or negative number to represent each phrase.

1. a gain of 34 yd

2. a loss of 12 lb

3. a raise of $30

The numbers 1, 2, 3,... together with ⁻1, ⁻2, ⁻3,... and 0 are called **integers.** You can represent integers as points on a number line.

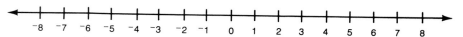

Two numbers that are the same distance from 0 on a number line but on different sides of 0 are called **opposites.** The **absolute value** of a number is its distance from 0 on a number line.

example 2

Write the opposite of each number.
Find the absolute value of each number.

a. ⁻3

b. 9

c. 0

solution

a. ⁻3 is the same distance from 0 as 3, but on the opposite side. The opposite of ⁻3 is 3. ⁻3 is 3 units from 0.

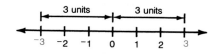

The absolute value of ⁻3 is 3. You write $|{-3}| = 3$.

b. The opposite of 9 is ⁻9. The absolute value of 9 is 9, or $|9| = 9$.

c. The opposite of 0 is 0. The absolute value of 0 is 0, or $|0| = 0$.

your turn

Write the opposite of each number.

4. ⁻6   **5.** 8   **6.** ⁻1   **7.** ⁻8   **8.** 5

Find the absolute value of each number.

9. ⁻3   **10.** 7   **11.** ⁻11   **12.** ⁻19   **13.** 15

Integers can be compared by using a number line. The greater integer is always to the right of the lesser integer on a number line.

example 3

Compare. Replace each __?__ with < or >. Use the number line given below.

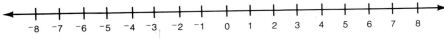

a. ⁻5 _?_ ⁻3   **b.** 3 _?_ ⁻2   **c.** ⁻4 _?_ ⁻6

solution

a. ⁻5 is *to the left of* ⁻3 on the number line.
⁻5 *is less than* ⁻3, or ⁻5 < ⁻3.

b. 3 is *to the right of* ⁻2 on the number line.
3 *is greater than* ⁻2, or 3 > ⁻2.

c. ⁻4 is *to the right of* ⁻6 on the number line.
⁻4 *is greater than* ⁻6, or ⁻4 > ⁻6.

your turn

Compare. Replace each __?__ with < or >. Use a number line if needed.

14. 4 _?_ ⁻1   **15.** ⁻3 _?_ 0   **16.** ⁻5 _?_ 5   **17.** ⁻4 _?_ ⁻2

practice *exercises*

practice for example 1 (page 442)

Write a positive or negative number to represent each phrase.

1. a loss of $8   **2.** 10°F below zero   **3.** 50 ft above sea level

4. a gain of $20   **5.** 35 ft below sea level   **6.** 43°F above zero

Write the opposite of each number.

7. $^-12$ **8.** $^-5$ **9.** 3   **10.** 11   **11.** $^-15$ **12.** 17

Find the absolute value of each number.

13. $^-8$ **14.** $^-13$ **15.** 13   **16.** 10   **17.** $^-6$ **18.** 1

Compare. Replace each __?__ with < or >. Use a number line if needed.

19. $^-7$ __?__ $^-11$ **20.** 8 __?__ 13   **21.** 0 __?__ $^-2$ **22.** 5 __?__ $^-6$

23. $^-16$ __?__ $^-15$ **24.** $^-4$ __?__ 0   **25.** 8 __?__ $^-8$ **26.** $^-2$ __?__ 1

Match each phrase to the appropriate integer.

27. the opposite of $^-9$ **28.** negative 9   **A.** 9

29. the absolute value of 9   **30.** positive 9   **B.** $^-9$

31. the opposite of 9   **32.** the absolute value of $^-9$

Write each set of integers in order from least to greatest.

33. $^-5$, 0, $^-3$, 5, $^-4$ **34.** 5, 8, $^-11$, $^-8$, 0   **35.** $^-1$, $^-14$, $^-9$, 2, 1

36. $^-14$, 17, 23, $^-21$, $^-6$ **37.** $^-8$, $^-12$, 11, 1, 0   **38.** $^-31$, $^-28$, $^-50$, 2, 6

Compare. Replace each __?__ with <, >, or =.

39. $|3|$ __?__ $|^-2|$ **40.** $|17|$ __?__ $^-17$ **41.** $|^-6|$ __?__ $|^-9|$ **42.** $|13|$ __?__ $|^-13|$

43. $|5|$ __?__ $|^-10|$ **44.** $|0|$ __?__ 0   **45.** $|3|$ __?__ $|^-3|$ **46.** $|8|$ __?__ $|^-7|$

47. Name all the integers that have an absolute value of 2.

48. The lowest point in the United States is 282 ft below sea level. Write an integer to represent this quantity.

review exercises

Find each sum.

1. 34 + 86   **2.** 47 + 59   **3.** 322 + 77   **4.** 199 + 147

5. 5.07 + 6.38   **6.** 5.74 + 13.6   **7.** 12.02 + 16.29   **8.** 11.9 + 5.37

9. $\frac{4}{5} + \frac{2}{5}$ **10.** $\frac{3}{4} + \frac{2}{3}$ **11.** $\frac{5}{8} + \frac{5}{6}$ **12.** $\frac{1}{3} + \frac{5}{7}$

20-2 ADDING INTEGERS

You can use arrows on a number line to represent the addition of two integers.

example 1

Use a number line to find each sum: a. $^-2 + 5$ b. $4 + {}^-6$

solution

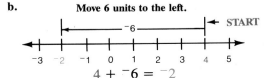

a.   **Move 5 units to the right.**

$$^-2 + 5 = 3$$

b.   **Move 6 units to the left.**

$$4 + {}^-6 = {}^-2$$

your turn

Use a number line to find each sum.

1. $2 + 7$ 2. $^-5 + 4$ 3. $6 + {}^-3$ 4. $^-2 + {}^-4$

     You can also add two integers by following some simple rules. The rules that you use depend on whether the integers have the same signs or different signs.

     To add two integers with the *same* signs, follow this procedure.

1. Find the absolute value of each integer.
2. Add the absolute values.
3. Give the sum the same sign as the two integers.

example 2

a. $9 + 7 = 16$ b. $^-7 + {}^-4 = {}^-11$

your turn

Find each sum.

5. $9 + 3$ 6. $7 + 6$ 7. $8 + 12$

8. $^-6 + {}^-8$ 9. $^-5 + {}^-7$ 10. $^-9 + {}^-6$

     To add two integers with *different* signs, follow this procedure.

1. Find the absolute value of each integer.
2. Subtract the lesser absolute value from the greater absolute value.
3. Give the sum the same sign as the integer with the greater absolute value.

Integers 445

example 3

Find each sum.

a. ⁻7 + 5

b. 8 + ⁻8

solution

a. |⁻7| = 7
|5| = 5
7 − 5 = 2 ⟵ |⁻7| > |5|
⁻7 + 5 = ⁻2 ⟵ The sum is negative.

b. |8| = 8
|⁻8| = 8 ⟵ **same absolute value**
8 − 8 = 0
8 + ⁻8 = 0 ⟵ **The sum of a number and its opposite is 0.**

your turn

Find each sum.

11. 9 + ⁻7   **12.** 4 + ⁻4   **13.** 10 + ⁻2
14. ⁻6 + 3   **15.** ⁻5 + 2   **16.** ⁻9 + 9

practice exercises

practice for example 1 *(page 445)*

Use a number line to find each sum.

1. 1 + 8   **2.** 4 + ⁻2   **3.** ⁻8 + 4   **4.** 5 + 3
5. 3 + ⁻3   **6.** 5 + ⁻7   **7.** ⁻4 + ⁻4   **8.** ⁻6 + ⁻2

practice for example 2 *(page 445)*

Find each sum.

9. 7 + 8   **10.** 4 + 9   **11.** 6 + 4   **12.** 5 + 8
13. 3 + 11   **14.** 5 + 14   **15.** 22 + 18   **16.** 0 + 33
17. ⁻2 + ⁻2   **18.** ⁻8 + ⁻5   **19.** ⁻3 + ⁻7   **20.** ⁻4 + ⁻9
21. ⁻6 + ⁻10   **22.** ⁻9 + ⁻8   **23.** ⁻11 + ⁻5   **24.** ⁻16 + 0

practice for example 3 *(page 446)*

Find each sum.

25. ⁻8 + 4   **26.** 4 + ⁻1   **27.** ⁻6 + 6   **28.** ⁻9 + 2
29. ⁻5 + 4   **30.** 11 + ⁻11   **31.** 6 + ⁻7   **32.** 8 + ⁻4
33. ⁻3 + 6   **34.** 12 + ⁻9   **35.** ⁻10 + 15   **36.** 16 + ⁻11
37. 15 + ⁻3   **38.** ⁻7 + 13   **39.** ⁻14 + 8   **40.** 6 + ⁻18

mixed practice (pages 445–446)

Find each sum.

41. 6 + 9   **42.** 7 + ⁻7   **43.** 6 + ⁻8

44. ⁻13 + 13   **45.** 3 + ⁻8   **46.** ⁻2 + ⁻14

47. 27 + ⁻13   **48.** ⁻29 + 0   **49.** ⁻23 + ⁻5

50. ⁻15 + ⁻17   **51.** 16 + ⁻16   **52.** 34 + 17

53. ⁻5 + ⁻4 + ⁻2   **54.** ⁻1 + 17 + ⁻12   **55.** ⁻15 + 15 + ⁻9

56. ⁻4 + ⁻8 + ⁻9   **57.** 14 + 9 + ⁻11   **58.** ⁻9 + ⁻7 + ⁻6

59. The temperature was 8°F below zero at midnight. By 7:00 A.M. it had risen 19°F. What was the temperature at 7:00 A.M.?

60. On three plays, a running back gained 18 yd, gained 9 yd, and lost 29 yd. What was the total number of yards for the three plays?

review exercises

Find each difference.

1. 37 − 14   **2.** 52 − 29   **3.** 64 − 48

4. 241 − 159   **5.** 6.84 − 4.72   **6.** 5.03 − 3.64

7. 4.59 − 1.04   **8.** 3.06 − 2.7   **9.** 7.8 − 4.37

10. $\frac{7}{8} - \frac{3}{8}$ **11.** $\frac{9}{10} - \frac{3}{5}$ **12.** $\frac{11}{12} - \frac{5}{6}$

mental math

When you add three or more integers mentally, look at all the addends before beginning. Don't just add from left to right.

Look for opposites.

     7 + 8 + ⁻7
     7 + ⁻7 = 0
     0 + 8 = 8

Add positive and negative numbers separately.

16 + ⁻25 + 23 + ⁻5 + ⁻10
16 + 23 = 39   ⁻25 + ⁻5 + ⁻10 = ⁻40
         39 + ⁻40 = ⁻1

Add mentally.

1. 5 + ⁻9 + 4 + 9   **2.** ⁻7 + 4 + ⁻3 + 4   **3.** 10 + 8 + ⁻12 + ⁻8

4. 15 + ⁻3 + 12 + ⁻4   **5.** 17 + ⁻19 + ⁻17 + 9   **6.** 19 + ⁻18 + 21 + ⁻1 + ⁻17

20-3 SUBTRACTING INTEGERS

The highest point in New Orleans is 15 ft *above* sea level. The lowest point is 4 ft *below* sea level. If you subtract 15 − ⁻4, you find that the difference between their altitudes is 19 ft.

$$15 - {}^-4 = 15 + 4 = 19$$

To subtract integers, use the following rule.

To subtract an integer, add its opposite.

example 1

Write a related addition.

a. 4 − 14

b. ⁻5 − ⁻13

solution

a. $4 - 14 = 4 + {}^-14$ ◄── **Subtracting 14 is the same as adding ⁻14.**

b. ${}^-5 - {}^-13 = {}^-5 + 13$ ◄── **Subtracting ⁻13 is the same as adding 13.**

your turn

Write a related addition.

1. 7 − 24

2. ⁻8 − 6

3. 5 − ⁻18

4. ⁻6 − ⁻13

example 2

Find each difference.

a. 5 − 16

b. ⁻9 − 2

c. 0 − ⁻7

d. ⁻3 − ⁻1

solution

a. $5 - 16$
  $= 5 + {}^-16$
  $= {}^-11$

b. ${}^-9 - 2$
  $= {}^-9 + {}^-2$
  $= {}^-11$

c. $0 - {}^-7$
  $= 0 + 7$
  $= 7$

d. ${}^-3 - {}^-1$
  $= {}^-3 + 1$
  $= {}^-2$

your turn

Find each difference.

5. ⁻5 − ⁻14

6. 0 − ⁻10

7. 3 − 11

8. ⁻9 − 20

practice *exercises*

practice for example 1 *(page 448)*

Write a related addition.

1. $6 - 17$
2. $12 - {}^-6$
3. $0 - {}^-13$
4. ${}^-7 - 2$
5. ${}^-10 - {}^-8$
6. $2 - {}^-23$
7. ${}^-2 - 23$
8. $15 - {}^-6$

practice for example 2 *(page 448)*

Find each difference.

9. ${}^-7 - 13$
10. $4 - {}^-12$
11. ${}^-14 - 0$
12. $0 - {}^-14$
13. ${}^-8 - {}^-5$
14. $13 - 13$
15. $8 - {}^-5$
16. ${}^-7 - 7$

mixed practice *(page 448)*

Copy and complete the chart.

	Subtraction	Related Addition	Answer
17.	$17 - 29$	?	?
18.	${}^-20 - {}^-15$	?	?
19.	$0 - {}^-43$	?	?
20.	?	${}^-6 + {}^-3$	?
21.	?	$5 + {}^-30$	?
22.	?	$10 + 24$	?

23. At 4:00 P.M. the temperature was 16°F above zero. By 11:00 P.M. the temperature had dropped 21°F. What was the temperature at 11:00 P.M.?

24. A mine elevator was 58 ft below the surface. It then went down another 77 ft. How far below the surface was the elevator then?

review *exercises*

Find each product.

1. 3×15
2. 19×7
3. 24×8
4. 21×6
5. 17×12
6. 27×15
7. 1.7×3.2
8. 6.4×2.8
9. 5.4×3.7
10. 3.8×2.9
11. 7.7×8.4
12. 6.7×9.3
13. $\frac{5}{8} \times \frac{2}{3}$
14. $\frac{3}{7} \times \frac{4}{5}$
15. $\frac{5}{9} \times \frac{2}{3}$
16. $\frac{3}{4} \times \frac{5}{7}$

20-4 MULTIPLYING INTEGERS

Consider the patterns in the tables below.

$3 \times 4 = 12$
$2 \times 4 = 8$ ← Both factors are positive. The product is positive.
$1 \times 4 = 4$

$0 \times 4 = 0$

$^-1 \times 4 = ^-4$
$^-2 \times 4 = ^-8$ ← One factor is negative. One factor is positive. The product is negative.
$^-3 \times 4 = ^-12$

$3 \times ^-4 = ^-12$
$2 \times ^-4 = ^-8$ ← One factor is positive. One factor is negative. The product is negative.
$1 \times ^-4 = ^-4$

$0 \times ^-4 = 0$

$^-1 \times ^-4 = 4$
$^-2 \times ^-4 = 8$ ← Both factors are negative. The product is positive.
$^-3 \times ^-4 = 12$

The patterns above suggest the following rules for multiplying integers.

The product of two positive integers or two negative integers is positive.
The product of a positive integer and a negative integer is negative.

example 1

Find each product.

a. $6 \times ^-2 = ^-12$
b. $^-5 \times 8 = ^-40$
c. $^-3 \times ^-17 = 51$
d. $4 \times 12 = 48$

your turn

Find each product.

1. $2 \times ^-9$
2. $^-9 \times ^-8$
3. $0 \times ^-7$
4. 5×13
5. $^-6 \times 5$
6. 11×0

example 2

Find each product.

a. $^-4 \times ^-5 \times ^-3$
$20 \times ^-3$ ← Multiply two integers at a time.
$^-60$

b. $^-6 \times 5 \times ^-3 \times 3$
$^-30 \times ^-3 \times 3$
90×3
270

your turn

Find each product.

7. $^-2 \times 6 \times ^-7$
8. $^-8 \times ^-5 \times ^-7$
9. $^-4 \times 3 \times ^-6 \times 5$
10. $13 \times ^-4 \times ^-9 \times ^-2$

example 3

Find each answer.

a. $(^-4)^2$ **b.** $(^-5)^3$ **c.** $(^-6)^1$ **d.** $(^-3)^0$

solution

a. $(^-4)^2 = {}^-4 \times {}^-4 = 16$
b. $(^-5)^3 = {}^-5 \times {}^-5 \times {}^-5 = {}^-125$
c. $(^-6)^1 = {}^-6$ ⬅ **Any number to the first power is equal to itself.**
d. $(^-3)^0 = 1$ ⬅ **Any nonzero number to the zero power is equal to 1.**

your turn

Find each answer.

11. $(^-9)^2$ **12.** $(^-4)^3$ **13.** $(^-7)^0$
14. $(^-10)^1$ **15.** $(^-2)^4$ **16.** $(^-6)^2$

practice exercises

practice for example 1 (page 450)

Find each product.

1. $^-9 \times 3$ **2.** 3×7 **3.** $7 \times {}^-6$ **4.** $^-5 \times {}^-5$
5. $^-6 \times {}^-1$ **6.** $0 \times {}^-9$ **7.** 4×18 **8.** $^-4 \times 16$
9. $^-8 \times 17$ **10.** $^-12 \times {}^-8$ **11.** $^-13 \times 0$ **12.** $^-15 \times 7$
13. 5×11 **14.** $^-17 \times {}^-14$ **15.** $12 \times {}^-12$ **16.** 18×0

practice for example 2 (page 450)

Find each product.

17. $^-1 \times {}^-4 \times {}^-7$ **18.** $4 \times {}^-2 \times {}^-3$ **19.** $^-2 \times 9 \times 2$
20. $^-3 \times {}^-2 \times 7$ **21.** $4 \times 6 \times 3$ **22.** $^-2 \times 0 \times {}^-8$
23. $^-2 \times {}^-4 \times {}^-3 \times {}^-5$ **24.** $3 \times {}^-9 \times {}^-5 \times 4$ **25.** $^-2 \times {}^-7 \times {}^-5 \times 6$
26. $7 \times 9 \times 4 \times 6$ **27.** $8 \times 5 \times {}^-3 \times 1$ **28.** $6 \times {}^-5 \times 0 \times 9$

practice for example 3 (page 451)

Find each answer.

29. $(^-2)^3$ **30.** $(^-5)^2$ **31.** $(^-8)^2$ **32.** $(^-9)^1$ **33.** $(^-6)^0$ **34.** $(^-1)^3$
35. $(^-7)^2$ **36.** $(^-3)^4$ **37.** $(^-1)^0$ **38.** $(^-1)^2$ **39.** $(^-2)^5$ **40.** $(^-4)^4$

mixed practice (pages 450–451)

Find each product.

41. $^-14 \times 11$

42. $^-7 \times ^-2 \times ^-8$

43. $3 \times ^-17 \times 0$

44. $7 \times ^-8 \times 11$

45. $^-9 \times ^-16$

46. $6 \times ^-4 \times 5 \times 2$

47. $^-5 \times ^-3 \times 4 \times 7$

48. $3 \times ^-3 \times ^-2$

49. 14×18

50. $(^-9)^3$

51. $(^-3)^3$

52. $^-19 \times 6$

53. $7 \times ^-17$

54. $(^-6)^3$

55. $(^-2)^4$

56. $^-8 \times ^-5 \times ^-1 \times 2$

57. During an experiment, the temperature of a solution dropped 4 degrees every hour. How many degrees had it dropped after 17 h?

58. A submarine started on the surface and made 5 dives. Each dive took it 38 m farther down. How far below sea level was it after the fifth dive?

review exercises

Find each quotient.

1. $108 \div 6$

2. $76 \div 4$

3. $105 \div 3$

4. $125 \div 5$

5. $24.8 \div 4$

6. $37.8 \div 2$

7. $74.5 \div 5$

8. $91.7 \div 7$

9. $\frac{5}{8} \div \frac{3}{4}$

10. $\frac{7}{10} \div \frac{4}{5}$

11. $\frac{7}{12} \div \frac{5}{6}$

12. $\frac{8}{9} \div \frac{2}{3}$

puzzle corner

The rules for a game state that you get 7 points for each correct answer and lose 5 points for each incorrect answer. If you answer 24 questions and still have 0 points, how many questions did you answer correctly?

20-5 DIVIDING INTEGERS

You can divide integers by using the relation between division and multiplication. The quotient in a division is a factor in the related multiplication, as shown below.

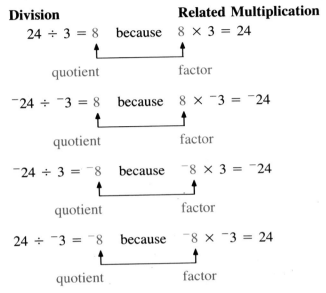

Division		Related Multiplication
$24 \div 3 = 8$	because	$8 \times 3 = 24$
quotient		factor
$^-24 \div ^-3 = 8$	because	$8 \times ^-3 = ^-24$
quotient		factor
$^-24 \div 3 = ^-8$	because	$^-8 \times 3 = ^-24$
quotient		factor
$24 \div ^-3 = ^-8$	because	$^-8 \times ^-3 = 24$
quotient		factor

The examples above suggest the following rules for dividing integers.

The quotient of two positive integers or two negative integers is positive.
The quotient of a positive integer and a negative integer is negative.

example 1

Find each quotient.

a. $28 \div 7$ **b.** $^-40 \div ^-5$ **c.** $^-36 \div 4$ **d.** $30 \div ^-6$

solution

a. $28 \div 7 = 4$ **b.** $^-40 \div ^-5 = 8$ **c.** $^-36 \div 4 = ^-9$ **d.** $30 \div ^-6 = ^-5$

your turn

Find each quotient.

1. $27 \div 3$ **2.** $^-20 \div ^-2$ **3.** $56 \div ^-8$ **4.** $^-72 \div 9$

Recall that when 0 is divided by any nonzero number, the quotient is 0. When you divide by 0, the quotient is *undefined*.

example 2

Tell whether the quotient is *positive*, *negative*, *zero*, or *undefined*.

a. ⁻32 ÷ 8

b. ⁻12 ÷ 0

c. 0 ÷ ⁻4

d. ⁻50 ÷ ⁻5

solution

a. negative

b. undefined

c. zero

d. positive

your turn

Tell whether the quotient is *positive*, *negative*, *zero*, or *undefined*.

5. 25 ÷ ⁻5

6. 0 ÷ ⁻10

7. ⁻22 ÷ ⁻2

8. ⁻5 ÷ 0

practice *exercises*

practice for example 1 *(page 453)*

Find each quotient.

1. 24 ÷ ⁻4

2. ⁻36 ÷ ⁻6

3. ⁻81 ÷ ⁻9

4. 42 ÷ ⁻7

5. 27 ÷ ⁻3

6. 45 ÷ 9

7. 63 ÷ ⁻3

8. ⁻48 ÷ 2

9. 18 ÷ 3

10. 44 ÷ 4

11. ⁻26 ÷ 2

12. ⁻36 ÷ 9

13. ⁻21 ÷ ⁻3

14. ⁻54 ÷ ⁻9

15. 45 ÷ ⁻3

16. 78 ÷ ⁻6

practice for example 2 *(page 454)*

Tell whether the quotient is *positive*, *negative*, *zero*, or *undefined*.

17. 0 ÷ ⁻9

18. ⁻52 ÷ ⁻4

19. ⁻1 ÷ 0

20. ⁻60 ÷ 6

21. 33 ÷ ⁻3

22. 0 ÷ 5

23. 120 ÷ 10

24. ⁻37 ÷ 0

mixed practice *(pages 453–454)*

Copy and complete the chart.

	Division		Related Multiplication
25.	⁻18 ÷ ⁻3 = 6	because	__?__ × ⁻3 = ⁻18
26.	80 ÷ ⁻8 = __?__	because	__?__ × ⁻8 = 80
27.	0 ÷ ⁻6 = __?__	because	__?__ × ⁻6 = 0
28.	⁻24 ÷ 2 = __?__	because	__?__ × 2 = ⁻24
29.	56 ÷ ⁻4 = __?__	because	__?__ × ⁻4 = 56
30.	49 ÷ ⁻7 = __?__	because	__?__ × ⁻7 = 49

Find each quotient.

31. $^-57 \div 3$ 32. $^-65 \div \,^-5$

33. $0 \div \,^-7$ 34. $^-40 \div \,^-2$

35. $140 \div 7$ 36. $^-36 \div 0$

37. $^-150 \div 6$ 38. $^-84 \div \,^-4$

39. $0 \div \,^-6$ 40. $91 \div \,^-7$

41. $108 \div 9$ 42. $54 \div 0$

43. A hot air balloon descended 207 ft in 9 min. On average, how many feet did it descend in one minute?

44. June is playing a game in which each black card has a value of 5 and each red card has a value of $^-4$. If the total of June's red cards is $^-140$, how many red cards has she drawn?

review *exercises*

Find each answer.

1. What is 30% of 420?   2. What is 4% of 125?

3. 12 is 25% of what number?   4. 18 is 8% of what number?

5. What percent of 300 is 75?   6. What percent of 45 is 27?

calculator corner

Some calculators have a ⊞ key. You enter a number and then push the ⊞ key to make the number negative.

     The ⊞ key can be used to find sums, differences, products, and quotients.

example   a. Find the sum: $^-23 + 16$ b. Find the product: $^-15 \times \,^-4$

solution   a. 23 ⊞ + 16 = $^-7$ b. 15 ⊞ × 4 ⊞ = 60

Use a calculator to find each answer.

1. $7 + \,^-17$ 2. $^-12 + 19$ 3. $^-27 + \,^-14$ 4. $16 + \,^-24$

5. $^-13 - 10$ 6. $^-15 - \,^-8$ 7. $26 - \,^-18$ 8. $^-16 - 24$

9. $^-12 \times 7$ 10. $16 \times \,^-5$ 11. $^-19 \times \,^-4$ 12. $14 \times \,^-8$

13. $^-84 \div \,^-7$ 14. $^-65 \div 5$ 15. $^-114 \div 6$ 16. $108 \div \,^-9$

20-6 SIMPLIFYING THE PROBLEM

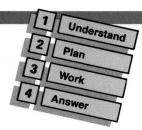

1 Understand
2 Plan
3 Work
4 Answer

When a problem seems very complicated or time-consuming, you may find it helpful to *simplify* the problem. One way to simplify is to reword the problem using simpler numbers. Solving the simpler problem may then help you solve the original problem.

example

Find the sum: $1 + 3 + 5 + \cdots + 45 + 47 + 49$

solution

Step 1   Given: the odd numbers from 1 to 49
Find: the sum

Step 2   There are 25 odd numbers from 1 to 49.

Solve a *series* of simpler problems.
- Find the sum of the first 2 odd numbers.
- Find the sum of the first 3 odd numbers.
- Find the sum of the first 4 odd numbers.
- Find the sum of the first 5 odd numbers.

Organize the simpler problems in a table.
Look for a pattern.

Step 3

Number of Odd Numbers	Addition	Sum	Pattern
2	1 + 3	4	$2^2 = 4$
3	1 + 3 + 5	9	$3^2 = 9$
4	1 + 3 + 5 + 7	16	$4^2 = 16$
5	1 + 3 + 5 + 7 + 9	25	$5^2 = 25$

Step 4   The pattern shows that (number of odd numbers)^2 = sum.
So the sum of the first 25 odd numbers is $(25)^2 = 625$.

Therefore, $1 + 3 + 5 + \cdots + 45 + 47 + 49 = 625$.

problems

1. Find the sum of the first 6 odd numbers.
2. Find the sum of the first 16 odd numbers.
3. Find the sum: $1 + 3 + 5 + \cdots + 95 + 97 + 99$
4. Find the sum: $5 + 7 + 9 + \cdots + 45 + 47 + 49$

5. The Hold-It Warehouse stacks crates using the triangular pattern shown at the right. The top row always has one crate. Each row always has two fewer crates than the row below it.

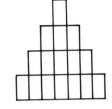

   a. How many crates are in a stack that has 24 rows?
   b. How many crates are in a stack if the bottom row has 39 crates?

6. Marie is having a party. The first time the doorbell rings, three guests arrive. Each time the doorbell rings after that, a group arrives that has two more guests than the preceding group.

   a. How many guests arrive on the eighth ring?
   b. If the doorbell rings 10 times, how many guests are attending the party?

7. Ten people are attending a meeting. Each person shakes hands with each of the others exactly once. What is the total number of handshakes that are exchanged?

8. If you are allowed to make 3 straight cuts, you can cut a pie into 7 pieces when you make the cuts as shown at the right. What is the greatest number of pieces you can get if you are allowed to make 6 straight cuts?

review exercises

1. Cans of tennis balls cost $3.98 each. How many can you buy with $25?

2. Frank has three different pairs of slacks, three different shirts, and two different sweaters. How many different combinations of shirts and slacks can he make?

3. Mrs. Garcia bought $4\frac{1}{4}$ yd of fabric costing $8 per yard and $3\frac{7}{8}$ yd of fabric costing $5 per yard. Choose the letter of the best estimate of the amount she paid altogether.

   a. $20   b. $32
   c. $52   d. $100

SKILL REVIEW

Write a positive or negative number to represent each phrase.

1. 19 ft above sea level
2. a gain of $39
3. 5°F below zero **20-1**

Write the opposite of each number.

4. $^-13$
5. $^-10$
6. 4
7. $^-8$
8. 0

Find the absolute value of each number.

9. 4
10. 0
11. $^-9$
12. 12
13. $^-2$

Compare. Replace each __?__ with < or >.

14. $^-6$ __?__ 0
15. $^-8$ __?__ $^-2$
16. 1 __?__ $^-5$
17. $^-7$ __?__ 3
18. 0 __?__ 7
19. 4 __?__ $^-2$
20. $^-5$ __?__ $^-6$
21. $^-9$ __?__ $^-3$

Find each sum.

22. $^-12 + {}^-7$
23. $14 + {}^-8$
24. $6 + {}^-15$
25. $14 + 7$ **20-2**
26. $16 + 9$
27. $^-3 + 3$
28. $^-17 + 8$
29. $^-13 + {}^-9$

30. Bill lost 35 points during the first round of a game. He gained 15 points during the second round. What was his score at the end of the second round?

Find each difference.

31. $15 - {}^-5$
32. $8 - 17$
33. $0 - 6$
34. $0 - {}^-6$ **20-3**
35. $^-4 - {}^-11$
36. $^-9 - 12$
37. $^-7 - {}^-7$
38. $5 - {}^-5$

Find each product.

39. $^-7 \times 12$
40. $^-6 \times {}^-3$
41. $0 \times {}^-9$ **20-4**
42. $5 \times {}^-7$
43. $^-2 \times {}^-5 \times 3$
44. $6 \times {}^-4 \times 3$
45. $(^-2)^6$
46. $(^-3)^4$
47. $(^-5)^1$

Find each quotient.

48. $^-24 \div 6$
49. $^-48 \div {}^-6$
50. $0 \div {}^-7$
51. $54 \div 9$ **20-5**
52. $^-12 \div 0$
53. $21 \div {}^-3$
54. $35 \div 5$
55. $^-36 \div 6$

Solve.

56. The first row of a theater has 5 seats. Each succeeding row has 2 more seats than the row in front of it. There are 28 rows in all. How many seats are in the theater? **20-6**

20-7 TEMPERATURE

Temperature can be measured in degrees Fahrenheit (°F) or degrees Celsius (°C). The thermometers at the right show some common temperatures on the Fahrenheit and Celsius scales.

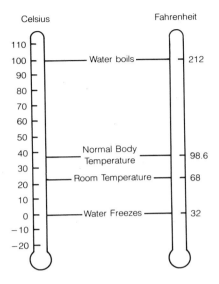

example

Select the more reasonable unit. Choose °F or °C.

a. The temperature of a glass of cold juice is about 40 __?__.

b. The air temperature on a warm summer day is about 30 __?__.

solution

a. °F   **b.** °C

exercises

Select the more reasonable unit. Choose °F or °C.

1. freezing point of water: 32 __?__
2. boiling point of water: 100 __?__
3. normal body temperature: 37 __?__
4. a cup of hot tea: 160 __?__
5. need to turn on the air conditioner: 26 __?__
6. need to turn on the heat: 60 __?__

Choose the temperature better suited to the given situation.

7. outdoor swimming
   a. 90°F   **b.** 90°C
8. water in a fish bowl
   a. 24°F   **b.** 24°C
9. making a snow sculpture
   a. ⁻1°F   **b.** ⁻1°C
10. a hot oven
    a. 350°F   **b.** 350°C

20-8 WIND-CHILL FACTOR

People often feel colder on a windy day because the moisture on their skin evaporates. The **wind-chill factor** is the temperature that results from a combination of actual air temperature and wind speed.

Wind-Chill Chart

Wind speed (mi/h)	Actual Air Temperature (°F)						
	⁻30	⁻20	⁻10	0	10	20	30
5	⁻36	⁻26	⁻15	⁻5	7	19	27
10	⁻58	⁻46	⁻34	⁻22	⁻9	3	16
15	⁻72	⁻58	⁻45	⁻31	⁻18	⁻5	9
20	⁻81	⁻67	⁻53	⁻39	⁻24	⁻10	4
25	⁻88	⁻74	⁻59	⁻44	⁻29	⁻15	1

example

The actual air temperature is 20°F. The wind speed is 25 mi/h.

a. Find the wind-chill factor.   **b.** How much colder does the wind make it feel?

solution

a. Read down the wind speed column to 25 mi/h. Read across to the column headed by 20°F. The wind-chill factor is ⁻15°F.

b. Subtract to find the difference:
20 − ⁻15 = 20 + 15 = 35
It feels 35°F colder due to the wind.

exercises

a. **Find the wind-chill factor for the given temperature and wind speed.**

b. **How much colder does the wind make it feel?**

1. 20°F, 20 mi/h   **2.** 10°F, 15 mi/h   **3.** ⁻10°F, 10 mi/h

Choose the set of conditions that would make you feel colder.

4. **a.** 20°F; 10 mi/h wind   **5.** **a.** 0°F; 15 mi/h wind
    b. 30°F; 20 mi/h wind   **b.** 10°F; 25 mi/h wind

6. The temperature is 20°F. The wind speed changes from 10 mi/h to 25 mi/h. How many degrees does the temperature seem to drop?

7. Suppose the wind speed is 20 mi/h and the actual air temperature is 15°F. Use the chart to estimate the wind-chill factor.

CHAPTER REVIEW

vocabulary vo·cab·u·lar·y

Choose the correct word to complete each sentence.

1. Numbers greater than zero are *(positive, negative)* numbers.
2. $|5|$ is read as "the *(opposite, absolute value)* of 5."
3. The numbers ..., ⁻2, ⁻1, 0, 1, 2, ... are called *(whole numbers, integers)*.
4. On a number line, the greater of two numbers is to the *(right, left)*.

skills

Write a positive or negative number to represent each phrase.

5. a loss of $38
6. 24°F above zero
7. a gain of $52
8. 5°C below zero

For each number, find:
a. **the opposite**   b. **the absolute value**

9. 14   10. ⁻17   11. ⁻20   12. 0   13. 22

Compare. Replace each __?__ with < or >.

14. 0 _?_ ⁻5   15. ⁻15 _?_ ⁻12   16. 6 _?_ ⁻10

Find each answer.

17. ⁻8 + 14   18. ⁻7 − 10   19. 13 − ⁻9   20. ⁻5 × 11
21. (⁻7)³   22. ⁻39 ÷ ⁻3   23. ⁻4 × ⁻15   24. 9 + ⁻9
25. 8 − ⁻8   26. 42 ÷ ⁻7   27. 6 × ⁻6   28. (⁻8)²
29. 25 ÷ 0   30. 12 − 15   31. ⁻56 ÷ 8   32. 17 + ⁻8

Solve.

33. The temperature at 1:00 A.M. was ⁻11°F. By 1:00 P.M. the temperature had risen 19°F. What was the temperature at 1:00 P.M.?
34. Find the sum: 3 + 5 + 7 + · · · + 95 + 97 + 99
35. Water freezes at 32°F. Mercury freezes at ⁻38°F. Find the difference between these two temperatures.
36. Use the chart on page 460. The actual air temperature is 0°F. The wind speed is 15 mi/h. Find the wind-chill factor.

CHAPTER TEST

Write a positive or negative number to represent each phrase.

1. a dive of 52 m
2. an increase of $44
3. a rise of 47 ft
4. a drop of 23°F

20-1

Write the opposite of each number.

5. 2   6. 0   7. 16   8. $^-15$ 9. $^-18$

Find the absolute value of each number.

10. 7   11. 0   12. 23   13. $^-10$ 14. $^-14$

Compare. Replace each _?_ with < or >.

15. $^-8$ _?_ $^-10$ 16. 2 _?_ $^-7$ 17. $^-4$ _?_ 0   18. $^-9$ _?_ 5

Find each sum.

19. $^-13 + {^-6}$ 20. $^-8 + 16$ 21. $9 + {^-15}$ 22. $^-5 + 5$ **20-2**

Find each difference.

23. $^-3 - {^-3}$ 24. $^-11 - 4$ 25. $5 - 17$ 26. $9 - {^-6}$ **20-3**

Find each product.

27. $^-8 \times {^-5}$ 28. $6 \times {^-9}$ 29. $(^-5)^4$ 30. $^-7 \times 4$ **20-4**

Find each quotient.

31. $^-16 \div {^-2}$ 32. $0 \div {^-3}$

33. $18 \div {^-6}$ 34. $14 \div 0$

20-5

Solve.

35. Find the sum: $3 + 5 + 7 + \cdots + 995 + 997 + 999$ **20-6**

36. In a store display, cans of tomatoes are stacked so that the bottom row has 15 cans. Each row above has 2 fewer cans than the row below. The top row has one can. How many cans are there in the display?

37. The average winter temperature at the North Pole is $^-30°F$. The average summer temperature is 50°F. Find the difference between these two temperatures.   **20-7**

38. Use the chart on page 460. The actual air temperature is $^-20°F$. The wind speed is 10 mi/h. Find the wind-chill factor.   **20-8**

A rock climber must possess a good sense of balance. In solving an equation, too, it is important to keep the two sides in balance.

CHAPTER 21

SOLVING EQUATIONS

463

21-1 SOLVING EQUATIONS: ADDITION AND SUBTRACTION

An **equation** is a statement that two numbers or quantities are equal. A **solution** of an equation involving one variable is a value of the variable that makes the equation true.

To **solve** an equation, you must get the variable alone on one *side* of the equals sign. You do this by using *inverse operations* to "undo" the operations in the equation.

To solve an equation that involves addition or subtraction, use the following method.

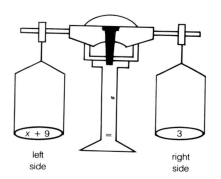

If *a number has been added* to the variable, *you subtract* that number from both sides.

If *a number has been subtracted* from the variable, *you add* that number to both sides.

example 1

Solve: $x + 9 = 3$

$$x + 9 = 3$$
$$x + 9 - 9 = 3 - 9 \quad \longleftarrow \text{Subtract 9 from both sides.}$$
$$x = {}^-6 \quad \longleftarrow \text{The solution is } {}^-6.$$

Check:

$$x + 9 = 3 \quad \longleftarrow \text{original equation}$$
$${}^-6 + 9 \overset{?}{=} 3 \quad \longleftarrow \text{Replace } x \text{ with } {}^-6.$$
$$3 = 3 \checkmark$$

your turn

Solve each equation. Check your answers.

1. $b + 42 = 80$
2. $53 = x + 14$
3. $32 + y = {}^-14$
4. ${}^-15 = z + 35$

example 2

Solve: ${}^-15 = c - 6$

$${}^-15 = c - 6$$
$${}^-15 + 6 = c - 6 + 6 \quad \longleftarrow \text{Add 6 to both sides.}$$
$${}^-9 = c \quad \longleftarrow \text{The solution is } {}^-9.$$

Check:

$${}^-15 = c - 6 \quad \longleftarrow \text{original equation}$$
$${}^-15 \overset{?}{=} {}^-9 - 6 \quad \longleftarrow \text{Replace } c \text{ with } {}^-9.$$
$${}^-15 = {}^-15 \checkmark$$

your turn

Solve each equation. Check your answers.

5. $c - 36 = 15$
6. $64 = x - 9$
7. $b - 8 = {}^-14$
8. ${}^-24 = y - 12$

practice *exercises*

practice for example 1 (page 464)

Solve each equation. Check your answers.

1. $27 = b + 37$
2. $a + 15 = 52$
3. $x + 19 = 31$
4. $n + 26 = 14$
5. $25 + c = {}^-36$
6. $^-49 = x + 36$

practice for example 2 (page 464)

Solve each equation. Check your answers.

7. $b - 15 = 7$
8. $n - 8 = 4$
9. $16 = x - 13$
10. $^-4 = n - 3$
11. $m - 25 = {}^-30$
12. $n - 16 = {}^-12$

mixed practice (page 464)

Solve each equation. Check your answers.

13. $n + 7 = {}^-6$
14. $24 = m - 7$
15. $^-3 = x + 16$
16. $9 + c = {}^-14$
17. $m - 16 = 24$
18. $x - 8 = {}^-3$
19. $54 = x + 37$
20. $n - 15 = 21$
21. $k - 25 = {}^-25$
22. $b - 6 = {}^-9$
23. $14 = x - 8$
24. $n - 16 = {}^-14$
25. $^-37 = 53 + b$
26. $y - 32 = 0$
27. $x - 12 = 12$
28. $^-9 = x + 6$
29. $m - 15 = {}^-8$
30. $36 + a = 12$

review *exercises*

Write the reciprocal of each number.

1. $\frac{3}{4}$
2. $\frac{1}{5}$
3. 6
4. 1
5. $\frac{8}{7}$
6. $2\frac{2}{3}$

Find each product or quotient.

7. $^-8 \times 2$
8. $^-4 \times {}^-11$
9. 7×13
10. $9 \times {}^-12$
11. $72 \div {}^-9$
12. $^-64 \div 8$
13. $75 \div 5$
14. $^-110 \div {}^-2$

Evaluate each expression when $x = 12$ and $y = {}^-6$.

15. ^-3x
16. ^-4y
17. $\frac{x}{-2}$
18. $\frac{y}{-3}$

19. A wall tile weighs $\frac{3}{8}$ lb. How much would 100 tiles weigh?
20. A recipe calls for $\frac{3}{4}$ c of chopped celery. If you wanted to triple the recipe, how many cups of chopped celery would you need?

Solving Equations 465

21-2 SOLVING EQUATIONS: MULTIPLICATION AND DIVISION

Ed is buying a stereo for $756. He will pay for it in 12 equal payments. Ed uses the equation $12n = 756$ to find that each payment will be $63.

$$12n = 756$$
$$\frac{12n}{12} = \frac{756}{12}$$
$$n = 63$$

　　When you solve multiplication or division equations, you again use *inverse operations*. To solve an equation involving multiplication or division, use the following method.

If *the variable has been multiplied* by a number, *you divide* both sides by that number.

If *the variable has been divided* by a number, *you multiply* both sides by that number.

example 1

Solve: $^-3a = 114$

$$^-3a = 114$$
$$\frac{^-3a}{^-3} = \frac{114}{^-3}$$ ⬅ **Divide both sides by $^-3$.**
$$a = {}^-38$$ ⬅ **The solution is $^-38$.**

Check: $^-3a = 114$ ⬅ **original equation**
$$^-3(^-38) \overset{?}{=} 114$$ ⬅ **Replace a with $^-38$.**
$$114 = 114 \checkmark$$

your turn

Solve each equation. Check your answers.

1. $8n = 144$　　　　**2.** $78 = 2x$　　　　**3.** $^-3n = 57$　　　　**4.** $^-64 = {}^-4c$

example 2

Solve: $\frac{x}{4} = 11$

$$\frac{x}{4} = 11$$
$$4 \cdot \frac{x}{4} = 4 \cdot 11$$ ⬅ **Multiply both sides by 4.**
$$x = 44$$ ⬅ **The solution is 44.**

Check: $\frac{x}{4} = 11$ ⬅ **original equation**
$$\frac{44}{4} \overset{?}{=} 11$$ ⬅ **Replace x with 44.**
$$11 = 11 \checkmark$$

your turn

Solve each equation. Check your answers.

5. $\frac{c}{2} = 8$　　　　**6.** $13 = \frac{n}{5}$　　　　**7.** $\frac{x}{^-6} = 9$　　　　**8.** $^-7 = \frac{a}{^-8}$

In some equations, the variable is multiplied by a fraction. To solve these equations, you *multiply both sides by the reciprocal* of the fraction.

example 3

Solve: $\frac{3}{4}x = 18$

$\frac{3}{4}x = 18$

$\frac{4}{3} \cdot \frac{3}{4}x = \frac{4}{3} \cdot 18$ ⟵ **Multiply both sides by** $\frac{4}{3}$.

$1 \cdot x = 24$

$x = 24$ ⟵ **The solution is 24.**

Check: $\quad \frac{3}{4}x = 18$ ⟵ **original equation**

$\frac{3}{4}(24) \stackrel{?}{=} 18$ ⟵ **Replace x with 24.**

$18 = 18 \checkmark$

your turn

Solve each equation. Check your answers.

9. $\frac{2}{5}y = 6$ **10.** $9 = \frac{3}{4}c$ **11.** $\frac{3}{8}n = {}^{-}24$ **12.** $^{-}16 = \frac{1}{5}x$

practice exercises

practice for example 1 (page 466)

Solve each equation. Check your answers.

1. $5a = {}^{-}30$ **2.** $7n = 42$ **3.** $^{-}36 = {}^{-}2y$ **4.** $32 = {}^{-}8y$

5. $3x = {}^{-}75$ **6.** $^{-}5b = {}^{-}45$ **7.** $^{-}63 = 9n$ **8.** $51 = 3y$

practice for example 2 (page 466)

Solve each equation. Check your answers.

9. $10 = \frac{b}{5}$ **10.** $^{-}20 = \frac{c}{7}$ **11.** $\frac{a}{^{-}4} = 16$ **12.** $\frac{c}{3} = 28$

13. $\frac{w}{^{-}3} = {}^{-}12$ **14.** $\frac{a}{^{-}6} = {}^{-}15$ **15.** $24 = \frac{x}{4}$ **16.** $^{-}31 = \frac{b}{2}$

practice for example 3 (page 467)

Solve each equation. Check your answers.

17. $\frac{4}{5}c = {}^{-}12$ **18.** $\frac{2}{7}m = 14$ **19.** $^{-}24 = \frac{2}{3}a$ **20.** $7 = \frac{1}{9}b$

21. $^{-}15 = \frac{5}{6}y$ **22.** $24 = \frac{3}{7}m$ **23.** $\frac{1}{3}z = {}^{-}18$ **24.** $\frac{3}{4}x = {}^{-}12$

Solve each equation. Check your answers.

25. $^-10c = ^-30$
26. $^-28 = \frac{n}{3}$
27. $\frac{3}{4}y = ^-24$
28. $\frac{1}{5}x = ^-21$

29. $^-5n = ^-210$
30. $\frac{b}{2} = ^-19$
31. $120 = \frac{n}{4}$
32. $9y = 9$

33. $^-3n = 0$
34. $16x = ^-16$
35. $^-36 = \frac{3}{5}b$
36. $\frac{n}{5} = 0$

37. $\frac{x}{^-3} = 55$
38. $\frac{n}{2} = ^-30$
39. $2n = ^-30$
40. $^-3n = ^-57$

41. $^-14k = ^-14$
42. $0 = 7n$
43. $\frac{1}{5}y = 6$
44. $5b = 115$

45. $^-20 = \frac{n}{^-4}$
46. $^-3n = 111$
47. $\frac{c}{^-9} = ^-45$
48. $\frac{2}{5}y = ^-18$

review exercises

Evaluate each expression when $a = 16$ and $b = ^-8$.

1. $2a + 1$
2. $2b + 1$
3. $3b - 1$
4. $5a - 1$

5. $\frac{a}{4} + 7$
6. $\frac{b}{4} + 7$
7. $\frac{a}{2} - 10$
8. $\frac{b}{2} - 6$

9. Mount Everest is 29,028 ft high. Mount McKinley is 20,320 ft high. Mount Whitney is 14,495 ft high. How much higher is Mount Everest than Mount Whitney?

10. Ellen earns $375 per week. How much does she earn in a year?

mental math

You can use mental math two ways to solve simple equations.
Solve $2a = ^-6$.
Think: $2 \times ^-3 = ^-6$, so $a = ^-3$ or   *Think:* $^-6 \div 2 = ^-3$, so $a = ^-3$.

Use mental math to solve.

1. $\frac{c}{2} = 6$
2. $\frac{x}{5} = ^-10$
3. $\frac{a}{^-2} = ^-5$
4. $\frac{s}{^-3} = 6$

5. $4n = 36$
6. $3y = ^-12$
7. $^-5m = 20$
8. $^-2g = ^-24$

9. $r + 9 = 11$
10. $b + ^-2 = ^-10$
11. $n + ^-3 = ^-9$
12. $8 + x = 20$

13. $k - 5 = 2$
14. $t - 8 = ^-8$
15. $d + 5 = ^-5$
16. $s - 2 = ^-3$

21-3 SOLVING TWO-STEP EQUATIONS

Many equations involve two operations. To solve these equations you first undo any addition or subtraction. Then you undo any multiplication or division. Use the following method to solve these equations.

1. Add the same number to or subtract the same number from both sides.
2. Multiply or divide both sides by the same nonzero number.

example 1

Solve: $^-3n + 10 = 64$

$$^-3n + 10 = 64$$
$$^-3n + 10 - 10 = 64 - 10 \longleftarrow \text{ Subtract 10 from both sides.}$$
$$^-3n = 54$$
$$\frac{^-3n}{^-3} = \frac{54}{^-3} \longleftarrow \text{ Divide both sides by } ^-3.$$
$$n = ^-18 \longleftarrow \text{ The solution is } ^-18.$$

Check: $^-3n + 10 = 64$
$$^-3(^-18) + 10 \stackrel{?}{=} 64$$
$$54 + 10 \stackrel{?}{=} 64$$
$$64 = 64 \checkmark$$

your turn

Solve each equation. Check your answers.

1. $2a + 9 = 25$

2. $59 = ^-4x + 7$

3. $6x - 2 = ^-14$

example 2

Solve: $\frac{x}{3} + 5 = 12$

$$\frac{x}{3} + 5 = 12$$
$$\frac{x}{3} + 5 - 5 = 12 - 5 \longleftarrow \text{ Subtract 5 from both sides.}$$
$$\frac{x}{3} = 7$$
$$3 \cdot \frac{x}{3} = 3 \cdot 7 \longleftarrow \text{ Multiply both sides by 3.}$$
$$x = 21 \longleftarrow \text{ The solution is 21.}$$

Check: $\frac{x}{3} + 5 = 12$
$$\frac{21}{3} + 5 \stackrel{?}{=} 12$$
$$7 + 5 \stackrel{?}{=} 12$$
$$12 = 12 \checkmark$$

your turn

Solve each equation. Check your answers.

4. $\frac{x}{3} - 2 = 10$

5. $\frac{n}{5} + 7 = 4$

6. $^-12 = \frac{b}{2} - 5$

example 3

Solve: $\frac{2}{3}x + 7 = {}^-13$

$$\frac{2}{3}x + 7 = {}^-13$$

$$\frac{2}{3}x + 7 - 7 = {}^-13 - 7 \longleftarrow \text{Subtract 7 from both sides.}$$

$$\frac{2}{3}x = {}^-20$$

$$\frac{3}{2} \cdot \frac{2}{3}x = \frac{3}{2}({}^-20) \longleftarrow \text{Multiply both sides by } \frac{3}{2}.$$

$$x = {}^-30 \longleftarrow \text{The solution is } {}^-30.$$

Check:
$$\frac{2}{3}x + 7 = {}^-13$$
$$\frac{2}{3}({}^-30) + 7 \stackrel{?}{=} {}^-13$$
$$^-20 + 7 \stackrel{?}{=} {}^-13$$
$$^-13 = {}^-13 \checkmark$$

your turn

Solve each equation. Check your answers.

7. $\frac{3}{4}x + 7 = 22$

8. $\frac{5}{6}z - 5 = {}^-30$

9. $^-9 = \frac{2}{5}c + 11$

practice exercises

practice for example 1 *(page 469)*

Solve each equation. Check your answers.

1. $7c + 8 = 50$

2. $^-7 = 2x + 9$

3. $8n - 7 = 41$

4. $27 = 4c - 5$

5. $39 = {}^-5b + 9$

6. $^-6n - 7 = 23$

practice for example 2 *(page 469)*

Solve each equation. Check your answers.

7. $\frac{y}{4} + 7 = 13$

8. $24 = \frac{n}{2} - 8$

9. $^-12 = \frac{c}{4} - 6$

10. $\frac{b}{5} + 6 = {}^-9$

11. $\frac{x}{3} - 7 = {}^-15$

12. $^-8 = \frac{z}{5} + 4$

practice for example 3 *(page 470)*

Solve each equation. Check your answers.

13. $\frac{2}{3}n - 5 = 11$

14. $\frac{3}{4}y + 6 = {}^-12$

15. $^-24 = \frac{2}{5}x - 4$

16. $^-13 = \frac{7}{8}n - 6$

17. $\frac{4}{5}z + 4 = {}^-12$

18. $12 = \frac{3}{7}x - 9$

mixed practice (pages 469–470)

Solve each equation. Check your answers.

19. $^-5n - 1 = {}^-21$ **20.** $^-5x - 2 = 18$ **21.** $^-15 = 5n + 20$

22. $60 = \frac{4}{7}x + 8$ **23.** $\frac{c}{4} + 8 = 12$ **24.** $\frac{y}{2} + 4 = 18$

25. $30 = {}^-6n - 12$ **26.** $100 = 4c + 16$ **27.** $^-10 = {}^-2n - 18$

28. $^-6m - 15 = {}^-45$ **29.** $\frac{5}{6}n + 7 = {}^-33$ **30.** $\frac{y}{3} + 4 = {}^-15$

review *exercises*

Find each answer.

1. 3^4 **2.** 7^3 **3.** 4^2 **4.** $2^3 \times 3^4$ **5.** $5^2 \times 9^1$ **6.** $3^0 \times 6^3$

7. Lee bought 24 sheets of plywood at \$2.59 each and 8 two-by-fours at \$1.79 each. How much did Lee spend altogether?

8. Dana's monthly auto expenses are \$198 for an auto loan, \$78 for gas, \$35 for insurance, and \$20 for maintenance. How much does Dana spend for auto expenses each year?

calculator corner

You can solve equations with greater numbers by using a calculator.

example   Solve: $12x + 16 = 340$

solution $12x + 16 - 16 = 340 - 16$ ⬅ **Use a calculator to subtract.**

$$\frac{12x}{12} = \frac{324}{12}$$ ⬅ **Use a calculator to divide.**

$$x = 27$$ ⬅ **The solution is 27.**

Solve each equation by using a calculator.

1. $3x + 73 = 214$ **2.** $m + 764 = 1128$ **3.** $^-4b - 44 = 244$

4. $c - 67 = {}^-913$ **5.** $5x - 20 = 80$ **6.** $12x = {}^-372$

For each equation, tell whether you would solve using *mental math* or a *calculator*. Then solve.

7. $\frac{x}{2} + 9 = 9$ **8.** $\frac{x}{25} - 19 = 28$ **9.** $\frac{z}{^-10} = 8$

10. $4z + 2 = 6$ **11.** $a + 89 = 28$ **12.** $5n = 50$

21-4 USING EQUATIONS

You can solve some word problems by using an equation. To use this strategy, you must first choose a variable to represent the unknown number. You then use this variable to write an equation that represents the facts of the problem.

example

Rosario bought a computer system for $989. He made a $149 down payment and paid the remaining amount in 7 equal payments. What was the amount of each payment?

solution

Step 1   Given: $989 total cost
$149 down payment
7 equal payments

Find: amount of each payment

Step 2   Write an equation to show that the sum of the 7 equal payments and the $149 down payment is $989. Let the variable n represent the unknown amount of each payment.

7	times	amount of each payment	plus	$149	is	$989
↓	↓	↓	↓	↓	↓	↓
7	×	n	+	149	=	989

Step 3 $7n + 149 = 989$ ◄── Subtract 149 from both sides.
$7n = 840$ ◄── Divide both sides by 7.
$n = 120$ ◄── The solution is 120.

Step 4   *Check:* $7(120) + 149 \stackrel{?}{=} 989$ ◄── Replace n with 120.
$840 + 149 \stackrel{?}{=} 989$
$989 = 989 \checkmark$

Each payment was $120.

problems

Solve by using an equation.

1. Manuel earned $176 last week. If he earned $58 on the weekend, how much did he earn on the weekdays?

2. Martha loaned 19 records to friends. If she has 64 records left, how many records did she have before she loaned some to her friends?

3. A computer printer prints 9 pages in one minute. How long will it take to print 126 pages?

4. Leon made 4 equal payments for a magazine subscription. If each payment was $12, how much did the magazine subscription cost?

5. Rachel pays her auto insurance in 7 equal payments of $53 each. How much does Rachel pay for auto insurance?

6. Lee Ann jogs the same number of miles on each of 6 days. The other day of the week she jogs 8 mi. If Lee Ann jogs 44 mi each week, how many miles does she jog on each of the other 6 days?

7. Doris bought 4 bags of fertilizer and one bag of grass seed. The bag of grass seed weighs 20 lb. If the total weight of the grass seed and the fertilizer is 160 lb, how much does each bag of fertilizer weigh?

8. At 5:00 A.M. the temperature was ⁻7°F. The temperature rose an equal number of degrees each hour for the next 8 h until it reached 17°F. What was the number of degrees that the temperature rose each hour?

review exercises

1. Bill bought 4 cups of yogurt at $.59 each and 2 packages of cheese at $1.69 each. How much did Bill pay altogether?

2. Sally has 220 marbles. She puts the same number of marbles in each of 6 jars. If she has 4 marbles left, how many marbles are there in each jar?

3. Marty sleeps 8 h each day. On school days, he spends 6 h at school and 2 h doing homework. How many hours in a seven-day week does he have for other activities?

4. On January 1 Deana deposits 1¢ in her savings bank. Each day after that she plans to deposit 2¢ more than she did on the preceding day. What is the total amount that she plans to deposit in January?

5. Millie earns $1955 each month. How much does Millie earn in a year?

21-5 THE COORDINATE PLANE

The grid at the right is a **coordinate plane.** The *horizontal* number line is the **x-axis.** The *vertical* number line is the **y-axis.** The *axes* meet at point *O*, which is called the **origin.**

Any point on a coordinate plane can be assigned an **ordered pair** of numbers. The *first* number of an ordered pair is the **x-coordinate.** The *second* number is the **y-coordinate.** The origin has coordinates (0, 0).

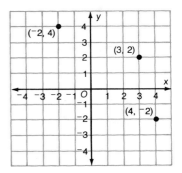

example 1

Give the coordinates of each point.

a. *A*　　　**b.** *B*

solution

a. Start at the origin. Point *A* is 1 unit right (positive) and 3 units up (positive). The coordinates are (1, 3).

b. Start at the origin. Point *B* is 2 units left (negative) and 3 units down (negative). The coordinates are ($^-$2, $^-$3).

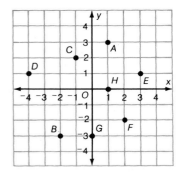

your turn

Give the coordinates of each point.

1. *C*　　　　**2.** *D*　　　　**3.** *E*　　　　**4.** *F*　　　　**5.** *G*　　　　**6.** *H*

The point *R* with coordinates (3, $^-$4) can be represented by *R*(3, $^-$4).

example 2

Graph *R*(3, $^-$4) on a coordinate plane.

solution

Start at the origin. Move 3 units to the right on the *x*-axis. Then move 4 units down.

your turn

Graph each point on a coordinate plane.

7. *T*(6, $^-$3)　　　**8.** *U*($^-$4, $^-$1)　　　**9.** *V*(2, 0)　　　**10.** *W*($^-$3, 6)

practice *exercises*

practice for example 1 (page 474)

Give the coordinates of each point.

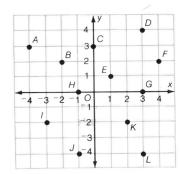

1. A
2. B
3. C
4. D
5. E
6. F
7. G
8. H
9. I
10. J
11. K
12. L

practice for example 2 (page 474)

Graph each point on a coordinate plane.

13. $M(5, 4)$
14. $N(^-3, 5)$
15. $O(0, 0)$
16. $P(5, ^-3)$
17. $Q(0, ^-2)$
18. $R(4, 1)$
19. $S(^-1, ^-5)$
20. $T(^-4, 6)$

mixed practice (page 474)

Match each location to the correct ordered pair.

21. 8 units right, 3 units down
22. 7 units left
23. 8 units right, 3 units up
24. 7 units down
25. 8 units left, 3 units down
26. 7 units right
27. 8 units left, 3 units up
28. 7 units up

A. $(0, 7)$
B. $(7, 0)$
C. $(8, 3)$
D. $(^-8, ^-3)$
E. $(^-7, 0)$
F. $(0, ^-7)$
G. $(^-8, 3)$
H. $(8, ^-3)$

29. Suzanne bicycled 5 blocks west, 8 blocks north, 11 blocks east, and 4 blocks south. If Suzanne's starting point is considered to be the origin, what are her final coordinates?

30. Doris drove 3 mi north from her house. She then drove 2 mi east, 6 mi south, 5 mi west, 3 mi north, and 3 mi east. If Doris's house is the origin, what are her final coordinates?

review *exercises*

Evaluate each expression when $x = ^-8$, $y = 2$, and $z = 4$.

1. xy
2. yz
3. xz
4. xyz
5. $\dfrac{x}{y}$
6. $\dfrac{x}{z}$
7. $\dfrac{0}{x}$
8. $\dfrac{yz}{x}$

21-6 GRAPHING EQUATIONS

Some equations contain two variables. A **solution** of such an equation is any ordered pair of values of the variables that makes the equation true.

example 1

Find three solutions of $y = 3x + 2$. Use $^-2$, 0, 2 as values for x.

solution

x	y = 3x + 2	y	solution
$^-2$	$y = 3(^-2) + 2$	$^-4$	$(^-2, ^-4)$
0	$y = 3(0) + 2$	2	$(0, 2)$
2	$y = 3(2) + 2$	8	$(2, 8)$

← Make a table of ordered pairs.

your turn

Find three solutions of each equation. Use $^-2$, 0, 2 as values for x.

1. $y = 2x + 5$ **2.** $y = {}^-4x + 7$ **3.** $y = {}^-3x - 4$

The **graph of an equation** is all points whose coordinates are solutions of the equation. To graph an equation like $y = 3x + 2$, use the following method.

1. Make a table of ordered pairs.
2. Graph the ordered pairs as points on a coordinate plane.
3. Connect the points with a straight line.

example 2

Graph the equation $y = 2x + 1$.

solution

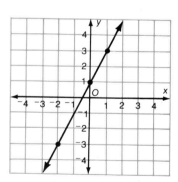

x	y = 2x + 1	y	solution
$^-2$	$y = 2(^-2) + 1$	$^-3$	$(^-2, ^-3)$
0	$y = 2(0) + 1$	1	$(0, 1)$
1	$y = 2(1) + 1$	3	$(1, 3)$

← Choose $^-2$, 0, 1 as values for x.

your turn

Graph each equation.

4. $y = 4x + 1$ **5.** $y = 3x - 1$ **6.** $y = {}^-2x + 4$

practice exercises

practice for example 1 *(page 476)*

Find three solutions of each equation. Use ⁻2, 0, 2, as values for x.

1. $y = 3x + 5$
2. $y = x - 9$
3. $y = 5x + 3$
4. $y = {}^-2x + 1$
5. $y = {}^-4x - 6$
6. $y = {}^-5x - 4$

practice for example 2 *(page 476)*

Graph each equation.

7. $y = 4x - 2$
8. $y = x + 4$
9. $y = 5x + 2$
10. $y = {}^-3x + 3$
11. $y = {}^-2x - 1$
12. $y = {}^-3x + 1$

mixed practice *(page 476)*

Graph each equation using the given values of x.

13. $y = 2x - 4$; ⁻3, ⁻1, 0, 1, 3
14. $y = x - 3$; 2, 4, 6, 8, 10
15. $y = {}^-4x + 2$; ⁻2, ⁻1, 0, 1, 2
16. $y = {}^-3x - 1$; ⁻1, 0, 1, 2, 3
17. $y = \frac{x}{2} + 5$; ⁻4, ⁻2, 0, 2, 4
18. $y = \frac{2}{3}x + 4$; ⁻9, ⁻6, ⁻3, 0, 3

review exercises

Solve each equation.

1. $50t = 400$
2. $360 = 12w$
3. $41 = m - 19$
4. $2l + 48 = 120$
5. $\frac{h}{2} = 28$
6. $4s = {}^-64$
7. $x + 180 = 98$
8. $5 = \frac{n}{3} - 10$

9. Bill earns $8.50 per hour. He works 8 h each day. If Bill works 5 days each week, how much does he earn each week?

10. Marita bought a skirt for $18.95 and 2 T-shirts for $6.75 each. She gave the sales clerk a $50 bill. What was the amount of change that she received?

Puzzle Corner

Raymond ate 100 grapes in 5 days. Each day he ate 6 more grapes than the day before. How many grapes did he eat on each of the 5 days?

SKILL REVIEW

Solve each equation. Check your answers.

1. $x + 19 = 41$
2. $13 = z + 27$
3. $14 + c = {}^-11$ **21-1**
4. $y - 12 = 14$
5. $a - 15 = {}^-8$
6. ${}^-24 = m - 19$

7. $3x = 51$
8. ${}^-5y = {}^-85$
9. ${}^-84 = 7z$ **21-2**

10. $\frac{c}{6} = 14$
11. $21 = \frac{3}{4}a$
12. $\frac{n}{3} = {}^-17$

13. $4y + 15 = {}^-5$
14. $3z + 11 = 47$
15. $41 = 6a - 13$ **21-3**

16. $\frac{m}{7} + 20 = 9$
17. $3 = \frac{n}{9} - 8$
18. $\frac{3}{5}x + 17 = 2$

Solve by using an equation.

19. A photocopy machine makes 8 copies in one minute. How many   **21-4** minutes will it take to make 96 copies?

20. Lisa bought 6 cases of computer paper. She also bought $13 worth of other office supplies. If the total bill was $121, what was the cost of each case of computer paper?

Use the coordinate plane at the right.
Give the coordinates of each point.

21. A
22. B
23. C
24. D
25. E
26. F

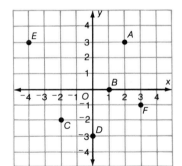

21-5

Graph each point on a coordinate plane.

27. $R(5, 4)$
28. $S({}^-3, {}^-1)$
29. $T(4, 0)$
30. $U(0, {}^-5)$

Find three solutions of each equation.
Use ${}^-2, 0, 2$ as values for x.

31. $y = 2x + 1$
32. $y = 4x + 3$
33. $y = 3x - 2$ **21-6**
34. $y = 5x - 4$
35. $y = {}^-2x + 5$
36. $y = {}^-3x - 1$

Graph each equation.

37. $y = {}^-3x - 4$
38. $y = {}^-2x + 3$
39. $y = {}^-4x - 5$
40. $y = 2x + 2$
41. $y = 4x$
42. $y = x - 3$

21-7 USING FORMULAS

A **formula** is an equation that describes a relationship between two or more quantities. Often each quantity is represented by a variable. The variable used is often the first letter of the word it represents. For example, we often use the following formula for distance.

$$\text{Distance} = \text{rate} \times \text{time}$$
$$D = r \times t$$
$$D = rt$$

You can use what you know about solving equations to work with formulas.

example

How long will it take an airplane traveling at 800 km/h to travel 2800 km?

solution

Write the formula for distance and replace the variables with the numbers they represent.

$$D = rt$$

Replace D with 2800. ➡ $2800 = 800t$ ⬅ **Replace r with 800.**

$$\frac{2800}{800} = \frac{800t}{800}$$ ⬅ **Divide both sides by 800.**

$$3.5 = t$$

It will take 3.5 h for the plane to travel 2800 km.

exercises

1. A cyclist traveled 80 mi at a rate of 20 mi/h. How long did it take?

2. It took Lyle 2.4 h to hike 18 km. How fast was he walking?

3. Elizabeth drove 135 mi in 2.5 h. How fast was she driving?

4. A cheetah can run at a maximum rate of 70 mi/h. If a cheetah could run 7 mi at this rate, how long would it take?

The chart shows some familiar formulas.

Formula in Words	Symbols
interest = principal × rate × time	$I = Prt$
amount financed = cash price − down payment	$F = c - d$
cost = number of items × price per item	$C = np$
batting average = $\frac{\text{hits}}{\text{at bats}}$	$avg = \frac{h}{b}$
miles per gallon = $\frac{\text{miles}}{\text{gallons}}$	$mi/gal = \frac{mi}{gal}$

Use the chart above. Solve.

5. Pat buys 12 buttons at $.19 each. How much does she spend for the buttons?

6. Nader Hassan drove 300 mi and used 12.5 gal of gasoline. How many miles did he average per gallon of gasoline?

7. Karina hopes to earn $900 interest on her $5000 investment in the next three years. What interest rate must she get?

8. How long would it take $800 invested at a 6% interest rate to earn $192 in interest?

9. In one season, Rosco Hobson had a batting average of 0.300. Rosco was at bat 540 times. Find the number of hits he had.

10. A car with a 25-gal gas tank gets 13 mi/gal. How far can the car go on a full tank of gas?

11. Luke Van Hoven has $25. How many paperback books can he buy at $6.25 apiece?

12. Harriet Hosmer had 122 hits in 425 times at bat. Find her batting average, rounded to the nearest thousandth.

13. Sherry bought 12 pens for $21.48. Find the price of one pen.

14. Gary Stevens bought a house for $121,000. His down payment was $56,000. How much did he finance?

15. Max earned $495 in interest in 2 years. His interest rate was 5.5%. Find the amount he invested.

16. A jumbo jet traveling at 600 mi/h can complete the trip from New York to London in 5.8 h.

    a. Find the air distance from New York to London.

    b. The Concorde travels at 1340 mi/h. Find the time for the Concorde to travel from New York to London. Round to the nearest tenth of an hour.

21-8 LONGITUDE AND LATITUDE

We use **longitude** and **latitude** to locate points on Earth's surface.

Lines of longitude run north and south. Longitude is measured in degrees east (E) or west (W) of the **prime meridian.**

Lines of latitude run east and west, parallel to the **equator.** Latitude is measured in degrees north (N) or south (S) of the equator.

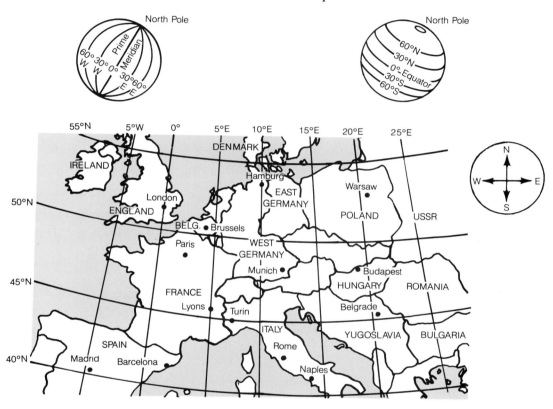

example 1

To estimate the longitude and latitude of Paris, France, look at the map.
Longitude: Paris is between 0° and 5°E. The longitude is about 2°E.
Latitude: Paris is between 45°N and 50°N. The latitude is about 48°N.
Paris is located at about 2°E longitude, 48°N latitude.

your turn

Estimate the longitude and latitude of each city.

1. Rome, Italy

2. Madrid, Spain

example 2

To find which country contains the point 3°W longitude, 52°N latitude, start at the prime meridian and move west about 3°.
Move up a bit past the 50°N line to about 52°N.
The point 3°W longitude, 52°N latitude is in England.

your turn

Use the map on page 481. Find the country in which each point is located.

3. 20°E longitude, 47°N latitude

4. 7°W longitude, 53°N latitude

practice exercises

practice for example 1 (page 481)

Use the map on page 481. Estimate the longitude and latitude of each city.

1. Turin, Italy

2. Lyons, France

3. Brussels, Belgium

4. Warsaw, Poland

5. London, England

6. Budapest, Hungary

practice for example 2 (page 482)

Use the map on page 481. Find the country in which each point is located.

7. 5°W longitude, 42°N latitude

8. 20°E longitude, 51°N latitude

9. 8°E longitude, 57°N latitude

10. 3°E longitude, 48°N latitude

mixed practice (pages 481–482)

Use the globes and the map on page 481.

11. Which is farther north?
   a. Belgrade, Yugoslavia
   b. 2°E longitude, 44°N latitude

12. Which is closer to the prime meridian?
   a. Munich, West Germany
   b. 20°E longitude, 45°N latitude

13. Which is farther south?
   a. 20°W longitude, 60°S latitude
   b. 70°E longitude, 22°S latitude

14. Use a globe or map to estimate the latitude and longitude of your community. Find cities in two other countries that are on the same line of latitude as your community.

CHAPTER REVIEW

vocabulary vo·cab·u·lar·y

Choose the correct word to complete each sentence.

1. A(n) (*solution, equation*) is a statement that two numbers or quantities are equal.
2. On a coordinate plane, the vertical number line is the (*x-axis, y-axis*).
3. The first number in an ordered pair is the (*x-coordinate, y-coordinate*).
4. On a coordinate plane, the axes meet at the (*origin, coordinate*).

skills

Solve each equation. Check your answers.

5. $x - 14 = 3$

6. $19 = z + 5$

7. $3a = 57$

8. $\frac{c}{8} = 6$

9. $^-3y + 17 = 8$

10. $5d = {}^-65$

11. $\frac{3}{4}c = {}^-36$

12. $x - 11 = {}^-25$

13. $27 = {}^-2y + 11$

14. $\frac{z}{4} = {}^-16$

15. $^-72 = {}^-6a$

16. $\frac{2}{3}x + 9 = 33$

Solve by using an equation.

17. Kwan bought 7 boxes of pencils. He then bought 8 loose pencils. If Kwan bought 92 pencils in all, how many pencils were in each box?

18. Linda earns $8 per hour. Last week she earned $256. How many hours did she work?

Graph each point on a coordinate plane.

19. $R(3, {}^-6)$

20. $S({}^-2, 5)$

21. $T(0, {}^-4)$

22. $U({}^-3, 0)$

Graph each equation.

23. $y = {}^-2x + 2$

24. $y = x - 4$

25. $y = 3x - 2$

26. Use the formula from the chart on page 480. Jonathan and Diane invested $1500 for 1 year. They received $90 interest. What was the interest rate?

27. Use the map on page 481. Estimate the longitude and the latitude of Barcelona, Spain.

CHAPTER TEST

Solve each equation. Check your answers.

1. $x + 13 = 9$

2. $4 = y + 18$

3. $a + 7 = {}^-18$ **21-1**

4. $z - 5 = 15$

5. $c - 11 = {}^-6$

6. ${}^-14 = x - 3$

7. $6a = 96$

8. $76 = {}^-4c$

9. $5d = {}^-85$ **21-2**

10. $\frac{x}{7} = 28$

11. $\frac{z}{9} = 45$

12. $30 = \frac{5}{6}a$

13. $2y + 11 = 13$

14. $5z - 9 = {}^-29$

15. $\frac{m}{3} + 6 = {}^-18$ **21-3**

16. $12 = \frac{c}{4} - 12$

17. $\frac{4}{5}d + 7 = 23$

18. $\frac{3}{4}y - 8 = {}^-26$

Solve by using an equation.

19. Mary jogs the same number of miles every day of the week. If she jogs 42 mi each week, how many miles does she jog each day?   **21-4**

20. Tom bought 4 tires for his car. After a discount of $44 Tom paid $184 for the tires. How much did each tire cost before the discount?

Use the coordinate plane at the right.
Give the coordinates of each point.

21. R

22. S

23. T

24. U

25. V

26. W

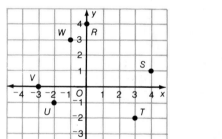

   21-5

Graph each point on a coordinate plane.

27. $E(2, 5)$

28. $F({}^-6, 4)$

29. $G(3, {}^-3)$

30. $H(0, {}^-6)$

Find three solutions of each equation. Use ${}^-3, 0, 3$ as values for x.

31. $y = x + 5$

32. $y = 2x - 4$

33. $y = {}^-3x$ **21-6**

Graph each equation.

34. $y = x - 7$

35. $y = 4x - 6$

36. $y = 2x + 1$

37. A train travels 390 mi in 6 h. Find the speed of the train.   **21-7**

38. Use the map on page 481. Estimate the longitude and the latitude of Hamburg, West Germany.   **21-8**

Building a house requires many special skills. In computing amounts and costs of materials, formulas for perimeter and area are very useful.

CHAPTER 22

PERIMETER AND AREA

485

22-1 POINTS, LINES, PLANES, AND ANGLES

A **point** is an exact location in space.

Point A

A **line** is a set of points that extends without end in opposite directions.

Line AB, written $\overleftrightarrow{AB}$

A **ray** is a part of a line. It has one **endpoint** and extends without end in one direction. When you name a ray, the endpoint is named first.

Ray XY, written $\overrightarrow{XY}$

A **line segment** is a part of a line. It consists of two endpoints and all the points between them.

Line segment RS, written $\overline{RS}$

A **plane** is a set of points on a flat surface that extends without end.

Plane F

An **angle** is formed by two rays that have the same endpoint. The endpoint is called the **vertex** of the angle. The rays are called the **sides**. When you name an angle, the vertex is the middle letter.

Angle PQR, written $\angle PQR$

example 1

Make a drawing to represent each of the following.

a. $\overleftrightarrow{RS}$ b. $\overline{PQ}$ c. $\overrightarrow{ST}$ d. $\angle XYZ$

solution

a.   b.   c.   d.

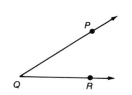

your turn

Make a drawing to represent each of the following.

1. point D 2. $\overleftrightarrow{EF}$ 3. $\overleftrightarrow{UV}$ 4. $\overline{ST}$ 5. $\angle EFG$ 6. plane R

Angles are measured in units called **degrees** (°). To measure or draw an angle you use a **protractor.**

example 2

a. To measure ∠ABC using a protractor, use the following method.
   1. Put the center of the protractor on the vertex (B).
   2. Place the 0° mark on one side ($\overrightarrow{BC}$).
   3. Read the number where the other side ($\overrightarrow{BA}$) crosses the scale.

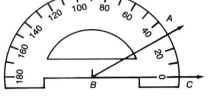

The measure of ∠ABC is 30°, written m∠ABC = 30°.

b. To draw ∠RST with a measure of 40°, use the following method.
   1. Draw a ray ($\overrightarrow{ST}$) to represent one side.
   2. Place the center of the protractor on the endpoint (S) with the 0° mark on the ray.
   3. Mark the number of degrees (40°) and remove the protractor.
   4. Draw a ray ($\overrightarrow{SR}$) through the mark.

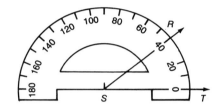

your turn

Use a protractor to measure each angle.

7.
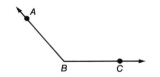

8.

9.
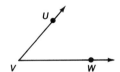

Use a protractor to draw an angle of the given measure.

10. 25°   11. 75°   12. 150°

An angle may be classified by its measure.

A **square corner** indicates a right angle.

A **right angle** has a measure of 90°.

smaller than a right angle

An **acute angle** has a measure between 0° and 90°.

larger than a right angle

An **obtuse angle** has a measure between 90° and 180°.

Two lines that meet in one point are called **intersecting lines.**
Lines that intersect to form right angles are called **perpendicular lines.**
Lines in a plane that do not intersect are called **parallel lines.**

example 3

Tell whether each angle is *acute, right,* or *obtuse*.

a.

b.

c.

Tell whether the lines are *parallel, perpendicular,* or *neither*.

d.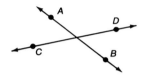

e.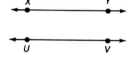

f.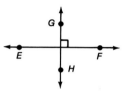

solution

a. obtuse

b. acute

c. right

d. neither

e. parallel ← **You may write $\overleftrightarrow{XY} \parallel \overleftrightarrow{UV}$.**

f. perpendicular ← **You may write $\overleftrightarrow{EF} \perp \overleftrightarrow{GH}$.**

your turn

Tell whether each angle is *acute, right,* or *obtuse*.

13.

14.

15.

Tell whether the lines are *parallel, perpendicular,* or *neither*.

16.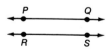

17.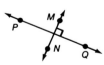

18.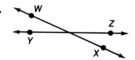

practice exercises

practice for example 1 *(page 486)*

Make a drawing to represent each of the following.

1. point F 2. $\angle RST$ 3. $\overleftrightarrow{GH}$ 4. $\overrightarrow{PQ}$ 5. $\overline{CD}$ 6. plane W

Use a protractor to measure each angle.

7. 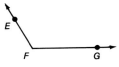   8. 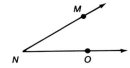   9.

Use a protractor to draw an angle of the given measure.

10. 30°   11. 45°   12. 60°   13. 90°   14. 120°   15. 135°

Tell whether each angle is *acute*, *right*, or *obtuse*.

16.    17. 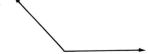   18.

Tell whether the lines are *parallel*, *perpendicular*, or *neither*.

19.   20. 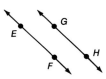   21.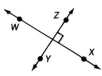

Use the figure at the right.

22. Name two parallel lines.
23. Name two perpendicular lines.
24. Name four rays with endpoint E.
25. Give the measure of $\angle AEB$.
26. Name two acute angles.
27. Name two right angles.

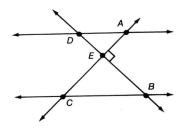

review exercises

Solve each equation.

1. $^-10 = x + 5$
2. $a - 7 = 7$
3. $^-4y = 96$
4. $^-3a + 8 = 32$
5. $\frac{z}{6} = {}^-6$
6. $\frac{2}{3}c = 18$
7. $\frac{x}{5} - 11 = 6$
8. $\frac{3}{5}y + 4 = {}^-8$

22-2 POLYGONS

A **polygon** is a closed plane figure formed by joining three or more line segments *at their endpoints*. Exactly two line segments meet at each endpoint. The line segments are called **sides** of the polygon. The points where the sides intersect are called **vertices** (plural of vertex).

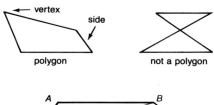

A line segment that joins two vertices *and is not a side* is called a **diagonal.** In polygon *ABCD*, shown at the right, $\overline{BD}$ is a diagonal.

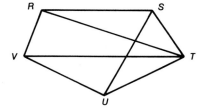

---

example 1

Use the figure at the right to name as many of the following as are shown.

a. sides   **b.** vertices   **c.** diagonals

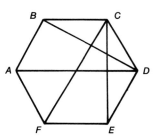

solution

a. $\overline{RS}, \overline{ST}, \overline{TU}, \overline{UV}, \overline{VR}$ **b.** *R, S, T, U, V*   **c.** $\overline{SU}, \overline{RT}, \overline{VT}$

your turn

Use the figure at the right to name as many of the following as are shown.

1. sides   **2.** vertices   **3.** diagonals

You name a polygon by its number of sides.

triangle	quadrilateral	pentagon	hexagon	octagon
3 sides	4 sides	5 sides	6 sides	8 sides

Two line segments are **congruent** if they have the same length. Two angles are **congruent** if they have the same measure. A **regular polygon** is a polygon with all its sides congruent and all its angles congruent.

example 2

Name each polygon. Tell whether it is *regular* or *not regular*.

 a. The marks show congruent sides and congruent angles.

hexagon, regular

b.

quadrilateral, not regular

your turn

Name each polygon. Tell whether it is *regular* or *not regular*.

4.

5.

6.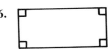

Quadrilaterals can be classified according to their properties.

trapezoid — one pair of parallel sides

parallelogram — two pairs of parallel sides

The opposite sides and the opposite angles of a parallelogram are congruent.

Some parallelograms have special names.

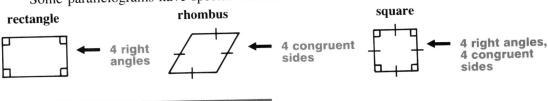

rectangle — 4 right angles

rhombus — 4 congruent sides

square — 4 right angles, 4 congruent sides

example 3

Name each quadrilateral.

a.

rhombus

b.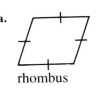

rectangle

c.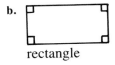

trapezoid

your turn

Name each quadrilateral.

7.

8.

9.

practice exercises

practice for example 1 (page 490)

Use the figure at the right to name as many of the following as are shown.

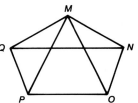

1. sides
2. vertices
3. diagonals

practice for example 2 (page 491)

Name each polygon. Tell whether it is *regular* or *not regular*.

4.

5.

6.

7.

practice for example 3 (page 491)

Name each quadrilateral.

8.

9.

10.

11.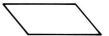

mixed practice (pages 490–491)

Name each polygon in the figure at the right. Use the name that identifies each polygon *most* accurately.

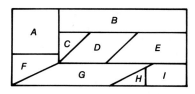

12. *A*
13. *B*
14. *C*
15. *D*
16. *E*
17. *F*
18. *G*
19. *H*
20. *I*

review exercises

Complete.

1. 24 ft = __?__ in.
2. 14 pt = __?__ qt
3. 50 oz = __?__ lb __?__ oz
4. 80 cm = __?__ mm
5. 400 mL = __?__ L
6. 12.5 kg = __?__ g

7. A bowling ball has a mass of 7255 g. How many kilograms is this?
8. Sandy works 40 h per week. If Sandy works 50 weeks per year and earns $19,000, how much does Sandy earn per hour?

22-3 PERIMETER

The distance around a polygon is called its **perimeter** (*P*). To find the perimeter of a polygon, you add the lengths of all its sides.

example 1

Find the perimeter of the polygon shown at the right.

solution

$P = 5 + 7 + 2 + 9$

$P = 23$ .... The perimeter is 23 in.

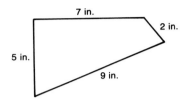

your turn

Find the perimeter of each polygon.

1. 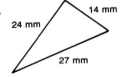   **2.** 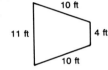   **3.**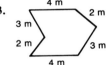

To find the perimeter of a rectangle or a square you can use one of these *formulas*.

rectangle
$P = 2 \times \text{length} + 2 \times \text{width}$
$P = 2l + 2w$

square
$P = 4 \times \text{length of one side}$
$P = 4s$

example 2

Use a formula to find the perimeter of each polygon.

a. rectangle with $l = 32$ ft and $w = 25$ ft

b. square with $s = 5$ m

solution

a. $P = 2l + 2w$
$P = 2(32) + 2(25)$
$P = 64 + 50 = 114$ The perimeter is 114 ft.

b. $P = 4s$
$P = 4(5)$
$P = 20$ The perimeter is 20 m.

your turn

Use a formula to find the perimeter of each polygon.

4. rectangle with $l = 6$ ft and $w = 2$ ft

5. square with $s = 3$ cm

practice *exercises*

practice for example 1 *(page 493)*

Find the perimeter of each polygon.

1.
4 ft
3 ft   5 ft

2.
3 in.
8 in.
8 in.
3 in.

3.
9 mm
9 mm   9 mm
9 mm   9 mm
9 mm

4.
5 m
2 m   4 m
6 m

practice for example 2 *(page 493)*

Use a formula to find the perimeter of each polygon.

5. square with $s = 8$ cm

6. rectangle with $l = 10$ m and $w = 4$ m

7. rectangle with $l = 13$ yd and $w = 7$ yd

8. square with $s = 7$ in.

mixed practice *(page 493)*

Find the perimeter of each polygon. Use a formula when possible.

9. triangle with sides that measure 9 m, 12 m, and 15 m

10. square with a side that measures 13 ft

11. trapezoid with sides that measure 8 in., 7 in., 8 in., and 12 in.

12. parallelogram with sides that measure 6 cm, 9 cm, 6 cm, and 9 cm

13. rectangle with length 14.4 m and width 7.2 m

14. regular pentagon with a side that measures 9.6 yd

15. A tennis court is a rectangle with length 26 yd and width 12 yd.
     Find its perimeter.

16. A baseball diamond is a square with a side that measures 90 ft.
     Find its perimeter.

review *exercises*

Evaluate each expression when $a = 4$, $b = 6$, and $c = 9$.

1. ac

2. b^2

3. a^2c

4. $5c^2$

5. $\frac{b}{2} + a$

6. $c + \frac{b}{3}$

7. $2c - \frac{a}{2}$

8. $ab + c$

9. $ab - c$

10. a^4

11. $a^2 + b^2$

12. ab^2

22-4 CIRCLES AND CIRCUMFERENCE

A **circle** is the set of all points in a plane that are the same distance from a given point in the plane. The given point is the **center** of the circle. A line segment that joins the center with any point on the circle is a **radius** (plural: *radii*). The circle shown, with center O, is called circle O.

A line segment joining any two points on a circle is a **chord.** A chord that contains the center of a circle is a **diameter.** A diameter is twice as long as a radius.

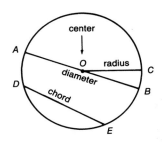

example 1

Use the figure above. Name as many of the following as are shown.

a. the circle   b. radii   c. diameters   d. chords

solution

a. circle O b. $\overline{OA}, \overline{OB}, \overline{OC}$ c. $\overline{AB}$ d. $\overline{AB}, \overline{DE}$

your turn

Use the figure at the right. Name as many of the following as are shown.

1. the circle
2. radii
3. diameters
4. chords

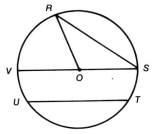

The distance around a circle is called its **circumference** (C). When the circumference of a circle is divided by the length of its diameter (d), the quotient is always the same number. This number is represented by the Greek letter π (read "pi"). Therefore:

$$C \div d = \pi$$
$$C = \pi d$$

Since a diameter is twice as long as a radius (r), you can also write:

$$C = 2\pi r$$

To find the circumference of a circle you can use either 3.14 or $\frac{22}{7}$ as an *approximate* value for π. The value $\frac{22}{7}$ is often used when the diameter is a multiple of 7.

example 2

Find the circumference of each circle.

a. diameter = 12 cm (Use $\pi \approx 3.14$.)

b. radius = 14 in. (Use $\pi \approx \frac{22}{7}$.)

solution

a. $C = \pi d$

$C \approx 3.14 \times 12$

$C \approx 37.68$

The circumference is approximately 37.68 cm.

b. $C = 2\pi r$

$C \approx 2(\frac{22}{7})(14)$

$C \approx 88$

The circumference is approximately 88 in.

your turn

Find the circumference of each circle.

5. diameter = 8 mm (Use $\pi \approx 3.14$.)

6. radius = 16 m (Use $\pi \approx 3.14$.)

7. diameter = 7 ft (Use $\pi \approx \frac{22}{7}$.)

8. radius = 28 in. (Use $\pi \approx \frac{22}{7}$.)

practice exercises

practice for example 1 (page 495)

Use the figure at the right. Name as many of the following as are shown.

1. the circle

2. radii

3. diameters

4. chords

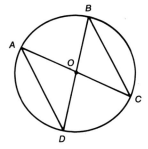

practice for example 2 (page 496)

Find the circumference of each circle. Use $\pi \approx 3.14$.

5. diameter = 5 cm

6. diameter = 9 mm

7. diameter = 14 ft

8. radius = 13 in.

9. radius = 4 m

10. radius = 15 in.

Find the circumference of each circle. Use $\pi \approx \frac{22}{7}$.

11. diameter = 21 ft

12. diameter = 35 yd

13. diameter = 77 cm

14. radius = 49 in.

15. radius = 70 ft

16. radius = $10\frac{1}{2}$ yd

Find the circumference of each circle. Use π ≈ 3.14.

17.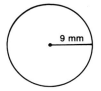
9 mm

18.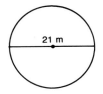
21 m

19.
17 cm

20.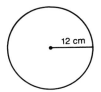
12 cm

21.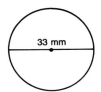
33 mm

22.
20 m

Complete the chart. Use π ≈ 22/7.

	23.	24.	25.	26.	27.	28.
radius	35 ft	21 in.	?	?	?	?
diameter	?	?	56 yd	35 in.	?	?
circumference	?	?	?	?	198 ft	264 yd

29. The diameter of a child's swimming pool is about 110 cm. Find its approximate circumference. Use π ≈ 3.14.

30. The radius of a satellite dish is 6 ft. Find its approximate circumference. Use π ≈ 3.14.

review exercises

Compare. Replace each __?__ with >, <, or =.

1. 7185 __?__ 7158
2. 984 __?__ 9840
3. 60,922 __?__ 69,022
4. 31.2 __?__ 3.12
5. 6.90 __?__ 6.9
6. 0.052 __?__ 0.502

22-5 AREA OF RECTANGLES, SQUARES, AND PARALLELOGRAMS

The **area** (*A*) of a figure is the amount of surface it covers. Area is measured in square units. Some common units of area are listed below.

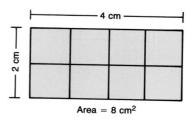

Area = 8 cm²

U.S. Customary

square inches (in.²)
square feet (ft²)
square yards (yd²)
square miles (mi²)

Metric

square millimeters (mm²)
square centimeters (cm²)
square meters (m²)
square kilometers (km²)

To find the area of a rectangle or a square you could count the number of square units inside it. Frequently it is easier to use a formula.

rectangle

$A = lw$

square

$A = s \times s = s^2$

example 1

Find the area of the rectangle and the square.

a.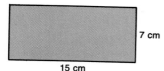

b.

solution

a. $A = lw$
   $A = 15 \times 7$
   $A = 105$
   The area is 105 cm².

b. $A = s^2$
   $A = 6^2$
   $A = 36$
   The area is 36 ft².

your turn

Find the area of each rectangle and each square.

1.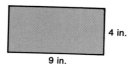

2.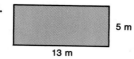

3.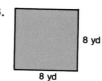

4.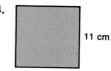

You can find the area of a parallelogram by using this formula.

$$\text{Area} = \text{base} \times \text{height}$$
$$A = bh$$

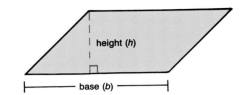

example 2

Find the area of each parallelogram.

a.

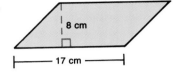

b.

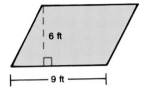

solution

a. $A = bh$
$A = 17 \times 8$
$A = 136$
The area is 136 cm^2.

b. $A = bh$
$A = 9 \times 6$
$A = 54$
The area is 54 ft^2.

your turn

Find the area of each parallelogram.

5.

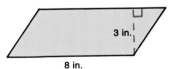

6.

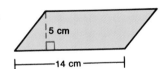

practice exercises

practice for example 1 (page 498)

Find the area of each rectangle and each square.

1.

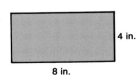

2.

3.

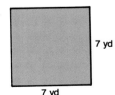

4.

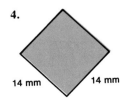

Find the area of each parallelogram.

5.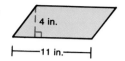

6.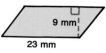

7.

8.

mixed practice (pages 498–499)

Find the area of each figure.

9. square with side 15 m

10. parallelogram with base 14 mm and height 9 mm

11. rectangle with length 17 ft and width 5 ft

12. square with side 18.7 in.

Complete.

13. rectangle: $A = 144 \text{ ft}^2$, $w = 8$ ft, $l = \underline{\ ?\ }$ ft

14. rectangle: $A = 288 \text{ cm}^2$, $l = 48$ cm, $w = \underline{\ ?\ }$ cm

15. parallelogram: $A = 243 \text{ m}^2$, $b = 9$ m, $h = \underline{\ ?\ }$ m

16. parallelogram: $A = 221 \text{ in.}^2$, $h = 17$ in., $b = \underline{\ ?\ }$ in.

17. The base of the Great Pyramid of Cheops is a square with a side that measures 230 m. Find the area of the base of the pyramid.

18. An ice skating rink is a rectangle with length 66 yd and width 33 yd. Find its area.

review *exercises*

Find each answer.

1. $2\frac{1}{10} \div 3$

2. $5\frac{3}{4} + 1\frac{2}{3}$

3. $3\frac{1}{3} \times 4\frac{1}{5}$

4. $3\frac{1}{4} - 2\frac{2}{5}$

5. 7.8×0.5

6. $9 - 3.2$

7. $0.6 \div 7.5$

8. $\$.40 + \$1.29 + \$5$

puzzle corner

1. Draw two rectangles that have the same area, but different perimeters.

2. Draw two rectangles that have the same perimeter, but different areas.

22-6 AREA OF TRIANGLES AND TRAPEZOIDS

A diagonal of a parallelogram divides it into two triangles, as shown at the right. The area of each triangle is half the area of the parallelogram.

You can find the formula for the area of a triangle by multiplying the formula for the area of a parallelogram by one half.

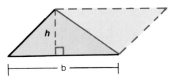

A (parallelogram) $= bh$

A (triangle) $= \frac{1}{2}bh$

example 1

Find the area of each triangle.

a.
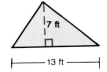

b.
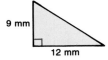

c.
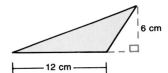

solution

a. $A = \frac{1}{2}bh$

$A = \frac{1}{2} \times 13 \times 7$

$A = 45\frac{1}{2}$

The area is $45\frac{1}{2}$ ft².

b. $A = \frac{1}{2}bh$

$A = \frac{1}{2} \times 12 \times 9$

$A = 54$

The area is 54 mm².

c. $A = \frac{1}{2}bh$

$A = \frac{1}{2} \times 12 \times 6$

$A = 36$

The area is 36 cm².

your turn

Find the area of each triangle.

1.
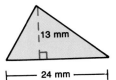

2.
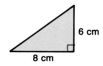

3.
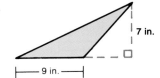

To find the area of a trapezoid, you first find the sum of the lengths of the parallel sides, or **bases.** You then multiply this sum by half the height, as shown at the right.

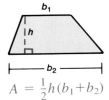

$A = \frac{1}{2}h(b_1 + b_2)$

example 2

Find the area of each trapezoid.

a.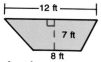

b.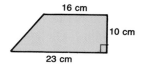

solution

a. $A = \frac{1}{2}h(b_1+b_2)$

$A = \frac{1}{2} \times 7 \times (8 + 12)$

$A = \frac{1}{2} \times 7 \times 20$

$A = 70$

The area is 70 ft².

b. $A = \frac{1}{2}h(b_1+b_2)$

$A = \frac{1}{2} \times 10 \times (16 + 23)$

$A = \frac{1}{2} \times 10 \times 39$

$A = 195$

The area is 195 cm².

your turn

Find the area of each trapezoid.

4.

5.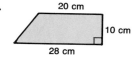

6.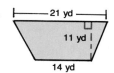

practice exercises

practice for example 1 (page 501)

Find the area of each triangle.

1.

2.

3.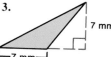

4.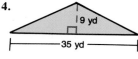

practice for example 2 (page 502)

Find the area of each trapezoid.

5.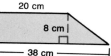

6.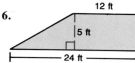

7.

8.

Find the area of each figure.

9. triangle with a base that measures 14 cm and height 11 cm
10. triangle with a base that measures 18 m and height 24 m
11. triangle with a base that measures 42 in. and height 24.7 in.
12. triangle with a base that measures 20.4 ft and height 13 ft
13. trapezoid with bases that measure 30 cm and 45 cm, and height 14 cm
14. trapezoid with bases that measure 24 ft and 31 ft, and height 16 ft
15. The height of a triangular sail is 20 ft. The base measures 9 ft. Find the area of the sail.
16. A park is shaped like a trapezoid. The parallel sides are 260 yd long and 430 yd long. The distance between the parallel sides is 180 yd. Find the area of the park.

review *exercises*

Is the first number divisible by the second number? Write *Yes* or *No*.

1. 640; 5   2. 321; 2   3. 8599; 3
4. 18,392; 4 5. 445; 10   6. 6104; 8

mental math

Sometimes you can check the reasonableness of a perimeter or area by estimating mentally.

18.8 cm

Square
Area $\stackrel{?}{=}$ 353.44 cm²
Perimeter $\stackrel{?}{=}$ 752 cm

Think: Each side is about 20 cm long.
$A \approx 20 \times 20$, or 400. So 353.44 cm² is *reasonable*.
$P \approx 4 \times 20$, or 80. So 752 cm is *not reasonable*.

Estimate mentally to determine if the given perimeter or area is *reasonable* or *not reasonable*.

1.
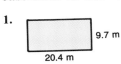
9.7 m
20.4 m
Rectangle
Perimeter $\stackrel{?}{=}$ 198 m

2.
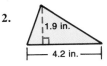
1.9 in.
4.2 in.
Triangle
Area $\stackrel{?}{=}$ 3.99 in.²

3.
5.1 ft
18.8 ft
Parallelogram
Area $\stackrel{?}{=}$ 197.4 ft²

4.
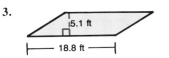
9.5 m
Square
Area $\stackrel{?}{=}$ 902.5 m²
Perimeter $\stackrel{?}{=}$ 38 m

22-7 AREA OF CIRCLES AND COMPOSITE FIGURES

Suppose you divide a circle into equal parts, as shown at the right. You can then rearrange these parts to form a figure that looks like a parallelogram. The area of this "parallelogram" is equal to the area of the circle.

To find a formula for the area of a circle, begin with the area of the "parallelogram."

$A = b \times h$

$A = \frac{1}{2}C \times r$ ← base $= \frac{1}{2}C$ and height $= r$

$A = \frac{1}{2}(2\pi r) \times r$ ← Recall that $C = 2\pi r$.

$A = \pi r \times r$

$A = \pi r^2$ ← formula for the area of a circle

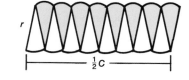

example 1

Find the area of each circle.

a. radius = 4 cm (Use $\pi \approx 3.14$.)

b. radius = 7 in. (Use $\pi \approx \frac{22}{7}$.)

solution

a. $A = \pi r^2$

$A \approx 3.14 \times 4^2$

$A \approx 3.14 \times 16$

$A \approx 50.24$

The area is approximately 50.24 cm².

b. $A = \pi r^2$

$A \approx \frac{22}{7} \times 7^2$

$A \approx \frac{22}{7} \times 49$

$A \approx 154$

The area is approximately 154 in.²

your turn

Find the area of each circle.

1. radius = 9 m (Use $\pi \approx 3.14$.)

2. radius = 28 ft (Use $\pi \approx \frac{22}{7}$.)

To find the area of a circle when you know the diameter, first multiply the diameter by one half.

---

example 2

Find the area of each circle.

a. diameter = 10 m (Use $\pi \approx 3.14$.)

b. diameter = 28 ft (Use $\pi \approx \frac{22}{7}$.)

solution

a. $A = \pi r^2$

$A \approx 3.14 \times 5^2 \longleftarrow r = 10 \times \frac{1}{2} = 5$

$A \approx 3.14 \times 25$

$A \approx 78.5$

The area is approximately 78.5 m².

b. $A = \pi r^2$

$A \approx \frac{22}{7} \times 14^2 \longleftarrow r = 28 \times \frac{1}{2} = 14$

$A \approx \frac{22}{7} \times 196$

$A \approx 616$

The area is approximately 616 ft².

your turn

Find the area of each circle.

3. diameter = 24 cm (Use $\pi \approx 3.14$.)

4. diameter = 42 in. (Use $\pi \approx \frac{22}{7}$.)

A **composite figure** is a polygon that is made up of other polygons. To find the area of a composite figure, you divide it into polygons whose areas you know how to find, and then find the sum of the areas.

---

example 3

Find the area of the figure at the right.

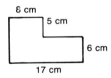

solution

Divide the figure into two rectangles. Label them I and II.

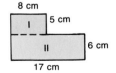

$A(I) = lw = 8 \times 5 = 40$
$A(II) = lw = 17 \times 6 = 102$
$A(I) + A(II) = 40 + 102 = 142$ The area is 142 cm².

your turn

Find the area of each figure.

5.

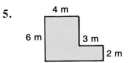

6.

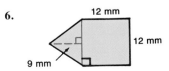

practice exercises

practice for example 1 (page 504)

Find the area of each circle.

1. radius = 8 cm (Use $\pi \approx 3.14$.)
3. radius = 56 in. (Use $\pi \approx \frac{22}{7}$.)

2. radius = 18 m (Use $\pi \approx 3.14$.)
4. radius = 77 ft (Use $\pi \approx \frac{22}{7}$.)

practice for example 2 (page 505)

Find the area of each circle.

5. diameter = 60 cm (Use $\pi \approx 3.14$.)
7. diameter = 14 ft (Use $\pi \approx \frac{22}{7}$.)

6. diameter = 48 mm (Use $\pi \approx 3.14$.)
8. diameter = 28 yd (Use $\pi \approx \frac{22}{7}$.)

practice for example 3 (page 505)

Find the area of each figure.

9.
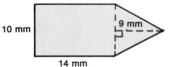

10.
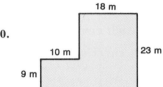

11.
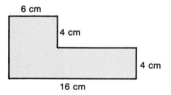

12.
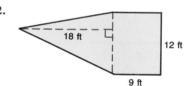

mixed practice (pages 504–505)

Find the area of each circle. Use $\pi \approx 3.14$.

13.

14.

15.

16.

Find the area of each circle. Use $\pi \approx \frac{22}{7}$.

17.

18.

19.

20.

Find the area of each figure.

21.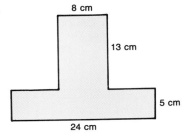

22.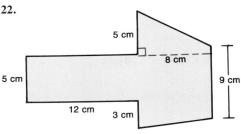

23. The diameter of Stonehenge in England is 156 ft. Find the area of the ground enclosed by Stonehenge. Use $\pi \approx 3.14$.

24. The radius of the Pantheon in Rome is about 71 ft. Find the area of the floor of the Pantheon. Use $\pi \approx 3.14$.

review exercises

Estimate.

1. 50% of $58.95
2. 25% of $77.98
3. 33% of $73.99
4. 67% of 154
5. 49% of 306
6. 76% of 16.5
7. 26.5% of $475
8. 35% of $185

Find each answer.

9. $2 \times 12 + 2 \times 8$
10. $2(12 + 2) + 8$
11. $7 \times 4 - 6 \div 2$
12. $4 + 3 \times 8 - 6$

calculator corner

Some calculators have a $\boxed{\pi}$ key. You can use this key to find the circumference and the area of a circle.

example Find the circumference and the area of a circle with radius 5 cm.

solution $C = \pi d \approx \boxed{\pi} \times 10 \approx 31.415927$ ⟵ **Many calculators use 3.1415927 for π.**

$A = \pi r^2 \approx \boxed{\pi} \times 5 \times 5 \approx 78.539816$

Use a calculator to find the circumference and the area of each circle.

1. radius = 9 m
2. radius = 5.8 in.
3. radius = 2.7 ft
4. diameter = 15 yd
5. diameter = 9 cm
6. diameter = 38 mm

22-8 MAKING A DIAGRAM

1 Understand
2 Plan
3 Work
4 Answer

Some problems can be solved by using a **Venn diagram.**
This special kind of diagram shows the relationship between
two or more groups of people, animals, or objects.

example

Three hundred people returning from a trip to Europe were asked which
countries they had visited. 158 had been to England, 188 had been to
France, and 148 had been to Italy. 97 had visited both England and
France, 73 had visited England and Italy, 100 had visited France and
Italy, and 57 had visited all three countries.

a. How many visited England, but not Italy or France?

b. How many visited France, but not Italy?

solution

Draw a Venn diagram. Begin with a rectangle that
represents the 300 people. Draw three overlapping
circles to represent the people who visited each of
the three countries.

    Working outward from the middle region, fill
in the number of people who visited each combination of countries.

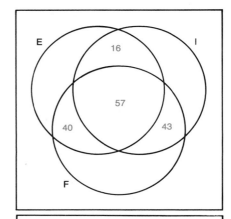

All three countries: 57

E and F, not I: $97 - 57 = 40$ ◄— **E = England**
                               I = Italy
E and I, not F: $73 - 57 = 16$ **F = France**
F and I, not E: $100 - 57 = 43$

E, not F, not I: $158 - (40 + 57 + 16) = 45$
I, not E, not F: $148 - (16 + 57 + 43) = 32$
F, not E, not I: $188 - (40 + 57 + 43) = 48$

Now add all the numbers in the circles.

$45 + 16 + 32 + 40 + 57 + 43 + 48 = 281$
$300 - 281 = 19$

So 19 people visited none of the three countries.

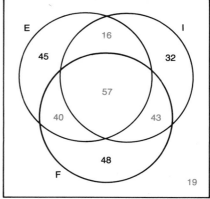

a. Forty-five people visited England, but not Italy
    or France.

b. $40 + 48 = 88$
    Eighty-eight people visited France, but not Italy.

problems

1. There are 160 freshmen at Central High School. Sixty of them study French, 82 study Spanish, and 6 study both languages. How many of the freshmen study neither French nor Spanish?

2. Of 200 people surveyed, 120 people watch the early television newscast, 85 people watch the late newscast, and 40 people watch both. How many watch neither?

3. One hundred high school boys were asked which sports they play. Of them, 30 play basketball, 32 baseball, and 39 football. Eleven play both basketball and football, 12 play basketball and baseball, 9 play football and baseball, and 5 play all three sports.
   a. How many play none of the three sports?
   b. How many play only football?
   c. How many play basketball and baseball, but not football?

4. Of 110 students surveyed, 34 study Spanish, 40 study French, 15 study German, 8 study both Spanish and French, 4 study Spanish and German, 3 study French and German, and 1 studies all three.
   a. How many of the students do not study any of the languages?
   b. How many study only French?
   c. How many study Spanish or French, but not German?

5. In a survey 600 people were asked their two favorite colors. Of them, 450 chose red as one of their favorites, 372 chose blue, and 10 chose neither red nor blue.
   a. How many people liked both colors?
      Hint: (I + III) + (II + III) − (I + II + III) = III
   b. How many people liked red, but not blue?

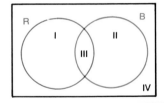

review *exercises*

1. Two points *determine* 1 line. Three points that do not lie on the same line determine 3 lines, as shown at the right. Four points, no 3 of which lie on the same line, determine 6 lines. How many lines are determined by 9 points?

Points	2	3	4	5
Lines	1	3	6	10

2. Paul, Larry, and Rita vacationed in Paris, London, and Rome. Each person went to a different city, and no one went to the city that begins with the same letter as that person's name. Larry did not go to Paris. Who went where?

SKILL REVIEW

Use the figure at the right.

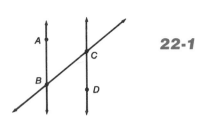

1. Name three line segments.
2. Name two rays.
3. Name two parallel lines.
4. Use a protractor to measure $\angle ABC$.

22-1

Name each polygon. Tell whether it is *regular* or *not regular*.

5.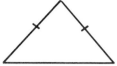

6.

7.

22-2

Find the perimeter of each polygon.

8. triangle with sides that measure 12 in., 20 in., and 16 in.
9. rectangle with length 6 m and width 2 m

22-3

Use the figure at the right to answer the following.

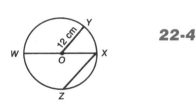

10. Name all chords that are shown.
11. Name all radii that are shown.
12. Name all diameters that are shown.
13. Find the circumference. Use $\pi \approx 3.14$.

22-4

Find the area of each figure.

14. rectangle with length 11 cm and width 5 cm
15. square with side that measures 14 m

22-5

16. triangle with a base that measures 19 ft and height 10 ft
17. trapezoid with bases that measure 15 mm and 7 mm, and height 4 mm

22-6

18. circle with diameter 22 cm; Use $\pi \approx 3.14$.
19. circle with radius 21 ft; Use $\pi \approx \frac{22}{7}$.

22-7

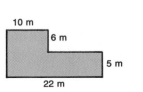

20. Find the area of the figure at the right.

21. Of the 80 diners in Emilio's restaurant Saturday night, 37 had seafood, 31 had beef, and 4 had both beef and seafood. How many had neither beef nor seafood?

22-8

22-9 HOME IMPROVEMENTS

Many contractors estimate the cost of home improve-
ments based on the actual size of the project.

example

A contractor estimates the cost of constructing a deck
at $12/ft². Estimate the cost of the deck shown at the right.

solution

Find the total area in square feet:

$A(\text{I}) = 5 \times 3 = 15$ (ft²)
$A(\text{II}) = 9 \times 5 = 45$ (ft²)
$A(\text{I}) + A(\text{II}) = 15 + 45 = 60$ (ft²)

Multiply by the cost per square foot: $60 \times \$12 = \$720$

The deck will cost about $720.

exercises

Use $12/ft² to estimate the cost of each deck. Use $\pi \approx 3.14$ in Exercise 3.

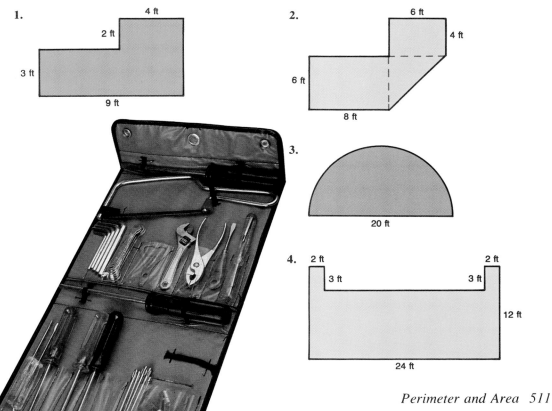

1. 4 ft, 2 ft, 3 ft, 9 ft

2. 6 ft, 4 ft, 6 ft, 8 ft

3. 20 ft

4. 2 ft, 3 ft, 2 ft, 3 ft, 12 ft, 24 ft

22-10 CONSTRUCTING CIRCLE GRAPHS

You can construct circle graphs to display data expressed as percents. The whole circle represents 100% of the data. You can divide the circle into wedges, or **sectors,** that represent the parts of the data. The sum of the angles formed by the sectors is 360°. To find the measure of each angle, write the percent as a decimal and multiply by 360°.

example

Construct a circle graph to display the given information.

United States Energy Sources

oil	natural gas	coal	other
49%	25%	20%	6%

solution

- Multiply to find the number of degrees for each sector. Round each number of degrees to the nearest whole number.

  oil: $0.49 \times 360° = 176.4° \approx 176°$

  gas: $0.25 \times 360° = 90°$

  coal: $0.20 \times 360° = 72°$

  other: $0.06 \times 360° = 21.6° \approx 22°$

- Draw a circle and any radius.

- Use a protractor to draw the angle for each sector.

- Label each sector and give the graph a title.

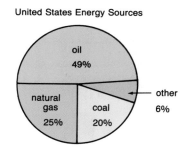

United States Energy Sources

exercises

Construct a circle graph to display the given information.

1. **World Population**

Asia	64%
Africa	12%
Europe	10%
North America	8%
South America	6%

2. **Area of the Great Lakes**

Superior	34%
Huron	24%
Michigan	24%
Erie	10%
Ontario	8%

3. **Federal Income from Taxes**

Personal Income Tax	44%
Social Security	32%
Corporate Income Tax	9%
Excise Tax	6%
Other	9%

4. **Sources of City Income**

State Aid	30%
Property Tax	26%
Federal Aid	15%
Sales Tax	10%
Other Taxes	19%

5. **Restricted Driver's License Minimum Age by State**

Fourteen Years	26%
Fifteen Years	24%
Sixteen Years	50%

6. **XYZ Co. Employee Commuter Methods**

Mass Transit	67%
Automobile	17%
Walk	10%
Car Pool	6%

7. **City Expenditures**

Education	16%
Police and Fire	15%
Public Welfare	12%
Health	8%
Urban Renewal	6%
Streets	4%
Other	39%

8. **Birth States of Presidents**

Virginia	21%
Ohio	18%
New York	10%
Massachusetts	8%
North Carolina	5%
Texas	5%
Vermont	5%
Other	28%

CONTRACTOR

Jane Gasko is a contractor. She must estimate the amounts of materials needed to do a job. She estimates the amount of paint by finding the area, subtracting a 10% *allowance* for doors and windows, and using the table at the right.

Type of coverage	Coverage for 1 gal
light	300 ft²
medium	250 ft²
heavy	200 ft²

example

Matt wants one coat of paint on the front of his house. Medium coverage is needed. Use the drawing at the right to estimate the number of gallons of paint he needs to buy.

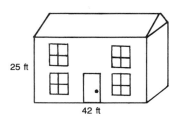

25 ft

42 ft

solution

Find the area: $42 \times 25 = 1050$ (ft²)
Find the allowance: $0.1 \times 1050 = 105$ (ft²)   ◄— **Write 10% as 0.1.**
Subtract: $1050 - 105 = 945$ (ft²)
Use the table: $945 \div 250 = 3.78$

Since Matt needs *more than* 3 gal of paint, he must buy 4 gal.

exercises

1. A wall is 75 ft high and 55 ft wide. There are six windows. Estimate the amount of paint needed for each.

   a. heavy coverage   **b.** light coverage

2. The front of Deneen's house needs medium coverage. Use the diagram at the right to estimate the number of gallons required.

   6 ft

   18 ft

   18 ft

3. Choose a room in your house you would like to paint. Use a tape measure to find the dimensions of the walls. Estimate how much paint you would need to buy.

CHAPTER REVIEW

vocabulary vo·cab·u·lar·y

Choose the correct word to complete each sentence.

1. A (*ray, line segment*) is a part of a line with two endpoints.
2. An (*acute, obtuse*) angle has a measure between 0° and 90°.

skills

Make a drawing to represent each of the following.

3. $\overrightarrow{AB}$
4. $\overline{XY}$
5. $\overleftrightarrow{BC}$
6. $\angle NOP$

Find the perimeter of each polygon.

7. triangle with sides that measure 25 cm, 17 cm, and 23 cm
8. rectangle with length 23 m and width 12 m

Use the figure at the right.

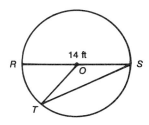

9. Name all chords that are shown.
10. Name all radii that are shown.
11. Find the circumference. Use $\pi \approx 3.14$.
12. Find the area. Use $\pi \approx \frac{22}{7}$.

Find the area of each figure.

13. triangle with a base that measures 18 m and height 6 m
14. rectangle with length 16 ft and width 7 ft
15. trapezoid with bases that measure 17 in. and 10 in., and height 10 in.
16. Estimate the cost of a square deck whose side measures 17 ft. Assume the deck will cost about $12/ft².
17. Kym's Fruit Market had 450 customers on Friday. 295 customers bought apples and 220 bought oranges. If 92 customers bought both apples and oranges, how many customers bought neither?
18. Construct a circle graph to display the given information.

Preferred Music of East High School Students

Rock	Country	Jazz	Classical	Other
40%	30%	15%	10%	5%

CHAPTER TEST

Use the figure at the right.

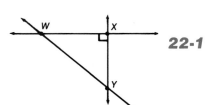

1. Name a right angle.
2. Name two perpendicular lines.
3. Use a protractor to measure ∠*XWY*.

22-1

Name each polygon. Tell whether it is *regular* or *not regular*.

4.   5.   6.

22-2

Find the perimeter of each polygon.

7. rectangle with length 15 in. and width 9 in.   8. square with side 16 ft

22-3

Use the figure at the right.

9. Name all radii that are shown.
10. Name all diameters that are shown.
11. Find the circumference. Use $\pi \approx \frac{22}{7}$.

22-4

Find the area of each figure.

12. square with a side that measures 21 cm

22-5

13. parallelogram with a base that measures 15 mm and height 9 mm
14. triangle with a base that measures 17 m and height 8 m

22-6

15. trapezoid with bases that measure 29 in. and 15 in., and height 14 in.
16. circle with diameter 24 cm; Use $\pi \approx 3.14$.

22-7

17. circle with radius 42 in.; Use $\pi \approx \frac{22}{7}$.
18. Find the area of the figure at the right.

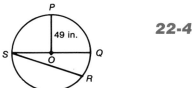

19. There are thirty students in Mr. Inouye's homeroom.
    Fifteen own a dog, nine own a cat, and four own both
    a dog and a cat. How many own neither a dog nor a cat?

22-8

20. Estimate the cost of a circular deck with radius 5 ft. Assume the
    deck will cost about \$12/ft². Use $\pi \approx 3.14$.

22-9

21. Construct a circle graph to display the given information.

22-10

Goldman Family Budget

Housing	Food	Clothing	Savings	Other
28%	22%	10%	15%	25%

Although these balls vary greatly in size, they are all spheres. The same formula can be used to find the volume of each one.

CHAPTER 23

SURFACE AREA AND VOLUME

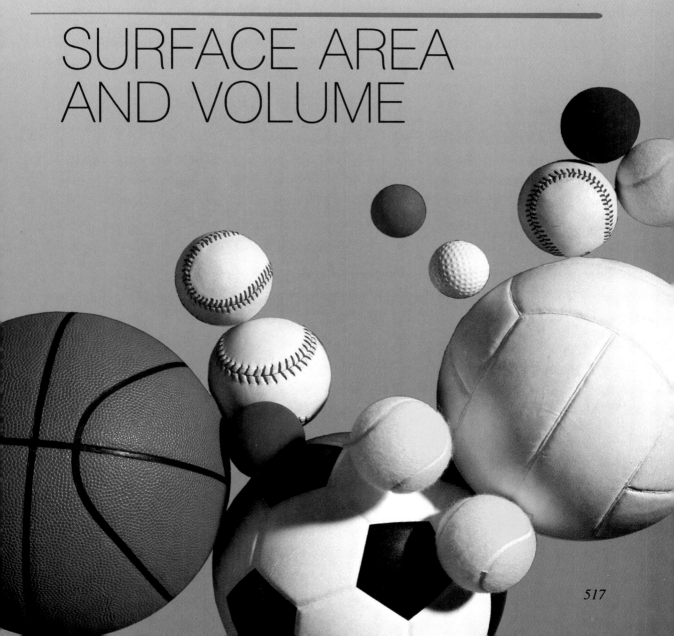

23-1 IDENTIFYING SPACE FIGURES

Three-dimensional figures that enclose part of space are called **space figures.**

A **polyhedron** is a space figure with flat surfaces. The flat surfaces are called **faces.** Two faces intersect at an **edge.** Three or more edges intersect at a **vertex.**

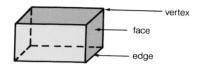

A **prism** is a polyhedron with two identical, parallel **bases.** The bases must be polygons. The other faces are parallelograms. A prism is named by the shape of its bases.

A **pyramid** is a polyhedron with one base. The base must be a polygon. The other faces of the pyramid are triangles. A pyramid is named by the shape of its base.

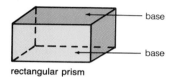

rectangular prism

triangular prism

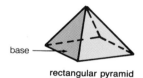

rectangular pyramid

hexagonal pyramid

cube

← A *cube* is a rectangular prism all of whose faces are squares. The length of each edge is the same.

example 1

Name each polyhedron. Give the number of faces, edges, and vertices.

a.

triangular pyramid
4 faces, 6 edges, 4 vertices

b.

hexagonal pyramid
7 faces, 12 edges, 7 vertices

c.

pentagonal prism
7 faces, 15 edges, 10 vertices

your turn

Name each polyhedron. Give the number of faces, edges, and vertices.

1.
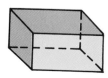

2.

3.
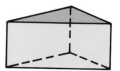

Some space figures are *not* polyhedrons. They have curved surfaces.

A **cylinder** has two identical, parallel, circular bases.

A **cone** has one circular base and one vertex.

A **sphere** is the set of all points in space that are the same distance from a given point called the **center.**

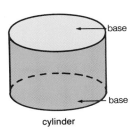

cylinder

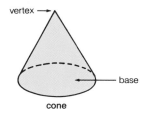

cone

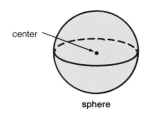

sphere

example 2

Name each space figure.

a.

cone

b.

sphere

c.

cylinder

your turn

Name each space figure.

4.

5.

6.

practice exercises

practice for example 1 (page 518)

Name each polyhedron. Give the number of faces, edges, and vertices.

1.

2.

3.

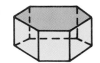

4.

Name each space figure.

5.

6.

7.

8.

Use the clues and the drawings on pages 518 and 519 to identify each space figure.

9. It has 6 square faces.

10. It has 4 triangular faces.

11. It has 8 edges and 5 faces.
One face is a rectangle.

12. It has 1 rectangular base.
The other four faces are triangles.

13. It has no edges.
It has no bases.

14. It has no vertices.
It has 2 bases.

15. It is a polyhedron.
It has 4 vertices.

16. It is a polyhedron.
It has 5 vertices.

17. It has 6 vertices.
It has 5 faces.

18. It has 5 faces.
It has 9 edges.

Copy and complete the chart.

	Polyhedron	Number of Faces (F)	Number of Vertices (V)	Number of Edges (E)	F + V − E
19.	rectangular prism	?	?	?	?
20.	triangular prism	?	?	?	?
21.	rectangular pyramid	?	?	?	?
22.	triangular pyramid	?	?	?	?

review exercises

Find the area of each figure. When appropriate, use $\pi \approx 3.14$.

1. rectangle with length 8 m and width 4 m

2. rectangle with length 14 ft and width 9 ft

3. square with side 13 in.

4. square with side 21 cm

5. circle with radius 15 cm

6. circle with diameter 44 mm

23-2 SURFACE AREA

The **surface area** of a polyhedron is the sum of the areas of its faces.

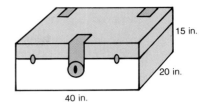

example 1

Find the surface area of the rectangular prism shown at the right.

solution

The faces of the rectangular prism are six rectangles. To find the area of each face, use the following formula.

$$A = l \times w$$

Add the areas of the six rectangular faces to find the surface area.

top: $A = 40 \times 20 = 800$

bottom: $A = 40 \times 20 = 800$

front: $A = 40 \times 15 = 600$

back: $A = 40 \times 15 = 600$

left side: $A = 20 \times 15 = 300$

right side: $A = 20 \times 15 = \underline{300}$

Total: 3400

The surface area is 3400 in.^{2}.

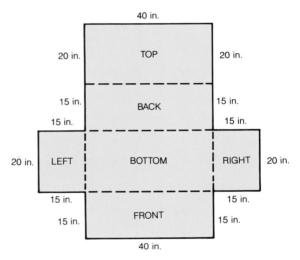

your turn

Find the surface area of each rectangular prism.

1.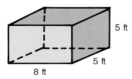

2.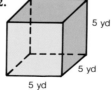

3.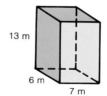

The surface area of a cylinder is the sum of the areas of its two circular bases and its curved surface.

example 2

Find the surface area of the cylinder shown at the right. Use π ≈ 3.14.

solution

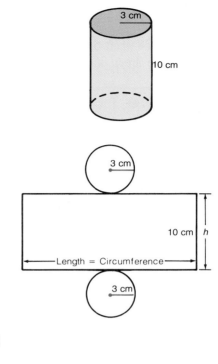

Each base of a cylinder is a circle. To find the area of each base, use the formula for the area of a circle.

$$A = \pi r^2 \approx 3.14 \times 3^2 = 28.26$$

The curved surface is like a label on a soup can. When unrolled, it forms a rectangle. To find the area of the curved surface, use the formula for the area of a rectangle ($A = lw$). Then substitute $2\pi r$ (circumference of the base) for l, and h (height of the cylinder) for w.

$$A = 2\pi rh \approx 2 \times 3.14 \times 3 \times 10 = 188.4$$

Add the three areas to find the surface area.

top base + bottom base + curved surface
   28.26   +   28.26   +   188.4   = 244.92

The surface area is approximately 244.92 cm².

your turn

Find the surface area of each cylinder.

4. Use π ≈ 3.14.

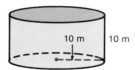

5. Use π ≈ 3.14.

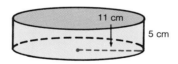

6. Use π ≈ $\frac{22}{7}$.

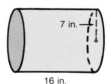

practice exercises

practice for example 1 (page 521)

Find the surface area of each rectangular prism.

1.

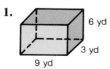

2.

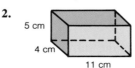

3.

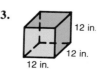

practice for example 2 (page 522)

Find the surface area of each cylinder.

4. Use $\pi \approx 3.14$.

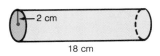

2 cm

18 cm

5. Use $\pi \approx \frac{22}{7}$.

7 ft

14 ft

6. Use $\pi \approx \frac{22}{7}$.

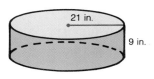

21 in.

9 in.

mixed practice (pages 521–522)

Find the surface area of each space figure. When appropriate, use $\pi \approx 3.14$.

7.

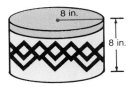

8 in.

8 in.

8.

SPAGHETTI

3 in.

10 in.

1 in.

9.

5 in.

10 in.

Boots

15 in.

10.

8 cm

SOUP

10 cm

11.

4 in.

4 in.

4 in.

12.

5 cm

TUNA

5 cm

13.

7 cm

7 cm

7 cm

14.

WORLD
FACTS

19 cm

4 cm

13 cm

15.

3 in.

Peanut
Butter

5 in.

16. What is the surface area of an aluminum can with height 11 cm and radius 4 cm? Use $\pi \approx 3.14$.

17. What is the surface area of a footstool shaped like a rectangular prism with length 25 in., width 12 in., and height 15 in.?

review exercises

Evaluate each expression when $a = 2$, $b = 5$, and $c = 9$.

1. bc **2.** ac **3.** b^2 **4.** a^2 **5.** ab^2

6. b^2c **7.** abc **8.** a^3 **9.** ab^3 **10.** a^3c

23-3 VOLUME OF RECTANGULAR PRISMS

The **volume** (V) of a space figure is the amount of space inside it. Volume is measured in cubic units. Some common units of volume are listed below.

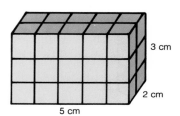

one cubic centimeter
1 cm³

U.S. Customary	**Metric**
cubic inches (in.³)	cubic millimeters (mm³)
cubic feet (ft³)	cubic centimeters (cm³)
cubic yards (yd³)	cubic meters (m³)

One way to find the volume of a rectangular prism is to count the number of cubic units.

example 1

Find the volume of the rectangular prism shown at the right.

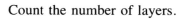

solution

Count the number of cubic centimeters in the top layer.

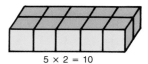

$5 \times 2 = 10$

Count the number of layers.

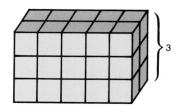

3

Multiply.

$$V = 10 \times 3 = 30$$

The volume is 30 cm³.

your turn

Find the volume of each rectangular prism.

1.
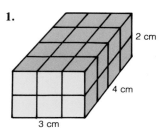

2 cm
4 cm
3 cm

2.

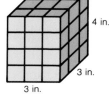

4 in.
3 in.
3 in.

3.
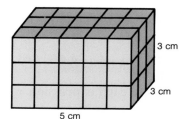

3 cm
3 cm
5 cm

You can also find the volume of a rectangular prism by finding the product of the area of its base (B) and height (h).
$$V = Bh$$
Because the base is a rectangle, you can replace B with lw.
$$V = lwh$$

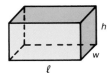

example 2

Find the volume of each rectangular prism.

a.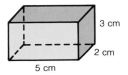

b.

solution

a. $V = lwh$
$V = 5 \times 2 \times 3$ ◀ Replace l with 5, w with 2, and h with 3.
$V = 30$
The volume is 30 cm³.

b. $V = lwh$
$V = 6 \times 6 \times 6$ ◀ Replace l with 6, w with 6, and h with 6.
$V = 216$
The volume is 216 ft³.

your turn

Find the volume of each rectangular prism.

4.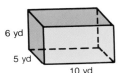

5.

6.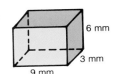

practice exercises

practice for example 1 (page 524)

Find the volume of each rectangular prism.

1.

2.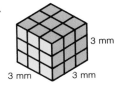

3.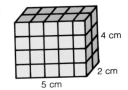

Find the volume of each rectangular prism.

4.
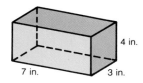
4 in.
7 in.   3 in.

5.

9 ft
9 ft   9 ft

6.
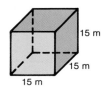
15 m
15 m
15 m

mixed practice (pages 524–525)

Find the volume of each rectangular prism.

7.
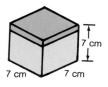
7 cm
7 cm   7 cm

8.
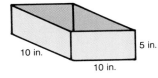
10 in.   5 in.
10 in.

9.
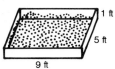
1 ft
5 ft
9 ft

10.
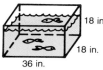
18 in.
18 in.
36 in.

11.
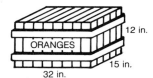
12 in.
ORANGES
32 in.   15 in.

12.
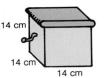
14 cm
14 cm
14 cm

13. A classroom is 20 ft wide, 30 ft long, and 12 ft high. If there are 24 students and one teacher in the room, how many cubic feet of space are available for each person?

14. There are 231 in.^{3} of water in one gallon. An aquarium is 42 in. long, 20 in. wide, and 22 in. high. How many gallons can it hold?

review *exercises*

Write each number in scientific notation.

1. 79   2. 85,000   3. 635   4. 940,000,000

Write the numeral form of each number.

5. 3.9×10^2 6. 6.5×10^6 7. 6.03×10^{12} 8. 7.15×10^1

puzzle corner

Show how to make four identical triangles using six straws of equal length that touch only at their tips.

23-4 VOLUME OF CYLINDERS

To find the volume of a cylinder, you multiply the
area of the base (B) by the height (h).

$$V = Bh$$

Because the base is a circle, you can replace B in this
formula with πr^2.

$$V = \pi r^2 h$$

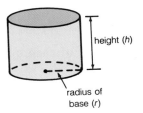

example 1

**Find the volume of the cylinder shown at the right.
Use $\pi \approx 3.14$.**

solution

$V = \pi r^2 h$

$V \approx 3.14(8^2)(20)$ ◄── **Replace r with 8
and h with 20.**

$V \approx 4019.2$

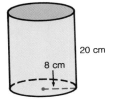

The volume is approximately 4019.2 cm³.

your turn

**Find the volume of each
cylinder. Use $\pi \approx 3.14$.**

1.

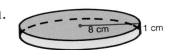

2.

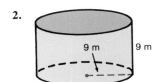

example 2

**Find the volume of the cylinder shown at
the right. Use $\pi \approx \frac{22}{7}$.**

solution

$V = \pi r^2 h$

$V \approx \frac{22}{7}(21^2)(20)$ ◄── **Replace r with
$\frac{1}{2} \times 42$, or 21.**

$V \approx 27{,}720$

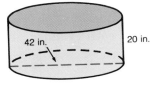

The volume is approximately 27,720 in.³.

your turn

**Find the volume of each
cylinder. Use $\pi \approx \frac{22}{7}$.**

3.

4.

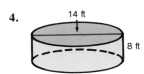

Surface Area and Volume 527

practice exercises

practice for example 1 (page 527)

Find the volume of each cylinder. Use π ≈ 3.14.

1.
6 cm   12 cm

2.
5 ft   7 ft

3.
2 ft   22 ft

4.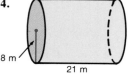
8 m   21 m

5.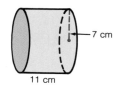
7 cm   11 cm

6.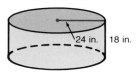
24 in.   18 in.

practice for example 2 (page 527)

Find the volume of each cylinder. Use π ≈ $\frac{22}{7}$.

7.
4 cm   7 cm

8.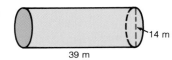
14 m   39 m

9.
42 yd   2 yd

10.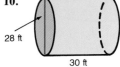
28 ft   30 ft

11.
8 in.   35 in.

12.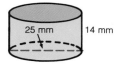
25 mm   14 mm

mixed practice (page 527)

Find the volume of each cylinder. Use π ≈ 3.14.

13.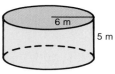
6 m   5 m

14.
15 m   135 m

15.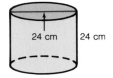
24 cm   24 cm

Find the volume of each cylinder. Use π ≈ $\frac{22}{7}$.

16.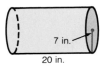
7 in.   20 in.

17.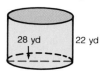
28 yd   22 yd

18.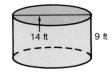
14 ft   9 ft

19. A silo in the shape of a cylinder has radius 8 ft and height 28 ft. Find its volume. Use $\pi \approx \frac{22}{7}$.

20. A railroad tank car is in the shape of a cylinder. Its diameter is 4 m and its length is 14 m. Find its volume. Use $\pi \approx 3.14$.

review exercises

Write each percent as a fraction in lowest terms.

1. 35%
2. 40%
3. 5.4%
4. $\frac{1}{2}\%$
5. $1\frac{1}{4}\%$
6. $87\frac{1}{2}\%$

Write each fraction as a percent.

7. $\frac{83}{100}$
8. $\frac{3}{50}$
9. $\frac{7}{40}$
10. $\frac{3}{4}$
11. $\frac{2}{3}$
12. $\frac{5}{8}$

mental math

Find each answer mentally.

1. $54 + 28$
2. $47 + 36$
3. $4 \times 17 \times 25$
4. $5 \times 42 \times 2$
5. 8×99
6. 4×299
7. $64 + 99$
8. $436 - 299$
9. $27.6 - 5.9$
10. $\$4.79 + \$3.99$
11. $\$3.25 + \$6.40$
12. $4 \times \$2.25$
13. 62×50
14. $4820 \div 5$
15. 25% of 400
16. 10% of 350
17. $5\overline{)625}$
18. $2\overline{)4876}$
19. $0.2\overline{)2.4}$
20. $0.05\overline{)30}$
21. $\frac{3}{10} \times \$40$
22. $\frac{2}{3} \times 18$
23. $10 \div \frac{1}{5}$
24. $5 - 2\frac{3}{4}$

25. $\frac{1}{4} + \frac{6}{7} + \frac{3}{4}$
26. $14 + {}^{-}3 + {}^{-}14 + 13$
27. $12 + {}^{-}6 + 5 + {}^{-}4$

28. 30 is what percent of 60?
29. What percent of 300 is 100?

30. Estimate a 15% tip for a meal costing $11.95.

Mentally estimate the mean.

31. 74, 73, 77, 76, 75, 77
32. 9.4, 9.1, 9.3, 8.6, 8.9

Mentally estimate.

33. $88 + 89 + 91 + 91 + 89 + 93$
34. $5.2 + 4.9 + 5.71 + 4.891$

23-5 VOLUME OF RECTANGULAR PYRAMIDS AND CONES

Suppose you empty a pyramid filled with water into a prism with the same base and height. You will find that the prism is only one-third full.

Now suppose you empty a cone filled with water into a cylinder with the same base and height. You will find that the cylinder is only one-third full.

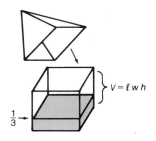

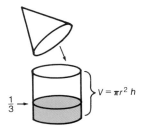

To find the volume of a rectangular pyramid or a cone, you use the following formulas.

rectangular pyramid

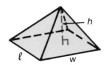

$V = \frac{1}{3}lwh$

cone

$V = \frac{1}{3}\pi r^2 h$

example 1

Find the volume of the pyramid shown at the right.

solution

$V = \frac{1}{3}lwh$

$V = \frac{1}{3}(12)(8)(10)$ ⬅ **Replace ℓ with 12, w with 8, and h with 10.**

$V = 320$

The volume is 320 cm³.

your turn

Find the volume of each pyramid.

1.

2.

example 2

Find the volume of each cone.

a. Use $\pi \approx 3.14$.

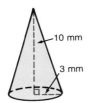
10 mm
3 mm

b. Use $\pi \approx \frac{22}{7}$.

12 in.
14 in.

solution

a. $V = \frac{1}{3}\pi r^2 h$

$V \approx \frac{1}{3}(3.14)(3^2)(10)$ ◀— **Replace _r_ with 3 and _h_ with 10.**

$V \approx 94.2$

The volume is approximately 94.2 mm³.

b. $V = \frac{1}{3}\pi r^2 h$

$V \approx \frac{1}{3}(\frac{22}{7})(7^2)(12)$ ◀— **Replace _r_ with $\frac{1}{2} \times 14$, or 7, and _h_ with 12.**

$V \approx 616$

The volume is approximately 616 in.³.

your turn

Find the volume of each cone.

3. Use $\pi \approx 3.14$.

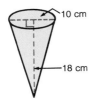
10 cm
18 cm

4. Use $\pi \approx \frac{22}{7}$.

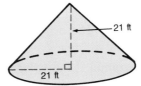
21 ft
21 ft

practice exercises

practice for example 1 (page 530)

Find the volume of each pyramid.

1.

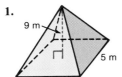
9 m
5 m
7 m

2.

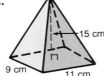
15 cm
9 cm
11 cm

3.

3 ft
3 ft
3 ft

Surface Area and Volume 531

practice for example 2 (page 531)

Find the volume of each cone.

4. Use π ≈ 3.14.

19 m
6 m

5. Use π ≈ 3.14.

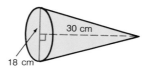
30 cm
18 cm

6. Use π ≈ $\frac{22}{7}$.

14 ft
3 ft

mixed practice (pages 530–531)

Find the volume of each space figure. When appropriate, use π ≈ 3.14.

7.

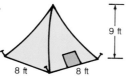
9 ft
8 ft   8 ft

8.

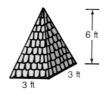
6 ft
3 ft
3 ft

9.

6 m
12 m

10.

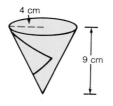
4 cm
9 cm

11.

144 m
215 m   215 m

12.

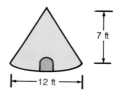
7 ft
12 ft

13. In Egypt, the Great Pyramid of Cheops has a square base with sides that each measure 252 yd. The original height of the pyramid was 160 yd. Find the original volume.

14. Find the height of a pyramid if the volume is 50 cm³ and the base is a square, 5 cm on a side.

review exercises

Find the area of each figure.

1. a rectangle with length 12 m and width 4 m

2. a triangle with a base that measures 6.2 cm and height 8 cm

3.

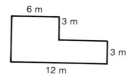
6 m
3 m
3 m
12 m

4.

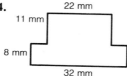
22 mm
11 mm
8 mm
32 mm

23-6 VOLUME OF SPHERES AND COMPOSITE FIGURES

A line segment that joins the center of a sphere to any point on the sphere is a **radius** (*r*). A line segment that joins any two points on a sphere and passes through the center of the sphere is a **diameter** (*d*).

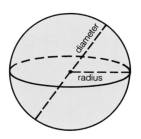

To find the volume of any sphere, you use the following formula.

$$V = \frac{4}{3}\pi r^3$$

example 1

Find the volume of each sphere. Use π ≈ 3.14.

a.

6 m

b.

18 cm

solution

a. $V = \frac{4}{3}\pi r^3$

$V \approx \frac{4}{3}(3.14)(6^3)$ ◄── **Replace *r* with 6.**

$V \approx 904.32$

The volume is approximately 904.32 m³.

b. $V = \frac{4}{3}\pi r^3$

$V \approx \frac{4}{3}(3.14)(9^3)$ ◄── **Replace *r* with $\frac{1}{2}$ × 18, or 9.**

$V \approx 3052.08$

The volume is approximately 3052.08 cm³.

your turn

Find the volume of each sphere. Use π ≈ 3.14.

1.

21 mm

2.

24 cm

Some space figures are a combination of polyhedrons, cylinders, cones, or spheres. To find the volume of these **composite space figures,** you add the volumes of the space figures that compose them.

example 2

Find the volume of the space figure shown at the right.

solution

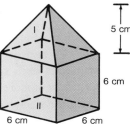

Divide the space figure into a rectangular pyramid
and a cube. Label them I and II.

$V(I) = \frac{1}{3}lwh = \frac{1}{3}(6)(6)(5) = 60$

$V(II) = lwh = (6)(6)(6) = 216$

$V(I) + V(II) = 60 + 216 = 276$

The volume is 276 cm³.

your turn

Find the volume of each space figure. When appropriate, use $\pi \approx 3.14$.

3.
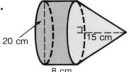

4.
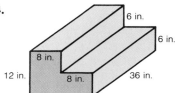

practice *exercises*

practice for example 1 (page 533)

Find the volume of each sphere. Use $\pi \approx 3.14$.

1.

2.

3.

4.

practice for example 2 (page 534)

Find the volume of each space figure. When appropriate, use $\pi \approx 3.14$.

5.
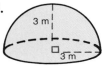

6.
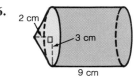

7.
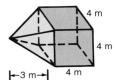

mixed practice (pages 533–534)

Find the volume of each space figure. When appropriate, use $\pi \approx 3.14$.

8. sphere with radius 30 m

9. sphere with radius 18 cm

10. sphere with diameter 60 m

11. sphere with diameter 36 cm

12. sphere with radius 12 m

13. sphere with radius 36 cm

14.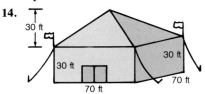

15.

16. A hot air balloon is shaped like a sphere with diameter 9 m. Find its volume. Use $\pi \approx 3.14$.

review *exercises*

Find each answer.

1. $10 + 5 \times 3$

2. $15 - 7 \times 2$

3. $24 \div 4 + 6$

4. $18 \div (6 \div 2)$

5. $5(17 - 6)$

6. $(9 + 6) \div (7 - 4)$

calculator corner

Some calculators have a M+ key that adds the number in the display to the memory. Pressing the MR key displays the number in memory. A calculator with these keys may be helpful in solving problems with composite figures.

example Find the volume of the figure at the right.

solution Total Volume = V(prism) + V(pyramid)

40 × 32 × 21 = M+ ← **This puts V(prism) in memory.**

40 × 32 × 15 ÷ 3 = M+ MR ← **M+ adds V(pyramid) to memory.**
MR displays the sum of the volumes.

Display: 33280   The total volume is 33,280 ft³.

Use a calculator to find the volume of each space figure.

1.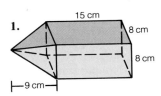

2.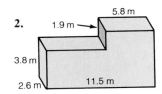

SKILL REVIEW

Name each space figure. If the figure is a polyhedron, give the
number of faces, edges, and vertices.

1.

2.

3.

4.

23-1

Find the surface area of each
space figure. When appro-
priate, use $\pi \approx \frac{22}{7}$.

5.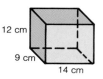

12 cm
9 cm
14 cm

6.

7 in.
14 in.

23-2

Find the volume of each
rectangular prism.

7.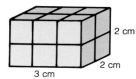

2 cm
2 cm
3 cm

8.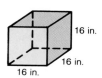

16 in.
16 in.
16 in.

23-3

9. A railroad box car shaped like a rectangular prism has length 48 ft,
width 10 ft, and height 12 ft. Find its volume.

Find the volume of each
cylinder. Use $\pi \approx \frac{22}{7}$.

10.

7 m
17 m

11.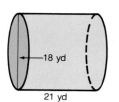

18 yd
21 yd

23-4

Find the volume of each
space figure. When appro-
priate, use $\pi \approx 3.14$.

12.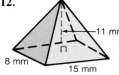

11 mm
8 mm
15 mm

13.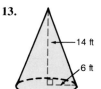

14 ft
6 ft

23-5

Find the volume of each
space figure. Use $\pi \approx 3.14$.

14.

24 cm

15.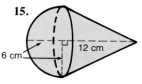

6 cm
12 cm

23-6

16. A natural gas storage tank is a sphere with diameter 24 m. Find its
volume. Use $\pi \approx 3.14$.

23-7 BUYING WALLPAPER

Wallpaper is bought on rolls that contain approximately 36 ft². Due to cutting and trimming, only about 30 ft² of this is usable. To wallpaper a room, you need to plan how much wallpaper to buy.

example

Frank plans to wallpaper his living room. The room is 16 ft long, 12 ft wide, and 7 ft high. It has 4 windows and 2 doors. How many rolls of wallpaper should he buy?

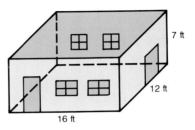

solution

- Multiply the perimeter of the room by the height.
  Perimeter = 2 × 16 + 2 × 12 = 56 (ft)
  Wall area = 56 × 7 = 392 (ft²)

- Divide the wall area by 30, the number of usable square feet on a roll.
  392 ÷ 30 ≈ 13.1 (rolls)

- Subtract one roll for every two openings (doors and windows).
  4 windows and 2 doors are 6 openings.
  6 openings mean 3 rolls.
  13.1 − 3 = 10.1

Since Frank needs more than 10 rolls, he should round up to the next whole number. Frank should buy 11 rolls of wallpaper.

exercises

Find how many rolls of wallpaper are needed for each room.

1. dining room
   14 ft long, 12 ft wide, 7 ft high
   1 door, 3 windows

2. bedroom
   10 ft long, 8 ft wide, 8 ft high
   2 doors, 2 windows

3. bedroom
   15 ft long, 9 ft wide, 8 ft high
   3 doors, 3 windows

4. living room
   22 ft long, 16 ft wide, 7 ft high
   3 doors, 5 windows

5. hallway
   24 ft long, 4 ft wide, 7 ft high
   6 doors

6. family room
   16 ft long, 11 ft wide, 8 ft high
   1 door, 4 windows

DESIGN DRAFTER

As a design drafter, Charlotte Gezen must calculate the weight of a part before it is made. She does this by using a chart to find the *density* of the material of the part.

Material	Density	
steel	490 lb/ft³	0.28 lb/in.³
marble	168 lb/ft³	0.01 lb/in.³
copper	558 lb/ft³	0.323 lb/in.³
gold	1211 lb/ft³	0.701 lb/in.³
nickel	553 lb/ft³	0.32 lb/in.³

example

A model of a steel beam that will be used as a roof support is shown at the right. Find the weight of the beam.

solution

Find the volume: $V = l \times w \times h$
$$= 20 \times 0.5 \times 1$$
$$= 10 \ (ft^3)$$

From the table, the density of steel is 490 lb/ft³.
Use the formula: weight = volume × density
$$= 10 \times 490$$
$$= 4900$$

The weight of the beam is 4900 lb.

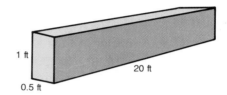

1 ft
20 ft
0.5 ft

exercises

Solve. Use a calculator if you have one.

1. A rectangular steel beam has length 30 ft, width 0.25 ft, and height 1 ft. Find its weight.

2. A cylindrical marble column has diameter 2 ft and height 20 ft. Find its weight. Use $\pi \approx 3.14$.

3. A jeweler made two models of the Great Pyramid. One model is copper and the other is gold. Each model has a square base, 5 in. on a side. Each model is 3 in. tall. Find the weight of each model.

4. A spherical ball bearing has a diameter of 1.5 in. Find its weight if it is made from nickel. Find its weight if it is made from steel. Use $\pi \approx 3.14$. Round each answer to the nearest hundredth.

CHAPTER REVIEW

vocabulary vo·cab·u·lar·y

Choose the correct word to complete each sentence.

1. A (*polyhedron, cylinder*) is a space figure with flat surfaces.
2. A (*pyramid, cone*) has one circular base and one vertex.

skills

Name each space figure. If the figure is a polyhedron, give the
number of faces, edges, and vertices.

3.    4.   5.   6.

Find the surface area of each
space figure. When appro-
priate, use $\pi \approx \frac{22}{7}$.

7.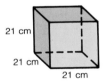
21 cm
21 cm
21 cm

8.
14 ft
7 ft

Find the volume of each
space figure.

9.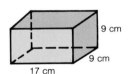
9 cm
9 cm
17 cm

10.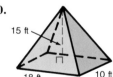
15 ft
18 ft   10 ft

Find the volume of each
space figure. Use $\pi \approx \frac{22}{7}$.

11.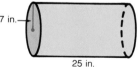
7 in.
25 in.

12.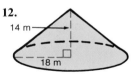
14 m
18 m

Find the volume of each
space figure. Use $\pi \approx 3.14$.

13.
21 mm

14.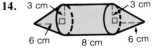
3 cm   3 cm
6 cm   8 cm   6 cm

15. How many rolls of wallpaper would you need for a room 18 ft long,
14 ft wide, and 8 ft high if the room has 2 doors and 4 windows?

CHAPTER TEST

Name each space figure. If the figure is a polyhedron, give the number of faces, edges, and vertices.

1.   2.   3.   4.   **23-1**

Find the surface area of each space figure. When appropriate, use $\pi \approx \frac{22}{7}$.

5.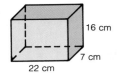

16 cm
7 cm
22 cm

6.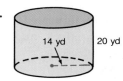

14 yd 20 yd

23-2

Find the volume of each rectangular prism.

7.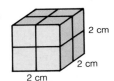

2 cm
2 cm
2 cm

8.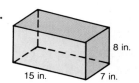

8 in.
15 in. 7 in.

23-3

Find the volume of each cylinder. Use $\pi \approx \frac{22}{7}$.

9.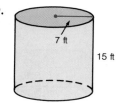

7 ft
15 ft

10.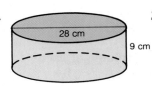

28 cm
9 cm

23-4

Find the volume of each space figure. When appropriate, use $\pi \approx 3.14$.

11.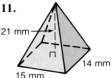

21 mm
14 mm
15 mm

12.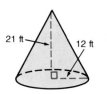

21 ft 12 ft

23-5

Find the volume of each space figure. Use $\pi \approx 3.14$.

13.

60 cm

14.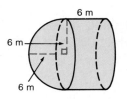

6 m
6 m
6 m

23-6

15. Find how many rolls of wallpaper you would need for a hallway that is 20 ft long, 4 ft wide, and 8 ft high. The hallway has 6 doors.

23-7

The triangular shape of these sails makes it possible for them to use the force of the wind efficiently.

CHAPTER 24

TRIANGLES

24-1 FACTS ABOUT TRIANGLES

In Chapter 22 you saw that quadrilaterals may be classified by their properties. In this lesson, you will see that triangles also have special classifications.

Triangles may be classified by their sides.

scalene triangle   **isosceles triangle**   **equilateral triangle**

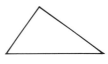   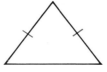

no congruent sides   two congruent sides   three congruent sides

Triangles may also be classified by their angles.

acute triangle   **right triangle**   **obtuse triangle**

three acute angles   one right angle   one obtuse angle

example 1

Classify each triangle first by its sides and then by its angles.

a.

two congruent sides → *isosceles* triangle
one right angle → *right* triangle

b.

no congruent sides → *scalene* triangle
three acute angles → *acute* triangle

your turn

Classify each triangle first by its sides and then by its angles.

1.   2.   3.

Suppose that you draw a large triangle on a piece of paper and cut the triangle out. You then tear off the three corners of the triangle and arrange them as shown at the right. No matter what type of triangle you choose, you will find that the three angles combine to form a **straight angle.** Since the measure of a straight angle is 180°, you have demonstrated the following.

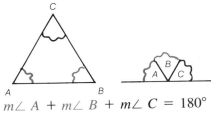

The sum of the measures of the angles of any triangle is 180°.

$$m\angle A + m\angle B + m\angle C = 180°$$

example 2

Find the missing angle measure in the triangle shown at the right.

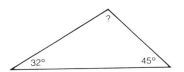

solution

The sum of the measures of the angles of any triangle is 180°.

$32° + 45° = 77°$ ⬅ **Add the two known measures.**

$180° - 77° = 103°$ ⬅ **Subtract the sum from 180°.**

The missing angle measure is 103°.

your turn

Find the missing angle measure in each triangle.

4.
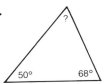

5.

6.

practice exercises

practice for example 1 (page 542)

Classify each triangle first by its sides and then by its angles.

1.

2.

3.

4.
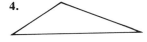

Find the missing angle measure in each triangle.

5.

6.

7.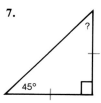

8.

mixed practice (pages 542–543)

The measures of two angles of a triangle are given. Find the measure of the third angle. Then classify each triangle by its angles.

9. 67°, 41°

10. 10°, 120°

11. 60°, 65°

12. 30°, 30°

13. 115°, 46°

14. 38°, 52°

15. 15°, 89°

16. 37°, 86°

17. One property of an equilateral triangle is that it has three congruent angles. Find the measure of each angle of an equilateral triangle.

18. One property of an isosceles triangle is that it has two congruent angles. If one angle of an isosceles triangle has a measure of 110°, find the measures of the other two angles.

review *exercises*

Tell whether each proportion is *true* or *false*.

1. $\frac{8}{12} = \frac{3}{4}$

2. $\frac{4}{10} = \frac{2}{5}$

3. $\frac{12}{20} = \frac{9}{15}$

4. $\frac{5}{8} = \frac{16}{24}$

Solve each proportion.

5. $\frac{x}{12} = \frac{3}{4}$

6. $\frac{a}{18} = \frac{5}{6}$

7. $\frac{6}{7} = \frac{24}{c}$

8. $\frac{9}{8} = \frac{36}{z}$

mental math

Write as a fraction in lowest terms.

1. 20%

2. 0.5

3. 0.75

4. 60%

5. $66\frac{2}{3}\%$

6. $12\frac{1}{2}\%$

Write as a percent.

7. 0.4

8. 0.375

9. $\frac{1}{10}$

10. $\frac{1}{4}$

11. $\frac{2}{5}$

12. $\frac{1}{3}$

24-2 SIMILAR TRIANGLES

Triangles that have the same shape are called **similar** triangles. If two triangles are similar, their *corresponding angles* are congruent. Their *corresponding sides* are **proportional**. This means that the ratios of the lengths of corresponding sides are equal.

   If the lengths of corresponding sides are in a 1 to 1 ratio, the triangles are **congruent**. Congruent triangles have the same shape *and* the same size.

example 1

In each pair, tell whether the triangles are *similar* or *not similar*. If the triangles are similar, tell whether they are *congruent* or *not congruent*.

a.

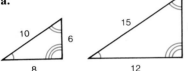

b.

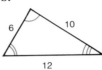

solution

a. Corresponding angles are congruent.

   Corresponding sides: $\dfrac{\text{first triangle}}{\text{second triangle}} \rightarrow \dfrac{10}{15} = \dfrac{2}{3}$ $\dfrac{6}{9} = \dfrac{2}{3}$ $\dfrac{8}{12} = \dfrac{2}{3}$

   The ratio of the lengths of the sides is 2 to 3. The triangles are *similar*. Since the ratio *is not* 1 to 1, the triangles are *not congruent*.

b. Corresponding angles are congruent.

   Corresponding sides: $\dfrac{\text{first triangle}}{\text{second triangle}} \rightarrow \dfrac{6}{6} = \dfrac{1}{1}$ $\dfrac{10}{10} = \dfrac{1}{1}$ $\dfrac{12}{12} = \dfrac{1}{1}$

   The ratio of the lengths of the sides is 1 to 1. The triangles are *similar*. Since the ratio *is* 1 to 1, the triangles are *congruent*.

your turn

In each pair, tell whether the triangles are *similar* or *not similar*. If the triangles are similar, tell whether they are *congruent* or *not congruent*.

1.

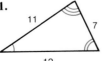 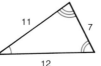

2.

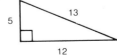

example 2

**The triangles are similar.
Find the missing length.**

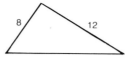 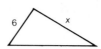

solution

Find the ratio of the known lengths of corresponding sides.

$$\frac{\text{first triangle} \rightarrow}{\text{second triangle} \rightarrow} \frac{8}{6} = \frac{4}{3}$$ ← **Write the ratio in lowest terms.**

Set up and solve a proportion involving the unknown length.

$$\frac{\text{first triangle} \rightarrow}{\text{second triangle} \rightarrow} \frac{4}{3} = \frac{12}{x}$$

$$4x = 36$$
$$x = 9 \qquad \text{The missing length is 9.}$$

your turn

In each pair, the triangles are similar. Find the missing length.

3.

4.

practice exercises

practice for example 1 (page 545)

**In each pair, tell whether the triangles are *similar* or *not similar*. If the
triangles are similar, tell whether they are *congruent* or *not congruent*.**

1.

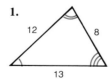 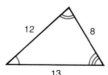

2.

3.

4.

 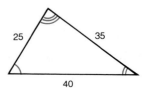

In each pair, the triangles are similar. Find the missing length.

5.

6.

7.

8.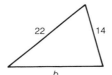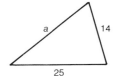

mixed practice (pages 545–546)

In each pair, the triangles are similar. Find the missing lengths. Then tell whether the triangles are *congruent* or *not congruent*.

9.

10.

11.

12.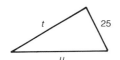

Tell whether each statement is *true* or *false*. If the statement is false, sketch a pair of triangles that explains your answer.

13. All equilateral triangles are similar. **14.** All equilateral triangles are congruent.

15. All right triangles are similar. **16.** All isosceles triangles are similar.

review exercises

Evaluate each expression when $a = 2$, $b = 5$, and $c = 6$.

1. a^3 **2.** c^2 **3.** $4b^2$ **4.** $7a^4$ **5.** a^2bc^3

Write each decimal as a fraction in lowest terms.

6. 0.4 **7.** 0.94 **8.** 0.203 **9.** 0.404 **10.** 0.875

24-3 SQUARES AND SQUARE ROOTS

Each side of the square at the right has a length of 4 units. When you use the formula that you learned in Chapter 22, you find that the area of the square is 16 square units. For this reason, the expression 4^2 is often read *four squared*.

$$A = s^2$$
$$= 4^2$$
$$= 16$$

4 units
4 units

The **square** of 4 is 16.
$$4^2 = 16$$

The **square root** of 16 is 4.
$$\sqrt{16} = 4$$ ← The symbol $\sqrt{}$ is called the *radical sign*.

example 1

Find each square root: **a.** $\sqrt{64}$ **b.** $\sqrt{0}$

solution

a. Since $8 \times 8 = 64$, $\sqrt{64} = 8$.   **b.** Since $0 \times 0 = 0$, $\sqrt{0} = 0$.

your turn

Find each square root.

1. $\sqrt{4}$ 2. $\sqrt{36}$ 3. $\sqrt{81}$ 4. $\sqrt{144}$

A number like 16 or 36 is called a **perfect square** because its square root is a whole number. If a number is not a perfect square, you may be able to use a table like the one on the facing page to find its *approximate* square root. Because the table includes squares of the numbers, you can also use it to find square roots of some greater numbers.

example 2

Use the table on page 549 to find each square root: **a.** $\sqrt{32}$ **b.** $\sqrt{4356}$

solution

a. Find 32 in the *No.* (number) column. Find the number across from 32 in the *Square Root* column: 5.657
$$\sqrt{32} \approx 5.657$$

b. Find 4356 in the *Square* column. Find the number across from 4356 in the *No.* column: 66
$$\sqrt{4356} = 66$$

your turn

Use the table on page 549 to find each square root.

5. $\sqrt{22}$ 6. $\sqrt{84}$ 7. $\sqrt{961}$ 8. $\sqrt{2809}$

Table of Squares and Square Roots

NO.	SQUARE	SQUARE ROOT	NO.	SQUARE	SQUARE ROOT	NO.	SQUARE	SQUARE ROOT
1	1	1.000	51	2,601	7.141	101	10,201	10.050
2	4	1.414	52	2,704	7.211	102	10,404	10.100
3	9	1.732	53	2,809	7.280	103	10,609	10.149
4	16	2.000	54	2,916	7.348	104	10,816	10.198
5	25	2.236	55	3,025	7.416	105	11,025	10.247
6	36	2.449	56	3,136	7.483	106	11,236	10.296
7	49	2.646	57	3,249	7.550	107	11,449	10.344
8	64	2.828	58	3,364	7.616	108	11,664	10.392
9	81	3.000	59	3,481	7.681	109	11,881	10.440
10	100	3.162	60	3,600	7.746	110	12,100	10.488
11	121	3.317	61	3,721	7.810	111	12,321	10.536
12	144	3.464	62	3,844	7.874	112	12,544	10.583
13	169	3.606	63	3,969	7.937	113	12,769	10.630
14	196	3.742	64	4,096	8.000	114	12,996	10.677
15	225	3.873	65	4,225	8.062	115	13,225	10.724
16	256	4.000	66	4,356	8.124	116	13,456	10.770
17	289	4.123	67	4,489	8.185	117	13,689	10.817
18	324	4.243	68	4,624	8.246	118	13,924	10.863
19	361	4.359	69	4,761	8.307	119	14,161	10.909
20	400	4.472	70	4,900	8.367	120	14,400	10.954
21	441	4.583	71	5,041	8.426	121	14,641	11.000
22	484	4.690	72	5,184	8.485	122	14,884	11.045
23	529	4.796	73	5,329	8.544	123	15,129	11.091
24	576	4.899	74	5,476	8.602	124	15,376	11.136
25	625	5.000	75	5,625	8.660	125	15,625	11.180
26	676	5.099	76	5,776	8.718	126	15,876	11.225
27	729	5.196	77	5,929	8.775	127	16,129	11.269
28	784	5.292	78	6,084	8.832	128	16,384	11.314
29	841	5.385	79	6,241	8.888	129	16,641	11.358
30	900	5.477	80	6,400	8.944	130	16,900	11.402
31	961	5.568	81	6,561	9.000	131	17,161	11.446
32	1,024	5.657	82	6,724	9.055	132	17,424	11.489
33	1,089	5.745	83	6,889	9.110	133	17,689	11.533
34	1,156	5.831	84	7,056	9.165	134	17,956	11.576
35	1,225	5.916	85	7,225	9.220	135	18,225	11.619
36	1,296	6.000	86	7,396	9.274	136	18,496	11.662
37	1,369	6.083	87	7,569	9.327	137	18,769	11.705
38	1,444	6.164	88	7,744	9.381	138	19,044	11.747
39	1,521	6.245	89	7,921	9.434	139	19,321	11.790
40	1,600	6.325	90	8,100	9.487	140	19,600	11.832
41	1,681	6.403	91	8,281	9.539	141	19,881	11.874
42	1,764	6.481	92	8,464	9.592	142	20,164	11.916
43	1,849	6.557	93	8,649	9.644	143	20,449	11.958
44	1,936	6.633	94	8,836	9.695	144	20,736	12.000
45	2,025	6.708	95	9,025	9.747	145	21,025	12.042
46	2,116	6.782	96	9,216	9.798	146	21,316	12.083
47	2,209	6.856	97	9,409	9.849	147	21,609	12.124
48	2,304	6.928	98	9,604	9.899	148	21,904	12.166
49	2,401	7.000	99	9,801	9.950	149	22,201	12.207
50	2,500	7.071	100	10,000	10.000	150	22,500	12.247

practice exercises

practice for example 1 (page 548)

Find each square root.

1. $\sqrt{9}$ 2. $\sqrt{49}$ 3. $\sqrt{1}$ 4. $\sqrt{25}$ 5. $\sqrt{100}$ 6. $\sqrt{121}$

practice for example 2 (page 548)

Use the table on page 549 to find each square root.

7. $\sqrt{13}$ 8. $\sqrt{71}$ 9. $\sqrt{109}$ 10. $\sqrt{841}$ 11. $\sqrt{7744}$ 12. $\sqrt{13,225}$

mixed practice (page 548)

Find each square root. Use the table on page 549, if necessary.

13. $\sqrt{225}$ 14. $\sqrt{20}$ 15. $\sqrt{103}$ 16. $\sqrt{131}$ 17. $\sqrt{8100}$ 18. $\sqrt{11,025}$
19. $\sqrt{625}$ 20. $\sqrt{55}$ 21. $\sqrt{1849}$ 22. $\sqrt{5776}$ 23. $\sqrt{90}$ 24. $\sqrt{11,664}$

Complete.

25.   32 is between 25 and 36.
$\sqrt{32}$ is between $\sqrt{25}$ and $\sqrt{36}$.
So $\sqrt{32}$ is between __?__ and __?__.

26.   92 is between 81 and 100.
$\sqrt{92}$ is between $\sqrt{81}$ and $\sqrt{100}$.
So $\sqrt{92}$ is between __?__ and __?__.

27. The area of a square is 2916 cm². Find the length of a side.
28. The area of a square is 126 cm². Find the approximate length of a side.

review exercises

Solve each equation.

1. $x +\ ^-12 = 14$ 2. $z - 9 = 2$ 3. $^-4y = 68$

4. $\frac{n}{4} = 13$ 5. $5x - 11 = 19$ 6. $\frac{2}{3}z + 6 = 18$

PUZZLE CORNER

Find the number of triangles in the figure at the right.

24-4 THE PYTHAGOREAN THEOREM

In a right triangle, the side opposite the right angle is called the **hypotenuse** (c). The hypotenuse is always the longest side. The other sides (a and b) are called **legs.**

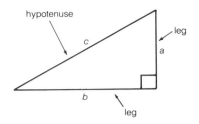

Over 2500 years ago, the Greek mathematician Pythagoras proved the following property relating the lengths of the sides of a right triangle. This property is called the **Pythagorean Theorem.**

For any right triangle, the square of the length of the hypotenuse is equal to the sum of the squares of the lengths of the two legs.

$$c^2 = a^2 + b^2$$

The Pythagorean Theorem is true *only* for right triangles. You can use the theorem to check if a triangle is a right triangle.

example 1

The lengths of the sides of a triangle are given. Tell whether the triangle is *a right triangle* or is *not a right triangle*.

a. 5, 8, 11

b. 9, 12, 15

solution

a.
$$c^2 \stackrel{?}{=} a^2 + b^2$$
$$11^2 \stackrel{?}{=} 5^2 + 8^2 \quad \longleftarrow \text{Substitute the greatest value for c.}$$
$$121 \stackrel{?}{=} 25 + 64$$
$$121 \neq 89 \quad \textit{not a right triangle}$$

b.
$$c^2 \stackrel{?}{=} a^2 + b^2$$
$$15^2 \stackrel{?}{=} 9^2 + 12^2$$
$$225 \stackrel{?}{=} 81 + 144$$
$$225 = 225 \quad \textit{right triangle}$$

your turn

The lengths of the sides of a triangle are given. Tell whether the triangle is *a right triangle* or is *not a right triangle*.

1. 6, 8, 10

2. 3, 5, 7

3. 7, 40, 41

If you know the lengths of two sides of a right triangle, you can use the Pythagorean Theorem to find the length of the third side.

example 2

Find the missing length. If necessary, round answers to the nearest tenth.

a.

b.

solution

a. $c^2 = a^2 + b^2$
$c^2 = 6^2 + 9^2$
$c^2 = 36 + 81$
$c^2 = 117$
$c = \sqrt{117} \approx 10.817$ ◀ **Use the table on page 549.**
The length of the hypotenuse is about 10.8 cm.

b. $c^2 = a^2 + b^2$
$13^2 = a^2 + 12^2$
$169 = a^2 + 144$ ◀ **Subtract 144 from both sides.**
$25 = a^2$
$a = \sqrt{25} = 5$
The length of the leg is 5 ft.

your turn

Find the missing length. If necessary, round answers to the nearest tenth.

4. **5.** 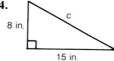 **6.** 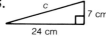 **7.**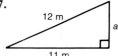

practice exercises

practice for example 1 (page 551)

The lengths of the sides of a triangle are given. Tell whether the triangle is *a right triangle* or is *not a right triangle*.

1. 8, 12, 14   **2.** 12, 16, 20   **3.** 5, 12, 13

4. 6, 9, 14   **5.** 7, 24, 25   **6.** 16, 30, 34

practice for example 2 (page 552)

Find the missing length. If necessary, round answers to the nearest tenth.

7. **8.** 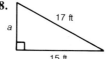 **9.** **10.**

Find the missing length.

11.
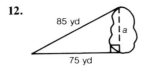
25 ft   24 ft
b

12.
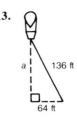
85 yd
a
75 yd

13.

a   136 ft
64 ft

Solve. Making a drawing may be helpful.

14. A rectangular park has length 116 m and width 87 m. Find the length of a diagonal walk across the park.

15. A support wire from the top of a radio tower is 100 ft long. It is anchored at a spot 60 ft from the base of the tower. Find the height of the radio tower.

review *exercises*

Find each answer.

1. What number is 8% of 400?

2. What percent of 87 is 29?

3. 25% of what number is 18?

4. 75% of 1.6 is what number?

5. 90 is what percent of 54?

6. 5 is 0.2% of what number?

7. 15% of 18 is what number?

8. 140% of what number is 119?

9. What number is $66\frac{2}{3}\%$ of 36?

10. $8\frac{1}{2}\%$ of 200 is what number?

calculator corner

Many calculators have a square root key $\boxed{\checkmark}$. Other calculators may also have a square key $\boxed{x^2}$ to find the second power of a number.

example   Use a calculator to find $\sqrt{3.6}$ and $(3.6)^2$.

solution   Enter 3.6 $\boxed{\checkmark}$ = .   Enter 3.6 $\boxed{x^2}$ = .
The answer is 1.8973666.   The answer is 12.96.

Use a calculator to find each square root or square.

1. $\sqrt{8.1}$ 2. $\sqrt{4.9}$ 3. $\sqrt{0.64}$ 4. $(4.7)^2$ 5. $(8.3)^2$ 6. $(5.08)^2$

24-5 MAKING A MODEL

1 Understand
2 Plan
3 Work
4 Answer

Sometimes it is difficult to visualize a problem that involves a space figure. In cases like these, it may be helpful to make a **model** of the figure in the problem. One way to make a model of a three-dimensional figure is to begin with a *two-dimensional* pattern.

example

Imagine that you could fold each pattern along the dashed lines. Which pattern could you fold to form the space figure shown at the left below?

a.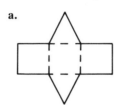

b.

c.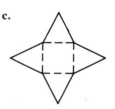

solution

The space figure is a square pyramid. It has a square base and four triangular faces. The pattern that you could fold to form this figure is (c).

problems

Imagine that you could fold each pattern along the dashed lines. Which pattern could you fold to form the space figure shown at the left below?

1.

a.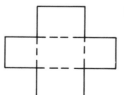

b.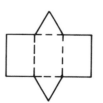

c.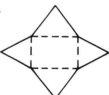

2.

a.

b.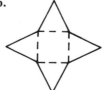

c.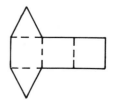

Identify the space figure that would be formed if you folded each pattern.

3.

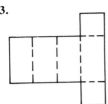

4.

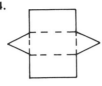

5.

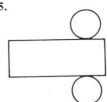

A. cylinder
B. cone
C. rectangular prism
D. triangular prism

Each of the following patterns could be folded along the dashed lines to make a cube. If the pattern were folded, which numbered face would appear directly opposite the face marked ★?

6.

7.

8.

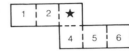

9.

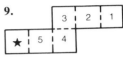

Could the given pattern be folded along the dashed lines to make a cube? Write *Yes* or *No*.

10.

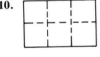

11.

12.

13.

14.

15.

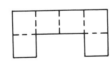

16.

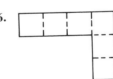

17.

18. There are eleven *different* patterns of six squares that could be folded to make a cube. Sketch the eleven patterns on a sheet of grid paper.

review exercises

1. Look for a pattern. Then write the next three numbers:
   1, 4, 9, 16, 25, 36, _?_, _?_, _?_

2. In how many different ways can three postage stamps be torn from a sheet of stamps so that the three stamps are still attached to one another?

SKILL REVIEW

Classify each triangle first by its sides and then by its angles.

1.
2.
3.

24-1

The measures of two angles of a triangle are given. Find the measure of the third angle.

4. 47°, 39°
5. 56°, 81°
6. 24°, 34°
7. 107°, 43°

In each pair, tell whether the triangles are *similar* or *not similar*. If the triangles are similar, tell whether they are *congruent* or *not congruent*.

8.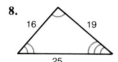
9.

24-2

In each pair, the triangles are similar. Find the missing length.

10.
11.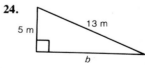

Find each square root. Use the table on page 549, if necessary.

12. $\sqrt{1600}$
13. $\sqrt{10}$
14. $\sqrt{2}$
15. $\sqrt{3600}$ **24-3**
16. $\sqrt{94}$
17. $\sqrt{3249}$
18. $\sqrt{12,100}$
19. $\sqrt{133}$

The lengths of the sides of a triangle are given. Tell whether the triangle is *a right triangle* or is *not a right triangle*.

20. 27, 36, 45
21. 18, 80, 82
22. 11, 40, 41 **24-4**

Find the missing length. If necessary, round answers to the nearest tenth.

23.
24.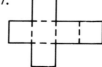

Identify the space figure that would be formed by folding each pattern.

25.
26.
27.

A. cube **24-5**
B. cone
C. cylinder
D. square pyramid

24-6 INDIRECT MEASUREMENT

Sometimes it is impossible to measure a distance directly. In such cases, you may be able to use similar triangles to make an **indirect measurement.**

example

Cheryl is 156 cm tall. When her shadow is 210 cm long, the shadow of a tree is 350 cm long. The triangles formed by Cheryl and her shadow and the tree and its shadow are similar. Use this information to find the height of the tree.

solution

- Make a drawing.

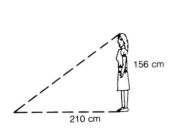

156 cm

210 cm

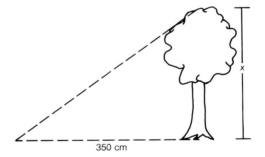

350 cm

- Find the ratio of the known lengths of corresponding sides.

$$\frac{\text{first triangle} \rightarrow}{\text{second triangle} \rightarrow} \frac{210}{350} = \frac{3}{5} \quad \longleftarrow \text{ Write the ratio in lowest terms.}$$

- Set up and solve a proportion involving the unknown length.

$$\frac{\text{first triangle} \rightarrow}{\text{second triangle} \rightarrow} \frac{3}{5} = \frac{156}{x}$$
$$3x = 5 \times 156$$
$$\frac{3x}{3} = \frac{780}{3}$$
$$x = 260$$

The tree is 260 cm tall.

exercises

Solve by using similar triangles.

1. When Zack's shadow is 8 ft long, the shadow of a flagpole is 20 ft long. Zack is 6 ft tall. How tall is the pole?

2. A 10-ft pillar casts a shadow that is 12 ft long. At the same time, a telephone pole casts a shadow that is 18 ft long. Find the height of the pole.

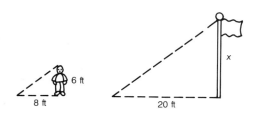 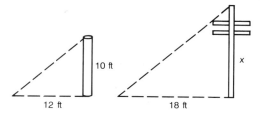

3. A 50-cm ruler casts a shadow that is 56 cm long. At the same time, a fence post casts a shadow 196 cm long. Find the height of the post.

4. A flagpole is 40 ft tall. When its shadow is 20 ft long, the shadow of a building is 30 ft long. How tall is the building?

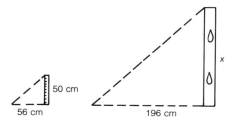 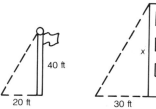

Solve by using similar triangles. Make a drawing.

5. Leona is 168 cm tall. When her shadow is 170 cm long, the shadow of a tree is 680 cm long. How tall is the tree?

6. Alf is 180 cm tall. When his shadow is 36 cm long, a tree casts a shadow that is 125 cm long. How tall is the tree?

7. Sally is 5 ft tall. When Sally's shadow is 3 ft long, the shadow of a television tower is 63 ft long. How tall is the television tower?

8. A highway road sign is 270 cm tall. When it casts a shadow that is 390 cm long, a bridge over the highway casts a shadow that is 650 cm long. Find the height of the bridge.

9. When Ralph's shadow is 290 cm long, the shadow of a giraffe is 580 cm long. If Ralph is 185 cm tall, how tall is the giraffe?

10. A fence post is 4 ft tall and casts a shadow that is 5 ft long. At the same time an electric tower casts a shadow that is 135 ft long. Find the height of the tower.

CHAPTER REVIEW

vocabulary vo·cab·u·lar·y

Choose the correct word to complete each sentence.

1. A triangle with three congruent sides is (*equilateral, scalene*).
2. Triangles that have the same shape, but not the same size, are (*congruent, similar*).

skills

Classify each triangle first by its sides and then by its angles.

 3.  4.   5.

The measures of two angles of a triangle are given. Find the measure of the third angle.

6. 63°, 21°   7. 49°, 68°   8. 94°, 81°   9. 119°, 27°

In each pair, the triangles are similar. Find the missing length.

10.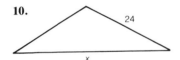

11.

Find each square root. Use the table on page 549, if necessary.

12. $\sqrt{2500}$ 13. $\sqrt{87}$ 14. $\sqrt{130}$ 15. $\sqrt{3969}$ 16. $\sqrt{8281}$

Find the missing length. If necessary, round answers to the nearest tenth.

17. 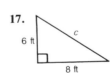   18.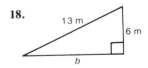

The lengths of the sides of a triangle are given. Tell whether the triangle is *a right triangle* or is *not a right triangle*.

19. 14, 48, 50   20. 15, 30, 34   21. 10, 24, 27

Could the given pattern be folded along the dashed lines to make a cube? Write *Yes* or *No*.

22. 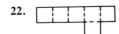   23. 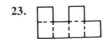   24.    25.

26. Miguel is 6 ft tall. When his shadow is 2 ft long, the shadow of a telephone pole is 8 ft long. Find the height of the pole.

CHAPTER TEST

Classify each triangle first by its sides and then by its angles.

1.
2.
3.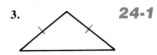

24-1

The measures of two angles of a triangle are given. Find the measure of the third angle.

4. 17°, 81°
5. 47°, 35°
6. 90°, 43°
7. 124°, 19°

In each pair, tell whether the triangles are *similar* or *not similar*. If the triangles are similar, tell whether they are *congruent* or *not congruent*.

8.
9.

24-2

In each pair, the triangles are similar. Find the missing length.

10.
11.

Find each square root. Use the table on page 549, if necessary.

12. $\sqrt{4900}$
13. $\sqrt{72}$
14. $\sqrt{101}$
15. $\sqrt{20,736}$ **24-3**

Find the missing length. If necessary, round answers to the nearest tenth.

16.
17.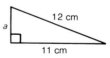

24-4

18. Imagine that you could fold each pattern. Which pattern could you fold to form the space figure at the left?

24-5

a.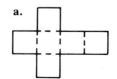
b.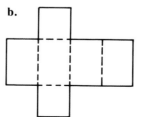
c.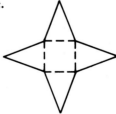

19. When Edward's shadow is 3 m long, the shadow of a building is 27 m long. Edward is 2 m tall. Find the height of the building.

24-6

Logo

Logo is a computer language that is often taught in schools. It uses a small triangle called a **turtle** to draw pictures, or **graphics.** The turtle draws a picture by following your commands to turn and move. Some of the turtle graphics **commands** are listed at the right.

Command	Short Form
home	HOME
forward	FD
back	BK
right	RT
left	LT

The HOME command brings the turtle to home position, as shown at the right. Notice that the turtle points to the top of the screen.

The FD and BK commands tell the turtle how to move. For example, starting from the home position, FD 6 instructs the turtle to move *forward* 6 steps. BK 4 means move *back* 4 steps.

The RT and LT commands tell the turtle to turn either right or left. The command RT 90 instructs the turtle to turn *right* 90 degrees. To turn *left,* use the LT command.

Home Position

RT 90

exercises

Use grid paper to draw the path of the turtle and its position after completing each set of commands.
Assume that the turtle starts in the home position.

1. BK 6   2. FD 11   3. FD 3   4. BK 15

5. FD 8 LT 45 BK 12

6. BK 10 LT 90 FD 10

7. FD 3 RT 90 FD 4 RT 135 FD 5

8. BK 6 RT 90 FD 9 LT 90 FD 6 LT 90 FD 9

9. Replace each __?__ with the command that will instruct the turtle to draw the picture at the right.

    FD 4 __?__ 90 __?__ 6 RT 45
    FD 4 __?__ 45 FD 1 __?__ 90 __?__ 9

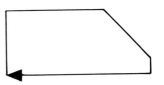

10. Write a set of Logo commands that will produce a rectangle.

Triangles 561

COMPETENCY TEST

Choose the letter of the correct answer.

1. Find the sum. $^-21 + 4$

   A. $^-17$
   B. 17
   C. $^-25$
   D. 25

2. When the shadow of a pole is 12 ft long, the shadow of a tree is 85 ft long. The pole is 8 ft tall. About how tall is the tree?

   A. about 11 ft
   B. about 57 ft
   C. about 64 ft
   D. about 128 ft

3. Find the volume of a rectangular prism with $l = 34$ m, $w = 12$ m, and $h = 85$ m.

   A. 131 m^3
   B. 262 m^3
   C. 11,560 m^3
   D. 34,680 m^3

4. Match the location to the ordered pair.

   5 units left, 3 units up

   A. $(^-5, 3)$ B. $(5, ^-3)$
   C. $(5, 3)$ D. $(^-5, ^-3)$

5. Solve. $3t + 7 = ^-5$

   A. $t = ^-12$
   B. $t = ^-36$
   C. $t = ^-4$
   D. $t = \frac{2}{3}$

6. Find the difference. $^-8 - ^-23$

   A. $^-15$
   B. 15
   C. $^-31$
   D. 31

7. 36% of the workers in a town work in manufacturing. You want to draw a circle graph describing the work force. Approximately what angle should you use for the manufacturing sector?

   A. about 3°   B. about 10°
   C. about 36°   D. about 130°

8. Two angles of a triangle measure 84° and 39°. Find the measure of the third angle.

   A. 123°
   B. 57°
   C. 96°
   D. 141°

9. Aziz rode his bicycle 30 mi in $2\frac{1}{2}$ h. Find his average speed.

   A. 12 mi/h   B. 18 mi/h
   C. 30 mi/h   D. 75 mi/h

10. Choose the true statement.

    A. $\angle$ AED is obtuse.
    B. $\angle$ ACB is acute.
    C. $\overleftrightarrow{BD} \perp \overleftrightarrow{AE}$
    D. $\overleftrightarrow{AB} \parallel \overleftrightarrow{DB}$

ALGEBRA AND GEOMETRY

11. Find the product. $^-48 \times {^-3}$

- A. 16
- B. $^-16$
- C. $^-144$
- D. 144

12. Find the area of a rectangle with length 15 cm and height 6 cm.

- A. 21 cm
- B. 42 cm
- C. 90 cm^2
- D. 180 cm^2

13. Choose the best word to describe the figure.

- A. polyhedron
- B. polygon
- C. pyramid
- D. cone

14. Find the surface area. Use $\pi \approx 3.14$.

- A. 1177.5 cm^2
- B. 471 cm^2
- C. 235.5 cm^2
- D. 628 cm^2

5 cm

15 cm

15. The triangles are similar. Find x.

- A. $x = 16\frac{2}{3}$
- B. $x = 24$
- C. $x = 30$
- D. $x = 54$

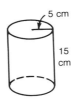

30   24   20   16

36   x

16. Find the quotient. $^-70 \div 14$

- A. 5
- B. $^-5$
- C. $^-56$
- D. $^-84$

17. Find the circumference of a circle with radius 3 cm. Use $\pi \approx 3.14$.

- A. 28.26 cm
- B. 56.52 cm
- C. 9.42 cm
- D. 18.84 cm

18. Find the volume. Use $\pi \approx \frac{22}{7}$.

- A. 3696 ft^3
- B. 1232 ft^3
- C. 1056 ft^3
- D. 352 ft^3

24 ft

7 ft

19. A club had \$132 in the treasury. The dues from 8 new members raised the amount to \$232. Find the dues for each member.

- A. \$12.50   B. \$45.50
- C. \$16.50   D. \$29

20. Choose the figure that represents the term $\overleftrightarrow{AB}$.

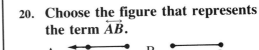

A. A B B. A B

C. A B D. A B

CUMULATIVE REVIEW CHAPTERS 1–24

Find each answer.

1. $^-7 + 2$
2. $8765 - 4339$
3. 3.25×0.004
4. $19\overline{)785}$

5. $^-4 \times 5 \times {}^-6$
6. $12 + 8 \div 2$
7. $\$12.35 + \$9.28$
8. $^-105 \div 7$

9. $^-8 + {}^-3$
10. $5\frac{1}{8} \div 2\frac{3}{4}$
11. $3\frac{4}{7} \times 2\frac{1}{3}$
12. $^-9 - {}^-12$

13. What percent of 225 is 108?
14. Write in simplest form: 32 ft 5 in. − 12 ft 8 in.

Estimate.

15. 4218×6756
16. $7239 + 6094 + 9228$
17. 65% of 26,986

18. $2.91\overline{)885.624}$
19. $\frac{13}{25} \times 807$
20. $19\frac{5}{6} - 9\frac{11}{13}$

Solve each equation.

21. $3b = {}^-9$
22. $x + 4 = {}^-4$
23. $\frac{2}{3}a = 12$
24. $^-5t + 4 = 9$

Write in order from least to greatest.

25. $\frac{5}{8}, \frac{7}{12}, \frac{5}{9}, \frac{2}{3}$
26. $^-3, {}^-5, 2, 0, {}^-1$
27. $2.73, 2.073, 2.37, 2.337$

28. Find the mean, median, and mode(s): 145, 312, 98, 77, 188, 98
29. Four pencils cost 82¢ and 3 erasers cost 89¢. About how much will two of each cost?
30. Find the perimeter of a rectangle with length 18 in. and width 8 in.
31. Find the volume of a cylinder with radius 2 cm and height 10 cm. Use $\pi \approx 3.14$.
32. Find the area of a square with sides 8 ft long.
33. Find the circumference of a circle with diameter 21 in. Use $\pi \approx \frac{22}{7}$.
34. Graph the equation $y = 2x + 3$.
35. A bowl contains 5 red apples, 4 yellow apples, and 3 green apples. Dennis takes one without looking. Then Theresa takes one, also without looking. Find the probability they both pick yellow.
36. Two angles of a triangle measure 52° and 91°. Find the measure of the third angle.
37. Is the triangle with sides of lengths 8, 13, and 15 a right triangle?
38. Monthly sales in July were $15,000. The monthly sales for August were $18,000. Find the percent of increase.

table of measures

Time

60 seconds (s) = 1 minute (min)	365 days
60 minutes = 1 hour (h)	52 weeks (approx.) } = 1 year
24 hours = 1 day	12 months
7 days = 1 week	10 years = 1 decade
4 weeks (approx.) = 1 month	100 years = 1 century

Metric

Length

10 millimeters (mm) = 1 centimeter (cm)

100 cm } = 1 meter (m)
1000 mm }

1000 m = 1 kilometer (km)

Area

100 square millimeters = 1 square centimeter
(mm^2)   (cm^2)

10,000 cm^2 = 1 square meter (m^2)

10,000 m^2 = 1 hectare (ha)

Volume

1000 cubic millimeters = 1 cubic centimeter
(mm^3)   (cm^3)

1,000,000 cm^3 = 1 cubic meter (m^3)

Liquid Capacity

1000 milliliters (mL) = 1 liter (L)

1000 L = 1 kiloliter (kL)

Mass

1000 milligrams (mg) = 1 gram (g)

1000 g = 1 kilogram (kg)

1000 kg = 1 metric ton (t)

Temperature–Degrees Celsius (°C)

0°C = freezing point of water

37°C = normal body temperature

100°C = boiling point of water

United States Customary

Length

12 inches (in.) = 1 foot (ft)

36 in. }
3 ft } = 1 yard (yd)

5280 ft }
1760 yd } = 1 mile (mi)

Area

144 square inches (in.^{2}) = 1 square foot (ft^2)

9 ft^2 = 1 square yard (yd^2)

43,560 ft^2 }
4840 yd^2 } = 1 acre (A)

Volume

1728 cubic inches (in.^{3}) = 1 cubic foot (ft^3)

27 ft^3 = 1 cubic yard (yd^3)

Liquid Capacity

8 fluid ounces (fl oz) = 1 cup (c)

2 c = 1 pint (pt)

2 pt = 1 quart (qt)

4 qt = 1 gallon (gal)

Weight

16 ounces (oz) = 1 pound (lb)

2000 lb = 1 ton (t)

Temperature–Degrees Fahrenheit (°F)

32°F = freezing point of water

98.6°F = normal body temperature

212°F = boiling point of water

Write the word form of each number.

1. 208,004   2. 8,005,100   3. 705,343,090   4. 6,040,000,300   *1-1*

Write the numeral form of each number.

5. 3 million, 400   6. 7 thousand, 21

7. two hundred seventy-three billion, nine hundred six million, fifty-three

8. five hundred two billion, eleven thousand, three hundred fifty-one

Find each sum.

9. $31 + $14 + $33   10. 475 + 912 + 84   *1-2*

11. 5112 + 846 + 83,401   12. 632 + 380 + 706

13. 999 + 23 + 95 + 909   14. $436 + $91 + $64

15. 45 + 63 + 77 + 122   16. 3091 + 527 + 469 + 33

17. Della has 874 stamps from England, 56 stamps from Italy, and 239 stamps from Canada. How many stamps has she altogether?

Estimate by adjusting the sum of the front-end digits.

18. 629 + 170 + 308 + 590   19. 701 + 313 + 26 + 902   *1-3*

20. 26,910 + 425 + 33,084   21. 13,423 + 82,491 + 3498

22. 1761 + 613 + 343 + 2390   23. $749 + $15 + $810 + $32

Find each difference.

24. 796 − 215   25. $530 − $218   26. 8000 − 2495   *1-4*

27. $17,020 − $6373   28. 61,735 − 997   29. 19,243 − 196

30. 27,904 − 8647   31. 72,597 − 66,988   32. 10,000 − 6809

33. A football stadium seats 70,000 people. There were 66,789 tickets sold for the game. How many tickets remained?

Write each phrase as a variable expression. Use t as the variable.

34. fifty increased by a number   35. twelve less than a number   *1-5*

36. a number decreased by 24   37. a number reduced by 7

38. 88 more than a number   39. the total of a number and 4

Evaluate each expression when $r = 6$, $s = 12$, and $t = 32$.

40. $1000 - s$ 41. $r + s$ 42. $t + 46 + t$ 43. $s + t + r$ *1-6*

44. $t - 19$ 45. $55 - t$ 46. $r + r + t$ 47. $76 + t + r$

extra practice

CHAPTER 2

Round to the place of the underlined digit.

1. 5̲7   **2.** 1̲97   **3.** 84̲36   **4.** 6̲299   **2-1**

5. 96,̲508   **6.** 38,1̲53   **7.** \$1,9̲92,147   **8.** 39,̲550,333

Estimate by rounding to the place of the leading digit.

9. $442 + 297$ **10.** $3724 + 6182$ **11.** $725 - 184$ **2-2**

12. $8741 - 3573$ **13.** $\$619 + \$316 + \$84$ **14.** $\$1124 + \$1742 + \$25$

Estimate by rounding to appropriate digits.

15. $\$329 - \$268$ **16.** $\$574 - \$46$ **17.** $\$1834 - \$1714$

18. $7845 - 274$ **19.** $\$29,065 - \$4536$ **20.** $62,591 - 57,299$

Compare. Replace each __?__ with >, <, or =.

21. 5724 __?__ 57,240   **22.** 9020 __?__ 9200   **23.** 8450 __?__ 8045   **2-3**

24. 39,723 __?__ 39,723   **25.** 3470 __?__ 3047   **26.** 9235 __?__ 9240

27. 1647 __?__ 1746   **28.** 394 __?__ 493   **29.** 34,210 __?__ 34,201

30. 16,465 __?__ 160,465   **31.** 10,000 __?__ 9999   **32.** 2,065,741 __?__ 2,065,741

33. Draw a bar graph to display the given information.   **2-4**

Allderdice High Fund Raiser

Class	Freshmen	Sophomores	Juniors	Seniors
Number of T-shirts	380	179	463	510

34. Draw a line graph to display the given information.   **2-5**

Parkvale Savings Customers

Morning Hour	8:00	9:00	10:00	11:00	12:00
Number of Customers	50	35	65	80	70

Answer the question in red.

35. Six apples cost \$1. How much change will you receive?   **2-6**
What missing fact is needed?

36. Find the total of 6498 and 10,422.
Is the answer 3924 reasonable?

Find each product.

1. 7×300
2. 10×500
3. 40×200
4. 30×70
5. 600×400
6. $500 \times 13,000$
7. 6000×900
8. 800×200

Find each product.

9. $\$3 \times 49$
10. 4×222
11. 7×325
12. $5 \times \$733$
13. 9×3806
14. 3×1426
15. $8 \times \$42,807$
16. 4×7256

Estimate each product.

17. 6×29
18. $4 \times \$782$
19. $5 \times \$1954$
20. 7×4120

21. For the upcoming concert, one ticket costs \$23. Estimate the cost of 8 tickets to the concert.

Find each product.

22. 13×15
23. 22×81
24. 16×451
25. 16×729
26. 62×702
27. 27×950
28. 45×372
29. 82×507

Estimate each product. Write whether the estimate is an *overestimate*, an *underestimate*, or if you *can't tell*.

30. 82×23
31. 87×529
32. 69×52
33. 77×58

34. A crowd of 8967 people gathered at the stadium to attend a rally. Admission to the event cost \$18. About how much money was raised by this rally?

Find each product. Check the reasonableness of your answer.

35. 132×133
36. 561×794
37. 905×281
38. 475×174
39. 139×235
40. 203×632
41. 791×246
42. 364×973
43. 276×1086
44. 914×3836
45. 107×9612
46. 884×1345

Use the properties of multiplication to find each product.

47. 402×596
48. 649×212
49. $8 \times 21 \times 5$
50. $2 \times 17 \times 5$
51. $20 \times 63 \times 5$
52. 102×16
53. 6×999
54. 4×198

Evaluate each expression when $a = 4$, $b = 5$, $c = 9$, and $d = 0$.

55. $3c$
56. $5ad$
57. $20bc$
58. $2ab$
59. $36c$
60. $12acd$
61. $11ac$
62. $17bd$
63. $30cd$
64. $70ac$

Find each quotient.

1. $4\overline{)\$652}$
2. $9\overline{)8262}$
3. $6\overline{)\$2442}$
4. $3\overline{)5536}$

5. $1209 \div 3$
6. $1118 \div 9$
7. $6314 \div 7$
8. $\$39,200 \div 8$

Use compatible numbers to estimate.

9. $5\overline{)592}$
10. $8\overline{)\$7164}$
11. $6\overline{)47,391}$
12. $19\overline{)39,464}$

13. $\$3719 \div 12$
14. $5372 \div 87$
15. $26,537 \div 88$
16. $34,972 \div 473$

Find each quotient. Check the reasonableness of your answer.

17. $58\overline{)1853}$
18. $92\overline{)\$6164}$
19. $57\overline{)1145}$
20. $24\overline{)\$1776}$

21. $5785 \div 19$
22. $3842 \div 54$
23. $63,840 \div 22$
24. $\$3484 \div 52$

Find each quotient. Check the reasonableness of your answer.

25. $530\overline{)9010}$
26. $416\overline{)\$3744}$
27. $367\overline{)23,488}$
28. $592\overline{)35,788}$

29. $8316 \div 213$
30. $7995 \div 205$
31. $\$60,632 \div 583$
32. $92,717 \div 437$

Evaluate each expression when $a = 24$, $b = 4$, and $c = 8$.

33. $\frac{16}{c}$
34. $\frac{c}{b}$
35. $\frac{0}{c}$
36. $\frac{a}{b}$
37. $\frac{216}{a}$
38. $\frac{c}{0}$

39. $\frac{a}{6}$
40. $\frac{12}{b}$
41. $\frac{c}{1}$
42. $\frac{72}{a}$
43. $\frac{c}{c}$
44. $\frac{232}{c}$

Write each phrase as a variable expression. Use n as the variable.

45. a number times 13
46. a number divided by 8
47. a number, halved
48. the product of a number and 7
49. a number shared equally by 5
50. 757 times a number
51. a number, quadrupled
52. a quarter of a number

Solve.

53. If one admission to the amusement park costs $16, how much will it cost for 7 people to enter the park?

54. A company's profits of $351,880 are to be shared equally by 38 stockholders. How much money will each stockholder get?

55. If John's yearly budget for record albums is $250, how many $7 albums can he buy in a year? How much money is left over?

56. There are twelve months in a year. How many months are there in 89 years?

Find each answer.

1. $4 + 2 \times 6$
2. $8(98 + 2)$
3. $15 - 3 \times 4$

5-1

4. $36 \div 9 + 20 \times 2$
5. $32 - 10 + 4 \times 12$
6. $15 + 12(37 - 29) - 16$

Evaluate each expression when $x = 8$, $y = 12$, and $z = 5$.

7. $20 - 2x$
8. $z + 4y$
9. $5y - x$
10. $3y + 2x$

11. $3x - y$
12. $\frac{24}{x} + z$
13. $19 - \frac{y}{4}$
14. $3x - \frac{20}{z}$

15. Jane arrived at the camera store with $40. She purchased 7 rolls of film at $4 each and 3 lens caps at $2 each. How much money did she have left?

Is the first number divisible by the second number? Write *Yes* or *No*.

16. 140; 5
17. 121; 2
18. 614; 10
19. 1256; 8

5-2

20. 5256; 4
21. 466; 3
22. 8442; 9
23. 891; 3

Write the prime factorization of each number.

24. 35
25. 45
26. 128
27. 200
28. 140
29. 330

5-3

Find the GCF.

30. 24 and 40
31. 45 and 75
32. 7 and 42
33. 50 and 28

34. 84 and 28
35. 13 and 91
36. 36 and 120
37. 45 and 23

Find the LCM.

38. 8 and 6
39. 18 and 24
40. 7 and 12
41. 5 and 40

5-4

42. 4, 5, and 6
43. 4, 10, and 16
44. 2, 7, and 9
45. 6, 15, and 20

46. One case of milk contains 24 cartons, and one case of paper cups contains 100 cups. What is the least number of cartons and cups that you can buy to get an equal number of each?

Find each answer.

47. 7^3
48. 2^4
49. 5^0
50. 1^7
51. 10^5
52. 3^4

5-5

53. $5^1 \times 8^2$
54. $6^2 \times 2^5$
55. $3^2 \times 4^3$
56. 5×10^3

Evaluate each expression when $m = 4$, $n = 5$, and $p = 10$.

57. m^3
58. $3n^2$
59. $37m^0$
60. $2n^3$
61. mp^2

5-6

62. $6m^2$
63. $7n^0p$
64. np^4
65. $6m^3n$
66. m^2p^3

Write a fraction that names the shaded part of each region or set.

1.
2.
3.
4.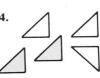

6-1

Write a fraction that answers the question.

5. What part of a year is five months?

6. What part of an hour is fifty-nine minutes?

Replace each __?__ with the number that will make the fractions equivalent.

7. $\frac{4}{4} = \frac{?}{10}$ 8. $\frac{3}{4} = \frac{?}{12}$ 9. $\frac{5}{20} = \frac{1}{?}$ 10. $\frac{0}{8} = \frac{?}{10}$ **6-2**

Write each fraction in lowest terms.

11. $\frac{12}{16}$ 12. $\frac{24}{40}$ 13. $\frac{6}{60}$ 14. $\frac{100}{900}$ 15. $\frac{27}{36}$ 16. $\frac{125}{150}$ **6-3**

Compare. Replace each __?__ with >, <, or =.

17. $\frac{7}{8} \underline{\ ?\ } \frac{5}{8}$ 18. $\frac{3}{4} \underline{\ ?\ } \frac{15}{20}$ 19. $\frac{4}{5} \underline{\ ?\ } \frac{5}{6}$ 20. $\frac{3}{8} \underline{\ ?\ } \frac{5}{12}$ **6-4**

Write a simpler fraction as an estimate of each fraction.

21. $\frac{10}{71}$ 22. $\frac{102}{396}$ 23. $\frac{21}{29}$ 24. $\frac{41}{62}$ 25. $\frac{51}{98}$ 26. $\frac{16}{33}$ **6-5**

Write as a fraction in lowest terms.

27. $7\frac{2}{3}$ 28. $6\frac{1}{2}$ 29. $11\frac{5}{7}$ 30. $10\frac{4}{6}$ 31. $4\frac{8}{10}$ 32. $15\frac{3}{6}$ **6-6**

Write as a whole number or a mixed number in lowest terms.

33. $\frac{10}{7}$ 34. $\frac{60}{5}$ 35. $\frac{42}{4}$ 36. $\frac{33}{15}$ 37. $\frac{101}{10}$ 38. $\frac{121}{11}$

Solve.

6-7

39. Karl bought two sweaters for $14 each, a pair of jeans for $25, and sneakers for $32. He gave the cashier a $100 bill. How much change did he receive?

Write each product in lowest terms.

1. $\frac{1}{5} \times \frac{3}{4}$　　2. $6 \times \frac{1}{10}$　　3. $\frac{3}{7} \times \frac{1}{9}$　　4. $\frac{1}{5} \times \frac{7}{9}$　　5. $\frac{5}{6} \times \frac{2}{11}$　　**7-1**

6. $\frac{5}{14} \times \frac{21}{25}$　　7. $\frac{3}{4} \times \frac{8}{15}$　　8. $9 \times \frac{5}{6}$　　9. $\frac{5}{9} \times 81$　　10. $\frac{1}{7} \times 7$

Estimate using compatible numbers.

11. $119 \times \frac{25}{99}$　　12. $32 \times \frac{16}{49}$　　13. $\frac{19}{31} \times 9$　　14. $199 \times \frac{24}{49}$

Estimate.

15. $2\frac{5}{6} \times 8\frac{1}{10}$　　16. $3\frac{1}{3} \times 5\frac{1}{4}$　　17. $7\frac{1}{2} \times 6\frac{5}{7}$　　18. $1\frac{2}{3} \times 3\frac{8}{9}$　　**7-2**

19. $\frac{1}{4} \times 23\frac{5}{8}$　　20. $11\frac{2}{3} \times \frac{1}{5}$　　21. $\frac{8}{25} \times 9\frac{1}{6}$　　22. $10\frac{7}{8} \times \frac{6}{11}$

Write each product in lowest terms.

23. $6 \times 4\frac{1}{3}$　　24. $5 \times 1\frac{1}{2}$　　25. $6\frac{1}{5} \times \frac{2}{3}$　　26. $5\frac{1}{4} \times \frac{8}{9}$　　**7-3**

27. $1\frac{3}{7} \times \frac{7}{10}$　　28. $12 \times 6\frac{1}{6}$　　29. $4\frac{2}{3} \times 2\frac{4}{7}$　　30. $2\frac{1}{10} \times 1\frac{1}{2}$

31. A gas tank holds $12\frac{1}{2}$ gal (gallons). If it is three-fourths full, how many gallons of gas are in the tank?

Write each quotient in lowest terms.

32. $\frac{9}{10} \div \frac{3}{10}$　　33. $\frac{2}{3} \div \frac{4}{9}$　　34. $\frac{5}{7} \div \frac{20}{21}$　　35. $\frac{4}{11} \div \frac{1}{2}$　　**7-4**

36. $\frac{1}{2} \div 10$　　37. $10 \div \frac{1}{3}$　　38. $6 \div \frac{4}{5}$　　39. $\frac{2}{3} \div 5$

40. $2\frac{4}{5} \div 2$　　41. $4 \div 1\frac{1}{3}$　　42. $6\frac{2}{3} \div \frac{5}{6}$　　43. $5\frac{1}{5} \div 8\frac{2}{3}$　　**7-5**

44. $1\frac{1}{9} \div 2\frac{1}{2}$　　45. $11\frac{2}{3} \div 1\frac{2}{5}$　　46. $10 \div \frac{1}{10}$　　47. $6\frac{9}{10} \div \frac{1}{2}$

48. Erika works part-time in a grocery store. Last week she worked $10\frac{3}{4}$ h and was paid \$86. How much was she paid per hour?

Estimate using compatible numbers.

49. $5\frac{4}{5} \div 1\frac{7}{8}$　　50. $30\frac{1}{3} \div 9\frac{3}{5}$　　51. $7\frac{1}{4} \div \frac{11}{23}$　　52. $1\frac{1}{9} \div \frac{9}{40}$

Write each sum or difference in lowest terms.

1. $\frac{3}{7} + \frac{2}{7}$　　2. $\frac{3}{8} + \frac{1}{8}$　　3. $\frac{5}{8} - \frac{3}{8}$　　4. $\frac{7}{10} + \frac{9}{10}$　　5. $\frac{33}{40} + \frac{9}{40}$ **8-1**

6. $\frac{1}{12} + \frac{3}{4}$　　7. $\frac{2}{5} + \frac{1}{6}$　　8. $\frac{7}{8} - \frac{3}{4}$　　9. $\frac{4}{7} + \frac{10}{21}$　　10. $\frac{1}{4} - \frac{1}{15}$ **8-2**

11. Kelly spends $\frac{1}{3}$ of her allowance on records and $\frac{2}{5}$ of her allowance on clothes. What fraction of her allowance is spent on these items?

Estimate by rounding.

12. $5\frac{4}{5} + 3\frac{7}{8}$　　13. $9\frac{1}{10} + 6\frac{3}{4}$　　14. $12\frac{1}{8} - 3\frac{1}{2}$　　15. $24\frac{1}{2} - 23\frac{3}{8}$ **8-3**

Estimate by adding the whole numbers, and then adjusting.

16. $4\frac{1}{3} + 1\frac{5}{9} + 3\frac{1}{10}$　　17. $2\frac{7}{15} + 5\frac{21}{40} + 7\frac{1}{9}$　　18. $9\frac{5}{6} + \frac{1}{10} + 3\frac{9}{11}$

Write each sum in lowest terms.

19. $6\frac{4}{9} + 1\frac{1}{9}$　　20. $7\frac{3}{10} + 2\frac{1}{10}$　　21. $5\frac{1}{2} + 4\frac{1}{3}$　　22. $9\frac{1}{5} + 6\frac{4}{5}$ **8-4**

23. $4\frac{4}{15} + 1\frac{4}{5}$　　24. $3\frac{2}{3} + 6\frac{3}{4}$　　25. $6\frac{5}{12} + 4\frac{1}{10}$　　26. $3\frac{7}{12} + 6\frac{13}{18}$

Write each difference in lowest terms.

27. $6\frac{5}{7} - 2\frac{2}{7}$　　28. $4\frac{3}{8} - 4\frac{1}{8}$　　29. $3\frac{5}{14} - 1\frac{2}{7}$　　30. $26\frac{7}{24} - 6\frac{1}{8}$ **8-5**

31. $10\frac{3}{4} - 1\frac{2}{9}$　　32. $3\frac{2}{5} - 2\frac{3}{10}$　　33. $14\frac{5}{8} - 5\frac{1}{20}$　　34. $6\frac{3}{4} - 5\frac{2}{7}$

35. $2\frac{1}{3} - 1\frac{2}{3}$　　36. $5\frac{1}{2} - 3\frac{3}{4}$　　37. $6\frac{1}{4} - 2\frac{5}{6}$　　38. $7\frac{2}{5} - 3\frac{1}{2}$ **8-6**

39. $18\frac{2}{5} - 7\frac{3}{4}$　　40. $1 - \frac{6}{11}$　　41. $17 - \frac{5}{9}$　　42. $10 - 6\frac{1}{3}$

43. The maximum recorded life span of a chimpanzee is $44\frac{1}{2}$ years, and the maximum recorded life span of a monkey is $34\frac{3}{4}$ years. How much greater is the life span of the chimpanzee?

Look for a pattern. Then write the next three numbers.

8-7

44. 23, 31, 39, 47, 55, __?__, __?__, __?__

45. $\frac{1}{3}$, 1, $\frac{5}{3}$, $\frac{7}{3}$, 3, __?__, __?__, __?__

Complete.

1. 20 ft = __?__ in.   **2.** 15 ft = __?__ in.   **3.** 72 in. = __?__ ft   **9-1**

4. 90 ft = __?__ yd   **5.** 4 mi = __?__ ft   **6.** 52,800 ft = __?__ mi

7. 6 yd 3 in. = __?__ in.   **8.** 76 in. = __?__ ft __?__ in.

9. 22 ft = __?__ yd __?__ ft   **10.** 72 mi 10 yd = __?__ yd

Measure the length of each object to the nearest $\frac{1}{16}$ inch.

11.    **12.** 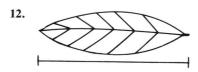   **9-2**

Complete.

13. 5 lb = __?__ oz   **14.** 48 oz = __?__ lb   **15.** 8000 lb = __?__ t   **9-3**

16. 12 t = __?__ lb   **17.** 112 oz = __?__ lb   **18.** 40,000 lb = __?__ t

19. 39 oz = __?__ lb __?__ oz   **20.** 5 lb 1 oz = __?__ oz

21. 2200 lb = __?__ t __?__ lb   **22.** 4 t 10 lb = __?__ lb

23. 10 gal = __?__ pt   **24.** 40 qt = __?__ gal   **25.** 6 qt = __?__ pt   **9-4**

26. 48 fl oz = __?__ c   **27.** 12 c = __?__ pt   **28.** 17 pt = __?__ c

29. 14 fl oz = __?__ c __?__ fl oz   **30.** 2 gal 3 qt = __?__ qt

31. 4 gal 3 pt = __?__ pt   **32.** 17 c = __?__ pt __?__ c

33. Bonnie buys 1 qt of juice three times a week. Bob buys 1 gal of juice once a week. Who buys more juice in one week?

Write each sum or difference in simplest form.

34. 4 ft 3 in. + 7 ft 6 in.   **35.** 6 yd 2 ft − 3 yd   **9-5**

36. 145 lb 9 oz + 14 lb 3 oz   **37.** 14 gal 3 qt − 2 gal 1 qt

38. 6 gal 2 qt + 3 qt   **39.** 1 ft 8 in. + 7 ft 6 in.

40. 4 t 1500 lb + 3 t 1500 lb   **41.** 1 qt 1 pt + 1 pt

42. 13 ft 4 in. − 2 ft 10 in.   **43.** 3 lb 3 oz − 13 oz

44. 4 mi 1000 yd − 2 mi 760 yd   **45.** 5 gal − 1 gal 1 qt

46. Andrew's height was 5 ft 11 in. when he entered the ninth grade. At the end of the school year his height was 6 ft 2 in. How much taller was Andrew at the end of the school year?

Write the word form of each decimal.

1. 0.2   **2.** 16.81   **3.** 3.006   **4.** 960.06   **10-1**

Write the numeral form of each decimal.

5. 6 tenths   **6.** 9 and 56 hundredths

7. three hundred eighty-nine and four ten-thousandths

8. fifty-two thousand and five hundred twenty-three thousandths

Round to the place of the underlined digit.

9. 4<u>8</u>.7   **10.** 11.<u>9</u>82   **11.** 0.86<u>1</u>3   **12.** 1.<u>0</u>09   **10-2**
13. $1<u>6</u>.72   **14.** 47.6<u>3</u>29   **15.** 502.6<u>9</u>5   **16.** $597<u>1</u>.65

Compare. Replace each __?__ with >, <, or =.

17. 4.06 __?__ 4.059   **18.** 15.6175 __?__ 15.6182   **19.** 1.2 __?__ 1.20   **10-3**
20. 172.963 __?__ 172.0963   **21.** 6.27 __?__ 6.269   **22.** 17.999 __?__ 18

23. List the following grade point averages from least to greatest:
2.21, 2.1, 2.3, 2.02, 2, 2.16

Write each decimal as a fraction or mixed number in lowest terms.

24. 0.7   **25.** 0.92   **26.** 0.075   **27.** 0.444   **28.** 1.7   **10-4**
29. 6.25   **30.** 25.11   **31.** 7.999   **32.** 6.003   **33.** 194.04

**Write each fraction or mixed number as a decimal. If the decimal is
a repeating decimal, round it to the nearest hundredth.**

34. $\frac{7}{10}$ **35.** $\frac{1}{5}$ **36.** $9\frac{3}{25}$ **37.** $11\frac{13}{20}$ **38.** $50\frac{13}{40}$ **39.** $\frac{7}{9}$ **10-5**

40. $\frac{4}{9}$ **41.** $\frac{7}{11}$ **42.** $4\frac{17}{20}$ **43.** $\frac{13}{18}$ **44.** $7\frac{5}{9}$ **45.** $2\frac{8}{15}$

Estimate each decimal as a simple fraction.

46. 0.106   **47.** 0.664   **48.** 0.8124   **49.** 0.506   **50.** 0.327

**If possible, solve. If it is not possible to solve, tell what additional
information is needed.**

51. Mrs. Levy bought 3 cans of peas at $.34 each and 4 cans of corn.   **10-6**
She gave the cashier $5. How much change did she receive?

52. Ian drove 321 mi in his new car. He used 13 gal of gasoline priced
at $1.04 per gallon. How much money did he spend on gasoline?

Find each sum.

1. $4.3 + 3.5$
2. $2.5 + 1.9$
3. $7.6 + 2.8$ *11-1*
4. $8.41 + 0.9$
5. $\$19.06 + \$3.46$
6. $\$6.35 + \$8.87$
7. $0.581 + 0.9306$
8. $39 + 14.6 + 1.47$
9. $1.81 + 0.005$
10. $3.24 + 11.6 + 2.9$
11. $16.1 + 0.707 + 8.2$
12. $53.4 + 6.21 + 5$

13. Pat spent $17.99 for a sweater and $9.50 for a belt. How much did he spend for these two items?

Estimate by adjusting the sum of the front-end digits.

14. $\$4.75 + \$6.21$
15. $258.6 + 543.4$ *11-2*
16. $2.35 + 3.19 + 0.96$
17. $3.7 + 9.07 + 6.26 + 5.889$

Estimate by rounding.

18. $0.461 + 0.8395$
19. $0.036 + 0.041$
20. $241.17 + 270.68$
21. $0.346 + 0.76 + 0.4238$

22. On the first three days of backpacking, Carol hiked 4.9 km (kilometers), 7.3 km, and 7.8 km. About how far did she hike in the three days?

Find each difference.

23. $6.9 - 5.4$
24. $\$5.49 - \$2.75$
25. $5.623 - 2.374$ *11-3*
26. $\$27.88 - \$1.60$
27. $53.47 - 20.6$
28. $20.94 - 7.368$
29. $\$19 - \$4.65$
30. $23 - 1.07$
31. $770 - 0.996$
32. $0.0073 - 0.0064$
33. $571.8 - 92$
34. $100 - 9.3071$

35. In a bicycle race, Paul beat Matt by 3.07 min. If Matt's time was 53.7 min, what was Paul's time?

Estimate by rounding to the place of the leading digit.

36. $\$72.79 - \$21.80$
37. $0.637 - 0.478$
38. $6.3 - 2.792$ *11-4*
39. $0.52 - 0.315$
40. $76.72 - 8.16$
41. $0.0693 - 0.0091$

Estimate by rounding to appropriate digits.

42. $12.6 - 10.7$
43. $\$47.62 - \$3.12$
44. $113.2 - 76.5$
45. $0.649 - 0.5701$
46. $1495.23 - 985.07$
47. $0.7856 - 0.0316$

48. Ryan opened a checking account with $141.12 and then wrote a check for $9.88. Estimate the amount left in his account.

Find each product.

12-1

1. 5.234×2
2. $\$46.35 \times 5$
3. 42×3.2
4. 1.56×9
5. 12×9.3
6. $\$4.39 \times 15$
7. $\$.04 \times 326$
8. 90×0.06
9. $\$37.54 \times 18$
10. 12×0.004
11. $\$3.02 \times 53$
12. 2.007×19

13. Lisa earns $4.35 per hour, and she works 18 h every week. Find her weekly pay.

Find each product.

12-2

14. 10×62.91
15. 100×0.236
16. 10×0.05
17. 67.9496×10
18. 1000×96.57
19. 6.703×10
20. 6.2×100
21. 1000×2.01
22. 100×62.5
23. 96.01×1000
24. 365.6×100
25. 0.09×1000

Find each product. If necessary, round to the nearest cent.

12-3

26. 5.7×2.1
27. 66.42×3.47
28. 8.2×3.9
29. $\$42.31 \times 0.6$
30. 1.7×42.76
31. 0.0602×0.4
32. $\$30.72 \times 6.39$
33. 0.05×0.06
34. 0.7×0.004
35. $602.3 \times \$1.05$
36. 0.5×16.4
37. 1503.4×100.6

38. Find the cost of 3.25 lb of cheese priced at $2.80 per pound.

Estimate by rounding.

12-4

39. 807×2.1
40. 7.16×39.5
41. 483×0.0096
42. $\$28.24 \times 4.8$
43. $\$7.69 \times 0.19$
44. 0.285×868.57

Estimate using compatible numbers.

45. 0.322×598
46. 0.09×1712
47. 0.263×398
48. 0.019×5100
49. 0.659×3590
50. 997×0.513

12-5

51. Mrs. Murphy earned $314.20 per week for 2 years. About how much money did she earn altogether? Choose the letter of the best estimate.
    a. $15,000　　b. $3000　　c. $30,000　　d. $7000
52. Estimate the cost of lunch for 62 people at a cost of $4.95 per person.
53. West High School has 784 students. About one fourth of them are juniors. Estimate the number of juniors.

Find each quotient. If necessary, round to the nearest thousandth.

13-1

1. $3\overline{)6.93}$
2. $7\overline{)3.78}$
3. $16\overline{)44.8}$
4. $9\overline{)44}$
5. $5\overline{)3.4}$
6. $9\overline{)54.63}$
7. $32\overline{)33.28}$
8. $25\overline{)0.08}$
9. $\$24.72 \div 12$
10. $2 \div 25$
11. $\$326.16 \div 9$
12. $2.493 \div 7$
13. $0.6 \div 14$
14. $10.2 \div 7$
15. $25.5 \div 11$
16. $75.91 \div 12$

17. A case of apple juice containing 12 cans costs $20.76. What is the price of each can?

Find each quotient.

13-2

18. $16.4 \div 10$
19. $357.22 \div 100$
20. $\$4.30 \div 10$
21. $14.6 \div 1000$
22. $655 \div 100$
23. $9.02 \div 10$
24. $0.935 \div 100$
25. $0.74 \div 100$
26. $\$5 \div 100$
27. $316.9 \div 1000$
28. $300 \div 1000$
29. $\$12,600 \div 10$

30. If a 10-lb bag of potatoes costs $8.90, what is the cost per pound?

Find each quotient. If necessary, round to the nearest thousandth.

13-3

31. $1.3\overline{)3.9}$
32. $0.2\overline{)16.8}$
33. $1.2\overline{)0.636}$
34. $1.3\overline{)1.17}$
35. $2.5\overline{)15}$
36. $0.6\overline{)9.12}$
37. $1.4\overline{)0.63}$
38. $0.04\overline{)3.605}$
39. $16.92 \div 0.012$
40. $44.94 \div 10.5$
41. $0.009 \div 0.04$
42. $52 \div 0.001$
43. $0.3 \div 0.7$
44. $18 \div 0.0003$
45. $6.004 \div 5.1$
46. $0.0009 \div 0.11$

Estimate.

13-4

47. $5.1\overline{)201.4}$
48. $1.9\overline{)6805.11}$
49. $9.86\overline{)89.7}$
50. $7.05\overline{)48.7}$
51. $\$71.85 \div 9.2$
52. $241.2 \div 0.299$
53. $1.51 \div 0.29$
54. $341.9 \div 0.05$
55. $3634.6 \div 0.59$
56. $1154.1 \div 31.7$
57. $159.7 \div 0.4$
58. $0.449 \div 0.089$

Write the numeral form of each number.

13-5

59. 2×10^2
60. 5×10^8
61. 1.3×10^3
62. 6.79×10^2
63. 5.03×10^3
64. 9.2×10^1
65. 8.35×10^1
66. 3.964×10^{10}
67. 1.965×10^5
68. 4.65×10^8
69. 3×10^6
70. 4.32974×10^7

Write in scientific notation.

71. 300
72. 7000
73. $100,000$
74. 9638
75. $800,000,000$
76. $10,300,000$
77. 25
78. $9,006,000$
79. $820,000$
80. 650
81. 17
82. $39,700$

Select the most reasonable unit. Choose mm, cm, m, or km.

1. length of a staple: 12 __?__   **2.** width of a room: 9 __?__   *14-1*

3. length of a car: 4.5 __?__   **4.** length of a paperback book: 170 __?__

5. length of a toothbrush: 15 __?__   **6.** distance from Seattle to Atlanta: 4000 __?__

Measure the length of each object in: a. centimeters   b. millimeters

7.    **8.**    *14-2*

Complete.

9. 40 cm = __?__ mm   **10.** 20 km = __?__ m   **11.** 17 m = __?__ mm   *14-3*

12. 5.9 cm = __?__ mm   **13.** 602.5 m = __?__ cm   **14.** 3.7 m = __?__ mm

15. 900 mm = __?__ cm   **16.** 7000 m = __?__ km   **17.** 93 mm = __?__ cm

18. 51 cm = __?__ m   **19.** 32.7 m = __?__ km   **20.** 15.3 km = __?__ m

Select the more reasonable unit. Choose L or mL.

21. capacity of a can of juice: 400 __?__   **22.** capacity of a gas tank: 40 __?__   *14-4*

23. capacity of a fish bowl: 5 __?__   **24.** capacity of a tea kettle: 2 __?__

Complete.

25. 5000 mL = __?__ L   **26.** 17 L = __?__ mL   **27.** 1500 mL = __?__ L

28. 0.15 L = __?__ mL   **29.** 3.2 L = __?__ mL   **30.** 16 mL = __?__ L

Select the most reasonable unit. Choose mg, g, or kg.

31. mass of an orange: 300 __?__   **32.** mass of a bumble bee: 2 __?__   *14-5*

33. mass of a notebook: 425 __?__   **34.** mass of a piano: 300 __?__

Complete.

35. 60 g = __?__ mg   **36.** 4000 g = __?__ kg   **37.** 20 mg = __?__ g

38. 7.5 g = __?__ mg   **39.** 5.9 g = __?__ kg   **40.** 3.8 mg = __?__ g

Make a drawing to picture the problem. Then solve.

41. Jason leaves his house and jogs 4 blocks due north, 2 blocks due   *14-6*
east, 3 blocks due south, and 2 blocks due west. Where is Jason in
relation to his house?

Write each ratio as a fraction in lowest terms.

1. 5 to 80
2. 22 to 55
3. 25 : 150
4. 16 : 36   *15-1*
5. 45 : 20
6. 13 to 52
7. 56 to 338
8. 81 : 180
9. 4 in. to 3 ft
10. 45 min to 2 h
11. 60 m to 3 mm
12. 1 cm to 7 mm
13. 7 days : 4 weeks
14. 80 cm : 2 m

Write the unit rate.

15. $125 for 5 h
16. 72 mi in 2 h
17. 165 mi on 5 gal   *15-2*
18. $4.68 for 3 lb
19. 276 pages in 4 h
20. $170 for 40 h
21. $18 for 4 tickets
22. 7.8 yd for 2 dresses
23. 135 mi in 4 h
24. 293.4 mi on 9 gal
25. $174.30 for 6 issues
26. $154 in 28 days

Solve each proportion.

27. $\dfrac{5}{7} = \dfrac{15}{x}$
28. $\dfrac{4}{6} = \dfrac{a}{30}$
29. $\dfrac{y}{3} = \dfrac{36}{27}$
30. $\dfrac{15}{z} = \dfrac{20}{32}$ *15-3*

31. $\dfrac{10}{30} = \dfrac{7}{x}$
32. $\dfrac{2}{10} = \dfrac{s}{15}$
33. $\dfrac{15}{n} = \dfrac{6}{2}$
34. $\dfrac{12}{c} = \dfrac{9}{15}$

35. $\dfrac{2}{4} = \dfrac{9}{t}$
36. $\dfrac{y}{8} = \dfrac{15}{5}$
37. $\dfrac{12}{n} = \dfrac{840}{700}$
38. $\dfrac{48}{16} = \dfrac{6}{a}$

Solve using a proportion.

39. If 3 apples cost $.54, find the cost of 8 apples.   *15-4*
40. Denise takes 30 min to type 4 pages. How long would it take her to type 6 pages?
41. In a parking lot, the ratio of sports cars to station wagons is 3 : 4. There are 15 sports cars. How many station wagons are there?
42. In a survey, the ratio of teenagers to middle-aged adults was 8 : 5. There were 30 middle-aged adults in the survey. How many teenagers were there?

An architect built a model of an apartment building. The scale is 1 in. : 4 ft.

43. The model's height is 15 in. What is the actual building's height?   *15-5*
44. The actual building's width is 100 ft. What is the model's width?
45. If an actual window will be 4 ft high, what is the corresponding window height on the model?
46. The actual front steps will be 6 ft wide. What is the width of the steps on the model?

Write a percent to represent the shaded part of each region.

1. 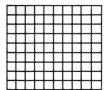   **2.** 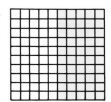   **3.** 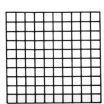   **4.** 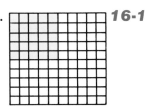 *16-1*

Write each percent as a decimal. Write each decimal as a percent.

5. 32%   **6.** 40%   **7.** 2%   **8.** 5.6%   **9.** 115%   *16-2*
10. 0.75   **11.** 0.142   **12.** 0.01   **13.** 0.3   **14.** 1.95

Write each percent as a fraction in lowest terms.

15. 93%   **16.** 82%   **17.** 16%   **18.** 9.2%   **19.** 11.5%   *16-3*
20. 22.8%   **21.** 0.5%   **22.** $\frac{7}{10}$%   **23.** $\frac{4}{7}$%   **24.** $6\frac{2}{5}$%

Write each fraction as a percent.

25. $\frac{3}{10}$ **26.** $\frac{57}{100}$ **27.** $\frac{1}{4}$ **28.** $\frac{11}{25}$ **29.** $\frac{1}{5}$ **30.** $\frac{9}{50}$ *16-4*
31. $\frac{7}{20}$ **32.** $\frac{1}{8}$ **33.** $\frac{2}{15}$ **34.** $\frac{7}{12}$ **35.** $\frac{27}{40}$ **36.** $\frac{1}{30}$

Find each answer.

37. 10% of 35 is what number?   **38.** 8% of 15 is what number?   *16-5*
39. What number is 20% of 45?   **40.** 60% of 75 is what number?
41. What number is $12\frac{1}{2}$% of 56?   **42.** $66\frac{2}{3}$% of 810 is what number?
43. 60% of 1005 is what number?   **44.** What number is $87\frac{1}{2}$% of 800?

Estimate.

45. 51% of $38   **46.** 74% of $803   **47.** 34% of 587   *16-6*
48. 5.9% of 4103   **49.** 11.1% of $9.99   **50.** 29.3% of $358

51. Talbot City has a butcher, a brewer, and a baker. These three jobs   *16-7*
are held by a Mr. Butcher, a Mr. Brewer, and a Mr. Baker, but no
man holds the job matching his last name. If you know that
Mr. Brewer is not the baker, find the last name of the butcher.

Find each answer.

1. 6 is what percent of 25?   **2.** 9 is what percent of 20?

3. What percent of 16 is 4?   **4.** What percent of 50 is 42?

5. 3 is what percent of 4?   **6.** 1 is what percent of 12?

7. What percent of 6 is 30?   **8.** 150 is what percent of 40?

9. Tim expected to sell his old car for $1500. He actually received only $1200 for the car. What percent of the expected price did he receive?

Find each answer.

10. 10% of what number is 13?   **11.** 17 is 50% of what number?

12. 15% of what number is 9?   **13.** 22 is 4% of what number?

14. 81 is 75% of what number?   **15.** 20% of what number is 17?

16. $33\frac{1}{3}$% of what number is 8?   **17.** 35 is $12\frac{1}{2}$% of what number?

18. The Bears won 72% of their games this season. If they won 18 games, how many games did they play?

Find each answer using a proportion.

19. What number is 25% of 32?   **20.** 7% of 50 is what number?

21. 30% of 70 is what number?   **22.** What number is 160% of 30?

23. What percent of 28 is 7?   **24.** 12 is what percent of 96?

25. What percent of 160 is 32?   **26.** 300 is what percent of 40?

27. 5.4 is 5% of what number?   **28.** 5 is 250% of what number?

29. 12 is 48% of what number?   **30.** 18 is 120% of what number?

Tell whether there is an *increase* or a *decrease*.
Then find the percent of increase or decrease.

31. original cost = 50 kg   **32.** original weight = 20 g
new cost = 57 kg   new weight = 27 g

33. original number = 120   **34.** original salary = $15,000
new number = 90   new salary = $14,550

35. original length = 3 cm   **36.** original weight = 4600 kg
new length = 5 cm   new weight = 4646 kg

37. original capacity = 4 L   **38.** original price = $800
new capacity = 6 L   new price = $628

Make a frequency table for the data.

18-1

1. **Student Ages**

15	16	15	17
16	15	18	16
14	18	15	17
18	14	16	16
17	16	15	16

2. **Student SAT Scores**

450	640	530	340
410	320	690	680
470	700	490	580
760	410	550	380
510	620	740	480

(Use intervals such as 301–400.)

Find the mean, median, and mode(s). If necessary, round the mean to the nearest tenth or cent.

18-2

3. 7, 4, 9, 8, 7
5. 88, 45, 67, 72, 45
7. 5, 6, 8, 8, 7, 4, 8, 9

4. $41, $51, $39, $45
6. 1.5, 2.5, 1.7, 3.9
8. $18, $22, $31, $45, $26, $42

Use the pictograph to answer the questions.

18-3

9. How many reference books are in the library?
10. What kind of book has twice as many copies as the biography books?
11. How many books are in the library altogether?
12. How many more fiction books are there than social studies books?

Use the circle graph to answer the questions.

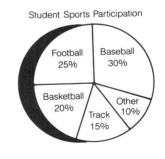

18-4

13. What fraction of the students surveyed participated in basketball?
14. If there were 200 students in the survey, how many played baseball? How many participated in track?
15. If there were 40 football players in the survey, find the total number of students in the survey.

18-5

16. Ann has 18 nickels and dimes altogether. Their total value is $1.25. How many nickels does she have?
17. The senior class sold 36 magazine subscriptions, some for $6 and the rest for $8. They collected $256. Find the number of $6 subscriptions sold.

Find the number of possible outcomes.

19-1

1. choosing a number from 1 to 5 and tossing a nickel

2. selecting a wallet; color: black, brown, tan; type: leather, vinyl

3. buying a painting; frame: silver, gold; size: small, medium, large

4. planning a one-week vacation from a choice of 6 weeks and 4 destinations

In how many different ways can each of the following happen?

19-2

5. seating 7 students in 7 chairs

6. assigning 4 chores to 4 people

7. creating a two-letter "word" from the letters in the word EDITOR

8. arranging a visit to 4 out of 10 museum exhibits

Find the number represented by each factorial.

9. 3!

10. 8!

11. 5!

12. A penny is tossed. Find P(tails).

19-3

13. A number cube is rolled. Find P(number < 5).

A card is drawn at random from a box containing 5 white, 7 green, 2 black, and 4 yellow cards. Find each probability.

14. P(white)

15. P(not yellow)

16. P(black or green)

Two tokens are drawn at random from those shown at the right. The first token is replaced before the second one is drawn. Find each probability.

17. P(2, then D)

18. P(not white, then A)

19. P(vowel, then blue)

20. P(two white)

19-4

Two tokens are drawn at random from those shown at the right. The first token is *not* replaced before the second one is drawn. Find each probability.

21. P(B, then 3)

22. P(4, then not blue)

23. P(white, then a number)

24. P(two blue)

25. A token is drawn at random from those shown above, and then it is replaced. Find the number of times that an odd number is expected to occur in 140 selections.

19-5

26. Out of 28 cars sold by a car dealer in one week, 8 were silver. How many of the next 350 cars sold would the dealer expect to be silver?

Write the opposite of each number.

1. 7   2. $^-$32   3. 15   4. $^-$19   5. 6   6. 0   **20-1**

Find the absolute value of each number.

7. 11   8. $^-$55   9. 0   10. $^-$3   11. 16   12. $^-$53

Compare. Replace each $\underline{\ ?\ }$ with >, <, or =.

13. 6 $\underline{\ ?\ }$ 9   14. $^-$3 $\underline{\ ?\ }$ $^-$5   15. 2 $\underline{\ ?\ }$ $^-$2   16. 0 $\underline{\ ?\ }$ $^-$3

17. 0 $\underline{\ ?\ }$ 5   18. $^-$6 $\underline{\ ?\ }$ 4   19. $^-$12 $\underline{\ ?\ }$ $^-$16   20. 12 $\underline{\ ?\ }$ 10

21. The hottest temperature on the surface of the planet Jupiter is 184°F below zero. Write an integer to represent this quantity.

Find each answer.

22. 13 + 4   23. $^-$13 + $^-$4   24. $^-$4 + 0   25. $^-$5 + 6   **20-2**

26. $^-$9 + $^-$3   27. $^-$7 + 6   28. 14 + $^-$3   29. $^-$11 + 21

30. 54 + $^-$10   31. $^-$6 + 9 + $^-$5   32. $^-$3 + 7 + 9   33. 4 + $^-$6 + $^-$14

34. $^-$2 − 5   35. $^-$1 − $^-$6   36. $^-$4 − 11   37. 7 − 9   **20-3**

38. 0 − 16   39. $^-$3 − $^-$5   40. 4 − $^-$4   41. 16 − 25

42. $^-$15 − 14   43. 31 − 50   44. $^-$32 − 0   45. $^-$22 − 5

46. $^-$3 × $^-$5   47. 4 × $^-$6   48. $^-$20 × 0   49. $^-$5 × 25   **20-4**

50. $^-$8 × $^-$5 × $^-$4   51. $^-$7 × 9 × $^-$5   52. 9 × $^-$1 × 0   53. 6 × 7 × $^-$9

54. $(^-4)^2$ 55. $(^-6)^1$ 56. $(^-3)^4$ 57. $(^-9)^0$

58. $^-$35 ÷ $^-$5   59. 0 ÷ $^-$2   60. $^-$100 ÷ 2   61. 5 ÷ $^-$5   **20-5**

62. $^-$96 ÷ $^-$48   63. $^-$17 ÷ 0   64. $^-$64 ÷ 4   65. $^-$200 ÷ $^-$4

66. $^-$75 ÷ $^-$3   67. 81 ÷ $^-$9   68. $^-$3 ÷ 0   69. 85 ÷ $^-$5

70. An elevator descended 7 floors in 49 seconds. How long does it take the elevator to descend one floor?

Find each sum.

71. 1 + 3 + 5 + . . . + 39   72. 1 + 3 + 5 + . . . + 25   **20-6**

73. 1 + 3 + 5 + . . . + 31   74. 1 + 3 + 5 + . . . + 79

75. 3 + 5 + 7 + . . . + 49   76. 3 + 5 + 7 + . . . + 21

77. 5 + 7 + 9 + . . . + 25   78. 5 + 7 + 9 + . . . + 101

Solve each equation. Check your answers.

1. $x + 6 = 11$ **2.** $54 = j + 6$ **3.** $y - 8 = 12$ **21-1**

4. $31 = y - 16$ **5.** $b - 9 = 5$ **6.** $^-7 = x + 20$

7. $3y = 81$ **8.** $^-72 = 8x$ **9.** $^-5a = ^-30$ **21-2**

10. $\frac{x}{6} = 12$ **11.** $\frac{h}{9} = ^-1$ **12.** $\frac{3}{8}x = 21$

13. $6y + 5 = 17$ **14.** $2b + 7 = ^-9$ **15.** $15 = 5x - 10$ **21-3**

16. $\frac{1}{3}x + 5 = 17$ **17.** $\frac{1}{4}x - 6 = ^-4$ **18.** $7 = \frac{2}{5}y + 3$

Solve by using an equation.

19. A high-speed printer can print 4 pages in one minute. How many   **21-4**
minutes will it take to print 52 pages?

20. Luis bought 8 boxes of computer paper and one ribbon. If the
ribbon cost $3 and the total bill was $59, what was the cost of
each box of computer paper?

Use the coordinate plane at the right.
Give the coordinates of each point.

21. A **22.** B **23.** C

24. D **25.** E **26.** F **21-5**

27. G **28.** H **29.** J

Graph each point on a coordinate plane.

30. $A(0,0)$ **31.** $B(2,0)$ **32.** $C(3,2)$

33. $D(^-3,4)$ **34.** $E(2,^-1)$ **35.** $F(0,^-4)$

36. $G(^-1,^-3)$ **37.** $H(^-4,^-2)$ **38.** $J(^-2,2)$

Find three solutions of each equation. Use $^-2, 0, 2$ as values for x.

39. $y = 3x + 4$ **40.** $y = ^-4x + 5$ **41.** $y = 5x - 6$ **42.** $y = 2x$ **21-6**

43. $y = ^-3x$ **44.** $y = x + 11$ **45.** $y = ^-6x$ **46.** $y = ^-2x + 2$

Graph each equation.

47. $y = x$ **48.** $y = 5x$ **49.** $y = x - 3$ **50.** $y = 2x + 3$

51. $y = ^-4x + 1$ **52.** $y = 2x - 3$ **53.** $y = ^-2x - 1$ **54.** $y = ^-3x + 4$

Make a drawing to represent each of the following.

1. $\overline{BF}$ 2. $\overrightarrow{AM}$ 3. plane M 4. $\angle OPF$ 5. point S 6. $\overleftrightarrow{ET}$ **22-1**

Use a protractor to draw an angle of the given measure.

7. $20°$ 8. $80°$ 9. $110°$ 10. $160°$ 11. $5°$ 12. $45°$

Name each polygon. Tell whether it is *regular* or *not regular*.

13.   14.   15.   16. **22-2**

Find the perimeter of each polygon.

17. square with $s = 10$ cm   18. square with $s = 11$ ft   **22-3**
19. rectangle with $l = 2$ m, $w = 9$ m   20. rectangle with $l = 8$ m, $w = 12$ m

Find the circumference of each circle.

21. diameter = 10 mm (Use $\pi \approx 3.14$.)   22. radius = 4 ft (Use $\pi \approx 3.14$.)   **22-4**
23. diameter = 14 cm (Use $\pi \approx \frac{22}{7}$.)   24. radius = 28 in. (Use $\pi \approx \frac{22}{7}$.)

Find the area of each figure.

25. 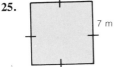   26. 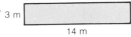   27. 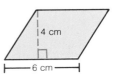   **22-5**

28.   29.   30. 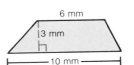   **22-6**

31. Use $\pi \approx \frac{22}{7}$.   32. Use $\pi \approx 3.14$.   33. 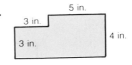   **22-7**

34. A cafeteria served lunch to 80 students. 56 of the students drank milk, 39 drank juice, and 28 drank both milk and juice. How many students drank neither?   **22-8**

Name each space figure. If the figure is a polyhedron, give the number of faces, edges, and vertices.

1.
2.
3.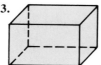
4.

23-1

Find the surface area of each space figure. When appropriate, use $\pi \approx 3.14$.

5.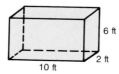
6.
7.

23-2

Find the volume of each space figure. When appropriate, use $\pi \approx 3.14$.

8.
9.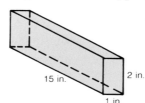
10.

23-3

11.
12.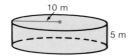
13.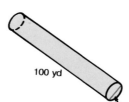

23-4

14.
15.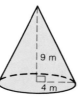
16.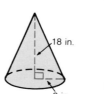

23-5

17.
18.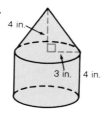
19.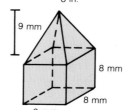

23-6

The measures of two angles of a triangle are given.
Find the measure of the third angle.

1. 54°, 23°   2. 64°, 49°   3. 13°, 28°   4. 5°, 95°   **24-1**
5. 45°, 45°   6. 60°, 60°   7. 34°, 111°   8. 49°, 103°

Each pair of triangles is similar. Find the missing length.

9.
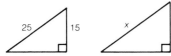   10.   **24-2**

11.    12.

Find each square root. Use the table on page 549, if necessary.

13. $\sqrt{43}$ 14. $\sqrt{1369}$ 15. $\sqrt{138}$ 16. $\sqrt{4900}$ **24-3**

Find the missing length. If necessary, round answers to the nearest tenth.

17. 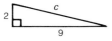   18.   19.   20. 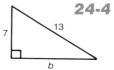   **24-4**

21. 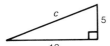   22.    23.   24.

Identify the space figure that would be formed if each pattern
could be folded.

25.   26. 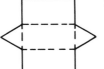   27. 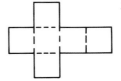   28. 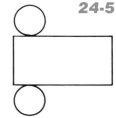   **24-5**

glossary

absolute value (p. 442): The distance of a number from 0 on a number line.

acute angle (p. 487): An angle that has a measure between 0° and 90°.

acute triangle (p. 542): A triangle with three acute angles.

addends (p. 5): Numbers that are combined by the operation of addition. In $6 + 3 = 9$, 6 and 3 are addends.

angle (p. 486): A figure formed by two rays that have the same endpoint.

area (p. 498): The amount of surface that a plane figure covers.

associative property of addition (p. 6): Changing the grouping of the addends does not change the sum.
$$(2 + 3) + 4 = 2 + (3 + 4)$$

associative property of multiplication (p. 59): Changing the grouping of the factors does not change the product.
$$(4 \times 5) \times 2 = 4 \times (5 \times 2)$$

average (p. 90): The result of dividing the sum of two or more numbers by the number of addends.

axes (p. 34): The two number lines, one horizontal and one vertical, used to display numerical facts in a graph.

bar graph (p. 34): A display of numerical facts in which the lengths of bars are used to compare numbers.

base of a power (p. 104): A number that is used as a factor a given number of times. In 5^4, 5 is the base.

budget (p. 415): A plan for allocating money.

Celsius scale (p. 459): A system of measuring temperature in which the boiling point of water is 100° and the freezing point of water is 0°.

center of a circle (p. 495): The point inside the circle that is the same distance from all points of the circle.

chord (p. 495): A line segment joining any two points on a circle.

circle (p. 495): The set of all points in a plane that are the same distance from a given point in the plane.

circle graph (pp. 407, 513): A graph that shows the relationship of data expressed as percents or parts of a whole.

circumference (p. 495): The distance around a circle.

cluster (p. 254): To be grouped about a central number or item.

commission (p. 385): An amount of money earned based on a percent of total sales.

common denominator (p. 126): The fractions $\frac{5}{11}$ and $\frac{9}{11}$ have 11 as their common denominator.

common factor (p. 100): A number that is a factor of two or more numbers. 7 is a common factor of 14 and 63.

common multiple (p. 102): A number that is a multiple of two or more given numbers. 30 is a common multiple of 2, 5, and 6.

commutative property of addition (p. 6): Numbers may be added in any order.
$$2 + 5 = 5 + 2$$

commutative property of multiplication (p. 59): Numbers may be multiplied in any order.

$$4 \times 3 = 3 \times 4$$

compatible numbers (pp. 73, 144): Numbers that multiply or divide easily, used in estimating.

composite figure (pp. 505, 533): An irregularly shaped figure that can be divided into simpler figures.

composite number (p. 100): A number that has more than two factors.

compound interest (p. 364): Interest paid both on the principal and on the interest previously earned.

cone (p. 519): A space figure with one circular base and one vertex.

congruent angles (p. 490): Two or more angles that have the same measure.

congruent line segments (p. 490): Two or more line segments that have the same length.

congruent triangles (p. 545): Triangles that have the same shape and size.

coordinate plane (p. 474): A plane divided into sections by a horizontal and a vertical number line.

coordinates of a point (p. 474): The numbers in the ordered pair that locate a point on the coordinate plane.

counting principle (p. 420): In probability, the total number of possible outcomes is the product of the number of choices for each step.

cross products (p. 121): For the fractions $\frac{3}{4}$ and $\frac{15}{20}$, 3×20 and 4×15 are cross products.

cube (p. 518): A rectangular prism all of whose faces are squares.

cylinder (p. 519): A space figure with two identical, parallel circular faces.

d

data (p. 398): A collection of numerical facts.

decimal (p. 212): A number written with a decimal point and digits to the right of the ones' place. 0.23 and 14.5 are decimals.

deductions (p. 266): Amounts of money subtracted from a worker's earnings.

degree (p. 487): A unit of angle measure.

denominator (p. 118): In the fraction $\frac{5}{8}$, 8 is the denominator.

dependent events (p. 427): Events in which the occurrence of one event affects the occurrence of another event.

diagonal of a polygon (p. 490): A line segment that joins two vertices of a polygon and is not a side.

diameter of a circle (p. 495): A chord that passes through the center of the circle.

difference (p. 10): The result of subtracting one number from another. In $17 - 9 = 8$, 8 is the difference.

digit (p. 2): In our number system, one of the symbols 0, 1, 2, 3, 4, 5, 6, 7, 8, 9.

discount (p. 386): An amount of money subtracted from the regular price.

distributive property (p. 60): Numbers inside a pair of parentheses may be multiplied by a factor outside the parentheses as follows.

$$4 \times (5 + 2) = (4 \times 5) + (4 \times 2)$$
$$= 20 + 8 = 28$$

dividend (p. 70): A number that is divided by another number.

divisible (p. 97): A number is divisible by a second number if the remainder is zero when the first number is divided by the second.

divisor (p. 70): The number by which another number is divided.

e

edge of a polyhedron (p. 518): The intersection of two faces of the polyhedron (a line segment).

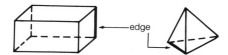

elapsed time (p. 43): The amount of time between the start and the end of an event.

equation (p. 464): A statement that two numbers or quantities are equal.

equivalent fractions (p. 121): Fractions that name the same number.

equilateral triangle (p. 542): A triangle with three congruent sides.

evaluate (p. 16): To find the value of a variable expression when the variables are replaced by given values.

even number (p. 99): A number that is divisible by 2.

event (p. 424): A set of outcomes.

exponent (p. 104): A number used to show how many times another number is to be used as a factor. In 3^5, 5 is the exponent.

exponential form (p. 104): A short form of writing a multiplication in which all the factors are the same. 4^3 is the exponential form of $4 \times 4 \times 4$.

f

face of a polyhedron (p. 518): Any one of its surfaces.

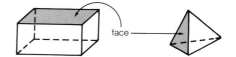

factor (p. 100): When one number is divisible by a second number, the second number is a factor of the first. 3 is a factor of 15.

factored form of a power (p. 106): The expression written as the product of its factors. The factored form of n^4 is $n \times n \times n \times n$.

factorial (p. 422): A notation for the product of a number and all nonzero whole numbers less than the given number.

$$4! = 4 \times 3 \times 2 \times 1 = 24$$

factors (p. 48): Numbers that are multiplied to give a product. In $7 \times 9 = 63$, 7 and 9 are factors.

Fahrenheit scale (p. 459): A system of measuring temperature in which the boiling point of water is 212° and the freezing point of water is 32°.

formula (p. 479): An equation that describes a relationship between two or more quantities.

fraction (p. 118): A number written in the form $\frac{a}{b}$, where $b \neq 0$. $\frac{2}{5}$ and $\frac{8}{3}$ are fractions.

g

graph (p. 34): A picture that displays and compares numerical facts.

graph of an equation (p. 476): All points whose coordinates are solutions of the equation.

greatest common factor (p. 100): The greatest number that is a factor of two or more numbers. 9 is the greatest common factor of 27 and 45.

gross pay (p. 265): The sum of regular and overtime earnings.

h

hexagon (p. 490): A six-sided polygon.

horizontal axis (p. 34): *See* axes.

hypotenuse (p. 551): The side opposite the right angle in a right triangle.

i

independent events (p. 427): Events in which the occurrence of one event does not affect the occurrence of another event.

integers (p. 442): The numbers . . . , ⁻3, ⁻2, ⁻1, 0, 1, 2, . . .

interest (p. 363): Money paid for the use of borrowed money.

intersecting lines (p. 488): Two or more lines that meet in one point.

inverse operations (p. 10): Operations that "undo" each other. Addition and subtraction are inverse operations.

isosceles triangle (p. 542): A triangle with two congruent sides.

l

leading digit (pp. 27, 215): The first nonzero digit of a whole number or a decimal.

least common denominator (LCD) (p. 126): The least common multiple of the denominators of two or more fractions.

least common multiple (LCM) (p. 102): The least positive number that is a multiple of two or more nonzero numbers. 40 is the LCM of 10 and 8.

legs (p. 551): The sides of a right triangle that form the right angle.

line (p. 486): A set of points that extends without end in opposite directions. Two points determine a line.

line graph (p. 37): A display of numerical facts that uses line segments to show both amount and direction of change.

line segment (p. 486): A part of a line that consists of two endpoints and all the points between them.

lowest terms (p. 124): A fraction is in lowest terms if the greatest common factor of the numerator and the denominator is 1.

m

mean (average) (p. 401): The sum of the items in a set of data divided by the number of items.

median (p. 401): The middle number (or the mean of the two middle numbers) of a set of data arranged in numerical order.

mixed number (p. 131): A number that consists of both a whole number and a fraction. $5\frac{3}{8}$ is a mixed number.

mode (p. 401): The number that appears most often in a set of data.

multiple (p. 102): When a number is multiplied by a nonzero whole number, the product is a multiple of the given number.

n

negative numbers (p. 442): Numbers less than zero.

net pay (p. 266): A worker's earnings after deductions have been subtracted.

numerator (p. 118): In the fraction $\frac{5}{8}$, 5 is the numerator.

o

obtuse angle (p. 487): An angle that has a measure between 90° and 180°.

obtuse triangle (p. 542): A triangle with one obtuse angle.

octagon (p. 490): An eight-sided polygon.

odd number (p. 99): A number that is not divisible by 2.

odds (p. 434): The ratio of the number of favorable outcomes to the number of unfavorable outcomes of an event.

opposites (p. 442): Two numbers that are the same distance from 0 on a number line, but on different sides of 0. 8 and ⁻8 are opposites.

ordered pair (p. 474): A pair of numbers such as (3, ⁻5) in which the order of the numbers is important.

origin (p. 474): The point on a coordinate plane where the x-axis and the y-axis meet.

outcome (p. 420): A possible result. One outcome of tossing a penny is *heads*.

p

parallel lines (p. 488): Lines in a plane that do not intersect.

parallelogram (p. 491): A quadrilateral with two pairs of parallel sides.

pentagon (p. 490): A five-sided polygon.

percent (p. 346): A notation that represents a ratio that compares a number to 100.
$$4\% = \frac{4}{100} = 0.04$$

percent of increase or decrease (p. 381): A percent comparing an amount of change to an original amount.

perfect square (p. 548): A number whose square root is a whole number.

perimeter (p. 493): The distance around a polygon.

permutation (p. 422): An arrangement of objects in a particular order.

perpendicular lines (p. 488): Lines that intersect to form right angles.

pi (π) (p. 495): A symbol representing the quotient when the circumference of a circle is divided by the length of the diameter, approximated by either $\frac{22}{7}$ or 3.14.

pictograph (p. 404): A way of displaying data in which a picture symbol represents a specified number of items.

place value (p. 2): The value given to the place where a digit appears in a number.

plane (p. 486): A set of points on a flat surface that extends without end.

point (p. 486): An exact location in space.

polygon (p. 490): A plane figure formed by joining three or more line segments at their endpoints.

polyhedron (p. 518): A space figure with flat surfaces.

positive numbers (p. 442): Numbers greater than zero.

power of a number (p. 104): The result of multiplying a number by itself a given number of times. 8, or 2^3, is the third power of 2.

prime factorization (p. 100): The process of writing a whole number as the product of prime numbers.

prime number (p. 100): A whole number greater than 1 that has only itself and 1 as factors.

principal (p. 363): An amount of money that is borrowed.

prism (p. 518): A polyhedron with two identical and parallel polygons as its bases and parallelograms as its other faces.

probability (p. 424): The chance that an event will occur, calculated by finding the ratio of the number of favorable outcomes to the number of possible outcomes of the event.

product (p. 48): The result of multiplying two or more numbers. The product of 5 and 7 is 35.

proportion (p. 329): A statement that two ratios are equal.

protractor (p. 487): An instrument used in measuring and drawing angles.

pyramid (p. 518): A polyhedron with any polygon as its base and triangles as its other faces.

Pythagorean Theorem (p. 551): For any right triangle, the square of the length of the hypotenuse is equal to the sum of the squares of the lengths of the two legs.

q

quadrilateral (p. 490): A four-sided polygon.

quotient (p. 70): The result of dividing one number by another. In $36 \div 4 = 9$, 9 is the quotient.

r

radical sign (p. 548): The symbol, $\sqrt{}$, used to denote the square root of a number. $\sqrt{49} = 7$

radius of a circle (p. 495): A line segment that joins the center of the circle with any point on the circle.

range (p. 398): The difference between the greatest number and the least number in a set of data.

rate (p. 327): A ratio that compares two unlike measures.

ratio (p. 324): A comparison of two numbers by division.

ray (p. 486): A part of a line that has one endpoint and extends without end in one direction.

reciprocals (p. 152): Two numbers whose product is 1. 7 and $\frac{1}{7}$ are reciprocals.

rectangle (p. 491): A parallelogram with four right angles.

regular polygon (p. 490): A polygon with all sides congruent and all angles congruent.

remainder (p. 70): The whole number left after one number is divided by another number.

$$\begin{array}{r} 4 \text{ R3} \\ 5\overline{)23} \\ 20 \\ \hline 3 \end{array}$$ — remainder

repeating decimal (p. 223): A decimal in which a digit or block of digits repeats endlessly. 0.666 . . . is a repeating decimal.

rhombus (p. 491): A parallelogram with all sides congruent.

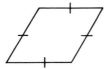

right angle (p. 487): An angle that has a measure of 90°.

right triangle (p. 542): A triangle with one right angle.

s

scale drawing (p. 335): A drawing that shows the correct shape of an object but usually is different in size.

scalene triangle (p. 542): A triangle with no congruent sides.

scientific notation (p. 284): A number written as the product of a power of 10 and a number that is at least 1 but less than 10. 3.7×10^3 is written in scientific notation.

sides of an angle (p. 486): The two rays that form the angle.

sides of a polygon (p. 490): The line segments that form the polygon.

similar triangles (p. 545): Triangles that have the same shape.

solve an equation (p. 464): Find a value of a variable that makes the equation true.

space figure (p. 518): A three-dimensional figure that encloses part of space.

sphere (p. 519): The set of all points in space that are the same distance from a given point called the center.

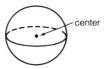

square (p. 491): A parallelogram with four right angles and all sides congruent.

square of a number (p. 548): The result when a number is used as a factor twice. 25 is the square of 5.

square root of a number (p. 548): One of the two equal factors of a number. 6 is the square root of 36.

statistics (p. 398): The branch of mathematics that deals with organizing and analyzing data.

straight angle (p. 543): An angle that has a measure of 180°.

sum (p. 5): The result of adding two or more numbers. The sum of 5 and 9 is 14.

surface area of a space figure (p. 521): The sum of the areas of all surfaces of the figure.

t

terms of a proportion (p. 329): The numbers used in forming the proportion. In $\frac{3}{20} = \frac{15}{100}$, the terms are 3, 20, 15, and 100.

trapezoid (p. 491): A quadrilateral with only one pair of parallel sides.

tree diagram (p. 420): In probability, a display that is used to count the number of possible outcomes.

triangle (p. 490): A three-sided polygon.

u

unit price (p. 314): The cost of one unit of a particular item, expressed in terms of the unit in which the product is generally measured.

unit rate (p. 327): A rate for one unit of a given quantity. Miles per hour is a unit rate.

V

variable (p. 13): A letter or other symbol used to represent a number.

variable expression (p. 13): An expression that contains one or more variables. *3abx* is a variable expression.

Venn diagram (p. 508): A diagram that shows the relationship between two or more groups of items.

vertex of an angle (p. 486): The endpoint of the two rays that form the angle.

vertex of a polyhedron (p. 518): The point where three or more edges of the polyhedron intersect.

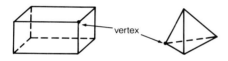

vertex of a polygon (p. 490): The point where two sides of the figure intersect.

vertical axis (p. 34): *See* axes.

volume (p. 524): The amount of space inside a space figure.

W

whole numbers (p. 2): The numbers 0, 1, 2, 3, and so on.

X

x-axis (p. 474): The horizontal number line in a coordinate plane.

x-coordinate (p. 474): The first number of an ordered pair.

Y

y-axis (p. 474): The vertical number line in a coordinate plane.

y-coordinate (p. 474): The second number of an ordered pair.

index

of a number, 355–359
and proportions, 378–380
Perimeter, 493–494
Permutation, 422–423
Perpendicular lines, 488
Pi (π), 495
Pictograph, 404–406
Pint, 197
Place value, 2, 212
Plane, 486
Point, 486
  coordinates of, 474
Poll, taking a, 433
Polygon, 490–492
  perimeter of, 493
Polyhedron, 518
  surface area of, 521
Population, 433
Pound, 195
Power,
  factored form of, 106
  of an integer, 451
  of a variable, 106
  of a whole number, 104
  zero, 104, 451
Prediction, 429–431
Price
  comparing, 316
  sale, 386
  unit, 314–315, 316
Prime factorization, 100
Prime number, 100
Principal, in money, 363
Prism, 518
  rectangular, 518, 521,
    524–525
  surface area of, 521–523
  volume of, 524–526
Probability, 420–433
Problem solving, four–step
  method, 86
Problem Solving Strategies
  choosing the correct operation,
    86–87
  displaying information,
    410–411
  identifying patterns, 182–183
  identifying too much or too
    little information, 226–227
  making a diagram, 508–509
  making a model, 554–555
  simplifying the problem,
    456–457
  understanding the problem,
    40–41

using drawings, 308–309
using estimation, 262–263
using equations, 472–473
using logical reasoning,
  360–361
using more than one
  operation, 134–135
using proportions, 332–334
Product, 48
  partial, 53, 56
  See also Multiplication.
Properties. *See under names of
  specific properties.*
Proportion, 329–334
  in problem solving, 332–334
  solving a, 329–331
Protractor, 487
Puzzle Corner, 15, 39, 52, 85,
  107, 120, 151, 178, 198, 217,
  236, 256, 276, 307, 326, 352,
  380, 400, 423, 452, 477, 500,
  526, 550
Pyramid, 518
  volume of, 530–532
Pythagorean Theorem, 551–553

q

Quadrilateral, 490
  classification of, 491
Quart, 197
Quotient, 70
  undefined, 453
  zeros in, 71, 274, 277
  See also Division.

r

Radius
  of a circle, 495
  of a sphere, 533
Range of a set of data, 398
Rate, 327–328
  in borrowing money, 363
  commission, 385
  discount, 386
  unit, 327
Ratio, 324–326
  equal, 329
Ray, 486
Reciprocal, 152
Rectangle, 491
  area of, 498
  perimeter of, 493

Rectangular prism, 518
  surface area of, 521–523
  volume of, 524–526
Remainder in division, 70
Renaming
  in addition, 5, 199–200, 234
  in comparing fractions, 126
  in multiplication, 50
  in subtraction, 10, 11, 179,
    180, 199–200, 239
Repeating decimal, 223
Reviews
  chapter, *See* Chapter Review.
  cumulative, 116, 210, 322,
    396, 440, 564
  skill, *See* Skill Review.
Rhombus, 491
Right angle, 487
Right triangle, 542
Rounding
  of decimal quotients, 275, 280
  of decimals, 215–217, 223,
    237, 260, 275, 280
  of mixed numbers, 147, 171
  of money numbers, 216, 258
  of whole numbers, 26–31

s

Salary, annual, 287
Sales tax, 368
Sample, 433
Savings account, 364–365
Scale
  of a drawing/model, 335–337
  of a graph, 34, 37
  on a map, 340–342
Scientific notation, 284–285
Short division, 72
Similar triangles, 545–547
Simple interest, 363
Skill Review, 18, 42, 64, 88,
  108, 136, 158, 184, 202, 228,
  244, 264, 286, 310, 338, 362,
  384, 412, 432, 458, 478, 510,
  536, 556
Social security tax, 266
Solving equations
  by addition or subtraction,
    464–465
  by multiplication or division,
    466–468
  two operations, 469–471
  two variables, 476
Space figure, 518–520

Sphere, 519
  volume of, 533–535
Spreadsheets,
  electronic, 393
Square, 491
  area of, 498
  perimeter of, 493
Square of a number, 548
  table of, 549
Square root(s), 548
  table of, 549
Statistics, 397–418
  misleading, 413
Subtraction
  checking, 10, 239
  of decimals, 239–243
  estimation in, 171–172
  of fractions, 166–172
  of integers, 448–449
  of measurement expressions,
    199–201
  of mixed numbers, 171–172,
    176–181
  in solving equations, 464–465
  of whole numbers, 10–12
  words and phrases, 13
Sum, 5, 48
  See also Addition.
Surface area, 521–523
Symbols
  approximately equal to, 223
  equality/inequality, 32, 121
Symmetry, 236

t

u

v

w

x y z

credits

Cover Design—Group Four Design
Cover Photograph—Jon Chomitz
Mechanical Art—Anco/Boston
Illustrations—Linda Phinney

Photographs

1 Jon Chomitz 4 Rick Stewart/Focus West
8 Macdonald Photography/The Picture Cube
10 Tom Tracy 19 Paul Von Stroheim/Stock Shop
20 Mark Segal/Click/Chicago 22 Index/Stock
25 Stan Ries/The Picture Cube 29 Bruce Coleman,
Inc. 37 Peter Chapman 38 Animals Animals/
Earth Scenes © 1988/E. R. Degginger 43 James
Ballard 44 Peter Chapman 47 Don Gray/F-Stop
51 Focus West 55 Jamie Tanaka/
Bruce Coleman, Inc. 56 Peter Chapman 60 Peter
Chapman 61 Michael Furman/Stock Market
65 Warren Morgan/Focus on Sports 66 John
Zoiner/Peter Arnold, Inc. 69 Jon Chomitz 71 Philip
John Bailey/The Picture Cube 73 Frank Siteman
76 Carole Jacobson/Journalism Services, Inc.
79 Peter Chapman 85 Elliott Varner Smith
86 Richard Gross/Stock Imagery 89 Peter Chapman
90 Eric Roth/The Picture Cube 93 Ken O'Donoghue
95 Tadd Goodale 106 Harry Hartman/Bruce
Coleman, Inc. 109 Animals Animals/Earth Scenes
© 1988/Richard Kolar 110 Raymond D. Barnes/
Click/Chicago 113 Stacy Pick/Uniphoto 117 Gregg
Eisman/Ligature, Inc. 121 Peter Chapman 124 Tim
Schultz/Click/Chicago 129 Tim Schultz/Bruce
Coleman, Inc. 130 Peter Chapman 133 Photoedit/
Tony Freeman 134 Bob Kramer 135 Photoedit/
James Shaffer 137 Tom Tracy/Stock Shop 138 Cary
Wolinsky/Stock Boston 138–139 Peter Chapman
140 The Picture Cube 143 H. Armstrong Roberts
147 Marmel Studios/FPG 149 Jeffry Myers/Stock
Boston 155 Harold Stucker/Stock Shop
159 Dan McCoy/Rainbow 160 Greg Eisman
161, 162 Photoedit/Mark Richards
165 Index/Stock 168 Ted Detoy/Stock Market
173 George Dritsas/Light Images 176 Tommy
Noonan/Uniphoto 177 Tom Tracy 181 Francisco
Erize/Bruce Coleman, Inc. 185 Index/Stock
186 Michal Heron 189 Ken O'Donoghue 193 (top
and bottom) Peter Chapman 194 (top) Tadd Goodale
194 (middle-left, center and right, bottom) Peter
Chapman 201 Focus on Sports 202 Mike Blake
203 Wide World 204 Adam Smith
Productions/Click/Chicago 206 (left) Peter Chapman
206 (right) Tadd Goodale 207 Michal Heron
211 Focus on Sports 215 Presse-Foto/Stock Shop
219 Berntson/Stock Shop 220 Photoedit/Tony
Freeman 225 Santa Cruz Seaside Co. 226 Peter
Chapman 229 Photoedit/Tony Freeman 230 Bob
Clarke/Index/Stock 233 Jon Chomitz 237 Peter
Chapman 241 Peter Chapman 242 John
Eastcott/Yva Momatiuk/The Image Works
245 Charles Gupton/Stock Market 246 Casio

247 Ken O'Donoghue 248 Pick/Webber/Stock
Boston 251 Jeff Albertson/The Picture Cube
252 Len Sheravin/Click/Chicago 258 Peter Chapman
260 H. Armstrong Roberts 262 Camerique
265 Richard Dunoff/Stock Market 267 Camerique
270 Rising Stock 273 Mitch Kezar/Uniphoto
278 Walter Chandoha 281 Joan Sake/Bruce
Coleman, Inc. 282 Plessner International/Stock Shop
287 Peter Chapman 288 Camerique 290 Charles
Gupton/Stock Market 293 Ken O'Donoghue
294 Reibel/Levine/Sportschrome 295 (top) Peter
Chapman 295 (bottom) Tadd Goodale 297 Peter
Chapman 298 clockwise from the top; (3 photos)
Peter Chapman, (2 photos) Mike Blake, Tadd Goodale,
Mike Blake, Tadd Goodale, Mike Blake 302 Lou
Jones 304 Photoedit/James Shaffer 305 Animals
Animals/Earth Scenes © 1988/D. R. Specker
307 (bottom) James Ballard 307 (top) Peter
Chapman 311 Peter Chapman 314 George
Harrison/Bruce Coleman, Inc. 315 James Ballard
316 Charles Gupton/Uniphoto 323 Jon Chomitz
327 Lee Foster/Bruce Coleman, Inc. 332 Paul
Johnson 336 Peter Vadnai/Stock Market 339 John
Dominisi/Wheeler Pictures 345 Vince Streano/Click/
Chicago 352 Jim Pickerell/Click/Chicago 360 James
Ballard 363 Rick Friedman/The Picture Cube
364 Andy Brilliant 365 Andy Brilliant/The Picture
Cube 368 Stuart Cohen/Stock Boston 371 Mark
Antman/The Image Works 372 Focus on Sports
381 Bob Kramer 385 Michal Heron 387 Solomon/
Martin/FPG 390 C.P. Marketing/FPG 393 COMSTOCK,
INC./Robert Houser 397 Rick Stewart/Focus West
404 Walter Chandoha 409 James Ballard/Ligature
410 James Ballard 413 Peter Chapman 415 Jim
Pickerell/Click/Chicago 416 (bottom) Larry Mulvehill/
Photo Researchers 416 (top) L. L. T. Rhodes/Click/
Chicago 419 © Leonard Lee Rue III/
After-Image 1987 430 Mark Phillips/Shostal
Associates 433 Dennie Cody/FPG
434 Scott Berner/Stock Shop 437 (top) Joseph
Nettis/Photo Researchers 437 (bottom) Southern
Stock Photos 441 Eugen Gebhardt/Stock Shop
448 Frank Fisher/Gamma-Liaison 452 C. B. Jones/
Taurus 455 Bob Taylor/Stock Shop 457 Peter
Chapman 459 Zviki-Eshe/Stock Market 460 Bob
Kramer 463 Bildagentur Mauritius/Stock Shop
466 Wynn Miller/Stock Shop 472 (top) T. Qing/FPG
472 (bottom) © Steve Murray/After-Image 1988
473 © Steve Murray/After-Image 1988 475 Maega/
Stock Shop 479 Plessner International/Stock Shop
485 Tom Ross/Index/Stock 497 Bilagentur Mauritius/
Stock Shop 500 Frank Fisher/Gamma-Liaison
503 Group III Kerr/Uniphoto 504 John Marshall
511 David Frazier/Stock Market 512 Peter Arnold,
Inc. 514 Jeff Apoian/Nawrocki Stock 517 Jon
Chomitz 529 Bob Daemmrich/Stock Boston
537 Will Campbell/FPG 538 COMSTOCK, INC./Tom
Grill 541 Plessner International/Stock Shop
545 Tom Tracy/Stock Shop 551 Bill Gallery/Stock
Boston 557 Marmel Studios/Stock Market

answers to your turn exercises

CHAPTER 1

Page 2 **1.** 30,000,000 **2.** 4,000,000,000 **3.** 800,000 **4.** 6 **5.** 50,000,000 **6.** 0

Page 3 **7.** eighty-four million, five hundred two thousand, three **8.** thirty-six billion, five hundred twenty-four million, eight hundred thousand **9.** seventeen billion, four hundred thirteen million, nine hundred thirty-four thousand, two hundred twenty-eight **10.** 518 billion, 329 million, 70 thousand, 4 **11.** 21 billion, 753 million, 3 thousand, 916 **12.** 102 billion, 763 million, 94 thousand, 251 **13.** 107,049,543,006 **14.** 69,004,337 **15.** 97,000,050,008 **16.** 1,005,012

Page 5 **1.** 7688 **2.** 43,867 **3.** $132,202 **4.** $3448 **5.** 117 **6.** 990 **7.** $789 **8.** $6953 **9.** 209 **10.** 233

Page 6 **11.** 19 **12.** 27 **13.** 27 **14.** 37 **15.** 187 **16.** 740

Page 8 **1.** about 5000 **2.** about 100,000 **3.** about 800,000 **4.** about 80 **5.** about 1000 **6.** about 9000

Page 9 **7.** about 1000 **8.** about 9000 **9.** about 9000 **10.** about 60,000

Page 10 **1.** 2253 **2.** 5645 **3.** $8796 **4.** $27,651 **5.** 271 **6.** 2421 **7.** $542 **8.** $73,558

Page 11 **9.** 471 **10.** 70,028 **11.** 467 **12.** 3974

Page 13 **1.** 84 **2.** 32 **3.** 77 **4.** 72 **5.** $x - 60$ **6.** $x + 500$ **7.** $x + 18$ **8.** $70 - x$

Page 16 **1.** 111 **2.** 17 **3.** 152 **4.** 132 **5.** 21 **6.** 71 **7.** 32 **8.** 80

CHAPTER 2

Page 26 **1.** 5300 **2.** 820 **3.** $16,000 **4.** $100

Page 27 **5.** 2000 **6.** $40,000 **7.** 4000 **8.** $80,000 **9.** 50 **10.** $3000 **11.** $1000 **12.** 9000

Page 29 **1.** about 8000 **2.** about 3000 **3.** about $90,000 **4.** about $6000

Page 30 **5.** about 100 **6.** about 9000 **7.** about $8000 **8.** about $820,000

Page 32 **1.** > **2.** < **3.** = **4.** 749; 873; 891 **5.** $473; $4654; $4739 **6.** 60,322; 61,428; 61,824

Page 34 **1.** 11 **2.** hockey, tennis **3.** about 4000 km **4.** about 2500 km **5.** about 2000 km **6.** about 3500 km

Page 35 **7.**

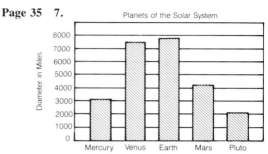

Page 37 **1.** about 51 million **2.** 1975 and 1980

Page 38 **3.**

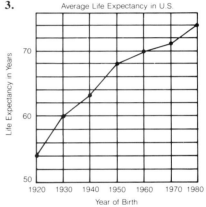

Page 40 **1.** number of plates **2.** cost of the shirt **3.** reasonable **4.** not reasonable

CHAPTER 3

Page 48 **1.** 60 + 60 + 60 + 60 + 60 + 60 + 60 = 420 **2.** 900 + 900 + 900 + 900 + 900 + 900 = 5400 **3.** 8000 + 8000 + 8000 + 8000 + 8000 + 8000 + 8000 + 8000 = 64,000 **4.** 5000 + 5000 + 5000 + 5000 = 20,000 **5.** 60 **6.** 4500 **7.** 80,000 **8.** 3,000,000

Page 50 **1.** $86 **2.** 390 **3.** 5768 **4.** $424,352 **5.** 2485 **6.** 47,384 **7.** $545,058 **8.** $155,084

Page 51 **9.** about 480 **10.** about 4500 **11.** about $30,000 **12.** about $280,000

Page 53 **1.** 324 **2.** 2967 **3.** 36,022 **4.** 59,070 **5.** 2888 **6.** 1026 **7.** 4761 **8.** 85,173

Page 54   9.   about 3200; overestimate
10.   about 12,000; can't tell   11.   about 18,000;
can't tell   12.   about 4800; underestimate

Page 56   1.   172,752   2.   103,675
3.   2,177,812   4.   2,648,397

Page 57   5.   629,280   6.   419,625   7.   471,177

Page 59   1.   685,602   2.   417,768   3.   413,256
4.   232,362   5.   8400   6.   990   7.   2800   8.   900

Page 60   9.   365   10.   276   11.   396   12.   588
13.   384   14.   291   15.   1456   16.   1992

Page 62   1.   7(2), 7 · 2   2.   35(4), 35 × 4
3.   9 · 11, 9 × 11   4.   28 × 6, 28 · 6   5.   0
6.   800   7.   224   8.   0

CHAPTER 4

Page 70   1.   282   2. $511   3.   1125 R4
4.   1547 R3

Page 71   5. $39   6.   894 R2   7. $471
8.   2567 R2   9.   604   10. $210   11.   5040 R4
12.   9006 R2

Page 73   1.   about 700   2.   about 900   3.   about
600   4.   about 9000   5.   about 80   6.   about 600
7.   about 200   8.   about 50

Page 75   1.   19   2. $91   3.   770 R17   4.   856 R48
5.   29 R13   6.   58 R5   7.   64 R33   8.   65 R14

Page 76   9.   101 R64   10.   425 R21
11.   1074 R3   12.   663 R58

Page 78   1.   185   2. $54   3.   1971 R291
4. $344   5.   339 R134   6.   581 R165

Page 79   7.   501 R87   8.   282 R170   9.   54 R501

Page 81   1. $4\overline{)84}$; $\frac{84}{4}$ 2.   108 ÷ 9; $\frac{108}{9}$
3.   145 ÷ 5; $5\overline{)145}$ 4. $16\overline{)512}$; $\frac{512}{16}$ 5.   9
6.   14   7.   6   8.   3   9.   5

Page 83   1.   944   2.   57   3.   201   4.   72
5.   11y   6. $\frac{84}{y}$ 7.   4y   8. $\frac{y}{10}$
Page 84   9.   y − 14   10. $\frac{y}{14}$ 11.   y + 20   12.   20y

CHAPTER 5

Page 94   1.   14   2.   22   3.   17   4.   5   5.   5
6.   490   7.   13   8.   20

Page 95   9.   10   10.   128   11.   40   12.   5

Page 97   1.   yes; no; no   2.   no; no; yes
3.   yes; yes; yes   4.   no; no; no   5.   no; no; yes
6.   yes; no; no

Page 98   7.   yes; yes   8.   yes; yes   9.   no; no
10.   no; no   11.   yes; no   12.   yes; no   13.   yes;
no   14.   no; no   15.   yes; yes   16.   yes; yes

Page 100   1.   2 × 5   2.   2 × 2 × 5   3.   2 × 3 × 5
4.   2 × 2 × 2 × 2   5.   2 × 19   6.   3 × 3 × 5

Page 101   7.   12   8.   4   9.   9   10.   3

Page 102   Answers may vary. Likely answers are
given.   1.   4, 8, 12, 16, 20, 24   2.   5, 10, 15,
20, 25, 30   3.   10, 20, 30, 40, 50, 60   4.   2, 4,
6, 8, 10, 12   5.   40   6.   48   7.   126   8.   36

Page 104   1.   81   2.   216   3.   32   4.   81
5.   25,000

Page 105   6.   1   7.   12   8.   7   9.   9   10.   32

Page 106   1.   z · z · z · z · z   2.   9 · m · m · m
3.   7 · r · s · s   4.   4 · x · x · y · y   5.   125
6.   100   7.   2000   8.   500

CHAPTER 6

Page 118   1. $\frac{5}{7}$ 2. $\frac{5}{8}$ 3. $\frac{3}{7}$

Page 119   4. $\frac{2}{6}$ 5. $\frac{2}{5}$ 6. $\frac{3}{4}$ 7. $\frac{2}{7}$ 8. $\frac{19}{60}$
9. $\frac{1}{12}$ 10. $\frac{11}{60}$

Page 121   1.   equivalent   2.   equivalent   3.   not
equivalent   4.   not equivalent

Page 122   5.   40   6.   21   7.   22   8.   45   9.   9
10.   6   11.   50   12.   13

Page 124   1.   no   2.   yes   3.   no   4.   no   5. $\frac{2}{3}$
6. $\frac{3}{4}$ 7. $\frac{2}{7}$ 8. $\frac{4}{9}$

Page 126   1.   >   2.   =   3.   <   4.   =   5.   <
6.   >

Page 127   7. $\frac{1}{4}, \frac{3}{7}, \frac{1}{2}$ 8. $\frac{3}{4}, \frac{7}{5}, \frac{5}{2}$ 9. $\frac{5}{22}, \frac{6}{11}, \frac{3}{2}$

Page 129   1.   about $\frac{1}{5}$ 2.   about $\frac{1}{3}$ 3.   about $\frac{1}{4}$
4.   about $\frac{1}{7}$ 5.   about $\frac{2}{5}$ 6.   about $\frac{2}{3}$ 7.   1   8.   0
9.   1   10. $\frac{1}{2}$

Page 131   1. $\frac{7}{2}$ 2. $\frac{19}{12}$ 3. $\frac{111}{20}$ 4. $\frac{40}{3}$ 5. $\frac{9}{2}$
6. $\frac{25}{3}$ 7. $1\frac{5}{7}$ 8.   2   9. $6\frac{4}{5}$ 10. $8\frac{1}{2}$ 11.   1
12. $6\frac{1}{2}$

Page 132   13.   >   14.   =   15.   >   16.   >

Page 138   1.   two   2.   one half note

Page 139   3.   one half note   4.   one eighth note

CHAPTER 7

Page 144   1. $\frac{1}{6}$ 2. $\frac{2}{9}$ 3. $\frac{4}{7}$ 4.   6   5. $\frac{9}{16}$
6. $\frac{3}{4}$ 7. $\frac{1}{5}$ 8. $1\frac{1}{3}$

Page 145   9.   about 30   10.   about 100
11.   about 50   12.   about 40

Page 147   1.   about 15   2.   about 3
3.   about 35   4.   about 100   5.   about 3
6.   about 4   7.   about 15   8.   about 20

Page 149   1.   72   2.   21   3. $11\frac{1}{2}$ 4. $37\frac{1}{2}$

Page 150   5.   9   6.   3   7. $3\frac{5}{6}$ 8. $4\frac{2}{3}$

Page 152 **1.** $\frac{8}{3}$ **2.** $\frac{7}{4}$ **3.** $\frac{1}{10}$ **4.** no reciprocal **5.** $\frac{4}{9}$ **6.** $\frac{13}{37}$

Page 153 **7.** $\frac{5}{6}$ **8.** $1\frac{7}{11}$ **9.** $\frac{1}{8}$ **10.** $1\frac{1}{35}$ **11.** 9 **12.** 40 **13.** $\frac{3}{35}$ **14.** $\frac{1}{12}$

Page 155 **1.** $2\frac{1}{7}$ **2.** 3 **3.** $\frac{2}{9}$ **4.** $4\frac{1}{8}$ **5.** $\frac{8}{11}$ **6.** $\frac{5}{9}$ **7.** $37\frac{1}{3}$ **8.** $\frac{8}{161}$

Page 156 **9.** about 4 **10.** about 6 **11.** about 100 **12.** about 20

Page 160 **1.** $1\frac{1}{4}$ c **2.** $\frac{5}{8}$ c **3.** $2\frac{1}{2}$ tsp **4.** $\frac{5}{8}$ tsp

Page 161 **5.** $\frac{1}{8}$ lb **6.** $\frac{7}{8}$ lb **7.** $\frac{1}{12}$ c **8.** $\frac{3}{8}$ tsp

CHAPTER 8

Page 166 **1.** $\frac{16}{19}$ **2.** $\frac{2}{11}$ **3.** $\frac{6}{7}$ **4.** $\frac{2}{3}$ **5.** 1 **6.** $1\frac{1}{9}$ **7.** $1\frac{4}{11}$ **8.** $1\frac{1}{2}$

Page 168 **1.** $\frac{3}{4}$ **2.** $\frac{29}{35}$ **3.** $1\frac{8}{15}$ **4.** $1\frac{1}{22}$

Page 169 **5.** $\frac{7}{10}$ **6.** $\frac{1}{36}$ **7.** $\frac{8}{21}$ **8.** $\frac{1}{33}$

Page 171 **1.** about 5 **2.** about 11 **3.** about 11 **4.** about 5 **5.** about 5 **6.** about 4 **7.** about 12

Page 173 **1.** $5\frac{7}{8}$ **2.** $2\frac{5}{6}$ **3.** $17\frac{1}{2}$ **4.** $8\frac{1}{3}$

Page 174 **5.** 16 **6.** $10\frac{1}{8}$ **7.** $5\frac{7}{18}$ **8.** $17\frac{2}{15}$

Page 176 **1.** $2\frac{3}{5}$ **2.** 2 **3.** $1\frac{1}{5}$ **4.** $55\frac{1}{3}$

Page 177 **5.** $4\frac{7}{36}$ **6.** $6\frac{1}{12}$ **7.** $2\frac{1}{6}$ **8.** $\frac{1}{5}$

Page 179 **1.** $\frac{2}{3}$ **2.** $4\frac{5}{8}$ **3.** $\frac{17}{20}$ **4.** $8\frac{4}{9}$

Page 180 **5.** $\frac{5}{6}$ **6.** $\frac{1}{3}$ **7.** $1\frac{3}{7}$ **8.** $5\frac{5}{8}$

CHAPTER 9

Page 190 **1.** 360 **2.** 864 **3.** 9 **4.** 2; 21 **5.** 311 **6.** 3; 720

Page 192 **1.** 3 in. **2.** 5 in.

Page 193 **3.** $1\frac{11}{16}$ in. **4.** $2\frac{1}{2}$ in.

Page 195 **1.** 14,000 **2.** 96 **3.** 3 **4.** 6900 **5.** 141 **6.** 11; 4

Page 197 **1.** 48 **2.** 6 **3.** 6 **4.** 37 **5.** 7 **6.** 8; 1

Page 199 **1.** 24 yd 7 in. **2.** 6 gal 1 qt **3.** 172 t 37 lb **4.** 14 ft 1 in. **5.** 32 gal **6.** 8 t 143 lb

Page 200 **7.** 1 pt 1 c **8.** 83 lb 5 oz **9.** 3 mi 1728 yd

CHAPTER 10

Page 212 **1.** 0.04 **2.** 0.2 **3.** 0.0001 **4.** 0 **5.** 0.004 **6.** 0.000008

Page 213 **7.** one hundred seventy-six and ninety-five hundredths **8.** nine and seven thousand three hundred seventeen ten-thousandths **9.** three hundred five thousandths **10.** 385 and 9 tenths **11.** 49 and 631 thousandths **12.** 71 ten-thousandths **13.** 0.5321 **14.** 22.0007 **15.** 392.46 **16.** 3.041

Page 215 **1.** 12.1 **2.** 0.420 **3.** 0.08 **4.** 25 **5.** 0.03 **6.** 1 **7.** 1.0 **8.** 0.005

Page 216 **9.** $20 **10.** $14 **11.** $1.10 **12.** $7.67

Page 218 **1.** < **2.** > **3.** = **4.** 2.09; 2.54; 2.89 **5.** 0.203; 0.31; 0.312 **6.** 0.033; 0.33; 0.333 **7.** 9.801; 9.81; 9.981

Page 221 **1.** $\frac{9}{10}$ **2.** $\frac{221}{1000}$ **3.** $\frac{2}{5}$ **4.** $\frac{6}{25}$ **5.** $\frac{33}{40}$ **6.** $\frac{307}{1000}$ **7.** $9\frac{7}{10}$ **8.** $44\frac{2}{25}$ **9.** $293\frac{4}{5}$ **10.** $90\frac{63}{100}$ **11.** $5\frac{11}{500}$ **12.** $15\frac{713}{1000}$

Page 223 **1.** 0.8 **2.** 0.24 **3.** 0.175 **4.** 2.5 **5.** 0.33 **6.** 0.44 **7.** 0.28 **8.** 0.82

Page 224 **9.** $\frac{1}{2}$ **10.** $\frac{9}{10}$ **11.** $\frac{1}{3}$ **12.** $\frac{2}{5}$

CHAPTER 11

Page 234 **1.** 5.1 **2.** 72.92 **3.** $200.04 **4.** 43.413 **5.** $33.89 **6.** 6.11 **7.** 45.617

Page 235 **8.** 16 **9.** 5.37 **10.** 8 **11.** $7.47 **12.** 22.59 **13.** 639.328

Page 237 **1.** about 1100 **2.** about 60 **3.** about $7.50 **4.** about $110 **5.** about 1.1 **6.** about $140 **7.** about 0.12

Page 239 **1.** 1.2 **2.** 8.54 **3.** $1.95 **4.** 0.064 **5.** 3.91 **6.** 2.281 **7.** 0.212 **8.** 59.9935

Page 240 **9.** 26.8 **10.** 3.75 **11.** $13.90 **12.** 0.997

Page 242 **1.** about 700 **2.** about $70 **3.** about 2000 **4.** about 10 **5.** about 4.2 **6.** about 0.8

Page 246 **1.** 1 $10 bill, 2 quarters **2.** 4 $1 bills, 3 quarters, 2 dimes, 3 pennies **3.** 3 quarters, 3 pennies **4.** 1 $20 bill, 1 $1 bill, 3 quarters, 1 penny **5.** 1 quarter **6.** 1 penny, 1 nickel, 1 quarter, 4 $1 bills

CHAPTER 12

Page 252 **1.** 7.941 **2.** 111.6 **3.** $189.36 **4.** $106.75

Page 253 **5.** 1.33 **6.** 289.8 **7.** 19.35 **8.** $329.96 **9.** 0.027 **10.** 45 **11.** 124 **12.** $1512.50

Page 255 **1.** 7.52 **2.** 723.4 **3.** 1475 **4.** 149.6 **5.** 4010 **6.** 88,880 **7.** 3100 **8.** 6550

Page 257 **1.** 2.64 **2.** 0.884 **3.** 1.8084 **4.** 33.072 **5.** 0.0024 **6.** 0.0003 **7.** 0.03 **8.** 0.04

Page 258 **9.** $3.75 **10.** $26.46 **11.** $57.53 **12.** $17.66

Page 260 **1.** about 360 **2.** about 30,000 **3.** about 4 **4.** about 0.2 **5.** about 180 **6.** about 900 **7.** about 1000 **8.** about 35

CHAPTER 13

Page 274 **1.** 1.9 **2.** 0.936 **3.** $2.23 **4.** 7.75

Page 275 **5.** 0.08 **6.** 2.006 **7.** $8.09 **8.** $3.10 **9.** 5.9 **10.** 8.09 **11.** 0.278 **12.** 4.663

Page 277 **1.** 19.82 **2.** 0.5703 **3.** 0.1852 **4.** 4.229 **5.** 0.046 **6.** 0.0075 **7.** 0.0387 **8.** 0.041

Page 279 **1.** 5 **2.** 7.13 **3.** 4.4 **4.** 5 **5.** 210 **6.** 53.75 **7.** 230 **8.** 130

Page 280 **9.** 2.5 **10.** 0.48 **11.** 1.43 **12.** 18.889

Page 282 **1.** about 3 **2.** about 6 **3.** about $200 **4.** about 50 **5.** about 15 **6.** about $60 **7.** about 900 **8.** about 700 **9.** about 700 **10.** about 0.2 **11.** about 4 **12.** about 45

Page 284 **1.** 3.35×10^4 **2.** 2.5×10^7 **3.** 3.749×10^2 **4.** 7.6×10^1 **5.** 359 **6.** 12,850,000,000 **7.** 7000 **8.** 2,000,000,000

Page 288 **1.** $1931.40 **2.** $546.84

Page 289 **3.** $397.77 **4.** $92.64

CHAPTER 14

Page 294 **1.** m **2.** km **3.** km

Page 295 **4.** cm **5.** mm **6.** cm

Page 297 **1.** 6 cm **2.** 2 cm

Page 298 **3. a.** 16 mm **b.** 1.6 cm **4. a.** 24 mm **b.** 2.4 cm

Page 300 **1.** 50 **2.** 4000 **3.** 30,000 **4.** 820 **5.** 3400 **6.** 1290

Page 301 **7.** 8 **8.** 20 **9.** 42 **10.** 3.7 **11.** 370 **12.** 2.98

Page 303 **1.** mL **2.** L **3.** 9000 **4.** 11 **5.** 3200 **6.** 0.04

Page 305 **1.** mg **2.** kg **3.** g **4.** mg **5.** kg

Page 306 **6.** 8000 **7.** 3 **8.** 60,000 **9.** 0.076 **10.** 5930 **11.** 4.5

Page 312 **1.** 5219 **2.** 8337 **3.** 1233 **4.** 1106

Page 314 **1.** $.16/daisy **2.** $.03/g

Page 315 **3.** $.008/g **4.** $.002/g

CHAPTER 15

Page 324 **1.** $\frac{4}{5}$ **2.** $\frac{25}{36}$ **3.** $\frac{5}{1}$ **4.** $\frac{1}{5}$ **5.** $\frac{9}{5}$ **6.** $\frac{1}{4}$ **7.** $\frac{5}{9}$ **8.** $\frac{36}{25}$ **9.** $\frac{36}{115}$ **10.** $\frac{5}{23}$

Page 325 **11.** $\frac{2}{9}$ **12.** $\frac{2}{1}$ **13.** $\frac{1}{8}$ **14.** $\frac{10}{21}$

Page 327 **1.** $5/h **2.** $28/shirt **3.** 30 mi/gal **4.** 4 mi/min **5.** $13.75/h **6.** $5.60/record **7.** $22.50/lb **8.** $.22/stamp

Page 329 **1.** true **2.** false **3.** true **4.** true

Page 330 **5.** 15 **6.** 20 **7.** 28 **8.** 45

Page 332 **1.** $3.20 **2.** $1.34

Page 333 **3.** 100 **4.** 12

Page 335 **1.** 15 ft; 10 ft **2.** $17\frac{1}{2}$ ft; 10 ft **3.** 15 ft; $12\frac{1}{2}$ ft **4.** 10 ft; $8\frac{3}{4}$ ft

Page 336 **5.** 12 in. **6.** $6\frac{1}{2}$ in.

Page 341 **1.** about 42 mi **2.** about 53 mi **3.** about 35 mi **4.** about 15 mi **5.** about 10 mi **6.** about 40 mi

CHAPTER 16

Page 346 **1.** 10% **2.** 21% **3.** 100% **4.** 6% **5.** 79% **6.** 94% **7.** 23%

Page 348 **1.** 0.67 **2.** 0.05 **3.** 0.023 **4.** 2.3 **5.** $0.66\frac{2}{3}$ **6.** 58% **7.** 5.5% **8.** 70% **9.** $14\frac{1}{8}$% **10.** 375%

Page 350 **1.** $\frac{31}{100}$ **2.** $\frac{9}{20}$ **3.** $\frac{18}{25}$ **4.** $\frac{27}{100}$ **5.** $1\frac{1}{5}$ **6.** $\frac{163}{1000}$ **7.** $\frac{9}{40}$ **8.** $\frac{1}{8}$ **9.** $\frac{1}{125}$ **10.** $\frac{1}{2000}$

Page 351 **11.** $\frac{1}{200}$ **12.** $\frac{1}{125}$ **13.** $\frac{1}{6}$ **14.** $\frac{87}{400}$ **15.** $\frac{29}{125}$

Page 353 **1.** 80% **2.** 45% **3.** 75% **4.** 70% **5.** $16\frac{2}{3}$% **6.** $22\frac{2}{9}$% **7.** $62\frac{1}{2}$% **8.** $33\frac{1}{3}$%

Page 355 **1.** 44.46 **2.** 68.85 **3.** 0.378 **4.** 47.52 **5.** 104 **6.** 21 **7.** $38\frac{1}{2}$ **8.** 78

Page 356 **9.** 0.2; $\frac{1}{5}$ **10.** 0.75; $\frac{3}{4}$ **11.** 0.333...; $\frac{1}{3}$ **12.** 0.375; $\frac{3}{8}$

Page 358 **1.** about 300 **2.** about $50 **3.** about $600 **4.** about 60 **5.** about 42 **6.** about 2.5 **7.** about $35 **8.** about $5400

CHAPTER 17

Page 372 **1.** 20% **2.** 5% **3.** 200% **4.** 150%

Page 373 **5.** $26\frac{1}{4}$% **6.** $7\frac{1}{2}$% **7.** $66\frac{2}{3}$% **8.** $58\frac{1}{3}$% **9.** $10\frac{1}{2}$% **10.** $18\frac{3}{4}$%

Page 375 **1.** 75 **2.** 300 **3.** 360 **4.** 3000

Page 376 **5.** 12 **6.** 25 **7.** 135 **8.** 136

Page 378 **1.** 165 **2.** 50 **3.** 14.4 **4.** 17.5 **5.** 60% **6.** 220% **7.** 9% **8.** $2\frac{1}{2}$%

Page 379 **9.** 80 **10.** 45 **11.** 2400 **12.** 2

Page 381 **1.** 30% **2.** 8% **3.** $33\frac{1}{3}$% **4.** $12\frac{1}{2}$%

Page 382 **5.** 25% **6.** 5% **7.** $37\frac{1}{2}$% **8.** $66\frac{2}{3}$%

Page 386 **1.** $8; $24 **2.** $4; $16 **3.** $12; $28 **4.** $6.25; $43.75

Page 387 **5.** 30% **6.** 25% **7.** 35% **8.** $37\frac{1}{2}$%

CHAPTER 18

Page 398
1. Scores (%)

Score	Tally	Freq.
60	II	2
65		0
70	卌	5
75	卌 IIII	9
80	卌 I	6
85	III	3
90	I	1
95	II	2

2. Games Attended

No.	Tally	Freq.
0	II	2
1	I	1
2	I	1
3	I	1
4	III	3
5	IIII	4
6	III	3
7	卌	5

Page 399
3. Scores (%)

Score	Tally	Freq.
51–60	II	2
61–70	卌	5
71–80	卌 IIII	9
81–90	卌 III	8
91–100	IIII	4

4. Heights (ft)

Height	Tally	Freq.
300–399	卌	5
400–499	卌	5
500–599	III	3
600–699	IIII	4
700–799	II	2
800–899	I	1

Page 401 **1.** 30; 31; 26 **2.** 0.62; 0.775; none **3.** 26; 16; 12 **4.** 3.8; 3.7; 3.7 and 4.5

Page 402 **5.** $3.83 **6.** 4.9

Page 404 **1.** about 32 hours **2.** about 30 hours **3.** women 55 and over **4.** about 4 hours more

Page 405
5.

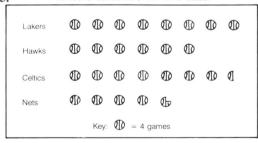

Number of Games Won, First Half of Season

Key: = 4 games

Page 407 **1.** $\frac{3}{10}$ **2.** 95 **3.** 17% **4.** $160 **5.** $600

CHAPTER 19

Page 420 **1.** 12 **2.** 8 **3.** 40 **4.** 6

Page 422 **1.** 6 **2.** 5040 **3.** 30 **4.** 336

Page 424 **1.** $\frac{1}{8}$ **2.** $\frac{7}{8}$ **3.** 1 **4.** $\frac{1}{4}$

Page 425 **5.** $\frac{1}{2}$ **6.** $\frac{5}{8}$ **7.** $\frac{3}{4}$

Page 427 **1.** $\frac{5}{48}$ **2.** $\frac{1}{9}$ **3.** $\frac{1}{11}$ **4.** $\frac{5}{33}$

Page 429 **1.** about 12 **2.** about 15 **3.** about 125 **4.** about 300

CHAPTER 20

Page 442 **1.** 34 **2.** ⁻12 **3.** 30

Page 443 **4.** 6 **5.** ⁻8 **6.** 1 **7.** 8 **8.** ⁻5 **9.** 3 **10.** 7 **11.** 11 **12.** 19 **13.** 15 **14.** > **15.** < **16.** < **17.** <

Page 445 **1.** 9 **2.** ⁻1 **3.** 3 **4.** ⁻6 **5.** 12 **6.** 13 **7.** 20 **8.** ⁻14 **9.** ⁻12 **10.** ⁻15

Page 446 **11.** 2 **12.** 0 **13.** 8 **14.** ⁻3 **15.** ⁻3 **16.** 0

Page 448 **1.** 7 + ⁻24 **2.** ⁻8 + ⁻6 **3.** 5 + 18 **4.** ⁻6 + 13 **5.** 9 **6.** 10 **7.** ⁻8 **8.** ⁻29

Page 450 **1.** ⁻18 **2.** 72 **3.** 0 **4.** 65 **5.** ⁻30 **6.** 0 **7.** 84 **8.** ⁻280 **9.** 360 **10.** ⁻936

Page 451 **11.** 81 **12.** ⁻64 **13.** 1 **14.** ⁻10 **15.** 16 **16.** 36

Page 453 **1.** 9 **2.** 10 **3.** ⁻7 **4.** ⁻8

Page 454 **5.** negative **6.** zero **7.** positive **8.** undefined

CHAPTER 21

Page 464 **1.** 38 **2.** 39 **3.** ⁻46 **4.** ⁻50 **5.** 51 **6.** 73 **7.** ⁻6 **8.** ⁻12

Page 466 **1.** 18 **2.** 39 **3.** ⁻19 **4.** 16 **5.** 16 **6.** 65 **7.** ⁻54 **8.** 56

Page 467 **9.** 15 **10.** 12 **11.** ⁻64 **12.** ⁻80

Page 469 **1.** 8 **2.** ⁻13 **3.** ⁻2 **4.** 36 **5.** ⁻15 **6.** ⁻14

Page 470 **7.** 20 **8.** ⁻30 **9.** ⁻50

Page 474
1. (⁻1, 2)
2. (⁻4, 1)
3. (3, 1)
4. (2, ⁻2)
5. (0, ⁻3)
6. (1, 0)

7-10.

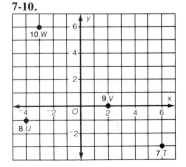

Page 476 **1.** (⁻2, 1), (0, 5), (2, 9)
2. (⁻2, 15), (0, 7), (2, ⁻1)
3. (⁻2, 2), (0, ⁻4), (2, ⁻10)
4.   **5.**   **6.**

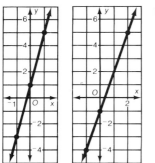 

Page 481 **1.** about 12° E, 43° N
2. about 5° W, 40° N

Page 482 **3.** Hungary **4.** Ireland

CHAPTER 22

Page 486 **1.**

2.

3.   **4.**

5.   **6.**

 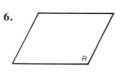

Page 487 **7.** 130° **8.** 90° **9.** 50°
10.   **11.**

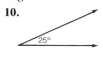

12.

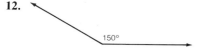

Page 488 **13.** acute **14.** obtuse **15.** right
16. parallel **17.** perpendicular **18.** neither

Page 490 **1.** $\overline{AB}, \overline{BC}, \overline{CD}, \overline{DE}, \overline{EF}, \overline{AF}$
2. A, B, C, D, E, F **3.** $\overline{BD}, \overline{AD}, \overline{CE}, \overline{CF}$

Page 491 **4.** pentagon, not regular **5.** pentagon, regular **6.** quadrilateral, not regular
7. parallelogram **8.** trapezoid **9.** square

Page 493 **1.** 65 mm **2.** 35 ft **3.** 18 m
4. 16 ft **5.** 12 cm

Page 495 **1.** circle O **2.** $\overline{OR}, \overline{OS}, \overline{OV}$ **3.** $\overline{VS}$
4. $\overline{RS}, \overline{VS}, \overline{UT}$

Page 496 **5.** 25.12 mm **6.** 100.48 m **7.** 22 ft
8. 176 in.

Page 498 **1.** 36 in.² **2.** 65 m² **3.** 64 yd²
4. 121 cm²

Page 499 **5.** 24 in.² **6.** 70 cm²

Page 501 **1.** 156 mm² **2.** 24 cm² **3.** 31½ in.²

Page 502 **4.** 294 mm² **5.** 240 cm² **6.** 192½ yd²

Page 504 **1.** 254.34 m² **2.** 2464 ft²

Page 505 **3.** 452.16 cm² **4.** 1386 in.²
5. 30 m² **6.** 198 mm²

CHAPTER 23

Page 518 **1.** rectangular prism; 6,12,8 **2.** pentagonal pyramid; 6,10,6 **3.** triangular prism; 5,9,6

Page 519 **4.** sphere **5.** cylinder **6.** cone

Page 521 **1.** 210 ft² **2.** 150 yd² **3.** 422 m²

Page 522 **4.** 1256 m² **5.** 1105.28 cm²
6. 1012 in.²

Page 524 **1.** 24 cm³ **2.** 36 in.³ **3.** 45 cm³

Page 525 **4.** 300 yd³ **5.** 125 in.³ **6.** 162 mm³

Page 527 **1.** 200.96 cm³ **2.** 2289.06 m³
3. 550 in.³ **4.** 1232 ft³

Page 530 **1.** 256 yd³ **2.** 462 m³

Page 531 **3.** 471 cm³ **4.** 9702 ft³

Page 533 **1.** 38,772.72 mm³ **2.** 7234.56 cm³

Page 534 **3.** 4082 cm³ **4.** 5184 in.³

CHAPTER 24

Page 542 **1.** isosceles; obtuse **2.** equilateral; acute **3.** scalene; right

Page 543 **4.** 62° **5.** 35° **6.** 32°

Page 545 **1.** similar; congruent **2.** not similar

Page 546 **3.** 16 **4.** 8

Page 548 **1.** 2 **2.** 6 **3.** 9 **4.** 12 **5.** 4.690
6. 9.165 **7.** 31 **8.** 53

Page 551 **1.** right triangle **2.** not a right triangle
3. not a right triangle

Page 552 **4.** 17 in. **5.** 25 cm **6.** 11.3 ft
7. 4.8 m

answers to selected exercises

CHAPTER 1

Pages 3–4 Practice Exercises 1. 500
3. 800,000 **5.** 1000 **7.** 80,000 **9.** three hundred fifteen **11.** twenty-seven thousand, nine hundred twenty-one **13.** four million, nine hundred twenty-five thousand, sixteen **15.** two hundred one billion, nine hundred eighty-seven million **17.** 1 million, 6 thousand, 3 **19.** 87 billion, 294 thousand, 36 **21.** 9 thousand, 81 **23.** 2 billion, 200 million **25.** 9,040,056 **27.** 5073 **29.** 273,906,000,004 **31.** E **33.** F **35.** D **37.** 3 billion, 339 million, 756 thousand, 324

Page 4 Review Exercises 1. 15 **3.** 17
5. 14 **7.** 13 **9.** 11 **11.** 11

Pages 6–7 Practice Exercises 1. 789
3. 91,494 **5.** $100,190 **7.** $1112 **9.** 258
11. $868 **13.** 466 **15.** 27 **17.** 130 **19.** 88
21. 1109 **23.** $664 **25.** 74,417 **27.** $68,602
29. 269 **31.** 430 **33.** 2000 **35.** $110
37. $70 **39.** $2088 **41.** 98

Page 7 Review Exercises 1. 8 **3.** 800
5. 600,000 **7.** 20,000,000

Page 9 Practice Exercises 1. about 800
3. about 8000 **5.** about 110,000 **7.** about 1300 **9.** about 60,000 **11.** about 18,000 **13.** about 1300 **15.** about $800 **17.** about 1200 **19.** about $70,000 **21.** gold charm and quartz watch

Page 9 Review Exercises 1. 5 **3.** 8 **5.** 8
7. 9 **9.** 9 **11.** 6

Pages 11–12 Practice Exercises 1. 84
3. $1048 **5.** 5888 **7.** $56,399 **9.** 345
11. $415 **13.** 62,172 **15.** $39,019 **17.** 285
19. 7159 **21.** 6436 **23.** $3174 **25.** $7186
27. $56,109 **29.** 190 **31.** $7286 **33.** 5051
35. $52,110 **37.** 49 **39.** 839 **41.** 143
43. $2250 **45.** $4818 **47.** $5887
49. 1,372,677

Page 12 Review Exercises 1. 131 **3.** 179
5. 59,205 **7.** $5704 **9.** 53,613 **11.** 27

Pages 14–15 Practice Exercises 1. 68 **3.** 3
5. 47 **7.** 36 **9.** 231 **11.** 44 **13.** $y + 17$
15. $y - 7$ **17.** $y + 53$ **19.** $19 - y$ **21.** $y + 9$
23. $46 - y$ **25.** B **27.** B **29.** A **31.** C
33. A **35.** a number increased by 81; the sum of a number and 81; 81 more than a number **37.** 14 increased by a number; the sum of 14 and a number; a number more than 14 **39.** $t + 13$ **41.** $q - 6$

Page 15 Review Exercises 1. six thousand, thirty-two **3.** one hundred twenty-one million, forty-three thousand, two hundred **5.** 24,360 **7.** $3422

Page 17 Practice Exercises 1. 27 **3.** 62
5. 94 **7.** 88 **9.** 140 **11.** 147 **13.** 55
15. 51 **17.** 21 **19.** 91 **21.** 116 **23.** 66
25. 104 **27.** 4 **29.** 329 **31.** 830 **33.** 101
35. 138 **37.** 187 **39.** 168 **41.** 19 **43.** 400
45. 381 **47.** 538

Page 17 Review Exercises 1. 1741 **3.** $5578
5. 33 **7.** blouse and sweater

Page 18 Skill Review 1. 3000 **3.** 800
5. D **7.** A **9.** 151 **11.** 6280 **13.** 6168
15. 2104 **17.** about 15,000 **19.** about 1300
21. 1185 **23.** 3564 **25.** 83,743 **27.** C
29. A **31.** 353 **33.** 29 **35.** 132 **37.** 246

Page 19 Exercises 1. 2710 mi **3.** 1517 mi
5. 1488 mi **7.** Go through St. Louis.

Page 20 Exercises 1. 3846 mi **3.** 4315 mi
5. 9913 mi **7.** 3135 mi **9.** Yes, the sum 1690 + 1445 + 1714 is about 5000.

Page 21 Exercises 1. 9:00 P.M. **3.** 7:00 A.M.
5. 11:30 P.M. **7.** 7:25 P.M.

Page 23 Chapter Review 1. difference **3.** B
5. D **7.** 99 **9.** $3778 **11.** 210 **13.** about 70,000 **15.** $z - 42$ **17.** 35 **19.** 285
21. 2189 mi **23.** 4334 mi

CHAPTER 2

Pages 27–28 Practice Exercises 1. 20
3. $500 **5.** 28,000 **7.** $5000 **9.** 3000
11. $20,000 **13.** 3100 **15.** 5000 **17.** 30
19. 1000 **21.** $9000 **23.** $30,000 **25.** 40
27. 390 **29.** 4300 **31.** 1000 **33.** $4000
35. $40,000 **39.** 9700

Page 28 Review Exercises 1. about 1100
3. about 1000 **5.** about 1100

Pages 30–31 Practice Exercises 1. about 110
3. about 30,000 **5.** about $700 **7.** about $1300 **9.** about 3,000,000 **11.** about $1000
13. about 900 **15.** about $3000 **17.** about 70,000 **19.** about $1,100,000 **21.** about 13,000
23. about 60,000 **25.** about $8100 **27.** about 600 **29.** b **31.** a, b, c **33.** about $33,000

Page 31 Review Exercises 1. 800 **3.** 400,000
5. 56,694 **7.** $112 **9.** 125 **11.** 385

Page 33 Practice Exercises 1. > **3.** <
5. < **7.** 160; 177; 284 **9.** 122,550; 122,585;
122,654 **11.** $417; $4151; $4157 **13.** false
15. true **17.** true **19.** 300; 302; 326; 362
21. $764; $5674; $5921; $50,677
23. about 150,000; less than **25.** Judy

Page 33 Review Exercises 1. 105,000
3. 12,350,000 **5.** 2400 **7.** 85,000

Pages 35–36 Practice Exercises 1. 12 **3.** 15
5. Bears, Lions **7.** about 7000 m **9.** about
6000 m **11.** Kilimanjaro, McKinley **15.** Pacific
13.

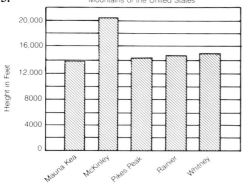
Mountains of the United States

Page 36 Review Exercises 1. 32 million,
427 thousand, 18 **3.** 1 million, 791
5. 7 thousand, 869 **7.** 14 million, 460

Pages 38–39 Practice Exercises 1. 40 **3.** 34
5. 45 **7.** decrease **9.** 1940 and 1950
11. **15.** line graph

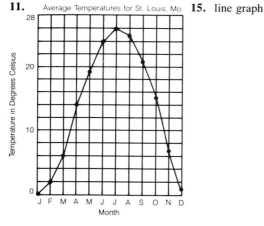
Average Temperatures for St. Louis, Mo.

Page 39 Review Exercises 1. about 20,000
3. about 8000 **5.** about 41,000 **7.** about 1100

Page 41 Problems 1. amount of money that
you have **3.** unreasonable **5.** number of
weekly payments **7.** no

Page 41 Review Exercises 1. 226,000,000
3. 30,000,004,000 **5.** 447,086,973
7. 92,000,007,421

Page 42 Skill Review 1. 60 **3.** $600
5. about 900 **7.** about 600 **9.** > **11.** 462;
487; 591 **13.** 49,216; 50,216; 57,489
15.

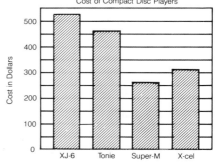
Cost of Compact Disc Players

17.

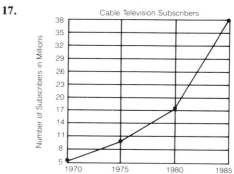
Cable Television Subscribers

19. number of hours that she babysat

Page 43 Exercises 1. 9 h 18 min **3.** 7 h
5. 18 h 41 min **7.** 12 h **9.** 5 min
11. 6 h 15 min

Page 44 Exercises 1. about 5 min **3.** about
20 min **5.** rolls **7.** 1:00 P.M.

Page 45 Chapter Review 1. is greater than
3. 480 **5.** $105,000 **7.** b **9.** true **11.** false
13. about 300 **17.** 7 h 55 min
15.

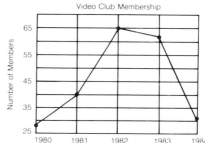
Video Club Membership

CHAPTER 3

Page 49 Practice Exercises 1. 20 + 20 + 20 + 20 = 80 **3.** 800 + 800 = 1600 **5.** 800 + 800 + 800 + 800 + 800 + 800 = 4800 **7.** 400 + 400 + 400 + 400 + 400 = 2000 **9.** 3000 + 3000 + 3000 + 3000 = 12,000 **11.** 5000 + 5000 = 10,000 **13.** 180 **15.** 4000 **17.** 56,000 **19.** 360,000 **21.** 120,000 **23.** 300,000 **25.** 4,500,000 **27.** 2,400,000 **29.** 150 **31.** 2100 **33.** 36,000 **35.** 360 **37.** 720,000 **39.** 28,000,000 **41.** $240,000

Page 49 Review Exercises 1. 72 **3.** 28 **5.** 56 **7.** 24 **9.** 60 **11.** 72 **13.** 32 **15.** 81 **17.** 45 **19.** 64

Pages 51–52 Practice Exercises 1. 48 **3.** $2607 **5.** $3717 **7.** 266,042 **9.** $694 **11.** 14,804 **13.** $533,472 **15.** about 300 **17.** about $500 **19.** about $500,000 **21.** 365 **23.** $294 **25.** 5067 **27.** $40,175 **29.** 9380 **31.** 417,264 **33.** 220 **35.** $696 **37.** 848 **39.** $3493 **41.** 6320 **43.** 9935 **45.** 36,072 **47.** 182,676 **49.** about 450 **51.** reasonable **53.** unreasonable; 316 **55.** unreasonable; 867

Page 52 Review Exercises 1. 2318 **3.** $221 **5.** 3308 **7.** 1670

Pages 54–55 Practice Exercises 1. 1325 **3.** 2576 **5.** 1513 **7.** 15,566 **9.** 19,136 **11.** 7533 **13.** 2054 **15.** 420 **17.** 12,189 **19.** 19,520 **21.** about 7200; can't tell **23.** about 2700; can't tell **25.** about 4000; overestimate **27.** about 18,000; overestimate **29.** about 10,000; can't tell **31.** 1273 **33.** 3366 **35.** 2136 **37.** 4144 **39.** 819 **41.** 38,493 **43.** 39,294 **45.** 45,612 **47.** 9591 **49.** 19,893 **51.** a **53.** b **55.** b **57.** about $400

Page 55 Review Exercises 1. 1427 **3.** 4795 **5.** 82,973 **7.** about 130,000 **9.** about 3600

Pages 57–58 Practice Exercises 1. 81,795 **3.** 423,864 **5.** 366,595 **7.** 550,338 **9.** 2,285,976 **11.** 85,527 **13.** 114,513 **15.** 187,875 **17.** 3,582,408 **19.** 3,345,272 **21.** 1,822,568 **23.** 256,500 **25.** 821,493 **27.** 293,760 **29.** 450,518 **31.** 1,479,318 **33.** 890,340 **35.** c **37.** c **39.** 638,620 miles

Page 58 Review Exercises 1. about 700 **3.** about 500 **5.** about 800 **7.** about 1100

Pages 60–61 Practice Exercises 1. 265,174 **3.** 483,070 **5.** 454,152 **7.** 277,872 **9.** 2580 **11.** 1120 **13.** 1600 **15.** 3060 **17.** 490 **19.** 420 **21.** 132 **23.** 297 **25.** 3992 **27.** 2135 **29.** 19,998 **31.** 468 **33.** 150 **35.** 133 **37.** 6321 **39.** 4048 **41.** 160 **43.** 8973 **45.** 119,140 **47.** $594

Page 61 Review Exercises 1. 256 **3.** 4463 **5.** 453,522 **7.** 51,295 **9.** 46,773

Page 63 Practice Exercises 1. 3 · 7, 3(7) **3.** 18(42), 18 × 42 **5.** 28 · 97, 28 × 97 **7.** 43 × 139, 43(139) **9.** 25 **11.** 18 **13.** 45 **15.** 0 **17.** 0 **19.** 3 · x, 3(x), (3)x **21.** r · s, r(s), (r)s **23.** p · q, pq, (p)q **25.** xy, (x)y, x(y) **27.** 152 **29.** 252 **31.** 0 **33.** 48 **35.** 3696 **37.** 440

Page 63 Review Exercises 1. < **3.** > **5.** < **7.** 31,744 frames

Page 64 Skill Review 1. 60 + 60 + 60 = 180 **3.** 4000 + 4000 + 4000 + 4000 = 16,000 **5.** 200 **7.** 360,000 **9.** 108 **11.** $2529 **13.** about 210 **15.** about 20,000 **17.** $6375 **19.** 3024 **21.** 21,983 **23.** about 4800; overestimate **25.** about 63,000; overestimate **27.** 212,364 **29.** 4,005,312 **31.** 7200 **33.** 608 **35.** 686 **37.** 3 × 42, 3(42) **39.** 9 · 28, 9(28) **41.** 280 **43.** 0

Page 65 Exercises 1. 580 **3.** 145 **5.** 610

Page 67 Chapter Review 1. product **3.** 80 **5.** 1500 **7.** 630,000 **9.** about 300 **11.** about 5000 **13.** 756 **15.** 34,823 **17.** 1,228,315 **19.** c **21.** 5400 **23.** 306,765 **25.** 576 **27.** 5085 **29.** 270

CHAPTER 4

Pages 71–72 Practice Exercises 1. 123 **3.** $429 **5.** 2622 R1 **7.** 2265 **9.** 31 **11.** $91 **13.** 3122 R1 **15.** 3624 **17.** 102 **19.** $270 **21.** 2036 R3 **23.** 2005 R3 **25.** 66 **27.** 22 **29.** 98 R3 **31.** 34 R1 **33.** 1728 R3 **35.** 16,680 **37.** 17 tables

Page 72 Review Exercises 1. about 1600 **3.** about 2400 **5.** about 10,000 **7.** about 10,000

Page 74 Practice Exercises 1. about 300 **3.** about 900 **5.** about 7000 **7.** about 2000 **9.** about 80 **11.** about 700 **13.** about 120 **15.** about 30 **17.** about 90 **19.** about 5 **21.** about 300 **23.** about 600 **25.** about 70 **27.** about 80 **29.** a **31.** d **33.** b **35.** d **37.** b **39.** about $30 each

Page 74 Review Exercises 1. 778,000 **3.** 4,090,000 **5.** 10,000 **7.** 9,400,000

Pages 76–77 Practice Exercises 1. 83
3. $118 **5.** 641 R17 **7.** $1122 **9.** 92
11. 277 R1 **13.** 315 **15.** 2726 R30
17. 356 R8 **19.** 108 R22 **21.** 414 R60
23. 495 R39 **25.** 214 **27.** 240 R1
29. 203 R11 **31.** 1018 R3 **33.** 2008
35. 3516 **37.** d **39.** c **41.** a **43.** a **45.** a
47. c **49.** about $70

Page 77 Review Exercises 1. 986 **3.** 1027
5. 412 **7.** 3268 **9.** 3285 **11.** 16,967
13. 1264 R2 **15.** 806 R4 **17.** < **19.** <
21. < **23.** >

Pages 79–80 Practice Exercises 1. 2 **3.** $11
5. 326 **7.** 8 R573 **9.** $264 **11.** 597 R550
13. 5 R279 **15.** 326 R18 **17.** 91 R388
19. b **21.** a **23.** reasonable **25.** unreasonable; 106 R514 **27.** unreasonable; 199 R230
29. 96 boxes

Page 80 Review Exercises 1. 6(36); 6 · 36
3. 42(31); 42 × 31 **5.** 54(107); 54 · 107
7. 59(241); 59 · 241 **9.** 145 **11.** 120 **13.** 39
15. 68

Page 82 Practice Exercises 1. $6\overline{)54}$; 54 ÷ 6
3. 140 ÷ 7; $\frac{140}{7}$ **5.** $\frac{756}{36}$, 756 ÷ 36

7. $15\overline{)1665}$; $\frac{1665}{15}$ **9.** 11 **11.** 15 **13.** 5
15. undefined **17.** 20 **19.** 5 **21.** 8 **23.** 1
25. 2 **27.** 4 **29.** 10 **31.** 0 **33.** 36 **35.** 6
37. $x\overline{)24}$; 24 ÷ x **39.** $\frac{a}{9}$; $9\overline{)a}$ **41.** $\frac{y}{16}$; y ÷ 16
43. x ÷ m; $\frac{x}{m}$

Page 82 Review Exercises 1. w − 38
3. w + 29 **5.** w + 7

Pages 84–85 Practice Exercises 1. 144

3. 57 **5.** 5 **7.** 202 **9.** 11x **11.** $\frac{84}{x}$ **13.** 2x

15. 3x **17.** b − 64 **19.** 80 + b **21.** $\frac{52}{b}$
23. 31b **25.** D **27.** B **29.** E **31.** B
33. D **35.** 40 **37.** 10 **39.** 80

Page 85 Review Exercises 1. 226 **3.** 3841
5. 222 **7.** 1358 **9.** 1548 **11.** 190,404
13. 24 **15.** 86

Page 87 Problems 1. 8 in. **3.** $19
5. $52,250 **7.** $208 **9.** 23,500
11. 410 desks; $110 left

Page 87 Review Exercises 1. 167 **3.** 317
5. 483 **7.** 255 **9.** 166 **11.** 173 **13.** 930
15. 596 **17.** 2933 **19.** 28,236

Page 88 Skill Review 1. 621 **3.** 2021
5. $6021 **7.** about 4000 **9.** about $2000
11. about $3000 **13.** 501 R9 **15.** 589 R51
17. 886 R66 **19.** 3 **21.** 95 R136 **23.** $1120

25. $4\overline{)62}$; 62 ÷ 4 **27.** $\frac{72}{9}$; $9\overline{)72}$ **29.** 8 **31.** 8
33. 33 **35.** 384 **37.** 37x **39.** 3x
41. $2812

Page 89 Exercises 1. 32 **3.** 480 **5.** 60
7. about 121 weeks **9.** about 1 century

Page 90 Exercises 1. $41 **3.** $27 **5.** $7
7. $8 **9. a.** Jan: $379; Feb: $354; Mar: $391;
Apr: $392 **b.** $379

Page 91 Chapter Review 1. quotient
3. multiply **5.** 3141 R2 **7.** 9672 R8
9. 80 R33 **11.** $8402 **13.** 66 R32 **15.** 656
17. about $600 **19.** about 2000 **21.** 4 **23.** 6

25. 64 **27.** 416 **29.** $\frac{82}{y}$ **31.** 12y **33.** $42

35. $71

CHAPTER 5

Pages 95–96 Practice Exercises 1. 16 **3.** 4
5. 26 **7.** 1 **9.** 25 **11.** 10 **13.** 6 **15.** 60
17. 2 **19.** 94 **21.** 132 **23.** 15 **25.** 27
27. 30 **29.** 10 **31.** 18 **33.** 55 **35.** 20
37. 3 **39.** 86 **41.** 31 **43.** 16 **45.** 55 **47.** $36

Page 96 Review Exercises 1. 15 **3.** 9
5. 21 **7.** 2

Pages 98–99 Practice Exercises 1. no; no; no
3. no; no; yes **5.** yes; no; no **7.** no; no; no
9. no; no; no **11.** yes; no; no **13.** yes; yes
15. yes; yes **17.** yes; no **19.** no; no **21.** no;
no **23.** yes; yes **25.** no; no **27.** yes; yes
29. no; no **31.** yes **33.** no **35.** no **37.** no
39. even **41.** odd **43.** odd **45.** no; yes; no; yes

Page 99 Review Exercises 1. 57,285 **3.** 101
5. 6126 **7.** 6200

Page 101 Practice Exercises 1. 3 × 7
3. 2 × 2 × 2 × 5 **5.** 3 × 3 × 3 × 3 **7.** 3 ×
3 × 5 × 5 **9.** 2 × 5 × 11 **11.** 2 × 2 × 2 ×
3 × 3 × 5 **13.** 3 **15.** 3 **17.** 1 **19.** 8
21. 2 **23.** 4 **25.** prime **27.** composite
29. composite **31.** prime **33.** composite
35. composite **37.** 2, 3, 5, 7, 11, 13, 17, 19

Page 101 Review Exercises 1. 4800
3. 280,000 **5.** 320,000 **7.** 400,000 **9.** $198

Page 103 Practice Exercises 1. 3, 6, 9, 12,
15, 18 **3.** 11, 22, 33, 44, 55, 66 **5.** 18, 36,
54, 72, 90, 108 **7.** 50 **9.** 12 **11.** 48
13. 15 **15.** 30 **17.** 90 **19.** 42, 48, 54, 60,
66, 72, 78, 84, 90, 96 **21.** 728 **23.** 300 of each

Page 103 Review Exercises 1. 64 **3.** 125
5. 64 **7.** 144

Page 105 Practice Exercises 1. 49 **3.** 16
5. 729 **7.** 729 **9.** 640,000 **11.** 1 **13.** 8
15. 34 **17.** 4 **19.** 18 **21.** 7^4 **23.** 10^3

25. 9^3 27. 4^4 29. 64 31. 1 33. 3 35. 196
37. 1,250,000 39. 200,000,000; 200 million

Page 105 Review Exercises 1. 32 3. 23
5. 33 7. 16

Page 107 Practice Exercises 1. $b \cdot b \cdot b \cdot b$
3. $3 \cdot a \cdot a$ 5. $b \cdot b \cdot c \cdot c \cdot c \cdot c$
7. $b \cdot b \cdot b \cdot c$ 9. $6 \cdot a \cdot a \cdot b \cdot b$ 11. 1000
13. 81 15. 75 17. 900 19. 10,000 21. y^5
23. $5 \cdot a \cdot a \cdot b$ 25. 81 27. 80 29. 90

Page 107 Review Exercises 1. about 50
3. about 70 5. about 70 7. $828

Page 108 Skill Review 1. 22 3. 19 5. 100
7. 15 9. 21 11. 100 13. yes 15. no
17. no 19. 9 21. $2 \times 2 \times 2 \times 3 \times 3$
23. 9 25. 13 27. 280 29. 60 of each
31. 121 33. 6 35. 8 37. 72 39. 8
41. 18 43. 400 45. 8100

Page 109 Exercises 1. 3456 3. 72
5. 15,552 7. 9 9. 3 11. 6 13. 720 flowers

Page 110 Exercises 1. 16 3. 10 5. 260
7. 2 issues 9. $273,600

Page 111 Chapter Review 1. prime 3. 12
5. 10 7. yes 9. no 11. no 13. $2 \times 3 \times 3$
15. $2 \times 5 \times 7$ 17. $2 \times 3 \times 3 \times 3$
19. 10 21. 6 23. 48 25. 72 27. 16
29. 16 31. 625 33. 750 35. 1872

CHAPTER 6

Pages 119–120 Practice Exercises 1. $\frac{1}{4}$ 3. $\frac{3}{6}$
5. $\frac{2}{5}$ 7. $\frac{4}{12}$ 9. $\frac{7}{12}$ 11. $\frac{5}{7}$ 13. $\frac{3}{4}$ 15. $\frac{3}{6}$
17. $\frac{2}{5}$ 19. $\frac{3}{6}$ 21. $\frac{4}{11}$ 23. $\frac{3}{7}$

Page 120 Review Exercises 1. 16 3. 36
5. 9 7. 240 9. 12

Pages 122–123 Practice Exercises 1. not
equivalent 3. not equivalent 5. equivalent
7. equivalent 9. 6 11. 63 13. 81 15. 110
17. 8 19. 3 21. 8 23. 5 25. 4 27. 1
29. 5 31. 24 33. 16; 4; 2

Page 123 Review Exercises 1. yes 3. no
5. yes 7. yes 9. 7 11. 11 13. $200

Page 125 Practice Exercises 1. yes 3. no
5. yes 7. yes 9. no 11. no 13. $\frac{1}{4}$ 15. $\frac{2}{11}$
17. $\frac{3}{4}$ 19. $\frac{7}{10}$ 21. $\frac{1}{5}$ 23. $\frac{6}{7}$ 25. $\frac{1}{25}$ 27. $\frac{1}{10}$
29. $\frac{5}{7}$ 31. $\frac{1}{12}$ 33. $\frac{4}{5}$ 35. $\frac{9}{100}$ 37. $\frac{4}{7}$

Page 125 Review Exercises 1. < 3. >
5. = 7. > 9. 42 11. 36

Pages 127–128 Practice Exercises 1. >
3. < 5. > 7. < 9. = 11. = 13. =

15. > 17. $\frac{1}{5}, \frac{2}{5}, \frac{1}{2}$ 19. $\frac{1}{2}, \frac{7}{10}, \frac{4}{5}$ 21. $\frac{2}{25}, \frac{1}{10}, \frac{7}{50}$,
$\frac{11}{20}$ 23. > 25. < 27. = 29. > 31. true
33. false 35. true 37. true 39. practicing
plays, looking at game films, lifting weights, jogging

Page 128 Review Exercises 1. about 80
3. about 2000 5. about 40 7. about 70

Page 130 Practice Exercises 1. about $\frac{1}{2}$
3. about $\frac{1}{6}$ 5. about $\frac{1}{3}$ 7. about $\frac{2}{3}$ 9. about $\frac{3}{4}$
11. about $\frac{1}{8}$ 13. 1 15. 0 17. 1 19. $\frac{1}{2}$
21. 0 23. $\frac{1}{2}$ 25. a 27. e 29. d 31. e
33. b 35. c 37. about $\frac{1}{4}$ 39. about $\frac{1}{2}$

Page 130 Review Exercises 1. $\frac{3}{8}$ 3. $\frac{7}{8}$ 5. $\frac{2}{3}$

Pages 132–133 Practice Exercises 1. $\frac{51}{5}$
3. $\frac{8}{7}$ 5. $\frac{117}{10}$ 7. $\frac{139}{9}$ 9. $\frac{100}{3}$ 11. $\frac{83}{9}$ 13. $4\frac{1}{8}$
15. $5\frac{3}{8}$ 17. $12\frac{2}{5}$ 19. 128 21. $7\frac{15}{17}$ 23. $24\frac{6}{35}$
25. > 27. > 29. < 31. > 33. 23
35. 1 37. 1 39. 5 41. $2\frac{1}{5}, 2\frac{5}{6}, 5\frac{2}{5}, 5\frac{6}{7}$
43. $8\frac{2}{3}, 8\frac{1}{2}, 8\frac{6}{11}, 8\frac{6}{10}$ 45. $1\frac{1}{2}, \frac{5}{2}, 2\frac{4}{6}, \frac{16}{3}$ 47. 33

Page 133 Review Exercises 1. 6417 3. 3876
5. 89 7. 216 9. 34

Page 135 Problems 1. $17 3. 75 5. $622
7. 90° F

Page 135 Review Exercises 1. 144 3. 27

Page 136 Skill Review 1. $\frac{1}{4}$ 3. $\frac{4}{7}$ 5. $\frac{3}{12}$
7. 12 9. 11 11. $\frac{1}{4}$ 13. $\frac{3}{7}$ 15. $\frac{1}{9}$ 17. <
19. < 21. about $\frac{1}{6}$ 23. about $\frac{1}{3}$ 25. about $\frac{1}{4}$
27. $\frac{15}{4}$ 29. $\frac{97}{10}$ 31. $\frac{49}{4}$ 33. $5\frac{2}{5}$ 35. 5
37. $7\frac{4}{7}$ 39. $98

Page 137 Exercises 1. about $\frac{1}{8}$ 3. about $\frac{1}{3}$
5. about 2 h

Pages 139–140 Practice Exercises 1. two
3. four 5. one quarter note 7. one quarter
note 9. one half note 11. one half note
13. one eighth note 15. yes

Page 141 Chapter Review 1. numerator
3. $\frac{27}{60}$ 5. not equivalent 7. equivalent 9. $\frac{19}{28}$,
$\frac{5}{7}, \frac{3}{4}, \frac{6}{7}$ 11. $\frac{20}{3}$ 13. $\frac{49}{4}$ 15. $\frac{80}{7}$ 17. 1 19. $\frac{1}{2}$
21. $\frac{1}{2}$ 23. $7\frac{1}{4}$ 25. 7 27. 8 31. about 4 h

CHAPTER 7

Pages 145–146 Practice Exercises 1. $\frac{1}{20}$
3. $\frac{3}{7}$ 5. $2\frac{1}{8}$ 7. 4 9. $\frac{18}{65}$ 11. $\frac{7}{16}$ 13. $\frac{1}{7}$
15. $\frac{10}{21}$ 17. $1\frac{1}{2}$ 19. 34 21. about 30
23. about 15 25. about 10 27. about 4
29. $\frac{8}{81}$ 31. $\frac{3}{5}$ 33. 9 35. 0 37. $\frac{1}{12}$
39. about 100 41. about 50 43. about 250
45. about 60 47. $24

Page 146 Review Exercises 1. 2360
3. 11,000 5. 312,000 7. 200,100
9. 2,500,000 11. 14,400,000

Page 148 Practice Exercises 1. about 4
3. about 28 **5.** about 36 **7.** about 88
9. about 3 **11.** about 2 **13.** about 30
15. about 25 **17.** about 14 **19.** about 5
21. about 5 **23.** about 4 **25.** about 6
27. about 2 **29.** about 16 mi

Page 148 Review Exercises 1. $\frac{13}{4}$ **3.** $\frac{38}{3}$
5. $\frac{8}{3}$ **7.** 72 **9.** 170 **11.** 900 **13.** 31,372

Pages 150–151 Practice Exercises 1. 24
3. 36 **5.** 28 **7.** $6\frac{1}{2}$ **9.** $5\frac{3}{5}$ **11.** $24\frac{3}{4}$
13. $16\frac{1}{5}$ **15.** 156 **17.** $\frac{11}{14}$ **19.** $2\frac{1}{2}$ **21.** $1\frac{1}{6}$
23. $\frac{11}{18}$ **25.** $26\frac{2}{3}$ **27.** $4\frac{8}{15}$ **29.** $1\frac{10}{11}$ **31.** 22
33. $1\frac{1}{3}$ **35.** 20 **37.** 33 **39.** $2\frac{4}{5}$ **41.** 8
43. $1\frac{1}{3}$ **45.** $3\frac{1}{3}$ **47.** 52 **49.** $\frac{1}{2}$ **51.** $37\frac{1}{2}$
53. $2\frac{7}{9}$ **55.** $8\frac{17}{24}$ **57.** 2 **59.** 12 **61.** \$9

Page 151 Review Exercises 1. 2509 **3.** 62
5. 26 **7.** 1298 **9.** about 1200 **11.** about
5400 **13.** about 40,000 **15.** about 280,000

Pages 153–154 Practice Exercises 1. 2
3. $\frac{1}{13}$ **5.** $\frac{19}{16}$ **7.** $\frac{8}{9}$ **9.** $\frac{33}{71}$ **11.** $\frac{4}{15}$ **13.** $\frac{6}{17}$
15. $1\frac{2}{3}$ **17.** $\frac{3}{7}$ **19.** 1 **21.** $1\frac{2}{7}$ **23.** 1 **25.** 10
27. $\frac{7}{96}$ **29.** $\frac{1}{78}$ **31.** $\frac{3}{4}$ **33.** $1\frac{1}{3}$ **35.** 1 **37.** $1\frac{4}{5}$
39. $1\frac{1}{2}$ **41.** $\frac{49}{64}$ **43.** $\frac{1}{24}$ **45.** greater than 1
47. equal to 1 **49.** $\frac{1}{12}$ gal

Page 154 Review Exercises 1. $\frac{92}{21}$ **3.** $\frac{71}{12}$
5. $\frac{26}{7}$ **7.** $4\frac{3}{4}$ **9.** $6\frac{1}{2}$ **11.** $61\frac{1}{2}$

Pages 156–157 Practice Exercises 1. $2\frac{4}{11}$
3. $2\frac{4}{9}$ **5.** $1\frac{2}{3}$ **7.** 1 **9.** $\frac{24}{35}$ **11.** 2 **13.** $3\frac{1}{3}$
15. $\frac{1}{6}$ **17.** $\frac{1}{2}$ **19.** $28\frac{10}{11}$ **21.** about 1
23. about 2 **25.** about 5 **27.** about 3
29. about 15 **31.** $1\frac{9}{11}$ **33.** $2\frac{8}{9}$ **35.** $\frac{3}{14}$ **37.** $\frac{1}{2}$
39. $1\frac{1}{5}$ **41.** about 2 **43.** about 20 **45.** about
6 **47.** about 2 **49.** \$8

Page 157 Review Exercises 1. about 900
3. about 7000 **5.** about 700 **7.** about 16,000

Page 158 Skill Review 1. $\frac{1}{15}$ **3.** $\frac{2}{33}$ **5.** $\frac{7}{9}$
7. $\frac{5}{6}$ **9.** $\frac{14}{27}$ **11.** $\frac{18}{121}$ **13.** 40 students
15. about 20 **17.** about 27 **19.** about 33
21. about 10 **23.** 36 **25.** $25\frac{2}{3}$ **27.** 24
29. 100 **31.** 18 **33.** $\frac{1}{8}$ **35.** $1\frac{1}{5}$ **37.** 1
39. $1\frac{11}{49}$ **41.** $1\frac{43}{44}$ **43.** 5 **45.** $\frac{45}{64}$ **47.** about 2
49. about 1

Pages 161–162 Practice Exercises 1. 48 oz
3. $1\frac{1}{2}$ tsp **5.** 5 c **7.** $12\frac{1}{2}$ tbsp **9.** $1\frac{1}{4}$ c
11. $2\frac{1}{2}$ tbsp **13.** $\frac{1}{2}$ tbsp **15.** $1\frac{1}{2}$ tsp **17.** $3\frac{3}{4}$ tbsp
19. $2\frac{5}{8}$ c **21.** 1 c **23.** $1\frac{1}{4}$ c **25.** 4 tsp **27.** 4 c

Page 163 Chapter Review 1. reciprocals
3. $\frac{3}{14}$ **5.** $\frac{28}{45}$ **7.** $1\frac{1}{3}$ **9.** $5\frac{5}{6}$ **11.** 29 **13.** $4\frac{1}{2}$
15. $3\frac{1}{9}$ **17.** $1\frac{11}{45}$ **19.** about 2 **21.** about 1
23. about 2 **25.** about 14 **27.** $\frac{1}{12}$ **29.** $\frac{5}{24}$
31. $\frac{3}{5}$ **33.** $\frac{3}{4}$ **35.** $\frac{2}{15}$ **37.** $3\frac{9}{10}$ **39.** 82
41. 2 c

CHAPTER 8

Page 167 Practice Exercises 1. $\frac{7}{9}$ **3.** $\frac{1}{6}$
5. $\frac{9}{10}$ **7.** $\frac{1}{2}$ **9.** $\frac{1}{3}$ **11.** 1 **13.** $1\frac{6}{17}$ **15.** $1\frac{4}{7}$
17. $1\frac{3}{4}$ **19.** 1 **21.** $\frac{1}{25}$ **23.** $\frac{3}{4}$ **25.** $1\frac{10}{19}$ **27.** 1
29. $\frac{1}{9}$ **31.** 1 **33.** $\frac{5}{8}$ lb

Page 167 Review Exercises 1. 8 **3.** 9 **5.** 3
7. 6 **9.** 20 **11.** 63

Pages 169–170 Practice Exercises 1. $\frac{11}{14}$
3. $\frac{3}{5}$ **5.** $1\frac{17}{36}$ **7.** $1\frac{25}{56}$ **9.** $1\frac{1}{15}$ **11.** $\frac{1}{6}$ **13.** $\frac{1}{2}$
15. $\frac{11}{24}$ **17.** $\frac{17}{42}$ **19.** $\frac{15}{34}$ **21.** $\frac{19}{20}$ **23.** $\frac{1}{60}$
25. $1\frac{4}{15}$ **27.** $\frac{87}{100}$ **29.** $\frac{1}{18}$ **31.** $\frac{1}{4}$ **33.** 1 **35.** $\frac{3}{4}$

Page 170 Review Exercises 1. $\frac{1}{3}$ **3.** $\frac{1}{2}$ **5.** $\frac{1}{3}$
7. about 12 **9.** about 15

Page 172 Practice Exercises 1. about 3
3. about 3 **5.** about 10 **7.** about 3 **9.** about
6 **11.** about 12 **13.** about 21 **15.** about 12
17. about 10 **19.** less **21.** about 10 gal
23. about 2 gal

Page 172 Review Exercises 1. 11 **3.** 22 **5.** 25

Pages 174–175 Practice Exercises 1. $2\frac{2}{3}$
3. $4\frac{6}{13}$ **5.** $12\frac{5}{18}$ **7.** $9\frac{13}{22}$ **9.** $15\frac{11}{14}$ **11.** $5\frac{19}{30}$
13. 6 **15.** $5\frac{3}{8}$ **17.** $10\frac{8}{55}$ **19.** $10\frac{7}{9}$ **21.** $5\frac{1}{4}$
23. $11\frac{1}{6}$ **25.** $6\frac{1}{12}$ **27.** 4 **29.** $9\frac{7}{24}$ **31.** $40\frac{23}{32}$
33. $17\frac{43}{90}$ **35.** $13\frac{5}{12}$ h

Page 175 Review Exercises 1. yes **3.** no
5. 17,005,149 **7.** 9046

Pages 177–178 Practice Exercises 1. $3\frac{1}{3}$
3. 5 **5.** $\frac{1}{2}$ **7.** $2\frac{1}{2}$ **9.** $4\frac{1}{3}$ **11.** $1\frac{1}{8}$ **13.** $\frac{1}{4}$
15. $4\frac{7}{15}$ **17.** $\frac{1}{6}$ **19.** $6\frac{3}{28}$ **21.** $5\frac{1}{12}$ **23.** 2
25. $3\frac{11}{18}$ **27.** $6\frac{5}{8}$ **29.** $3\frac{5}{14}$ **31.** $6\frac{3}{25}$ **33.** $7\frac{33}{70}$
35. 4 **37.** $3\frac{1}{6}$ **39.** $2\frac{1}{2}$

Page 178 Review Exercises 1. about \$900
3. about 21,000 **5.** about 700 **7.** about 8000
9. about 15 **11.** about 3 **13.** about 5
15. about 7 **17.** about \$1200

Pages 180–181 Practice Exercises 1. $12\frac{1}{2}$
3. $4\frac{8}{9}$ **5.** $3\frac{11}{18}$ **7.** $2\frac{1}{3}$ **9.** $1\frac{5}{24}$ **11.** $1\frac{11}{14}$ **13.** $\frac{8}{9}$
15. $\frac{5}{8}$ **17.** $\frac{7}{8}$ **19.** $11\frac{1}{3}$ **21.** $9\frac{3}{5}$ **23.** $12\frac{2}{3}$
25. $9\frac{1}{2}$ **27.** $1\frac{3}{8}$ **29.** $5\frac{5}{6}$ **31.** $2\frac{1}{4}$ **33.** $1\frac{2}{3}$
35. $6\frac{31}{42}$ **37.** $3\frac{1}{2}$ games

Page 181 Review Exercises 1. 157
3. 36,888 **5.** 88,000 **7.** 2703 **9.** $\frac{2}{9}$ **11.** $\frac{7}{12}$
13. $3\frac{7}{12}$ **15.** 15

Pages 182–183 Problems 1. 40, 46, 52
3. 32, 128, 512 **5.** 26, 37, 50 **7.** 15, 13, 19
9. $\frac{3}{2}, \frac{7}{4}, 2$ **11.** $\frac{81}{4}, \frac{243}{8}, \frac{729}{16}$ **13.** 27, 162, 81
15. 600, 3600, 25,200 **17.** $\frac{7}{5}, \frac{13}{5}, \frac{6}{5}$ **19.** 156
21. 6:30 P.M.

Page 183 Review Exercises 1. 426 **3.** 34, 55, 89

Page 184   Skill Review   1. $\frac{5}{7}$ **3.** $\frac{1}{3}$ **5.** $1\frac{4}{41}$
7. $1\frac{5}{14}$ **9.** $1\frac{1}{10}$ **11.** $1\frac{11}{20}$ h **13.** about 12
15. about 9 **17.** about 13 **19.** $6\frac{5}{6}$ **21.** $15\frac{7}{20}$
23. $10\frac{1}{12}$ **25.** $7\frac{7}{12}$ h **27.** $2\frac{5}{8}$ **29.** $3\frac{7}{18}$
31. $4\frac{19}{39}$ **33.** $\frac{34}{...}$ **35.** $\frac{3}{4}$ gal **37.** 720, 5040, 40,320

Page 185   Exercises   1. $8\frac{1}{2}$ h **3.** $7\frac{3}{4}$ h **5.** $8\frac{3}{4}$ h
7. $22\frac{1}{2}$ h

Page 187   Chapter Review   1. least common
multiple **3.** $\frac{1}{2}$ **5.** $1\frac{11}{36}$ **7.** $8\frac{1}{2}$ **9.** $\frac{1}{26}$ **11.** $\frac{7}{20}$
13. $5\frac{2}{15}$ **15.** $5\frac{2}{3}$ **17.** $19\frac{11}{20}$ **19.** $2\frac{38}{39}$ **21.** $7\frac{38}{63}$
23. $\frac{11}{24}$ **25.** about 2 **27.** about 11 **29.** $\frac{5}{8}$ h
31. $\frac{8}{3}, \frac{16}{3}, \frac{32}{3}$

CHAPTER 9

Page 191   Practice Exercises   1. 120 **3.** 633
5. 15 **7.** 14 **9.** 5; 3 **11.** 1; 720 **13.** 40
15. 9; 3 **17.** 26,407 **19.** 8800; 26,400;
316,800 **21.** 26 mi **23.** 7 ft **25.** 15 ft
27. 16,280 yd

Page 191   Review Exercises   1. 8 **3.** 24
5. 33 **7.** 4 **9.** 6000 **11.** 30,000,000

Pages 193–194   Practice Exercises   1. 4 in.
3. 3 in. **5.** $2\frac{1}{8}$ in. **7.** $2\frac{1}{8}$ in. **9.** $1\frac{1}{4}$ in.
17. 9 in. **19.** Answers will vary.

Page 194   Review Exercises   1. about 20
3. about 2 **5.** about 2 **7.** about 4

Page 196   Practice Exercises   1. 32 **3.** 5
5. 6 **7.** 4800 **9.** 207 **11.** 101; 14
13. 22,000 **15.** 13; 8 **17.** 2; 308 **19.** =
21. > **23.** < **25.** 11,000 lb

Page 196   Review Exercises   1. 17,514
3. 146 **5.** 126 **7.** 29,896

Page 198   Practice Exercises   1. 2 **3.** 28
5. 10 **7.** 3; 3 **9.** 11 **11.** 6; 1 **13.** 22
15. 31 **17.** 9 **19.** a **21.** b **23.** 36 qt

Page 198   Review Exercises   1. 2 · 5
3. 5 · 5 · 5 **5.** 2 · 2 · 5 · 5

Pages 200–201   Practice Exercises   1. 6 ft 11 in.
3. 2 ft 4 in. **5.** 28 gal 2 qt **7.** 86 mi 409 ft
9. 39 yd 1 ft **11.** 77 gal **13.** 28 yd 23 in.
15. 18 t 110 lb **17.** 2 ft 9 in. **19.** 8 gal 2 qt
21. 21 mi 1751 yd **23.** 2 qt 1 pt **25.** 8 lb 11 oz
27. 3 yd 1 ft **29.** 13 gal **31.** 56 lb 11 oz
33. 11 ft 3 in. **35.** 6 gal 3 qt **37.** 11 pt, or
1 gal 3 pt

Page 201   Review Exercises   1. 640 **3.** 6600
5. 396,000 **7.** 790,000 **9.** 11,000,000
11. 112,289,000

Page 202   Skill Review   1. 29,920 **3.** 31,886
5. 7 in. **7.** $1\frac{9}{16}$ in. **9.** 11 **11.** 133 **13.** >

15. 3000 lb **17.** 2; 1 **19.** 1536 fl oz
21. 6 ft 5 in. **23.** 10 gal 2 qt **25.** 5 mi 1756 yd
27. 8 gal

Page 203   Exercises   1. 1071 in. **3.** no; 23 ft
short **5.** 36,760 yd

Page 205   Chapter Review   1. weight **3.** 90 ft
5. 4 t **13.** 2 **15.** 3620 **17.** 12,040
19. 43 **21.** 10 ft 10 in. **23.** 44 t 500 lb
25. 7 lb 6 oz **27.** 10 qt 1 pt **29.** 14 gal 1 qt
31. 15 yd **33.** 2500 lb

CHAPTER 10

Pages 213–214   Practice Exercises   1. 0.04
3. 0.0005 **5.** 0.001 **7.** 0 **9.** one and six
tenths **11.** eight and five hundredths **13.** ninety-
eight hundredths **15.** four hundred fifteen and
five hundred two thousandths **17.** 7 and 3 tenths
19. 10 and 2 ten-thousandths **21.** 907 thousandths **23.** 761 and 25 hundredths **25.** 0.64
27. 192.03 **29.** 14.1 **31.** 603.036 **33.** 3
35. 2 **37.** 1 **39.** 0.00007 **41.** 0 **43.** 0.005
45. thirty-eight and forty-four hundredths

Page 214   Review Exercises   1. 500 **3.** 8730
5. 3500 **7.** 100 **9.** 7000

Pages 216–217   Practice Exercises   1. 0.3
3. 8.1 **5.** 2.80 **7.** 30 **9.** 0.8 **11.** 0.09
13. 0.002 **15.** $1 **17.** $320 **19.** $30
21. $27 **23.** $.37 **25.** $5.00 **27.** $5.56
29. $3.33 **31.** 1.1 **33.** 0.01 **35.** 9.71
37. 351.17 **39.** 0.3 **41.** 4.580 **43.** 7.00
45. $.47 **47.** a, d **49.** 102.9

Page 217   Review Exercises   1. < **3.** >
5. > **7.** $\frac{2}{3}$ **9.** 250 **11.** 96 **13.** $\frac{1}{3}$

Pages 219–220   Practice Exercises   1. >
3. = **5.** < **7.** > **9.** < **11.** < **13.** 0.52;
1.95; 2.25 **15.** 4.05; 4.5; 4.51 **17.** 1.023;
3.102; 3.201 **19.** 0.506; 0.56; 0.566 **21.** false
23. true **25.** true **27.** false **29.** true
31. true **33.** 1.38; 3.18; 8.13; 11.13 **35.** 3.63;
3.66; 6.30; 6.36 **37.** 11.05; 11.15; 11.5; 11.75;
12.1; 12.25; 12.5; 12.55

Page 220   Review Exercises   1. three and fifty-
seven hundredths **3.** one hundred three and four
hundred thirty-six thousandths **5.** four and sixty-
nine thousandths **7.** nine and two hundred thirty-
one ten-thousandths **9.** 14 **11.** 89 **13.** 7810
15. 6756

Page 222   Practice Exercises   1. $\frac{3}{10}$ **3.** $\frac{1}{2}$
5. $\frac{31}{50}$ **7.** $\frac{7}{100}$ **9.** $\frac{21}{100}$ **11.** $5\frac{21}{100}$ **13.** $1\frac{17}{100}$
15. $46\frac{897}{1000}$ **17.** $17\frac{17}{20}$ **19.** $55\frac{63}{100}$ **21.** $\frac{77}{500}$
23. $8\frac{101}{200}$ **25.** $16\frac{941}{1000}$ **27.** $\frac{43}{50}$ **29.** $\frac{9}{1000}$
31. 0.13; $\frac{13}{100}$ **33.** 0.26; $\frac{13}{50}$

Page 222 Review Exercises 1. $\frac{1}{2}$ 3. $\frac{1}{3}$ 5. $\frac{3}{5}$ 7. $\frac{1}{10}$ 9. $\frac{1}{2}$ 11. 79

Pages 224–225 Practice Exercises 1. 0.9 3. 0.125 5. 0.25 7. 0.875 9. 4.4 11. 3.04 13. 0.11 15. 0.83 17. 0.73 19. 0.39 21. 0.61 23. $\frac{1}{2}$ 25. $\frac{1}{4}$ 27. $\frac{3}{4}$ 29. $\frac{2}{3}$ 31. $\frac{1}{2}$ 33. 0.5 35. 0.33 37. 0.57 39. 3.56 41. 0.72 43. C 45. D 47. A 49. A

Page 225 Review Exercises 1. 2.8 3. 0.434 5. 0.67 7. $10

Page 227 Problems 1. 64 in. 3. You need the cost of the ball. 5. $58 7. $12

Page 227 Review Exercises 1. 32 mi/gal 3. You need to know the cost of the socks.

Page 228 Skill Review 1. seventy-nine hundredths 3. four and two hundred fifty-nine thousandths 5. two hundred ninety-five and ninety-five hundredths 7. four thousand, six hundred seventy-seven and one tenth 9. 0.8 11. 0.1 13. $36 15. = 17. > 19. $\frac{17}{100}$ 21. $7\frac{1}{4}$ 23. $36\frac{111}{1000}$ 25. $94\frac{26}{125}$ 27. 0.2 29. 7.17 31. 0.18 33. 0.875 35. $\frac{2}{3}$ 37. $\frac{1}{2}$ 39. $\frac{1}{5}$ 41. $\frac{1}{3}$ 43. 3 points

Page 229 Exercises 1. Twenty-eight and $\frac{43}{100}$ dollars 3. One hundred twenty-seven and $\frac{98}{100}$ dollars 5. Five hundred seventy-seven and $\frac{9}{100}$ dollars 7. Freda Harte 9. groceries 11. $42.17

Page 230 Exercises 1. 3,500,000 3. 219,300,000,000 5. 75,900,000 7. $5,900,000,000 9. $45,100,000 11. million 13. million 15. > 17. >

Page 231 Chapter Review 1. repeating 3. 0 5. 0.000002 7. $4.12 9. $9.23 11. true 13. false 15. $\frac{1}{10}$ 17. $3\frac{12}{25}$ 19. 0.7 21. 0.22 23. 0.83 25. 0.375 27. 0.53 31. Four and $\frac{87}{100}$ dollars 33. Sixty and $\frac{1}{100}$ dollars 35. 7.9

CHAPTER 11

Pages 235–236 Practice Exercises 1. 0.9 3. $18.20 5. 103.547 7. 13.501 9. 14.14 11. 9.143 13. $71.57 15. $1.00 17. 11.5 19. $37.01 21. 16.9 23. $23 25. 24.645 27. 0.1132 29. $54.38 31. 53 33. 17.991 35. 18.42 37. 4.408 39. 13.1313 41. 2.25 43. 9.27 45. 47.01 in.

Page 236 Review Exercises 1. about 1000 3. about 80,000 5. about 9000 7. about $1100 9. about $100,000

Page 238 Practice Exercises 1. about 90 3. about 1100 5. about 600 7. about 25 9. about 90 11. about 1.1 13. about 600

15. about $20 17. about 800 19. about 40 21. b 23. c 25. about 900 mi

Page 238 Review Exercises 1. 214 3. $630 5. $34,076 7. 36

Pages 240–241 Practice Exercises 1. 0.6 3. 2.4 5. 0.4 7. $4.49 9. 0.638 11. 3.1006 13. 0.39 15. 2.35 17. 4.31 19. 9.994 21. 6.171 23. 1.006 25. 1.6 27. 4.8 29. 3.92 31. $14.41 33. 4.075 35. 1.819 37. $1.09 39. 0.027 41. 18.3 43. $.98 45. $1.97 47. 94.192 49. 27.956 51. 2.801 53. 7.8 55. 6.41 57. 6.31

Page 241 Review Exercises 1. about 300 3. about 3000 5. about $100 7. about 5000

Page 243 Practice Exercises 1. about $70 3. about 0.4 5. about $10 7. about 300 9. about $80 11. about $30 13. about $30 15. about $6 17. about 0.4 19. about $3000

Page 243 Review Exercises 1. 2400 3. 240,000 5. 147,718 7. 47,472

Page 244 Skill Review 1. 47.6 3. $94.60 5. $61 7. 86.245 9. $7.43 11. about $8 13. about 1.5 15. about $60 17. about 0.9 19. about $1300 21. 7.9 23. 12.01 25. $64.54 27. 0.512 29. 3.8386 31. about 10 33. about 40 35. about $400 37. about 3400

Page 245 Exercises 1. $1763.26 3. $483.05 5. $1901.80

Page 247 Practice Exercises 1. 1 $5 bill, 2 $1 bills, 1 quarter 3. 1 $20 bill, 1 $5 bill, 1 dime, 1 nickel 5. 2 quarters, 1 dime, 1 penny 7. 4 $1 bills 9. correct 11. 1 $5 bill, 3 $1 bills 13. 4 $1 bills, 5 dimes; 4 $1 bills, 10 nickels 15. Answers may vary: 1 $10 bill, 7 dimes, 1 nickel, 1 penny; 1 $10 bill, 5 dimes, 5 nickels, 1 penny

Page 249 Chapter Review 1. sum 3. 57.6 5. $29.48 7. 7.2309 9. 70.6085 11. 1.063 13. 14.75 15. about $130 17. about 80 19. about 200 21. about $45 23. about $10 25. $1481.09 27. 3 pennies, 2 dimes, 1 quarter

CHAPTER 12

Pages 253–254 Practice Exercises 1. 9.6 3. 3.588 5. $27.55 7. $3744.63 9. 49.2 11. 50.18 13. 417.41 15. $27.56 17. 0.035 19. 60 21. 102 23. $176.70 25. 35.892 27. $163.97 29. 4.281 31. 301.15 33. 0.12 35. $21.30 37. 145.86 39. $247.76 41. $95.46 43. 0.06 45. 480 oz

Page 254 Review Exercises 1. 0.003

3. 0.07 **5.** 0.2 **7.** 0.0006 **9.** 2800
11. 4,200,000 **13.** 210,000 **15.** 4500

Page 256 Practice Exercises 1. 1.25
3. 2175 **5.** 887.7 **7.** 7447.1 **9.** 820
11. 690 **13.** 19,100 **15.** 3090 **17.** 8853.6
19. 219.9 **21.** 4822 **23.** 6600 **25.** 586
27. 950 **29.** 6750 **31.** 120 **33.** $290

Page 256 Review Exercises 1. 16,950
3. 20,794 **5.** 104,160 **7.** 833,426 **9.** 6.7
11. 296.0 **13.** 3.5 **15.** 68.7

Pages 258–259 Practice Exercises 1. 6.84
3. 1.386 **5.** 1.4299 **7.** 9.3906 **9.** 3.4072
11. 2.4768 **13.** 0.0048 **15.** 0.0042 **17.** 0.03
19. 0.003 **21.** 0.004 **23.** 0.0318 **25.** $48.75
27. $.24 **29.** $2.60 **31.** $.27 **33.** 0.16
35. 0.006 **37.** 0.4382 **39.** 96.975
41. $67.53 **43.** $52.55 **45.** 0.0012
47. $88.74 **49.** 75 **51.** 4.24 **53.** $20.63

Page 259 Review Exercises 1. about 12,000
3. about $16,000 **5.** 50 **7.** 0.5 **9.** about $\frac{1}{2}$
11. about $\frac{2}{3}$

Page 261 Practice Exercises 1. about $12
3. about 18 **5.** about 2700 **7.** about 9
9. about 100 **11.** about 2000 **13.** about 600
15. about 450 **17.** about $700 **19.** about 150
21. about 90 **23.** b **25.** b **27.** 99.10
29. 0.08320 **31.** 62.23 **33.** about $320

Page 261 Review Exercises 1. 2×3
3. 5×11 **5.** $2 \times 2 \times 2$ **7.** $2 \times 5 \times 5$
9. $2 \times 2 \times 2 \times 3$ **11.** $2 \times 2 \times 2 \times 3 \times 5$

Pages 262–263 Problems 1. c **3.** b
5. about $120,000 **7.** about 180 bricks
9. about $1.20

Page 263 Review Exercises 1. not reasonable
3. reasonable

Page 264 Skill Review 1. 3.6 **3.** 2.7
5. 65.88 **7.** $85.50 **9.** $113.43 **11.** 5252.8
13. 6.44 **15.** 6.8 **17.** 17 **19.** 80 lb
21. $12.80 **23.** 1.92 **25.** $3.80 **27.** 0.0008
29. 2.205 **31.** 0.0035 **33.** about $10
35. about 540 **37.** about 10,000 **39.** about
3000 **41.** about 120 **43.** about 300 **45.** b

Page 265 Exercises 1. $404.80 **3.** $195
5. $311.50 **7.** $504 **9.** $360.75

Page 267 Exercises 1. $206.65; $582.25
3. $135.46; $345.31 **5.** $799.76 **7.** $813.80
9. $7840.04 **11.** $1969.76

Page 269 Exercises 1. $30.00, $5.25, $35.25,
$4.00, $39.25 **3.** $109.50

Page 271 Chapter Review 1. product
3. 36.3 **5.** 0.012 **7.** 30.6 **9.** 50 **11.** 12.5
13. 1400 **15.** 0.2052 **17.** $8.49 **19.** $27.78

21. about 1000 **23.** about 210 **25.** about $20
27. about 100 **29.** about 600 **31.** about 40
33. c **35.** $415 **37.** $61.35

CHAPTER 13

Pages 275–276 Practice Exercises 1. 51.19
3. 2.5 **5.** 0.264 **7.** $.71 **9.** 3.07 **11.** 6.04
13. $7.50 **15.** 0.207 **17.** 0.7 **19.** 5.98
21. 0.189 **23.** 0.467 **25.** 4.51 **27.** 5.05
29. 12.5 **31.** 9.333 **33.** 0.009 **35.** 0.409
37. $24.10 **39.** 41.55 **41.** $.17

Page 276 Review Exercises 1. 442.2
3. 4150 **5.** 3800 **7.** 6.6 **9.** 0.75
11. 0.375 **13.** 0.07 **15.** 0.0625

Page 278 Practice Exercises 1. 60.34
3. 1.9564 **5.** 1.6403 **7.** 18.25 **9.** 0.215
11. $.65 **13.** 0.0139 **15.** 0.079 **17.** 0.0002
19. 0.026 **21.** 0.04 **23.** 0.0078 **25.** 0.43
27. 0.03 **29.** 0.1036 **31.** 0.0225 **33.** 28.456
35. 4.951 **37.** 0.066 **39.** 0.324 **41.** $1.15

Page 278 Review Exercises 1. 338 **3.** 2
5. 65 **7.** 500

Pages 280–281 Practice Exercises 1. 2
3. 5.3 **5.** 112 **7.** 0.51 **9.** 37.5 **11.** 44
13. 9.375 **15.** 200 **17.** 1.2 **19.** 157.14
21. 1.143 **23.** 0.28 **25.** 1.875 **27.** 4.1
29. 4.667 **31.** 10 **33.** 2.533 **35.** 0.714
37. 6.7 **39.** 0.21 **41.** 62.5 **43.** about 3.4 times

Page 281 Review Exercises 1. about 700
3. about 80 **5.** about 60 **7.** about 80

Page 283 Practice Exercises 1. about 10
3. about 6 **5.** about $5 **7.** about 20
9. about 2 **11.** about 7 **13.** about 150
15. about 0.5 **17.** about 250 **19.** about 1000
21. about 3 **23.** about 400 **25.** about 100
27. about 4 **29.** about 0.5 **31.** about 500
33. about $6 **35.** about 70

Page 283 Review Exercises 1. 100 **3.** 2468
5. 650 **7.** 8000 **9.** 1.85 **11.** 5.946

Page 285 Practice Exercises 1. 8.9×10^5
3. 3×10^8 **5.** 4.126×10^2 **7.** 5.1×10^1
9. 1,600,000 **11.** 80,000,000 **13.** 4608
15. 32.63 **17.** no **19.** no **21.** 4.02×10^7 km

Page 285 Review Exercises 1. $\frac{1}{4}$ **3.** $\frac{5}{6}$ **5.** $\frac{11}{14}$

Page 286 Skill Review 1. 3.629 **3.** $2.50
5. 2.833 **7.** 6.72 **9.** 6.04 **11.** 1.023
13. 1.007 **15.** 19.692 **17.** 26.08 **19.** 1.8267
21. 0.02 **23.** 0.0892 **25.** 0.671 **27.** 0.86
29. $4 **31.** 31 **33.** 64 **35.** 112.333
37. 11.111 **39.** 1.429 **41.** 203.75 **43.** about 100
45. about 50 **47.** about 3000 **49.** about 700

51. 2480 **53.** 31.15 **55.** 40,200 **57.** 71,400,000
59. 500,000 **61.** 45,230 **63.** 1.917×10^{10}
65. 3.651×10^3 **67.** 5.089×10^2
69. 4×10^9 **71.** 6.594×10^4

Page 287 Exercises 1. $1312.50 **3.** $2708.33
5. $225 **7.** $525.77 **9.** $336.54 **11.** $609.62

Page 289 Practice Exercises 1. $900
3. $1305 **5.** $176.28 **7.** $144.67
9. $1138.12 **11.** $1016; $151.46

Page 291 Chapter Review 1. quotient
3. 0.35 **5.** 6.25 **7.** $14.50 **9.** 0.009
11. 11.362 **13.** 0.4226 **15.** 522.1 **17.** 777
19. 63 **21.** about 6 **23.** about 5 **25.** about
7000 **27.** about 650 **29.** D **31.** A **33.** B
35. $8.50 **37.** $1014 **39.** $216.24

CHAPTER 14

Pages 295–296 Practice Exercises 1. m
3. m **5.** cm **7.** mm **9.** mm **11.** km
13. cm **15.** km **17.** 2 m **19.** 2 mm
21. 150 cm **23.** 1.4 m **25.** 0.2 cm

Page 296 Review Exercises 1. 24 **3.** 32
5. 192 **7.** 2 **9.** < **11.** >

Pages 298–299 Practice Exercises 1. 4 cm
3. 3 cm **5. a.** 35 mm **b.** 3.5 cm
7. a. 76 mm **b.** 7.6 cm **9.** 40 mm, 4 cm
11. 75 mm, 7.5 cm **13.** 120 mm, 12 cm
21. AC **23.** same distance

Page 299 Review Exercises 1. 176 **3.** 0.024
5. < **7.** >

Pages 301–302 Practice Exercises 1. 4000
3. 4900 **5.** 2300 **7.** 4 **9.** 38 **11.** 0.058
13. 580 **15.** 0.35 **17.** 860 **19.** = **21.** <
23. > **25.** < **27.** 5400 m **29.** 0.345 km

Page 302 Review Exercises 1. 25,710
3. 390 **5.** 10.25 **7.** 17,266 **9.** 24 **11.** $\frac{5}{12}$

Page 304 Practice Exercises 1. mL **3.** L
5. 8200 **7.** 4.5 **9.** 0.3 **11.** < **13.** >
15. < **17.** 0.8 L **19.** about 21 glasses

Page 304 Review Exercises 1. $3\frac{1}{9}$ **3.** $2\frac{2}{9}$
5. 0.35 **7.** $0.\overline{2}$ **9.** $330

Pages 306–307 Practice Exercises 1. g
3. kg **5.** kg **7.** 380,000 **9.** 2.5 **11.** 1600
13. > **15.** < **17.** < **19.** c **21.** b
23. 1600 g **25.** 1440 g, 1.44 kg

Page 307 Review Exercises 1. 0.034 **3.** 48
5. 50 **7.** 8300 **9.** 0.22 **11.** 34,000

Pages 308–309 Problems 1. 3 blocks due
south **3.** 4 blocks due west **5.** 12

Page 309 Review Exercises 1. $1889.75
3. 45, 42, 126

Page 310 Skill Review 1. 20 m **3.** 600 km
5. a. 3.8 cm **b.** 38 mm **7.** 340 **9.** 40,000
11. 4.78 **13.** mL **15.** L **17.** 420 mL, 4 L,
4200 mL, 4.5 L **19.** 2 mg **21.** 1.3 kg **23.** <
25. = **27.** = **29.** 2 blocks due south

Page 311 Exercises 1. $.24 **3.** $1.44
5. $.60 **7.** $.81

Page 313 Practice Exercises 1. 3995
3. 1875 **5.** 1685 kW · h **7.** 1156 kW · h
9. 1092 kW · h

Page 315 Practice Exercises 1. $.47/L
3. $.73/bulb **5.** $.06/g **7.** $.002/g
9. $.007/g **11.** $.002/mL **13.** $.001/g
15. $.56/kg **17.** $.38/bar

Page 316 Exercises 1. 2.5 kg **3.** 1.4 kg
5. 0.7 kg **7.** Answers will vary.

Page 317 Chapter Review 1. meter **7.** 0.47
9. 350 **11.** 0.06 **13.** true **15.** true
17. a. $2.10/kg, better buy **b.** $2.82/kg
19. $161.76

CHAPTER 15

Pages 325–326 Practice Exercises 1. $\frac{3}{5}$ **3.** $\frac{5}{4}$
5. $\frac{2}{3}$ **7.** $\frac{9}{31}$ **9.** $\frac{9}{100}$ **11.** $\frac{1}{100}$ **13.** $\frac{1}{4}$ **15.** $\frac{5}{7}$;
5:7 **17.** 8:15; 8 to 15 **19.** $\frac{13}{22}$; 13 to 22
21. 50:1; $\frac{50}{1}$ **23.** $\frac{1}{3}$ **25.** $\frac{3}{1}$ **27.** $\frac{1}{4}$ **29.** $\frac{2}{1}$
31. $\frac{3}{1}$ **33.** $\frac{15}{1}$ **35.** $\frac{11}{1}$

Page 326 Review Exercises 1. $\frac{1}{3}$ **3.** $\frac{3}{4}$ **5.** $\frac{1}{3}$
7. 32 **9.** 7 **11.** 3000 **13.** 16 **15.** 15
17. 50.15 **19.** 1.26 **21.** 0.008 **23.** 10.65

Page 328 Practice Exercises 1. 24 mi/gal
3. 80 words/min **5.** 4 cm/day **7.** 62.5 km/h
9. $480.50/week **11.** 3.5 h/class **13.** 375 mi/day
15. 5 tokens/ride **17.** $3.75/ticket **19.** 0.2 L/child
21. 12 boxes/carton **23.** $29/day **25.** Sylvia

Page 328 Review Exercises 1. not equivalent
3. not equivalent **5.** equivalent **7.** not equivalent **9.** 10 **11.** 1

Pages 330–331 Practice Exercises 1. true
3. false **5.** true **7.** false **9.** true **11.** true
13. 10 **15.** 40 **17.** 80 **19.** 9 **21.** 320
23. 6 **25.** $\frac{12}{7} = \frac{24}{14}$ **27.** $\frac{k}{9} = \frac{1}{3}$
29. 6:21 = 2:7 **31.** 10:r = 15:6 **33.** 12
35. 256 **37.** 18 **39.** 2 **41.** neither

Page 331 Review Exercises 1. 0.32 **3.** 40.2
5. 115.25 **7.** 27,068

Pages 333–334 Problems 1. $.40 **3.** 135
5. 270 **7.** 10 **9.** 70 **11.** 3600 **13.** $580

Page 334 Review Exercises 1. $33 **3.** $39.80

Pages 336–337 Practice Exercises 1. 6 ft; 3 ft
3. 5 ft; 3 ft **5.** 5 ft; 1 ft **7.** $5\frac{1}{2}$ in. **9.** 6 in.
11. 30 cm **13.** 2 ft

Page 337 Review Exercises 1. about 50
3. about $700 **5.** about 16 **7.** about $630
9. about $110 **11.** 81 **13.** 108 **15.** 567

Page 338 Skill Review 1. $\frac{5}{3}$ **3.** $\frac{1}{4}$ **5.** $\frac{80}{1}$
7. $\frac{3}{10}$ **9.** 43 to 77; $\frac{43}{77}$ **11.** 14:33; 14 to 33
13. 62 km/h **15.** $3.16/lb **17.** 80 words/min
19. false **21.** true **23.** 16 **25.** 3
27. $32.94 **29.** 312 lb **31.** $2\frac{1}{2}$ ft

Pages 341–342 Practice Exercises 1. about
32 mi **3.** about 37 mi **5.** about 24 mi **7.** about
58 mi **9.** about $1\frac{3}{8}$ mi **11.** about 2 mi
13. about $\frac{5}{8}$ mi **15.** about 120 mi **17.** about
80 mi **19.** about 100 mi **21.** about 63 mi

Page 343 Chapter Review 1. ratio **3.** $\frac{8}{25}$
5. $\frac{1}{8}$ **7.** $\frac{1}{1000}$ **9.** $\frac{3}{190}$ **11.** 28 to 21; $\frac{28}{21}$
13. 7 to 13; 7:13 **15.** $.23/oz **17.** 16 m/s
19. 8 **21.** 1 **23.** 7 **25.** 8 **27.** $1.68
29. about 80 **31.** about 25 km

CHAPTER 16

Page 347 Practice Exercises 1. 32% **3.** 47%
5. 17% **7.** 62% **9.** 10% **11.** 23.7%
13. 37% **15.** $75\frac{3}{4}\%$ **17.** 94% **19.** 65%
21. Erica: 26%; Joel: 35%; Randall: 17%; Gena:
22%

Page 347 Review Exercises 1. 50.42
3. 97.5 **5.** 1,045,000 **7.** 1.63

Page 349 Practice Exercises 1. 0.27
3. 0.265 **5.** 0.0732 **7.** 1.41 **9.** 0.003
11. $0.08\frac{1}{2}$ **13.** 43% **15.** 4% **17.** 61.6%
19. 234% **21.** 170% **23.** $12\frac{1}{2}\%$ **25.** 0.94
27. 23% **29.** 0.875 **31.** 190% **33.** 53.1%
35. $0.37\frac{1}{2}$ **37.** 0.04

Page 349 Review Exercises 1. $\frac{43}{100}$ **3.** $\frac{11}{50}$
5. $5\frac{1}{25}$ **7.** line graph

Pages 351–352 Practice Exercises 1. $\frac{49}{100}$
3. $\frac{4}{5}$ **5.** $\frac{3}{20}$ **7.** $\frac{3}{4}$ **9.** $\frac{99}{100}$ **11.** $1\frac{1}{10}$ **13.** $\frac{13}{1000}$
15. $\frac{79}{250}$ **17.** $\frac{3}{100}$ **19.** $\frac{3}{200}$ **21.** $\frac{7}{10,000}$ **23.** $\frac{11}{400}$
25. $\frac{7}{800}$ **27.** $\frac{3}{350}$ **29.** $\frac{11}{400}$ **31.** $\frac{1}{3}$ **33.** $\frac{3}{8}$
35. $\frac{199}{200}$ **37.** $\frac{47}{100}$ **39.** $\frac{77}{100}$ **41.** 1 **43.** $\frac{3}{500}$
45. $\frac{111}{500}$ **47.** $2\frac{3}{4}$ **49.** $\frac{1}{250}$ **51.** $\frac{19}{900}$ **53.** 0.75;
$0.33\frac{1}{3}$; 0.2 **55.** $\frac{1}{4}$

Page 352 Review Exercises 1. 0.6
3. 0.0625 **5.** 170 **7.** 0.05

Page 354 Practice Exercises 1. 40% **3.** 52%
5. 95% **7.** $83\frac{1}{3}\%$ **9.** $2\frac{1}{2}\%$ **11.** $91\frac{2}{3}\%$
13. 30% **15.** 85% **17.** $68\frac{3}{4}\%$ **19.** $66\frac{2}{3}\%$

Page 354 Review Exercises 1. 84 **3.** 0 **5.** 1

Pages 356–357 Practice Exercises 1. 0.58
3. 4.64 **5.** 75 **7.** 168 **9.** 240 **11.** $115\frac{1}{2}$
13. 0.1; $\frac{1}{10}$ **15.** 0.6; $\frac{3}{5}$ **17.** 0.125; $\frac{1}{8}$ **19.** 25

21. 21.4 **23.** 100 **25.** 20% **27.** 75%
29. $33\frac{1}{3}\%$ **31.** 32

Page 357 Review Exercises 1. about 50
3. about 7 **5.** about 90 **7.** about 90

Page 358 Practice Exercises 1. about $75
3. about 160 **5.** about 70 **7.** about $8
9. about 240 **11.** about $6 **13.** about $7.20
15. about $15 **17.** about $3.60 **19.** about 14
21. about $45 **23.** about $150 **25.** about 1000
27. about $6 **29.** about $140 **31.** about 240
33. about 900

Page 359 Review Exercises 1. 1; 6 **3.** 2; 12
5. 3; 18 **7.** 5; 30

Pages 360–361 Problems 1. Sol **3.** Rita:
left; Chris: right; Lyn: center **5.** Anne: Chicago;
Barry: Anchorage; Carol: Denver; David: Boston

Page 361 Review Exercises 1. 576
3. Miguel: lawyer; Jeff: doctor; Renee: engineer

Page 362 Skill Review 1. 26% **3.** 48%
5. 12% **7.** 0.16 **9.** 86% **11.** 1.4%
13. $0.53\frac{1}{2}$ **15.** $6\frac{5}{8}\%$ **17.** $\frac{13}{20}$ **19.** $\frac{3}{200}$ **21.** $\frac{13}{200}$
23. $\frac{1}{250}$ **25.** $2\frac{1}{4}$ **27.** 70% **29.** 56%
31. $12\frac{1}{2}\%$ **33.** $66\frac{2}{3}\%$ **35.** $41\frac{2}{3}\%$ **37.** 5
39. 7.65 **41.** 22 **43.** 85.05 **45.** 8.4
47. about $90 **49.** about $4 **51.** about $25
53. Barbara: Aruba; Tom: Bermuda; Amy: Tahiti

Page 363 Exercises 1. $46.15 **3.** $270
5. $27; $927

Page 365 Exercises 1. $10; $210; $10.50;
$220.50 **3.** $33; $2433; $33.45; $2466.45
5. $658.05; $13,498.05; $691.78; $14,189.83
7. $3060.63 **9.** $10,150; $10,302.25
11. $4280.37

Page 367 Exercises 1. $42 **3.** $72 **5.** $66
7. at least $540 but less than $550

Page 368 Exercises 1. $.52; $13.47 **3.** $.79;
$16.54 **5.** $3.12; $51.09 **7.** about $126

Page 369 Chapter Review 1. ratio **3.** 0.93
5. 14.5% **7.** 0.037 **9.** $\frac{67}{100}$ **11.** 4 **13.** $\frac{427}{1000}$
15. 82% **17.** $16\frac{2}{3}\%$ **19.** $43\frac{3}{4}\%$ **21.** 349.2
23. 9.3 **25.** about 80 **27.** about $2.10
29. $66 **31.** $54

CHAPTER 17

Pages 373–374 Practice Exercises 1. 60%
3. 5% **5.** 200% **7.** 150% **9.** $62\frac{1}{2}\%$
11. $83\frac{1}{3}\%$ **13.** $56\frac{2}{3}\%$ **15.** $8\frac{1}{3}\%$ **17.** 44%
19. $33\frac{1}{3}\%$ **21.** 150% **23.** $3\frac{1}{3}\%$ **25.** 75%

Page 374 Review Exercises 1. 0.5; $\frac{1}{2}$
3. 0.375; $\frac{3}{8}$ **5.** 0.6; $\frac{3}{5}$ **7.** 0.25; $\frac{1}{4}$ **9.** 0.875; $\frac{7}{8}$

Pages 376–377 Practice Exercises 1. 200
3. 900 **5.** 136 **7.** 2744 **9.** 1000 **11.** 300
13. 64 **15.** 48 **17.** 56 **19.** 440 **21.** 200
23. 419 **25.** 350 **27.** 7000 **29.** 6160

Page 377 Review Exercises 1. 1 **3.** 16
5. 20 **7.** 120 **9.** about 8 **11.** about 20
13. about 150 **15.** about 8 **17.** about 23

Page 379–380 Practice Exercises 1. 562.5
3. 528 **5.** 8 **7.** 1.65 **9.** 45 **11.** 25%
13. 125% **15.** $66\frac{2}{3}$% **17.** 6% **19.** $12\frac{1}{2}$%
21. 700 **23.** 1 **25.** 2500 **27.** 7 **29.** 432
31. 2000 **33.** 250% **35.** 13 **37.** 9000 books
39. 1500 people

Page 380 Review Exercises 1. 559
3. 222.21 **5.** $5\frac{13}{24}$ **7.** $\frac{23}{50}$ **9.** 800 **11.** 22.1
13. $\frac{5}{14}$ **15.** $1\frac{1}{2}$

Pages 382–383 Practice Exercises 1. 6%
3. 20% **5.** 65% **7.** $66\frac{2}{3}$% **9.** 28%
11. $16\frac{2}{3}$% **13.** 2% **15.** $33\frac{1}{3}$% **17.** increase;
25% **19.** decrease; $12\frac{1}{2}$% **21.** decrease; 7%
23. decrease; $62\frac{1}{2}$% **25.** $83\frac{1}{3}$%

Page 383 Review Exercises 1. $\frac{27}{100}$ **3.** $3\frac{37}{50}$
5. $77\frac{4}{5}$ **7.** $\frac{24}{25}$ **9.** = **11.** > **13.** < **15.** <

Page 384 Skill Review 1. 88% **3.** 140%
5. $81\frac{1}{4}$% **7.** $1\frac{3}{8}$% **9.** $14\frac{1}{2}$% **11.** 136
13. 64 **15.** 800 **17.** 1120 **19.** 60
21. 7680 employees **23.** 25% **25.** 6 **27.** 6.2
29. 200% **31.** 180 **33.** decrease; $37\frac{1}{2}$%
35. increase; 10% **37.** increase; 8%

Page 385 Exercises 1. $1430.55 **3.** $491.40
5. $3432

Pages 387–388 Practice Exercises 1. $63;
$147 **3.** $7.50; $42.50 **5.** 50% **7.** 35%
9. $8.50; $25.50 **11.** $1.60; $14.40
13. 25%; $18 **15.** 25% **17.** $23.80

Page 389 Exercises 1. $15.04; $.23
3. $55.44; $.83 **5.** $23.80

Page 391 Chapter Review 1. decrease
3. 175% **5.** 280 **7.** 400% **9.** 425 **11.** 8%
13. 64 **15.** 88 **17.** 85 **19.** increase; 35%
23. $420 **25.** $3.69

CHAPTER 18

Pages 399–400 Practice Exercises
3. Calories

Number	Tally	Freq.
200–249	II	2
250–299	ЖНТ IIII	9
300–349	ЖНТ II	7
350–399	II	2

5. Ages of Students

Age	Tally	Freq.
14	I	1
15	ЖНТ ЖНТ	10
16	ЖНТ II	7
17	IIII	4
18	II	2

7. 4 **9.** 167

Page 400 Review Exercises 1. about 40 mi/h
3. about 15 mi/h **5.** cheetah **7.** antelope,
cheetah, ostrich

Pages 402–403 Practice Exercises 1. 71; 72;
none **3.** 5.5; 5; 4 and 5 **5.** 3.6; 3.5; 2.5
7. 24.5; 15; 15 **9.** 8.4; 8.8; 7.3 and 9.3
11. $59.33 **13.** 6.7 **15.** 17.8; 19; 19
17. 59.3; 66.5; 63 and 70 **19.** 116.6; 111; none
21. $70,000 **23.** $12,500 **25.** median
27. 6.8 oz

Page 403 Review Exercises 1. $41 **3.** $40\frac{1}{4}$
5. Friday

Pages 405–406 Practice Exercises
1. about $20,000,000 **3.** 1975
7. 56 **13.**
9. yellow
11. $4\frac{1}{4}$

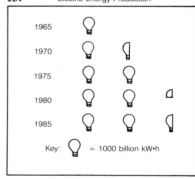

Electric Energy Production

1965
1970
1975
1980
1985

Key: = 1000 billion kW•h

Page 406 Review Exercises 1. 70 **3.** 28
5. 260

Pages 408–409 Practice Exercises 1. $\frac{1}{10}$
3. 55% **5.** 43 **7.** 624 **9.** 25% **11.** housing
and food **13.** $315 **15.** $125 **17.** Asia
19. Antarctica **21.** Asia and Africa **23.** about
17.6 million square miles

Page 409 Review Exercises
1.

Distance from the Sun

Distance (Millions of Miles)

200
160
120
80
40
0

Earth   Mars   Mercury   Venus

Page 411 Problems 1. 16 **3.** 15 $1 bills,
5 $5 bills **5.** 26 nickels, 7 dimes **7.** 10¢, 20¢,
25¢, 30¢, 35¢, 45¢, 50¢, 55¢, 60¢, 70¢, 75¢, 80¢,
85¢, 95¢, $1.05 **9.** 12

Page 411 Review Exercises 1. about 14 s

Page 412 Skill Review
3. 70; 70; 60 **5.** 5.7; 5; 5 and 7 **7.** 3.5; 4;
0 and 5 **9.** about 225 **11.** about 150 **13.** $\frac{1}{5}$
15. 334

Page 413 Exercises
1.

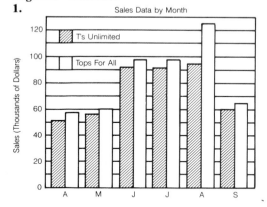

Sales Data by Month

Page 414 Exercises 1. $128.00 **3.** $313.75
5. $356.25 **7.** $478.00

Page 416 Exercises 1. about $50 **3.** about
$90 **5.** about $50 **7.** about $20 **9.** about $50
11. about $90 **13.** about $50 **15.** about $40

Page 417 Chapter Review 1. mean
3. Games Played

Games	Tally	Frequency
2	I	1
3	I	1
4	II	2
5	ℍℍ	5
6	ℍℍ II	7
7	ℍℍ III	8

5. 80; 80; 75
7.

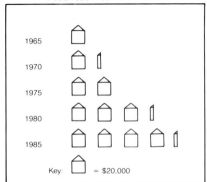

Median Sale Price of a New Home

1965

1970

1975

1980

1985

Key: ⌂ = $20,000

9. $1,320,000,000 **11.** Yes. **13.** about $20

CHAPTER 19

Page 421 Practice Exercises 1. 12 **3.** 9
5. 10 **7.** 48 **9.** 8 **11.** 40 **13.** 32

Page 421 Review Exercises 1. $5\frac{7}{18}$ **3.** 7.676
5. 518.7 **7.** $3\frac{22}{49}$

Page 423 Practice Exercises 1. 120 **3.** 720
5. 20 **7.** 720 **9.** 5040 **11.** 210 **13.** 2
15. 3,628,800

Page 423 Review Exercises 1. $\frac{3}{4}$ **3.** $\frac{5}{6}$
5. $\frac{11}{20}$ **7.** $\frac{2}{3}$ **9.** $\frac{6}{17}$ **11.** $\frac{5}{6}$

Pages 425–426 Practice Exercises 1. $\frac{1}{6}$ **3.** 0
5. $\frac{5}{6}$ **7.** $\frac{3}{7}$ **9.** $\frac{5}{7}$ **11.** $\frac{5}{6}$ **13.** $\frac{1}{3}$ **15.** $\frac{1}{5}$
17. $\frac{9}{10}$ **19.** 0 **21.** $\frac{1}{50}$ **23.** $\frac{1}{10}$; 10%

Page 426 Review Exercises 1. 3.75×10^2
3. 8×10^5 **5.** 4.152×10^6 **7.** 4.8913×10^3
9. 6200 **11.** 6 **13.** 35 **15.** 4; 10
17. 11,500 **19.** 6.5 **21.** 0.46 **23.** 2.85

Page 428 Practice Exercises 1. $\frac{1}{30}$ **3.** $\frac{4}{15}$ **5.** $\frac{2}{15}$
7. $\frac{1}{15}$ **9.** $\frac{2}{225}$ **11.** $\frac{4}{9}$ **13.** $\frac{1}{105}$ **15.** $\frac{1}{105}$ **17.** $\frac{3}{52}$

Page 428 Review Exercises 1. 150 **3.** $101\frac{9}{11}$

Pages 430–431 Practice Exercises 1. about 15
3. about 25 **5.** about 112 **7.** about 152
9. about 30 **11.** about 22 **13.** about 27
15. about 60 **17.** about 8 **19.** about 112

Page 431 Review Exercises 1. about 1000
3. about 21,000 **5.** about 700 **7.** about 10
9. about 6 **11.** about 2 **13.** 25 **15.** 3000
17. 3600

Page 432 Skill Review 1. 15 **3.** 40,320
5. 24 **7.** $\frac{1}{6}$ **9.** $\frac{1}{2}$ **11.** $\frac{1}{48}$ **13.** $\frac{1}{2}$ **15.** $\frac{1}{28}$
17. $\frac{5}{56}$ **19.** about 25

Page 433 Exercises 1. $\frac{12}{25}$ **3.** about 57,600
5. 200 **7.** about 14,850

Page 434 Exercises 1. 5 to 9 **3.** 9 to 5
5. 1 to 5 **7.** 5 to 1 **9.** $\frac{2}{15}$

Page 435 Chapter Review 1. outcomes
3. 12 **5.** 720 **7.** 24 **9.** $\frac{1}{2}$ **11.** $\frac{1}{49}$
13. about 5 **15.** about 4% **17.** 1 to 6

CHAPTER 20

Pages 443–444 Practice Exercises 1. ⁻8
3. 50 **5.** ⁻35 **7.** 12 **9.** ⁻3 **11.** 15 **13.** 8
15. 13 **17.** 6 **19.** > **21.** > **23.** < **25.** >
27. A **29.** A **31.** B **33.** ⁻5, ⁻4, ⁻3, 0, 5
35. ⁻14, ⁻9, ⁻1, 1, 2 **37.** ⁻12, ⁻8, 0, 1, 11
39. > **41.** < **43.** < **45.** = **47.** ⁻2, 2

Page 444   Review Exercises   1. 120 **3.** 399
5. 11.45 **7.** 28.31 **9.** $1\frac{1}{5}$ **11.** $1\frac{11}{24}$

Pages 446–447   Practice Exercises

1. 9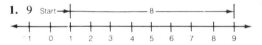

3. ⁻4
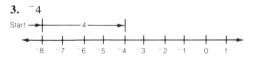

5. 0

7. ⁻8

9. 15 **11.** 10 **13.** 14 **15.** 40 **17.** ⁻4
19. ⁻10 **21.** ⁻16 **23.** ⁻16 **25.** ⁻4 **27.** 0
29. ⁻1 **31.** ⁻1 **33.** 3 **35.** 5 **37.** 12
39. ⁻6 **41.** 15 **43.** ⁻2 **45.** ⁻5 **47.** 14
49. ⁻28 **51.** 0 **53.** ⁻11 **55.** ⁻9 **57.** 12
59. 11°F

Page 447   Review Exercises   1. 23 **3.** 16
5. 2.12 **7.** 3.55 **9.** 3.43 **11.** $\frac{3}{10}$

Page 449   Practice Exercises   1. 6 + ⁻17
3. 0 + 13 **5.** ⁻10 + 8 **7.** ⁻2 + ⁻23 **9.** ⁻20
11. ⁻14 **13.** ⁻3 **15.** 13 **17.** 17 + ⁻29; ⁻12
19. 0 + 43; 43 **21.** 5 – 30; ⁻25 **23.** ⁻5°F

Page 449   Review Exercises   1. 45 **3.** 192
5. 204 **7.** 5.44 **9.** 19.98 **11.** 64.68 **13.** $\frac{5}{12}$
15. $\frac{10}{27}$

Pages 451–452   Practice Exercises   1. ⁻27
3. ⁻42 **5.** 6 **7.** 72 **9.** ⁻136 **11.** 0
13. 55 **15.** ⁻144 **17.** ⁻28 **19.** ⁻36
21. 72 **23.** 120 **25.** ⁻420 **27.** ⁻120
29. ⁻8 **31.** 64 **33.** 1 **35.** 49 **37.** 1
39. ⁻32 **41.** ⁻154 **43.** 0 **45.** 144 **47.** 420
49. 252 **51.** ⁻27 **53.** ⁻119 **55.** 16 **57.** 68°

Page 452   Review Exercises   1. 18 **3.** 35
5. 6.2 **7.** 14.9 **9.** $\frac{5}{6}$ **11.** $\frac{7}{10}$

Pages 454–455   Practice Exercises   1. ⁻6
3. 9 **5.** ⁻9 **7.** ⁻21 **9.** 6 **11.** ⁻13 **13.** 7
15. ⁻15 **17.** zero **19.** undefined **21.** negative **23.** positive **25.** 6 **27.** 0; 0 **29.** ⁻14;
⁻14 **31.** ⁻19 **33.** 0 **35.** 20 **37.** ⁻25
39. 0 **41.** 12 **43.** 23 ft

Page 455   Review Exercises   1. 126 **3.** 48
5. 25%

Pages 456–457   Problems   1. 36 **3.** 2500
5. a. 576 crates **b.** 400 crates
7. 45 handshakes

Page 457   Review Exercises   1. 6 cans **3.** c

Page 458   Skill Review   1. 19 **3.** ⁻5 **5.** 10
7. 8 **9.** 4 **11.** 9 **13.** 2 **15.** < **17.** <
19. > **21.** < **23.** 6 **25.** 21 **27.** 0
29. ⁻22 **31.** 20 **33.** ⁻6 **35.** 7 **37.** 0
39. ⁻84 **41.** 0 **43.** 30 **45.** 64 **47.** ⁻5
49. 8 **51.** 6 **53.** ⁻7 **55.** ⁻6

Page 459   Exercises   1. °F **3.** °C **5.** °C
7. a **9.** b

Page 460   Exercises   1. ⁻10°F; 30°F
3. ⁻34°F; 24°F **5.** a **7.** about ⁻17°F

Page 461   Chapter Review   1. positive **3.** integers **5.** ⁻38 **7.** 52 **9.** ⁻14; 14 **11.** 20;
20 **13.** ⁻22; 22 **15.** < **17.** 6 **19.** 22
21. ⁻343 **23.** 60 **25.** 16 **27.** ⁻36 **29.** undefined **31.** ⁻7 **33.** 8°F **35.** 70°F

CHAPTER 21

Page 465   Practice Exercises   1. ⁻10 **3.** 12
5. ⁻61 **7.** 22 **9.** 29 **11.** ⁻5 **13.** ⁻13
15. ⁻19 **17.** 40 **19.** 17 **21.** 0 **23.** 22
25. ⁻90 **27.** 24 **29.** 7

Page 465   Review Exercises   1. $\frac{4}{3}$ **3.** $\frac{1}{6}$ **5.** $\frac{7}{8}$
7. ⁻16 **9.** 91 **11.** ⁻8 **13.** 15 **15.** ⁻36
17. ⁻6 **19.** $37\frac{1}{2}$ lb

Pages 467–468   Practice Exercises   1. ⁻6
3. 18 **5.** ⁻25 **7.** ⁻7 **9.** 50 **11.** ⁻64
13. 36 **15.** 96 **17.** ⁻15 **19.** ⁻36 **21.** ⁻18
23. ⁻54 **25.** 3 **27.** ⁻32 **29.** 42 **31.** 480
33. 0 **35.** ⁻60 **37.** ⁻165 **39.** ⁻15 **41.** 1
43. 30 **45.** 80 **47.** 405

Page 468   Review Exercises   1. 33 **3.** ⁻25
5. 11 **7.** ⁻2 **9.** 14,533 ft

Pages 470–471   Practice Exercises   1. 6 **3.** 6
5. ⁻6 **7.** 24 **9.** ⁻24 **11.** ⁻24 **13.** 24
15. ⁻50 **17.** ⁻20 **19.** 4 **21.** ⁻7 **23.** 16
25. ⁻7 **27.** ⁻4 **29.** ⁻48

Page 471   Review Exercises   1. 81 **3.** 16
5. 225 **7.** $76.48

Page 473   Problems   1. $118 **3.** 14 min
5. $371 **7.** 35 lb

Page 473   Review Exercises   1. $5.74 **3.** 72 h
5. $23,460

Page 475   Practice Exercises   1. ($^-$4, 3)
3. (0, 3) **5.** (1, 1) **7.** (3, 0) **9.** ($^-$3, $^-$2)
11. (2, $^-$2)

13.–20.

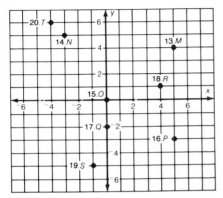

21. H **23.** C **25.** D **27.** G **29.** (6, 4)

Page 475   Review Exercises   1. $^-$16 **3.** $^-$32
5. $^-$4 **7.** 0

Page 477   Practice Exercises   1. ($^-$2, $^-$1),
(0, 5), (2, 11) **3.** ($^-$2, $^-$7), (0, 3), (2, 13)
5. ($^-$2, 2), (0, $^-$6), (2, $^-$14)

7.

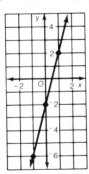

11.

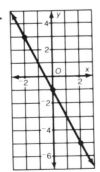

17.

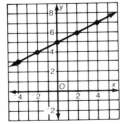

Page 477   Review Exercises   1. 8 **3.** 60
5. 56 **7.** $^-$82 **9.** $340

Page 478   Skill Review   1. 22 **2.** $^-$14
3. $^-$25 **4.** 26 **5.** 7 **6.** $^-$5 **7.** 17 **8.** 17
9. $^-$12 **10.** 84 **11.** 28 **12.** $^-$51 **13.** $^-$5
14. 12 **15.** 9 **16.** $^-$77 **17.** 99 **18.** $^-$25
19. 12 min **20.** $18 **21.** (2, 3) **22.** (1, 0)
23. ($^-$2, $^-$2) **24.** (0, $^-$3) **25.** ($^-$4, 3)
26. (3, $^-$1) **31.** ($^-$2, $^-$3), (0, 1), (2, 5)
32. ($^-$2, $^-$5), (0, 3), (2, 11) **33.** ($^-$2, $^-$8),
(0, $^-$2), (2, 4) **34.** ($^-$2, $^-$14), (0, $^-$4), (2, 6)
35. ($^-$2, 9), (0, 5), (2, 1) **36.** ($^-$2, 5), (0, $^-$1),
(2, $^-$7)

39.

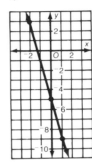

41.

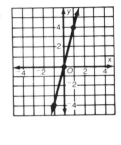

Pages 479–480   Exercises   1. 4 h **3.** 54 mi/h
5. $2.28 **7.** 6% **9.** 162 hits **11.** 4 books
13. $1.79 **15.** $4500

Page 482   Practice Exercises   1. about 7°E,
45°N **3.** about 4°E, 51°N **5.** about 0°, 52°N
7. Spain **9.** Denmark **11.** a **13.** a

Page 483   Chapter Review   1. equation
2. *y*-axis **3.** *x*-coordinate **4.** origin **5.** 17
6. 14 **7.** 19 **8.** 48 **9.** 3 **10.** $^-$13
11. $^-$48 **12.** $^-$14 **13.** $^-$8 **14.** $^-$64
15. 12 **16.** 36 **17.** 12 pencils **18.** 32 h

19.–22.

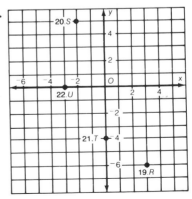

23. 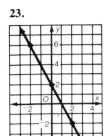 **25.**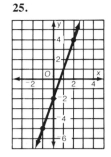

27. about 2° E, 42° N

CHAPTER 22

Pages 488–489   Practice Exercises   1. • F

3.
G   H

5.
C   D

7. 120°   **9.** 90°

11. 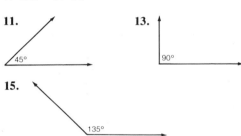   **13.**

45°   90°

15.

135°

17. obtuse   **19.** neither   **21.** perpendicular
23. $\overrightarrow{AC}$, $\overrightarrow{BD}$ **25.** 90°   **27.** Answers may vary.
∠BEC, ∠DEC, ∠AED, ∠BEA

Page 489   Review Exercises   1. ⁻15   **3.** ⁻24
5. ⁻36   **7.** 85

Page 492   Practice Exercises   1. $\overline{MN}$, $\overline{NO}$, $\overline{OP}$,
$\overline{PQ}$, $\overline{QM}$ **3.** $\overline{QN}$, $\overline{MP}$, $\overline{MO}$ **5.** pentagon, not
regular   **7.** octagon, regular   **9.** rhombus
11. parallelogram   **13.** rectangle   **15.** rhombus
17. trapezoid   **19.** triangle

Page 492   Review Exercises   1. 288   **3.** 3, 2
5. 0.4   **7.** 7.255 kg

Page 494   Practice Exercises   1. 12 ft
3. 54 mm   **5.** 32 cm   **7.** 40 yd   **9.** 36 m
11. 35 in.   **13.** 43.2 m   **15.** 76 yd

Page 494   Review Exercises   1. 36   **3.** 144
5. 7   **7.** 16   **9.** 15   **11.** 52

Pages 496–497   Practice Exercises   1. circle O
3. $\overline{AC}$, $\overline{BD}$ **5.** 15.7 cm   **7.** 43.96 ft

9. 25.12 m   **11.** 66 ft   **13.** 242 cm
15. 440 ft   **17.** 56.52 mm   **19.** 53.38 cm
21. 103.62 mm   **23.** 70 ft; 220 ft   **25.** 28 yd;
176 yd   **27.** $31\frac{1}{2}$ ft; 63 ft   **29.** 345.4 cm

Page 497   Review Exercises   1. >   **3.** <   **5.** =

Pages 499–500   Practice Exercises   1. 32 in.²
3. 49 yd²   **5.** 44 in.²   **7.** 120 cm²   **9.** 225 m²
11. 85 ft²   **13.** 18   **15.** 27   **17.** 52,900 m²

Page 500   Review Exercises   1. $\frac{7}{10}$ **3.** 14
5. 3.9   **7.** 0.08

Pages 502–503   Practice Exercises   1. 30 m²
3. 24.5 mm²   **5.** 232 cm²   **7.** $103\frac{1}{2}$ yd²
9. 77 cm²   **11.** 518.7 in.²   **13.** 525 cm²
15. 90 ft²

Page 503   Review Exercises   1. yes   **3.** no
5. no

Pages 506–507 Practice Exercises 1. 200.96 cm²
3. 9856 in.²   **5.** 2826 cm²   **7.** 154 ft²
9. 185 mm²   **11.** 88 cm²   **13.** 1384.74 m²
15. 314 mm²   **17.** 7546 ft²   **19.** 154 m²
21. 224 cm²   **23.** 19,103.76 ft²

Page 507   Review Exercises   1. about $30
3. about $25   **5.** about 150   **7.** about $120
9. 40   **11.** 25

Page 509   Problems   1. 24   **3. a.** 26   **b.** 24
c. 7   **5. a.** 232   **b.** 218

Page 509   Review Exercises   1. 36

Page 510   Skill Review   1. $\overline{AB}$, $\overline{BC}$, $\overline{CD}$
3. $\overleftrightarrow{AB}$, $\overleftrightarrow{CD}$ **5.** triangle, not regular
7. octagon, regular   **9.** 16 m   **11.** $\overrightarrow{OY}$, $\overrightarrow{OW}$, $\overrightarrow{OX}$
13. 75.36 cm   **15.** 196 m²   **17.** 44 mm²
19. 1386 ft²   **21.** 16

Page 511   Exercises   1. about $420   **3.** about
$1884

Page 513   Exercises
1.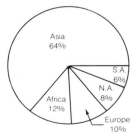

World Population

Asia
64%

S.A.
6%
N.A.
8%

Africa
12%

Europe
10%

3.

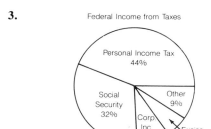

Federal Income from Taxes

Personal Income Tax 44%

Social Security 32%

Corp. Inc. 9%

Other 9%

Excise 6%

Page 515 Chapter Review 1. line segment
3. ●———————●
   A   B
5. ←—●————●——→
      B   C

7. 65 cm **9.** $\overline{RS}$, $\overline{ST}$ **11.** 43.96 ft **13.** 54 m^2
15. 135 in.^{2} **17.** 27

CHAPTER 23

Pages 519–520 Practice Exercises 1. rectangular prism; 6,12,8 **3.** hexagonal prism; 8,18,12
5. cone **7.** cylinder **9.** cube **11.** rectangular pyramid **13.** sphere **15.** triangular pyramid
17. triangular prism **19.** 6,8,12,2 **21.** 5,5,8,2

Page 520 Review Exercises 1. 32 m^2 **3.** 169 in.^{2}
5. 706.5 cm^2

Pages 522–523 Practice Exercises 1. 198 yd^2
3. 864 in.^{2} **5.** 924 ft^2 **7.** 803.84 in.^{2}
9. 550 in.^{2} **11.** 96 in.^{2} **13.** 294 cm^2
15. 61.23 in.^{2} **17.** 1710 in.^{2}

Page 523 Review Exercises 1. 45 **3.** 25
5. 50 **7.** 90 **9.** 250

Pages 525–526 Practice Exercises 1. 12 ft^3
3. 40 cm^3 **5.** 729 ft^3 **7.** 343 cm^3
9. 45 ft^3 **11.** 5760 in.^{3} **13.** 288 ft^3

Page 526 Review Exercises 1. 7.9×10^1
3. 6.35×10^2 **5.** 390 **7.** 6,030,000,000,000

Pages 528–529 Practice Exercises 1. 1356.48 cm^3
3. 276.32 ft^3 **5.** 1692.46 cm^3 **7.** 88 cm^3
9. 2772 yd^3 **11.** 1760 in.^{3} **13.** 565.2 m^3
15. 10,851.84 cm^3 **17.** 13,552 yd^3
19. 5632 ft^3

Page 529 Review Exercises 1. $\frac{7}{20}$ **3.** $\frac{27}{500}$
5. $\frac{1}{80}$ **7.** 83% **9.** 17.5% **11.** $66\frac{2}{3}\%$

Pages 531–532 Practice Exercises 1. 105 m^3
3. 9 ft^3 **5.** 2543.4 cm^3 **7.** 192 ft^3
9. 113.04 m^3 **11.** 2,218,800 m^3
13. 3,386,880 yd^3

Page 532 Review Exercises 1. 48 m^2
3. 54 m^2

Pages 534–535 Practice Exercises 1. 113.04 cm^3
3. 904,320 cm^3 **5.** 56.52 m^3 **7.** 80 m^3
9. 24,416.64 cm^3 **11.** 24,416.64 cm^3
13. 195,333.12 cm^3 **15.** 452.16 in.^{3}

Page 535 Review Exercises 1. 25 **3.** 12
5. 55

Page 536 Skill Review 1. triangular pyramid;
4,6,4 **3.** cylinder **5.** 804 cm^2 **7.** 12 cm^3
9. 5760 ft^3 **11.** 5346 yd^3 **13.** 527.52 ft^3
15. 904.32 cm^3

Page 537 Exercises 1. 11 **3.** 10 **5.** 11

Page 539 Chapter Review 1. polyhedron
3. rectangular pyramid; 5,8,5 **5.** cone
7. 2646 cm^2 **9.** 1377 cm^3 **11.** 3850 in.^{3}
13. 38,772.72 mm^3 **15.** 15

CHAPTER 24

Pages 543–544 Practice Exercises 1. isosceles; right **3.** isosceles; acute **5.** 60° **7.** 45°
9. 72°; acute **11.** 55°; acute **13.** 19°; obtuse
15. 76°; acute **17.** 60°, 60°, 60°

Page 544 Review Exercises 1. false **3.** true
5. 9 **7.** 28

Pages 546–547 Practice Exercises 1. similar; congruent **3.** similar; not congruent **5.** 8 **7.** 9
9. $y = 12$, $x = 5$; not congruent **11.** $g = 48$,
$h = 40$; not congruent **13.** true **15.** false

Page 547 Review Exercises 1. 8 **3.** 100
5. 4320 **7.** $\frac{47}{50}$ **9.** $\frac{101}{250}$

Page 550 Practice Exercises 1. 3 **3.** 1
5. 10 **7.** 3.606 **9.** 10.440 **11.** 88 **13.** 15
15. 10.149 **17.** 90 **19.** 25 **21.** 43
23. 9.487 **25.** 5; 6 **27.** 54 cm

Page 550 Review Exercises 1. 26 **3.** ⁻17 **5.** 6

Pages 552–553 Practice Exercises 1. not a right triangle **3.** right triangle **5.** right triangle
7. 20 m **9.** 10.7 in. **11.** 7 ft **13.** 120 ft
15. 80 ft

Page 553 Review Exercises 1. 32 **3.** 72
5. $166\frac{2}{3}\%$ **7.** 2.7 **9.** 24

Pages 554–555 Problems 1. b **3.** C **5.** A
7. 1 **9.** 4 **11.** Yes **13.** No **15.** No
17. No

Page 555 Review Exercises 1. 49, 64, 81

Page 556 Skill Review 1. equilateral; acute
3. isosceles; obtuse **5.** 43° **7.** 30° **9.** similar; not congruent **11.** 12 **13.** 3.162 **15.** 60
17. 57 **19.** 11.533 **21.** right triangle
23. 9.9 cm **25.** D **27.** A

5. 672 cm   7. 105 ft   9. 370 cm

Page 559   Chapter Review   1. equilateral
3. isosceles; right   **5.** equilateral; acute   **7.** 63°
9. 34°   **11.** 15   **13.** 9.327   **15.** 63   **17.** 10 ft
19. right triangle   **21.** not a right triangle
23. No   **25.** Yes

Extra Practice

Chapter 1, page 566   1. two hundred eight
thousand, four   **3.** seven hundred five million,
three hundred forty-three thousand, ninety
5. 3,000,400   **7.** 273,906,000,053   **9.** $78
11. 89,359   **13.** 2026   **15.** 307   **17.** 1169
19. about 1900   **21.** about 100,000   **23.** about
$1600   **25.** $312   **27.** $10,647   **29.** 19,047
31. 5609   **33.** 3211   **35.** $t - 12$ **37.** $t - 7$
39. $t + 4$ **41.** 18   **43.** 50   **45.** 23   **47.** 114

Chapter 2, page 567   1. 60   **3.** 8400
5. 97,000   **7.** $2,000,000   **9.** about 700
11. about 500   **13.** about $1000   **15.** about $60
17. about $100   **19.** about $24,000   **21.** <
23. >   **25.** >   **27.** <   **29.** >   **31.** >
35. amount of money that you gave the salesperson

Chapter 3, page 568   1. 2100   **3.** 8000
5. 240,000   **7.** 5,400,000   **9.** $147   **11.** 2275
13. 34,254   **15.** $342,456   **17.** about 180
19. about $10,000   **21.** about $160   **23.** 1782
25. 11,664   **27.** 25,650   **29.** 41,574
31. about 45,000; can't tell   **33.** about 4800;
overestimate   **35.** 17,556   **37.** 254,305
39. 32,665   **41.** 194,586   **43.** 299,736
45. 1,028,484   **47.** 239,592   **49.** 840
51. 6300   **53.** 5994   **55.** 27   **57.** 900
59. 324   **61.** 396   **63.** 0

Chapter 4, page 569   1. $163   **3.** $407
5. 403   **7.** 902   **9.** about 120   **11.** about 8000
13. about $300   **15.** about 300   **17.** 31 R55
19. 20 R5   **21.** 304 R9   **23.** 2901 R18
25. 17   **27.** 64   **29.** 39 R9   **31.** $104   **33.** 2
35. 0   **37.** 9   **39.** 4   **41.** 8   **43.** 1   **45.** $13n$
47. $\frac{n}{2}$ **49.** $\frac{n}{5}$ **51.** $4n$ **53.** $112   **55.** 35; $5

Chapter 5, page 570   1. 16   **3.** 3   **5.** 70
7. 4   **9.** 52   **11.** 12   **13.** 16   **15.** $6
17. No   **19.** Yes   **21.** No   **23.** Yes
25. $3 \cdot 3 \cdot 5$ **27.** $2 \cdot 2 \cdot 2 \cdot 5 \cdot 5$
29. $2 \cdot 3 \cdot 5 \cdot 11$ **31.** 15   **33.** 2   **35.** 13
37. 1   **39.** 72   **41.** 40   **43.** 80   **45.** 60
47. 343   **49.** 1   **51.** 100,000   **53.** 320
55. 576   **57.** 64   **59.** 37   **61.** 400   **63.** 70
65. 1920

Chapter 6, page 571   1. $\frac{3}{4}$ **3.** $\frac{5}{8}$ **5.** $\frac{5}{12}$
7. 10   **9.** 4   **11.** $\frac{3}{4}$ **13.** $\frac{1}{10}$ **15.** $\frac{3}{4}$ **17.** >
19. <   **21.** $\frac{1}{7}$ **23.** $\frac{2}{3}$ **25.** $\frac{1}{2}$ **27.** $2\frac{3}{8}$ **29.** $\frac{82}{7}$
31. $\frac{24}{5}$ **33.** $1\frac{3}{7}$ **35.** $10\frac{1}{2}$ **37.** $10\frac{1}{10}$ **39.** $15

Chapter 7, page 572   1. $\frac{3}{20}$ **3.** $\frac{1}{21}$ **5.** $\frac{5}{33}$
7. $\frac{2}{5}$ **9.** 45   **11.** about 30   **13.** about 6
15. about 24   **17.** about 56   **19.** about 6
21. about 3   **23.** 26   **25.** $4\frac{2}{15}$ **27.** 1   **29.** 12
31. $9\frac{3}{8}$ gal   **33.** $1\frac{1}{2}$ **35.** $\frac{8}{11}$ **37.** 30   **39.** $\frac{2}{15}$
41. 3   **43.** $\frac{3}{5}$ **45.** $8\frac{1}{3}$ **47.** $13\frac{4}{5}$ **49.** about 3
51. about 14

Chapter 8, page 573   1. $\frac{5}{7}$ **3.** $\frac{1}{4}$ **5.** $1\frac{1}{20}$
7. $\frac{17}{30}$ **9.** $1\frac{1}{21}$ **11.** $\frac{11}{15}$ **13.** about 16
15. about 2   **17.** about 15   **19.** $7\frac{5}{9}$ **21.** $9\frac{5}{6}$
23. $6\frac{1}{15}$ **25.** $10\frac{31}{60}$ **27.** $4\frac{3}{8}$ **29.** $2\frac{1}{14}$ **31.** $9\frac{19}{36}$
33. $9\frac{23}{40}$ **35.** $\frac{2}{3}$ **37.** $3\frac{5}{12}$ **39.** $10\frac{13}{20}$ **41.** $16\frac{4}{9}$
43. $9\frac{3}{4}$ years   **45.** $\frac{11}{3}, \frac{13}{3}, 5$

Chapter 9, page 574   1. 240   **3.** 6   **5.** 21,120
7. 219   **9.** 7; 1   **11.** $1\frac{7}{16}$ in.   **13.** 80   **15.** 4
17. 7   **19.** 2; 7   **21.** 1; 200   **23.** 80   **25.** 12
27. 6   **29.** 1; 6   **31.** 35   **33.** Bob
35. 3 yd 2 ft   **37.** 12 gal 2 qt   **39.** 9 ft 2 in.
41. 2 qt   **43.** 2 lb 6 oz   **45.** 3 gal 3 qt

Chapter 10, page 575   1. two tenths   **3.** three
and six thousandths   **5.** 0.6   **7.** 389.0004
9. 49   **11.** 0.861   **13.** $17   **15.** 502.70
17. >   **19.** =   **21.** >   **23.** 2, 2.02, 2.1, 2.16,
2.21, 2.3   **25.** $\frac{23}{25}$ **27.** $\frac{111}{250}$ **29.** $6\frac{1}{4}$ **31.** $7\frac{999}{1000}$
33. $194\frac{1}{25}$ **35.** 0.2   **37.** 11.65   **39.** 0.78
41. 0.64   **43.** 0.72   **45.** 2.53   **47.** about $\frac{2}{3}$
49. about $\frac{1}{2}$ **51.** You need to know the cost of a
can of corn.

Chapter 11, page 576   1. 7.8   **3.** 10.4
5. $22.52   **7.** 1.5116   **9.** 1.815   **11.** 25.007
13. $27.49   **15.** about 800   **17.** about 25
19. about 0.08   **21.** about 1.5   **23.** 1.5
25. 3.249   **27.** 32.87   **29.** $14.35
31. 769.004   **33.** 479.8   **35.** 50.63 min
37. about 0.1   **39.** about 0.2   **41.** about 0.06
43. about $45   **45.** about 0.08   **47.** about 0.76

Chapter 12, page 577   1. 10.468   **3.** 134.4
5. 111.6   **7.** $13.04   **9.** $675.72   **11.** $160.06
13. $78.30   **15.** 23.6   **17.** 679.496   **19.** 67.03
21. 2010   **23.** 96,010   **25.** 90   **27.** 230.4774
29. $25.39   **31.** 0.02408   **33.** 0.003
35. $632.42   **37.** 151,242.04   **39.** about 1600
41. about 5   **43.** about $1.60   **45.** about 200
47. about 100   **49.** about 2400   **51.** c
53. about 200

Chapter 13, page 578   1. 2.31   **3.** 2.8
5. 0.68   **7.** 1.04   **9.** $2.06   **11.** $36.24
13. 0.043   **15.** 2.318   **17.** $1.73   **19.** 3.5722
21. 0.0146   **23.** 0.902   **25.** 0.0074

27. 0.3169 **29.** $1260 **31.** 3 **33.** 0.53
35. 6 **37.** 0.45 **39.** 1410 **41.** 0.225
43. 0.429 **45.** 1.177 **47.** about 40
49. about 9 **51.** about $8 **53.** about 5
55. about 6000 **57.** about 400 **59.** 200
61. 1300 **63.** 5030 **65.** 83.5 **67.** 196,500
69. 3,000,000 **71.** 3×10^2 **73.** 1×10^5
75. 8×10^8 **77.** 2.5×10^1 **79.** 8.2×10^5
81. 1.7×10^1

Chapter 14, page 579 1. mm **3.** m **5.** cm
7. 4.3 cm; 43 mm **9.** 400 **11.** 17,000
13. 60,250 **15.** 90 **17.** 9.3 **19.** 0.0327
21. mL **23.** L **25.** 5 **27.** 1.5 **29.** 3200
31. g **33.** g **35.** 60,000 **37.** 0.02
39. 0.0059 **41.** 1 block due north

Chapter 15, page 580 1. $\frac{1}{16}$ **3.** $\frac{1}{6}$ **5.** $\frac{9}{4}$
7. $\frac{28}{169}$ **9.** $\frac{1}{9}$ **11.** $\frac{20,000}{1}$ **13.** $\frac{1}{4}$ **15.** $25/h
17. 33 mi/gal **19.** 69 pages/h **21.** $4.50/ticket
23. 33.75 mi/h **25.** $29.05/issue **27.** 21
29. 4 **31.** 21 **33.** 5 **35.** 18 **37.** 10
39. $1.44 **41.** 20 **43.** 60 ft **45.** 1 in.

Chapter 16, page 581 1. 3% **3.** 10%
5. 0.32 **7.** 0.02 **9.** 1.15 **11.** 14.2%
13. 30% **15.** $\frac{93}{100}$ **17.** $\frac{4}{25}$ **19.** $\frac{23}{200}$ **21.** $\frac{1}{200}$
23. $\frac{1}{175}$ **25.** 30% **27.** 25% **29.** 20%
31. 35% **33.** $13\frac{1}{3}$% **35.** $67\frac{1}{2}$% **37.** 3.5
39. 9 **41.** 7 **43.** 603 **45.** about $20
47. about 200 **49.** about $1 **51.** Brewer

Chapter 17, page 582 1. 24% **3.** 25%
5. 75% **7.** 500% **9.** 80% **11.** 34
13. 550 **15.** 85 **17.** 280 **19.** 8 **21.** 21
23. 25% **25.** 20% **27.** 108 **29.** 25 **31.** increase; 14% **33.** decrease; 25% **35.** increase;
$66\frac{2}{3}$% **37.** increase; 50%

Chapter 18, page 583
1. Student Ages

Age	Tally	Freq.
14	II	2
15	IIII	5
16	IIII II	7
17	III	3
18	III	3

3. 7; 7; 7
5. 63.4; 67; 45
7. 6.9; 7.5; 8

9. about 100 **11.** about 1700 **13.** $\frac{1}{5}$
15. 160 **17.** 16

Chapter 19, page 584 1. 10 **3.** 6 **5.** 5040
7. 30 **9.** 6 **11.** 120 **13.** $\frac{2}{3}$ **15.** $\frac{7}{9}$ **17.** $\frac{1}{64}$
19. $\frac{1}{16}$ **21.** $\frac{1}{56}$ **23.** $\frac{2}{7}$ **25.** about 35

Chapter 20, page 585 1. ⁻7 **3.** ⁻15 **5.** ⁻6
7. 11 **9.** 0 **11.** 16 **13.** < **15.** > **17.** <

19. > **21.** ⁻184 **23.** ⁻17 **25.** 1 **27.** ⁻1
29. 10 **31.** ⁻2 **33.** ⁻16 **35.** 5 **37.** ⁻2
39. 2 **41.** ⁻9 **43.** ⁻19 **45.** ⁻27 **47.** ⁻24
49. ⁻125 **51.** 315 **53.** ⁻378 **55.** ⁻6
57. 1 **59.** 0 **61.** ⁻1 **63.** undefined **65.** 50
67. ⁻9 **69.** ⁻17 **71.** 400 **73.** 256 **75.** 624
77. 165

Chapter 21, page 586 1. 5 **3.** 20 **5.** 14
7. 27 **9.** 6 **11.** ⁻9 **13.** 2 **15.** 5 **17.** 8
19. 13 min **21.** (3, 2) **23.** (4, ⁻3)
25. (⁻3, 0) **27.** (⁻4, 4) **29.** (⁻2, 3)
39. (⁻2, ⁻2), (0, 4), (2, 10) **41.** (⁻2, ⁻16),
(0, ⁻6), (2, 4) **43.** (⁻2, 6), (0, 0), (2, ⁻6)
45. (⁻2, 12), (0, 0), (2, ⁻12)
49. 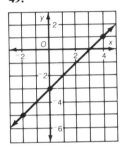 **51.**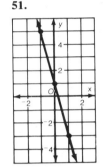

Chapter 22, page 587 1.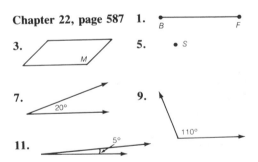
3. **5.** •S
7. 20° **9.** 110°
11. 5°

13. pentagon; not regular **15.** quadrilateral;
not regular **17.** 40 cm **19.** 22 m
21. 31.4 mm **23.** 44 cm **25.** 49 m² **27.** 24 cm²
29. 15 yd² **31.** 616 mm² **33.** 29 in.²

Chapter 23, page 588 1. cube; 6; 12; 8
3. rectangular prism; 6; 12; 8 **5.** 184 ft²
7. 301.44 mm² **9.** 30 in.³ **11.** 904.32 ft³
13. 6358.5 yd³ **15.** 150.72 m³
17. 3052.08 in.³ **19.** 704 mm³

Chapter 24, page 589 1. 103° **3.** 139°
5. 90° **7.** 35° **9.** 30 **11.** 18 **13.** 6.557
15. 11.747 **17.** 9.2 **19.** 8 **21.** 13 **23.** 9.9
25. triangular pyramid **27.** cube